D1219160

DEMCO

OUR TIMES

OUR TIMES

The Age of Elizabeth II

A. N. WILSON

Farrar, Straus and Giroux
New York

In Memory of

HUGH MONTGOMERY-MASSINGBERD

Farrar, Straus and Giroux
18 West 18th Street, New York 10011

Printed in the United States of America
Originally published in 2008 by Hutchinson, Great Britain
Published in the United States by Farrar, Straus and Giroux
First American edition, 2010

Grateful acknowledgement is made for permission to reprint the following material:
Lines from 'Knowing Me' by Benjamin Zaphaniah from *Too Black, Too Strong* (Bloodax Books, 2001), reproduced with permission.
'Lebanon government joins forces with bid to have Blair tried in Scotland for war crimes': Article reproduced with the permission of *The Sunday Herald*, Glasgow, © 2008 Herald & Times Group; Byline: Neil Mackay; *The Sunday Herald*; Publication Date: Sunday 06 August 2006.

Library of Congress Cataloging-in-Publication Data
Wilson, A. N., 1950–
      Our times : the age of Elizabeth II / A. N. Wilson.— 1st American ed.
      p.   cm.
      "Originally published in 2008 by Hutchinson, an imprint of Random House Books, Great Britain"—T.p. verso.
      Includes bibliographical references and index.
      ISBN-13: 978-0-374-22820-0 (hardcover : alk. paper)
      ISBN-10: 0-374-22820-5 (hardcover : alk. paper)
      1. Great Britain—History—Elizabeth II, 1952–   2. Great Britain—Social conditions—1945–   3. Great Britain—Intellectual life—1945–   I. Title.

DA592.W4674 2010
941.085—dc22
                                                                        2009015652

www.fsgbooks.com

1   3   5   7   9   10   8   6   4   2

Contents

CONTENTS

Part Five The Lady

Part Six Mr Major's Britain

Part Seven The Project

Illustrations

Acknowledgements

This book could not have been written without visits to The Public Record Office at Kew, Lambeth Palace Library, the British Library, the London Library, and the Marylebone Public Library. Grateful thanks to the staff at all these institutions. Hilary Lowinger at *Private Eye* magazine was very helpful, as was Ian Hislop. Thanks, also, to Harry Boyle and A. D. Harvey and Jonathan Cecil for allowing me to pick their brains. Sue Freestone and Gillon Aitken were begetters of the book, and among its more helpful midwives, I must acknowledge and thank Caroline Gascoigne, James Nightingale – as ever, a tower of strength, and a great picture researcher too – Emma Mitchell and Richard Collins. Before anyone saw the finished product it had been typed and retyped by Amy Boyle – a very special thanks to her. Douglas Matthews provided the index.

OUR TIMES

Introduction

Queen Elizabeth II succeeded her father George VI on 6 February 1952. This story is not about her, but it covers the years of her reign which, at the time of writing, looks as if it might well rival that of Queen Victoria in longevity. (Victoria reigned for more than sixty-three years.) Already, the reign of Elizabeth II has encompassed so much change and has witnessed so many remarkable achievements that it makes her seem almost like a time traveller, spanning not just six decades, but whole centuries. The Britain of the early 1950s is so utterly different from Britain in 2008, when I lay down my pen, that it is bizarre to think that we have had the same Head of State as we did when rationing was still in force, and when Churchill was still Prime Minister.

But was this Queen's reign, like that of Victoria, a time of British success, or of failure? Will this, the second Elizabethan era, compare favourably with that of her great-great grandmother's or not? The Age of Victoria was one in which Britain became the greatest world power. At the beginning of Victoria's reign, the first waves of industrial and technological revolution had put Britain into a position in which she had no rivals in the fields of invention and industrial productivity. It only needed free trade – which came about as a result of repealing tariffs on imported grain, the so-called Corn Laws – for an amazing bonanza to take place.

Thereafter, for half a century, until Germany was united and began to catch up, there was no country on earth to match Britain's wealth-producing capacity. At the same time, thanks to a combination of commercial enterprise, and a genuine desire to help the peoples of Asia and Africa, the British Empire came into being.

Nearly all this prowess, in terms of riches and political power, had evaporated by the time our own Queen Elizabeth came to the throne. Britain was not the true victor in the Second World War – it was the Soviet Union and America that emerged as the superpowers in the new global order. Indeed, the war (1939–45) against Hitler ruined Britain financially. At the time of Elizabeth II's accession, there was a housing crisis – with many people living in slums, and others housed in prefabs which were an enterprising, and surprisingly comfortable, response to the shortage, but which look to the eyes of hindsight like huts in a Toy Town. There were fuel shortages. The nationalisation of coal and steel industries by the post-war Labour government guaranteed that industrial expansion in Britain would fall catastrophically behind her international competitors, and labour relations were deplorable for the first quarter century of the reign – until Margaret Thatcher did the cruel but necessary thing and hammered the trades unions. When one considers the cold, the poverty, the sheer misery of post-war austerity Britain and compares it with the Britain of today, it is hard not to believe that an improvement has been accomplished which, in its way, is as amazing as anything the Victorians brought about. The standard of living of the average British family in 1952, when a twenty-five-year-old Princess Elizabeth succeeded to the throne, would seem harsh today even to Romanians or the poorest of the East Germans. Few families could afford to drink alcohol except on special occasions. Wine was unheard of – except on Christmas Day. Elizabeth David had not yet revolutionised the British palate and most of the food on offer in restaurants and hotels – assuming you were lucky enough to be able to afford it – was unpalatable. Foreign holidays were for the few, and even they were restricted in the amount of money that could be taken abroad, so that it was all but impossible to travel abroad for more than ten days without running out of cash. A quarter of British homes had inadequate sanitary arrangements, outdoor lavatories, and bathrooms shared with neighbours.

Over half the adult population over the age of thirty had no teeth – it was the received wisdom among dentists that it was better for your health to have dentures. The unhappily married stayed unhappy, unless they wished to go through the considerable expense and humiliation of a divorce, in which there always had to be a guilty party, and farcical scenes had to be enacted in hotel rooms with retired prostitutes, witnessed by private detectives, in order to provide the evidence of adultery.

Homosexuals were treated as diseased beings, and until the recommendations of the Wolfenden Report were passed into law – which did not happen fully until 1967 – two men over the age of twenty-one were in breach of the law even if they shared a bed in complete privacy.

The Lord Chamberlain still exercised censorship over the stage, and until the pantomimic *Lady Chatterley* trial of 1960, the law made no distinction between works of literature which dealt frankly with sexual matters and sordid pornography.

So, when we look back at the reign of Elizabeth II, and recognise the improvements in living standards, and the enormous increase in national prosperity, and in sexual liberty, it would be perverse not to rejoice.

Consider also the change in the position of women. For the first twenty-five years of the Queen's reign, it was perfectly permissible for employers to pay women markedly less for doing the same jobs as men, and there were many jobs to which only very privileged women could aspire.

Before 1967, the only abortionists a woman was likely to meet were Vera Drakes with knitting needles, and before the advent of the Pill many women felt enslaved by marriage and family life.

By the beginning of the twenty-first century there existed a Britain which did not persecute unmarried mothers, did not hang those who may (or may not) have committed a murder, and did not compel the poor to live in slums. Though its overburdened health service was badly run and there were newspaper stories every week of dirty, badly run hospitals, this should not blind us to the extraordinary advances in medical science and the standards of medical care, which enabled many cancer patients to be cured, which can offer life-saving heart surgery which would have been undreamed of in 1953, and which allowed the ageing population to replace hips and knee joints at the taxpayers' expense.

The second Elizabethan Age was a period in which the majority of the British basked in comfort, security and luxury. And if from time to time security was threatened – by IRA bombs, by the Brixton riots, or by Islamist terror – what was this compared to the wars which previous generations endured, with the British cities, and London especially, being nightly bombarded in the Blitz, and two generations, 1914–18 and 1939–45, seeing hundreds of thousands of civilians and service men and women killed in monstrous acts of war?

And yet, it would be a bold person who stood up and said that the reign of Elizabeth had been Britain's most glorious period. For the reign of Elizabeth is the one in which Britain effectively stopped being British.

The chief reason for this is mass immigration on a scale that has utterly transformed our nation. Governments needed cheap labour, and the first immigrants from the West Indies helped the expanding health service, the improved transport system and burgeoning industry.

Horrified by the older generation's racialism, the next generation built up a race relations industry in which discrimination on grounds of skin pigmentation became illegal. But meanwhile, for fear of being thought racist, successive governments allowed thousands of immigrants and their innumerable dependants, most of whom, far from bringing necessary skills, were a drain on the welfare system, or took jobs which could have been done by those already living here. That is particularly true of the past decade, in which immigration to Britain has taken place on a scale unprecedented in our nation's history. According to the government's own figures, hastily revised in 2007, 1.1 million have migrated to the UK since New Labour came to power – though according to former minister Frank Field the true figure may be as high as 1.6 million.

Though it is certainly true that some of these immigrants have helped Britain prosper, it is equally inescapable that they have changed the character and composition of whole areas of Britain – and not always for the better. Eager to be tolerant, governments did not insist that these immigrants learn the language or integrate properly.

Because the bulk of primary schools were Church of England, it seemed only fair – didn't it? – to have Muslim schools, too. This folly ignored the fact that Church of England did not mean narrowly Christian, it meant schools for all, which historically had been run by the Church. And by creating Muslim schools, governments allowed for the growth of a disaffected, 'radicalised' young Islamist population, many of whom are intent on destroying Britain itself.

But even if we set aside immigration for one moment, there have been many other ways in which Britain has not simply changed, but has radically undermined its very essence and nature during the course of Queen Elizabeth's reign.

Some would point to the way that Britain has sacrificed its national sovereignty to Europe. Others would highlight New Labour's tinkering with the constitution, the attempted abolition of the office of Lord Chancellor, and the mutilation of the House of Lords. That's before we even consider the virtual dissolution of the Church of England.

All these things are symptoms, rather than causes of a palpable fact: that the Britain of 6 February 1952 is not merely different from the Britain of today. It has ceased to exist.

If you list the austerities endured by our grandparents and parents in 1952, many would cheer the disappearance of their Britain. But with the collective nervous breakdown which followed the Suez debacle in 1956, and the end of Empire, the British gradually lost any sense of what it meant to be together as a nation.

That spirit of national identity which was so quickened by the Second World War dissipated itself during the 1960s and 1970s. Comprehensive education was meant to destroy the class system; instead it deepened class division by making anyone who could afford to – and many who scarcely can afford it – educate their children privately.

It was symptomatic of the times that so many of the best scientists and recent writers went abroad. The poet Geoffrey Hill lived much of his creative life out of England. From the late 1980s until 2006 he was at Boston University. Hill's crabbed, sometimes difficult verse, catches (he borrowed the phrase from one of his mentors, Samuel Taylor Coleridge) Platonic England.

Platonic England, house of solitudes,
rests in its laurels and its injured stone,
replete with complex fortunes that are gone,
beset by dynasties of moods and clouds.

The Britain he evokes, which is in part the West Midlands of his child-hood (his father was a policeman in Worcestershire) and in part the Mercia of King Offa, is morally damaged, aesthetically marred, histor-ically adrift. In some of the most successful of his poems, we feel him only just escaping the overpowering influence of Yeats. Sometimes, the breaks away are into obscurity too dense to be unprised. There is, however, a definite and palpable quality in his music, a sense of desolation, a voice of authority and greatness. It is a quality which has all but left us. At the beginning of our times, when T. S. Eliot and Evelyn Waugh were still alive, when Benjamin Britten had still to compose his greatest work, when Churchill, even in his decrepitude, was still Prime Minister, it was still possible to hope that the culture would cast up a few great ones from the general melee. As our times moved on, however, an infallible sign of the death of the culture was that no such figures emerged. For T. S. Eliot, we had Andrew Motion, for Winston Churchill, Jacqui Smith. When we consider the figures of the Victorian past in Britain, it is to evoke in the mind's eye figures who easily stand comparison with their world contem-poraries. Tolstoy commended Ruskin, for example. Though the two men never met, there would have been no sense, *had* Tolstoy made the *haj* to the Lake District to meet Ruskin, of a giant meeting a pigmy, but of *two* giants, one distinctively Russian, the other wholly British.

Yet when Aleksandr Solzhenitsyn came to Britain in 1976, there was a bleak sense that there was no one in the entire island who could match the profundity of his achievement, or the sheer awfulness of his life-experience. Solzhenitsyn's literary merits have been disputed by those with political axes to grind. The three best books – *One Day in the Life of Ivan Denisovich, Cancer Ward* and *The First Circle* – are simply tower-ingly bigger achievements than anything which British writers of our times have managed to piddle forth. 'A great writer is, so to speak, a second government. That's why no regime anywhere has ever loved its great writers, only its minor ones,' remarks one of the characters in *The First Circle*. When he came to Britain, he broadcast on BBC radio – on 23 March 1976. It was three years before Margaret Thatcher came to power. It was a while before Ronald Reagan had denounced the 'evil empire' of Soviet Communism, whose evil Solzhenitsyn had done so much to expose. He feared that the West was weakening and not resisting the still considerable might of the Kremlin's political influence. To that extent, his words quickly, and happily, became out of date. But in another sense, they remain just as apposite thirty and more years after he spoke them. For he was not simply speaking of the West's capacity to resist the Soviets. He was talking about the West losing its soul.

'And Great Britain – the kernel of the Western world as we have already called it – has experienced this sapping of its strength and will to an even greater degree, perhaps, than any other country. For some twenty years Britain's voice has not been heard in our planet; its character has gone, its freshness has faded. And Britain's position in the world today is of less significance than that of Romania, or even . . . Uganda.' The great Russian believed that the West had become 'enmeshed in our slavish worship of all that is pleasant, all that is comfortable, all that is material – we worship things, we worship products. Will we ever succeed in shaking off this burden, in giving free rein to the spirit that was breathed into us at birth, that spirit that distinguishes us from the animal world?'[1]

Some of the weaknesses of the West to which Solzhenitsyn drew attention were what disgusted the Islamic world when it contemplated the moral and spiritual bankruptcy of Europe and America. The resurgence of a violent Islam, not merely in the urban battlefields of Basra and Baghdad, but in the weaving towns of Yorkshire and on the London buses, can hardly be ignored. When terrorists strike, the indigenous population can feel justifiable anger, not only against the perpetrators but also against a political class which allowed the situation to come about in which such suicide-bombing fanatics could exist.

Then, however, a little time passes, as we begin to hear the voices of liberal commentary upon such tragic events. Then, we begin to see how far the culture has dissipated, how little, in fact, it any longer coheres, or even exists. Politicians, anxiously trying to make good the devastating folly of their predecessors, suggest ways in which we could force 'British values' upon disaffected young Muslims, while a former Lord Chief Justice thinks that things might be helped if all new immigrants, upon reaching the age of majority, were asked to swear an oath of allegiance to the Queen.

The roots of what has happened to us go much deeper than individual mistakes made by administrators within the last half-century. Solzhenitsyn made himself the butt of cynical abuse by asserting the belief that our troubles go back to the Enlightenment, and the eighteenth-century abandonment of religion. From the moment he came out of Russia, he expressed the belief that he would one day return. Political commentators smiled politely but believed that the monolith of Soviet Communism would never be shaken. His prophecy, however, came true, and he did go home. But though he returned, as an old Slavophile, who believed, with Dostoyevsky, that Mother Russia could find her soul by kneeling at the feet of Jesus, most Russians turned a deaf ear to him. His own culture was dissipating, under the influence of spiv capitalists, even more rapidly than it had done under the brutal atheist Stalinist and post-Stalinist state.

Our problems have been different in the West, but we have witnessed the same dissolution and dissipation of a common culture. Solzhenitsyn could hope for a revival in religious belief which would act as a cultural glue. Such ideas had been abandoned in Britain as long ago as the 1840s.[2] What united Britain was not so much religion as a shared sense of identity and purpose, a shared sense which had been quickened and strengthened by the experience of the Second World War. It was part of the national myth that during the heroic summer of 1940 Britain had stood alone against the rest of the world, but it was a myth which also happened to be true. When it did so, it had intact an Empire, a vast industrial base at home, an unwrecked landscape, unspoilt townscapes, a rail network, a national Church, a class system, almost all of which, within a decade of the war coming to an end, would have faded, or actually been forcibly removed.

Today, my Britain, the England of my mother and my father, no longer exists. This is a sentence which means something quite different, when written down in 2008, than it would have meant when written down half a century ago. Of course, history always moves on; and of course there is a tendency for an older generation is to think that change has been for the worse.

In our times, however, something much more radical has happened. This book is certainly not advancing the proposition that all changes in the last fifty years have been for the worse. In terms of physical wellbeing, of medical and dental care, of opportunities for travel and cultural enrichment, the changes in the last half-century for the great majority in Britain, and in the West generally, have been material improvements. But nearly all the major changes have been destructive of the common culture. One obvious example, taken from the very middle of our times, is the so-called Big Bang on 27 October 1986. Thereafter, more money came into London than at any period in its history. But, almost overnight, the City of London, that institution which had been central to the wealth of Britain as a nation from the late seventeenth century until our time, was no longer in the hands of British institutions or British families. Geographically, the Square Mile was still in the same place. The Thames still ran softly, but the song was no longer sung in English.

The great dome of St Paul's, emblem not only of Sir Christopher

Wren's belief in a rational, as well as a national Church, but also (from the famous photographs of its remaining through the smoke of the Blitz) an emblem of national solidity in the face of destructive threats from outside, this great dome itself was to be dwarfed by the huge American-style blocks and slabs which soared above the City's skyline, to the dismay of the Prince of Wales and others. Within its walls, the cathedral church of the Diocese of London had become the chief meeting place of a sect, rather than the seat of a national Church. The liturgy of 1662, which had been part of the inner music of English heads and English ears since it was first authorised, was discarded in the late 1960s, as was any claim by the Church to utter the Common Prayer of the nation. No longer answerable to Parliament, the Church had an assembly of its own, the General Synod, in which it could conduct divisive discussions from which there appeared to be no retreat – gay bishops? women priests? The delay of the disestablishment of the Church did not mean that disestablishment was not inevitable. And with disestablishment would come a further weakening of any bond which might hold the nation in an imaginative and cultural knot.

The Union between Scotland and England had been the beginning of the story of British Imperial greatness. Together, with occasional dramatic spats, the two nations had achieved remarkable feats – of statecraft, of philosophy, of engineering, of empire-building. In our times, like a married pair who wondered whether they had ever liked each other, they drift almost heedlessly towards separation, with a series of devolutionary measures which few of the electorate actually asked for, and probably even fewer actively desired.

Here, then, are three areas – the ownership of the wealth in the City of London, the status of the Established Church, and the very Union of Great Britain and Northern Ireland – whose status is palpably different at the end of our times from what it was at the beginning. These factors make Britain less British, even before you have begun to consider the influence of mass immigration and membership of the European Union, or of the more nebulous but no less observable isolation of groups, classes, ethnicities, within our borders. During the Second World War, and in the times of economic austerity thereafter, we were – yes, it made sense to use the first person plural – *we* were an entity. The young men, of whatever social class, did National Service together. Rich and poor had received identical rations, fairly shared. With the coming of prosperity – prosperity which almost everyone must surely have welcomed – the problems began. The inhabitants of the British archipelago became a collection of classes and races and individuals, living side by side and for the most part trying to ignore one another. The only thing, in fact, which the indigenous population still had in common with all their fellow aliens on the strange little archipelago was the Queen herself. And one suspects, as she continued to go about Britain meeting her subjects and shaking their hands, that she had come to feel a stranger there, too. What had happened was that Britain, having undergone a series of stupendous changes, most of them, if measured in purely economic terms, improvements, had ceased to be anybody's home.

PART ONE

Churchill and Eden

I

Old Western Man

The travellers trotted on, and as the sun began to sink towards the White Downs far away on the western horizon they came to Bywater by its wide pool, and there they had their first really painful shock. This was Frodo and Sam's own country, and they found out now that they cared about it more than any other place in the world. Many of the houses that they had known were missing. Some seemed to have been burned down. The pleasant row of old hobbit-holes in the bank in the north side of the Pool were deserted, and their little gardens that used to run down right to the water's edge were rank with weeds. Worse, there was a whole line of the ugly new houses all along The Pool Side, where the Hobbiton Road ran close to the bank. An avenue of trees had stood there. They were all gone. And looking with dismay up the road towards Bag End they saw a full chimney of brick in the distance. It was pouring out black smoke into the evening air.[1]

The Great War is over. The Ring of Power has been destroyed. As in Wagner's *Ring* cycle which is one of its primary analogues, *The Lord of the Rings* concludes with Middle-earth passing into the hands of the human race. The Dark Lord and his power were destroyed when the ring itself was thrown into the Cracks of Doom in the Land of Mordor where the shadows lie. The Elves of the High Kindred, together with Gandalf the Wizard, take ship at the Grey Havens and pass out of our world. The Shire, the comfortable, rural world of the Hobbits, will no doubt return to some kind of normality, but it has been wrecked during the war and it is difficult to believe, amiable and strong as old Sam Gamgee is, that the Shire will ever be quite the same.

The literary fortunes, and reputation, of the author of *The Lord of the Rings* find no parallel. Reviewing it for *The Nation* on 14 April 1956, Edmund Wilson, while dismissing J. R. R. Tolkien's (1892–1973) great work as 'balderdash' and 'literary trash', made the strikingly false prophecy that the book would appeal only to British literary taste.[2] Of all the works published in England during the early to mid-1950s, *The Lord of the Rings* made by far the most world-wide appeal, translated into dozens of languages and, even during the author's lifetime, becoming, among the Californian hippies of the late 1960s, a quasi-religious text. *Gandalf lives*, they proclaimed on their T-shirts.

Tolkien was an unlikely hippy guru. Of South African parentage (his father was a bank clerk) he was brought up in Birmingham, attended King Edward's School and Exeter College, Oxford. From an early age his passion was for language. As a child he had stared at the coal trucks bound for Wales and had been fascinated by the words painted upon them, so unlike the Germanic languages, English and Afrikaans and German, to which he had been accustomed – *Nantyglo, Senghenydd, Blaen Rhondda, Penrhwceiber* and *Tredegar*. Soon he was inventing languages with all their morphology and syntax, as well as imagining the mythologies they carried with them.[3]

Much of the epic which made him famous concerns a war in which ill-equipped, small individuals are pitted against forces of monstrous darkness. *The Lord of the Rings* is among the best war literature. Not only the vast battles, but the tiredness and hunger of the common solider on his long, wet, nocturnal marches are unforgettably recreated. Tolkien lost most of his school friends in the First World War and his epic is a story of unremitting loss and pessimism. As for almost all who fought in it, or lived through it, the First World War was the great calamity from which his generation never recovered. By the time of the Second, he was a professor of philology at Oxford, a medieval scholar of great brilliance. After decades of creating the private languages and mythology which had been part of his inner life since childhood, he had enjoyed, in 1937, the success of a children's story, *The Hobbit*, and by using the same characters but setting them against the mythic background he had for so long imagined, Tolkien, over a twelve-year slog, and against the demands of his teaching and research, had finished one of the great masterpieces of twentieth-century literature. Rayner Unwin, son of the publisher Stanley Unwin, collected the typescript on 19 September 1952. The first volume, *The Fellowship of the Ring*, was published in 1954, the next, *The Two Towers*, some time later in the same year, and *The Return of the King* in 1955. Many of the critics and pundits during those years would have shared Edmund Wilson's intellectually snobbish opinions – would have shared them, that is to say, if they had so much as noticed the books' publication. The BBC dramatised it in 1956, by the end of the decade it was beginning to be translated, but the phenomenal success, the sales of millions, did not take off until it was published in paperback in the United States of America in 1965.[4]

The popularity of the book among the young of that generation would surprise only those who saw a contrast between their appearance, and manner of life, and that of Tolkien himself. He was a reclusive, extremely conservative Roman Catholic of austere morals. They supposedly practised free love and wore flowers in their hair. But neither believed in the future. He had seen his world, the old world, wrecked by the perpetual fear that a Third World War might eliminate the world of nature itself, destroy the planet.

Tolkien stands toweringly above the new authors of the new Queen's reign. True, the old troupers – Ivy Compton-Burnett, P. G. Wodehouse and Agatha Christie – continued to write a slim volume each year as if to reassure their fans that the world they had created still existed on some plane. Of those who began to be published in the post–Second World War era, none has Tolkien's weight of pessimism or majesty of vision. He rightly dismissed the idea that his epic was an allegory. Otherwise Sauron would have to be a mere code for Hitler, and The Ring for the atomic bomb. The whole book is much bigger than any such trivial matching could ever suggest. It is a story of a world wrecked, gone forever, destroyed. No one supposes that Sam Gamgee and his wife, Rose, courageous as Sam has been, will ever repeat the glory, still less rise in his Hobbit life, to the levels of tragic grandeur known in the heroic days of Theoden, King of the Golden Hall, or of the cruel, majestic quasi-Byzantine courts of Gondor. Those glory times are forever over. Literature was left to perky, cheeky chappies, Lucky Jim setting fire to his bedding with cigarettes, finding Room at the Top by marrying the boss's daughter, wowing the avant-garde audiences of *Look Back in Anger* with his realism. Their antics did not really survive the decade in which they first appeared. They were ephemera.

Tolkien's friend Clive Staples Lewis (1898–1963) enjoyed fame on several levels (children's writer, radio evangelist) but wrote his most lasting work as a literary scholar. He, like Tolkien, had been through the First World War, and lived with a sense of finished cataclysm. On 11 May 1954, C. S. Lewis, after a lifetime at Oxford, was elected to a new chair at Cambridge, becoming Professor of Medieval and Renaissance English. His inaugural lecture, entitled 'De Descriptione Temporum', spoke of a great gulf between the modern world and everything, pagan and Christian, which had gone before. In the old world, as he saw it, rulers wanted to 'forestall or extinguish widespread excitement . . . They even prayed (in words that sound curiously old-fashioned), to be able to live "a peaceable life in all godliness and honesty" and "pass their time in rest and quietness". Now – instead of rulers, there were "leaders with" (I suppose) what people call "magnetism" or "personality".' Modern art was the first in history to be unintelligible – the Cubists, Picasso and T. S. Eliot are cited as examples. Did any of Lewis's Cambridge audience believe him when he said, 'I am not in the least concerned to decide whether this state of affairs is a good or a bad thing. I merely assert that it is a new thing'? Thirdly, he cites the un-christening of Europe. They now lived in a post-Christian age. Fourthly, the world was mechanised.

Lewis paraded himself as belonging to the last generation of Old Western Man, the last generation who had anything in common with Jane Austen or Sir Walter Scott. His was an unbroken tradition from Homer – 'I might almost say from the Epic of Gilgamesh' – to the modern world. 'Surely the gap between Professor Kyle and Thomas Browne is far wider than that between Gregory the Great and Virgil? Surely Seneca and Dr Johnson are closer together than Burton and Freud?'[5]

Was Lewis just posturing, or was there some element of truth in what he had to say? Was one of the reasons that Britain would find it so confusing to adapt to life in the post-war era not merely that it had lost an Empire, but that it had also, in common with the other countries of the West, lost contact not just with individual authors or works of art from the past, but with a shared self-defining culture? Certainly the days were already fast disappearing in the mid-fifties when a shared knowledge of Latin and Greek could be expected of European audiences. By the end of our times, when knowledge of even one play by Shakespeare was no longer required by public examiners of sixteen-year-olds, it might have been felt that some very radical change indeed had taken place.

In 1965, two years after Lewis died, A. J. P. Taylor, his old colleague at Magdalen College, Oxford, completed his superbly readable *English History 1914–1945*. This energetic story saw the Second World War as, among other things, the period when Britain had embraced modernity. 'Before the war Great Britain was still trying to revive the old staples. After it, she relied on new developing industries. Electricity, motor-cars, iron and steel, machine tools, nylons and chemicals were all set for expansion . . . The very spirit of the nation had changed.' He saw the heroes of the world wars not as the generals or the dictators, nor even Churchill, but the people of Britain themselves.

> Traditional values lost much of their force. Other values took their place. Imperial greatness was on the way out; the welfare state was on the way in. The British Empire declined; the condition of the people improved. Few now sang *Land of Hope and Glory*. Fewer even sang *England, Arise*. England had risen all the same.[6]

It is a magnificent ending for a book, written during the optimistic years of Harold Wilson's premiership by a popular and populist don who saw the world going his way. If social cohesion is measured in terms of 'motor-cars, iron and steel, machine tools, nylons and chemicals'[7] then Britain in the mid-1950s looked set for improvement. If societies, however, require shared mythologies, ideologies, folk memories, to help them cohere and to live through times of crisis, then perhaps the pessimism of Tolkien and Lewis was prophetic.

Throughout our period, the polarities expressed by these two positions become more and more irreconcilable. On the one hand politicians, economists, industrialists and *some* moralists point to ever-increasing prosperity, and greater freedoms. On the other there is the sense that the Shire has been wrecked, that a tall chimney is belching smoke into its previously unsullied air and that, at the same time, the old tales are being forgotten, the old songs no longer sung. Capitalism could produce just as effective a block on the past as could the faceless dictatorship of Orwell's *1984* where even the nursery rhyme 'Oranges and Lemons' is a distant, and a forbidden, memory.

Karl Popper's great work of social science, *The Open Society and Its Enemies*, was written in New Zealand during the Second World War. Born in Vienna in 1902, Popper had been a teenaged Marxist, but the emergence of the twentieth-century dictatorships filled him with distrust of utopianism. The two chief objects of his opprobrium were Plato, the utopian who had created in his *Republic* a prototype of totalitarian control, and Hegel, the godfather of Marx and Marxism. Popper looked forward to a post-war world in which, with the horrors of fascism behind them, Europeans could build an open society. The open society was not for Popper an alternative Utopia, it was something which was coming anyway: the only alternatives were hateful systems denying freedom.

> The lesson which we . . . should learn from Plato is the exact opposite of what he tries to teach us . . . Arresting political change is not the remedy; it can never bring happiness. We can never return to the alleged innocence and beauty of the closed society. Our dream of heaven cannot be realized on earth. Once we begin to rely upon our reason, and to use our power of criticism, once we feel the call of personal responsibilities, and with it, the responsibility of helping to advance knowledge we cannot return to a state of implicit submission to tribal magic.[8]

Popper was the prophet of our times, one of the most influential, not least because he was one of the most intelligible, philosophers. The structures of British society were not utopian artificial constructs such as Marxian or fascist societies were, but they were *closed*. They were hemmed in by the same shared tribal magic. Indeed, tribal magic was one of the things which strengthen closed societies and have no place in open ones.

One of Popper's contentions in his philosophy was that problems are never solved without producing more problems. The economic freedom of an open society necessitated our making a collective decision: how should a society protect the victims of a free market? Popper's answer was, broadly, social democracy: the ordering of society on more egalitarian or at least protective lines.

As well as being a social scientist of far-reaching influence, Popper was also the foremost philosopher of science in our times. What he himself found problematic, and which his critics found incoherent in his work, was in his theory of moral value. How could an open society embrace the future and abandon the tribal magic without losing a shared common set of values? Did not an open society ineluctably suggest that values should be or become relative?

Popper recognised the human need for a bit of tribal magic but could see it passing away. He found it helpful to divide his lucubrations about the nature of things into three worlds. World 1 was the world of physical objects, material things. World 2 was the world of the individual mind, the subjective world. What interested Popper the social scientist was World 3, the world of shared constructs, not necessarily *conscious* constructs, by which creatures lived together – spiders' webs, bees' hives, and in the human case, science, mathematics, music, art, ethical values. One might add religion, though Popper, like many thinkers of our times, had no time for religion.

Popper was influential but not so influential as to be responsible for the development of the open society in Britain. He analysed with percipience something which was inevitably going to happen, and proposed ways forward which were not original to himself. Closed societies, monist societies, aspired to, or actually possessed, rules which were accepted by the majority. Closed society rules seem to members of an open society intolerably narrow and harsh, as was seen in the later days of our times when open society people contemplated the world-view of their comparatively recent ancestors: or of closed societies within their midst, ostracising women taken in adultery, persecuting homosexuals, chastising children, or asserting the superiority of their own race or creed. These things, all natural or innocent in a closed society, became abhorrent to an open society as it discovered its limits.

This book is the story of how Britain had been a closed society and became an open one. The tribal magic which C. S. Lewis loved was something he could already see vanishing in 1954, just as Tolkien could see in his mythologies that the generation old enough to have fought in the First World War had witnessed its own version of a Twilight of the Gods.

It is more agreeable to live in an open society than in a closed one, just as it is more agreeable to live in a rich society than a poor one. It would be unnecessary to write such platitudes were it not for the fact that the greater the growth of liberty in the West and the greater the prosperity, the more troubled some people became. Marxists and ex-Marxists naturally felt aggrieved and looked around for examples – there were plenty to hand – of capitalism which had become corrupt, or which was helping to cut links with the past – while ignoring capitalism's innate tendency to make the majority of people richer. Religious people of almost all persuasions were troubled by the open society which questioned and doubted so many of its old certainties in the ethical sphere. Nostalgia – for old forms, old ceremony, old ways, old songs, old stories – what Tolkien embodied in *The Lord of the Rings* and Lewis saw embodied in Old Western Man – was justified, for there was never a period in history when the past, in the form, for example, of buildings and townscapes, in the form of marriage – and sexual – conventions, in the form of ethnic cohesion, was more swiftly and irrevocably swept away.

Britain as a political entity survived in this period, but it was to be less 'British'. Mass immigration, the injection of American culture, membership of the European Union were only three factors which warred on the sense of national identity. This sense of coming adrift from their moorings led many Britons to forms of collective mental pessimism: to a belief that overconsumption or overuse of earth's natural resources was leading to environmental disaster, for instance, or to a belief that the country had been swallowed up by America, by foreigners, by threats of various kinds. Many of these fears were not illogical in themselves, merely in the intensity with which they touched nerves, set off in the midst of demonstrable security and prosperity the sense that society was breaking up, that Britain was doomed.

Yet by 1986, Popper could conclude the postscript to the reissue of his autobiography, *Unended Quest*, by stating:

> Anyone who is prepared to compare seriously our life in our Western liberal democracies with life in other societies will be forced to agree that we have in Europe and North America, in Australia and New Zealand the best and most equitable societies that have ever existed in the whole course of human history.[9]

What was it, then, which convinced so many British men and women that the truth was otherwise – that there was more 'truth' in the pessimism of *The Lord of the Rings* than in the common-sense optimism of Popper? What were they nostalgic for? A. J. P. Taylor had perkily asserted that England had risen. What made so many of its inhabitants feel that it had sunk again? Whether the following pages find an answer, the phenomenon of a national malaise remained central to the British – perhaps to the Western – psyche throughout our times, as if, during a meal where everyone is eating, drinking and making merry, a sudden silence descends and a feeling grips the company without any obvious justification that *all is not well*.

2

Space and Spies

At a reception at the Soviet Embassy in Washington, DC, on 4 October 1957, an usher handed an urgent message to Walter Sullivan of the *New York Times*. He was to telephone his office. When he came back from the telephone, he pressed excitedly through the throng, to reveal to his fellow scientist, and fellow American, Richard Porter, the news – 'It's up!'[1]

He was referring to Sputnik, the polished aluminium sphere, no bigger than a basketball, which the Soviets had projected into orbit from the Baikonur Cosmodrome in Kazakhstan on 2 October. The sphere was now circumnavigating the planet at 18,000 mph, in an elliptical orbit which brought it to within 155 miles of the earth's surface at some points, and 500 miles at others.

Only in the nineteenth century, when European mankind abandoned the idea of a personal God or a visitable heaven, did the moon change its status. In all previous generations of human history, the moon had been a symbol, sometimes a goddess. Selene, the Greek moon, was a divinity who drove a chariot, and her love of Endymion, sung by John Keats, was the sign and type of the awakening of human imagination. The moon goddess was sometimes identified with Artemis or Diana the huntress. She controlled the fortunes of her votaries. She was mysterious, changing and changeable, and in some mythologies the actual cause of mutability itself. The Greeks had begun each year after the first appearance of the new moon at the summer solstice. The Romans divided the year into lunar months. Only in the prosaic industrial age of nineteenth-century capitalism did the moon cease to be a symbol of human dependency upon fate or the gods and become yet another territory to colonise, yet another problem for science to solve.

In 1865 Jules Verne had published his fantasy *From the Earth to the Moon*, in which the passengers on this space journey are shot by a giant cannon. It was in the post–Second World War world that Verne's fantasy seemed to be realisable. Vostok [the East] 1 was the first successful scheme for launching a man into space. It was in 1961 that the first man went into space – once again from Baikonur. Colonel Yuri Alexeyevich Gagarin, aged twenty-seven, was strapped into a tiny capsule 2.6 metres in diameter. He orbited the earth once, doing the trip in 1 hour 48 minutes. Of classically proportioned good looks, Gagarin was a hero not only in his own country but throughout the Western world, especially among the anti-American British young. His clean-shaven face, blown up to poster size, adorned the bedroom of many a teenaged suburban British girl. When his spacecraft landed, and he emerged in a potato field near Engels, he met an old peasant woman. This figure from the novels of a pre-revolutionary rural past was probably an old Orthodox *babushka* who believed that she was seeing an angel, but she allegedly framed her questions in science fiction terms:

> Peasant: Have you come from outer space?
> Gagarin: Just imagine it! I certainly have.
> Peasant: I was a bit scared. The man's clothes were strange and he just appeared out of the blue. Then I saw him smile, and his smile was so good that I forgot that I was scared.[2]

Whatever scientific purposes the space mission had supposedly fulfilled, its political significance was lost on no one. Before he set out, Colonel Gagarin had said, 'To be the first to do what generations have dreamed of, the first to blaze man's trail to the stars – name a task more complex than the one I am facing. I am not responsible to one man, or only to a score of people, or merely to all my colleagues. I am responsible to all of the Soviet people, to all mankind, to its present, to its future. And if in the face of all I am still ready for this mission, it is only because I am a Communist, inspired by the examples of unsurpassed heroism of my countrymen – the Soviet people.' His successful return vindicated not only him, as a hero, but the whole political system which underpinned it. Such was the success of Soviet suppression of information that it was universally supposed, both within and without the Iron Curtain countries, that Gagarin's triumph had come as a result of steady progress unmarred by disaster. There were in fact dozens of calamities. In October 1960, for example, when safety regulations were ignored trying to get a huge R-16 rocket to ignite, an explosion killed more than one hundred technicians, as well as Field Marshal Nedelin, but no one was informed. It was in fact the accident rate which eventually slowed down the pace of Soviet progress in space research and allowed the Americans to race ahead. In the first stages, however, in the 1950s, the ability to cover up mistakes was a help in the propaganda war, which the Americans appeared to be losing. And the comparative poverty of the Russians helped in the initial stages because they were compelled by necessity to keep their designs and equipment simple. Sergei Korolev, the great Soviet space scientist, used stainless steel, not aluminium or titanium, to build spaceships. They were fuelled by kerosene and liquid oxygen. They had to be small, and they were set simple objectives.

Like the Russians, the Americans from the first saw the space race as a political race for dominance. Whereas the old myth had the moon chasing a human being, and filling him with poetic imagination and dreams, the new myth saw man chasing the moon, overpowering the virgin huntress and enlisting her in the ideological battle between dialectical materialism and market capitalism, between Lenin and Abraham Lincoln, between a state which claimed possession of an individual's mind, while promising to nourish his or her body from cradle to the grave; and a state which proclaimed liberty but allowed the poor to die without health care or education, and which still permitted outright discrimination on grounds of race.

Speaking to a Joint Session of Congress on 25 May 1961, the new young President of the United States, John F. Kennedy, announced, 'I believe this nation should commit itself to achieving the goal, before this decade is out, of landing a man on the Moon and returning him safely to earth. No single space project in this period will be more impressive to mankind or more important for the long range exploration of space; and none will be so difficult or so expensive to accomplish.'[3]

Perhaps the most important word in Kennedy's second sentence was 'expensive'. The space race would become a chance for the Americans to bust the Soviets at the poker table. For the early 1960s, the two great monster powers were neck and neck in the space race. Trying to match the triumph of Colonel Gagarin, NASA sent Enos into space, the super-chimp who was representing the Americans, followed shortly thereafter by John Glenn, the first American human being to make the journey. In 1962, Scott Carpenter made three orbits, only to be trumped in 1963 by the daughter of a Russian tractor driver, Valentina Tereshkova, who became not only the first woman to have travelled in space but also to have notched up more hours in space in one journey in her craft, Vostok 6, than all the Americans had accomplished in the whole Mercury Programme, which had just been completed. This people's heroine did no fewer than forty-eight orbits in one trip. By 1965, however, the Americans were beginning to pull ahead, achieving longest times in space, and longest distances traversed. It was the Russians who produced the first pictures of the lunar surface, on 3 February 1966, prompting the Americans to speed up their Apollo Mission, the project actually to land on the moon. Apollo 1 in 1967 was a disaster, in which astronauts Edward White, Virgil Grissom and Roger Chaffee were incinerated. But then the Russian spaceship Soyuz [Union] suffered a comparable disaster, and a propaganda setback occurred in 1968 when, aged thirty-four, Yuri Gagarin was killed in a plane crash. By 1969, the crew of Apollo 11 was chosen: Neil Armstrong, Buzz Aldrin and Michael Collins. Apollo 10 was the dress rehearsal, which orbited the moon. In the mission of Apollo 11, from 16 to 24 July 1969, Columbia's CSMS Eagle flew for 8 days, 3 hours, 18 minutes and 35 seconds. It landed on the moon. On the day it did so, a bunch of flowers appeared on John F. Kennedy's grave in Arlington Cemetery, bearing the inscription, 'Mr President, the Eagle has landed'.[4]

At 9.56:20 Houston Daylight Time, on 20 July 1969, the thirty-eight-year-old Neil Alden Armstrong from Wapakoneta, Ohio, dropped back on to the footpad of his spacecraft and lifted his left foot backwards to test the lunar soil, making furrows in the dust with the toe of his boot. Selene, Phoebe, the inviolable goddess, had been violated. Rather like spirits who, when communicating from the other side through a medium, seem capable of expressing themselves only in banalities, Neil Armstrong said, 'That's one small step for [a] man, one giant leap for mankind.' Then Armstrong held the staff while Buzz Aldrin thrust the national flag of the United States into the surface of the moon to consummate the primary goal of the Apollo Program, the assertion of American dominance not merely of the earth but of the universe.[5]

The British never had the resources to be able to compete in such a momentous race. Britain was actually the fifth nation to put a satellite into polar orbit – the Prospero, which was launched in 1971. The Ministry of Defence gave it just £9 million. Its launcher, the Black Arrow, was distantly modelled on the V2 rockets which had rained down on London in 1944. Hydrogen peroxide, water with another oxygen atom added, will, when heated sufficiently, produce a magnificently inflammable gas. Engineers at the Royal Aircraft Establishment worked out that a three-stage rocket, based on the Black Knight rocket, could launch a satellite weighing up to 100kg into a 300-mile orbit. After two test launches and one failure, they succeeded in launching Prospero in 1971 from the Woomera Range in Australia. The satellite was to have been named Puck who, in Shakespeare, 'Put a girdle round the earth in forty minutes' but the aerospace minister Frederick Corfield did not trust himself to get the name right when announcing this British technological triumph to the House of Commons. It was renamed Prospero.

The clumsy gesture of American spacemen in helmets jabbing a flag-pole into the moon dust must have reminded many British television viewers of their own Victorian past. Just such gestures had been made one hundred years earlier, in unlikely and remote places in Africa and Asia, establishing the British dominance not only of territory but of the spirit of the times. In our times, Britain was reminded of her place.

A great intellectual and spiritual battle was in progress for the soul of the planet. As well as being the natural policeman and administrator of the world, Britain had been accustomed to thinking that it was the world's natural moral arbiter. The Second World War had only confirmed this British self-perception. Had not Britain 'stood alone' against the darkness, when the Soviet Union had briefly allied itself to Hitler and the United States had hedged its bets before entering the conflict? British values, British decency, British fair play had 'beaten' the vile doctrines of the National Socialists. The British continued to glorify the early years of the Second World War, when these simplified views of things could be seen to be, roughly speaking, true, and to play down the implications of the later years of the war, when Churchill was beginning to lose his grip, when the Americans and the Russians accomplished the business not only of beating Germany, but of bankrupting Britain and dismantling the Indian Empire as part of a condition of winning the war.

When the two giants themselves began the Cold War in the immediate post-war years, Britain was a little out of things. Of course, technically speaking, the British government and the British Foreign Office, whether the government was Attlee and his Labour Party, or Churchill and Eden with the Conservatives, was an ally of the Americans. But the metaphor of the space race was a powerful reminder of the fact that Britain could no longer afford to take part. And Suez heightened the sense Britain felt, not only that it was out of the running, but that perhaps America was not, after all, quite such a friend and ally as everyone had supposed in the days only a decade earlier, when Churchill, flown with the Victorian poet's vision, gazed across the Atlantic with the words, ' Westward, Look, the Land is bright!'

The British could not afford spaceships and rockets. The Union flag was never going to be planted on the moon, but in the ideological conflict between big clumsy market-led democracy and big brutal Marxist-Leninism, a certain breed of British could indulge in skills which they had perfected at their public schools: double-think, lying and treachery.

The double-think is especially important if we are to understand the spies, and the creepy-silly-undeveloped-schoolboy world they inhabited. The British government during the Second World War was for many British people an ideal. At the head of it was a Victorian aristocrat who was politically *sui generis*, who had belonged to two major political parties and been at home in neither, and who symbolised greatness, self-confidence and humour. But this great Churchill had presided over a government which was effectively Soviet in the degree of control which it had exercised over the people. For the first time since the Industrial Revolution, Britain had seen a fair distribution of food, through the ration systems. While the middle classes howled about powdered eggs, the working classes, for the first time, had protein and vitamins in their diet. Schooling and medicine, even before the Attlee revolution post-1945, had been planned for all the people along socialist lines. To these experiences of home-grown socialism must be added the military fact that, after Russia had been invaded by the Germans, the Red Army became Britain's greatest ally. The Red Army, just as much as Eisenhower's US forces, saved Europe from the Nazis. That was how a majority of British, taught by newsreels, saw things. There was therefore every reason for double-think about the Soviet–American Cold War.

In John le Carré's incomparable novels about espionage during the period, there is captured something more: the resentment at the loss of British power in the world fed into a hatred of America, which derived real satisfaction from the notion of joining forces with the only power in the world which could at that date plausibly challenge the military muscle and political influence of Washington.

In May 1951, the cover was blown on two British diplomats in the embassy at Washington – Guy Burgess and Donald Maclean. Burgess, an outrageous, boozy homosexual, and the snooty heterosexual Maclean both had many friends in London society. They were clubmen, diners out, known to 'everyone'. They had been recruited as Soviet agents when they were still undergraduates at Cambridge. Goronwy Rees, an Oxford academic who was involved heavily in the world of espionage (probably only as a spy for the West, rather than as a double agent), remembered a conversation with the Director of the Courtauld Institute of Art and Surveyor of the Queen's Pictures. This learned art historian believed that Burgess had been swayed by 'his violent anti-Americanism, his certainty that America would involve us all in a Third World War'. Burgess, according to the Courtauld director, was 'the Cambridge liberal conscience at its very best, reasonable, sensible, and firm in the faith that personal relations are the highest of all values'.[6]

The man who delivered this judgement to Goronwy Rees, sitting by the river bank near Oxford, was Anthony Blunt, himself a Soviet agent, whose cover was blown in 1964, but who was not publicly exposed, stripped of his knighthood and hounded by the press until November 1979, shortly after Margaret Thatcher became Prime Minister. By then Britain was a very different place and its relations with the rest of the world had altered considerably. In the 1950s, however, the exposure of the spies, educated at public schools and Cambridge, made a humiliating dent in the way Britons perceived themselves. The officer class had been vilified and hated by class warriors since the time of the First World War, but both world wars had created a sense of comradeship across the classes – something which was extended to some degree by the continuation of conscription to National Service for all British males aged eighteen and over. The defection of Burgess and Maclean, and the gossip, turning to common knowledge, that the Foreign Office and the Intelligence Services had been riddled with traitors, created a profound unease. Far from wishing to perpetuate their position of duty and privilege as the governing class, these public school boys had been engaged since the 1930s in passing secrets to the Russians. Many agents died in the field because of the treachery of Burgess and Maclean, and probably thanks to the activities of Kim Philby, a drunken journalist who joined his comrades in exile in Moscow in 1963. Blunt does not seem to have been personally responsible for any deaths. But the existence of the spies, and their class, gave the (accurate) impression that as it began to rot and die, the old Britain was actually corrupt at its centre. Just as Churchill himself as Prime Minister began to look and sound like a dissipated old soak, so, much further down the hierarchy of things, there were these men who used all their intelligence and skill to undermine, to destroy, to dissipate British strength. Their actual crimes, thrilling enough for lovers of espionage adventures, represented only a part of what made them disconcerting. Burgess, Blunt, Philby, Maclean and their army of less famous and distinguished traitors were not merely criminals. They were emblems of a national disease. Malcolm Muggeridge, who had himself worked in Intelligence, and who was no stranger to alcohol, described a drunken evening in Guy Burgess's flat at which were present, 'John Strachey, J. D. Bernal, Anthony Blunt, Guy Burgess, a whole revolutionary *Who's Who* . . . There was not so much a conspiracy around [Burgess] as just decay and dissolution. It was the end of a class, of a way of life; something that would be written in history books, like Gibbon on Heliogabalus, with wonder and perhaps hilarity, but still tinged with sadness as all endings are.'[7]

The ambivalence of the intellectual and academic classes about the Soviet Union is one of the most extraordinary features of the age. Those in Britain who had misguidedly supported the Italian or Spanish Fascists in the 1930s were well advised to keep the matter dark; and those who had expressed any sympathy with Hitler, even in the 1930s, long before any implementation either of war or genocide, remained social outcasts forever. Diana Mosley, for example, who had had conversations with Hitler before the war, and who refused in after times to deny that she had enjoyed them, was regarded as an embodiment of evil in most sections of the British press, even though in her autobiography, *A Life of Contrasts*, she made clear that she deplored the acts of war, and the extermination camps. Eric Hobsbawm, who joined the Communist Party while at King's College, Cambridge, in 1936–39, and was friends with Philby, Burgess and Maclean, merely said that the massacres perpetrated by Stalin were 'excessive'. Asked on Radio 4's *Desert Island Discs* in 1995 whether he thought the chance of bringing about a communist Utopia was worth any sacrifice, he said, 'Yes'. Even the sacrifice of millions of lives? 'That's what we felt when we fought the Second World War' was his reply. He was rewarded with professorial chairs of History at Birkbeck College, London, and at Cambridge and, in 1998, with the Companion of Honour. Far from being regarded as a malign intellectual eccentric, Hobsbawm was fawned upon by the London dinner-party circuit. His book *The Age of Revolution* was published by the bon vivant networker George Weidenfeld. His fellow academics, even if not themselves Marxists, could share the view of the Warden of Goldsmiths College, Ben Pimlott, that Hobsbawm 'thinks on a grand scale'. Dispassionate readers might ask in what sense the word 'think' is being used in such a sentence. 'We knew of the Volga famine in the early '20s,' Hobsbawn admitted, 'if not the early '30s. Thanks to the breakdown of the West, we had the illusion that even this brutal, experimental system was going to work better than the west. It was that or nothing.' When the Soviet Union collapsed, with all its secret police, its prison camps, its systematic intimidation and torture and suppression of free speech, Hobsbawm saw it as 'an unbelievable social and economic tragedy'.[8]

The treason of the spies was to be explained in part by youthful enthusiasm for a cause, in part (certainly for Burgess) by sheer anarchic malice. But the treason of the clerks – the treason of the academics – had a much more profound effect. They persisted in blinding themselves to the essential violence on which Marxist regimes had always established, and maintained power. Decades before the Hungarian Uprising of 1956, the nature of Leninism and Stalinism had been made clear. As long ago as 1923, the simplicity of it all had been explained by Bertie Wooster, when his friend Bingo Little dallies with a group known as the Red Dawn. 'Do you yearn for Revolution?' one of them asks Bertie. 'Well, I don't know that I exactly yearn. I mean to say, as far as I can make out, the whole nub of the scheme seems to be to massacre coves like me; and I don't mind owning I'm not frightfully keen on the idea.'[9] In February 2008 the MP Diane Abbott expressed the view on television that some people thought Mao had 'done more good than bad'. Rod Liddle remarked in the *Sunday Times*, 'There are two possible explanations for this. The first, and kindest, is that Ms Abbott is pig-ignorant. The second is that she is perfectly well aware of the millions upon millions of people Mao starved to death during his "Great Leap Forward" and the millions more who were killed or had their lives destroyed by his cultural revolution – but thinks that, by and large, these are trivialities, mere footnotes to history.'[10] Long after the collapse of the Soviet Union, and the death of

Mao Tse-tung in China, the most brutal forms of communism found their defenders in the university lecture halls of Britain. Like a headless chicken still capable of running round the yard, socialism enjoyed an afterlife in intellectual and academic circles when it had ceased to have any plausibility in the world of practical politics. It did much harm.

The Peter Simple column in the *Daily Telegraph* was one place where the antics of the fellow-travellers were treated with the angry derision they deserved. It was begun by Colin Welch in 1955. Welch was one of the many brilliant people of our times who chose to be a journalist. Steeped in European (especially German) literature and music, intellectually serious, emotionally chaotic, in earlier ages he would in all likelihood have been a don. He was partly a journalist as a gesture of opposition to the follies of the age. The same was true of Malcolm Muggeridge, his predecessor as deputy editor at the *Telegraph*, or Peregrine Worsthorne, another brilliant polemicist. Both Welch and Worsthorne were guided by the philosophy of Michael Oakeshott (1901–90), arguably the greatest British political philosopher of the twentieth century. Oakeshott stood in opposition not only to socialism, but to the unthinking commitment to 'the Enlightenment' from which socialism sprang – as his obituarist put it, 'the whole post-Enlightenment style of thought, according to which everything can be understood quasi-scientifically, and reduced to a set of clear-cut "problems" to which there must exist equally clear-cut solutions'. He once said, 'I am a member of no political party. I vote – if I have to vote – for the party which is likely to do the least harm. To that extent I am a Tory.' A fellow of Caius College, Cambridge, he became professor at the London School of Economics, in succession to the socialist Harold Laski, in 1951. 'When Oakeshott left Cambridge for Laski's chair at LSE, Laski's students were appalled. They listened with horror to his inaugural lecture which told them their hopes of a better world were false and their guides wiseacres.' Upon his retirement, he lived in a tiny cottage in Dorset, without heating; but he was no ascetic, enjoying wine, women and chain-smoking. His friend Worsthorne was influenced by his bohemianism as well as by his luminosity of thought. While professor at LSE, Oakeshott was the lodger of Perry Worsthorne and his beautiful French wife Claudie at Cardinal's Wharf, a rickety, elegant little house reputed to have been the residence of Christopher Wren when he was designing St Paul's. It is on Bankside and looks across the river directly to the cathedral. 'My only regret about Michael as a lodger was that I could never get him to talk about "Conservatism" in which I was supposed to be interested. "Leave talking about politics to the Left," he used to say. "They have nothing better to do." Yet in his way he was a guru. No piece of writing has ever influenced me as much as his famous essay Rationalism in Politics. By comparison, all the other political writers of the time – Laski, Cole, Bertrand Russell, not to say Marx – seemed vulgar and commonplace, not to say stuffy and pretentious.'[11]

It was to puncture this pretentiousness that 'Peter Simple' devoted himself. Colin Welch handed on the column in 1957 to Michael Wharton, a saturnine figure destined for legendary status in Fleet Street. Half his ancestors came from the gritty weaving towns of Yorkshire and the other half from the Jewish ghettoes of Russia. Wharton had a circle of wits to help him with the column – including Claudie Worsthorne, Dick West, Roy Kerridge, and his wife, Kate, whom in a bizarre manner he lost to Colin Welch, while remaining Welch's closest friend. No one could say that these upholders of Toryism in a vapid socialist world were great exemplars of bourgeois marital habits.

Wharton continued writing his Peter Simple columns over four decades, filing his last piece of copy shortly before his ninety-second birthday. The column was a mixture of comment and fantasy, peopled with a gallery of characters all too recognisable in the Britain of Macmillan, Heath, Harold Wilson and John Major. Many of them inhabit a bleak-sounding town, or, rather, conurbation, called Stretchford. Other towns in the Wharton world were the northern Soup Hales and Nerdley. Dr Spacely-Trellis, the go-ahead Bishop of Bevindon, or Dr Ellis Goth-Jones, the popular Medical Officer of Health for Stretchford, or Julian Birdbath the Man of Letters, were slightly more than mere types: they had a zany, Swiftian life of their own, and the humour of the columns was cumulative. Wharton's alternative universe – he often wrote as if he was inhabiting the Middle European domains of some Prince Bishop of the Holy Roman Empire – both did and did not resemble our own. His distaste for the objects of his satire never let up, nor did his inventiveness. One of his finest creations was undoubtedly Mrs Dutt-Pauker of Hampstead.

'I have hated Hampstead for her Left-wingery, but I have loved her for her strange, leafy soul. Nowhere in London are green thoughts so green, especially in a rainy June, when the grass grows high in her innumerable gardens tame and wild.' It is here that the walker comes across Mrs Dutt-Pauker's Queen Anne house, Marxmount. Wharton believed that near this house, in a densely wooded part of the Heath, was to be found 'a tribe of Left wing pygmies of cannibal habits and strong views on racial integration'.

'That would be the among the least of the perils I might have to face as I pushed on through the dense foliage or paused to eat my bread and cheese by some gay flowerbed, watched by indignant progressive eyes from a book-lined study or seized and dragged indoors to take part in a discussion on comprehensive education and the need for Socialist play-groups.'[12] One of the strangest things about the Britain of the last half-century was that, while socialist politicians vanished from the world stage in the 1980s, and from the House of Commons in the 1990s, Mrs Dutt-Pauker remained a perennial figure in British life, to be met, even in the twenty-first century, whenever there was a meeting of PEN or Amnesty International, and even to be heard occasionally on the political panel discussions on TV and radio. Though intellectually discredited, she was still welcome at college guest nights at Newnham and Somerville, her views less shakeable than the concrete walls and barbed-wire encampments erected by her heroes to enslave the human race.

This chapter's related themes, of the exploration of space and the British sympathisers with Soviet Communism, were to colour the following decades, which is why they have been treated here in a broad way, carrying us beyond the chronological sequence which will follow. The spies, and their friends in the academic and literary world, made little secret of their hostility to the country, and culture, which had given them birth. They hated Britain, as a political entity, and sided with its enemies. At the same time, they were often conservative in everything except their politics. Alan Bennett was to capture this paradox in his play about Guy Burgess, *An Englishman Abroad*, in which Guy Burgess, living in exile, persuades a visiting actress, Coral Browne, to order a suit for him at his Jermyn Street tailors when she returns to London. It is a charming play – beguilingly subversive. Browne manages to get Burgess's shoes copied from his shoemaker's last in St James's Street, and his suit made by the tailor. But she has difficulty in a different shop when she tries to order him pyjamas in the style he had always favoured.

The shop assistant refuses, and, as the stage direction says, 'Her Australian accent gets now more pronounced as she gets crosser' . . . 'You were happy to satisfy this client when he was one of the most notorious buggers in London and a drunkard into the bargain . . . But not any more. Oh, no. Because the gentleman in question has shown himself to have some principles, which aren't yours, and, as a matter of interest, aren't mine. But that's it, as far as you're concerned. No more jamas for him.'[13]

It is an electrifying moment dramatically, and a good deal less cloying than E. M. Forster's notorious claim that if forced to choose between betraying his friends and betraying his country, he hoped he would have the guts to betray his country. Plays do not have to state every point of view, so the audience can both savour the drama and notice the unfairness of Coral Browne/Alan Bennett's arguments. They don't allow for the possibility that the shop assistant's refusal to send comfortable and expensive pyjamas to a traitor could have been actually based not upon stuffiness, but upon principles of his own. Would Coral Browne, or Alan Bennett, have felt differently (if only slightly differently) about sending pyjamas to, let us say, Lord Haw Haw in prison? Or to Ribbentrop, who probably also shopped, when Ambassador in London, at the same Jermyn Street tailors and outfitters as had been patronised by Burgess? We are not told. But, as Bennett himself made plain, both in the play and in the Preface written in 1989, the issue was odder than that. 'I have put some of my own sentiments into Burgess's mouth. "I can say I love London. I can say I love England. I can't say I love my country, because I don't know what that means", is a fair statement of my own, and I imagine many people's positions.'[14] As a matter of observable fact, Alan Bennett was completely right. This was 'many people's positions', the more so as our times progressed. It was always easy, at any stage of the period, to notice extreme cases of alienation, whether it was the Cambridge-educated spies at the beginning of the 1950s or the Yorkshire-born Muslim terrorists of the twenty-first century. But what is striking is that so many other inhabitants of the archipelago felt like strangers here – or should that word be 'there'? By the end of the period, it was not simply political outsiders or immigrants who felt like 'displaced persons': it was part of the very nature of inhabiting these islands. The phrase 'my country' – which would have been perfectly intelligible in the middle of the nineteenth century – became harder to define towards the end of the twentieth. And if that is the case, then the beginnings of this dissolution – the disappearance of what made the phrase 'my country' translatable – had begun to happen in the post-war years. The treason of Guy Burgess and Donald Maclean can be seen in this setting to be symptoms of a generalised confusion rather than overt causes of destruction.

For all the extreme distastefulness of the spies and their attitude to their own country, and their adulation of a system of murder and repression which they wished to spread to the West, they had remarkably little permanent effect on Britain itself. One of the central political paradoxes of our times was encapsulated in this fact. Left-wingery of various colourings might have been considered normal thinking in university common rooms and literary salons. This might have led, and undoubtedly did lead, to many writers and speakers of influence to express unpatriotic sentiments; and it might have led, and undoubtedly did lead, to some disastrous economic policies when a supposedly left-wing government was eventually elected to power in 1963. But in terms of actual infiltration, the Soviet bloc had no influence upon Great Britain at all. Far more wide-ranging changes came to Britain as a result of American, than of Soviet, influence. There is a paradox here, which would see its full flowering in the early twenty-first century among the English 'neo-cons': namely that those British patriots who had supported the United States against the Soviet Union in the Cold War found themselves in a position of commending American influences which did far more than Russia to destroy the old British way of life. The brasher of the 'neo-cons' of later times would come to welcome this fact, and regard the building of Denver- or Pittsburgh-style skyscrapers in small English towns in as favourable a light as the arrival of American hamburger chains to replace the small independent café. But small-c conservatives were less sure. If a prime objection to the spies and the crypto-Reds was that they were trying to undermine what made Britain British, then could not the same accusation be levelled against Britain's greatest friend and ally?

This was one way of putting it. Another way of seeing things would be to suggest that, in the post-war trauma, Britain was undermining itself; it was changing willy-nilly. By this analysis, attempts to 'blame' Soviet agents, or American styles of cheap clothes and food and music, mistake the nature of the case. Neither the KGB, nor the Coca-Cola Company, were to be held responsible for something which was more mysterious, more general, a change which in another culture would have been seen as the will of the Fates, or the movement of History.

3

Other Gods

Britain had been changed completely by the war, but it took some while for the depth and range of the alteration to become apparent. The first and greatest of these changes was the economic one. Britain had gone from being one of the richest nations, not only in the world, but in history, to being a country which was bankrupt. It had great industrial, and fiscal, resources, and with the upturn in the world economy of the 1950s, Britain would gradually recover some of its economic, though never its political, strength. But in the immediate post-war years the stagnation of the economy, greatly exacerbated by the experiment of state socialism and nationalisation, disguised from the British some of the more lasting changes in national life.

Nearly all these changes appeared as benefits, but as each one was eagerly embraced, Britain left behind a little of that *esprit de corps* which had bound society together so remarkably during the war years. By banishing the ways in which they thought about themselves, the British became less of a group, more a collection of individuals. Not for nothing did the old God of the Hebrews tell His people: 'Ye shall not go after other gods, of the gods of the people which are round about you' (Deuteronomy 6: 14). In the 1950s the British hungrily, greedily, went after other gods, who supplied them with food, and sexual imagery and music which they voraciously devoured.

Before exploring this phenomenon, however, we should note a feature which contributed hugely to the slow return of wellbeing which coursed through frozen British veins after the hardships of war and socialist austerity.

Wars have always expedited technological advance. Archimedes invented the catapult for the Greek army – it was first used with devastating effect at the Battle of Syracuse in 265 BC. Chinese alchemists of the Han dynasty pioneered gunpowder because their military leaders were desperate to assert superiority over their enemies. During the Second World War, the numbers of those involved in the conflict, and the intensity of the fighting, meant that the technological advances were proportionately superior. Consider the development of antibiotics. It was when trying to find a way of combating the devastating post-war influenza pandemic of 1919 that Alexander Fleming had first made his discovery of penicillin. The mould which had grown accidentally during one of his laboratory experiments turned out to be lethal to streptococci, gonococci, meningococci and pneumococci. But having made the discovery, in 1928, Fleming never developed it. The penicillin notatum vanished very quickly in laboratory conditions and he had not the where-withal to develop it as a packaged pharmaceutical. It was only during the war, in Oxford, that the Australian Howard Florey and German émigré chemist Ernst Chain, together with Norman Huntley, read Fleming's paper and began to develop the idea of penicillin, testing it on laboratory mice infected with streptococci. When the idea was taken to America, it became possible, after 1944, for penicillin to be produced on a scale to deal with the many infected troops in field hospitals. It was the wonder drug which, as well as curing syphilis and gonorrhoea in a matter of weeks, was to go on to cure millions of patients who would previously have died – of meningitis, pneumonia and other curable diseases.

The existence of antibiotics, and the growth of the pharmaceutical industry, was a vital factor in the increased wellbeing of the post-war world. Another example of the beneficial effects of war on the advance of technology came out of the Manhattan Project, whose prime aim had been to develop nuclear weaponry, for use against – in the event – Japanese civilians. Unforeseen consequences of the research on the Manhattan Project, however, included radiation therapy for the treatment of cancer, as well as the nanotechnology which would, by the close of the twen-tieth century, transform the world – not only with laser surgery but with digital cameras, and advances in computer science which seemed like magic.[1]

Some of this technological revolution took years to develop, but oth-ers – of which antibiotics were the most conspicuous – began to change life from the 1950s onwards. Changes which can be seen with hindsight to be wholly beneficial do not always feel pleasant to the conservatively minded.

While Iris Murdoch wrote her bestsellers about emotional chaotics, and Francis Bacon painted his tormented canvases of deliberately skewed popes and unclothed females, these artworks gave out messages of violence and unrest. These were confusing times. 'Winter kept us warm.' Demobbed soldiers found it hard to adjust to civvie street. Likewise, many British people felt beleaguered, even wondering whether the victories of 1945 had been anything but illusory.

'Remember Magna Carta. Did she die in vain?' The words might have been the motto of these unhappy or bewildered Britons, who saw some-thing of themselves in the man who uttered them – Tony Hancock (1924–68).

With his Homburg hat, melancholic folds of flesh about his jowls and his doggy eyes, Hancock was a comic who reflected an image of Britain, more especially of England, to itself. Hancock, with his series of humiliations and whinges, was an only half-exaggerated version of what many Englishmen now felt about themselves and about their country. Hancock had come down in the world. In the very act of being born, he had managed to run to seed. His parents, Jack and Lily, had run a hotel in Bournemouth. Jack died when Hancock was eleven. A spell at the Berkshire public school Bradfield College, also *alma mater* to the author of *Watership Down*, Richard Adams, added a glimpse of another world which fed Hancock's archetypically English class chippiness. The war intervened when he was seventeen. His career in the RAF led him to Entertainments National Service Association (ENSA) tours, and to acts in the Ralph Reader Gang Shows.

His first peace-time job was at the Windmill Theatre in Soho, whose boast was 'we never closed'. Comedy turns punctuated the naked displays. This work led to contacts with radio producers and sketches on such standbys as *Workers' Playtime* and *Variety Bandbox*. What marked Hancock out was his petulance. His 'character' began to emerge in the series *Educating Archie*, as the tutor to a ventriloquial doll, operated by Peter Brough, called Archie Andrews. 'Flippin' Kids' was his catchphrase. It was in the autumn of 1954 that *Hancock's Half Hour* was given its first radio broadcast, scripted by that inspired pair Ray Galton and Alan Simpson. The show transferred to television in 1956 and was soon being watched by 23 per cent of the adult population.[2]

Galton and Simpson may be said to have invented the low-lit dramas of English *ennui* which John Osborne and Harold Pinter, a few years later, were to make highbrow. Pinter trod comparable territory to that explored first in *Hancock's Half Hour* and in the later incomparable Galton and Simpson series about the aspirations of a young rag and bone merchant living with his manipulative old father, *Steptoe and Son*. Galton and Simpson made Anthony Aloysius Hancock (the actor's real names were Anthony John) live at 23 Railway Cuttings, East Cheam. 'Hancock', his biographer tells us, 'was secretly in awe of Galton and Simpson's acute sense of what was risible about his pretensions' (his winemanship, for example), his hunger for education (encyclopaedias and potted histories of the world formed the basis of his reading) and his not always simulated grandeur of manner.

In the tragi-comic half-hour plays, Hancock was always on his offended dignity, unlike his coarse housemate Sid James, who in real life was cuckolding Hancock. Sid bore an incongruous resemblance to Benjamin Britten, whose operas, the greatest works of music of our times – *Billy Budd*, 1951, *Gloriana*, 1953, *The Turn of the Screw*, 1954 – were contemporaneous with *Hancock's Half Hour*.

Whether he was being a radio ham or a blood donor, or simply musing in 23 Railway Cuttings on the sadness of what might have been, Hancock was programmed, like his country, to failure and self-pity. One of his most touching failures – and it is only just a failure – was the feature film he made – *The Punch and Judy Man* (1962). In the film, his wife's desire to better herself, and the scorn they meet at the hands of the snooty middle-class elders of a seaside town, turns to farce. It is a self-parodying lament for a Britain which was doomed. Now, when we look at Hancock's eternally middle-aged face, even at photographs taken in the early 1950s when he was still young in years, we can see the self-destructive rage which in the summer of 1968 would lead to the overdose of barbiturates washed down with vodka in a Sydney flat. We can feel no surprise that so many of Hancock's contemporaries wanted not merely to change but to obliterate the sad old place which provided the backdrop for such hemmed-in existences.

'Go not after other gods' was not advice which many Britons could be expected to heed when allured by the temptations of Elizabeth David's gastronomic rhapsodies, or the sexual allure of Brigitte Bardot or Marilyn Monroe.

When Elizabeth David (1913–92) began to write her cookery articles for *Harper's Bazaar*, they must have read to many readers like fantasy. (When Ivy Compton-Burnett, a comfortably well-heeled maiden lady sharing her life with the upper-middle-class furniture historian Margaret Jourdain, was given a bottle of champagne at this period, she asked plaintively, 'D'you heat it?'[3]) Elizabeth David wrote of aubergines at a time when such a vegetable was not to be seen outside the more exotic street markets of Soho and the Food Hall of Selfridges where, when in London, she went shopping. She wrote of olive oil when most Britons still bought this commodity in tiny bottles from the chemist. It was for massaging babies and loosening ear wax, not for preparing salad.

Yet for all her sophistication, Elizabeth David was a woman of her time. She recommended the use of Knorr stock cubes, and she never saw the point of coffee: having developed a taste for Nescafé during the war, she 'never wished for anything better'.[4] But she was a revolutionary. She did more good for the British table and the British palate than anyone of the twentieth century. But, rather like her contemporary Lawrence Durrell, whose Alexandria novels enjoyed such a vogue in the fifties before being everlastingly forgotten, they looked always to abroad for their pleasure. Britain, as it discovered some time in the 1980s, partly thanks to the Prince of Wales, had a rich gastronomic tradition which had only been interrupted by the war. A Stilton cheese, or a good Cheddar, rivals any cheese in France. English strawberries or English peaches are as succulent and delicious as anything eaten in Greece to the sound of cicadas. But Elizabeth David showed no consciousness of the fact.

A Book of Mediterranean Food (published in 1950) had been much more than a collection of recipes. It was a manifesto, which on its opening page quoted Michel Boulestin's challenging view that 'It is not really an exaggeration to say that peace and happiness begin, geographically, where garlic is used in cooking.' In a Britain where food was still rationed (tea until 1952), and which in many quarters had all but forgotten how to cook, she evoked the smell and taste of another world – 'the oil, the saffron, the garlic, the pungent local wines; the aromatic perfume of rosemary, wild marjoram and basil . . . the brilliance of the market stalls piled high with pimentos, aubergines, tomatoes, olives, melons, figs . . . the great heaps of shiny fish, silver, vermilion, or tiger-striped, and those long needle fish whose bones mysteriously turn green when they are cooked'.

Her *Italian Food* was chosen by Evelyn Waugh as a favourite book of the year in the *Sunday Times* of 1954.[5] It was one of those books, together with her *French Country Cooking* and *French Provincial Cooking*, which were not merely collections of recipes, but sustained essays upon the delights of food, and evocations of the beautiful, colourful places where the recipes were born. Many copies of these books remained beside the beds of those, such as Evelyn Waugh, who admired their prose and the scents and tastes it evoked. Far more copies, however, were to be found in kitchens. Little by little, their pages would be stained with spatterings of tomato, oil and stock. Even by 1955, she could address the problem of availability in a reissue of *A Book of Mediterranean Food* in Penguin: 'So startlingly different is the food situation now as compared with only two years ago that I think there is scarcely a single ingredient, however exotic, mentioned in this book which cannot be obtained somewhere in this country'[6] . . . Philip Larkin, uncrowned laureate of provincial England, once remarked[7] that he knew the end of England had come when croissants reached Beverley in Yorkshire, though his friend Barbara Pym, whose sad, pinched little novels for and about church spinsters of both sexes he championed and enjoyed, liked to read Elizabeth David in bed. (Her books evoked the duller pleasures of preparing macaroni cheese and baked beans on toast.)

Elizabeth David herself came across in her books more as a voice, and a strongly held point of view, than a character – though we now know, from her biographers, the strengths and vulnerabilities of her personality. She never exploited the emergent medium of television to show off her skills, either as food historian or kitchen performer. Fanny Cradock showed no such diffidence. She took understandable pride in the fact that in 1956, before an audience of 6,500 *Daily Telegraph* readers in the Royal

Albert Hall, the Queen Mother said that she thought the post-war improvement in the standard of British cuisine was the responsibility of Fanny Cradock and her husband, Johnny.[8]

Cradock, who was guyed on the wireless comedy shows *Beyond Our Ken* and *Round the Horne* as Fanny Haddock, was one of those characteristic figures of our age who defied parody and whose own self-projection was far more ridiculous than anything satirists could devise. Her surgically lifted face gave her an expression of everlastingly indignant, frozen amazement, and she had been prepared to undergo plastic surgery on her nose when technicians told her it was 'too big' and was 'casting shadows over the food'. Although she expressed the aim (for which the Queen Mother was to applaud her) 'to make good cookery easy and fun for the post-war generation of housewives, who had grown up during the years of food shortages', there was never much sense – as there was in the televised cookery lessons of the bearded Philip Harben, for example – that viewers were expected actually to try the elaborate recipes, and table settings, upon which Mrs Cradock insisted. The pleasures of her programme, like those of Nigella Lawson in a later era, were voyeuristic rather than gastronomic. Fanny dressed for dinner before cooking it, and hovering at her side was Johnny Cradock, her third husband, a put-upon Old Harrovian who poured, and sometimes commented upon, the wine. Rather as in the case of Gilbert Harding, another television 'personality' of the same era, part of Cradock's appeal was her irascibility. 'I have always been extremely rude, and I have always got exactly what I wanted.'

The Cradocks, their accents and their clothes, were really a species of vaudeville as much as they were apostles of good food. Like their admirer Queen Elizabeth, they appeared to belong to the pre-war world of deference and camp fantasy which the Second World War and the Attlee government had effectively made obsolete. Like those who read Waugh's *Brideshead Revisited* – and even more, those who watched it televised in 1981 – the great majority of fans did not aspire to belong to the grandeur enacted.

Those who did still exist at the top of the social hierarchy could no doubt sniff, through all Fanny Cradock's grand phrases, the mothbally odours of the shabby genteel. The arcane rituals of the Season – presentation of debutantes at Buckingham Palace, Queen Charlotte's Ball, and all its attendant cocktail parties and dinners – continued throughout the post-war years until, in 1958, the Royal Family themselves decided that enough was enough. One thousand four hundred and forty-one debutantes were presented at Buckingham Palace in that last year, but a much smaller number remained in London to 'do' the Season. One of them,

Fiona MacCarthy, who wrote a witty account of the whole matter – *Last Curtsey* – made the telling point that the controlled mating rituals no longer corresponded to any form of reality. This was not how women of the period wished to find husbands. Many had already lost their virginity, and most wanted to do something more interesting with their lives than had been permitted to their mothers. Even if *The Female Eunuch* had yet to be written, 'there was a vociferous debate over the next few years on what it meant to be a woman'.[9]

Not only did the mothers of the debutantes seem to their daughters to be caught in a pointless trap of self-imposed limitations ('The generations of our mothers accepted they were wives and mothers and that was that'[10]), but they were also imprisoned – as their daughters for the most part did not entirely wish to be – by class.

For men, class differences were sometimes ironed out and sometimes exacerbated by National Service. Two years' military service was compulsory from 1947 (the National Service Bill) until 1962.[11] It was the last period in British history when male members of quite different classes were forced to be together. Evelyn Waugh's son Auberon remembered his period of training at Caterham as a time of 'simple physical torture – being made to run, with bursting lungs, round a track, carrying a Bren gun over my head as a form of punishment; after being injected with TAB (anti-typhus vaccine); being drilled in double time for half an hour in pyjamas to the latrine (or shithouse); being screamed at by a drill sergeant in front of the whole battalion for having dirty flesh on parade (a shaving cut) and doubled off the parade ground . . . The only useful lesson I learnt at Caterham concerned the resentment and hatred of large sections of the working class for such as myself.'[12]

There is no reason to doubt his testimony, though not everyone felt inspired by the hatred to devote a lifetime to class warfare. Nicholas Harman, an Etonian, later a journalist on *The Economist*, remembered being told at Caterham, by a Scouser in the barrack room, that he had been talking in his sleep. 'I said, "Really sorry, don't think so," and he said, "Well, it was either you or McGuinness, you both talk funny." Later, in Korea, Harman's platoon sergeant in the Royal Fusiliers, who during the Second World War had been a temporary captain in an Indian regiment, said he liked the British army because you could tell an officer even in the dark by the way he spoke.'[13]

Whether National Service inspired the young men to look forward to a bright future in which all classes could work together, or whether it fostered class resentment, perhaps depended upon the temperaments of those concerned. As a social phenomenon, it neatly mopped up a class of people whom Marx, in *Capital*, termed the lumpenproletariat – rendered in the charming translation of Eden and Cedar Paul 'the tatterdemalion or slum proletariat'. Marx divided the class into three – the able-bodied, the orphans and the pauper children, and the 'demoralized, the degenerate, the unemployable'.[14] In Leninist versions of the Marxist state, these people would find themselves in labour camps, or if possible exterminated. In Britain, throughout the nineteenth century, they had been cruelly dragooned into semi-slavery, either as factory hands or as domestic servants or foot soldiers. If they positively refused to work, they were consigned to the workhouse, and their life expectancy was extremely short, not more than forty years old in many cases.

The 1945 election had changed their position, and when National Service came to an end there would be removed the last disguise used by governments to hide the existence of these people from the rest. The only humane course of action was to pursue the optimistic course that those labelled 'demoralized degenerate and unemployable' by Karl Marx might, in a liberal democracy, be educated to a level where they would soon move on happy and equal terms with the rest. By 2008, after more than half a century of beneficent state education, 30,000 British school children per annum were leaving school with no qualifications at all.[15] In the fifty previous years, the rest of society would have been performing the optimistic and charitable task of sending these people to school, trying to persuade them to eat wholesome food, and extending their lives, in spite of their habits of smoking and drinking, to the point where they would require, along life's path, expensive prisons, hospitals and eventually old folks' care homes specially built for them. No public figure in our times ever quite learnt how to solve this problem, for those whose forebears, in harsher times, had led lives which were nasty, brutish and short. Almost no one in public life, in fact, was impolite enough to see it as a problem at all, though as the ranks of the lumpenproletariat in all senses swelled – becoming both more numerous and more obese – it was not a phenomenon which it was easy to ignore. The kindly minded lawmakers and formers of opinion of the period, not all of them socialists, hoped for some way of improving the lot of everyone in society, and would echo the aspiration of Miss Luke, the schoolmistress in an I. Compton-Burnett novel, who says, 'I have spent my life amongst educated and intelligent people . . . I pay the rightful homage of the highly civilized . . . to those whose lives are spent at the base of civilisation.'[16] There had never been a time in history when everyone else – from the working classes to the classes at the top of the economic scale – had been compelled through decency to live as if the 'unemployable' were just like everyone else. The experiment, or illusion (depending upon viewpoint), would colour the years which followed.

Certainly, after National Service was phased out, and the economic revival made evident the gaps between talents and opportunities, the artificially close social cohesion, which had been an unwonted feature of British life since the beginning of the Second World War, began to come apart.

An early warning signal came with the change in the musical scene. Rock 'n' roll was the expressive African American slang for sexual intercourse. The phrase soon became synonymous with music of a kind never heard before on this planet; music which, when amplified electrically, could be used to numb the senses, to subdue the critical faculties, even to torture non-Western enemies. In the 2002–7 invasion of Iraq, prisoners were tortured by constant exposure to loud rock music, a form of mental blasting which was the recreational physical-cum-mental background noise for a majority of Western young people. In the West, rock 'n' roll, and its various variations and descendants – rock, heavy metal, etc – became the music of the age. Bill Haley and His Comets exemplified the northern band rock 'n' roll which was initially the music's most popular form in England – though Memphis country rock, as popularised by Elvis Presley, would soon overtake it.[17] Having started as an innovation among black working-class American youth, rock music was destined to become the common lingua franca of our times, the noise coming from loudspeakers in every country on the planet. No other form of music has ever had this degree of universality. In every country where rock music became the norm, it drove out indigenous musical forms. It took a mere generation in Ireland, for example, for the extinction of songs which had been learnt over hundreds of years. Once the pied piper's rock muzak had been installed in an Irish bar, just as in a bar in Melbourne or Singapore or Buenos Aires or Swindon, the young would follow it, leaving behind the native tradition, the old stories and songs which had been inside the heads of their forefathers. Although fans of rock music do know the lyrics of their favourite numbers, they can never in their own, unamplified persons ever hope to reproduce the sound exactly. In all previous generations of the human race, music was collective and it was an activity. If you went to the pub or the music hall, you sang. You joined in. Rock music was the first purely passive musical form. It was something which happened to you. You gyrated and shook to it, as to the shamanic summons of a witch-doctor, but you could not exactly sing along to it. You were not part of the music, as you might when singing 'My Old Man Said Follow the Van' around the pub piano. You were the music's victim. And this was designedly so, since the 1950s was the first decade in which children and adolescents – now for the first time in history given the name of teenagers – had any money.

Previously, boys and girls of sixteen dressed as their parents dressed, and danced to the same music. Now, for anyone who chose to make money out of them, they could be offered special young persons' clothes, young persons' music.

Just as Elizabeth David tempted English palates with Mediterranean food, and English ears accustomed themselves to American music, so British sex symbols were required not to be attractive in themselves, so much as to be 'the British answer to Marilyn Monroe' – sometimes to Brigitte Bardot.

Diana Mary Fluck was born in the railway town of Swindon in 1931. As a teenager she had dated Desmond Morris, also from Swindon and later famous as the author of *The Naked Ape*, a zoologist and anthropologist. Her name was so obviously in danger of mispronunciation that she changed it to Diana Dors. After she became famous, she agreed to open a church fete in her native town. The vicar of Swindon, in his desperation to avoid just such a mispronunciation, was guided by a malign misfortune to avoid the wrong obscenity. 'Ladies and gentlemen, it is with great pleasure that I introduce to you our star guest. We all love her, especially as she is our local girl. I therefore feel it right to introduce her by her real name: Ladies and Gentlemen, please welcome the very lovely Miss Diana Clunt.'[18]

Her many films, and her occasional ventures into print, did not suggest coyness about sex. Films included *Good Time Girl* (1948), *Lady Godiva Rides Again* (1951), *Yield to the Night* (1956), *The Love Specialist* (1956) and many others, teetering off beyond the borders of suggestiveness with *Adventures of a Taxi Driver* and *Keep It Up Downstairs*.

What was striking about her was not her name, but the notion that in this era of history a rising English sex bomb had to model herself on foreigners. 'Things were complicated', she wrote in *For Adults Only*, 'as we all seemed to have double initials, such as B.B., in her [Brigitte Bardot's] case, D.D. in mine, M.M. as in Marilyn Monroe herself.'[19] It was Dors's misfortune to lack the smallest scintilla of Bardot's or Monroe's sex appeal. In spite of having dyed her hair blonde, and in spite of preparedness to show off enormous breasts, she had a coarse, puddingy face and no acting ability. 'Since I left school at thirteen I have been working for a certain standard of living' also seemed a spectacularly unsexy and joyless approach to stardom. 'Once I'd got it, I saw no reason to give it all up. Luxury is comfortable, it's good for you, it's luxurious.'[20]

Just as Swindon-born sex symbols now had to take their cue from Hollywood, so religious revival itself, were it ever to occur in the godless, post-war atmosphere of Britain, came from across the Atlantic. When Billy Graham came over to Britain in 1954, he addressed the largest religious congregation yet seen in the British Isles: 120,000 people, crowded into the Wembley Arena. For the previous three months, Billy Graham had conducted what amounted to a missionary campaign to convert England to a completely un-English form of religion. Although it was always his policy to advise converts to seek out the church of their own background, whether Methodist, Church of England or Roman Catholic, rather than enlisting them as recruits in his own Baptist Church, Billy's 1954 mission had an aim which went beyond the desire for the personal conversion of the sinner. He wanted England to become part of a universal religious resistance to the threats of world communism. He wanted England to become more like the middle- and working-class America which were the most fructiferous areas of Graham's vineyard. 'There will always be an England. But will it always be the England we have known?' he asked. 'The England of history has been an England whose life, both national and individual, was ever centred upon the things of God.'[21]

While there were some reasons for supporting this suggestion – the fact that the world had only the previous year witnessed an ancient coronation ceremony in which the young Queen was anointed with the oil of chrism by the former headmaster of Repton, the Archbishop of Canterbury, Geoffrey Fisher; the fact that bishops sat *ex officio* as members of the Upper House of Parliament; the fact that so many English schools were of a specifically religious foundation – it would be hard, since the 1689 Whig Revolution, to match Billy's words to the England of John Locke, of the four Georges, of Dickens, John Stuart Mill and Disraeli, of Marie Lloyd and Tony Hancock. Naturally, some inhabitants of these islands, once evangelised by the Celtic saints and later by Benedictine monks, had centred themselves upon 'the things of God'. But while individuals – including some of the individuals named above – were so centred, there remained a bedrock of British indifferentism, not merely in religion, but also in music: had not a German visitor deemed it *Das Land ohne Musik*? It was not a place where you wore your heart on your sleeve.

But for Billy, England had suffered something tragic in the war years of 1940–45. This was not the loss of its Imperial world power or the ruination of its exchequer, both of which had been the specific war aims of US President Roosevelt and US Treasury Secretary Henry Morgenthau Jnr, but something more nebulous. According to Graham, 'Through fear-haunted days and never-ending nights, the German bombs turned England's homes and churches into fire-blackened heaps of rubble. And when the war ended, a sense of frustration and disillusionment gripped England, and what Hitler's bomb could not do, Socialism with its accompanying evils shortly accomplished.'

There were voices raised against this interpretation of recent events. 'Apologize, Billy – or Stay Away,' called out the *Daily Herald*, when it reported these words of the evangelist on Saturday 20 February.[22] But Graham did not apologise. The fact that some members of the socialist Cabinet, such as Stafford Cripps and Frank Longford, had been Christians, whereas the present Prime Minister, old Sir Winston Churchill, was an unreconstituted Victorian unbeliever, was not allowed to get in the way of a piece of good rhetoric. Addressing an audience at Central Hall in Westminster shortly after his arrival, Billy announced: 'President Eisenhower was right when he said we must have a spiritual awakening if the Western World is to survive. And Sir Winston Churchill has said he wonders whether our problems have not got beyond our control – I am going to preach a gospel not of despair but of hope – hope for the individual, for society and for the world.'[23]

It was a time when any English boy or girl who wanted to be a cowboy emulated the somewhat anodyne Roy Rogers. The privileged child would even possess a fringed Roy Rogers hat, waistcoat and sheriff's badge, and a Roy Rogers CA-gun in a Roy Rogers holster. 'Roy Rogers is coming to London for the crusade,' said Dr Graham, 'at his own expense. He has a tremendous influence on boys and girls, and I think his Christian testimony is a wonderful opportunity of [sic] getting them interested in church and Sunday school.'

Did the Evangelical Alliance chaired by Major General D. J. Wilson-Haffendon ('Haffy') get quite what it had bargained for when it invited Dr Graham to England? Haffy was a Victorian throwback, as were most of those who still counted for anything in England, men such as the Archbishop of Canterbury, Dr Geoffrey Fisher, the Prime Minister, Sir Winston Churchill, or the Poet Laureate, John Masefield. Haffy had been a staff officer for thirty years in the Indian Army. He guaranteed that Billy Graham would, in the course of his visits, be given such dinners at the House of Commons, the Café Royal and Claridge's as might have graced the pages of a novel by Trollope. The Earls of Cottenham and Cavan, the Viscounts Bridgeman and Newport, the Bishops of Worcester and Barking were in attendance. Somehow, however, the particular brand of Christianity Dr Graham brought to England was not of a native kind. As the assemblies filled the seats at Harringay Arena, and eventually as the throngs grew at Wembley, Billy would introduce his fellow Americans who sat with him on the podium. Former US Air Force Senator Stuart Symington (Democrat) and Senator Styles Bridges (Republican). There, too, was the gigantic Don Morrow, a leading figure in American football now destined for the Presbyterian ministry.[24]

Perhaps only those who heard Billy Graham speak could imagine the effect. He was one of those orators of whom Bill Clinton in small, Adolf Hitler in large, degree were two, capable of swaying the emotions of crowds by something which seems close to hypnotism. During the latter part of the Harringay mission one of the organisers remarked that if Billy Graham ended his sermon by reading out the multiplication tables and then gave the invitation, the people would still come.[25] This was an allusion to the moment in every Billy Graham rally when, after the sermon, and the playing of 'mood music', the crowds are invited to swoon forward and give themselves to Christ, as the choir raised their voices . . .

> Blessed assurance, Jesus is mine
> This is my story, this is my song,
> Praising my Saviour, all the day long!

Compared with the millions who tuned in to *Hancock's Half Hour*, the thousands who gave themselves to Christ at Billy's rallies were small in number. But *The Economist*, on 22 May 1954, commented, 'The appeal is to emotion which, as every dictator knows, will snowball its way through a crowd. Yet Mr Graham does not produce mass hysteria, although he is certainly dramatic, as he lunges about the stage taking by turns the roles in the Fall of Adam and Eve . . . Anglican parsons will shudder at the thought they should emulate his technique even if they could. But though they rightly preserve the intellectual tradition that has always been theirs, they can hardly ignore the fact that it is Mr Graham who seems to be on the wavelength.'[26]

Was it possible that *The Economist* had alerted its readers to the social and historical significance of these rallies in London sports arenas? Great Britain was not on the verge of a religious revival. In fact, from the 1950s onwards, allegiance to any of the major Christian denominations, with occasional blips in the graph, would be in steady decline. There was, however, a distinct change in the air. The 'intellectual tradition' of which the 'Anglican parsons' formed a part was something which went back to the seventeenth century, when modern England truly began. To the period after the civil wars, and after the restoration of Charles II in 1660, belonged a crucial few decades in which were forged the political, economic, educational and religious fabric of the nation. The Church by law established, with the monarch as its Supreme Governor, chose to be Episcopal; and in the 1950s, the bishops, in their lawn sleeves, continued to sit in the House of Lords; the liturgy, framed in 1662, continued to be the only lawful form of service in established churches, and it was that to which the huge majority of parishes, schools and colleges adhered. The Bank of England, founded in the late seventeenth century, and the City of

London, with all its companies, and guilds, and the Stock Exchange, remained independently British, and was the source of the nation's wealth. That system of capital and credit allied to an essentially Whig-aristocrat form of government was the basis of the British success story, both in its European wars against first the Bourbons and later Napoleon, and in its colonial and Imperialist expansion across the globe. To this late seventeenth-century period, too, belonged the foundation of the Royal Society, the beginnings of modern science, the astounding advances in physics and chemistry made by the likes of Robert Boyle and Isaac Newton.

The ancient Greeks had, among the great range and succession of their divinities, worshipped two gods who represented fundamentally opposed principles of life. Many cultural historians saw in this tension, between the worship of the god Apollo, and the worship of Dionysus, a key to why Greece had excelled, both as the ancestor of modern political stability, the cauldron of notions of stable statecraft, and also the origin of the great European literature and the birth of tragedy. Apollo, whose epithet Phoebus means radiant, is always represented as a young athlete. His cult was associated with military and athletic training, with discipline, and with ideas of responsible citizenship. He was also the god of music, an art form which depends upon rules. When Marsyas the shepherd thought he could make art by 'letting it all hang out', he was forced to sacrifice himself to Apollo; he was flayed, his skin removed, a painful reminder to worshippers of the god that beauty and art, like political systems and military skill, come from discipline, order, degree. Apollo was the god who guided the hand of John Locke and the English Enlightenment, and who kept the British electorate voting for the 'boring' political parties, while the rest of Europe lurched from the extremes of fascism and communism. Apollo, too, guided the British idea of humour, which was based on irony, on doggedness, on courage in the face of overwhelming hostility, such as was demonstrated by Hitler in the 1939–45 war.

The god seen as representing an opposing principle to the orderliness of Apollo was the god of wine, Dionysus, known to the Romans as Bacchus. He was bisexual and bispecial, which is why he came to be seen as a type of Christ, the God-Man. Bacchus/Dionysus was both male and female, human/divine and animal. His followers worked themselves into frenzies. Rules, boundaries and systems, for Dionysus and his followers, existed in order to be transcended or destroyed. Human beings under the influence of drink, drugs or mass hysteria have become the servants of Dionysus. The Greeks channelled the worship of Dionysus to certain periods of the year (one of them, obviously, being the wine harvest) and to certain rituals, which included those of emotional chaos which came to be known as tragedy and comedy. Theatre was the creation of Dionysus.

Dionysus was a god who came and went. He was not always present. His cult in ancient Athens was evidence of the human need to explore, and expose, the sources of our fears, lusts, rages; to dramatise, and thereby come to terms with, the sexual and familial histories which we all carry about with us. But when the festival was over, the worshippers of Dionysus would go back to the altars of Apollo, to reason, to order, to grammar, to the punishment of wrongdoing and the discipline of mind, body and society.

England in the 1950s did not realise it, but it was in the process of closing down the temples of Apollo, and handing over its worship to Dionysus.

Behind all this, there existed a concept of self- and political control which was fundamental to the British Enlightenment. To Billy Graham, the great philosopher Bishop Butler might have said, as he said to John Wesley, 'Sir, the pretending to gifts of the Holy Ghost is a horrid thing, a very horrid thing.'[27]

4

A Portrait of Decay

We sometimes speak of corruption to mean that a government or a group of people is knowingly crooked and dishonest. But corruption is also something which happens to bodies which are dead. Britain in the final administration (1951–5) of Sir Winston Churchill was flyblown and stinking in this latter sense.

Britain was tired, old, in decay, as was its Prime Minister. In January 1954, Malcolm Muggeridge, the editor of the humorous periodical *Punch*, commissioned (Leslie Gilbert) Illingworth, the cartoonist, to draw Winston Churchill in his decrepitude and to have a caption indicating it was time he went. 'It's true, that edition,' Muggeridge mused, 'but there'll be accusations of bad taste.'[1]

Churchill was bitterly hurt. '*Punch* goes everywhere,' he moaned to his doctor. 'I shall have to retire if this sort of thing goes on . . . It isn't really a proper cartoon. You've seen it? There's malice in it. Look at my hands – I have beautiful hands.'[2]

It was true, added the doctor, Lord Moran, but he who had so often recorded for posterity Churchill with no trousers on, Churchill's big, white fat bottom, Churchill having strokes, Churchill coughing, Churchill wheezing, Churchill drunk, could not resist describing the cartoon. 'The eyes were dull and lifeless. There was no tone in the flaccid muscles. The jowl sagged. It was the expressionless mask of extreme old age.' Nor could the good doctor resist copying out Malcolm Muggeridge's 'malice', which compared old Churchill to the Byzantine Bellarus. 'By the time he had reached an advanced age . . . his splendid faculties began to falter. The spectacle of his thus clutching wearily at all the appurtenances and responsibilities of an authority he could no longer fully exercise was to his admirers infinitely sorrowful, and to his enemies infinitely derisory.'

Worse was to come when members of both Houses of Parliament raised money for Sir Winston's eightieth birthday. It was agreed that Graham Sutherland should be commissioned to paint Churchill's portrait. As the artist remembered matters, a memory not untinged with bitterness, he believed 'that the portrait was to be given to [Churchill] by both Houses on his 80th birthday *for his lifetime* and that after his death *it would revert to the House of Commons*. I was even shown places where it might hang.'[3]

After three sittings the old man was anxious to get a glimpse of the canvas. 'Come on. Be a sport. Don't forget I'm a fellow artist.' But when he saw the work, he immediately protested. 'Oh no, this won't do at all. I haven't a neckline like that. You must take an inch, nay, an inch and a half off.'[4]

Once the painting was complete, Churchill did his utmost not to exhibit the picture publicly. He wrote to Sutherland that 'the painting, however masterly in execution, is not suitable as a presentation from both Houses of Parliament . . . About the ceremony in Westminster Hall. This can go forward although it is sad there will be no portrait. They have a beautiful book which they have nearly all signed, to present to me, so that the ceremony will be complete in itself.'

In the event, Charles Doughty, the secretary of the Parliamentary Committee which commissioned the picture, went to Chartwell, Churchill's country home, and told him he had to accept the picture, and accept it publicly.

The eightieth birthday of the Prime Minister was on 30 November. Already *The Times* had published a photographic image of the portrait and the paper's art critic praised it, saying it was more successful than Sutherland's portraits of Lord Beaverbrook and Somerset Maugham. When Churchill accepted the gift on the podium he resorted, as he often did in life when threatened, to that very English shield, facetiousness:

> I doubt whether any of the modern democracies abroad has shown such a degree of kindness and generosity to a party politician who has not yet retired and may at any time be involved in controversy [laughter] . . . the portrait . . . [he turned theatrically to look at it] . . . is a striking example of *modern* art. [Yelps of philistine laughter and applause] It certainly combines force and candour. These are qualities which no active member of either House can do without or should fear to meet.[5]

The son of a former Lord Chancellor and himself one day destined to fill that office, Quintin Hogg MP, immediately leapt in with his comments: 'If I had my way, I'd throw Mr Graham Sutherland into the Thames. The portrait is a complete disgrace . . . Churchill has not got all that ink on his face – not since he left Harrow, at any rate.'[6] But those who had seen the man, and the picture, knew that Sutherland with his brush strokes had perceived the same truth as the cartoonist and the satirists had seen. Churchill was past it, which is what made him such a very apposite Prime Minister at this date.

When the Labour Party won the General Election of 1945, by an overall majority of 136 seats in the House of Commons, many were astounded.

The people of Britain had spoken so unambiguously, so clearly. They had dismissed the individual who for many, at the time and since, was 'the man who won the war' (and at the time of the election it was not quite over – the election was in July, the Americans bombed Hiroshima with an atomic bomb on 6 August); the 'greatest Englishman', Winston Churchill. They had voted in as their Prime Minister Clement Attlee, who seemed like a nonentity but who had a very clear, and a very clearly explained, programme. Clement Attlee and his team wanted the socialist government which had begun in wartime – state control of supplies of food and fuel and production – to continue in peacetime. His party was quite happy with the first great global consequence of America having entered the war on the side of the Allies – namely, the dismantlement of the British Empire. Attlee lost no time in negotiating the liberation of India from the Imperial straitjacket (as it was seen). It was surely only a matter of time before the other colonies, in Africa and Asia, followed suit. Britain, bankrupted by the war and deprived of her Empire, was in a position where she could not but choose to become a new thing. And surely the landslide election result had made it very clear what a majority of the electorate wanted. They wanted Britain to recognise that the strange story of its Empire, and its growth as a world power between the eighteenth and the mid-twentieth centuries, had been an historical aberration. She was only a north European Protestant archipelago, of tremendous resourcefulness, of great technological expertise, of deep cultural brilliance, but no longer an Imperial power. She was poised to become something a little like Sweden – a northern European socialist state, in which the major sources of supply and manufacture, as well as the health, education and welfare of the people, were paid for by high taxation and a centralised government.

After five years of it, however, the electorate made it plain that its wishes were very much less clear-cut. The appalling weather, the deep snows and frozen pipes of 1947, perhaps contributed to the feeling; the frequent runs on the pound, a metaphor which suggested a recurrent national indigestion, a universal feeling of faint sickness, made many people feel that the last thing they wished was to have their life savings and their income confiscated by the state, the more so, since there was not much evidence that the railways, as British Railways, ran any better than they did as LNER, LMS or the old Great Western. As the years went by, the nationalised coal and steel industries performed noticeably less well than their continental rivals. The National Health Service was deemed to be a success, but the more hypochondriacal everyone became, and the further medical and pharmaceutical research advanced, the less affordable it seemed.

So it was, that by the time that this book begins its story, the electorate of Great Britain and Northern Ireland had decided that it did not wish to be a northern socialist state such as Sweden. It re-elected the Conservative Party, whose leader was still the old war hero, Winston Churchill. Having watched the debacle when India was partitioned and over a million were killed in the fight between Muslim and Hindu, some conservative-minded people at home wondered whether the paternalistic old Empire had been such a cruel idea after all. Was there any need to abandon the African colonies, to which, especially in Kenya and Southern Rhodesia, so many ex-servicemen had taken their families for a new life after the war? Watching the chaos in the Middle East since the establishment of a 'State of Israel' and the growth of anti-Western populist movements in Egypt, did the British public want to retire altogether from the world scene? Did they not still possess, in the British Commonwealth of nations, a unique position of influence in the world? Was it not right, in spite of the shift of power to the United States, that Britain with all her wisdom, influence, historical links with Egypt, Malaya, Cyprus, Malta, Africa, should continue to play a role which was utterly unlike any other country?

So, Britain, by re-electing Winston Churchill, thought again about its own national identity. The old King died of lung cancer, and he was replaced by his beautiful, and completely mysterious, from birth to old age, daughter Elizabeth. It was inevitable that headline writers and cliché-mongers would seize upon the idea of a New Elizabethan Age, but . . . why not? Britain never completely resolved the irreconcilable differences concealed in the post-war elections: in 1945 they had wanted a benign socialism, in 1951 Imperialist nostalgia. Having just lived through the financial ruin of the war, the bankruptcy of the peace, the millions of deaths and bereavements, the misery of the austerity years in which a banana seemed a luxury, small wonder the British were confused about their identity.

Churchill's chief function, in his last spell in office, was symbolic. He was the Grand Old Man who had won the war, and as long as he was the Prime Minister it was possible for some of the electorate, at least, to nurse the illusion that Britain still enjoyed the power and prestige which it had known before that calamity.

Churchill was tired and old, however, and he had little or no control over the changes which were evident to anyone of his political acuity. At the end of November 1952, for example, he asked to be told the numbers of coloured people – as they were called in those days – who had entered Britain. He wanted to know where they lived; also, the number of 'coloured' students. Two days later, he asked in Cabinet whether the Post

Office was employing any 'coloured' workers, pointing out that 'there was some risk that difficult social problems would be created' if this turned out to be the case.[7] On 18 December 1952, he set up an inquiry to see how further immigration by 'coloured' people could be prevented, and whether they could be kept out of the civil service. When the report was ready, in February 1954, Churchill told the Cabinet that 'the continuing increase in the number of coloured people coming to this country and their presence here would sooner or later come to be resented by large sections of the British people'. But he agreed that it was 'too soon to take action' in the matter.[8]

He was reluctant to continue the policy, which he had inherited from the previous Labour administration, of granting African colonies their independence, and when forced to go ahead with allowing Kwame Nkrumah to become the Prime Minister of the Gold Coast (later Ghana) he wrote apologetically to the apartheid government of South Africa, 'I hope you recognise that the decisions taken about the Gold Coast are the consequences of what was done before we became responsible.'[9]

The blatant racism of the old war hero shocks a later generation. For this reason, it is convenient for historians to suggest that it was only 'extremists', such as Sir Oswald Mosley, who thought in this way. (Mosley tried to revive his old fascist thugs of pre-war days and stood for Notting Hill in the 1959 election.) It was in Notting Hill, where many blacks had settled, that the race riots had occurred in 1958. It is easy, and correct, to see Mosley as inflammatory. Less easy for the imagination to absorb is the fact that when it came to his views of black people, the leader of the British fascists had views which were commonplace for a white man of his generation. They were shared by Sir Winston Churchill. They were shared by the hero of El Alamein, General Montgomery (1887–1976). After the war, Clement Attlee as Prime Minister sent Monty to Africa to provide a confidential report on the suitability of giving the Africans self-government. It was a shock for the liberal-minded 'Clem' to be told by Monty, after a two-month 'fact-finding tour', that 'the African is a complete savage and is quite incapable of developing the country himself'. He recommended making the whole of sub-Saharan Africa into a British-controlled bulwark against communism, to be aligned with South Africa. His advice was only to come to light in 1999, and a fellow peer, Lord Chalfont, commented that 'his reputation is irredeemably damaged'.[10]

Churchill's attitudes to Europe were no more progressive than his ideas about 'coloured' people. Although Churchillian quotes on the European subject were often cited, as the British quarrelled among themselves about it in later years, it is hard to imagine him lining up with Jacques Delors or Tony Blair. True, in 1946 Churchill had airily spoken of the possibility of a United Europe, but in private he conceded that 'I have never thought that Britain . . . should become an integral part of a European Federation'. In 1950, at the Council of Europe in Strasbourg, he called for a United European Army to be formed against the Soviet Union, but by 1952 he was telling President Truman, 'I have been doubtful about a European Army . . . It will not fight if you remove all traces of nationalism. I love France and Belgium, but we cannot be reduced to that level.'[11]

The sad fact was that Illingworth, Muggeridge and Graham Sutherland had all seen what was abundantly obvious to his close colleagues. Harry Crookshank, Leader of the House, found him 'terribly drooling . . . fast losing his grip'.[12] Far from being the prophet who looked forward to the actual future – a multi-racial Britain which was part of the European Union, he had turned into a drooling old reactionary, always half tight, incapable of holding back the future he deplored.

If the aged figurehead was barely capable of fulfilling his symbolic duties, the new young Head of State was also to find herself the target of some hitherto unprecedented criticism.

The decline in deference is one of the most striking features of our times. Deference was always tinged with irony in Britain, as anyone can deduce from reading the novels of Sir Walter Scott or Dickens, where impertinent servants are often quicker-witted than their masters, and where haughtiness or arrogance in superiors is regularly lampooned. The class system existed, and until the 1950s it remained very largely unaltered, partly because of the irony which in some senses redeemed it.

There was one aspect of it all, however, which was largely untinged by irony, and that was the attitude of the public towards the monarchy. The Coronation on Tuesday 2 June 1953 had held the nation in thrall, filling television viewers with the sense that Britain in all its pride and greatness could be reborn. It was a triumphalist, but also a poignant ceremony, bringing memories of the late King, a dignified, dutiful figure whom almost everyone respected for his courage in reviving the monarchy after the Abdication crisis of 1936, and his leadership during the Second World War.

His daughter, Queen Elizabeth II, was enchantingly beautiful, and although in her public appearances she appeared to be shy and stilted, the public invested her with all their hopes for a better future. Her youth, her piety, her winning smile, her bright eyes, her young children, all excited a reverence which approached idolatry.

It was sometimes difficult to remember this in the later years of her reign, when even conservative newspapers were open in their scorn for her children, when her husband's tactless jokes or outbursts of bad temper became commonplace causes of embarrassment, and when the Queen herself could be lampooned as an ugly puppet on the television satirical show *Spitting Image*. By the time this show was shocking and amusing the nation, republicanism was spoken of as an alternative form of government, and chatted about on the BBC as a plausible alternative – though it never seemed to have appealed to more than about 20 per cent of the adult electorate.

The Queen had to learn, after the advent of 'satire' in the 1960s, that the age of deference was dead. But in the 1950s she was considered to be beyond criticism. This was demonstrated when a small-circulation journal, *National and English Review*, edited by a Conservative peer called Lord Altrincham, devoted its issue of August 1957 to an analysis of the institution of monarchy. Of the various articles, the one which attracted most attention was penned by Lord Altrincham himself, later, when he had renounced his peerage in order to stand unsuccessfully for Parliament, known as the writer John Grigg.

His article contrasted George V, whom he saw as an ideal constitutional monarch, and the shaper of the modern constitution, with the granddaughter, Elizabeth II. He considered it a great mistake that the Court was composed of tweedy, aristocratic types, rather than representing the racial and social range, not merely of Great Britain but of the Commonwealth of which she was the head. 'Crawfie, Sir Henry Marten, the London season, the race-course, the grouse-moor, canasta, and the occasional royal tour – all this would not have been good enough for Queen Elizabeth I!'[13]

What people found truly shocking in Altrincham's article was not so much his attack on the 'upper class twits' of the Court, as his personal description of Elizabeth II herself: 'She will not . . . achieve good results with her present style of speaking, which is frankly "a pain in the neck". Like her mother, she appears to be unable to string even a few sentences together without a written text . . . But even if the Queen feels compelled to read all her speeches, great and small, she must at least improve her method of reading them. With practice, even a prepared speech can be given an air of spontaneity.

'The subject-matter must also be endowed with a more authentic quality. George V, for instance, did not write his own speeches, yet they were always in character; they seemed to be a natural emanation from and expression of the man. Not so the present Queen's. The personality conveyed by the utterances which are put into her mouth is that of a priggish schoolgirl, captain of the hockey team, a prefect, and a recent candidate for Confirmation. It is not thus that she will be enabled to come into her own as an independent and distinctive character.'[14]

A torrent of denunciation descended upon Altrincham. 'What a cowardly bully you are,' one woman wrote to him. As he was emerging from Television House with Ludovic Kennedy on 6 August, Altrincham met with Mr B. K. Burbridge, who stepped forward from the crowd and smacked him hard in the face, shouting, 'Take that from the League of Empire Loyalists' (i.e. Mosleyites). In fining Mr Burbridge 20s. for his assault, the Chief Metropolitan Magistrate expressed sympathy for his motives: 'Ninety-five per cent of the population of this country were disgusted and offended by what was written,' he remarked, truthfully.

The Queen was unable to change her very distinctive character, though she was to conduct her duties as Head of State conscientiously and se-riously for over half a century after Lord Altrincham's article first appeared. As far as the composition of her Court was concerned, she did not heed his advice. At the end of the reign, it was still composed of aristocrats and canasta players, with no admixture from the Commonwealth, and no members of the middle or lower classes. The Queen remained doggedly, and to many people shockingly, badly educated. She displayed no knowledge of literature – old or new – no interest in serious music or the arts, no cleverness in an academic or ostentatious sense, though as time went on it would seem that she possessed myste-rious reserves of common sense. As time wore on, it would seem as if her notion of parenthood was remote, and cold, and her eldest son publicly criticised her for this – though the rather brisker Princess Anne would leap to the mother's defence. Her decision to send her sons to Gordonstoun was unredeemed folly. Stories regularly circulated of the Queen being, like many Englishwomen, more able to emote with animals than with members of her own species, and it would be fallacious to suggest that she ever excited warm affection from her people.

But there was something there. What it was would be extremely hard to define. Constitutional historians such as Lord Altrincham could, if they surveyed the whole of the Queen's reign, compare her unfavourably with George V. She was known to be agitated by the state of the Established Church – in this she was not alone as the years wore on, and it moved through a series of self-imposed crises. But she was generally considered powerless to intervene. Why? Was she not the Supreme Governor of the Church? She was deemed to be worried about the danger to the Union posed by Scottish nationalism, but once again she seemed to do nothing about it. She allowed some rum coves, and some actual criminals, to become peers of her realm – how closely did she question the Prime Ministers responsible for the elevation of these rogues? Would not George V have refused to allow the mangling of the House of Lords perpetrated by Tony Blair? Would that redoubtable monarch not have insisted upon a plausible alternative system being in place before the

Second Chamber was deprived of its hereditary element, and the red leather seats were filled with Blair's placemen and placewomen, some of whom had overtly bought their places?

All these things were the direct responsibility not of her advisers, not of anyone but the Head of State herself, and they are more serious criticisms than that her voice was a pain in the neck.

But she was one of those very mysterious people in history whose virtues consisted in what she was, not in what she did, and which easily overcame her drawbacks. One of these virtues was longevity. In a rapidly changing Britain, she remained the one fixed point, the one element of public life which did not change. Secondly, as was made clear on the rare occasions when she was known to broadcast her own words, rather than speeches written for her, she was a person of directness, simplicity, unfashionable Christian piety. Thirdly, she was a genuinely humble person. But these are lists of adjectives and qualities and they fail to convey what it is, about her and the institution they represent, that filled so many of her subjects with a feeling they nursed for no other public figure. At the time of her Golden Jubilee, after a disastrous period for the Royal Family, it was widely expected that the occasion would be a flop. Over a million people thronged the streets of London to see her on the balcony of Buckingham Palace – the largest crowd that had assembled since the victory celebrations at the end of the war. She was – a word once applied by her daughter-in-law to her butler – a rock.

Churchill's death in 1965 produced a great upswell of patriotic sentiment, personal admiration and nostalgia. Churchill in his last days as Prime Minister, however, was an embarrassment. It was perceived that the strongest of his appetites, stronger even than his need for brandy and cigars, was lust for power, and it outlasted his physical and mental capabilities – as the merciless diaries of his doctor recorded. Any suggestion that he was too old for the task, whether it came from colleagues or the press, would be treated as examples of disloyalty. 'He spoke bitterly of the folly of the Tories in rashly throwing away all he had to give.' (In fact, it was his son-in-law, Christopher Soames, who was urging the old man to retire. 'I think I can harangue the bastards for fifty minutes,' he said of what would be his last speech as leader to the Party Conference at Blackpool. 'If they try to get me out, I will resist.'[15]

'Poor Anthony will be relieved at this,' the old man remarked, after one of his many 'turns', but he continued to stay on in office, rather than allowing Anthony Eden, his chosen heir since 1940, to take over the leadership. Although he liked to praise Eden, Churchill also had grave doubts about his judgement, and worries about the younger man's state of health. In both areas, Churchill was right to be worried. On the very eve of his resignation, Churchill held a dinner for the Queen at Number 10 Downing Street. When the evening was over, his doctor went to see the old man in his bedroom. He was still wearing his Garter (of which he was a Knight), his Order of Merit and his knee-breeches. He sat silently and then suddenly blurted out, 'I don't believe Anthony can do it.'[16] The next day, wearing one of the last frock coats to be seen in London outside a theatrical outfitters, the grand old Victorian went to Buckingham Palace to kiss the Queen's hands and resign his office. Robert Anthony Eden, two months short of his fifty-eighth birthday, succeeded him as Prime Minister.

5

Suez

Eden, the only male British Prime Minister known to have varnished his fingernails, was easily the best-looking individual, of either sex, to occupy that office in the twentieth century. Many also regarded him as the most disastrous, though there is so much competition for the role that attempts to draw up an order of prime ministerial incompetence, during the period 1956 to the present day, would be invidious. Some now question whether he was dependent upon Benzedrine, as was rumoured during his time in office.

He took some sleeping pills called Sparine, but the medical records, now held at Birmingham University, suggest that it was not until his very last two weeks in office that he took Benzedrine.[1] Certainly, his health had not been good. For many years he had suffered from duodenal ulcers, and he followed a sparing diet. A grumbling appendix had been operated upon in 1948. He suffered from migraines and nervous collapses. In April 1953, Churchill had removed a cigar from his lips in order to ask his doctor whether it was true, 'What . . . they are saying about smoking and cancer of the lungs.' Moran replied, 'It is not proven.'[2] Meanwhile, Eden as Foreign Secretary was in agony with gallstones and on 12 April a botched operation at the London Clinic to remove his gallbladder led to his body being poisoned. High fever had followed and his life had been despaired of. Had it not been for an American doctor, Richard Cattell, who unblocked Eden's biliary duct and cured his jaundice, he would never have been Prime Minister at all.[3]

While these medical dramas unfolded in the life of a British Foreign Secretary, events were unfolding in Egypt which would be forever associated, not merely with the name of Eden, but also with the humiliation of Britain as a world power. On 18 June 1953, King Farouk had been forced to abdicate, and Egypt was declared a republic by General Mohammed Neguib. It was noted, by the Foreign Office and by those newspapers which concerned themselves with foreign affairs; but there were other events of greater moment in the world, of which a potential war in Indo-China, economic troubles in Western Europe and French fears about a resurgent West Germany were themselves less obviously and urgently worrying than the escalation of the Cold War between the United States and the Soviet Union.

Churchill, as an old Imperialist, had supported to the end of his premiership a heavy commitment of British troops to the Suez Canal Zone. Eden, more aware of the way the world was moving, had negotiated with the Egyptians and the Americans a slow withdrawal of these British forces over a twenty-month period. Churchill was dismayed by Eden's attitude to America. 'We must never get out of step with the Americans – *never*', was Churchill's line.[4]

Eden extracted from John Foster Dulles, the US Secretary of State, the undertaking that America would keep the Canal open, whatever happened, and that it would support British interests in the region. The Americans, however, disliked Eden, partly because of his cosying up to the Chinese in Indo-China, and his success in diffusing the crisis there. General Neguib, meanwhile, had lost popularity in Egypt, owing to his too conciliatory attitude towards the British, in particular over their continued occupation of the Sudan – scene of the Battle of Omdurman where in 1898 Churchill had taken part in the famous cavalry charge. By October 1954, Neguib's position had been taken by a much younger and more radical figure, Colonel Gamal Abdel Nasser.

Eden's policy in the Middle East had really centred upon Jordan and Iraq, two Arab powers sympathetic to British interests. The policy was complicated on the one hand by British support for the fledgling State of Israel (established only in 1948 against huge opposition from the Arab world). General Sir John Glubb – 'Glubb Pasha' – was the commander of the Jordanian Arab Legion, committed to fighting Israel if that country attacked Jordan. The Saudis also looked threateningly at Jordan, and were trying to undermine the Hashemite monarchy in Baghdad. In this confused scene, in which the King of Jordan could be made to seem like a puppet of the British Imperialists, Colonel Nasser, young, dynamic, fiery, and backed by Saudi money and Russian armaments, kept up non-stop vituperative propaganda against the British. On the radio from Cairo, he reiterated, with clear and loud voice, that the destruction of Israel was the overriding purpose, not only of Egypt, but of the entire Arab world.

Clearly, the Jordanian royal family were rattled, and in March 1956 Glubb Pasha was sacked. Eden, sensing the hand of Nasser threatening Britain's former allies in Amman, urged a joint Anglo-American move against the government of Egypt, blocking sterling balances held by the Egyptian government, imposing economic sanctions and withdrawing aid for the Aswan Dam. John Foster Dulles did indeed put a stop to aid for the Aswan Dam project, but this was as far as the Americans were prepared to commit themselves.

There was an inherent paradox in the whole position of Britain in the Middle East. On the one hand, it was committed, through the Tripartite Declaration of 1950, to fight Israel if Israeli forces crossed the Syrian or

Jordanian borders. The British Foreign Office was then, as it would remain for decades, basically 'pro-Arab' and anti-Jewish. And yet Nasser's behaviour over the Suez Canal put Eden in the position of lining up with Israel against its Arab enemies.

Buried in the British psyche was the link which the Suez Canal forged between the Mediterranean and the Arabian Sea and the Indian Ocean. It was the short passage to India, it was the stylish short cut for those with white faces to lord it over those with brown faces; it was this canal in which Disraeli had negotiated with such panache a British share, paid for with cheap loans from the House of Rothschild, a souvenir of the heyday of Imperial British glory. And on 25 July 1956, Colonel Nasser announced that the Canal had been nationalised by the Egyptian government.

Speaking to his people, Nasser told them that '120,000 Egyptians had died in forced labour while digging the canal'. It was a distressing statistic, even though it was drawn from the pages of Herodotus (died 425 BC) and referred to an attempt to dig a canal in the seventh century before Christ. In fact, in the ten years of the digging of the nineteenth-century canal 1,394 paid Egyptian employees died.[5] Medical supervision had been of a Western standard and the death rate among the canal workers during that period was lower than the Egyptian national average on other building sites. Nasser, however, and his millions of Arab supporters, saw the Canal, and the contemporary British attitude towards it, as a symbol of an outmoded European colonialist attitude towards the peoples of the Middle East. The question was, would the British rise to the bait, or would they seek some other way out of the crisis? For the Russians, watching the crisis develop, the questions were slightly different, but no less momentous. Would the Russian support of Nasser, and other potential anti-Western governments in Africa and Asia, strengthen the hand of the Soviet Union in its Cold War against the Western powers? Would Britain (in Suez primarily, but by implication elsewhere) obey the letter of international law, or would it 'go it alone' in an attempt to open the Canal and assert its strength? And if it did so, without obeying the letter of United Nations resolutions, would this strengthen the Soviet Union when *it* chose to deal with satellite states within the Iron Curtain whom its masters in Moscow deemed to be recalcitrant? For if Britain chose to 'discipline' Egypt, what was to stop Russia doing the same for Hungary, in its attempts to have a more democratic, less Stalinist form of communist state?

The Suez crisis resolved itself into three broad phases: first, a period of negotiation, with other nations of the world; secondly, a period of military action; thirdly, a British withdrawal from Egypt, and the ruin of Eden's political career.

President Nasser assured the international community, and all those who might use the waterway for lawful trade, that there was no question of closing the Suez Canal. The Western powers were unimpressed, and on 2 August, the Foreign Ministers of the United States (Dulles), Britain (Selwyn Lloyd) and France (acting Foreign Minister Gazier) met in London to establish an international agency which would administer the safe passage of traffic in the Canal. The Soviet Union sent a representative to the conference, as did India; Egypt and Greece declined to be represented – Greece at this time having its own difficulties with Britain over the future of Cyprus. In all, twenty-two nations were represented at the conference. The American plan, publicly backed by Dulles, was for the creation of an international Suez Canal Board to be associated with the UN. President Eisenhower was very much against military action, and certainly against UK or French independent military action. Privately, however, when staying at Hatfield with Lord Salisbury, Dulles confided his ambivalence about Suez. Speaking *à deux* with Eden, Dulles admitted that Eisenhower was against military action, but that he, as Secretary of State, 'did not want to know' British military plans.[6] Eden, who did not enjoy a cordial relationship with Dulles, nevertheless drew the conclusion that Britain could count on American moral support, should he decide to take military action. This was a fatal mistake, and showed the truth of Churchill's advice 'We must never get out of step with the Americans'. Another feature of the whole affair was that the British diplomats, crucially Sir Roger Makins in Washington and Gladwyn Jebb in Paris, were kept in the dark by Eden about his true intentions. The first conference ended, then, with a broad resolution, led by Dulles, to set up a Suez 'users' association' to protect the interests of the twenty or so nations involved.

For the month of August, attention was diverted from Egypt by the terrorist activities of the Greek Cypriots, led – at first furtively, later openly – by Archbishop Makarios. If the Greeks succeeded in driving the British out of Cyprus, and the Egyptians sent them away from North Africa, it would become more obvious than ever that the days of the British Empire were definitely over. To an older generation of Imperialists, it had been clear that if the British ceased to administer India and Ireland, the days of its Empire would rapidly dissolve. Hindsight finds this obvious, but at the time of Suez, only a little more than a decade after the end of the Second World War, things looked different. The Dominions of the British Commonwealth – Canada, Australia, New Zealand and South Africa – were all in various ways happy to be ruled under the British Crown. They looked to the Queen as their Head of State, and she, much more than the generality of her politicians, persisted in believing in the

Commonwealth as a useful political entity. Meanwhile, in 1956, not merely the island of Cyprus, but also the Gold Coast, Nigeria, Somaliland (with Italian Somaliland, later Somalia), Sierra Leone, Tanganyika, Uganda, Kenya and the Gambia, Northern and Southern Rhodesia were still part of the British Empire: that is, most of the African continent. In addition, Jamaica and other islands of the West Indies, and Malaya in the Far East, were still part of the Empire. What had begun in a previous century as a supreme trading advantage had developed into a crippling financial burden which Britain could not afford. In August 1955, 10 per cent of Britain's gross national product was spent upon defence. It reckoned on sustaining more than 800,000 servicemen. Plans were under way, long before Suez, to get rid of the Empire. (In September, while the powers were discussing the future of the Suez Canal, the Colonial Secretary went to the Governor of the Gold Coast, proposing that the country be granted independence on 6 March 1957 and all the African countries named above, with the exception of Southern Rhodesia, would follow in the next decade.)

In the autumn, as people returned from summer holidays, and political parties and trades unions assembled for their conferences, there was a general consensus on the left that the government should not intervene militarily in Egypt. Troops had been mobilising and it was no secret that Eden favoured a military option. He saw Nasser as an Arab Mussolini, and the seizure of the Canal as a repetition of those acts of brigandry in the 1930s – Mussolini's invasion of Abyssinia, Hitler's carving up of Czechoslovakia – which, because they went unchecked, 'led to' the Second World War. Eden, who, with Churchill, had regarded negotiated peace as 'appeasement' and an encouragement to aggression, was bound to think in this way. Not to do so would, by implication, suggest that the 50–70 million victims of the Second World War had died in vain.[7]

Matters in the Middle East were soon to change radically, in any event, as a result of the acts of open hostility between Israel and her immediate neighbours. While in London, Selwyn Lloyd tried to establish the ground rules by which the Suez Canal Users' Association might actually work in practice. Dulles, back in the US, gave a press conference which seemed to backtrack from any suggestion of unconditional support for Britain. While these uncertainties persisted, there were outbreaks of firing along the Israeli–Jordanian border and the British government, in compliance with its treaty obligations, gave warning to Israel that British forces were committed to come to the aid of King Hussein.[8]

But in fact, on 14 October, General Maurice Challe, Deputy Chief of Staff of the French Air Force, had gone to see Eden with a secret plan devised with his own prime minister, Guy Mollet: that the English and the French should ally themselves with Israel and tacitly disre-gard the treaty obligations into which they had entered with Jordan, Syria, Iraq and other Arab powers. On 29 October, Israeli troops crossed the Sinai Desert with the aim of wiping out the Fedayeen bases in the Suez Peninsula. The Tripartite Powers (Britain, France and the US) warned that it would take 'immediate action' *against* Israel, and insisted that Israeli forces be moved back at least ten miles from the Canal Zone.

What happened next is, on the face of things, puzzling. Israel immediately complied with the Tripartite Declaration, that if withdrawal had not happened within twelve hours Anglo-French forces would inter-vene. On 30 October, Hugh Gaitskell, leader of the Labour Party, asked the Prime Minister in the House of Commons whether he could give an undertaking that no military action would take place until the whole matter had been referred to the Security Council of the United Nations. Eden replied 'with regret' that he could give no such undertaking. When Egypt rejected the Anglo-French ultimatum, British and French bombers flew over Egyptian military targets – on 31 October – and bombing began. (The US had already condemned Israel in the Security Council as the aggressor in this conflict.) On 2 November, Israeli forces won a signifi-cant victory over the Egyptian army in the Sinai Peninsula; British and French bombers had largely wiped out the Russian-built Egyptian air force, on the ground.

While the General Assembly of the UN called for an immediate cease-fire, and a withdrawal of Israeli, French and British troops from Egypt, Eden defended his position. In a broadcast of 3 November, he asked, 'Should we have put the matter to the Security Council and left it at that? Should we have been content to wait and see if they would act? How long would this have taken?' The sole purpose of British and French policy, he said, was to separate the warring armies of Egypt and Israel, and to do the work which the UN had failed to do. To the Crown Prince of Baghdad he repeated that 'the sole purpose of the intervention of British forces is to put a stop to hostilities between Israel and Egypt . . . We hear that the Israeli forces intend to abide by our latest request not to advance further than ten miles from the Canal although the gates of Egypt [does he mean Cairo?] are now open to them. This is at least some-thing gained and I hope it will soon be apparent to the world that our action was the only one which could have brought about this result. As soon as we have occupied the key points on the Canal, we shall ask the Israelis to withdraw from the Egyptian territory.'

In the light of what the Americans subsequently tried to do in the Middle East in the late twentieth and early twenty-first centuries, it was indeed 'ironic' that President Eisenhower and Secretary of State Dulles did not support Eden's policy, even if they found him unappealing as a character. Eisenhower later told Richard Nixon that Suez was 'his major foreign policy mistake'.[9] Keeping the peace between Israel and her neighbours; tacit support for the survival of Israel as a political entity; wooing of pro-Western oil-rich Arab powers against radical or Islamist anti-Western governments: . . . if viewed from the perspective of later 'neo-con' politics, Eden's intervention in Suez looks like a resolute piece of realpolitik.

In a letter to his Constituency Association, dated 3 November, Sir Winston Churchill expressed wholehearted approval of Eden's policy, and added, 'I am confident that our American friends will come to realize, not for the first time, we have acted independently for the common good.' Whatever the private truth of this optimistic assertion, the American President, who was on the eve of going to the polls in an election, was not going to commit himself to any support for the Anglo-French action. Indeed, he denounced it as being 'in error'.[10]

Dwight Eisenhower, the great 'Ike', whose slow handling of the occupation of Europe in 1944–45 had guaranteed the enslavement to Soviet tyranny of all the peoples of East Germany, Czechoslovakia, Poland, Hungary and Yugoslavia, was now engaged in a clumsy global war against 'communism' – by which he chiefly meant that very Soviet tyranny his own military blunders had empowered. He had no wish to antagonise those members of the Security Council, including the oil-rich Saudis – who had condemned the Anglo-French action. If Britain further humiliated and bankrupted itself on the world stage it would be no disaster in the eyes of this President who followed Roosevelt and Truman in earnestly wishing for the dismantlement of the last vestiges of the British Empire. So Churchill's hope for American support over Suez was misplaced; misplaced, too, would have been any hope of American help for the Hungarians, who saw the Soviet tanks roll into the streets of Budapest without a single military threat from the great enemy of communism. 'The eyes of the world are upon you,' Ike had said to the US forces occupying Europe in June 1944. 'The hopes and prayers of liberty-loving people everywhere march with you.'

The letters to *The Times* caught the mood of the country, with a great majority opposing the military intervention, and more than one correspondent being aghast that the Suez crisis should have averted attention from the tragedy in Budapest. On 4 November, Malcolm Muggeridge and Robert Speaight – the actor who had immortalised T. S. Eliot's Becket in *Murder in the Cathedral* – wrote from the Garrick Club, 'The bitter division in public opinion provoked by the British intervention in the

Middle East has already had one disastrous consequence. It has deflected popular attention from the far more important struggle in Hungary. A week ago the feelings of the British people were fused in a single flame of admiration for the courage and apparent success of the Hungarian revolt. Now, that success seems threatened by Russian treachery and brute force, and Hungary has appealed to the West . . . It is the first, and perhaps will prove the only opportunity to reverse the calamitous decisions of Yalta' . . . (That is, the conference at which a decrepit, drunken Churchill discovered that Roosevelt, himself on the verge of death, had in effect agreed to let Stalin gobble up Eastern Europe when the war against Hitler had been won) . . . 'The Prime Minister has told us that 50 million tons of British shipping are at stake in his dispute with President Nasser. What is at stake in central Europe are rather more than 50 million souls. It may be objected that it is not so easy to help the Hungarians; to this excuse they are entitled to reply that it was not so easy to help themselves.'[11]

On the same day, 6 November, *The Times* published a letter from the daughter of a former Prime Minister, Asquith – Lady Violet Bonham Carter – 'I am one of millions who watching the martyrdom of Hungary and listening yesterday to the transmission of her agonizing appeals for help (immediately followed by our 'successful bombings' of Egyptian 'targets') have felt a humiliation, shame, and anger which are beyond expression . . . We cannot order Soviet Russia to obey the edict of the United Nations which we ourselves have defied, nor to withdraw her tanks and guns from Hungary while we are bombing and invading Egypt. Today we are standing in the dock with Russia . . . Never in my lifetime has our name stood so low in the eyes of the world. Never have we stood so ingloriously alone.'[12]

Lady Violet, pillar of the Liberal Party and mouther of all the familiar Liberal world-views, might have recalled that Churchill, whom she loved and idolised, had achieved the height of his fame when Britain, only sixteen years earlier, had been alone – if not ingloriously alone. While some, such as Muggeridge, deplored the Suez action because it shattered national unity, and others, such as Lady Violet, because it offended against the laws of the UN and – perhaps the same thing in Lady Violet's eyes – morality, there were others who deplored it simply because it was unpopular, with Arabs, Russians, Americans and others.

But although the bulk of the press, the Labour Party and that equally influential party, the left-leaning London dinner party, were all against Suez, together with the rent-a-mob of poets, dons, clergy and ankle-socked female graduates who deplored British action, they did not necessarily constitute the majority of *unexpressed* public opinion. Roy Harrod, the

Keynesian economist of Christ Church, Oxford, and tutor to generations of future economists, believed that 'the more level-headed British, whom I believe to be in the majority though not the most vocal' supported the 'notable act of courage and statesmanship' displayed by the government.

By 6 November, both the Israeli and the Egyptian governments had agreed to an unconditional ceasefire, and the Anglo-French occupying forces had agreed to withdraw and hand over, if necessary, to a UN peace-keeping force.

The background to this had, however, been politically and economically humiliating to Britain. The Canal was blocked. A run on the pound had developed and some 15 per cent of Britain's gold reserves had vanished. The Machiavellian Chancellor of the Exchequer, Harold Macmillan, who had supported the Suez venture from the outset, now reversed his position. He was told that the pound could only be supported with a loan from the International Monetary Fund, and that this loan, which would come from the United States, was dependent upon the ceasefire being immediate, and British troops withdrawing.

Had Macmillan still been Foreign Secretary, he would have been implicated, as were Prime Minister Eden and Foreign Secretary Selwyn Lloyd, in every stage of the debacle. As it was, he could convey to his friends in the United States (his wife's late nephew, heir to the Dukedom of Devonshire, had been married to Kathleen 'Kick' Kennedy, sister of the future President) that he had never been a keen supporter of the Suez enterprise and was now in favour of British withdrawal.

Brendan Bracken wrote to Beaverbrook on 7 December, 'Macmillan is telling journalists that he intends to retire from politics' rather than serve under his great rival, Rab Butler. 'His real intentions are to push his boss out of Number 10 and he has a fair following in the Tory Party.' American academic opinion veers to the view that, at this stage of the Suez drama, Macmillan was actually in touch, directly or indirectly, with Eisenhower. 'It appeared that Eisenhower, and certainly Macmillan, were attempting to ease Eden from power.'[13] Another has observed that 'although documentation is not clear cut' — and of course, Macmillan would have been much too clever to leave documentation — 'there is sufficient evidence to suggest that Washington was heavily involved behind the scenes'.[14]

Those who write or speak of the Suez fiasco sometimes overlook the fact that, from a military point of view, it was a success; Nasser's forces were defeated, and had an Anglo-French force remained in the area, to occupy the entire zone, they would have brought 'peace and order to the Middle East' to use Roy Harrod's phrase. But Eden, and England, were victims of the Fates, or the Americans. Had Britain been at the zenith of power, a bad press at home, and a divided Cabinet, would not have led to a failure of nerve such as occurred after the Egyptian and Israeli ceasefire. This could have been hailed as a triumph for the decisive military astuteness of France and Britain who had acted, if not according to the letter of the UN, then at least in accordance with its spirit. They could have claimed, as Eden did, that they intended only to bring peace and stability to the region, to silence the incitements to war and mayhem, and the destruction of Israel, coming from Nasser, and to establish that there is still a place in the world for nations acting as policemen to brigand states. But such words as Eden might have attempted along these lines were drowned out by a chorus of anti-war feeling at home and anti-British sentiment abroad.

By 22 December, six weeks after their dispatch, the last British troops were withdrawn from the Suez area. His nerves and health in tatters, Eden had become a pariah-politician who could do no right. On 23 November, Eden and his wife flew for a three-week holiday at Goldeneye, Jamaica, at the house of his friend Ann Fleming and her husband, the inventor of James Bond. The hideaway 'is much patronized by tax evaders and affluent idlers', complained Jock Colville, Churchill's private secretary. 'With petrol and oil rationed again in England, the retreat of the Prime Minister to a parasites' paradise seemed to rank prominently in the annals of ministerial follies.'[15]

It was on another cruise, a recuperative journey to New Zealand the following year, after his resignation, that Eden found himself on board the *Britannic*. The waiters and stewards rigged up a boxing ring and Eden awarded the prize to the best pugilist, two bottles of beer and two hours' overtime bonus. The winning steward was John Prescott who, when Deputy Prime Minister to Tony Blair, would notoriously land a punch during an election campaign.

On 3 December, the Foreign Secretary Selwyn Lloyd told the House of Commons of the ceasefire. 'We have stopped a small war and prevented a large one. The force which we temporarily interposed between the combatants is now to be relieved by an international force . . . Responsibility for securing a settlement of the long-term problems of the area has now been placed squarely on the shoulders of the United Nations.'[16]

Britain was publicly announcing that it was no longer the policeman of the world. The American response was immediate, and positive. As soon as conditional withdrawal of British and French troops from Egypt was announced, the American oil companies shipped 200,000 barrels of oil to an oil-starved Britain. The American Export-Import Bank announced that a loan of $500 million would be made available on easy terms and the International Monetary Fund approved a British drawing of $561 million. There could have been no more transparent and humiliating demonstration. If the British acted alone, without the President's permission, they went bust. If they toed the American line, they became solvent once more.[17] When he came back from his holiday, Eden confronted the question posed by a predecessor as Prime Minister, Clement Attlee: namely, whether the British and French governments had had prior warning of the Israeli invasion of Egypt. With Eden's recovery from ill health, Attlee wrote, 'the country may reasonably ask that he should put an end . . . to an uncertainty which cannot fail to be damaging to the national interest'.

A hasty cover-up operation began. Two middle-ranking Foreign Office people were told to put together a file of all the sensitive papers on Suez and deliver it to the Cabinet Secretary, Norman Brook. The papers were never seen again. Meanwhile, at Chequers, the name of General Challe, who had come there to discuss the Israeli plot with Eden, was scratched out of the visitors' book, to be replaced by the name of some minor official. When confronted in Parliament, Eden was faced with the choice of admitting that he had known in advance of the Israeli invasion, or of lying. He chose to lie.

'I want to say this on the question of foreknowledge, and to say it quite bluntly to the House, that there was not foreknowledge that Israel would attack Egypt – there was not. But there was something else. There was – we knew it perfectly well – a risk of it, and in the event of a risk of it, certain discussions and conversations took place as, I think, was absolutely right, and as, I think, anybody would do.'[18] Eden knew that both Mollet and Ben-Gurion, the Prime Minister of Israel, were in a position to demonstrate the untruth of what he was saying. Although they did not land him in any embarrassment while he was Prime Minister, they both gave their own accurate version of events afterwards. Worse, Macmillan and Butler both knew that he was lying to the House of Commons. In later times, the mendacity of a Prime Minister at the Dispatch Box was something which the electorate would take for granted, but Eden was living at the tail end of England's Glory. He went to Lord Salisbury ('Bobbety') on 5 January 1957 to tell him that he was resigning for reasons of ill health. There were no elections for the position of Conservative Party leader in those days. Bobbety, the grand old man of the Party, merely canvassed the Cabinet for their views, giving them the choice of R. A. Butler or Harold Macmillan. As each man came into his room, he was asked, 'Hawold or Wab?' Only one opted for Wab. And so – such was the way of these things – on 10 January 1957, Harold Macmillan became the Prime Minister.

PART TWO

Macmillan

6

Supermac

Harold Macmillan's appearance – the hooded eyes, the moustache, the irregular and discoloured teeth, the element of parody in dress sense – frequently gave rise to a feeling of distrust. Impressions that he cut a risible figure were disconcertingly replaced by the sense that the joke, whatever it was, might after all be at the mocker's expense, that Macmillan had contrived his appearance, voice, manner as a comedic mask behind which to conceal either a different self, or, like the Sphinx, the secret of emptiness, the secret that there was no secret to hide.

Visiting a collective farm outside Kiev, he donned plus fours, 'as if he were at Chatsworth'.[1] Such a game would no doubt have delighted the son-in-law of the 9th Duke of Devonshire (which Macmillan was), and yet true blue Tories, who saw him always as one who was eager to sell the pass, remembered that he advised his nephew, the 11th Duke, to abandon Chatsworth.[2] He sensibly ignored the advice. Macmillan, to those of instinctively conservative reaction, is the Prime Minister who would not do anything to save the Doric arch at Euston Station, allowing the plansters, as John Betjeman called them, to demolish that magnificent Greek-revival London terminus, and erect a characterless, ugly replacement. His lofty comment was 'only dying countries tried to preserve the symbols of their past'.[3]

Then again, hardened monetarists look back upon the Keynesian Macmillan era as one of disaster. Macmillan's worst economic memories were of Stockton-on-Tees, his first constituency in the 1930s, when he had seen the terrible effects of economic recession. 'It was his instinct to be rebellious against the restrictive actions of the Treasury – he never liked the Treasury. "What is wrong with inflation, Derry?" I'd reply, "You're thinking of your constituents in the 1930s?" "Yes – I'm thinking of the under-use of resources – let's over-use them!" He believed in import controls, but the Treasury wouldn't let him.'[4] These are the recollections of his second Chancellor of the Exchequer, Derick Heathcoat-Amory. His first Chancellor, Peter Thorneycroft, resigned on 6 January 1958, together with the Economic Secretary to the Treasury, Nigel Birch, and the Financial Secretary, J. Enoch Powell. They had all urged, following a disastrous run on the pound, that there must be swingeing cuts in welfare and public spending if disastrous inflation were to be avoided. Macmillan, who was about to go on a long tour of the Commonwealth when the Treasury men hatched their attack, dismissed it as 'a little local difficulty'.[5] Later he would even pretend not to remember Thorneycroft's identity – 'that man who looked like an English butler, with the nice Italian wife – I forget his name'. Some believed that Macmillan had come to power, not merely by the normal Machiavellian ploys of lobbying and undermining his rivals, but by making secret deals with the Americans. One of his fiercest critics, Alan Clark, in *The Tories*,[6] went so far as to say that 'Macmillan's contact with George Humphrey (US Secretary of the Treasury) bordered on the treasonable . . . Macmillan now set about mobilising his American contacts.'

Shadier than his dealings with the Americans in 1956 had been Macmillan's unaccountable role in the handing over of White Russians and Cossacks to the Soviet authorities at Klagenfurt (British-occupied Austria) in May 1945. By the terms of the Yalta Agreement, the Soviets had no claims upon Russian émigrés who had escaped their wrecked country after the Revolution and Civil War. Into this category most certainly fell three White Army generals (Krasnov, Shkuro and Kilech-Ghirey), together with a number of people such as Olga Rotova, a Yugoslav citizen, who had *never been Soviet citizens*, being held by 36 Infantry Brigade commanded by Brigadier Geoffrey Musson – under the overall control of Lieutenant General Charles Keightley, of the 5 Corps of the 8th Army. Churchill, as Prime Minister, and Lord Alexander of Tunis (Supreme Allied Commander in the Mediterranean) had specifically ordered Keightley not to surrender the Cossacks and non-Soviet citizens to the Red Army. Harold Macmillan flew in to Klagenfurt from Caserta on 13 May 1945 to discuss Soviet proposals. He was the government minister resident at AFHQ (Allied Force Headquarters). The next day, evidently on Macmillan's instructions, Keightley lied to Alexander, in a telegram, saying the 40,000 or so contained a 'large number of Soviet nationals' whom they had been forced to repatriate. On 26 May Brigadier Musson ordered all his battalion commanders holding Cossacks in the Drau Valley to send *all* their Cossacks back, regardless of citizenship. The Cossacks were 'handed over' with violence and entirely against not only their will but international law. Together with their wives and children, they were forced into trucks at bayonet point. 'It was a great grief to me', Macmillan recorded in his memoirs, 'that there was no other course open.'

In 1957, Khrushchev allowed a tiny trickle of Cossacks who had managed to survive the camps in the Arctic Circle and Siberia to leave Russia. Only a few score, of the thousands imprisoned, came out, clutching their non-Russian passports. One of them, Captain Anatol

Petrovsky, wrote, appealing to the Prime Minister, reminding him that the British Military Command had known he was not a Soviet citizen when they handed him over for twelve years of starvation, freezing cold and enforced slavery in the mines of Siberia and Vorkuta. He was by then living as an invalid and a displaced person and wondered if the Prime Minister would be prepared to compensate him. He received an impersonal reply from the Foreign Office: 'I am directed to refer to your letter of the 4th of September to the Prime Minister . . . A thorough examination of the facts led to the conclusion that no action could be taken to assist the persons named in your letter.'[7]

Those who vilified Macmillan's memory did so usually from a position of the doctrinal right. They often attributed to him powers which perhaps no British politician at this date actually possessed. Because they regretted the increased power of America; the dissolution of the British Empire in Africa; the failure of Britain to prevent the collapse of Iraq, or the heightening of conflict in the Middle East between Jew and Arab, between 'moderate' or pro-Western Arabs and Islamists; the loss of Cyprus as a Mediterranean British base; and the segregation of the island into Greek and Turkish halves; they attributed these ills to the deviousness or anti-Toryism of the Prime Minister. Likewise, at home, the chaos of labour relations, the inflationary wage demands made by trades union 'barons', the 'liberalisation' of life in areas as diverse as capital punishment, or sexual mores, were blamed on 'Supermac', either because he was too weak to prevent them, or because he anarchistically or seditiously wished to undermine the country by promoting them. Another way of seeing him, however, this man of masks, was as one who regretted the loss of old values, but who did not really believe in the power of politics alone to preserve them.

Macmillan's premiership lasted from January 1958 to October 1963. It was a period of quite extraordinarily rapid change, both in Britain and abroad. He resigned hurriedly because he believed that a minor prostate condition was potentially fatal. His estimation of himself was captured in his judgement – 'That illness was a sad blow for me. Without being conceited, it was a catastrophe for the party.'[8] Much was made of the fact that, even from his hospital bed, Macmillan attempted to control the succession. The two likeliest contenders were the irrepressibly foolish Quintin Hogg, who had inherited the title of Lord Hailsham from his father, the founder of the London Polytechnic, and R. A. Butler, Macmillan's Home Secretary. At the last minute, 'Supermac' lost faith in Hogg, and told the Queen that she should appoint the 14th Earl of Home as the new Prime Minister.

Whatever Mac saw in Home, it is clear what he saw in Hogg. 'Those who clamour for Butler and Home are really not so much shocked by Hogg's oddities as by his honesty. He belongs both to this strange modern age of space and science and to the great past – of classical learning and Christian life. This is what they instinctively dislike.'9

This is a description that could also be applied to Harold Macmillan. In old age, with a characteristic mixture of Edwardian drawl and simple camp, he meditated upon the sad marriage of Quintin Hogg, whose wife betrayed him during the war with a member of the Free French. 'He came back on leave, and found her in bed – both of them, so it was a hard thing for him, such a sweet boy. No, he's suffered . . . he was a gentleman and a Christian.'10

Macmillan's own life was clouded by a wife's infidelity. Unlike Hogg, who put away his own wife instantly, citing the Gospel of Matthew in his defence – 'Saving for the cause of adultery!'11 – Mac turned a blind eye to the long love affair with his fellow Conservative MP Bob Boothby.

Although 'everyone knew' about the liaison, he was late in coming to the news. When a friend, during a railway journey in 1929, made an allusion to Lady Dorothy and Boothby which was inescapable in its meaning, Macmillan was on the point of reaching for the luggage in the rack above his head. The news so surprised him that he fell backwards on to the carriage floor and fainted.12

Boothby was popular with the public, largely because of his association with Churchill. He had been among the Conservative MPs who stood beside 'Winston' in the wilderness years of the 1930s and who opposed the policy of appeasing the brigand states of Europe. In the 1950s and 1960s as television became popular, he was a natural for discussions and chat shows. His spotted bow ties and aristocratic method of delivery reminded audiences of his Churchillian credentials. He was a character, a cove, a card. The development of eroticism in his life, he described in his twilit years to an old friend – 'I began with handkerchieves, progressed to boys, then found women attractive, then back to boys again, and now I find consolation once more with handkerchieves.'13 This remark was made after his marriage, in August 1967, to Wanda Senna, the daughter of a Sardinian import-export wholesaler. 'I don't need friends. I've got lots of friends. What I want is a wife,' the sixty-seven-year-old told the thirty-four-year-old beauty. His first marriage, in 1935, to Diana Cavendish, had lasted a matter of months, until his affair with Dorothy Macmillan (a cousin of his wife's) became known. The association with the East End gang leader Ronnie Kray demonstrated the range of Boothby's social and erotic sympathies. 'Once you get into the clutches of that family, by God, you haven't a hope. They are the most tenacious family in Britain.' He was speaking in 1973 to a *Sunday Times* journalist, Susan Barnes, who married the Foreign Secretary Antony Crosland. But he was referring to the Cavendishes rather than to the Krays.[14] The Krays, as Ronnie's obituarist was to put it, 'brought to the hitherto parochial British criminal scene a taste of American organised crime'.[15] The twin brothers, Reggie and Ronnie, controlled pubs and clubs by protection rackets. They were skilled blackmailers and, as amateur boxing champions, adepts of violence. They never lost a fight until they turned professional at sixteen. In 1950 they were charged with brutal assault and then − a common feature of cases involving the brothers − the witnesses retracted their statements. They were eventually to be put on trial for the murder of George Cornell and Jack 'The Hat' McVitie. They had lured McVitie to a flat in Stoke Newington in October 1967. Urged on by psychopathic Ronnie, Reggie stabbed McVitie, pinning him to the floor through the throat. The violence of the attack caused McVitie's liver to fall out. The twins were imprisoned at Parkhurst; Ronnie, having been certified insane, was transferred to Broadmoor.

From his prison cell in 1988 Reg was able to become as moralistic as any Disgusted Reader of a conservative broadsheet. 'It's a different world now to what it was in 1969 when we went down. It's a different criminal world too − it's far more deadly. Then it was dog eat dog − criminals waging war against other criminals. Old ladies didn't get attacked by vicious thugs in those days. Young girls didn't get raped in broad daylight. Coppers didn't get kicked and punched and spat on at football matches. There was a kind of respect for people in those days.' So much respect, indeed, was there, that even when on the run from the police in 1968, Reggie had found the time to go to the Starlight Club in Highbury, demanded £1,000 on the spot from a man called Fields, and, when he didn't pay up, 'shot him through the leg and left one of the Firm to smash his face in'.[16] Ah, happy, innocent days.

Before and after their imprisonment, the Krays enjoyed mingling with the more raffish figures in showbiz and on the fringes of society. Blonde women such as Diana Dors (her husband, Alan Lake, was another criminal) and Barbara Windsor, were part of their circle, though never a temptation to Ronnie. 'I'm not a poof; I'm a homosexual,' he would explain. He seduced the East End boys he recruited as spies and he held parties which were regarded as 'sophisticated'. It was at one such party that Ronnie Kray encountered Bob Boothby.

On 11 July 1964 the *Sunday Mirror* proprietor Cecil King, editor-in-chief Hugh Cudlipp and editor Reginald Payne published a banner headline: 'Peer and a Gangster: Yard Probe Public Men at Seaside

Parties'. The paper announced that 'a top level Scotland Yard investigation into the alleged homosexual relationship between a prominent peer and a leading thug in the London underworld has been ordered by the Metropolitan Police Commissioner Sir Joseph Simpson'.[17] On the Monday following, there arrived a photograph of Boothby in his flat sitting on his sofa next to Kray. The following Sunday the paper published the photograph.

Boothby tried to bluff it out. He even went so far as to ask the openly gay MP Tom Driberg the identity of the well-known peer who was alleged to have had an affair with the well-known thug. 'I'm sorry, Bob, it's you' was the reply.[18] Boothby went to see Gerald Gardiner QC, a future Lord Chancellor, who advised him to consult the Mr Tulkinghorn of our times, Arnold Goodman. We can only assume that Boothby lied to both his legal advisers. On 31 July he wrote the following letter to *The Times*:

Sir,

On July 17th I returned to London from France and I found, to my amazement, that Parliament, Fleet Street and other informed quarters in London were seething with rumours that I have a homosexual relationship with a leading thug in the underworld involved in a West End protection racket; that I have been to 'all-male' Mayfair parties with him; that I have been photographed with him in a compromising position on a sofa; that a homosexual relationship exists between me, some East End gangsters and a number of clergymen in Brighton; that some people who know of these relationships are being blackmailed; and that Scotland Yard have for months been watching meetings between me and the underworld thug, and have investigated all these matters and reported on them to the Commissioner of the Metropolitan Police.

I have, for many years, appeared on radio and television programmes; and, for this reason alone, my name might reasonably be described as 'a household name', as it has been in the *Sunday Mirror*. On many occasions I have been photographed, at their request, with people who have claimed to be 'fans' of mine; and on one occasion I was photographed, with my full consent, in my flat (which is also my office) with a gentleman who came to see me, accompanied by two friends, in order to ask me to take an active part in a business venture which seemed to me to be of interest and importance. After careful consideration I turned down this request, on the ground that my existing commitments prevented me from taking on anything more, and my letter of refusal is in his possession.

I have since been told that some years ago the person concerned was convicted of a criminal offence; but I knew then, and know now, nothing of this. So far as I am concerned, anyone is welcome to see or to publish any photographs that have ever been taken of me.

I am satisfied that the source of all these sinister rumours is the *Sunday Mirror* and the *Daily Mirror*. I am not a homosexual.* I have not been to a Mayfair party of any kind for more than 20 years.* I have met the man who is alleged to be a 'king of the underworld' only three times, on business matters;* and then by appointment in my flat, at his request, and in the company of other people.

I have never been to a party in Brighton with gangsters – still less clergymen. No one has ever tried to blackmail me. The police say that they have not watched any meetings, or conducted any investigations, or made any reports to the Home Secretary connected with me. In short, the whole affair is a tissue of atrocious lies.

I am not by nature thin-skinned; but this sort of thing makes a mockery of any decent kind of life, public or private, in what is still supposed to be a civilised country. It is, in my submission, intolerable that any man should be put into the cruel dilemma of having either to remain silent while such rumours spread, or considerably to increase the circulation of certain newspapers by publicly denying them. If either the *Sunday Mirror* or the *Daily Mirror* is in possession of a shred of evidence – documentary or photographic – against me, let them print it and take the consequences. I am sending a copy of this to both.

Your obedient servant
Boothby

(*In the previous paragraphs, the phrases followed by an asterisk are demonstrable falsehoods.)

In 1964 £40,000, one of the largest sums ever paid in compensation for a libel, was paid to Boothby and the editor of the *Sunday Mirror* was sacked. It was a good demonstration of the powers of the libel laws to intimidate journalists. After the debacle of the Profumo affair, issuing writs for libel was the most usual way employed by rich villains to muzzle the press. The cost of bringing such proceedings to court, and the possibility that, even if the case were successful, a judge might not award full costs, guaranteed that only the rich and powerful could use this law to protect themselves. Boothby won his case by committing perjury.[19] He wrote to his QC, Gerald Gardiner, on 10 August 1964 – 'We were lucky in having Mr Goodman's help, as he is one of the shrewdest bargainers in the business. It is, I think, the fastest and largest settlement of the kind ever made. So it should have been.'[20]

Whether you believe that Ronnie Kray and Boothby had no sexual relationship, there were many who would raise an eyebrow at Ron's description: 'It was strictly a business relationship which later became a friendship – a friendship based on the fact that we had both been so badly smeared by the national press.'[21] It was a bizarre business relationship. It was a good example of how small Britain was, and how, as in the *roman-fleuve* of Anthony Powell, the unlikeliest characters turned out to know one another. Not that Powell ever touched upon the criminal underworld. For that the reader would be directed to the raffish novels of Simon Raven. Nevertheless, a colourful figure such as Boothby, even if he did not attend very many of the Krays' parties, provides a link between, on the one hand, a Prime Minister and one of the great ducal families, with, on the other hand, hatchet men and protection racketeers.

The relationship with Dorothy Macmillan had begun as long ago as 1929 and remained the dominant one throughout her life. 'It was Dorothy who seduced Boothby and dominated him. He not only fulfilled her sexually, but gave her the fun, glamour and exciting company that her husband was unable to do.'[22] Though Lady Dorothy begged her husband for a divorce he refused to allow her emotional satisfaction to come in the way of his political career. But, by the time that ambition had been satisfied and Harold Macmillan was Prime Minister (aged sixty-three), Macmillan and his wife had become friends, and indeed, they returned from the Commonwealth tour of 1958 as a sort of Darby and Joan. None would have guessed, from her substantial appearance (comparisons were made with the comic actress Margaret Rutherford) or her aristocratic contempt for conventions, of the strange emotional secrets the Macmillans shared. At Birch Grove, the Macmillans' country house, the police patrolled the gardens by night before the visit of General de Gaulle, and were disturbed to note a light bobbing about outside the house. They were surprised to find the Prime Minister's wife, wearing only a slip and gumboots, a miner's lamp on her forehead and two hot-water bottles strapped to her ample midriff – 'I got a bit behind with the bedding out'.[23] Confronted by CND demonstrators, she leaned from her car window to tell them what she thought. 'Where did you learn that language, m'lady?' asked her chauffeur. 'From the grooms.' As with her husband, however, there was surely a strong element of self-consciousness in all the cultivated eccentricities, as when she turned up in a television studio wearing her old tweed skirt beneath, but a clean silk shirt, adorned with important Cavendish jewels on her top – the only part, as she observed, which would be seen by the audiences at home.

It was surely the playfulness of the Macmillans which made them charming. When J. Enoch Powell scornfully dismissed Harold Macmillan as an actor manager, he was observing a set of qualities which he disliked, but which are probably necessary in public life. What mysteriously seems to have happened to Britain during the Macmillan era is that the artifices by which, hitherto, public life was carried on, were stripped away – in the names of truth, or subversion, or the unmasking of hypocrisy, or simple mischief. It was the time when the Island of Apollo truly became the Island of Dionysus. The Macmillans, with their divergent public and private masks, their firm sense of a distinction between the two, were appropriate rulers during such a transition, yet they could not have envisaged in their wildest nightmares in 1957, the things which would come to pass by 1963.

In foreign policy Macmillan faced three enormous and unavoidable questions, which can be summarised in three words – America, Commonwealth, Europe. The Suez debacle had left Anglo-American relations all but shattered. For Macmillan, whose mother was American, and who had enjoyed the comradeship of General Eisenhower during the Second World War, the Anglo-American alliance was the natural bedrock on which Britain's foreign policy must be constructed, the more so since the Empire was in rapid dissolution, and her position *vis-à-vis* Europe was, at best, ambivalent. It was obvious that, since the end of the Second World War, Britain had all but lost its status as a world power. If it was to maintain any position of influence in the world, any sense of itself as worthy of its place on the Security Council of the United Nations, it could only do so as a special ally of the United States.

These are the years (Eisenhower's presidency lasted until 1961, when he was succeeded by John F. Kennedy) when the Cold War between the United States and the Soviet Union very nearly escalated into actual war; and when the ever-volatile Middle East saw crises which, in the case of the Lebanon, literally demanded American intervention, and in the cases of Egypt, Israel and Iraq and Jordan required American steerage against Russian intervention. They were delicate times in which Britain had no capacity, post-Suez, to act directly, but in which the restraining word here, the patient extra negotiation there, the piece of local or diplomatic experience in another area could be seen, with hindsight, to have made a difference.

Macmillan's meeting with Eisenhower in Bermuda within weeks of taking office went some way towards overcoming the distrust which had grown up between the two nations over Suez. When, the following year, events in the Middle East became inflamed, the British and the Americans were able to work together; or, if not together, more closely than would have seemed possible during Eden's premiership. In May 1958, the President of the Lebanon, Camille Camoun, appealed for American help. Inspired by Nasser of Egypt, and with Russian armaments imported from Syria, the anti-Western opposition parties threatened Camoun's government, and the Lebanon, with civil war. The strongest ally the West had in the Middle East was Iraq, whose young King Faisal had been educated in Britain (like his Old Harrovian cousin the King of Jordan). In July, Faisal was killed at the age of twenty-three. It looked as if the Kingdom of Jordan would likewise be overthrown by a combination of Soviet-inspired communism, discontented Islamism and Nasser-induced bloody-mindedness. Within six hours the US 6th fleet was heading for Beirut. 'You are doing a Suez on me,' quipped Macmillan to Eisenhower by telephone.[24]

It was a good, bitter joke, underlying the essential irrationality of American foreign policy over the previous two years. Either they did accept the British (roughly speaking Imperialist) attitude to the region, namely that the West had a need, or even a duty, to police the Middle East, keeping its more 'extremist' elements under control, or they should have been prepared to leave it alone, with the inevitable consequence that the fledgling State of Israel would be devoured in its nest. The Foreign Office in London urged Macmillan to befriend the new government in Iraq, partly for the sake of peace, partly to ensure the West's continued access to the oil fields south of Basra. But it required some sleight of hand to be able to do this while retaining the friendship of Jordan, whose grief-stricken King, mourning the death of his royal cousin in Baghdad, felt let down by the British. Macmillan kept the 2 Parachute Brigade at Amman airport throughout the crisis to assure King Hussein that Britain would support Jordan against a comparable revolution to the one which toppled Faisal, but the American support for this particular part of the summer's Middle Eastern crises was lukewarm. Fifty years and more after those events, Britain and America had still not satisfactorily decided upon their role in the Middle East. The summer of 1958, however, in which Ike 'did a Suez' and intervened in the Lebanon to keep at bay the insurgents, had quickened the American sense of the nature of the problem.

The brinkmanship in American relations with Russia was, as far as world peace was concerned, more immediately alarming. In Eisenhower's last year in office, East and West seemed close to an agreement on the reduction in nuclear armaments. Khrushchev, the Russian leader, wanted to play the double game of reducing arms, and punishing the West by constant and not unjustified observations about the ever-increasing proliferation of American missile stations all over Northern Europe and the Mediterranean, and of the burgeoning espionage industry. John le Carré's novels of moral ambivalence and mutual distrust were the best things to emerge from the murky history of Cold War diplomacy. The closer the spymaster George Smiley came to unearthing Karla, his opposite number in Moscow, the finer seemed the lines, not only between the dirty tricks one side was prepared to play on the other, but also between the moral worth of either side's set of values. Indeed, the achievement of le Carré, best seen in retrospect when the Cold War was over, was the implication that what we were confronting here was an extraordinary case of displacement. While politicians on both sides moved from one particular summit meeting or diplomatic crisis to another; while agents in the field pulled off yet one more dirty trick, or double-crossed another opposite number, their activities, whose puerility seemed well coloured by the affinity so many of the English spies felt with school, and prep school at that, became emblematic of cultural identity crisis on both sides. Macmillan had the sense that there were not going to be many more politicians who could straddle 'this strange modern age of space and science' and 'the great past – of classical learning and Christian life'. If learning and Christianity were to be scuppered, what would come in their place? What stories would the West be able to tell itself, if it could not claim that its political institutions were the inspiration of Demosthenes, and its religious strength from the Church by law established? A similar sense, however, as the West would learn from reading the novels of Solzhenitsyn, possessed the Soviet mind, a sense that their creeds – in this case Marxist-Leninism – were based on a chimera in which nobody really believed. To hide from themselves their lack of self-belief, the superpowers moved to yet more violent displays of fundamentalist strength, as though the evaporation of faith – in the classical past, in Christianity, or in dialectical materialism – was not the fault of doubt within the soul, but from outside infiltration, the enemy at the gates.

In America's case, the gate at which the enemy lurked was Cuba. In the New Year of 1959, Fidel Castro had ousted the right-wing dictator Fulgencio Batista y Zaldívar and established, only a few miles across the water from Florida, a Marxist-Leninist state, equipped, armed and financed from Moscow. The new President, John F. Kennedy, fulfilling a plan which had been hatched by his predecessor, organised a landing at the Bay of Pigs in Cuba of a brigade of anti-Castro Cuban dissidents, trained in Florida. There were 1,500 men armed with American tanks and guns. They lasted just forty-eight hours before being captured by Castro's crack troops. By October of the following year, the Russians had installed medium-range offensive missiles in Cuba, with a range of 1,500 to 2,000 miles, and Kennedy contemplated an air strike to remove them. There was even talk of a full-scale invasion of Cuba to 'finish with Castro once and for all'. In the last week of October 1962, it looked as if the USA and the Soviet Union were preparing the ultimate horror, nuclear war, prompting Bertrand Russell's verdict that 'Kennedy and Macmillan are the wickedest people in the story of man'. Had the Russians not dismantled their missile bases in Cuba, the unthinkable holocaust could have happened. But if we are right in our analysis of what was going on in the psyche of both sides, a nuclear war was never going to happen. Armageddon occurs because the Reign of the Saints and the True Believers is about to begin, when differing certainties come to blows in the Last Battle. But the Cold War was fought not between fundamentalisms but between self-doubters posing as fundamentalists; not between certainties but between uncertainties. Both sides in the poker game knew they had almost worthless hands.

Cold War, bluff, confrontation, spying, arrests, threats, glooms, silences were to characterise the times, not battles, which had scarred the 1930s, the time of certainties.

The emblem of the pointless stalemate was the Berlin Wall.

Although many Western intellectuals persisted in the belief that communism was a plausible economic-political philosophy and the Soviet Union its worthy guardian, those who were obliged to live beneath its murky shadow took a different view. As early as 1949, 59,245 East Germans had left the German Democratic Republic for the West. By 1953, 331,390 had left, and in Berlin, isolated behind the Iron Curtain, but, in its French, English and American sectors part of the Free West, the refugee crisis was not only a visible disgrace to the government of Walter Ulbricht, but also an administrative catastrophe. Who would heal, who would administer, who would teach the East Germans when, for example, 5,000 doctors and dentists had left the country by 1961, hundreds of scientists, many academics (the entire Law Faculty of the University of Leipzig)? In 1961 even Miss East Germany defected to the West. How could they stop the flow?

In spite of the West's enormous Intelligence Service, and its innumerable agents and double agents in the East, not one of them guessed what Ulbricht was going to do, even when, during a news conference about the refugee crisis, he darkly quipped, 'No one is going to build a wall.'[25]

In the early hours of 13 August 1961 Soviet and East German troops moved around the city, and the Westerners became conscious that some form of blockade was being erected at the inter-Berlin border. As light dawned, it became clear that a barbed-wire barrier had been erected, soon to be followed by the great concrete wall itself. Willy Brandt, Mayor of West Berlin, who had been on a train to Hanover the previous night, hurried back to the city by plane and went directly from Tempelhof to Potsdamer Platz. As he walked about among the quiet, shocked crowds, he was persistently asked, 'When are the Americans going to come?' The Wall was in flagrant violation of the Four Power status of post-war Berlin, as agreed by the United Nations. West Germans feared that the building of the Wall would be the prelude to the Soviet invasion of West Germany itself – a groundless fear as hindsight knows. It was assumed by the Germans that some action would be taken by the Western powers. Macmillan was telephoned the day after the Wall went up. He was having a golfing holiday in Scotland at the time, and he did not think it necessary to cut short his pleasure. 'Nobody is going to fight over Berlin,' he remarked. Nor would Adenauer leave Bonn to show solidarity with the people of Berlin.

President Kennedy, who sent his deputy president Lyndon Baines Johnson on a visit to Germany shortly after the Wall had been built, did not get around to visiting until June 1963, by which time East Germany was firmly and safely behind its concrete prison wall. His speechwriter was able to come up with a quotable sound bite: 'All free men, wherever they may live, are citizens of Berlin, and therefore as a free man, I take pride in the words, *Ich bin ein Berliner.*' Only he wasn't a Berliner, and those who were might have welcomed more support at the time. When Willy Brandt publicly declared the contents of his letter to Kennedy, back in 1961, imploring the West to do something, Kennedy was furious. THE WEST DOES NOTHING complained the newspaper *Bild.* Crowds of demonstrators massed in West Berlin displaying banners which read WE APPEAL TO THE WORLD . . . But it suited the world (or so the world supposed) to have a divided Germany. Still haunted by the spectres of the two world wars, the Western powers continued to believe, in the absence of a scintilla of evidence, that a strengthened Germany would turn into a militaristic Germany, or that a united Germany would somehow 'threaten' the West. The Soviets had urged restraint upon the East German authorities, which is why they asked for the Wall to be a barbed-wire barrier in the first instance in case American tanks and troops were moved in. Then, in all likelihood, the Soviets would have backed away. But Erich Honecker, First Secretary of the East German Communist Party, was a man who had clocked the Western idea. He had urged from the beginning that the Wall should be unassailable, and built of concrete. Nothing quite like it had ever been seen in history. Kennedy thought that the Wall was 'a hell of a lot better than a war'.

Apparently that was what most people supposed. The Americans and British, who, either separately or together, were prepared to rattle sabres in small countries such as the Lebanon or Jordan, had reverted to the old appeasement policies of the 1930s when it came to a power with muscle.

'The Berlin Wall', wrote the greatest historian of that city, 'sealed off the last escape route from what had now become a giant 100,000-square-kilometre prison called the German Democratic Republic.' In the le Carré-ish balancing game played by the foreign ministries and governments of Washington and London it was considered 'suitable', 'acceptable', 'preferable' that millions of human beings should be compelled to live in poverty, fear and servitude.

Macmillan was a much-travelled Prime Minister who saw his role primarily in terms of foreign affairs. Indeed, like subsequent Prime Ministers, he could even savour foreign problems, the more intractable or dangerous the better, since they enhanced his self-estimation as a statesman, whereas problems at home, ranging from day-to-day wage disputes with trades unions, to more general matters such as the implosion and ultimate collapse of Western culture itself, were less attractive. Within weeks of taking office, as has been said, he was off to Bermuda to 'mend the fences' with President Eisenhower. Six weeks during the wintry early months of 1958 were devoted to a tour of the Commonwealth – starting in India where, to Anthony Sampson, one of the journalists in his entourage, 'he seemed an apparition from the imperial past', with his dark blue suit in the blazing heat of Delhi airport, his Old Etonian tie and his shy, stilted manner. In fact, the Commonwealth tour was in many senses restorative. Always hypochondriac and prone to winter colds, he could escape the English winter. After a long period of estrangement from his wife he could become her friend, dependent, as the tour went on, to Pakistan, Ceylon, New Zealand and Australia, upon her exuberant and aristocratic ability to talk to strangers, and able to enjoy her company without the ever painful phenomenon of her disappearing, for a part of each month, to be with her lover Boothby.

Politically, moreover, the Commonwealth tour was wonderfully easy. Indeed, it was more in the nature of a royal progress than a political tour, since none of the problems facing the countries he visited were ones to which the British Prime Minister was being asked to provide a solution. India and Pakistan, sure enough, had their local difficulties, but since independence more than a decade ago, they were not looking to Westminster for the impossible business of decisions. As for the white Dominions of New Zealand and Australia, they possessed, at this date, almost no inhabitants who wished to be independent of the British Crown. They were parodies of Britain itself, without any of the threats to Britain's happiness or security – threats such as a collapse of labour relations, or housing shortages.

Never slow to note newspaper items about himself which could be construed in a favourable connotation, Macmillan quoted in his memoirs from a journalist – 'Whatever Macmillan may have done for the Commonwealth, the Commonwealth has certainly done for Macmillan.'

But it was not in the independent states of the Indian subcontinent, nor in the happily self-governing white Dominions, that the problems of British colonialism, or post-colonialism, were to be found. These boiled and festered in the vast continent upon which, until he became Prime Minister, Macmillan had never set foot: Africa.

Chronologically, the colonies of West Africa were the first to go the way of India and Pakistan, and achieve self-government. To many Africans at the time, as to the huge majority of everyone else in the world once history had unfolded, it was a transparent demographical fact that one day, majority rule, and rule by the indigenous population, would follow. In the late 1950s, however, this notion was by no means obvious, and was indeed hotly contested, especially in three African areas – in the huge, fertile, mineral-rich and beautiful East African Kenya; in the southern-central cluster known as the Central African Federation – Southern and Northern Rhodesia and Nyasaland – and South Africa. The more right-wing members of Macmillan's own Cabinet, most notably Lord Salisbury, as well as the white inhabitants of these regions, all believed that it was desirable, and possible, for white minority rule to continue in these areas. Successive British governments since the Second World War had displayed conflicting and contradictory policies over the matter. In 1957, then, the Gold Coast was granted independence and, as the newly named country of Ghana, it enjoyed an in many ways successful decade under the premiership of Dr Kwame Nkrumah, with a single-chamber, elected parliamentary system, and with local government conducted in four regional assemblies. Nigeria became independent in 1960, and in spite of much more complex tribal and religious divisions than those in Ghana, it enjoyed a measure of stability under Sir Abubakar Balewa. Sierra Leone, effectively independent since 1958, became formally so in 1961.

Kenyan nationalists, on the other side of the continent, could look forward to no such smooth handover of power from the hands of the white men. It had been the policy of the post-war Labour government in Westminster, as of the Conservative governments, to treat Kenya rather as if it were Australia or New Zealand, a fertile land in which whites from the old country could be encouraged to settle. British ex-servicemen had received money from Attlee's, Churchill's and Eden's exchequers to help them establish farms in Kenya. The colonisation of this hugely rich country was not, then, the inheritance of some casually made Victorian decision to settle the land with Europeans. It was a living colony, and the Imperialist expansion in East Africa was going on even as the British withdrew from India and from West Africa.

The resistance movement to all this came from the Kikuyu tribe, which formed about 20 per cent of the Kenyan population. Under the leadership of Jomo Kenyatta, they had pursued a course of terror, in the hope of driving the whites from Africa out of sheer horror. The secret Kikuyu society which committed itself to his murderous policy bore the name of Mau Mau.

The government in London had begun to recognise that Kenyan independence, and the end of white supremacy, was an inevitability, but they could not bring themselves to admit as much, either to the inhabitants of Kenya or to their own right wing. The Colonial Secretary, Alan Lennox-Boyd, as late as January 1959, could hold a conference in London in which he promised independence to the two other East African colonies – Tanganyika (independent 1961) and Uganda (1962) – while claiming that Kenyan independence would either not happen at all or was a long way off. Later that year, at Hola detention camp in Kenya, eleven Mau Mau detainees were beaten to death by the warders. It was initially claimed that they had died from lack of water. Lennox-Boyd was sacked and replaced by Iain Macleod, a very different sort of Conservative, who enraged his colleagues, and the white Kenyans, by stating the obvious – that Jomo Kenyatta the terrorist would be released from prison, and that majority rule in that country would soon become an inevitability. Kenya became independent on 12 December 1963. Some white settlers were richly compensated by British taxpayers' money and came home. Most of the 30,000 Europeans (compared with the five and a quarter million Africans) decided to stay on, unharmed by Kenyatta or his former Mau Mau fighters.

The weight of sheer majority, or the Law of Time, would make it inevitable that Africa would be ruled by Africans. But even this fact, becoming obvious to Macmillan and those around him, was not immediately apparent to those who lived in African countries, particularly those in the southern part of the continent. And here, if one is to paint a fair picture of history, it is necessary to think not of two groups – Africans who wanted independence at any cost, and white supremacists – but a third, comprising Africans and Europeans who found, particularly for example in Southern Rhodesia, that a system of law and order, in which more and more Africans were being educated, and entering upon responsibilities formerly exercised by whites, was perhaps preferable to a violent or sudden transition from all-European to all-African government.

And then again, further south there was the unique and extreme example of South Africa. When Macmillan arrived on the last lap of his African tour at Durban, he found sunburnt, happy whites, waving Union Jacks as they came from their tennis courts and their swimming pools. But he also found a group of black protesters who, adapting his own famous political cliché at home, carried banners which read, 'We've never had it so bad'.

As the move towards African independence spread across the continent, the southern African countries hardened in their colonial attitudes. In Rhodesia, the Law and Order Maintenance Bill, passed in 1960, greatly strengthened the hand of what was in effect an all-white one-party system of government, giving the authorities powers of press censorship which by European standards would have been fascist, and allowing brutal police treatment of suspects. In South Africa, things were more extreme. Though sixty years had passed since the Boer War, the old Dutch Boer religion had not gone away. Nor had resentment among the Afrikaans population at being pushed around by the British. South Africa was poised to leave the Commonwealth. Even as Macmillan visited them, Nelson Mandela with 155 others was on trial for treason. A month after Macmillan's visit, sixty-seven black demonstrators were shot at Sharpeville. And the danger, ever-present in Macmillan's mind (not least because so many members of his own party at home supported the right-wing line), was that Southern Rhodesia would follow the South African line and move towards white-ruled independence.

Speaking to the all-white South African Parliament in words written for him by a diplomat called David Hunt, Macmillan once again demonstrated the blurb writer's zest for the memorable cliché, with his famous Wind of Change speech:

Ever since the break-up of the Roman Empire one of the constant facts of political life in Europe has been the emergence of independent nations . . .
Today the same thing is happening in Africa, and the most striking of all the impressions I have formed since I left London a month ago is of the strength of this African national consciousness. In different places it takes different forms, but it is happening everywhere. The wind of change is blowing through this continent, and, whether we

like it or not, this growth of national consciousness is a political fact. We must all accept it as a fact and our national policies must take account of it.

To say that there was an element of humbug in the speech is not to deny that Macmillan, in common with many liberal-minded Englishmen of the period, was genuinely shocked by the system of apartheid, whereby, as in the United States, segregation between human beings on the grounds of skin pigmentation was formally written into the system. In Britain, segregation existed, and would go on existing, through the invisible veils of class snobbery, economic segregation and taboo. Macmillan and his kind would have been amazed had a group of blacks turned up on one of their shooting parties or at Pratt's Club, but the many unwritten rules of English society made such an event impossible to envisage. Therefore, when he met old Dr Verwoerd, the President of South Africa, who spelt such things out in print and made them into fixed laws, Macmillan was shocked, having the not especially original insight that for Verwoerd apartheid was 'more than a political philosophy, it was a religion; a religion based on the Old Testament rather than on the New'.[26] The Commonwealth Immigrants Bill, drawn up in February 1962, began with the assertion that 'Immigration officers will of course carry out their duties without regard to the race, colour or religion of Commonwealth citizens who may seek to enter the country', but no one had any doubt as to its aim, namely to limit the number of black people coming into the country. It was a piece of fine old British hypocrisy from first page to last, since it was carefully designed to keep out the blacks, while not being seen to do so. In the words of Macmillan's official biographer, Alastair Horne, 'one of the principal complications . . . was how to preserve non-discrimination while not closing the door on members of the "white" Commonwealth'.[27]

Quite apart from the ideological problems facing the Commonwealth, its economic relationship with the former mother country was to be the serious underlying question of the Macmillan years. Would trade with the Commonwealth be enough to sustain economic growth at home and allow Macmillan to purvey to the British people a situation in which, he could tell them they had 'never had it so good'?

When attacked for the cliché, and for the philosophy which lay behind it, by no less a person than Dr Fisher, Archbishop of Canterbury, Macmillan responded hotly and with passion. Fisher, at a sermon in Croydon of all places, said that it was 'a dreadful' phrase, and added some humbug of his own in which he wondered, 'will it always stay good if we do not keep our minds on the love of God?'[28]

Macmillan retorted, in a private letter:

I also share your view as a Churchman that the material condition of a people must by no means be the only criterion. Unless it has the spiritual values it will fail. Nevertheless it is the function of Governments to try to improve material conditions and I have always thought that the Church had supported us in this effort.

The attack on poverty, the attempts to clear the slums, to deal with low wages, to remove unemployment, all these were always impressed upon me by your great predecessor Dr Temple, as truly Christian duties. At any rate, when I put my mind back to the conditions of the great slums, with three million unemployed, with the means test, with the state of health and housing conditions, and indeed with the general level in which many of our people were condemned to live, I rejoice that it is now so good . . .

On my African tour [he was writing from Nigeria] I am more and more impressed by the need which I have always put strongly before the country, especially at the last General Election, for the 'good neighbour' policy, that is that they should use their growing material strength for the assistance of development overseas, especially in the Commonwealth. But I have also reminded them that they cannot do this out of poverty. They can only do it out of wealth.[29]

The burgeoning prosperity of post-war Europe, and the large free-trade area of the Common Market, was not something from which Britain could afford to exclude itself. Indeed, for some British observers, it was vital, if economic prosperity was to continue in Britain, that membership of the Common Market be sought as soon as possible. For others, however, Europe was a spectre to be dreaded: from the left, it was seen as a capitalist club, and from the right as a federalist trap which would neuter national sovereignty.

The Treaty of Rome was signed on 25 March 1957, at a moment when Britain was still reeling from the Suez debacle and the new Prime Minister was primarily concerned with repairing the wreckage of Anglo-American relations.

The signatories to the original treaty were those who, in different ways, had suffered defeat in the Second World War, who had known at first hand, and at far greater cost than the victors, the devastating effects of war, but who had also known, before the war, a much greater degree of short-term economic success than the *laissez-faire* economy of Britain. Germany (now only West Germany) and Italy had both had what could be termed state-enforced Keynesianism which had led to the conquest of unemployment, and a programme of public works – the building of modern road systems, railways and infrastructure which had no comparison in Britain. It was the aim of the former fascist countries of Italy and Germany, together with their satellites Belgium, Luxembourg and the Netherlands (which had been largely fascist in sympathy in the 1930s), to recover what had been achieved in the 1930s, without, naturally, a revival of the repressive structures of the police state. The other great inspiration of the European idealists was to bring about peace between France and Germany, whose conflicts since 1870 had led to the loss of so much European life. Here, once more, France, which had effectively been governed from Berlin from 1940 to 1944 – half directly under German occupation and half, in so-called Vichy France, under the satrapy of Marshal Pétain. Clearly, it was impossible so soon after the war to admit that the arrangement had been advantageous to France, especially since France was now under the benign dictatorship of General de Gaulle, whose Free French gesture had done little to further the defeat of the Third Reich but much to hearten those Frenchmen and women who felt the humiliations of the 1940–44 years. So it was that de Gaulle signed up to the Treaty of Rome, seeing it as a convenient way of enjoying the economic advantages of federalism while telling his electorate, and perhaps actually believing, that the new Common Market, with its ultimate aim of laying 'the foundation of an ever closer union among the peoples of Europe', was really a way of France dominating Europe without using military force.

It was perhaps not surprising that the basically fascist idea of a United Europe was not pursued by many British politicians in their election manifestos of 1959, the first election after the Treaty of Rome was signed. The only British politician who embraced the idea of 'Europe a Nation' with public enthusiasm was Sir Oswald Mosley, a fringe figure since his imprisonment during the Second World War under the 18B regulations, and, being natural flypaper for the crackpots, not a man likely to be brought back into the fold of either main party, even if he had shown signs of wishing this. Nevertheless, he was the first British politician to make public use of those arguments which would later be familiar on the lips of the 'pro-Europeans' in British politics, namely that in a competitive economic world it was no longer viable for small nation states to 'go it alone'. In *Europe: Faith and Plan – A Way Out from the Coming Crises* – Mosley asked, 'Can these relatively small, isolated, individual nations of Western Europe face for fifteen years on world markets the competition of America's normal production surplus, plus the deliberate market-breaking dumping of the Soviets at below European production costs?' No, because 'they are dependent on external supplies of raw materials for their industries . . . they are forced to pay for these necessities by exports sold in open competition in world markets, under conditions where they have no influence whatever'.[30]

The Macmillan government knew this as clearly as anyone, just as they were aware that from its very first beginnings, when the French and Germans turned potential industrial rivalry into a partnership which easily outstripped British coal and steel (hampered by industrial disputes and all the disadvantages of state-owned industry). The French and German Coal and Steel agreement, the brainchild of French Foreign Minister Robert Schumann and Jean Monnet, was the basis of an economic idea which was ineluctable for the Europeans.

For some parts of British industry, the advantages of joining in such a Common Market were, would be, huge. In other areas, where Britain was in touch with a bigger world market, there was no advantage, or positive disadvantage, which is why both sides of the political debate in Britain, between pro- and anti-Europeans, can always be made to sound perfectly plausible. Equally, however, the political-cum-mythological arguments for the Island Race to allow itself to be subsumed into a European Federalist idea, with loss of sovereignty and 'Britishness', has always been understandably abhorrent to the majority of British voters.

These differences would run like a great seismic fault line through the whole political history of Britain for the next half-century, dividing parties and individual minds (for most of the prominent British politicians changed their minds at least once about whether they were or were not Europeans).

Macmillan, as ever Janus-like, looked back to a time when Britain had 'influence in Europe' (that is, the period when he himself was in Italy at the end of the war watching a little wistfully as the Americans swept slowly through France and Germany but too slowly to stop Stalin swallowing up all the countries of Eastern Europe). A natural Francophile who had fought at the Battle of the Somme, he wanted to check what he feared would be undue German influence in Europe, and, naturally, it was a blow to him that General de Gaulle vetoed the British application to join the Common Market in 1962. He attributed this, probably quite rightly, not to any economic arguments, but to the fact that de Gaulle could not quite forgive Britain for its personal kindness to himself during the Second World War (Churchill had not only allowed de Gaulle to set up his Free French organisation in London but had actually suggested the medieval arrangement that the governments of

France and Britain should become one). Nor could de Gaulle tolerate a memory of France's humiliations in 1940. 'Things would have been easier,' he opined, 'if Southern England had been occupied by the Nazis – if we'd had Lloyd George for Pétain, then we would have been equal [i.e., with the French] . . . that's why [de Gaulle] found Adenauer, who'd also been occupied, an easier ally than me . . . I may be cynical, but I fear it's true – if Hitler had danced in London, we'd have had no trouble with de Gaulle.'[31]

Throughout Europe (though not, curiously enough, in the United States) societies in the last fifty years have followed a pattern: as prosperity increases, the conventions and rules of society have relaxed. Capital punishment was abolished; corporal punishment, whether of criminals or of children in schools or at home, came to be frowned upon; greater tolerance was shown towards sexual deviancy; abortion became more easily available; religious belief, or at any rate adherence to religious organisations, declined. R. A. Butler, thought by many to be the lost leader of the Conservative Party, or Macmillan's obvious successor when the time came, became Home Secretary in 1957. When he did so he was not an abolitionist, but he became so. (His wife, Molly, had been an abolitionist ever since her first husband, High Sheriff of Essex, had borne responsibility for hangings.)[32]

Butler was a canny if ultimately unsuccessful politician. He inherited the Homicide Act, 1957, from his predecessor, one which he described as 'rather curious' since it restricted the death penalty not to degrees of murder but to the imagined deterrent effect which any particular hanging would be deemed to have on the maintenance of law and order. He refused, for political reasons, to reopen the case of Timothy Evans, who had been hanged for the murder of his wife and child, and he refused to question, though he was deeply disturbed by, the case of Derek Bentley, who was hanged for a murder committed by his younger accomplice, Christopher Craig. Butler could see that to bring up the issue of capital punishment before an election was political folly. The majority of the public, in common with the right wing of the Conservative Party, loved hangings, and would not be impressed by a party which promised to abolish them. Therefore the whole matter was deferred throughout Macmillan's term of office. Butler and Macmillan, progressivists at heart (though Macmillan favoured capital punishment, he knew its abolition was one day an inevitability), therefore allowed hangings to continue, a good example in miniature of the untroubled attitude which politicians have towards life and death, when weighing in the balance a fellow mortal's existence and their own chance of re-election. Indeed, when Henry Brooke took over as Home Secretary there was no certainty at all that the death penalty would be abolished in the foreseeable future.

It was not until the Sexual Offences Act of 1967 that law permitted homosexual acts between two males, in private, and over the age of twenty-one. Abortion was still in most cases very difficult to obtain and was the preserve of the back-street amateur, with her knitting needles and bottles of gin. Divorce was difficult to obtain. Harold Macmillan managed to pay lip service to the march of progress without, on home territory, having to do much to expedite its advance.

There were two areas, however, in which historians can see that Macmillan's government definitely defined the future of Britain on the domestic front. The first was in the area of immigration, the second of transport.

Although the 1962 Commonwealth Immigrants Act was, as has been said, grossly hypocritical in regard to race, and although its aim was to limit the immigration into Britain by those who were called in those days 'coloured', the limits it imposed were slight and ineffectual. Harold Macmillan told his diary he had never seen the Commons 'in so hysterical a mood' since Suez when the Bill was debated. The Labour Party (who three years later, when themselves in power, brought in a much more restrictive Bill to curb immigration) claimed to be deeply shocked. Gaitskell called it a 'cruel and brutal anti-colour legislation'. ('Gaitskell is the kind of cad that only a gentleman can be,' thought Macmillan.[33]) For J. Enoch Powell and the right-wing conservatives, the Bill did not go nearly far enough in preventing West Indians and Asians from entering Britain. (There were fewer Africans in those days.)

Short of unimaginable acts of transportation which would indeed have been 'cruel and brutal', it is impossible to see how the process of immigration could, in fact, have been reversed. Aeroplanes and comparatively cheap travel had been invented. They could not be uninvented. There was a general movement of peoples across the face of the globe, and not just a move from Commonwealth countries to Britain. The increase of prosperity at home meant an increase in the labour market. The National Health Service, London Transport, British Railways and other huge employers had already, by the Macmillan era, come to depend upon cheap immigrant labour. But a mighty change it was, poised to alter the character of all the big British cities.

The second change which took place in the Macmillan era was the conscious decision by the government for Britain to stop being a railway nation and to become a car nation.

Here there truly was a choice, and the politicians unquestionably made the wrong one.

One of the great achievements of the Victorians, and a key reason for their economic domination of the world, was the setting up of a railway network which linked every part of the United Kingdom. At the peak of railway travel in 1914 there were over 20,000 miles of railways in Britain.[34] After the nationalisation of the railways by the Labour Party during the first Attlee government, there was obviously a fall in the profitability of the railways. Much of the stock was out of date. The British Transport Commission, chaired from 1953 to 1961 by General Sir Brian Robertson, proposed, surely sensibly, a wholesale modernisation of the railways.

Politicians, however, only see the short term. They were worried by repeated labour disputes on the railways. They saw that more and more freight was now carried by road, and they thought that the answer to this was not to improve the rail service but to follow the inevitably calamitous route of building more roads. (They did not see the truth that the more roads you build, the more traffic clogs them, with all the environmental calamities which follow.) Macmillan's Minister of Transport, Ernest Marples, believed that the British Transport Commission was 'incompetent' and that General Sir Brian Robertson should be sacked, to be replaced by a man who had 'one of the most able and fertile brains in the industrial and commercial world' – Dr Richard Beeching. Beeching was already in the pay of those who wished to make a huge killing by building a vast series of *Autobahns* all over Britain. Whether or not this was known to Macmillan, the Prime Minister met Beeching *à deux* on 10 May 1961.[35] He asked Beeching about the possibility of selling off railway property 'to finance modernisation'. Beeching was put in charge of modernising the railways. The trades unions were quite understandably and rightly immediately opposed to him. They were never consulted either by Macmillan or by Beeching about the proposals he had in mind. First, the closure of railway workshops where rolling stock and locomotives were made and repaired – the men who worked there never so much as warned in advance.

Beeching, who had now abolished the BTC and been declared Head of British Railways, told the Cabinet that they should be prepared to axe 70,000 jobs in the railways. 'Most of this reduction would be effected by normal wastage and control of recruitment.' On 27 March 1963, the Beeching Plan for the Railways was on sale at Her Majesty's Stationery Office, and Ernest Marples was crowing to the Commons that his government would provide 'an efficient, economic and well-balanced transport system for Great Britain'. The Beeching Plan, when put into effect, was to lead to the reduction of railway mileage from 17,500 in

1963 to 11,000 in 1975, only a little more than half the railway capacity enjoyed by Britain at the outbreak of the Great War.

Not only was rail travel comparatively cheap and environmentally friendly; not only were the fuels necessary to maintain it (coal in the 1950s and in the 1960s, diesel and electricity) all easily obtainable and limited within a government budget, but the railway network did link up Britain in a way which roads somehow do not, without destroying everything in their path. The journey by train from a city centre to a provincial town, changing to a branch line and emerging at the wooden, gas-lit platform of some remote 'halt' was, of course, the work of engineers and planners. But in spite of the deep hostility felt by some countrymen and old Tories to the development of the railways in the nineteenth century, the remarkable thing about the trains (which, of course, only passed through country districts every hour or so) was how tolerantly they left nature intact. To make comparable journeys by car requires roads, it requires garages built on by-passes, and it requires the noisy, ugly, polluting means of transport to be taken from the crowded city centre or town to the formerly unsullied bit of country. Beeching, and Macmillan with him, had made no corner of Britain entirely safe from the car. Railways could pass through hillside, fields and villages without, miraculously, destroying them and in most cases the coming of the railway (as evoked in the poetry of Edward Thomas or the crime novels of Michael Innes) actually seemed at home in the world of nature, as was witnessed by many a remote signal box or level crossing, heavy, in summer, with cow parsley and rose-bay willow herb, or swathed in autumn by cow-breathed fogs and river mist. After Macmillan, there were few parts of England where the noise of bird-song and insects chirruping is not drowned by the destructive hum of the distant *Autobahn*.

Commenting on his own preferred recreation, grouse-shooting, Macmillan commented, 'I think one of the reasons why one loves a holiday on the moors is that, in a confused and changing world, the picture in one's mind is not spoilt.

'If you go to Venice or Florence or Assisi you might as well be at Victoria Station – masses of tourists, chiefly Germans in shorts. If you go to Yorkshire or Scotland, the hills, the keepers, the farmers, the farmers' sons, the drivers are all the same; and (except for the coming of the Land Rover, etc) there is a sense of continuity.'[36] It is probably still possible to find such tranquillity in the Highlands of Scotland, and in parts of Yorkshire. In Macmillan's day, it was available to many British people in their own back gardens, and certainly in the landscapes of Devon, Gloucestershire, Suffolk, Lancashire, most of which have been irreparably ruined by roads – what he wistfully calls 'the coming of the Land Rover, etc'.

In the end, Macmillan's hypochondria, his sense of his own decay, allied to periods of self-doubt and black depression, became not merely a reason for his standing down, but also an emblem of what was happening to Britain itself. Macmillan was the ideal, the most expressive possibly, leader for Britain at this period, for a Britain which both had genuine links with the past, but links which were also fraudulent; a Britain which was genuinely cynical, yet wistfully holding on to faith; a Britain which was the sick man of Europe, but which was also a self-doubting hypochondriac who would make old bones.

Meanwhile, two duller, but equally devastating threads of destiny were being woven by the Norns to the Conservative Party's undoing. Both had to do with the party of Opposition.

The first was the sudden death of Hugh Gaitskell, leader of the Labour Party, on 18 January 1963. He was fifty-six years old. The disease which killed him, *lupus erythematosus*, had come upon him quite unexpectedly. As the 'right-wing' Labour leader, witty, eloquent, passionate, he looked bound to win the next election from the Conservatives. But would he have done so ('Gaitskell is the kind of cad that only a gentleman can be')? Would he really have given the impression, as his successor so audibly and visibly was able to do when the time came, that a vote for Labour was a vote not merely for a different party in government but in effect for a completely different Britain? After Gaitskell's death, the choice for the Labour leadership was between the right-wing candidate, a working-class man called George Brown, and a former Oxford don of lower-middle-class origins, James Harold Wilson. They chose Wilson, though both Wilson and Brown were well qualified to pick up Macmillan's comic mantle.

There was now absolutely no danger of the public feeling that the Labour Party was led, like the Conservatives, by a 'toff', and since these class matters were coming more and more to the fore, this was a vital ingredient in the Conservatives' downfall.

The Macmillan government, largely composed of uninspired old men, looked as if it was losing electoral support. At a by-election in March 1962, the Liberal candidate, Eric Lubbock, won the safe Tory seat of Orpington by 7,855. Another by-election loomed, this time in Leicester, and during the night when the poll was being counted, Macmillan panicked, deciding that there was a plot against him. ('Butler,' he told Selwyn Lloyd, with no evidence whatever, 'had been plotting to divide the party on the Common Market and bring him [Macmillan] down.')

So Macmillan sacked Lloyd as Chancellor, and six other Cabinet ministers, bringing in some slightly younger blood – Keith Joseph, Edward
Boyle and William Deedes among them. The ruthlessness of Macmillan's
gesture was immediately likened to Hitler's suppression of the Rohm
supporters in the SA in 1934 and dubbed the Night of the Long Knives.
Gilbert Longden MP (Conservative) during a censure debate on 26 July
congratulated the Prime Minister on keeping his head, when all around
him were losing theirs. It was obvious that the Conservatives were ready
for a spell in Opposition, and this would have been the case even if
Macmillan's government had not been assailed by the three phenomena
usually blamed for his demise – the exposure of a cypher clerk in the
British Embassy in Moscow, John Vassall, as a homosexual and a secret
Soviet agent; the scandal of John Profumo, Secretary of State for War,
being revealed to have had a brief affair with a young woman, Christine
Keeler. Another key event occurred on 31 July, just before the summer
recess of 1963. The Peerage Bill became law, as a result of the agita-
tions of the former Viscount Stansgate. When Anthony Wedgwood Benn,
MP for Bristol, inherited a viscountcy from his father, he was anxious
to be rid of it to continue his political career in the Commons. This
was the first step in the transformation of this moderate Social Democrat
Anthony Wedgwood Benn to Tony Benn, Trotskyite firebrand, darling
of radio audiences and People's Friend. It also enabled other hereditary
peers to nurse the undignified political aspirations which had hitherto
been open only to commoners. Quintin Hogg, who had inherited the
title bestowed on his father for founding the London Polytechnic
(Viscount Hailsham), and the 14th Earl of Home, who was able to
perform the office of Foreign Secretary from the House of Lords, were
both now in a position to succeed Macmillan, since it was felt in these
progressive times that, although such Prime Ministers as Lord Liverpool,
Lord Salisbury and Lord Rosebery had all managed to exercise their
duties from the Upper House, it was no longer appropriate in the age
of the Beatles and *What's My Line?*

When Macmillan developed very mild prostate troubles, he resigned
immediately. The Conservatives had no processes for electing their leader
but, if questioned, the majority would have supposed that, just as the
choice last time had been between Wab or Hawold, so now it would
be the turn of Wab with Quintin Hogg as a clownish alternative. They
had not reckoned upon Macmillan from his hospital bed concocting
the story for the Queen that the majority of people in the party wanted
Lord Home, who would soon be transmogrified into Sir Alec Douglas-
Home. Nor perhaps had anyone quite reckoned on Home's charm and

political astuteness, neither of which was lost upon the television-viewing electorate. The 1964 election was a close-run thing. If a mere nine hundred people in eight marginal constituencies had voted Conservative instead of Labour, then Douglas-Home's government would have survived.[37]

7

Mental Health and Suicides

When Naomi Campbell was asked by a journalist what she liked reading, the cultivated scribbler came away with the impression that the super-model had said 'Foucault': it subsequently appeared more likely that she had in fact uttered two words, the second of which was 'all'. Michel Foucault (1926–84) was undoubtedly one of the emblematic prophets of our times, and his *History of Madness*, first published in 1961, one of the most influential texts. Though Naomi Campbell might not have read, or heard of, Foucault, being too busy throwing scenes in restaurants and yelling at journalists, many of her more intellectually pretentious contemporaries at polytechnics and colleges throughout Britain would have absorbed the ideas of the Poitiers-born anarchist thinker: namely, that the very concept of reason was no more than an instrument of political control. For every conscientious student who had actually read Foucault, there would be ten thousand nerds who believed that the French savant has somehow or another rumbled a confidence trick being played upon the multitude. Foucault's 'philosophy' was a confirmation of the chippy paranoia which exists in the minds of many 'little people', namely that the policeman pacing reassuringly up and down at the end of the pave-ment, the nurse bustling unselfishly about the hospital ward, the doctor working long hours in the surgery, the prison warder keeping dangerous knifers, rapists and muggers from our doors at night are all engaged in a mysterious conspiracy to curtail our liberty. Refusing to recognise the obvious – that in a society without any restraints the weak would inevitably be exposed to attack, mockery, neglect – Foucault saw all restraint, and all convention, as essentially sinister. Foucault taught a whole generation to distrust authority, even when it appeared to be attempting to protect the weak from attack, or protecting the vulnerable from themselves.

The humorist Tony Hendra recollected: 'When I went up to Cambridge University in the early 1960s it was to complete my studies as a Benedictine monk . . . But then I bought a ticket for *Beyond the Fringe*. I went into the show a monk, and I emerged having completely lost my vocation. I didn't know things could be so funny. I didn't realise that authority was so absurd.'[1] The stage show, of comic sketches which had begun at the Edinburgh Fringe, and was repeated to outstanding acclaim on the stage at Cambridge and Brighton, as well as in London and New York, launched the careers of Jonathan Miller, Alan Bennett, Dudley Moore and Peter Cook. It first appeared at the Fortune Theatre in London on 10 May 1961, from which Michael Frayn dated the arrival in the capital of 'satire'. But by the standards of Pope and Swift, for example, or of the magazine *Private Eye*, *Beyond the Fringe* was hardly violent in its satirical abuse. What its first audiences found so liberating was that it refused to take *anything* seriously. As an early enthusiast, Bernard Levin, wrote: 'These four immortals take on such targets as the Prime Minister, Dr Verwoerd, Mr Mboya [the Kenyan African nationalist leader], the H-bomb, Mr Cousins' opposition to the H-bomb, capital punishment, patriotism, Shakespeare, the clergy, the linguistic philosophers, the Sunday-night religious television programmes, history, lunacy, and anti-semitism . . .' When it first happened, *Beyond the Fringe* caught its audiences by surprise. The young monk who was so bowled over by the show in Cambridge might have been unusual in wanting to be a monk; he was not unusual in finding *Beyond the Fringe* a revelation. Larkin, in his cycle clips in the 1950s, had presupposed that 'someone will forever be surprising/A hunger in himself to be more serious'.[2] *Beyond the Fringe* reminded the British of their equally strong need, felt at the beginning of the 1960s, to be more facetious. This ushered in much good comedy in the theatre, and some more alarming theatre in the supposedly serious worlds of academic medicine and psychiatric care. Even in the opening decade of the twenty-first century, a hostile review of a retranslation of Foucault's *History of Madness* could provoke extreme reactions.

Years after Foucault's death, psychiatrist and scholar Andrew Scull had the temerity to expose Foucault's many errors of historical fact. Foucault had claimed, for example, that 'it was in the buildings that had previously been both convents and monasteries that the majority of the great asylums of England . . . were set up'. Only one – the Bedlam, or Bethlehem Hospital, had such an origin and the great majority of English asylums were the products of the Enlightenment.[3]

Scull's book *Decarceration* is a devastating indictment of the care of mental patients 'in the community'. He claimed that the therapeutic effectiveness of much so-called anti-psychotic medicine – mainly the phenothiazines – had been greatly exaggerated. He was a Marxist who wrote from his own belief that the state had a duty to nurse and protect its vulnerable citizens. Studying the plight of mental patients in America and Britain who had been turned loose into the community, he noted that they were often living as down-and-outs, or being cared for by the Salvation Army. 'Yet more exist by preying on the less agile and wary, whether these be "ordinary" people trapped by poverty and circumstance in the inner city, or their fellow decarcerated deviants.'[4] Scull's review of the reissued Foucault excited some passionate defences of Foucault in the following issues of the *Times Literary Supplement*. Perhaps the fairest came from Bill Luckin of the Centre for the History of Science, Technology and Medicine, at the University of Manchester – 'Had it not been for Foucault, British and American social history under-graduates would still be plodding their way through stodgily Whiggish accounts of the history of penology, education and madness and much else. Better that these parts of the academic universe should have been theorized, under the pre-eminent influence of Foucault, than that students should have continued to be subjected to blandly non-problematic versions of the past . . .'[5]

Foucault's errors of fact did not trouble his many admirers, since they found in his pages one of the central doctrines of our times, namely that all authority is dangerous. For Foucault, one of the most expres-sive emblems of an Enlightenment society was Jeremy Bentham's Panopticon, the architectural control tower, designed by the Utilitarian philosopher for use in British prisons, and which would allow the authority to keep an eye on every aspect of the inmates' lives. For Foucault, the Panopticon was not merely a device for spying on crimi-nals. It was an architectural parable of the way that the closed societies of the recent European past imposed discipline on the populace, in schools, in factories and in hospitals.[6]

Foucault did not create the modern open society, in which sexual mores changed, in which punishment was no longer deemed appropriate for 'deviant' behaviour, but he was one of the most persistent and beguiling of arguers against restraint. The 1960s were rightly seen as times in which all manner of restraints were questioned. Foucault was the prophet of this questioning.

The manner in which societies care for the mentally ill reveals much. In primitive societies, mental illness could be seen as a form of diabolic posses-sion. In post-Enlightenment times, the most disturbing feature of madness was its assault upon order. The phrase was that a man or woman had 'lost their reason' – a terrible thing by any standard, but if your entire social and metaphysical system was, as you supposed, based on reason, madness was especially to be feared. Hence the post-Enlightenment view that those who had 'lost their reason' should be incarcerated. Violent crimes, and murders, and even thefts, tended not to be punished by imprisonment until the close of the nineteenth century. Floggings, hangings or transportation, or (same thing) pressing the criminals into military service were thought better ways of dealing with both crime and its causes. For the Victorians, who cared so deeply about financial probity and about the exercise of reason, incarceration was the appropriate treatment of the indigent and the insane. The workhouse was the place where they locked up the poor who had fallen upon hard times, whereas the debtors' gaol was for the more genteel Mr Dorrits and their families. The mad were housed in mental hospitals which dotted Great Britain until the mid to late twentieth century, great buildings, very often on the edge of towns, often referred to with a jokey mixture of dread and pity, by all the local inhabitants. The idea behind such institutions was a fundamentally kind one, namely that lunatics were not equipped to look after themselves, that they might do themselves and other people damage, and they were better off institutionalised. The actual treatment, however, could be harsh, since almost the only form of treatment allowed to the patients until the mid-twentieth century was restraint. Indeed, in publicly owned mental institutions very little was spent upon palliative medicine for the insane.

The early 1960s witnessed a peculiar combination of developments – firstly a vast growth in the pharmaceutical industry, leading many psychiatrists to believe that some forms of mental illness could be treated with drugs, and without recourse to incarceration; secondly, governments, pressed to expand other branches of public health care, saw an opportunity here to reduce expenditure; thirdly, there was a revolution in the way that mental health itself was regarded, and in writings of some psychiatrists, philosophers, or 'thinkers', the very concept of madness itself was questioned.

The development of pharmaceutical treatment of mental illness was an extraordinary breakthrough. Psychotic illness, especially schizophrenia, was considered by those orthodox medics who continued to believe in the existence of mental illness to be caused by an overactivity of dopamine in the brain. Dopamine is a natural transmitter, known as a neurotransmitter; it transmits messages between brain cells. A new drug, chlorpromazine, developed in Paris in 1953 (marketed as Largactil) blocked receptors in the brain, particularly dopamine. Aggression, delusions, hallucinations could all be held at bay or eliminated from a patient by merely swallowing a small pill. Psychosis, if not cured, could be contained.

This seemed like very good news for mental patients who had hitherto been compelled to face a lifetime of restraint, imprisoned in a Victorian lunatic asylum, sometimes wearing a straitjacket, or in later times simply zonked on heavy sedatives, usually paraldehyde. With judicious pill-swallowing, the nightmare could be over. It was good news, too, for the politicians who wished both to spend more money on the National Health Service and to save money where possible. Macmillan's Minister, subsequently Secretary of State for Health, J. Enoch Powell, had a grandiose spending plan. No wonder the Secretary of State for Health looked with joy at the prospect of closing the old lunatic asylums.

He overlooked, of course, some disturbing facts. Schizophrenics and others who might benefit from taking Largactil could not always be persuaded to take the pills, and if left to their own devices might well forget to do so. Largactil had side effects, making some patients sleepy or jaundiced. These problems could be worked out if the patients continued to have medical supervision and to have back-up care if they were 'released into the community' – i.e., let out of the lunatic asylums and expected to live like non-delusional, non-psychotic individuals. Almost no one existed who had been trained in the work of caring for such patients. There existed no halfway houses to assist psychotic patients to make a new life for themselves outside hospital. The state, in opting for pharmaceutical treatment of such patients, followed the trend of medicine throughout Western Europe and America, but they did nothing to help the vulnerable patients. Similar problems would be faced with the benzodiazepine Librium, which was first pioneered in 1960, and lithium, which was used in the treatment of manic depression.

This was to be a very good era for investment in the pharmaceuticals industry. The National Health Service provided a huge customer for the pills and potions manufacturers. Glaxo, the largest UK supplier of penicillin, had a ready-made market when the Health Service began in 1948 and made the shrewd decision to obtain licences from the USA (at great expense in the 1950s) to manufacture the new products which had been developed in America. It also pursued a policy of takeover of smaller UK companies – Allen and Hanbury's, Evans Medical Company, Edinburgh Pharmaceuticals (in 1962), the British Drug Houses Group in 1967, Farley's Infant Food in 1968. By the 1970s it was able to cancel its long-term agreements with Schering-Plough (to acquire US products) and acquire an American research laboratory of its own – Meyer Laboratories Inc of Florida.[7]

In the story of pharmaceuticals versus hospital care for mental health we see the beginnings of a phenomenon which would come out further in the open in Thatcher's Britain. That is, the alliance between market capitalism and what would once have been thought anarchism. In the place where money counts supremely, there ceases to be such a thing as society. The boom in the pharmaceutical industry preceded, and could be said to have created, the anarchist ideas of Foucault, who, while being the creature of this boom, probably thought of himself as deeply anticapitalist. We see here the germs of why the old left–right divisions over social and political issues gradually ceased to make sense in our times.

Whether the Secretary of State for Health in 1962 was ever to be prescribed anti-psychotic drugs himself is not vouchsafed by his biographers. He was undoubtedly one of the more interesting figures in British political history. J. Enoch Powell, only a short time later associated with fervently xenophobic views and with the desire to restrict immigration, had, as Health Secretary, been only too happy to fill 34 per cent of junior hospital posts with immigrant doctors and nurses.[8] The politicians of Powell's generation, as of almost all generations, were nonentities. With his long, vulpine, lopsided face, his somehow mean moustache, his curious cowlick of Brylcreemed hair swept back from a professorial brow, and his penetrating cold grey eyes, Powell stood out from all his colleagues; not least because of his Brummy accent. He had been a Fellow of Trinity College, Cambridge. Walter Hamilton, his tutor, said that Powell was the finest Greek scholar he had ever taught.[9] Powell became a Professor of Greek at Sydney University at the age of twenty-five, and he rose to the rank of brigadier (having enlisted in the Royal Warwickshire Regiment as a private). There was something about him which called out for attention. For whatever reason, however, whether being of a much lower social class than that from which brigadiers and Conservative Cabinet Ministers usually came (his parents were elementary school teachers), or whether because he was a much-indulged only child, the mere possession of remarkable abilities was never quite enough for him. He needed to go out on a limb.

Nobel Laureate, novelist and self-appointed sage, the dwarfish Elias Canetti, who had been compelled to leave Vienna after the rise of the Nazis, and who spent most of his post-war life in Hampstead, came across Powell in the 1950s. 'What immediately struck me about him was the Continental, one might almost say the Central European way he presented himself. He straightaway broached Nietzsche and Dante with me. Dante he quoted in Italian and at considerable length. The thing that attracted him about Dante was the explicitly partisan nature of it . . . "In Dante's time, people were burned at the stake . . . hatred of the enemy *burned*."'[10]

Once out in the street, having had their first conversation, Canetti asked Powell if he was upset by the British loss of India. 'He stopped in the middle of the street and beat his breast several times: "It hurts in here!"' Powell was a notable example of a type more often found among autodidacts than academics, namely a very clever person with no judgement. The desire to cut a dash, to hold improbable or paradoxical opinions always seemed stronger than the desire to submit his proud intellect to the judgement of a sensible majority. *Securus judicat orbis terrarum*, the tag from Saint Augustine which had eventually converted Newman to Catholicism, would have been a repellent one to Powell, who by the end of his life had accumulated a whole bundle of heterodox beliefs, including the view that the Earl of Oxford, rather than 'The Man of Stratford', wrote the plays of Shakespeare, and that the Gospels lied when they stated that Jesus had been crucified. Powell, a regular church-goer, believed, on no evidence, that Jesus had been stoned to death by the Jews, the customary penalty for blasphemy.

Whether or not Powell was himself deranged has often been discussed. As Health Secretary, he was enjoying his first real taste of administra-tive power, having resigned on a point of monetarist principle with Thorneycroft and Nigel Birch – and had been part of Macmillan's 'little local difficulty'. As Health Secretary he was in charge of the most unwieldy and expensive of government departments, and the arrival of pharmaceuticals, which could be prescribed to patients instead of expen-sive hospitalisation, seemed like an answer to a prayer. Largactil spelled the end of the lunatic asylums. In America, it was the monetarist governor of California, Ronald Reagan, and S. I. Hayakawa, psychologist, academic and US senator, who pioneered the policy of shunting the mentally ill from hospitals into 'community' facilities, clutching their packets of pills. In March 1962, at a conference of the National Association of Mental Health, it was pointed out that 'community care as it then stood was largely a fiction'.[11] Nevertheless, Powell believed that by closing 75,000 beds occupied by mental patients, he could launch a programme of improvement in care for the physically sick: '£500 million over a decade, building 90 new hospitals, drastically remodel 134 more and provide 356 further improvement schemes, each costing £100,000.'[12]

Powell's speech about the lunatic asylums was a sort of poem: 'There they stand, isolated, majestic, imperious, brooded over by the gigantic water-tower and chimney combined, rising, unmistakeable and daunting out of the countryside [sic] – the asylums which our forefathers built with such immense solidity . . . These . . . are the defences we have to storm.'[13]

By a strange conjunction, monetarist economic policies conjoined with the psychiatric fad of the times, namely that the mentally ill (many of them) did not need residential care. From this was a short step to believ-ing they did not need care at all, or that labelling one person mad and another sane was purely arbitrary.

The most famous charlatan to espouse the anti-psychiatric claptrap in Britain was R. D. Laing (1927–89). The son of working-class Presbyterians, he was born in Glasgow, and, clever product of the grammar school, studied medicine at Glasgow University. His interest in psychological medicine had begun in the army, where he worked in psychiatric units, and in 1956 he joined the Tavistock Clinic in London and himself underwent analysis. From 1962 to 1965 he established a therapeutic clinic at Kingsley Hall, where patients and doctors lived together, and where he experimented with the use of LSD. This group experiment was very much influenced by Jean-Paul Sartre, whose *Critique de la Raison Dialectique* was a key text for Laing[14] and which influenced Laing's own bestseller *The Divided Self* (1960), which sold 400,000 copies in paperback in Britain alone. He openly encouraged female patients to sleep with him, and the 'clinic' at Kingsley Hall more resembled a brothel run by lunatics than it did a place of healing.

Laing attacked not only the distinction between madness and sanity, and not only the use of restraint or pharmaceuticals to calm psychotic patients. Much more radically, he attacked any notion of mutual responsibility in relationships. He saw families, or 'family ghettoes' as he called them, as a mutual protection racket. Any human relationship which contained within it the anticipation of exchange – whether from wife and husband, parent and child – he regarded as a confidence trick. The only sort of relationship he seemed to sanction was that of worship (frequently turning to hatred) lavished upon him by his female patients. The difficult thing to grasp about Laing, when he is viewed from the safe distance of several decades, is that he was hugely influential. Peter Sedgwick, author of *Psycho Politics*, wrote in 1982, 'It is only four years since I walked into a gathering of 30 or 40 postgraduate trainees in social work, to introduce them to two parents of schizophrenic children, both of them activists with me in a local pressure group for the welfare of schizophrenia sufferers. Much to the surprise of the parents and myself, this audience of social-work trainees directed a barrage of hostile questions and comments at us. Was not psychiatric diagnosis just a matter of labelling awkward people, just like in Russia?'[15]

Laing was the prophet, but he was telling the generation now coming to adulthood what they wished to hear. Apollo was dead and Dionysus, with his whooping maenads, had taken control of the madhouse. His own childhood, during which he was beaten by a fierce mother who wanted to keep him from other children, had been replicated throughout Britain across the class system. Privately educated children were caned for the smallest offence, or no offence at all; working-class children were walloped. Discipline, during a period of austerity when there were few toys and food was in short supply, had been repressive to a degree. Laing was one of the prophets who led the way from this bondage to a promised land where there were no rules, no restraints, no commitments; and where all the old rights became wrongs. 'We are the fallen Sons of Prophecy', he told his disciplines, 'who have learned to die in the Spirit and be reborn in the Flesh.'[16]

If Laing was the Prophet of this first wave of the Age of Self-Indulgence, Sylvia Plath (1932–63) was its Martyr-Saint. Her short life story provided a Hammer Horrors version of the old Henry James theme, the American girl lured into the moral ambiguities of Old Europe. Born to academic parents, Plath attended Smith College, where she had already begun to write poems and stories. She won a Fulbright Scholarship which took her to Newnham College, Cambridge, and it was while in Cambridge that she met a young poet who had lately graduated, Ted Hughes (1930–98). They met in March 1956, and married that June, and were to have six intense years and two children together. He was a tall Heathcliff Yorkshireman, craggy-faced, instantly overpoweringly attractive to women, and incapable, throughout life, of monogamy. She, to all outward appearances, was a pretty, dyed-blonde American Hausfrau of (paternally) German origin. One who met her at this time likened her to a girl in the soap and deodorant advertisements of the 1940s and 1950s.[17] Their friend Al Alvarez recollected, 'Before my second marriage, I had an Australian girlfriend, who knew Ted, and she told me that when she first set eyes on him her knees went weak. "He looked like Jack Palance in *Shane*," she said. And I knew another woman, a psychoanalyst, who had such a strong reaction when she first met Ted – she told me this many years later – that she actually went to the bathroom and vomited.'[18] Plath was often silent in company. It was only after her melodramatic departure from this world, and the posthumous publication of her *Journals*, and her violent volume of poems, *Ariel*, that the nature of her turbulent imagination came to be known to the world. She was preternaturally possessive and jealous. 'Who knows who Ted's next book will be dedicated to? His navel. His penis.'[19] After one row, 'I had a sprained thumb, Ted bloody claw-marks for a week, and I remember hurling a glass with all my force across a dark room; instead of shattering the glass rebounded and remained intact: I got hit and saw stars – for the first time – blinding red and white stars exploding the black void of snarls and bitings . . . I have a violence in me that is hot as death-blood. I can kill myself – or I know it now – even kill another.'[20]

Before she first came to England, Plath had attempted suicide, and had a history of psycho-troubles. When Hughes fell in love with another woman, Assia Wevill, he and Plath separated. Hughes took a small flat in London, while remaining in their Devon farmhouse. Plath took a two-floor duplex flat in the house in 23 Fitzroy Road, Primrose Hill, which had once been the London residence of W. B. Yeats.

Not since 1947 had Britain known such a snow-bound, frozen winter as that of 1962–63. Alvarez described it:

The snow began just after Christmas and would not let up. By New Year the whole country had ground to a halt. The trains froze on the tracks, the abandoned trucks froze on the roads. The power stations, overloaded by million upon pathetic million of hopeless electric fires, broke down continually; not that the fires mattered, since the electricians were mostly out on strike. Water pipes froze solid; for a bath you had to scheme and cajole those rare friends with centrally heated houses, who became rarer and less friendly as the weeks dragged on. Doing the dishes became a major operation. The gastric rumble of water in outmoded plumbing was sweeter than the sound of mandolins. Weight for weight, plumbers were as expensive as smoked salmon and harder to find. The gas failed and Sunday roasts were raw. The lights failed and candles, of course, were unobtainable. Nerves failed and marriages crumbled. Finally, the heart failed. It seemed the cold would never end. Nag, nag, nag.[21]

It was in this cold spell, on 11 February 1963, that Sylvia Plath left a tray of bread and milk in the bedroom of her children, Frieda, almost three, and Nicholas, one. She went into the kitchen and folded a cloth inside the gas oven on which she laid her head. Alvarez maintained that she had intended the suicide to fail. She left a note with the name and telephone of her doctor, John Horder. The nanny who arrived to look after the children on Monday morning was unable to get into the flat, however, and Plath's downstairs neighbour, Trevor Thomas, had been knocked out by the gas, though he survived.[22]

In Hughes's view, or at least the view he developed with hindsight (written in 1986), 'the key factor in Sylvia's death, the mechanical factor, was the tranquiliser drug that was being administered to her by Dr Horder. Accounts of her death regularly find no place for this detail, which seems to me fairly important. In the diaries, she describes the terrible interval that came regularly between the point where one pill lost its effect and the next pill took hold – the matter of two hours which fell in the early morning. After her death, I learned from her mother that this particular drug had been tried on S., during her recovery from her first suicide attempt, and that it induced such an extreme suicidal reaction, in the gap between doses, that S.'s mother was warned never to allow it to be given to S. under any circumstances. Dr Horder knew nothing about this.'[23]

Assia Wevill had a daughter, Shura, by Hughes. When that relationship went wrong, Wevill, in imitation of Plath, took her own life, but unlike Plath, she took her daughter with her, murdering the child with sleeping pills before she killed herself.

It did not take long for Plath to be canonised in the campuses, first of America and then of Britain. She became in death what she had not been in life, a feminist and a man-hater. Her extraordinary poems became, for many of her shrill admirers, anti-male manifestos – 'Daddy, daddy, you bastard, I'm through', as she concluded one of the finest poems of our age.[24] Like Yeats in Auden's poem, Plath's gift survived it all, as did, eventually, Hughes's, though for most of his life he carried the burden not only of his private guilt and grief, and his concern for his children, but also the hatred of a whole generation of women who used Plath as a religious focus for their pent-up feelings of rage. The Hausfrau in the soap and deodorant ads had reached for her dagger. It was as if Lucille Ball had suddenly been cast as Medea or Lady Macbeth.

Suicide as a way out of misery will always remain an option for some. And yet, from the year of Plath's death until 1977, suicides were reduced by one-third in England and Wales. This very remarkable statistic was no coincidence. It was largely the responsibility of one heroic individual, a clergyman called Chad Varah (1911–2007). Varah was ordained in 1935, and one of his early tasks, as a curate at St Giles's, Lincoln, was to conduct a funeral in unconsecrated ground, since the dead person was a suicide. It was a thirteen-year-old girl who had killed herself because she had started to bleed between the legs and had thought she was suffering a terrible disease which she could not bring herself to talk about. When the mourners had left, Varah stared at her open grave, and said, 'Little girl, I never knew you, but you have changed my life. I promise you, that I will teach children what they need to know about sex, even if I get called a dirty old man.'[25] As vicar of St Paul's, Clapham Junction, he heard that there were three suicides a day in London, and he determined to do something about it. He became the vicar of the beautiful Wren church of St Stephen's Walbrook, in the City of London, a position which gave him in effect a sinecure. It was from this place, which had few parochial duties and no Sunday services, that he was able to launch his life's work. On 1 November 1953, with the memorable telephone number MAN 9000, he launched what was originally called the Good Samaritans, a helpline for the suicidal. Soon calls were coming in at a rate of one hundred a day. Volunteers were trained, and there was a strict rule that they were not allowed to attempt to convert any caller to any religious or philosophical viewpoint. They were listeners. He was married (to the world President of the Mother's Union) and he had five children. As well as working with the suicidal he gave himself to the related task of sex therapy. He was a man of his time, and his thinking evolved. In the 1960s, he was still advising homosexuals to meet a sufficiently pretty girl and perhaps undergo psychotherapy in order to be 'cured'. By the time he retired in 2003, he combined liturgical conservatism, loving the Prayer Book order of 1928, with heterodox opinions. (He was a firm believer, for example, in reincarnation.) He wrote for the sex magazine *Forum*, and he was a defence witness during the Linda Lovelace obscenity trial in the 1970s. When cross-examined by a barrister who reminded him of the Seventh Commandment, Varah replied, 'Why are you quoting this ancient desert lore at me?'[26] When one thinks of all the damage, some of it intentional, which is inflicted upon the world by politicians, it is refreshing to remember the life of Chad Varah, whose wisdom and kindness can be measured in terms of the dramatic decline in the suicide statistics during the time that the Samaritans began their work.

8

Lady Chatterley and Honest to God

Old Britain was a restricted place, where it was not possible to print, or say, or perform, anything you chose. The Britain coming to birth was a place which took it for granted that Freedom of Expression was not merely an inalienable right, but also one which had been around forever. Yet the Lord Chamberlain, in the first decade of Queen Elizabeth II's reign, still decreed what could or could not be performed on the stage, just as he had done in the reign of Queen Elizabeth I. Obscenity, a notoriously difficult thing to define, could be prosecuted, and sometimes was, as when Radclyffe Hall's harmless, and ungraphic, account of lesbian love had been condemned in 1928.

The case that made everyone realise the climate had changed, utterly and irrevocably, was that of *Regina* v. *Penguin Books Ltd*, heard in October 1960 at the Old Bailey. For some years, Roy Jenkins, Antony Lambton, Hugh Fraser, A. P. Herbert, Lord Birkett and others had been campaigning for a change in the Obscenity Laws, and in 1959 Roy Jenkins's Private Members' Bill was finally forced through Parliament and became law. This killed the Common Law which referred to 'Obscene Libel' and required the court, in a case of prosecution, to consider the book 'as a whole'. There could be no conviction if 'it is proved that publication of the article in question is justified as being for the public good on the ground that it is in the interests of science, literature, art or learning, or of other objects of general concern'.[1]

The Director of Public Prosecutions, since 1944, had been Sir Theobald Mathew (1898–1964). As the new Jenkins law was being drafted, Mathew had been summoned to inform the relevant Select Committee at the House of Commons. He recorded that he strongly disapproved of his department being placed in a position 'of being a censor of novels or other literary publications'. Mathew is usually cast as a villain by contemporary historians. Under his watch as DPP, for example, there was a colossal increase of prosecution of homosexuals. In the years 1940–44 (the year of Mathew's appointment) 1,631 men were prosecuted in 'cases of Unnatural Offences and Indecency with other males'. With Mathew in charge, the number of prosecutions rose to 2,814 in the next four-year period, and so on upwards in a steady spiral curve. In 1952 *alone* 5,425 men were prosecuted. Investigating the reasons for the sudden increase, Harford Montgomery Hyde, MP for North Belfast and author of *Other*

Love, noted that the Metropolitan Police Commissioner Sir John Nott-Bower was from 1953 particularly zealous in the application of the law. 'It is easier and incidentally safer and less troublesome to catch a homosexual than a burglar,' Hyde noted.[2] But he also felt constrained to mention that Sir Theobald Mathew was 'a devout and conscientious Catholic'.[3] One can't blame Mathew alone for attitudes which seem, from the perspective of a later age, not merely cruel but positively bizarre. After all, Lord Dawson of Penn, President of the Royal College of Physicians and physician in ordinary to every king since Edward VII, told the House of Lords, in July 1937, 'I am not at all sure that in the future it may not be regarded as an insufficiency disease . . . The more reasonable view is gradually being accepted that it . . . has one foot in the realm of disease and it is not wholly in the realm of crime.' Sir Theobald Mathew was not alone in his belief that it was a good idea to persecute homosexuals, nor in his view, once the Roy Jenkins bill had become law in 1959, that it was his job as Director of Public Prosecutions to suppress 'feelthy' literature.

Lady Chatterley's Lover, it is pretty generally agreed, was precisely the sort of book the Jenkins Act had hoped to protect from the philistine attentions of police and lawyers. It was transparently a book of aching seriousness, and the love affair which takes place between the wife of an impotent 'toff' and her earthy gamekeeper is one of the things, but not the only thing, in the book which demonstrates Lawrence's creed, which was essentially that of the great Victorian moralists Carlyle and Ruskin: namely, industrialised society, and modern 'values', had corrupted people, and that in order to find their true selves they needed to return to nature, and also (a detail more appealing to Lawrence than to Carlyle, it must be said) explore the unashamed enjoyment of sex. But the gamekeeper, Oliver Mellors, likes to use the word 'fuck' and it was this fact, quite apart from the number of times he indulges in the activity with her ladyship, which offended not merely the Director of Public Prosecutions, but also the Attorney-General, Sir Reginald Manningham-Buller (nicknamed Bullying-Manner by Bernard Levin and said to be the original of Anthony Powell's Widmerpool).

So it was that when Penguin Books, who had published all D. H. Lawrence's work hitherto, boldly published the unexpurgated *Lady Chatterley*, they were prosecuted. The senior Treasury Counsel, Mervyn Griffith-Jones QC, represented the Crown, and in his opening speech to the jury, before a single witness had been called, he lost his case. 'You may think that one of the ways in which you can test this book, and test it from the most liberal outlook, is to ask yourselves the question, when you have read it through, would you approve of your young sons, young daughters – because girls can read as well as boys – reading this book? Is it a book that you would have lying around in your own house?' The clumsy assurance that girls could be as literate as boys was bad enough. But he went on, drawing audible and of course unintended laughter from the jury – 'Is it a book that you would even wish your wife or your servants to read?'⁴

For the next five days, a succession of worthies from the literary and academic worlds appeared in court, to be coaxed by the intelligent defence counsels – Gerald Gardiner QC and Jeremy Hutchinson QC – to defend *Lady Chatterley*, or D. H. Lawrence, or both. Graham Hough, Helen Gardner, Rebecca West, E. M. Forster, Richard Hoggart, Anne Scott-James, Cecil Day-Lewis, Stephen Potter and others all came and offered their testimony. But, really, their work had already been done for them by Mervyn Griffith-Jones, asking whether it was a book which 'you would even wish your wife or your servants to read.' The world had spun on a little further than Mr Griffith-Jones, from the confines of his Inn of Court and his club, had quite realised. Few women by this date would have waited for their husband's permission before reading a book. None would like the suggestion that they would be depraved or corrupted or tempted to commit adultery because of Lawrence's novel, a work of genius with a number of profoundly ludicrous pages. The majority of British citizens since the Second World War made do without servants.

There would be some attempts, after the *Chatterley* trial, to revive prosecutions for Obscenity. Sir Theobald Mathew set in train an investigation into Mary McCarthy's *The Group*, for example, but every indication was that a prosecution would fail. The deliberately pornographic *Fanny Hill*, written in the eighteenth century, but published in our times by Mayflower Books, was prosecuted. The trial was in some senses a reprise of the *Chatterley* one, with Mervyn Griffith-Jones prosecuting and Jeremy Hutchinson defending. *Fanny Hill* and her publishers were found guilty, but the spirit of the times was against the judgement. The last successful case brought was that against Calder and Boyars, for publishing *Last Exit to Brooklyn* in 1966. The cricketing bishop, David Shepherd, came to give evidence against the book, largely it would seem because it displayed homosexuality in a favourable light. But the conviction was quashed in the Court of Appeal, and thereafter the custom of prosecuting books under the Obscene Publications Act fell into disuse. As Bernard Levin observed, '*Portnoy's Complaint* appeared unscathed in Britain and no question of prosecution arose . . . In the last months of the sixties, *Fanny Hill* was republished, unexpurgated. No prosecution followed; the authorities' surrender seemed, for the time being at least, to be complete.'⁵

Among the witnesses assembled to defend *Lady Chatterley's Lover* in Court No. 1 at the Old Bailey in October 1960 was the suffragan Bishop of Woolwich, Dr J. A. Robinson. He believed that the last two pages of Lawrence's book were 'a most moving advocacy of chastity'. Asked by the judge whether the novel portrayed the life of an immoral woman, the bishop had replied, 'It portrays the life of a woman in an immoral relationship, in so far as adultery is an immoral relationship.'⁶

Dr Robinson was a Cambridge don who had quite recently been lured from the academic life by the Bishop of Southwark, the Rt Revd Mervyn Stockwood, to see if there was any possibility of awakening the religious impulses of those who lived in the wastelands of post-war south London. Dr Robinson was on the face of things an unlikely populariser. His work had been chiefly on comparatively obscure themes of New Testament theology, and in particular on the German theologians who had attempted, in the inter-war years, to 'demythologise' the New Testament from an existentialist viewpoint. Rudolf Bultmann, in particular, had believed it was possible, if the reader made no attempt to read the Gospel narratives as historical, to be challenged on a personal level by the stories which the Gospels represented. The bishop, a tall, bald man with a parsonical voice, was the son of a distinguished theologian and Dean of Wells. He was a dyed-in-the-wool Church of England man, married to a pretty woman, with one son and three daughters, all of whom grew up to be great beauties. The *Chatterley* trial awoke in him an addiction to publicity. The following year, this mild-mannered man spoke out against capital punishment. There was nothing remarkable about this; probably the majority of practising Christians at this date opposed hanging. But the bishop chose to time his remarks for the Conservative Party Conference. The *Daily Sketch* wrote, 'The Bishop of Woolwich warned the Tories yesterday, "Don't support hanging. Capital punishment is on the way out," said the bishop.

'"There will be attempts to put the clock back – to extend the death penalty – in the motions at the Conservative Party conference this week," he said.'⁷

At any juncture during our times, the British press has had a small cast of characters whom it can produce when actual news material is thin. There is the badly behaved aristocrat, preferably had up at regular interval for motoring offences involving alcohol; there is the adulterous footballer; the various 'maverick' Members of Parliament who have no hope of real political advantage but who regard publicity as a very acceptable alternative to power and who can be relied upon to denounce their party leaders at any provocation or none. And there is the trendy bishop, preferably advocating practices and doctrines which will offend the sensibilities of the more narrow-minded or puritanical church-goer. In his views, there was probably little to separate Dr Robinson from many another mild English churchman who, like the Bishop of Stortford in P. G. Wodehouse, 'had been thinking of an article . . . on the subject of Miracles; . . . the tone he had taken, though in keeping with the trend of Modern Thought, had been tinged with something approaching scepticism'.[8] Dr Robinson, however, for all his donnish reserve, happily fell into the vacant seat of the 'Red Dean' of Canterbury (Hewlett Johnson, who believed that Stalin had established an Earthly Paradise) or the prosaically doubting Bishop of Birmingham, Barnes, who once described himself as 'a troubled theist' – a phrase which a careless but probably accurate sub-editor rendered in the next morning's newspaper as 'a troubled atheist'. After a bout of lumbago, the Bishop of Woolwich penned a very short paperback, which gave a distillation of his favourite German theologians, and offered it for publication to the small Christian publishing company of SCM. He wrote a good puff for his own book in the liberal Sunday newspaper the *Observer*, which bore the provocative headline OUR IMAGE OF GOD MUST GO.

He could not possibly have predicted the result. Three months after publication, 300,000 copies of *Honest to God* had been sold, and it was being translated into many languages.[9] Over a million copies were eventually sold.

Of the hundreds of letter-writers to newspapers, or to the bishop himself, or to the Archbishop of Canterbury, opinion was divided. Many felt Robinson's attempts to write theology for the masses were sheer heresy, questioning the very basis of what they considered to be Christianity itself. Others, however, felt that the bishop had provided fresh air to breathe: 'I am an ordinary struggling faithful member of the Church, middle-aged, with no brains. But I found myself overwhelmed with relief when I read *Honest to God*. Far from having a negative influence it has strengthened my faith in a personal God. I have read the book twice, and I did not find anything in it that could damage honest faith at all. It gave me a wonderful sense of joyful relief at being freed from something unreal and slightly false, something unrelated to one's innermost being, and unrelated to the created world . . . I have friends who feel just the same, and have found their faith renewed and strengthened by the Bishop of Woolwich's book.' This was only one of hundreds of letters to arrive on the desk of the Archbishop of Canterbury.

Among laymen who were obsessed by the book, and who wrote to the Archbishop about it, was Harold Macmillan. 'What impresses me', the Prime Minister wrote, 'with the exception of a few rather cheap witticisms, is the reverent approach which underlies the somewhat H. G. Wellsian style . . . It is of course very difficult for people of different generations to understand each other's problems and it may well be that for the youth of today we need different symbols; instead, for instance, of the traditional religious art, whether the grand and terrifying Byzantine mosaic, or the mild beauty of the Renaissance painting. For instance, a modern abstract painting of God might be more attractive to young people than the traditional form. Nevertheless, whichever it is, it is only a symbol, and whether God is represented as God the Father in conventional painting, or as a series of triangles and circles, it is still only an attempt to use the material to represent the infinite.'[10]

When, however, the Archbishop wrote a short pamphlet denouncing *Honest to God*, and restating a more orthodox theology, Macmillan wrote again, 'I think it is a mistake to bewilder people, and I am sure we shall all be very grateful to you for having written this booklet to try and help those who are distressed.'[11]

The Archbishop summoned the Bishop of Woolwich for an interview. Robinson remembered the Archbishop saying very little except, 'Well, now! Well now!' *ad infinitum*.[12] Ramsey's memorandum of the interview noted, 'I had a long talk with the Bishop of Woolwich on April 23 [1963]. I was grieved to find how lacking he is in responsibility; indeed, he seemed to me to be adolescent in his failure to grasp that actions have inevitable consequences and make inevitable impressions. He was "surprised" at things which should give no surprise at all to any intelligent adult. I thought he was in a good deal of a muddle spiritually and more in need of help than he realised [sic]; and his adolescent limitation extends to his own realm of theological discussion where he fails to see what meaning is inevitably conveyed by words and phrases. He did however ask my advice about what he should do. My advice to him was (i) to avoid constant publicity; (ii) to take opportunities of making clear his acceptance of orthodoxy, if he is conscientiously able to do so; but (iii) if he is asked how he reconciles acceptance of orthodoxy with the thesis of his book, I do not know how he can set about it.'

In later years, Bishop Robinson, who returned to Cambridge to become the Dean of Trinity College, so espoused orthodoxy as to become an advocate of the authenticity of the Turin Shroud, and he was somewhat penitent about having written *Honest to God*. The Archbishop, for his part, repented of having denounced the book, and felt he had panicked about nothing. The Most Reverend Arthur Michael Richard Ramsey (1904–88) was the hundredth Archbishop of Canterbury, and he was the appointment of Harold Macmillan. Ramsey was certainly one of the strangest occupants of that office, but also, perhaps, historically one of the most significant. If one of the features of our times is that Britain broke up, that it ceased being a monist society and became a pluralist society, then Michael Ramsey, who systematically and deliberately set in place the means to dismantle the Church of England, must be seen as a key player.

Ramsey was the son of a mathematics don at Magdalene College, Cambridge, and the brother of Frank Ramsey, a distinguished philosopher of mathematics who had been one of the early champions of Wittgenstein in England, and who died of jaundice at age twenty-six. The family was Congregationalist, but Ramsey was drawn to Anglo-Catholicism. He always held in balance his academic interests – he was Regius Professor of Divinity at Cambridge – and his priestly role, hearing confessions and offering spiritual advice to a wide range of men and women. A big, burly, bald man, he looked like a mad professor, and was much debilitated by depression. His extraordinary silences made conversation with him disconcerting. When his communist atheist sister was widowed, he drove to Oxford to sit with her and her children for half a day but did not utter a word.[13] He had the habit of repeating words or phrases in a trance-like chant. '"Baldock", Michael Ramsey once remarked out loud while driving home the morning after he had dined with the Cambridge Union and taken part in a debate. "Baldock. Baldock". He had raised his eyes from *The Times* and spotted the signpost as he entered this spectacularly uninteresting Hertfordshire town. "Baldock. Baldock". Again and again, in monotonous tones, the word "Baldock" was repeated. Had it triggered some childhood memory? Was it just the sound of the word he found mesmeric? Was he perhaps a little mad? He must have repeated the word "Baldock" thirteen or fourteen times. Even for someone in his company who knew him well, the experience was strangely unnerving.'[14]

It is hardly surprising that his predecessor, the brisk Geoffrey Fisher, who had been Michael Ramsey's headmaster when he was a boy at Repton, should have considered him an unsuitable successor. Fisher told Macmillan so in no uncertain terms. Macmillan replied, 'Well, Archbishop, you may have been Michael Ramsey's headmaster but you're not mine, and I intend to appoint Dr Ramsey, good afternoon.'[15]

Macmillan told Ramsey this story, and it poisoned relations between the Archbishop and his predecessor. Fisher was appointed to a life peerage and was always known by Ramsey as the Baron. The old Archbishop bombarded the new with letters of admonition and complaint, which Ramsey claimed he put into the waste-paper basket without reading. But he did not destroy them. The whole sorry correspondence is preserved in Lambeth Palace. 'It is ridiculous (and worse)', Fisher wrote, 'that we should be in this situation of frigid correspondence with no friendly correspondence. We ought to be able to laugh ourselves out of it, but we can't.'[16] When Fisher threatened to write to *The Times* complaining about the modern liturgy ('Series II') which Ramsey had allowed to be introduced, Ramsey wrote, 'It would cause resentment for you to criticize publicly Convocations and advise the House of Laity . . . *Please don't.* Yours etc. Michael.'[17] (Ramsey was slightly more tactful with his own successor, Donald Coggan, whom he nicknamed the Cog. 'I liked him,' he wrote of Coggan when he was still Bishop of Bradford, 'and was as yet unaware of his glaring deficiencies.'[18]

Ramsey was a mixture of the nonconformity of his family tradition, and the Anglo-Catholic priestly piety which had nourished him through a depressive adulthood. With the Church of England by law established, with its liturgy and canons still subject to Parliament, its bishops, clad in gaiters and top hats, still chosen by the Prime Minister, its role as a sort of spiritual topping to the Establishment, he had little or no sympathy. On one foreign tour, when the plane had been delayed, his press secretary found him lying on his bed with his hands clasped behind his head repeating again and again, 'I hate the Church of England.' 'It's a good job there's no one but me to hear you saying that,' his press officer said. 'Oh, but it's true,' was Ramsey's reply. 'I do hate the Church of England. Indeed I do.' When he was enthroned at Canterbury, he said, 'Here in England, the Church and State are linked together, and we use that link in serving the community. But in that service, and in rendering to God the things that are God's, we ask for a greater freedom in the ordering and in the urgent revising of our forms of worship. If the link of Church and State were broken, it would not be we who ask for this freedom who broke it, but those – if there be such – who denied that freedom to us.' When he retired in 1974, he publicly admitted, 'It would not be a grief to me to wake up and find that the English establishment was no more.'[19]

These sentiments would not seem remarkable on the lips of a bishop in any period of British history post-Ramsey. But this was a man who, as Bishop of Durham, had stood beside the Queen at her Coronation in Westminster Abbey when she was anointed by Headmaster Fisher. In 1953, it had really seemed as if everything in England was to carry on as it had done before the war.

Ramsey was one of those pivotal figures who saw that everything had in fact changed. In his years as Archbishop, the Established Church continued, officially, to exist. The Queen was still, officially, the Head of the Church of England. But with the establishment of the Church's own parliament, the General Synod, and the introduction of a wide range of modern liturgies to replace the Book of Common Prayer which had been the one authorised form of worship since the Restoration of Charles II, a very profound change had taken place. The Church of England was recognising that its claim to speak for everyone in England was a fiction. In 1961, 605 men were ordained to the priesthood of the Church of England. In 1970, the number had shrunk to 185. On Easter Sunday 1970, out of a population of 46 million, only 1.6 million members of the Church of England received Communion. By recognising the reality, Ramsey helped to speed the Church on its way to oblivion. Though bishops in their seventeenth-century lawn sleeves continued to sit in the House of Lords, and though the monarch continued each Maundy Thursday to go to a different cathedral to distribute Maundy Money, the reality of things was that the Established Church did not really any longer exist. A new sect, Anglicanism, had been born. And its democratic parliament, the Synod, encouraged the Anglicans to divide themselves into sects – Evangelicals, who followed a version of Billy Graham's American fundamentalism; the 'Catholics', some of whom liked the traditions of independent Anglican Catholicism such as nourished Ramsey; and some of whom were crypto-, or not so crypto, Roman Catholics. These things were the consequence, rather than the cause, of society becoming pluralist not monist, but they were a dramatic symptom of it. At the time of the Queen's Coronation, it still made a sort of sense to speak of Britain as a Christian country. At some stage it became post-Christian, and by the end of our times it was not Christian in itself at all, though there were Christians (and many other faith groups) within it. There was no longer a shared language of ceremony. The Prayer Book words with which English men and women performed their rites of initiation over infants, their marriages and their funerals, had been part of the common tongue for three hundred and more years. After Ramsey, this ceased to be so. 'In the midst of life we are in death' . . . 'with my body I thee worship' . . . 'the High Court of Parliament under our most religious and gracious Queen at this time assembled' . . . These phrases would soon have no resonance in the English ear. Even the clergy, perhaps especially the clergy, many of whom hated the old Prayer Book, would not recognise them. The cracks had begun to appear in the ice.

Honest to God did not cause the subsequent secularisation of Britain. It was an early signal that this secularisation was already in inexorable progress. Robinson, as a suffragan bishop in the bleak, poverty-stricken south London suburbs, became associated with what came to be known as South Bank Theology. One of the most dynamic young clergymen in the district was an Olympic athlete who was the Rector of Woolwich, the Revd Nicolas Stacey. When he arrived the congregation of the church was fifty. In eight years he managed to double it. He created a housing association; he had a discotheque in the crypt, but the huge majority of the people of Woolwich had no interest in the Church, or in religion. By the end of eight years, Stacey was completely disillusioned and felt a failure. He resigned his living and became the Deputy Director of Oxfam, subsequently doing great work for prisoners and AIDS sufferers. He continued, perhaps surprisingly, to believe in God, and to be a Christian priest, but he did not feel that the Church of England was equal to the task of persuading the people of Woolwich, or the people of Britain, to engage with the Gospel.

To many people, these voices of 'trendies' from the South Bank must have been very surprising. The Church of England had just been living through several decades which could be seen with hindsight to be its apogee, its glory days. Writers such as Rose Macaulay, John Betjeman, W. H. Auden, Dorothy L. Sayers and Charles Williams had been conspicuous members of this Church. The Queen had been crowned in a religious ceremony in which all the dignitaries were bishops and clergy of the Established Church, all of them men, many of them distinguished intellects.

Moreover, in the 1950s, the Church had been at the centre of one of the definitive political dramas of our times, namely the struggle against apartheid in South Africa. It was no accident that those Englishmen who spearheaded resistance to apartheid should have been Anglican monks who were rooted and grounded in a faith in the Incarnation, a belief that, since God chose to be man, there could be no distinction between people on account of gender, ethnicity or social status. A book written by one of these High Church monks, Trevor Huddleston's *Naught for Your Comfort*, published in 1956, had been enormously influential in opening the eyes of the world to the grievous state of things in South Africa.

It would seem that a Church which could field saintly prophets such as Raymond Raynes and Trevor Huddleston in South Africa, scholarly theological faculties such as could be found at the older universities, as well as bishops in the palaces and on the benches of the House of Lords, could not be in a stronger position. Yet the publication of *Honest to God* made many people wonder how much the Church any longer believed, and whether they really belonged to it.

Most parishes in the land continued to have a parson, who was allowed to live in a parsonage. However, from the 1960s onwards the Church pursued a policy of selling off its vicarages and rectories. The downward trend of church membership was relentless. On Easter Day 1939, 10 per cent of the population went to Communion. It had fallen to 6.5 per cent in 1960 and 5 per cent in 1968. Though some people continued to use churches for weddings and funerals, the numbers of those bringing children to be baptised as a matter of course plummeted. Within a decade of *Honest to God*, the churches in England were all huddling together, having discovered 'ecumenism'. Some of the Churches, such as the Methodists, were in serious danger of dying out altogether unless they merged with a larger body. In the coming decades, the Church would make various efforts to delude itself that the secularisation of the West was not terminal. There would be pockets of evangelical revival. Churches pursuing a Billy Graham style of religion would attract congregations in several hundreds, as opposed to Nicolas Stacey's 50 or 100. Such 'happy clappy' churches looked crowded, but a crowd of 250 or 300 was nothing compared to the tens of thousands, the millions, who never went near a church. After the decision to ordain women to the priesthood there was a temporary halt in the decline of 'vocations'; but many of those ordained were women in their twilight years, and it would seem likely that their arrival on the scene put off as many potential worshippers as it attracted. Even in the strange opening decade of the twenty-first century, when the peoples of the world turned more and more to religion, they did not turn to the Church of England. One of the most striking features of life in our times, in Britain, and in Western Europe generally, has been the decline of institutional Christianity – most especially in the Church of England and the Church of Rome. Societies define themselves historically in terms of tribal loyalty, in caste systems and in the shared cultic activities of religion. This would remain the case in Britain at certain key times of year, or at certain moments of national self-awareness. Royal funerals, or ceremonies for the remembrance of the slain in war, could continue for very many in Britain to summon forth a collective religious emotion, even if the 'religion' was of a kind difficult to classify in philosophical or theological terms. The life of the parish church, however, its weekly services and activities, completely failed to touch the average British citizen during this period. Indeed, accurately considered, Britain after the 1960s became a secular state. These things happened gradually, and there was perhaps no one defining moment. But surely something very like a defining moment was the televising of John Galsworthy's *The Forsyte Saga* on BBC in 1967. So completely gripped was the nation by the unfolding drama week by week that many vicars and their congregations abandoned Evensong, never to revive it. In 'Quires and Places where they sing', to use the old phrase, the service was still repeated daily, in cathedrals and colleges, to a prodigious variety of beautiful musical settings. But the familiar Sunday evening ritual in parish churches, with a few gathering to sing the evening hymns, and to hear again the prayer to Lighten Our Darkness – that was now over.

9

Profumo and After

On a blazingly hot summer's day in 1961, Nancy Astor stepped off the train at Didcot, into the back of a waiting taxi. It was a regular arrangement that the old lady should take the fast train from London, and the slightly longer drive to her magnificent country seat, Cliveden, rather than taking the stopping train to Taplow. Nancy Astor, who had been born in Danville, Virginia, in 1879, had married, aged eighteen, an alcoholic named Robert Shaw. Six years later, she divorced, and married William Waldorf Astor. ('I married beneath me – all women do.') Her extreme puritanism (she was an eager convert to Christian Science), her driving ambition, her old-fashioned American tendency to take a matriarchal view of the world, all made her the ideal candidate for that historic role – the first woman to sit as a British Member of Parliament (Conservative) at Westminster. The Astor millions helped, too. She had children, remarkably enough, given her repugnance for the human body and its functions. Bobbie Shaw, the son of the first marriage, grew up to be something of a liability, a homosexual alcoholic who was obliged to leave the Royal Horse Guards for being drunk on duty. Two years later, in 1931, he had been arrested for importuning and imprisoned for four months. It was with some alarm that one of her Astor sons heard that the old lady was writing her memoirs. It would, he blurted out, be too horrifying to tell the truth. In her Edwardian-Virginian voice, Nancy asked, 'What do you mean – horrifyin'?' 'Because you are so possessive. That's why we are all cases of arrested development; though I admit that Bobbie is the only one of us actually to have been arrested.'

Nancy Astor's husband, the second Viscount, died in 1952 and was succeeded by their son William (born 1907), a much-married Conservative MP. He inherited not only the 1916-created (purchased from the newly created Prime Minister Lloyd George) peerage, but also Cliveden, one of the most beautiful Victorian houses in England. Sir Charles Barry designed it in 1850, on the perfectly sited ruins of a seventeenth-century ducal residence. From the balustrades (which survive from that Duke of Buckingham's house) the eye looks down the thickly wooded banks of the Thames. In the foreground a perfect Italianate garden has been made, with flat lawns and parterres divided from one another by stone steps as each swoops downwards to the lush valley below. On the level of the house is a magnificent pavilion, and behind one of the garden walls, in what must have been a kitchen garden, is a swimming pool which even in the English climate makes a sun trap of Italianate degree.

To this beautiful place, on a beautiful summer's day, the Dowager Viscountess returned, since, of course, she had ignored the convention that Dowagers move out of the big house when their husbands die. She was still in residence at Cliveden, arresting her sons' development, just as she had been since she 'married beneath her'. To this place she had returned after winning her Commons seat – Plymouth – for refreshment and repose. Here, as the 1930s unfolded, and the Conservatives failed to address any of the issues which worried her – poor housing, poverty, drunkenness, bad education – she had uttered her despondent cry, 'I sometimes wonder whether I joined the right party.' (After the 1929 election, she had tried to get the fourteen other women MPs to join a Women's Party – under her leadership, naturally.) Here, too, as the 1930s passed by, she entertained those who came to be known by the contemptuous nickname (it was Evelyn Waugh's cousin, the communist Claud Cockburn, who coined it) 'The Cliveden Set'. Cockburn's idea had been that in the beautiful setting of Cliveden, upper class and rich politicians, journalists and men of influence met to plan the policy of appeasing Hitler – even of subverting the processes of democracy to bring in a government which positively favoured the European dictatorships. All sorts of politicians fetched up at her dinner table. One night, in 1930, a young Conservative called Frank Pakenham found himself seated beside the firebrand Chancellor of the Duchy of Lancaster (Labour), Oswald Mosley. Mosley expounded the view that cometh the hour, cometh the man. He said that after the dullness of such-and-such had emerged Gladstone; after the tedium of Lord Derby's 'Who? Who?' Cabinet had sprung the dynamic Disraeli . . . 'And,' added Mosley, his eyes agleam, 'after Ramsay MacDonald . . .'

Pakenham thought the ambition of this young – thirty-five-year-old – politician touching; could Mosley not *see*, what was obvious to Pakenham – that no political party would risk choosing as Prime Minister a man of such promiscuous sexual habits?

Did the household gods of the Astors remember this conversation thirty years later when Cliveden once more attracted the public attention? And do its three twentieth-century incarnations make Cliveden an emblem of how the country changed? In the thirties, the supposed scene of appeasement and sell-out; in the 1950s and early 1960s, the famous backdrop to scenes of Dionysian orgies; and in the 1980s and 1990s, a 'luxury hotel', a place for yuppies to burn off some of their excess money with elaborately cooked *cuisine minceur*, with individualised bath-robes, chocolates on the pillow and the peculiar air of unreality which such 'luxury' always superimposes?

But we have left Nancy Astor and the taxi driver, in the broiling sun of that afternoon in 1961. The driver crossed the gravel with her suitcase, entered the house by the front door – not something he would have done in one of the older houses in England – and into the large, dark, cool hall, an experience not unlike stepping into the scenes of one of the later novels of Henry James, where the tastes of Old Europe – heavy tapestry, polished ancient oak and cool stone floors – are sustained by American money. Nancy Astor thanked the man and drifted towards her apartments, but, before doing so, she told the man that he must go in search of refreshment.

'Do not drive home without drinkin' somethin'. If you want tea, go through that door – the green baize door in the corner, you'll come to a kinda back door. Walk along – you'll find the kitchen, say I sent you. Ask for a cup of tea, and you can take it out to the back and drink it in the garden.'

The man did as he was told, but he found the kitchen deserted and the back door open. There was, nevertheless, a teapot on the table, and so he helped himself to a cup, and, as instructed, he went out to the back of the house to find a bench to sit upon. Turning a corner by what looked like an outhouse or greenhouse, he found himself beside the swimming pool. He was not alone. Sitting around in the sunshine were about a dozen people, six young women of beauty, and six men. As he stared, and looked away, and stared again, the man felt a stab of incredulous horror. He crept away with his tea, and found a bench nearer the kitchen door. As he sat down he pondered what he had seen. Was it possible? Not only was it possible, it was unmistakable. He had just seen, sitting naked beside the pool in the company of what appeared to be a selection of tarts, a group of public men – a Cabinet Minister, a member of the Royal Family, and others – whom he had previously regarded as honourable figures, leaders, his social and political superiors.

The previous page is a blank, because that taxi driver, who told me the story, belonged to the old world. He named the men who sat around the pool, some of whom have never been named by the history books; but he only did so anecdotally. He never sold his remarkable story to a newspaper. What happened in the case of the Profumo affair, as it came to be known, was that hypocrisy, that last ragged garment with which the old governing classes could swathe themselves, was rudely snatched away. Matters which had never been mentioned in the press, unless they had been aired in court (hence the popularity, for *News of the World* readers, of lurid divorce hearings), could now be set down in print by newspapers prepared to risk the libel laws. Some time in 1929 David Lloyd George gave a dinner in a private room of a London hotel to which he invited a group of politicians supposedly at odds with one another. One of the younger men exclaimed, when he saw the guest list – 'This will lift the roof if it gets out.' 'Lloyd George replied with his ineffable dumpling expression: "My dear boy. If everything I have done in this hotel during the last forty years had got out, you have no idea how many times I would have had to retire from politics."'[1] A. J. P. Taylor thought six of the twentieth-century Prime Ministers (pre-1968) had committed adultery[2] – three presumably were Asquith, Lloyd George and MacDonald. The other three are harder to pin down. The point is, that although gossips and those in the Upper Ten [Thousand], as the Victorians called them, all 'knew' about such things, they were never aired in the newspapers. A distinction was maintained between the pleasures of private gossip and the baldness of public discourse.

The Profumo affair changed all that, and if it made for a more exciting press, and a more candid atmosphere, it also was a key factor in the diminishment of British political life. Post-Profumo, British politicians were noticeably less intelligent. What intelligent person would choose to enter a sphere of life where it was deemed legitimate for the popular press – and, in time, all newspapers, and even the BBC – to publicise love affairs and sexual indiscretions? It is arguable that for those who were thrust into public life either by insatiable ambition (the politicians) or by the accident of birth or marriage (the Royal Family) the scrutiny was actually intolerable, a fact which is surely one of the explanations for the psychological oddity of so many late twentieth-century, early twenty-first-century politicians and royal persons. In an ideal world, corrupt standards in public life would be purged by exposure. Dishonesty, sexual depravity, financial irregularity by public figures would result in their disgrace, and replacement by those who were pure, lovely and of good report. In the imperfect world we actually inhabit, the elimination of double standards resulted in the weakening of any standards at all. But in the early 1960s there was a public mood of impatience with the Old Gang who had ruled Britain since the war. Macmillan's pose as a remote Edwardian aristocrat was a source of as much irritation as admiration, and was the underlying reason for the vengeful moralistic public fury which led to the ruin of his Secretary of State for War, John Profumo.

The central figure in the story was Stephen Ward, an osteopath who practised in Wimpole Mews, the medical district of Marylebone. He had treated all manner of famous patients, including members of the Royal Family, Winston Churchill and his son Randolph, Nubar Gulbenkian, Danny Kaye, Sir Anthony Eden and Sir Malcolm Sargent. He had also – and here was how the tale began to unfold, treated Nancy, Lady Astor and her son Lord Astor. Ward was a frequent guest at Cliveden and, in return for a peppercorn rent, he kept a cottage on the estate as a weekend retreat.[3]

The osteopath was always surrounded by pretty young women, whom he was happy to introduce to friends. One of these was an extremely beautiful long-legged girl with long, rust-coloured hair who had begun modelling for *Tit-Bits* when she was fifteen (in March 1958), moved on to bare-breasted dancing at Murray's Cabaret Club in Beak Street, Soho. 'She was a nymphomaniac in the true sense of the term, in that she felt emotionally secure only when she was giving her body to someone . . . She once admitted that she would allow a man to use her in any way that pleased him as long as he did not want to kiss her on the lips.'[4] Her name was Christine Keeler.

She moved into Ward's flat, and became a regular visitor to the Cliveden cottage within days of meeting at Murray's Cabaret Club. They never had a sexual relationship. He kept her amused with constant jokes, he impressed her by his famous contacts, he was her rescuer. Ward introduced her to the friends who looked to him as a purveyor of young women. Among them was a bridge-playing naval attaché at the Soviet Embassy, Commander Yevgeny Ivanov. Another who met Keeler during a hot weekend round the swimming pool at Cliveden in July 1961 was John Profumo, an Old Harrovian, recently elevated by Macmillan to the post of Secretary of State for War. Ward was in the perfect position to be a blackmailer, or an agent for the Soviet Union. He was neither. He had merely allowed a situation to develop whereby a Soviet naval attaché and a Secretary of State for War were sharing, albeit unwittingly, the same mistress.

Then a crisis occurred. On 14 December 1962 a young West Indian called Johnny Edgecombe turned up at Ward's flat in Wimpole Mews and fired shots at the window. Inside were Christine Keeler and another of Ward's girls, Mandy Rice-Davies. Edgecombe had come round with a gun because Mandy had displaced him in her affections with another West Indian, one Lucky Gordon. Edgecombe was put on trial for the attempted murder of Keeler, and for possessing a firearm with intent to endanger life. He was acquitted on the murder charge – Keeler having absconded – but when the court learned of previous convictions for 'living on immoral earnings' and theft and drug possession, he was sent down for seven years.

By now, the rumours of Keeler's affair with Ivanov and Profumo was common knowledge. The satirical magazine *Private Eye* on 22 March, led the way with:

IDLE TALK
Reveals
Lunchtime O'Booze
Mr Silas Jones, a West Indian immigrant of no fixed abode, was today sentenced at the Old Bailey to twenty-four years' Preventive Detention for being in possession of an offensive water pistol.

The chief 'witness' in the case, gay fun-loving Miss Gaye Funloving, a twenty-one-year-old 'model', was not actually present in Court. She has, in fact, disappeared. It is believed that normally, in cases of this type, a Warrant is issued for the arrest of the missing witness.

'PARTIES'
One of Miss Funloving's close 'friends', Dr Spook of Harley Street, revealed last night that he could add nothing to what had already been insinuated.

Dr Spook is believed to have 'more than half the Cabinet on his list of patients'. He also has a 'weekend' cottage on the Berkshire estate of Lord ——, and is believed to have attended many 'parties' in the neighbourhood.

Among those it is believed have also attended 'parties' of this type are Mr Vladimir Bolokhov, the well-known Soviet spy attached to the Russian Embassy, and a well-known Cabinet Minister.

RESIGNATION?
Mr James Montesi, a well-known Cabinet Minister, was last night reported to have proffered his 'resignation' to the Prime Minister, on 'personal grounds'.

It is alleged that the Prime Minister refused to accept his alleged 'resignation'. Mr Montesi today denied the allegations that he had ever allegedly offered his alleged 'resignation' to the alleged 'Prime Minister'.[5]

Then, on the evening this story was printed, Colonel George Wigg (1900–83) rose in the House of Commons. Wigg was an old soldier, the eldest of six children of a dairyman from Ealing, west London. His appearance, elephantine ears, huge nose, bright, intelligent eyes, made him a gift to cartoonists. Poverty made it impossible to take up scholarships won in boyhood and he left school at fourteen, joined the Hampshire Regiment at eighteen and served in the regular army as a private soldier. The odious braying Tory MPs, when he was elected for Labour for the seat of Dudley, in 1945, liked to mock Wigg's struggles. 'Has not the time come,' asked Sir David Renton on one occasion, 'for the Hon. Member to be sent back to his regiment?'[6] It was a cruelly snobbish remark since in the Hampshire Regiment Wigg had never been promoted above the ranks. Only after war broke out did he become a lieutenant colonel in the Royal Army Education Corps. He had got on reasonably well with Profumo until 1962, when he began asking awkward questions about a British Army operation in Kuwait, to repel an invasion for Iraq. Though puffed as a 'model' operation, Wigg knew this was a lie. As many as 10 per cent of the troops were out of action through heat exhaustion. The replies given to Wigg by the Defence Minister were revealed by a subsequent Parliamentary Select Committee to be untrue. He used his questions as a launch pad for a wholesale criticism, quite justified, of the state of the British Army. He never forgave Profumo for trying to lie to him over Kuwait. When a cleric in the Admiralty called John Vassall was blackmailed by the Russians for homosexuality and subsequently exposed as an agent, Wigg received a mysterious anonymous telephone call – not to his own home but to the house of a friend he happened to be visiting.

'Forget about Vassall,' said the voice. 'You want to look at Profumo.'

So it was that Wigg could act the role of Profumo's nemesis in the Commons:

There is not an Hon. Member in the House, nor a journalist in the Press Gallery, nor do I believe there is a person in the Public Gallery who in the last few days has not heard rumour upon rumour involving a member of the Government Front Bench. The Press has got as near as it can – it has shown itself willing to wound but afraid to strike . . .

I rightly use the privilege of the House of Commons – that is what it is given to me for – to ask the Home Secretary, who is the senior member of the Government on the Treasury Bench now, to go to the Dispatch Box – he knows that the rumour to which I refer relates to Miss Christine Keeler and Miss Davies and a shooting by a West Indian – and, on behalf of the Government, categorically deny the truth of these rumours. On the other hand, if there is anything in them, I urge him to ask the Prime Minister to do what was not done in the Vassall case – set up a Select Committee so that these things can be dissipated, and the honour of the Minister concerned freed from the imputations and innuendoes that are being spread at the present time.[7]

Profumo came to the House of Commons and made a statement which was transparently false. *Private Eye* printed on its cover a picture of him sitting on a bed, with a balloon saying: 'And if *Private Eye* prints a picture of me on a bed, I'll sue them.' Profumo had told the Commons, 'there was no impropriety whatsoever in my acquaintanceship with Miss Keeler'. Then he had left the House and together with his wife, the actress Valerie Hobson (she had played the lead in *The King and I*), and the Queen Mother, had gone to the races. But the matter was not going to go away. Lucky Gordon came up for trial at the Old Bailey, charged with wounding Keeler in the street. Ward gave the Home Secretary evidence that Keeler and Profumo had been lovers. Profumo resigned.[8]

The Establishment exacted a grisly revenge upon Ward, the initiator of the disaster. The osteopath was himself put on trial, on 22 July 1963, for living off the immoral earnings of prostitutes; for procuring girls under the age of twenty-one to have illicit sexual intercourse; for procuring abortions; and for conspiring to keep a brothel. Ward was acquitted of procuring, but the jury, persuaded by the prosecution counsel Mervyn Griffith-Jones, found him guilty of poncing for Christine and Mandy – even though Christine denied being a prostitute. By then, Ward was in St Stephen's Hospital, having taken an overdose of Nembutal tablets. He died at 3.50 p.m. on 3 August. Six days later, the funeral took place at Mortlake Crematorium. Apart from a solitary wreath of roses from his family, there was one wreath made up of a hundred white carnations. It was from Kenneth Tynan; John Osborne; his wife, Penelope Gilliat; Annie Ross, the jazz singer; Dominic Elwes, who had stood bail for Ward; Arnold Wesker; and Joe Orton. Their card read simply

> To Stephen Ward
> Victim of Hypocrisy.

A postscript to the Profumo affair occurred in 1976 when George Wigg was charged by police while accosting women from his motor car as he drove slowly near Marble Arch. The magistrate acquitted him, not because he believed Wigg's denial, but because he considered that the 'kerb crawling' of which Wigg had accurately been accused did not amount to an offence.[9]

Profumo himself became the modern equivalent of a medieval penitent. He offered his services to Toynbee Hall, the settlement for the poor and needy in the East End, and thereafter commuted four days a week to help alcoholics, drug addicts, ex-convicts and the elderly.[10]

On the surface of things, it could be said that very little had happened. Some men had cheated on their wives with a number of compliant young women – even though the compliance was underwritten with cash, there was no suggestion of coercion. Despite the best endeavours of the press to say otherwise, no national security had been breached. But something had happened. Britain had changed. With their blundering, self-righteous rhetoric the politicians tried to put it into words. On television Lord Hailsham said, 'Of course, we have all been kicked in the stomach.' He then proceeded to kick Profumo, reminding him that he had 'lied and lied and lied – lied to his friends, lied to his family, lied to his colleagues, lied to his solicitor, lied to the House of Commons . . . This is a great national moral issue.'[11] Quite what the issue was, the politicians found it difficult to articulate. Harold Wilson, as the newly elected leader of the Labour Party, did his best in the debate in the Commons which followed Profumo's resignation. 'Saturday's paper told of an opportunist night-club proprietor who had offered Miss Christine Keeler – or should I refer to her as Christine Keeler Ltd – a night club job at a salary of £5,000 a week, and I say to the Prime Minister that there is something utterly nauseating about a system of society which pays a harlot twenty-five times as much as it pays its Prime Minister, 250 times as much as it pays its Members of Parliament, and 500 times as much as it pays some of its ministers of religion.'[12]

This economic approach to the question was certainly arresting, but what point did it make? As Dame Rebecca West pointed out in the next issue of the *Sunday Telegraph*, 'Nobody sensible would go to a night-club to see Members of Parliament coming down staircases dressed in sequins and tail-feathers unless there were at least 250 of them; you need a lot, as market gardeners cunningly say, to make a show.'[13]

Like the collapse of the Crown Prosecution of *Lady Chatterley*, the Profumo affair was one of the prime factors in making Britain a little less stuffy about sex. By the time newspaper readers had glutted themselves with the antics of Stephen Ward's distinguished clients, there seemed less case for public legislators telling others how to conduct their sexual lives. No one could say that the *Chatterley* case or the Profumo affair directly caused the liberalisation of divorce laws, the facilitation of legal abortion or the growth of tolerance towards homosexuals, but they played their part. More crucial than any part they played in the sexual revolution was the decline in deference, which was definitely hastened by Profumo, and the strengthening of the power of the press – and, with it, the medium of television. The laws of libel would be invoked, as they were by a succession of well-monied rogues over the next half-century, to cloak their misdemeanours. But after the Profumo case the press would be less timid about exposing not merely the sexual peccadilloes but all other aspects of the lives of public figures.

PART THREE

A Fourteenth Earl and a Fourteenth Mr Wilson

10

Enemies of Promise

'Mr Attlee had three Old Etonians in his cabinet. I have six. Things are twice as good under the Conservatives.' So said Harold Macmillan in 1959.[1] He could have added, as Anthony Sampson did in his *Anatomy of Britain*, that Eton had also educated eighteen out of the twenty-six dukes, and that it had produced Humphrey Lyttelton, Aldous Huxley, Lord Longford and Lord Dalton, a well-chosen list of names to indicate the Etonian range – Lyttelton a noted jazz musician and later a highly popular radio voice in a panel game called *I'm Sorry, I Haven't a Clue*; Huxley as a then modish, if now unfashionable, novelist; Longford and Dalton among other roles socialist politicians. Throughout the 1950s, Sampson showed in his *Anatomy* the high proportion of those entering the diplomatic service had been educated at public schools, a significant number at Eton. The same story could be replicated in the civil service, in the City and the greater financial institutions, and in the press. There was a strong Etonian mafia or Freemasonry in Britain, so much taken for granted among its members that they barely even noticed that it was there. Equally strong was resentment against it, especially among those men who were educated at other boarding schools.

Private Eye, for example, and with it a whole new school of journalism which materially changed the climate, was written largely by men educated at public schools which were not Eton. The magazine was in effect the continuation of a satirical journal begun at Shrewsbury School by Christopher Booker. He was the founder-editor of the *Eye*, and Richard Ingrams, who took over the editorship in an office coup only a year or so afterwards, Willie Rushton, one of the great cartoonists of the century, and the Trotskyite sage and idealist Paul Foot had all been together at Shrewsbury. Paul Foot left bruising accounts of the sadism of Anthony Chevenix-Trench, who enjoyed caning the bare buttocks of the prettier boys when they failed the ever-more-difficult Greek Unseens which he set them. Chevenix-Trench was a celebrated headmaster of Eton, who left under a cloud after the complaints made there. His behaviour at Shrewsbury quickened the hatred felt by the *Private Eye* Old Salopians for Eton. And when they were joined by Auberon Waugh, who had been sent by his father Evelyn to Downside Abbey, they were to encounter another yet more vitriolically anti-Etonian imagination.

Paradoxical as it may sound, however, it was the unfairness of their attacks on 'Baillie Vass' which made *Private Eye* such an effective force for good in Britain. Not since the days of the Regency when Cobbett wrote his *Register* had there been journalists who were prepared so frequently to risk the penalties of the law in order to tell the truth about what was going on in the country, and above all in the government. Wayland Young, author of what remains the best book on the Profumo affair, written in 1963, called *Private Eye* 'the bravest and often the most accurate, organ of opinion in the British Press'.[2] Whatever peculiar character traits fuelled these young men, they made the Establishment shake in its shoes. The weapons of cruelty and unfairness which they wielded would never have been so effective if they had weighed their words, or considered that a figure such as Alec Home was a decent man, whom they probably would have all liked if they had known him personally. Such feelings would have corrupted their purpose, which was a peculiarly English combination of frivolity and anger. The chief function of the magazine, from the beginning, was to make readers laugh. But it also made rogues sleep less easy in their beds, knowing that these young men were prepared to mock and unmask anyone, even if they were the Prime Minister, even if they were rich enough to sue them, and send them to prison.

From the beginning, *Private Eye* was a joint effort. Paul Foot was one of the very rare beings who genuinely hungered and thirsted after righteousness. A passionate atheist of the Shelley school, he had inherited enough of his Methodist West Country forebears' temperament to need a creed as well as goodness of heart to motivate him. He found it, bizarrely, in the life and doctrines of Trotsky. In spite of the nonsensical views of politics which this sometimes inspired, it taught Foot to distrust all the major political parties in Britain, and everyone who represented them. He was the champion of victims and injustice, and was prepared to spend hours, days, months, listening to telephone calls, answering letters, visiting prisons, nagging at lawyers, to reveal miscarriages of justice. He was a great journalist.

So, too, in a very different mould, was his friend Auberon Waugh, who began writing for *Private Eye* only in the early 1970s, but who deserves a mention here as one of the inspirational figures in the team. His politics would be hard to define; though he was a lifelong member of the Conservative Party, he was really an anarchist, who believed anyone who actually chose to go into politics had some psychological flaw. But the hero, and pirate king, of the *Private Eye* story was Richard Ingrams. Because the magazine was so entertaining, over so many years, it is easy to forget that he defied the libel laws and other intimidations to print stories which, especially in its early days, no newspaper would touch. It was entirely owing to the indomitable courage of Ingrams himself that many of these stories, about the conduct of government under Wilson, Heath, Callaghan and Thatcher, ever reached the public. John Betjeman had, certainly since the war, realised that one reason for the architectural wreckage of Britain was simple corruption. Plansters bribed local governments to give planning permission for the demolition of good, old architecture, and the erection of modernist blight. At the centre of one such scandal, which had the widest possible repercussions throughout the North East and in the London Borough of Wandsworth, was a corrupt architect and developer, John Poulson, together with his partner in crime, the Labour Party chieftain in Newcastle upon Tyne, T. Dan Smith.[3] They had sucked many into their maw, including the lazy old Reggie Maudling who had been in Poulson's pay but conveniently lost the relevant papers at the time of Poulson's bankruptcy in 1972. (Maudling's career was ruined.[4]) The web of corruption was so wide and so tightly woven that no ordinary newspaper would have risked, as Ingrams did, imprisonment in order to expose it.

The villainies of Jeremy Thorpe and Robert Maxwell were first aired in *Private Eye*. When no newspaper protested at the killing of unarmed Irish suspects in Gibraltar under the premiership of Thatcher, it was the *Eye* which did so. Without an editor who was cussed and weird and downright bloody-minded, as Ingrams was, the enterprise would either have folded, under the pressure of bullies such as James Goldsmith or Robert Maxwell, or it would have become bland. Paul Foot and Ingrams were once walking across the Berkshire Downs when Goldsmith's heaviest guns were firing. Foot said, 'What are you going to do about this Goldsmith thing? It's going to finish you. It's going to get you evicted from your house, and everything.' Ingrams just said, 'My main problem is how I'm going to attack him next.' This was a rare, reckless courage.

Ingrams nurtured many of the best talents in Fleet Street. Little by little, the atmosphere in Britain changed. Without deference, as has already been stated, much of the business of public life becomes impossible; and for that, with all the concomitant lessening of talent in politics, *Private Eye* must bear some of the responsibility. But when one considers the lists of Ingrams's targets and enemies, it is hard not to rejoice at all his victories and overlook the undoubted cruelty in the very nature of *Private Eye*, cruelty which often hit innocent targets. The other vein of the magazine, best represented when Ingrams was working in tandem with the actor and former Eton master John Wells ('Jawn'), was in parody. Ingrams's Wodehousian gifts were never better shown than in the 'Dear Bill' Letters, which he wrote with Wells, purporting to be letters from Denis Thatcher to Bill Deedes, and in the voluminous writings of that sentimental romancer Sylvie Krin, author of such Mills and Boon style accounts of the Royal Family as *Love in the Saddle* and *Heir of Sorrows*. Nor should one forget the poetical works of E. J. Thribb, aged 17½.

The enemies of Macmillan, and of his successor, were so intent upon making mischief, both at the time of Macmillan's resignation and in subsequent years, that the unsuitability of Home to the role of a mid-twentieth-century British Prime Minister was a given doctrine, seldom examined for its plausibility. In fact, given the choice between R. A. Butler and Quintin Hogg, Macmillan (and/or the Queen) made a sensible choice in selecting Home. It was a time of a singularly delicate international situation: the Cold War threatened to turn into actual war; the colonial and post-colonial situation in Africa, especially in Rhodesia, would have benefited neither from R. A. Butler's instinctive cowardice nor from Hogg's impulsive folly. So, after a tumultuous Conservative Party Conference in Blackpool, at which the leadership contenders made exhibitions of themselves, the Queen summoned the 14th Earl of Home and asked him to form an administration. Since 1923, it had been a received wisdom in the Conservative Party that the reason Lord Curzon, much the ablest candidate, failed to become Prime Minister was that he belonged to the Upper House. Home therefore set about renouncing his peerage, which he was able to do following Anthony Wedgwood Benn's renunciation of his viscountcy. As Sir Alec Douglas-Home, he contested the safe Tory seat of Kinross and West Perthshire, and he took his seat in the House of Commons on 8 November 1963.

It was an aristocratic *coup d'état*. True, the aristocracy, in such forms as Bobbety Cecil (Lord Salisbury), hovered in the wings of the Conservative Party, but it was an age since they had so blatantly shown their hand. 'The Tory Party is run by about five people,' said one leading member, 'and they all treat their followers with disdain: they're mostly Etonians, and Eton is good for disdain.'[5] But Sir Alec Douglas-Home did not treat people with disdain. He was a palpably decent person. He was vague: 'Moscow, Alec, Moscow', his wife had to keep reminding him on a visit to Russia as they came down the steps of an aeroplane, lest he 'should assume that he had just arrived in Washington or Peking or Rome'.[6] But he was also sharp-witted, and, given the attack which was unleashed upon him immediately by a hostile media, remarkably popular. He himself blamed the shortness of his tenure of office (barely a year) upon the influence of a new satirical TV show called *That Was The Week That Was*, compèred by a Cambridge-educated son of the Methodist manse named David Frost and directed by a sharp-tongued homosexual called Ned Sherrin (educated at Sexey's School, Bruton, Somerset). For them, as for most of the team of satirists they assembled – Bernard Levin, Roy Kinnear, Millicent Martin, and the rest – as for the *Private Eye* boys, who also wrote material for *That Was The Week*, there was something self-evidently risible in having an aristocrat as Prime Minister. The fact that he was diplomatically experienced counted for nothing. Nor did the fact that, because of a long period as a young man when he suffered from tuberculosis of the spine, he had spent over a year reading Marxist texts. He was thought to be the only member of the House of Commons who had read *Das Kapital*, and he was the author of an impressive, well-researched letter to Churchill in 1945, protesting at the disgraceful terms of the Yalta Agreement with Stalin, and protesting at the fate of the Eastern European countries at the end of the Second World War. Had a man with the same qualifications as Home been educated at a grammar school and spoken with a regional accent, the media would probably have been hailing him as supremely well equipped for office.

One of the paradoxical features of our times is not that the aristocracy has especially declined, either in wealth or in influence, but that it has been thought improper for this wealth and influence to be reflected in the political sphere.

As so often in his Polonius-like machinations, Macmillan had given out confusing signals. It was he who had anointed the 14th Earl of Home as his successor, and yet it was he who, with the 1958 Life Peerages Act, had undermined the hereditary principle itself. The great majority of those who accepted peerages for life were former members of the House of Commons.[7] For the remainder of the twentieth century, they sat in the Second Chamber together with the hereditary peers. It was not until 1999 with its House of Lords Reform Bill that the Blair government limited the numbers of hereditary peers permitted to be legislators to ninety-two.[8] Finally, their right to sit there was abolished altogether. Given the climate of the times, the wonder is that it took so long. Since Victorian times, radicals had been calling for the divorce between membership of the Upper House and membership of peerage of the realm. It took the government of New Labour fully to bring this to pass, though Macmillan had taken the first step. Between 1965 and 1983 no hereditary titles were created. Margaret Thatcher made three creations – an earldom (of Stockton) was given to Macmillan; a viscountcy apiece was given to George Thomas (Viscount Tonypandy) and William Whitelaw, neither of whom had male heirs. The paradox is, that in the fifty years since the Life Peerages Act, and the steady diminution of direct political power of the aristocracy, the old peerage has grown stronger in terms of wealth and private influence.

In 1989, the meritocratic *Sunday Times* published the first of its List of the Richest People in Britain. The political agenda of its proprietor, Rupert Murdoch, and its editor, Andrew Neil, was that Britain should become more like America, a place, supposedly, where birth counted for less than enterprise, and where it was possible for enterprising people to pull themselves up by their bootstraps. In fact, this is an illusory economic concept, a piece of myth. As an experienced historian of wealth, W. D. Rubinstein, has pointed out, the statistics all suggest one thing. The surest way to become rich is to inherit money. In the period 1809–1939, Rubinstein found only fifteen truly self-made millionaires; the rest had all started out with the help of inherited money.[9] In 1989, Andrew Neil, who had hoped to print a list of the new Thatcherite meritocracy, was able, it is true, to field some who had made their money out of motor racing or multi-storey car parks, but a quarter of the hundred listed were hereditary landowners. When Gladstone raised the richest man in Victorian England from a Marquessate in 1874, he made him the Duke of Westminster. In Thatcher's Britain of 1989, the richest man was still the Duke of Westminster. Many of the landed classes, who in real terms were prodigiously wealthy, did not appear on Andrew Neil's list because, in order to avoid confiscatory levels of taxation, they had formed their estates into trusts and limited companies which they did not, technically, own. So the list of the rich aristocrats in the *Sunday Times* tended to be those who lived chiefly off urban rents – figures such as the Duke of Westminster and Earl Cadogan. Even so, after the first ten years of the Rich List's history, well over a hundred members of the peerage and the landed gentry appeared in the list, none worth less than £20 million.[10]

At the time when Alec Douglas-Home was Prime Minister this was a state of things which the Labour Party and many others in Britain were actively determined to reverse. Harold Wilson had a stock of replies to hecklers. When he was in full flight, promising new and better schools, hospitals, roads, laboratories and all the blessings of modern life, some recalcitrant member of the audience called out, 'Where are you going to find the money to pay for it?' he would shout back, 'Out of Lord Carrington's pocket!'[11] It pleased the fans, but it was economic nonsense. Lord Carrington's pocket remained as full at the end of our times as it had been when Harold Wilson made the boast. There were many landed families who, in the mid-twentieth century, were obliged through poverty to abandon their ancient country houses, and sell their land, or donate it all to the National Trust. Those who survived, however, did so not necessarily because they had more grit or enterprise or other meritocratic virtues. They were simply much richer, and were determined to remain so. In the past in Britain it was deemed axiomatic that those who had the largest share of the nation's wealth should have the biggest say in determining the course of its affairs. This is still, broadly, the point of view in America, where presidential candidates either have to possess, or to find the support of, colossal fortunes merely to stand for election. In Britain in 1963, however, attitudes had so changed that the mere fact of belonging to the aristocracy was considered a disqualification for office. After Alec Home went, there would follow over forty years in which the 'toffs' in the Conservative Party either retreated from politics altogether or played backroom roles. It led to a situation where, for example, in the 1990s, so obviously brilliant a man and ruthlessly good a politician as Viscount Cranborne, who succeeded as 7th Marquess of Salisbury in 2003, was confined to fighting losing battles for the rights of the hereditary peers in the House of Lords, rather than use his talents for the wider good of the country. His is an extreme case, but there are many others where toffs were excluded from public life simply for being toffs. The growth of their wealth, and the diminishment of their political power, was one of the many symptoms of the dissolution of late twentieth-century society. Socialists of the Harold Wilson generation would have liked the government of Britain to be shared between intellectuals and trades unionists. Meritocrats of the Thatcher generation would have wanted it to be governed by businessmen. But the political structures of Britain, and its institutions, remained largely unchanged, and they were determined by the ownership of wealth and land, by the position of the older universities and the more prestigious private schools, and by Parliament itself. Since 1689, the system, the institutions, had been posited upon an aristocratic form of government. Under the Victorians, this system had evolved, to widen the franchise, but it had not become in any continental sense democratic. Nor would it, throughout our times. Proportional representation, the only truly democratic voting system, was not introduced in all the years 1953–2008, and the representatives sent to Parliament might have represented all the people but they only represented some 20 per cent of their actual opinions and political colouring.

What Britain was left with, by the end of the period, was the rump of an aristocratic system, with no aristocracy allowed to govern within it. Alec Home's short tenure of office was the end of an era when those trained through generations to belong to the 'governing classes' were actually allowed to govern.

In any event, 1963 was a brave moment for a 14th Earl to become Prime Minister, and from the very first the media were out not merely to mock, but to destroy him. When the *Aberdeen Evening Express* accidentally used a photograph of Home to illustrate a story about one Baillie Vass, one of *Private Eye*'s more baffling soubriquets was instantly born. Home became, in the eyes of that magazine, 'Baillie Vass, the notorious Scottish entrepreneur and confidence trickster'.[12] They printed more than one picture of him enthroned on the lavatory with his striped parliamentary trousers crumpled around his ankles. In September, his mere appearance in a photograph in the *Guardian* unleashed this comment: 'In a desperate attempt to win over the female voters Baillie Vass last week exposed himself in Downing Street in the presence of Mr Butler, and a photographer from the Grauniad. It is well known that the impudent Baillie pins his hopes of winning the election on women (our Political Correspondent writes) but it was not expected that he would stoop to such primitive stunts in order to gain their allegiance.'[13] The 'Election Issue' had a floppy gramophone record ('His Master's Vass') stuck to the cover. When removed, it revealed a photograph of Baillie Vass on the lavatory. He is surrounded by putti drawn by Gerald Scarfe, with the faces of R.A. Butler, Quintin Hogg, Edward Heath and another unrecognisable. The bubble coming from the Baillie's mouth is 'Put that record back AT ONCE'.[14]

What did they find so odious about him? Nine years after Home had stopped being Prime Minister, the magazine's diarist, Auberon Waugh, angered at being sacked from *The Times* by Baillie Vass's nephew Charles Douglas-Home, was still pursuing the campaign – in 1973 – reminding readers, 'Vass it was who stood up to be counted at Munich; who patiently got on with his needlework throughout the resulting World War when a bad back laid him low; who refused to be cowed by the tyrant Nasser at Suez; whose unswerving support for Michael Stewart emboldened that timid little man to see his peculiar Nigerian policy through; who keeps trying to sell black Rhodesians down the river, despite repeated discouragement. Sir Baillie Vass, at 89, is widely regarded as the most honourable man in British politics.'[15] One of the reasons Waugh's invectives in his *Private Eye Diaries* packed such a punch was that you did not know how much of it was meant. Probably, at the time of writing, drunk or half-drunk, he meant every word, as when he added, in the same *Diary* entry, 'I have always maintained that Churchill should have been hanged at the end of the last war – whether for specific war crimes, like the introduction of civilian bombing, or for Yalta, or merely to herald a return to the civilised standards of peace.'

Sir Alec Douglas-Home was actually an embodiment of such 'civilised standards'. He worried about 'whether democracy (one man, one vote) will last. Certainly it will relapse into some more authoritarian form of government unless the great majority are really well-educated in the basic facts of community and international living' . . . 'We've got a long way to go before we can say democracy is secure and stands on its feet.'[16]

He wanted to bring in legislation, such as Margaret Thatcher was to do, to democratise the trades unions. His short premiership was dominated by foreign affairs. In Cyprus, the Turks threatened to invade. Harold

Sir Winston Churchill makes a speech of thanks to MPs after being presented with a portrait of himself aged 80 by Graham Sutherland. Churchill was bitterly hurt by the picture, which revealed him – and by extension Britain – in a state of irreversible collapse.

J. R. R. Tolkien's epic *The Lord of the Rings* was not an allegory, but its bleak depiction of vanished civilisations and lost traditions matched what had happened to Europe after the Second World War.

Nemesis One. The Egyptian Prime Minister Gamal Nasser receives the adulation of the crowds for closing the Suez Canal. Although British, French and Israeli troops effected a victory over the Egyptians, the subsequent humiliation of Britain by America spelled the end of Britain as a world power.

Nemesis Two. England's prosperity and power in Victorian days was symbolized by the building of its railways. The decision of Harold Macmillan to allow Dr Richard Beeching to close more than half the railway mileage in Britain was environmentally, aesthetically and socially disastrous.

Dr Billy Graham, on his mission to Britain in 1954, addressed crowds of thousands. Those converted to his American evangelicalism had a strong influence on the Church of England.

The majority of Britons, perhaps, continued to share the chippiness, pessimism and offended dignity of Tony Hancock, seen here (*left*) with Sid James (*centre*) in an episode of the popular TV show *Hancock's Half Hour*.

Harold Macmillan with Yuri Gagarin, the first man in space. The Russian success in this field speeded up the symbolic rivalry of the superpowers, the USSR and the USA, in their fight to dominate not merely the world but the galaxy.

Harold Macmillan's marriage to Lady Dorothy Cavendish was a tragicomedy whose bizarre secrets were not known to the public during his administration.

Bob Boothby, wit, raconteur, TV personality and MP, was for many years the lover of the Prime Minister's wife, Lady Dorothy.

Boothby's name was also linked to that of Ronnie, one of the notorious Kray twins, whose violent gang controlled the East End of London. 'I'm not a poof,' Ronnie would explain, 'I'm a homosexual.' Here Reggie (*left*) and Ronnie are seen with their mother, Violet.

Health Secretary J. Enoch Powell was responsible for closing down many of the Victorian lunatic asylums. As Health Secretary he had pursued a policy of employing more and more nurses and hospital workers from the Commonwealth, but as a later demagogue, perhaps in penitence for what he had done as Secretary of State, he came to deplore the arrival of non-whites in such large numbers.

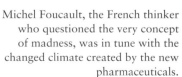

Michel Foucault, the French thinker who questioned the very concept of madness, was in tune with the changed climate created by the new pharmaceuticals.

John Profumo, Keeler's lover, and his wife, the actress Valerie Hobson, in the unwelcome light of publicity.

Christine Keeler had simultaneous affairs with the Secretary of State for War and an attaché at the Soviet Embassy. She initiated the collapse of the Conservative Government.

In the trial of *Lady Chatterley's Lover*, the Bishop of Woolwich (*left*) compared the act of sex with Holy Communion.

Conservative-Anarchist: Auberon Waugh, son of Evelyn, was one of the most brilliantly iconoclastic writers of the age.

Conservative-Anarchists: the Rolling Stones, in every way more talented than the Beatles, both threw over the traces and instantaneously became the Voice of Britain.

Conservative-Anarchist: Archbishop Ramsey ('I hate the Church of England') planted time bombs which would ensure its ultimate dissolution.

Wilson made a fool of himself in the Commons, demanding that Britain should send her 'heaviest tanks' to Cyprus, vehicles totally unsuited to the terrain, as to security operations, as Home was able gently to point out.

Wilson would follow Home's foreign policy almost to the letter – support for democratic governments in Africa, support for an independent Malaysia, continued negotiations with Rhodesia to try to persuade the white minority government to agree a programme of devolving power to the black majority, maintaining the transatlantic alliance, and yet not being totally subsumed by the US. This was the argument in favour of Britain possessing its own nuclear deterrent and being a member of NATO. 'It is not to man's credit,' Home said, 'that the peace is held by a balance of nuclear power but it is the fact of life and paradoxically the hope of life too.'[17]

Scarcely a month after Douglas-Home became Prime Minister, President John Fitzgerald Kennedy was assassinated – on 22 November in Dallas, Texas. He had been in office thirty-four months and he was forty-six years old. His assassin was Lee Harvey Oswald, a twenty-four-year-old former US Marine who was apprehended on the day of the murder and himself assassinated on 24 November, while being taken from Dallas gaol to a county prison. (His murderer was a nightclub owner called Jack Ruby.)

Kennedy died from a gunshot wound in the brain at 1.00 p.m. local time (7.00 p.m. Greenwich Mean Time). (On the same day died also Aldous Huxley and C. S. Lewis.) In the aircraft flying the body back to Washington, and with Kennedy's widow Jackie at his side, Vice President Lyndon Baines Johnson, aged fifty-five, took the oath of office as 36th President before Federal Judge Sarah Hughes, who was in tears. A stranger in a New York street, one of the innumerable vox pop interviews for television stations around the world, said he was younger than Kennedy, for whom he had not voted. He said he suddenly felt very old. He turned aside to weep.

The assassination of John F. Kennedy was an overwhelming shock, not only to the people of America, but to the world. The unknown young New Yorker who felt suddenly old and weepy encapsulated the mood of the quarter of a million people who filed past Kennedy's body in the rotunda of the Capitol, and of the mourners who came to the funeral – the Duke of Edinburgh, Sir Alec Douglas-Home, President de Gaulle, Dr Ludwig Erhard and the rest.

That Was The Week That Was had been unsparing, to date, in its attempts at bad-taste mockery of those set in authority. When they heard the news of Kennedy's death, on a Friday night, Ned Sherrin and David

Frost decided immediately that the next day's show should be a serious tribute. They devoted twenty minutes to saying that Kennedy was 'miraculous . . . an amazing man who seemed so utterly right for the job'. Millicent Martin sang 'His soul goes riding on', and they trundled out Dame Sybil Thorndike to recite a poem by Caryl Brahms – 'Yesterday the sun was shot out of your sky, Jackie'. The whole programme was, according to *Private Eye* Trotskyist Paul Foot, 'sickeningly sycophantic'.[18]

Kennedy was connected to Britain with much closer bonds than most American Presidents had been. His father had been Ambassador at the Court of St James before the war and though his gut-Irish anti-British view of the European situation had enraged those who saw him as a pro-Hitler isolationist, his clever, handsome children were part of society. Much to the horror of the Catholic Kennedys, Joe's daughter Kathleen (Kick) had married Billy Hartington, heir to the Duke of Devonshire; because the Devonshires would not countenance a Catholic wedding, the marriage took place at the Chelsea Register Office. Joe came to the wedding to give away his daughter, who was excommunicated, but most of the Kennedys stayed away. Hartington was killed in the war in September 1944. Kick was killed in a plane crash in the Rhône Valley on 13 May 1948. She was with her (married) lover Peter FitzWilliam, whom she had hoped to marry, but, since she died as the Marchioness of Hartington, she was buried in the family plot at Edensor, the model village adjoining Chatsworth. JOY SHE GAVE/JOY SHE HAS FOUND is her epitaph.[19] It was chosen by her mother-in-law, the Duchess. Her own mother refused to attend the funeral. An observer noted, 'the stricken face of old Joe Kennedy as he stood alone, unloved and despised, behind the coffin of his eldest daughter, and the hundreds of British friends who had adored her and now mourned her.'[20]

It was a scene which demonstrated how deeply the Kennedys had become a part of the very British class which the British themselves – among the satirists and opinion-forming intelligentsia – had decided was obsolete. Lady Dorothy Macmillan was Kick Kennedy's aunt by marriage. Jack Kennedy was not only an in-law but also the devoted friend of his sister's sister-in-law Debo. Nancy Mitford, Debo's eldest sister, wrote to another sister, Jessica, 'Our fast young sister went over that ocean & had long loving *tête à têtes* with your ruler. Andrew [11th Duke of Devonshire] says Kennedy is doing for sex what Eisenhower did for golf.'[21]

During the Kennedy years, the special relationship between Britain and the United States was a familial one.

This did not stop Jack Kennedy absorbing the information that the Profumo affair had finished not merely his 'Uncle Harold' but the Conservative government. Ambassador David Bruce in London had told

Kennedy by telegram, 'Macmillan's admission that he did not know what was going on at critical times was in circumstances pitiable and extremely damaging. He did not try to shirk responsibility, but on his own account did not give impression that he knew how to exercise it in unfolding developments of case on which nearly everyone in Parliament appeared to be better informed than the Prime Minister.'[22]

The Profumo affair had been slightly more than a spectator sport for the American President, as Ambassador Bruce may or may not have been aware. It was through an American businessman, Thomas Corbally, who was a friend of Stephen Ward, that Bruce (and, indeed, Macmillan) had first learnt of Commander Ivanov's involvement with Christine Keeler.[23] J. Edgar Hoover, head of the FBI, had also heard of Ivanov through an informant code-named Fedora, a KGB officer who had offered to work for the US. The FBI, the CIA and the OSI (Office of Special Investigations) had all taken an obsessive interest in what Christine Keeler and Mandy Rice-Davies had been up to during their stay at the Hotel Bedford in New York in July 1962 and whether they had – as was rumoured – slept with the President. The Attorney-General Robert Kennedy was interested enough in the possibility to look into it, although it seems inconceivable, had Jack Kennedy slept with Keeler, that she would have kept quiet about it afterwards.[24]

Inevitably, there were those who resisted the Kennedy cult, especially after the assassination of Bobby in 1968 threatened to turn them not merely into the royal, but also the holy family of America. Whether you see them as gangsters or idealists or both, however, the death of Jack Kennedy was a turning point. Conspiracy theories abound as to the motives and cause of the assassination. As far as Britain was concerned, there was a sense of youth having been violated, and this will undoubtedly have had its effect on the electorate in 1964 when by a narrow margin, and for the first time in thirteen years, Labour won the election. Harold Wilson might not seem with hindsight like the Voice of Youth, but he was the youngest man to date to become Prime Minister in the twentieth century. Labour took 44.1 per cent of the poll and 317 seats, the Conservatives 303 seats, and 43.4 per cent of the poll; the Liberals with 11.2 per cent won 9 seats. The electorate could hardly be said to have been decisive in their rejection of the 14th Earl, nor of what he stood for, but a change had been signalled. One of Home's ancestors was the Earl of Durham, known as Radical Jack because of his 'extreme' espousal of the cause of Chartism and universal suffrage at the beginning of the nineteenth century. The end was now heralded of a Britain which had continued, modified but not radically altered by the reforms of 1832, since the Whig Revolution of 1689.

II

The 14th Mr Wilson

'Wilson likes to have nonentities about him', Cecil King once wrote in his diary.[1] And you certainly see what he meant, when you consider that, upon taking office in 1964, he made Patrick Gordon Walker the Foreign Secretary (he had even lost his seat, Smethwick, in the General Election and must, even by the undistinguished standards of the period, be seen as one of the dullest holders of that office); or that the new Chancellor of the Exchequer was James Callaghan, a party apparatchik, who never had an idea in his life, and who was so uncertain of his powers that he often went next door to Number 10 to seek the Prime Minister's advice, often in carpet slippers, and sometimes in tears, late at night, so worrying did he find the task of managing the national economy.[2]

Seen from a slightly wider perspective, however, King's judgement will not stand up. Compared with the outgoing party, the new administration was richly filled with colourful personality. What had the Conservative Party to compare with George Brown, Wilson's rival for the Labour leadership after Gaitskell's death, and now presiding over the newly created Department of Economic Affairs? Born in Borough, Southwark, Brown had the appearance of a clever bird, instantly amiable, clever, passionate, with large, dark watery eyes and a voice which moved from bass to falsetto especially, a not infrequent occurrence, when he was drunk. A keen womaniser and Anglo-Catholic, not always enthusiasms which go together in a man, Brown was determined to keep the Labour Party on the Gaitskellite straight and narrow, but there was nothing straight or narrow about his approach. His biographer says that in the annals of the civil service there had been nothing like the creation of the DEA since the Middle Ages when 'Lords of Misrule . . . furnished with hobby horses, dragons, drums and gongs, were permitted, briefly, to take over the city, as a reminder to the anointed rulers, and the populace, of how thin is the line between order and chaos'.[3] Brown was only one of a whole brigade of brightly exaggerated characters who by no stretch of the imagination could be described as nonentities. There was the large, shambolic, bisexual (he had slept with W. H. Auden and had a shaky marital history) figure of Dick Crossman, a representative of the left-wing intellectuals, whom Wilson placed at the Department of Housing and Local Government. With his swept-back hair and Billy

Bunter specs he still resembled the firebrand don he had once been. Or there was the red-haired, theatrical figure of Barbara Castle, whose North Country accent and left-wing credentials became more exaggerated as she entered a television studio, someone who was halfway between being a journalist (like her husband, Ted) and an ideologue (like Michael Foot) and whose determination to make a career for herself in politics was manifested in dogged hard work and toe-curling exhibitionism. She began as Minister for Overseas Development, often a 'woman's job' in British politics, but was determined to make her mark on the domestic scene. Waiting in the wings, and destined to be Wilson's Home Secretary and Chancellor (though in the first administration only a Minister of Aviation), was the orotund, clever Welshman Roy Jenkins (Woy), whose Balliol bumptiousness and claret-marinaded dinner-party manners made no attempt to conceal high ambition. He had written some well-turned books about Asquith and about Sir Charles Dilke. He had been one of Gaitskell's closest courtiers, and some of his love affairs, notably with Gaitskell's mistress Ann Fleming, could be seen as useful career moves. The grandeur of his manner and pomposity of his aristocratic-high-table verbal mannerisms – the lisped 'r', the ever-stirring right hand, sometimes to emphasise a debating point, sometimes to feel along a hostess's thigh, could only have been an act, and anyone with a memory stretching back to his youth could remember his father as a trades unionist, later MP, who had been imprisoned in the General Strike, and Woy as the grammar-school boy from the Welsh Valleys. And what of Colonel George Wigg, whose sly question in the House of Commons had exposed the Profumo scandal, and who liked to feed the Prime Minister with troubling details of the plots against him, even when they did not exist? What of (in those days centrist and anti-left-wing) Anthony Wedgwood Benn, pop-eyed MP for Bristol, whose dinner table in Holland Park, subsidised by a millionaire American wife, provided a useful meeting place for the Prime Minister's supporters and 'Kitchen Cabinet'? What about the paunchy figure of the solicitor Arnold Goodman, dubbed by the satirists Lord Goodmanzee, who knew the secrets of all in high places and was fast to become an indispensable adviser to the Prime Minister? What of Wilson's bright-eyed, tall, toothy secretary, Marcia Williams?

No, Cecil King's word 'nonentities' is the wrong one. Indeed, all these tuppence-coloured puppets in the new toy theatre make the central character, Harold Wilson, seem the nonentity, not his entourage.

The smile which was drawn on to his round face was thin and unscrupulous. Smoking (he was seldom without a pipe) was a habit to which he had become addicted when at Oxford, during tutorials with

G. D. H. Cole, the leftist historian of the Labour Party. Wilson, however, was never really socialist, even though it suited him to pose as the 'candidate of the left' in his jockeying for position in the party. At Oxford, where he got a first class degree, and taught economics at New College (as a lecturer) and University College (as a research fellow), he was noted as a clever but not as a cultivated or charming man; nor as one, as so many of his contemporaries were, who was in the least drawn to the ideological debates of the times. Jenkins, even as a student, had been an anti-Marxian Social Democrat. When the great schism occurred in the Oxford Labour Club between Marxists and Social Democrats, with the huge majority veering to the extreme left, the Treasurer of the Marxists, Iris Murdoch, wrote a letter about the matter beginning, 'Comrade Jenkins', and he wrote back 'Dear Miss Murdoch'. Denis Healey, later to succeed Jenkins as Shadow Chancellor in 1972, like most clever people at that time was drawn not merely to the political drama of the age (the Spanish Civil War, the advance of fascism) but also to cultural experiment, eagerly devouring Samuel Beckett's *Murphy*. Crossman, as befitted a lover of W. H. Auden, thought of himself as a man of letters as well as a politico.

Wilson, who had never befriended any of these future colleagues in his student days, was, in spite of brief membership of the Oxford Labour Club, primarily a Liberal, who worked as the secretary to Lord Beveridge, Master of University College, on the drafting of the famous Beveridge Report, a blueprint for social change and improvement after the war. Whereas those destined to form his Cabinet had gone on, after war service, to move in a social circle in London which included writers, bohemian aristocrats, philosophers and musicians, Wilson had no social circle. This had nothing to do with class, though he liked, with his chippy denunciations of Gaitskell's Frognal Set, to imply that it had. Healey, Jenkins and the others were no grander than Wilson. He chose to marry a teenage sweetheart and to live a life of petit bourgeois quietness, eating cold pork pie and HP sauce while reading Dorothy L. Sayers detective stories. Arnold Goodman rightly categorised him as a philistine and 'half-educated'.[4] Where others in this new Labour government (which was what made the emergence on to the public scene of Castle, Jenkins, Healey, Crossman, Crosland, Longford et al. so entertaining) had a rounded life, Wilson's existence had revolved, since undergraduate days, around self-promotion pure and simple. He had met his wife, Gladys Mary Baldwin (no relation of the pre-war Prime Minister), at a tennis club in the Wirral when he was still a schoolboy. She was a shorthand typist at Lever Brothers, the daughter of a Congregationalist minister. Dissent was a bond between them, though she distinctly did not share her husband's political interest, and it was torture to Gladys, who later came to be known as Mary, when her husband entered Number 10.

Private Eye began a satirical 'Mrs Wilson's Diary', which made fun of the very qualities which had made the Wilsons popular with some elements in the electorate, namely their homeliness and Mary's belief that her parish magazine level doggerel verses were 'poetry'.

Mary Wilson's happiest times were spent at Lowenva, a prefabricated bungalow on the Scilly Isles which she had purchased in 1959. They visited the place with their two sons two or three times a year. These holidays, obviously enjoyed by all the family, make a contrast with the breaks which a later Labour Prime Minister, Tony Blair, enjoyed with his family, in the villas of the rich. But the marriage was not a happy one. There was a third element, ever present, which disrupted the possibility of harmony between Harold and Mary, and this was his desire to lead the party and the country. The embodiment of this ambition, as well as its most eager abetter, was his secretary Marcia. Bernard Donoughue, Wilson's Press Secretary in the 1970s, wrote, 'Harold and Marcia's relationship was one of great intensity and complexity . . . Its existence mattered to everyone who worked in Number 10 trying to serve the Prime Minister. It inevitably pervaded our lives, sometimes intruding merely as rumbles of distant thunder, sometimes striking centre stage like lightning. It was an influence which clearly met some deep need in Harold and may well have assisted him greatly in his rise to the top of British politics, providing the necessary aggression and jagged edge which was lacking in his own rather soft personality.'[5]

Inevitably, the relationship gave rise to ribald gossip. Donoughue and his Kitchen Cabinet Colleague Joe Haines had no doubts about the strength of her influence over Wilson, though they remained more puzzled by the means with which she continued to exercise her all-controlling spell. Perhaps none of the three men, neither Wilson, Haines nor Donoughue, in their quest for a secret to explain Marcia's power, took sufficient account of the obvious, namely her foul temper, a quality in women so disagreeable to men that many will do anything to appease it, in the hope that it will simply go away. Margaret Thatcher, to far greater effect than Marcia Williams, would use this very nasty characteristic to gain supreme mastery over an entire Cabinet. Perhaps Marcia also knew secrets about Harold Wilson's early dealings in the Soviet Union when he went on supposed trade delegations as a representative of Montague L. Meyer Ltd. 'Certainly in my hearing', Donoughue writes, 'Marcia threatened to "destroy" Wilson, tapping her handbag ominously (though I never saw its contents).'

These, then, were some of the 'nonentities' who now controlled Britain.
Those who had voted the Labour Party into power no doubt did so
because they wanted a more liberalised society in which the birching
of miscreants was no longer permitted, in which capital punishment
was abolished, in which the laws governing censorship, of the kind
which the *Chatterley* trial had made farcical, were overthrown, and in
which practising homosexual adults could live without the fear of the
policeman or, not always the same person, the blackmailer. These liber-
alisations in the law were effected. More important to the majority of
Labour voters was the hope that, with an increase in prosperity, the
poorest in society could receive a share of the benefit, not only with
improved wages and conditions of work, but also in housing, health
care and education. Some of these hopes were realised, but, alas, Harold
Wilson as an economics don from Oxford arrived with a whole fleet
of economic advisers such as Thomas Balogh, who in 1945 had seriously advised a Labour Party Conference that the dynamism of the
Soviet economy would give the USSR 'an absolute preponderance
economically over Western Europe'.[6] Thomas Balogh's fellow Hungarian Nicky Kaldor used to joke that 'every time he was called by
a foreign country to advise what changes should be made in its system of taxation, a revolution followed within a year or two'. Kaldor
and Balogh urged upon Wilson, as Roy Harrod had urged upon
Macmillan, a broadly Keynesian approach to state borrowing and to
inflation. Wilson never wished, any more than did Kaldor and Balogh,
to turn the country into a miniature Soviet Union, but their idea that
the Soviet programme represented an economic success story underpinned the disaster these men inflicted upon the British economy and
explained why such comparatively little progress was made in building
up a cleaner, better-housed, or better-educated Britain. The sheer
mismanagement of the economy by the economists is one of the tragi-
comic stories of the age.

Wilson was an adept at the art of politics, of persuading individuals
or groups within the Labour Party to support him, even if they felt ideologically or temperamentally disinclined to do so. He extended the same
mesmeric art over the electorate, and was the first Labour Prime Minister
to win three general elections for his party – quite a feat when one
considers the palpable mismanagement of national and international
affairs his administrations achieved. Part of the Wilson formula was based
on his own pleasant personality; for it is one of the paradoxes of political life that some of the most skilful practitioners in the unpleasant
tricks of the trade – manipulation, dissimulation, self-assertiveness and
a willingness to do down their closest friends and allies – could be

combined with a pleasant temperament. Wilson was liked, by electorate and colleagues, for the very simple reason that he was likeable. His cleverness was unthreatening, taking the form of prodigious memory feats, when it came to dates of speeches made by members of the party executive, for example, and a perfect recall of innumerable Gilbert and Sullivan lyrics. By sleight of hand – and this was the other great cause of his success and popularity – he discarded doctrine, indeed never had the smallest interest in it (by contrast with the ideologues of his party to right and left), in favour of a generalised belief in progress, and what in an earlier age had been called the March of Mind. Britain was marching forward to an exciting new classless era in which technology would transform everyone's lives. There was a hint of truth in this vision, though neither the classnessness which comes with economic liberalism nor the skills of technologists had the Labour Party to thank. Wilson, however, made it seem as if he was the driver of the bandwagon on which he had leapt aboard.

At the Labour Party Conference in Scarborough in 1963, the year before he had taken office, he had drawn the contrast between the class-bound, old-school-tie Conservative Party and the up-to-the-minute Labour Party, which was on the side of science and technology. Echoing Marx, he said, 'If there had never been a case for socialism before, automation would have created it. It is a choice between the blind imposition of technological advance, with all that means in terms of unemployment, and the conscious, planned purposive use of scientific progress to provide undreamed of living standards and the possibility of leisure ultimately on an unbelievable scale.'[7] In spite of Wilson's promises, however, of state-owned science-based factories to compete with private enterprise, the truth is that technological expertise and scientific cleverness do inevitably lead to a reduction in the workforce, and nearly all such progress in history has been independent of state subsidy or interference. His claim in that speech that Britain had become a team of Gentlemen in the world of Players who could not compete against the gloriously state-subsidised scientists of the Soviet Union conveniently overlooked the fact that, ever since 1945, there had been a steady brain drain of scientific and technological skill, usually from well-established universities, and the boffins and men in white coats had overwhelmingly chosen not to work in the scientific labs of the Gulag Archipelago but in the United States, where private money and private enterprise paid for infinitely better laboratories than were available in Europe, and gave double the salaries.[8]

Once he took office, however, Wilson did make good his promise to put state money into higher education on a scale hitherto unprecedented.

Wilson imaginatively invented the University of the Air, or the Open University as it came to be known, which enabled grown-ups to restart educational adventures which the intervention of jobs and family had made impossible. For many mature students, especially women who had never had the opportunity to take their studies further before their first pregnancy, the Open University was a gateway to learning which no previous establishment, except perhaps Birkbeck College London (which provides lectures in the evenings for mature students), had provided. Following the counsel of the Robbins Report in 1963, the Labour government provided grants for all students in higher education. There were thirty universities in 1962. By 1968 the number had risen to fifty-six. To the stolid 'civic' universities such as Birmingham, Reading, Leeds and Bristol were added the plate-glass powerhouses of modernity such as Sussex, East Anglia, Warwick and Lancaster, all built on greenfield sites, and quickly developing a campus 'ethos', a 'student life' comparable to the youth culture of France or the United States. This had its political and social consequences as we shall see, very little of which was reflected in the 'white heat of technology'. As busily as the new government built new places of higher learning – thirty polytechnics were commissioned by the Education and Science Department in 1967 – it worked diligently to destroy the solid groundwork of traditional schooling which would have made these new colleges into intellectual powerhouses. The man who commissioned the polytechnics, Antony Crosland, is known to history for one sentence – his ambition to 'destroy every fucking grammar school in England'. This is not to say that the development of comprehensive schools (about 60 per cent of British secondary pupils were educated in them by 1970, and about 90 per cent by 1980) was not introduced with the kindliest motives. Whether standards of numeracy, literacy, scientific knowledge or technological skill arose across the nation, and whether there was more chance for the clever children of the economically disadvantaged than in the old system, will remain a matter of debate. It is hard to imagine Roy Jenkins, Roy Hattersley, Margaret Thatcher, Denis Healey, Edward Heath or Harold Wilson himself having been quite as successful as they were had they not been educated in the despised grammar school tradition. But they all supported the comprehensivation of the system, Thatcher as Education Minister, in the hope that the opportunities they had enjoyed would be extended from the 25 or 30 per cent of those who attended grammar schools in 1944 to all.[9]

Wilson's distinctive contribution to the cultural debate, however, was not just to make higher education available to all but also to counteract the bias against science which had prevailed in British education ever since Matthew Arnold wrote *Culture and Anarchy*.

When Sylvia Plath was interviewed at Cambridge for her Fulbright Scholarship, she was asked her views of C. P. Snow. She had never read him, and felt ashamed, as if caught out not having read Tolstoy or Proust.

Charles Percy Snow (1905–80) is a vanished name today. The son of a clerk in a Leicester shoe factory, Snow proceeded from Leicester University, via London University, to Cambridge, where his work in the Cavendish Laboratory ended in failure. (Research into infra-red spectroscopy was based on an unsustainable intuition.) Having failed as a scientist, Snow threw himself into the pleasures of personal ambition and college intrigue (he was a Fellow of Christ's), preoccupations which he thinly disguised as fiction in his cardboardy novel sequence *Strangers and Brothers*. When Snow, who had advanced his literary career by marrying a good second-rank novelist, Pamela Hansford Johnson, delivered a lecture on 'The Two Cultures', he advanced the technocratic creed which he shared with Harold Wilson. He thought it sad that so few scientists read literature, but equally sad that literary folk did not know the second law of thermodynamics.

The response by F. R. Leavis, the closest thing modern Cambridge produced to Savonarola, was characteristic.

'The judgement I have to come out with is that not only is he not a genius; he is intellectually as undistinguished as it is possible to be.' Thus, Savonarola. But, Leavis went further and in this he was surely completely fair and absolutely accurate. 'If that were all, and Snow were merely negligible, there would be no need to say so in any insistent public way, and one wouldn't choose to do it. But . . . Snow is a portent. He is a portent in that, being in himself negligible, he has become for a vast public on both sides of the Atlantic a master-mind and a sage. His significance is that he has been accepted – or perhaps the point is better made by saying, "created"; he has been created an authoritative intellect by the cultural conditions manifested in his acceptance . . . he doesn't know what he means, and doesn't know he doesn't know.'[10] This completely deserved invective will be seen to apply to almost every sage, pundit, bestselling writer, poet and novelist of the age. When civilisations are in freefall, everything becomes inverted. It is the sages who say the most foolish things; those behaving with the deepest solemnity become like clowns. Snow's pompous, leaden belief in 'science' was, and would continue to be, widely entertained, and matched Harold Wilson's belief in the white heat of technology. The dangers inherent in industrial capitalist society, against which Carlyle and Ruskin had inveighed in the nineteenth century and D. H. Lawrence in the early years of the twentieth, were matters to which Snow and his many adherents were completely blind.

Leavis, a great critic, and, for all his undoubted absurdities, an obviously great man, denounced the political philosophy of our times. 'It is the world in which, even at the level of the intellectual weeklies, "standard of living" is an ultimate criterion, its raising an ultimate aim, a matter of wages and salaries and what you can buy with them, reduced hours of work, and the technological resources that make your increasing leisure worth having; so that productivity – the supremely important thing – must be kept on the rise, at whatever cost to protecting conservative habit.'[11]

Harold Macmillan had promised an ever increased 'standard of living'. Under Harold Wilson it was 'business as usual', with government borrowing more and more money which it was unable to recoup in taxes, high as these were. Meanwhile, such questions as soul, What We Live By, the value of human life itself on the planet, was forgotten in a scramble for votes, a lust for more and more kitchen gadgets and television programmes, and trips to by now wrecked foreign resorts, and a mindless belief in 'science'. Of all this, C. P. Snow was a worthy prophet and spokesperson.

Snow had his reward. Readers of his turgid novel sequence must often have wondered whether they were in an alternative universe, reading Powell's *Dance to the Music of Time* rewritten by the plodding yet aggressively ambitious anti-hero Widmerpool. Wilson ennobled Snow (just as Widmerpool is ennobled) with a life peerage. Snow joined the Wilson government as parliamentary secretary in the newly created Ministry of Technology.[12]

The room in the 'Corridors of Power' (like Harold Macmillan, whose family-owned business published him, Snow had a genius not only for using other people's clichés but for coining his own) and a title were not enough for the large-faced, hectoring, homburg-hatted Snow.

Writing from Millbank Tower on 11 December 1965, Widmerpool/Snow requested not merely a car, but also a chauffeur. 'I do not really want to worry the Prime Minister, when he is so very busy, but, hoping it is no great nuisance, I should like to trouble you a little with the matter of having an official car made available for my use . . . I do need to get around socially and otherwise more than most Parliamentary Secretaries and it would diminish my usefulness if I could not do this *freely* . . . The official car pool is helpful but when I make last-minute arrangements – and most of my arrangements are last minute – it often happens that they just do not have a car available. I hate being so heavy-footed over a matter like this but the sheer mechanics of driving are rather difficult just now.'[13]

'Human kind cannot bear very much reality.' And in the political sphere it takes a while for reality to sink in. Macmillan's six and a bit years as Prime Minister and Alec Douglas-Home's postscript had permitted these ageing men of the 1930s to nurse the illusion, as they negotiated with foreign statesman, that Britain's place in the world was still as it had been before the Suez fiasco. Harold Wilson would only be able to demonstrate to the world that Britain had become at best an impotent spectator of world events (as far as the American crusade against communism was concerned) and, at worst, a powerless 'leader of the Commonwealth' when the former colonies in Africa began the inevitable post-colonial backlashes.

Wilson's most conspicuous foreign policy failure was in Rhodesia. Ian Smith (1919–2007), the son of a Scottish butcher and cattle dealer who had come to Rhodesia in 1898, became Prime Minister on 13 April 1964. His political position was clear: 'the preservation of justice, civilization and Christianity' in Rhodesia by means of white-only government. Seeing the way that other African countries had gone, 'good old Smithy', as he was known by his supporters, saw no reason to appease world opinion just because the rest of the world was 'too corrupted, too prejudiced, too subverted to perceive the advantages that white rule gave to the peoples of Rhodesia'.[14] He asked Alec Douglas-Home to grant Rhodesia independence and the request was refused, unless Smith ended the policy of racial discrimination, and adopted a policy of majority rule.[15] Wilson's attempts to impose such ideas on good old Smithy were as unavailing as had been Home's. On Armistice Day 1965,[16] Ian Smith's government declared UDI – a Unilateral Declaration of Independence. They swore loyalty to the Queen, and continued to fly the Union flag, but they would no longer take orders from London. Smithy's government was composed of some distinctive figures, including the 7th Duke of Montrose, who had bought his 1,600-acre farm for 16s. per acre. Six foot five inches in height, the Duke opined, 'It is a common observation that the African is a bright and promising little fellow up to the age of puberty. He then becomes hopelessly inadequate and disappointing, and it is well known that this is due to his almost total obsession henceforth with matters of sex.'[17]

While Harold Wilson felt paralysed by the situation, the Archbishop of Canterbury expressed the view, 'If Britain has to take over the government and administration of Rhodesia, then the British government is bound to consider the use of force as the ultimate sanction. One could not quarrel with the use of force in such circumstances.'[18] There was an uproar, nearly all of it hostile, against the Archbishop. Several hundred white Rhodesians burnt their Bibles and sent the ashes to Lambeth Palace. An Anglican priest in the Low Veld wrote to the Archbishop to tell him his remarks had done more damage in five days than most could have done in five years.[19] One correspondent noted that, 'All Britain's emotions about a disappeared Empire and an ailing Commonwealth lie behind this story.'[20]

Wilson put economic pressure on the Smith regime. Rhodesia was expelled from the sterling area. Oil imports to Rhodesia were banned. For a small landlocked country dependent on foreign oil supplies and foreign trade, these should have been crippling blows. Wilson misread the courage and defiance of the white Rhodesians, and he did not realise that the South African and Portuguese governments would be only too happy to make fools of the United Kingdom by defying the sanctions. Wilson, five months after UDI, realised he was losing and summoned Smithy to talks on the British cruiser HMS *Tiger*, sailing emblematically, round and round in circles in the Mediterranean off Gibraltar.[21] Wilson caved in to Smith, offering to accept his idea of white majority rule until the end of the century, but this was not enough for Smithy's right-wing critics at home who wanted to introduce the Municipal Amendment Act (which passed into law in 1967) empowering municipalities to segregate parks, swimming pools, lavatories, hospitals, and to fade out any African representation in parliament. Rhodesia was destined to become a time warp of racial intolerance and neo-colonisation until Margaret Thatcher and Peter Carrington, at the Lancaster House Conference in 1979, gave the government of Zimbabwe to Robert Mugabe, leader of the ludicrously named National Democratic Party. Within twenty years, the most fertile country in Southern Africa was suffering from starvation, the economy was plagued by Weimar levels of inflation, Mugabe and pals grew rich while opposition politicians and journalists were tortured, killed and imprisoned. On 28 February 1979, Ian Smith had said to the Rhodesian parliament, 'History recalls many cases of once great nations which have decayed and crumbled into ignominy, but none which have collapsed with such rapidity and completeness as far as Great Britain is concerned. For us in Rhodesia, it was a tragic stroke of fate that we came in towards the tail end of Britain's expansion and civilisation in this world . . . Because of this, we lost out in gaining this thing called independence . . . Because of this, we have been left to the end, right to the bitter end, in that we have been dragged down in the morass of Britain's decadence and decline.'[22]

It was in 1962 that the Americans began their ill-starred attempt to shore up the corrupt regime of Ngo Dinh Diem in South Vietnam against the incursions of Vietcong troops from the communist North. Following the example of the British success in Malaya during the 1950s, the Americans attempted to isolate 'secure villages', in which government troops protected the peasantry from the ravages of the communist guerrillas. However, under Diem's generals, the villages had become little better than concentration camps, and it became clear that the Americans must choose between allowing Vietnam to go communist and intervening directly. By January 1962, the US had begun to fly helicopters to back up South Vietnamese forces. General de Gaulle advised President Kennedy to keep out. 'You will, step by step, be sucked into a bottomless military and political quagmire,' he sagely foretold. But Kennedy went in. By the time Harold Wilson had become the British Premier, and Kennedy had been assassinated, the new President, Lyndon Baines Johnson, was waist deep in the quagmire. US warships regularly patrolled the North Vietnamese coast, and on 2 August 1964 their destroyer the *Maddox* was attacked by three North Vietnamese torpedo boats. Air support from USS *Ticonderoga*, an aircraft carrier, led to an engagement. The *Maddox* was saved; one of the torpedo boats was sunk. President Johnson could see the incident in the Gulf of Tonkin as an 'unprovoked military action' by the communists, justifying sending in yet more troops and military hardware. By early 1965, about four-fifths of South Vietnam was under the control of the Vietcong guerrillas. They were only twenty miles from Saigon, the capital city; Johnson responded by escalating the war. By the end of the year in excess of 184,000 US troops were engaged in Vietnam and 1,350 military personnel had been killed in action.

The Vietnam War occupied a comparable position in the collective imagination of the 1960s to the Spanish Civil War in the 1930s, with the difference that it was much further away from Britain, and the leftists of various colourings who felt exercised by it did not send even a token brigade or two to fight their cause. Instead, they identified with the struggle of the American left by playing Joan Baez and Bob Dylan protest records, and by growing their hair longer.

Wilson had begun his career in the Labour Party with the statutory anti-American prejudices. 'Not a man, not a gun must be sent to defend the French in Indo-China,' he told a May Day rally in 1954, as the communist leader Ho Chi Minh was taking over what became North Vietnam. Yet as Prime Minister in 1965 he could tell the House of Commons (1 April 1965): 'So far as Her Majesty's Government are concerned, I repeat, that we have made absolutely plain our support for the American stand against Communist infiltration into South Vietnam . . . The people of South Vietnam, like the people of North Vietnam and every other area, are entitled to be able to lead their own lives free of terror, free from the danger of sudden death or from the threat of a Communist takeover, and the Government of South Vietnam are entitled to call in aid allies who could help in that purpose.'[23] Although *Private Eye* had a cover drawn by Gerald Scarfe showing Wilson applying his tongue to LBJ's rump,[24] the Wilson slyness saved him from some of the more abject and dangerous postures into which later British Prime Ministers would contort themselves before American Presidents. He resolutely refused Johnson's appeal for British troops to be sent to Vietnam, chiefly one must assume because he knew this would be electorally disastrous, and that the left of his party would not have tolerated it – such was their power in those days over their leader. Nevertheless, he did send 70,000 'peace-keeping' troops to Borneo and Sarawak to defend Malaysia. Johnson knew perfectly well that Britain, isolated in the world, and with no real power of its own, felt itself obliged to tag along behind America, however many mistakes in foreign policy it made. In exchange for using Britain as a launch pad for its nuclear missiles trained on Moscow, and as an ally in the United Nations and elsewhere against an increasingly horrified rest of the world, America could afford to lard the Prime Minister of the day, whoever he happened to be, with the statutory comparison with the old warlord. 'In you sir,' LBJ told Wilson in July 1966 after he had won a second term in office, 'England has a man of mettle, a new Churchill in her hour of crisis'[25] – the hour of crisis was, of course, a sterling crisis. Having spent his years in Opposition explaining to left-wing audiences that American domination of the British economy was disastrous, he immediately switched, when Prime Minister, to believing it to be necessary, as when the Chrysler Corporation bailed out the collapsing Rootes Motors which had been limping along under British management.[26] If American money could be found to pay the wages of British car 'workers', then it was worth defending the de-forestation of South Vietnam or the bombings of Hanoi, in which thousands of Vietnamese civilians got killed. Although he dissociated himself from the bombings, and carefully leaked an off-the-cuff remark to the effect 'Johnson's gone mad. We'll have to find a new ally'[27] – he knew perfectly well that no such ally existed.

Whatever the twists and turns of Harold Wilson's foreign policy might produce, he was able, in his second administration, to perform a comedic masterstroke by appointing George Brown to the Foreign Office. The appointment lasted nineteen Dionysian months, a period of particular happiness for cartoonists, headline writers, satirists and all who preferred to be amused by the antics, rather than concerned with the policies, of the Foreign Secretary. An early moment of joy came when Bill Lovelace, a photographer for the *Daily Express*, snapped the Foreign Secretary aboard the *Queen Mary*, on 22 September 1966, attempting a popular dance called the frug with New York publicist and cookbook author Miss

Barbara Kraus. Lovelace's photograph recorded George Brown, his eyes on a level with the bosomy front of the tall Miss Kraus. Though the eyes were on this level, they were closed and the picture captured him in a swaying posture, as though on the point of collapse. 'It's the end of my marriage,' Brown wailed, when he saw the *Express*. 'Sophie won't accept this, nor will the girls.'[28] In fact the long-suffering Sophie put up with her husband until, on Christmas Eve 1982, he left her for a much younger woman, his secretary Margaret Haines. (He died in 1985 of cirrhosis of the liver, having become a Roman Catholic.[29]) As Foreign Secretary, the moment on board ship with Barbara Kraus was only one of many incidents where the accident-prone George behaved according to type. Diplomatic niceties were not his style. There was the occasion in 1967 when the Belgian government – their Prime Minister, Chiefs of Staff, Foreign Minister, Defence Minister – held a banquet for Brown at the conclusion of a European tour. As the meal came to an end and the diners made to leave, Brown barred their way, standing in the main door of the dining room and waving his arms. 'Wait! I have something to say,' he told them. 'While you have all been wining and dining here to-night, who has been defending Europe? I'll tell you who's been defending Europe – the British Army. And where, you may ask, are the soldiers of the Belgian Army tonight? I'll tell you where the soldiers of the Belgian Army are. They're in the brothels of Brussels.' British Embassy staff hustled him away, while the Belgians stared, frozen with incredulous embarrassment.[30]

The incident which most endeared him to the Foreign Office, however, occurred during an official visit to Brazil during a diplomatic reception at the Brazilian President's Palace of the Dawn. A witness recalled, 'It was really beautiful – I think only the Latin Americans still do it that way: all the military officers were in full dress uniform, and the ambassadors were in court dress. Sumptuous is the word, and sparkling. As we entered, George made a bee-line for this gorgeously crimson-clad figure, and said, "Excuse me, but may I have the pleasure of this dance?" There was a terrible silence for a moment before the guest, who knew who he was, replied, "There are three reasons, Mr Brown, why I will not dance with you. The first, I fear, is that you've had a little too much to drink. The second is that this is not, as you seem to suppose, a waltz the orchestra is playing, but the Peruvian national anthem, for which you should be standing to attention. And the third reason why we may not dance, Mr Brown, is that I am the Cardinal Archbishop of Lima.'[31]

Ever since Kenya became independent in 1963, Jomo Kenyatta had committed his country to a racialist policy of 'Americanisation', putting the position of some 80,000 Kenyan Asians in question. The Conservative Home Secretary, Henry Brooke, said in that year that it would be 'out of the question' to deny these Kenyan Asians entry to Britain if they wished it. 'It would be tantamount to a denial of one of the basic rights of a citizen, namely to enter the country of which he is a citizen.'[32] By 1967, Kenyatta was making it clear to his Asian fellow Kenyans that they must leave. In the first two months of 1968, 13,000 arrived in Britain. The Labour Home Secretary, James Callaghan, reacted with panic and hastily introduced a bill to the House of Commons to restrict the entry of any more. Only 1,500 'non-patrial' (that is non-white Asians) from Kenya could be admitted *per year*, though it was permissible for as many white Kenyans as so desired to enter Britain.

These white Kenyans were referred to as British subjects, and their entry into Britain was referred to as 'welcome home', whereas Richard Crossman, for example, could refer to 'Kenyan Asians with British passports', as if there was something strange about these particular Kenyans possessing such documents. The reason for the government's panic, however, was clear enough. Britain, in common with other European countries, depended for their expanding economy on more and more cheap labour, particularly since the indigenous members of the white working class who had grown up since the war found menial work unattractive. The ineluctable growth of free trade, about which the socialist parties of Europe were sceptical, but the so-called right-wingers were optimistic, carried with it the natural consequence that many people, from all over the globe, would gravitate towards the expanding Western economies for work.

The paradox, politically, here was that those who most fervently embraced market economics, and the ideas of what came to be called monetarism, were likely, in social policy, to be conservatives who instinctively disliked the changes to national life which mass immigration inescapably brought with it. And many such monetarist conservatives were, like a good number of Little Englander socialists, and indeed human beings generally, racialist by instinct. By October 1961, 300,000 new immigrants had arrived in a decade: a fact which prompted the Commonwealth Immigration Act. But in that year alone, a further 130,000 migrants entered Britain. As the 1960s progressed, the proportion of dependants to active workers also went up. Whereas a high proportion of the early immigrants were adults who worked in the National Health Service and in public transport, by 1971 women and children made up three-quarters of the immigrant population.

Harold Macmillan had asked a special group of his Cabinet to form the Commonwealth Immigration Committee, and this group, which included Reginald Maudling and J. Enoch Powell, recommended that the annual migration should be limited to 45,000 – still a huge number if it were repeated year on year for decades.

Since that time, Macmillan and Home had gone, and the Conservative Party had elected as its leader a former *Church Times* journalist and organ scholar by the name of Edward Heath as its leader. Heath, who was to develop in rancorous old age into a sort of Social Democrat, had been the right-wing candidate in the leadership contest against Reginald Maudling. His right-wingery manifested itself in a deep commitment to Europe, a profound desire to sign Britain up to the European experiment, and hence to promote free trade. This led to his having a confrontational attitude to industrial relations – much more so than a man such as R. A. Butler. In the area of race relations, however, he was modern, and he did not wish to appease the racialist wings of his party. This attitude probably had the inevitable effect of making the wilder extremists break rank, as would occur memorably in Birmingham in April 1968.

J. Enoch Powell was an even more fervent free marketeer and mone-tarist than Heath ever was, and so the logic of his position would surely have led him to wanting as much immigration as possible. As the Secretary of State for Health in Macmillan's government and an astringent economiser, he had been only too happy to fill 34 per cent of junior hospital posts with immigrant doctors and nurses.[33]

But Powell's desire to be on a limb, to cut a dash, went hand in hand with a wish shared with almost all politicians – the wish to be popular. In April 1968, as the controversy about the Kenyan Asians gathered pace, and the towns of the West Midlands, such as Wolverhampton (which Powell represented in Parliament), filled up with immigrants from Pakistan and India and the West Indies, Powell was very well aware of how passion-ately the indigenous population felt betrayed in this matter by the governing classes. Powell, ever since the Labour governments had taken office, had attacked the 'New Model Army of gentlemen who know best' – a New Model Army which grew apace in England, with the ad-dition of many female members. And one of the things which the New Model Army most deplored was racial prejudice of any kind. It was when addressing the Birmingham Conservatives in April 1968 that Powell managed to deliver a speech which was calculated to cock a snook at the New Model Army, both within Labour's ranks and among the Shadow Cabinet – for Edward Heath was a gentleman who knew best if ever there was one.

'We must be mad,' Powell said, in his Brummy voice to his Brummy friends, 'literally mad as a nation to be permitting the annual inflow of some fifty thousand dependants, who are for the most part the material of the future growth of the immigrant-descended population. It is like watching a nation building its own funeral pyre.' It was a speech which drew upon the anecdotal evidence of his correspondents, including a somewhat mysterious lady in Northumberland who claimed that a woman in his own constituency in Wolverhampton was afraid to go out. 'She finds excreta pushed through her letter-box. When she goes to the shops, she is followed by children, charming wide-grinning piccaninnies. They cannot speak English, but one word they know. "Racialist" they chant. When the new Race Relations Bill is passed, this woman is convinced she will go to prison. And is she so wrong? I begin to wonder' . . . Powell did not make it clear why this woman could go to prison, or even whether she existed. When he was asked to identify the street in his constituency where the excreta had been posted through the door, he was unable to do so, and on a televised interview broadcast to coincide with the twenty-fifth anniversary of the speech he rather unimpressively claimed that he did not believe the world 'piccaninny' had any racial connotation. (If it hadn't, why were the piccaninnies chanting 'racialist'?)

Powell certainly did not emerge well from the episode of the speech, for which he was instantly sacked by Edward Heath from the Shadow Cabinet. And it would perhaps not be worth dwelling at such length upon this speech were it not for two remarkable things: one was the sibylline prophecy which it contained, and the other was the degree of popular response which it elicited.

The prophecy was drawn from Virgil, who was seen by the Middle Ages not just as a poet but also as a wizard. 'As I look ahead, I am filled with foreboding. Like the Roman, I seem to see the River Tiber foaming with much blood.'[34]

In 1987, Powell made the remark on television that 'If I had a regret, it was that I didn't quote Virgil in Latin, but then I didn't want to appear pedantic, so I took the Latin out and put in a translation. I probably ought to have stuck to the Latin . . . Nobody would have troubled to translate it.'

Like many of his remarks on the subject of the 'Rivers of Blood' speech, as it came to be known, this cluster of half-truths is puzzling. It surely was not just the quotation from Virgil which excited so much controversy. What about the assertion that 'in this country in fifteen or twenty years time, the black man will have the whip hand over the white man'? Powell's belief that an allusion to one of the best-known passages in the whole of European literature would have baffled every listener in the land, including newspaper editors and commentators who, like himself, had degrees in classics, also suggests arrogant solipsism on a titanic scale, as if Latin were a private language known only to himself. Others would have perhaps been less careless in their quotation. In Virgil's sixth book of the *Aeneid* (at that time a set text for Latin 'O' level and probably read by tens of thousands of boys and girls in Britain), the Cumaean sibyl, about to escort Aeneas to the underworld, foresees

> bella, horrida bella
> Et Thybrim multo spumantem sanguine cerno.
>
> (I see Wars, horrid wars, and the Tiber foaming with
>   much blood – *Aeneid* vi. 86).

A few days later in his house in South Eaton Place, Powell was found by his friend John Biffen MP 'preoccupied among his classical reference books'. 'I can't find the Roman,' Enoch remarked. He had realised that it was not 'the Roman' (which Roman? Virgil?) who had the vision of the Tiber foaming with blood, but the Sybil. Anyone can make a slip, but how strange for the classical professor to make such a very elementary howler, or for it to take him more than ten seconds to find the quotation to verify.

More important than the origin of a Latin quotation were two questions: whether the Wolverhampton seer's own prophecy came true – whether there were rivers of blood flowing through England as a result of huge numbers of immigrants; and, secondly, what the speech showed about the feelings of the indigenous population towards the immigrants.

If Powell had foretold that Islam was an uncompromising faith, and that the arrival of tens of thousands of Muslims into a Christian or post-Christian country would store up problems for the future, then there might be some justification for the assertion, often made to this day by bar-room experts, that 'Enoch got it right'. But Powell's speech was simply racist. He predicted that there would be a 'civil war' on racial lines. 'What's wrong with racism?' he candidly asked on television in 1995. 'Racism is the basis of a nationality.'[35]

Powell's intellectual and spiritual journey went forward in a series of strange leapfrog hops, in which, after a long spell of believing one thing, he suddenly believed the opposite. He had been a passionate imperialist. Then he had 'discovered' the doctrine that no sovereign parliament could have an Empire whose members were not represented in that assembly. (The Bostonians had discovered that during their Tea Party in 1773.) He was an atheist, and then, on a misty evening in autumn in Wolverhampton, he stepped back inside the Church. He had been a keen European – even

advocating a shared European army; and then the most eloquent exponent of the independence of the nation state. Had he lived longer, it is
conceivable that he would have seen what a very great number of people
have seen over the last fifty years: yes, the immigrations changed England
forever, but part of this change was a growing ability, among those of
different ethnic backgrounds, to live alongside one another without
conflict on anything like the scale Powell predicted. (The case of radical
Islam, which comes later in our story, is not unrelated to the prophecy
of the Wolverhampton Prophet, but it *is* different.)

This was not how it seemed at the time of Powell's speech in 1968. In
the ten days after he had made the speech, Powell received more than
100,000 letters, only 800 expressing disagreement with him. Diana
Spearman, editor of *New Society*, analysed the letters. Relatively few were
blatantly racist or unpleasant in tone. The huge proportion 'feared that
continued immigration was a threat to British culture and traditions'.
Spearman noted how many of the letters reflected a sense of 'alienation',
a feeling of distrust of the Establishment. 'The letters reflect the feeling
that *they* by their actions have produced problems for *us*, which do not
in any way affect *them* and which they are not doing anything to help
us solve. *Their* idea is to tell *us* what we must and must not do.'[36]

This feeling remains. It was the issue of immigration which exacerbated it. That of the European question (Common Market, European
Union) carried it on. During the next fifty years there would be a growing
sense that the New Model Army of gentlemen who know best, the New
Establishment, had detached itself from the general will of the electorate.
Up to this point, many voters felt common cause with the broad, amorphous coalitions of interest represented by one of the three chief political
parties. In the Harold Wilson era this began to change. The left would
begin its bid for dominance of the Labour Party, a struggle which took up
most of the next decade and ended in its defeat. Conservatives – those
who were truly conservative, and wanted England to stay as it was, or to
go back to the demographic, architectural or gastronomic conditions of
pre-war Britain – no longer had a voice in Heath's Conservative Party.

If your ordinary, instinctive Tory found no representation of his life-
view in the Conservative Party, there was an equal sense of betrayal
among those socialists who had been simple-hearted enough to hope
that Harold Wilson, once the candidate of Labour's left and torch-bearer
for Bevanism, would bring to pass a Socialist Britain. Paul Foot wrote,
'The two years of Labour government from March 1966 to March 1968
have seen the death of Harold Wilson, Yorkshire socialist and Moral
Crusader. Every one of his priorities have been reversed or abandoned.
Racialist minorities in Southern Africa have been appeased. The American

Government, with his support, have trebled their fire power in Vietnam. Programmes for overseas aid, housing, hospital building, school building, a minimum incomes guarantee have been abandoned or slashed . . .' And so on. His catalogue is a long one.[37]

This sense of impotence, of political parties 'knowing best', but not representing the aspirations of their natural supporters, was to be a characteristic of Britain for the next forty years, with the exception of Margaret Thatcher's first two terms of office. Those of naturally Conservative instincts were simply turned off politics altogether.

12

Ireland

In June 1966 Harold Wilson was still basking in his electoral triumph of three months earlier. True, he had his money worries – to devalue, or not to devalue the pound. True, the problems of Rhodesia still haunted him. And the possibility of a seamen's strike, inspired as the Prime Minister believed by communists, would scupper his prices and incomes policy.[1] Little could he have believed, however, that in this secular, modern, white-hot technology year of 1966 Britain was on the edge of a very different set of problems from across the Irish Channel – problems which would haunt all Wilson's successors to the close of the century. True, Wilson was aware of injustices towards the Catholic population of Northern Ireland and had expressed vague hopes that something would be done about them. The Prime Minister of Northern Ireland, Captain Terence O'Neill, had gone some way to trying to bring in moderate reforms, which had met with adamant resistance from the Protestant working classes.

Harold Wilson did not know Ireland and did not understand it. He would probably have reacted with something like indifference when informed that a body called the Free Presbyterian Church, led by its young founder, the Revd Ian Paisley (born 1926), intended to picket the Irish Presbyterians General Assembly in Belfast. With his tall, bulky gait, his brilliantined hair, his thick lips which seemed in their liquid sibilance positively to savour the anti-papalist insults which fell from them, with his strong Ulster brogue and his alarmingly powerful lungs, larynx and vocal chords, Paisley was an easy object of metropolitan mockery. Only imagine him at dinner with Roy Jenkins, or at a concert with Denis Healey. The Labour Cabinet, with their careers behind them as Oxford dons, could mock his educational background (the Ballymena Technical High School boy received his doctorate from the dubious source of Bob Jones University) – in marked contrast to Roy Jenkins's priding himself on his 'double' – honorary degrees from both Yale and Harvard.

For Paisley, the Irish Presbyterians, like the regular Ulster Unionists, were fudgers, who had betrayed their basic principles. He saw the Presbyterians as having sold out to modernist, wishy-washy interpretations of Scripture; he saw Captain O'Neill's party as being toadyish to Westminster, and too willing to kowtow to Roman Catholics. Why, only that Easter, Belfast, bastion city of Protestant independence, had been festooned with Irish tricolours, put up by Irish republicans. The government had done nothing to stop them! Paisley had responded by marching to the City Hall Cenotaph with 6,000 supporters. For the summer picket of the Presbyterian gathering the police were ready for them outside the Assembly Hall, but Paisley changed the route of his march. As they passed Cromac Square a mob of Catholics was waiting with bricks and metal objects. *The well-disciplined Protestants did not retaliate*, but the police became involved, a riot ensued – minor by the standards of Northern Ireland – and Paisley was arrested and given a prison sentence in Crumlin Road gaol. It was the young firebrand's political baptism.

J. Enoch Powell, an English politician who chose to involve himself in Irish politics, coined the phrase that all political careers end in failure. He did not live to see Paisley's career end in success, a success which defied all the received wisdom of moderates, all the believers in compromise, all the advocates of capturing the centre ground in order to attract people of good will from all shades of opinion. Party politics almost by its nature loses touch with the people they set out to represent. They called him, his followers, 'the big man', and this he was in all senses. He was always perfectly clear about his constituency: they were the Protestant working-class people of Ulster. When middle-class Presbyterianism began to squirt soda water into the mixture, Paisley simply started a new Church: the Free Presbyterians. When the Ulster Unionists, whose senior politicians tended to be landed, Anglican, with public school backgrounds and accents, seemed to be too willing to play London's tune or to give quarter to the Roman Catholics, Paisley was equally clear about the political way ahead. He founded his own party, the Democratic Unionist Party, rightly so-called because it reflected what its rank and file supporters actually believed. Paisley was the only person in modern Europe to have founded both a party and a Church. Though attempts were made to see him, like Sinn Fein, as the political wing of a violent or revolutionary movement, or at least to suggest that he colluded in violence on the loyalist side, no evidence was ever produced to substantiate such a claim. True, Paisley attended the funerals of those who had been violent in the Protestant cause. One of his followers once said that 'those who walked behind the coffins of IRA killers were showing support for their actions',[2] and if there is truth in that, then Paisley may be held to account for the company he kept, as for some of the people he represented. He certainly reacted hotly to any idea of the B-Specials being disarmed. (The B-Specials were police auxiliaries, wholly Protestant, and detested by the Catholics. When the B-Specials were abolished by the Westminster government, some of them became paramilitaries.[3]) If walking behind an IRA coffin proclaimed support for their activities, then the same can be said of walking behind UDF coffins. 'Don't let anyone disarm you,' Paisley told the B-Specials. In February 1981, when the British and Irish governments looked as if they were trying to solve the Northern Irish problem by the simple means of excluding the Northern Irish people from their deliberations, Paisley took five journalists to a secret location near Ballymena to see five hundred men in combat jackets with what were purported to be certificates for legally held firearms. The point was, these weapons *were* legally held. He and his followers were operating within the law. Sir Edward Carson had threatened violence in the event of the Protestant North being coerced into some Free State or Home Rule agreement with the rest of Ireland. One hundred thousand men had gathered on the shores of Belfast Lough to brandish guns on 23 September 1911 and hear Carson commit them to fighting, if necessary, to maintain the Union with Britain. While addressing a crowd in Portadown, Paisley 'brandished the bandolier which his father had worn as a member of Carson's UVF, an act which impressed upon those gathered the seriousness of the present situation and just what the price could be'.[4] No one could doubt the violence of Paisley's rhetoric – 'I believe the time has come when all Lundies [i.e., traitors], yellow bellies and all cowards must leave our ranks – and we shall fight to the death.'

When 'the Troubles' of modern times began, the bullying Protestants appeared to most dispassionate outside observers, as to the Westminster government, to be without moral excuse, and the put-upon Catholic minority in the North to be the ones who needed protection. (Hence the British government sending in troops to defend the Catholics against Protestant violence.) When the Catholic Civil Rights Movement was taken over by the IRA the political complexion of the situation altered radically. Neither the mainstream Northern Irish parties – the Catholic SDP, and the official Ulster Unionists – nor the governments of Dublin and Westminster quite knew how to cope with the IRA. When civilian casualties escalated, there was always the tendency for politicians – except Paisley – to buckle. There was therefore a supreme paradox about the Northern Irish story which, in our times, moved from cataclysmic violence to relative peace. So long as Dublin and Westminster appealed to 'reasonable' middle ground, the Northern Protestants knew that what they were in fact doing was trying to bring about a United Ireland behind their backs. Only when they stopped treating Paisley like a dangerous ranter, and recognised that he more than the official Unionists represented the fears and aspirations of the working-class Protestant majority, was the IRA terrified into serious cooperation. For thirty years the IRA appeared to dominate the story. 'We demand,' Paisley thundered, 'that the IRA be exterminated from Ulster . . . There are men willing to do the job of exterminating the IRA. Recruit them under the Crown and they will do it. If you refuse, we will have no other decision to make but to do it ourselves.'⁵ The English TV viewer, and perhaps the English politician, maybe thought this was some sort of absurd bluff, an attempt to become the Oliver Cromwell of East Belfast. The IRA platoons knew it wasn't bluff. If Northern Ireland moved towards a solution of its problems which was both just *and* democratic, it was thanks, far too late in the day, to two British Prime Ministers, Mr Major and Tony Blair, harnessing the Revd Dr Ian Paisley.

The province of Northern Ireland, its very existence as a political entity, bristles with paradox. It came into being after the First World War and as part of the peace settlement between Britain and the rest of Ireland which by then was known as the Irish Free State. The governance of Ireland had haunted and disturbed W. E. Gladstone: 'The long, vexed, and troubled relations between Great Britain and Ireland exhibit to us the one and only conspicuous failure of the political genius of our race to confront and master difficulty, and to obtain in a reasonable degree the main ends of civilised life.'⁶ Gladstone, as leader of the Liberal Party and Prime Minister, made three attempts to pass a Home Rule Bill through the House of Commons. This would have given Ireland, the whole island, the status of a Dependency, like Canada. The Irish would have their own parliament, run their own affairs, and yet owe allegiance to the British Crown. It was not what the out and out nationalists would have wanted but it was better than reliance upon Westminster. The first Home Rule Bill, 1886, was defeated in the Commons by 343 votes to 313 because the puritanical North Country Liberals were shocked by revelations about the adultery of the Irish nationalist leader Charles Parnell. The Second Bill of 1893 was passed in the Commons but thrown out by the Lords (overwhelmingly, a vote of 419 to 41). The Third Bill was also thrown out by the Lords but the new Parliament Act of 1911 allowed the Commons to overrule the Lords in matters of such importance and so it passed into law – in 1914, with the proviso that the Irish would put the whole matter on 'hold' during the First World War. The Prussian, the Russian, the Ottoman Empires fell, millions died. The British, French and Americans presided over the Treaty of Versailles, which if it had a central idea was the right of self-determination to be given to small nations, and then the British politicians realised that the problem of Ireland remained unsolved. Churchill had written, 'The mode of thought of men, the whole outlook on affairs, the groupings of parties, all encountered violent and tremendous changes in the deluge of the world, but as the deluge subsides and the waters fall we see the dreary steeples of Fermanagh and Tyrone emerging once again. The integrity of their quarrel is one of the few institutions that have been left unaltered in the cataclysm which has swept the world.'[7]

While the Catholic majority throughout the island of Ireland wanted independence, this desire was not shared by the Protestants of the North, whose ancestors had been transplanted Presbyterian Scots.

The outbreak of civil war in Ireland, the tragic story of Irish republicans killing *one another* over the issue of Irish partition, led eventually to a compromise which probably no one completely wanted. In 1922 the Irish Free State was established, but consisting only of twenty-six counties. The remaining six counties included the two mentioned by Churchill, Fermanagh and Tyrone, which were in fact predominantly Catholic. These six counties were the new province of Northern Ireland. Upon these people, predominantly Protestant, predominantly Scottish, overwhelmingly Unionist, the British government imposed Home Rule against their will. The twenty-six counties, the Free State, were independent. David Lloyd George, British Prime Minister, did not wish to do anything that could look, either to the new Irish government in Dublin, or to the United States, as if Britain were still trying to exercise power on the island of Ireland. So he set up the Stormont Assembly, and gave to the people of Northern Ireland their own Prime Minister, Cabinet, government.

The Unionist position had been stated eloquently in the House of Commons by Lord Robert Cecil in 1920 – 'We shall have this astounding position, that the only form of Home Rule which will exist in Ireland will be that which exists in Ulster ... Home Rule is to be established effectively only in that part of Ireland which hates and loathes the whole idea of Home Rule.'[8] The leader of the Irish Unionists, Sir Edward Carson, in the same debate had implored, 'She [Ulster] has always made the simple appeal to you to leave her alone and to treat her as you treat your own people and she would be perfectly satisfied. And I am bound to say that this breaking up and the giving to Ulster a Parliament may lead to many unforeseen consequences.'[9]

By creating 'Ulster', the British had indeed stored up unforeseen consequences. Forced against their will to have their own Free State, the Northern Protestants evolved, over the years 1922–68, a system of life in which the Catholics were second-class citizens. The constituency boundaries in Fermanagh, Tyrone and Londonderry were redrawn so that although these places were demographically predominantly Catholic, the Protestant candidates got elected to Stormont. Not for nothing was it in Ulster that the election joke 'Vote early, vote often' was coined. Discrimination against Catholics in the workplace was routine. The great shipbuilders Harland and Wolff had a policy of not employing Catholics.

Housing allocation was unfair. There was blatant discrimination in making local government appointments. Despite occasional suggestions that they should do something about it, the English politicians had invariably held back. The British government did not want, in the words of the Labour Home Secretary, James Callaghan, 'to get sucked into the Irish bog'.[10] Sucked in, however, they inevitably were.

On 12 August 1969 the Apprentice Boys' parade marched, as it had often done, through Londonderry. The Apprentice Boys were a largely working-class movement, political more than religious – less religious, say, than the Orange Order, which required its members to 'honour and diligently study the Holy Scriptures'[11] – and as time went on owing less and less allegiance to the Ulster Unionist Party. (In the 1920s the Apprentices had upper- and middle-class members; by 1974 they formally broke their ties with the UUP.[12])

The 1969 march through Londonderry was to commemorate the action of the Apprentice Boys who, against the advice of the bishop and the civil leaders of 1685, closed the gates of the city and kept out the army of James II, thereby, eventually, securing the defeat of the Catholic cause, the expulsion of the Catholic King to France, and the victory of William of Orange, William III, and the triumph in the whole of the British archipelago of those 'values' which had secured the growth of science, the progress of well-ordered Whiggish statecraft, the situation in the eighteenth and nineteenth centuries which had made Britain a palpably freer, happier and better ordered place than nations which had lived through the alternative – Bourbon absolutism, revolution, counter-revolution, communards, mutual distrust. The name of William of Orange, excluded from history syllabuses in British schools since the start of the Troubles, was not merely celebrated in Northern Ireland but throughout the United Kingdom, and the expulsion of James II was spoken of without irony in English as well as Northern Irish textbooks as the Glorious Revolution.

Naturally, the Apprentice Boys of 1969 were a provocation to the Catholics of Bogside in that city whose very name was a controversy (Catholics called it Derry). Gerrymandering ensured that this largely Catholic city was represented by Protestants in Stormont.[13] There followed a three-day siege of the Bogside, in which the Royal Ulster Constabulary were pelted with petrol bombs by the Catholics and then, aided by the B-Specials, they tried to break the forty-two barricades with which the Catholics had ringed themselves. The police began to fear that they were facing not a mere street fight, but an armed uprising. On 14 August, the head of the RUC Inspector General Joseph Anthony Peacock asked for the British Army to be deployed. Callaghan as Home Secretary agreed, and at around 5.00 p.m. the first soldiers of the Prince of Wales Regiment arrived on Londonderry's streets.

For the next thirty years, a bloody life unfolded for the soldiers deployed, and for the people foolhardy or unfortunate enough still to reside in the trouble spots of Northern Ireland, which were limited overwhelmingly to the border territories, and to the working-class districts of Londonderry and Belfast, and other towns. (Even at the height of the Troubles, the more genteel suburbs of Belfast seemed no more violent, and a good deal more beautiful, than those of Manchester or Birmingham.) If the British government had been merely dealing with a Catholic civil rights organisation, there might have been some hope of brokering a settlement, which gave justice to Catholics and appeased Protestant fears.

Even the Civil Rights Movement, however, was not all that it seemed. The first president of the Civil Rights Association, Betty Sinclair, was a Stalinist communist. She was succeeded by another communist, Edwina Stewart, who then gave place to a representative of another group, the People's Democracy, and their young leader, a graduate of the Queen's University, Belfast, called Bernadette Devlin, who was elected to Westminster as an MP for Mid Ulster in April 1969, at the age of twenty-one – the most youthful member of the Commons since William Pitt the Younger. Bernadette came just too early in feminist history to make an impact. Her demeanour in the House of Commons – crossing the Chamber and striking Reggie Maudling when Home Secretary was a high point – spilled over into farce. Was this because a largely male press, a largely male political Establishment, patronised her? Certainly. Did she confirm, with her appalling teeth, and wild hair, deep-seated anti-Irish prejudices? Without a doubt. Was her having a baby out of wedlock enough to ditch her career with her respectable Irish constituents and brand her in the British press as a brazen hussy? Yes, indeed – these were still the days of shotgun weddings and phrases like 'living in sin'. She was not destined to be the Countess Marcewiez or Maud Gonne of the 1970s; her career survived only one session of the British Parliament. The straitlaced Catholics who had voted her in voted her promptly out. She married, went to live in the South, had a family, took an interest in left-wing politics, was chairman, indeed, of the 'Independent Socialist Party', but Who's Who listed her recreations as 'walking, folk music, doing nothing'. Her place as the champion of Catholic Northern Irish poor would be taken by altogether more dangerous individuals.

The Irish Republican Army in 1969 was a group of people, or several groups, very different in outlook from those enthusiasts for the Celtic twilight, those patriots of both religions or none, those rebel daughters of country houses, those poets and soldiers who had either belonged to, or supported, the IRA at the time of the Easter Rising in Dublin in 1916. In the Republic of Ireland, it had settled down to a comparatively small collaboration of gangsters and political dreamers of the Marxian end of the spectrum, thousands of miles, ideologically, from the actual Irish men and women who had put Eamon de Valera in power. The coming, or renaissance, of the Troubles, should have been the ideal opportunity for the IRA to come to the aid of the beleaguered Irish nationalists of Derry, as they called it, and West Belfast, but while Bernadette Devlin, the Joan of Arc of the Civil Rights Movement, went to prison for her part in the Siege of Derry, the IRA were felt to have betrayed their natural working-class constituents. In 1967 the IRA Chief of Staff Cathal Goulding had, while not renouncing physical force, placed the importance upon creating 'a radical socialist agenda'. No wonder the graffiti began to appear on the riot-scarred walls – 'IRA – I ran away.'[14]

There followed, perhaps inevitably, a split between the official IRA and the Provisionals, or Provos. The officials were always uneasy about performing acts of violence which would harm 'civilians', seeing it as their task, when acts of murder were to be performed, to kill B-Specials, RUC officers and, when they arrived, British soldiers. The Provos as revolutionary Marxists believed that mayhem and fear would advance the revolution, though the incoherence of their aims was another ingredient in the Troubles. The aims of the (largely) peaceful Catholic republicans of the North were easily understood. A man such as Gerry Fitt, MP for West Belfast since 1966, was more troubling for the IRA – and for the Paisleyites – than it was for the British government. Gerry Fitt represented a minority in the narrow confines of Ulster, but if a poll had been taken which included British (let alone American, or world-wide) opinion, Fitt would have probably commanded an enormous *majority*. He wanted an alleviation of the injustices which had plagued Catholics in the North since 1922. He wanted fairness. He resigned as SDLP leader when it became clear how close his colleagues were getting to 'traditional nationalism', that is to the IRA. What Fitt could not get through persuasion, and the ballot box, he did not want. Some SDLP politicians were happy to talk peace and allow the men of violence to achieve their objectives for them.

Unlike some of his successors in the republican movement in the North, Fitt had an open contempt for the IRA, which was why they tried over and over again to kill him. He showed them, unlike the weasly John Hume, darling of TV political commentators in the 1980s and 1990s, no fear. Fitt, as a clever working-class Belfast man, was aware, as the Westminster politicians were not, of how complicated matters would become once the would-be Che Guevaras, the urban guerrillas of the Provisional IRA, entered the scene, with all their nonsensical confusions: their claim, for instance, upon which so much of their propaganda success in the United States was based, that the unfortunate British soldiers, who had been sent by an impulsive Home Secretary to stop Protestant mobs from lynching Catholics, were by contrast an army of 'occupation'.

When Mr Justice Scarman was appointed to report on the 'Battle of Bogside' he was shocked to read the Royal Ulster Constabulary log of the Derry events, in which he found that Bogsiders were referred to as 'the natives' in RUC radio reports.[15] But how could a Liberal English judge hope to disentangle what was going on in this terrible place? History had forced the mutually uncomprehending parties together into the arena. Whatever the motives of the Scottish settlers in Ulster in the seventeenth century, their twentieth-century descendants had not asked to be born into a divided island in which their political destiny, their very identity as people, was perceived to be under threat by Irish republicanism. (The secularisation of the South had not yet begun, which would mean, in the event of a united Ireland, the Ulster Protestants sending their children to Catholic primary schools, since the RC Church ran the primary schools.) 'So?' asked a secularised English nitwit of Iris Murdoch in the days of her Paisleyite fervour.[16] 'So,' she, whiskey-flown and flushing, retorted – 'would you be happy to send your children to a NAZI school?' If the Protestants were in an unenviable position, so too were the Catholics, who had not wanted the 1922 settlement and who, especially the inhabitants of Londonderry perhaps, felt themselves trapped by a whim of fate on the wrong side of a border, bullied, discriminated against, besieged.

Sympathy for both sides must be keen in the bosom of any but a biased observer. Sympathy for the British soldiers must also be deep, when the difficulty, or, to be more realistic, the downright impossibility of their task is considered. Once the Troubles had begun, it was generally agreed by the politicians that the presence of the troops was the sole factor in preventing the outbreak of civil war. The historian can afford the luxury of wondering whether this was in fact the case. (The prospect of either side 'winning' such a war would have been a terrible one.) Responsible politicians, and the senior army officers and intelligence officers they employed, could not take that risk. A political solution *had* to be found – one which would satisfy the fears of the working-class Catholics and Protestants, and which would not outrage public opinion in the Irish Republic and Britain. Until such a solution was found, the British soldier, hour by hour, month by month, had to keep the two warring communities apart, had to provide security for the police, had to do what he could to root out the arms of the guerrillas. Such rooting-out, once the explosions and shootings began in earnest, would play into the hands of the Marxist propagandists in the IRA making out the poor squaddie who searches a church hall, a terraced house or a farm for illegal weaponry to be a brutally insensitive invader. The routine security checks of cars at the borders increased this perception of the soldier as the enemy.

The soldier was hampered by the fact that in as much as he was representing a political point of view, it was the one point of view which, so far as Northern Irish people as a whole were concerned, was untenable, that their affairs were best settled by the English.

The true Unionist believed that Ulster was as much part of the United Kingdom as one of the English counties. 'I look forward to the time when the political battles of Northern Ireland are fought between Conservative and Labour . . . In the meantime [though], it will obviously continue for a long while on the present sectarian basis.' So said Reginald Maudling, who succeeded Callaghan as Home Secretary when the Conservatives won the General Election on the mainland in June 1970.[17] The pure Unionist belief led to some confusing analogies which dogged conservative, small and large C, thinking about Northern Ireland for a generation: the *Daily Telegraph* pundit T. E. Utley, a fervent defender of this position, had more influence, over other commentators and on politicians, than was desirable.

> Had British Governments simply proceeded on the assumption that Ulster was an integral part of the United Kingdom their response to violence there would have been fundamentally different. It is scarcely conceivable, for example, that in a state of civil disturbance in Britain large parts of Birmingham or Manchester would have been allowed for months on end to become rebel enclaves to which the police and the Army were denied access. It would have been quite incredible also that, at a time when the lawful authorities still had overwhelming force at their disposal, the leaders of a rebellion in Warwickshire or Lancashire would have been given safe conducts to London to discuss conditions of peace.[18]

Utley published these words in 1975. The key words which give the lie to his plausibility are the fourth, *simply*, and halfway through the paragraph, *Britain*. Nothing about the situation in Northern Ireland had been, or would be, simple. Some Unionists believed that Northern Ireland should be treated as if it were Warwickshire or Lancashire; nonetheless, they also spoke of it as detached from Britain as, of course, it was and ever should be. It would take thirty years to persuade British governments to stop thinking in this way and to adopt the saving double-think which saw that Ulster both was – and was not – British.

The two extremist wings of the explosive situation had seen this from the beginning. The Provos saw that the war which they intended to conduct to drive the British out of Ireland would be a long one. They had the good fortune to have established links with Colonel Muammar Gaddafi of Libya. An English tutor at Tripoli College, known to his Libyan handlers as Mister Eddie, was given the status of IRA Ambassador, with a splendid Italianate villa in the middle of Tripoli's embassy district. In the three years of the IRA–Libyan liaison, over $3.5 million ($10 million by 2002 values) was funnelled via banks in the City of London into the IRA's bank accounts. Mister Eddie, an IRA sympathiser rather than a full member, was to fall foul of the Provisionals when in 1974 he organised a conference between them and the loyalist paramilitaries the UDA (Ulster Defence Association) with the aim of discussing setting up an independent Northern Irish state. Mister Eddie foresaw the solution offered to, and accepted by, Paisley and the IRA leadership by Tony Blair thirty years later.[19] Since 'Mister Eddie's' plan would have eventually dissolved any need for the IRA to exist, it is not surprising that it was vigorously rejected.

At the time of the split in the IRA it probably had no more than forty to sixty members in the whole of Belfast. Among the families which joined the Provos was that of the Adamses. Grandfather Gerry Adams had fought alongside Michael Collins in the Irish Republican Brotherhood against the English in the pre-1922 war. Gerry, the father, had served an eight-year jail sentence after ambushing members of the RUC in 1942. Their son, also Gerry, had natural qualities of leadership, which showed themselves during the Easter Riots of 1970. Billy McKee, the new Provo Belfast commander, heard that riots had erupted in the Lower Falls Road and commanded his men to go to Ballymurphy and take on the British Army. It would have led to certain defeat at the hands of superior British firepower. Adams dragooned all McKee's men into a terraced house in West Belfast and held them at gunpoint. As one of them realised, 'Adams wanted ordinary people involved in the rioting as a way of radicalizing them.' The riots lasted four days. Thousands had appeared on the streets. On and off the riots repeated themselves all summer, and, by the end of it, the Ballymurphy IRA with Gerry Adams as its commander was the most militant in Belfast. Adams's position as the dominant figure in the IRA over the next thirty years was assured. In the general elections of June, which saw Harold Wilson's government defeated by the Conservative Party of Edward Heath, Ian Paisley defeated the official Unionist candidate and became the Member of Parliament for Bannside, Co. Antrim. He was now a figure not merely in the streets and conventicles of Ulster but in the national Parliament and on the national stage.

13

The 1960s

It was a violent decade, which saw the murder of John F. Kennedy, Robert Kennedy and Martin Luther King Jr. in the United States; the fatal stabbing of Prime Minister Hendrik Verwoerd in South Africa; and the grotesque murder of Sharon Tate with four friends in Beverly Hills, followed by the murder of Leno Lo Bianca in the same district. Charles Manson, a charismatic hippy, was found guilty of the crimes. It was the decade of the Vietnam War, in which the South Vietnamese lost 150,000 lives (400,000 wounded), the North Vietnamese 100,000 (300,000 wounded) and the United States military 45,941 (300,635 wounded). The reactions in Europe and America to the war were not all of a pacifist character. There was street fighting and rioting in London, Paris, Washington and Chicago. In Northern Ireland, the Troubles escalated and in Czechoslovakia (20 August 1968) Soviet tanks threatened a repeat of Hungary, 1956, when they entered Prague and brought to an end the benign reforms of Dubček. So for all the summer of love and the love-ins and the everlasting songs, it was a blood-spattered, confused time. Peter Weiss's 1964 play *The Persecution and Assassination of Jean-Paul Marat as Performed by the Inmates of the Asylum of Charenton under the Direction of the Marquis de Sade* was the archetype of the Theatre of Cruelty. The convulsions would seem to many apocalyptic, as if some rough beast were to be born, as in Yeats's horrific prophecy; perhaps as if Dostoyevsky too was right to have foreseen a time when, God having been discarded, anything would be deemed permissible.

In Britain, the practice of hanging criminals was discontinued. Revulsion against the ghoulish ritual had been growing ever since the Second World War, particularly in the prison service itself, where the doctor, the chaplain in full canonicals, and prison officers, together with the governor assembled to watch the hangman demonstrate his skills. Albert Pierrepoint (1905–92) was the most prolific exponent of the art. He had taken part in his first hanging when he assisted his uncle Tom hang Patrick McDermott at Mountjoy Prison in Dublin on 29 December 1932. He believed himself to be the swiftest in the business, executing James Inglis on 8 May 1951 at Strangeways Prison in Manchester in a mere seven seconds. In all, he executed an estimated 433 men and 17 women in the course of his career, including 200 war criminals at Hameln Prison in the British-controlled sector of Germany after the Second World

War, the celebrated pro-Nazis John Amery, who was hanged at Wandsworth in December 1945, and William Joyce, 'Lord Haw-Haw', the Irish-American Nazi broadcaster who, in spite of not being a British subject, was hanged for treason at Wandsworth on 4 January 1946. Pierrepont also hanged Derek Bentley (28 January 1953 at Wandsworth). Bentley, who had the mental age of eleven after a head injury sustained during the war, shot a policeman. He was out with Christopher Craig, who shouted out the words 'Let him have it!' before Bentley pulled the trigger. On 30 July 1998, the Appeal Court finally ruled (after forty-five years of campaigning by his father, sister Iris and, since Iris's death the previous year, by her daughter, Maria Bentley Dingwall) that his conviction was unsafe.

Pierrepont also hanged Timothy John Evans for murdering his wife at 10 Rillington Place in Notting Hill – a crime for which he was posthumously pardoned, when John Reginald Christie (hanged Pentonville Prison, 15 July 1953) was condemned for murdering seven women at that address. He also hanged the pathetic Ruth Ellis on 13 July 1955 at Holloway Prison; a mother of two who shot her lover in a crime passionnel, hers was a case which shocked the public and did much to alter the mood about capital punishment.

When Harold Wilson's first government came in, the death penalty was suspended; the Private Members' Bill to do so (sponsored by Sydney Silverman MP) received Royal Assent on 9 November 1965, suspending the death penalty for a period of five years and in effect abolishing it. The last two executions in Britain were carried out simultaneously in Walton and Strangeways prisons (the former in Liverpool) when Peter Anthony Alen and Gwynne Owen Evans (real name John Robson Walby) were hanged for the murder of a laundry man by the name of John West.

Even while these liberal laws were being passed in London, to the immense relief of Christians who questioned the legitimacy, and humanists who deplored the indecency, of hanging, murders were taking place.

Ian Brady worked at Burlington Warehouses, a big catalogue company in the middle of Manchester. Myra Hindley got a job there as a typist, and soon fell under Brady's hypnotic sexual allure. Quite early on in their relationship, he persuaded her to buy a tape recorder, then (1961) a newfangled device only recently on the market.

Hindley was not herself unintelligent (she'd turned down a place at a teacher training college because she wanted to start earning her living as a secretary) and Brady gave himself intellectual airs, reading Nietzsche and Wittgenstein, alongside Harold Robbins's *The Carpetbaggers*, with its message that rape and incest were exciting.[1] He liked playing a tape of Hitler's speeches. His copy of *The Life and Ideas of the Marquis de*

Sade is now preserved in the National Archives at Kew, because Hindley and Brady were the most notorious British murderers of the twentieth century.

He began with simple beating. She had discovered, once she became his lover, that he was a sadist and he easily initiated her into the ideas and appetites which that involved. They liked stalking unknown men in pubs and, when they found them in a darkened spot, giving them 'punishment' beatings. In bed, they fantasised about the perfect murder.[2] They got hold of a friend's van and enjoyed driving round contemplating their first murder. The killings were meticulously planned, with Brady carefully counting all the buttons on his clothes and listing all the items of clothing which would have to be burned when the deed was done. Their first victim was Pauline Reade, whom Myra Hindley had known since childhood, and whom they picked up as she was walking along the street in broad daylight. Brady raped her and killed her with a knife, and then Hindley drove them to the moors to bury the body. 'If you'd shown any signs of backing out you'd have ended up in the same hole as her,' he said. 'I know,' was her reply.[3] That was 12 July 1963.

Ten-year-old Lesley Ann Downey was probably the next victim. Once again, the murder was carefully planned in advance. They would find a victim and get 'it' to help carry some boxes to the back of the van. They found Lesley Ann at a fairground, as they staggered about with boxes of food and drink. Lesley Ann's cry – 'Please, Dad, no!' – was carefully recorded on the newfangled tape recorder. Myra turned up Radio Luxembourg to drown the noise while Brady raped the child. Brady photographed his victim, and the next day they drove to the moors to bury the body.

By the time they were brought to trial at Chester Assizes for what had come to be known as the 'Moors Murders', on 27 April 1966, the police knew of just three killings – Lesley Ann Downey and Edward Evans, aged seventeen, and Pauline Reade. Brady was also convicted of the murder of twelve-year-old John Kilbride. After the murderers had been imprisoned for life, it became clear that there were other victims.

Naturally the case excited interest, much of it extremely prurient. The tape recorder had enabled the jury, and those in the public gallery, to hear Brady and Hindley torturing their victim. Pamela Hansford Johnson, novelist wife of C. P. Snow, attended the trials and wrote a book[4] claiming that Brady and Hindley were the product of what had come to be known as the 'permissive' society.[4] But what society had ever permitted crimes such as theirs? Another writer, Emlyn Williams, the Welsh playwright, wrote an account of the murders, *Beyond Belief*, which must have left readers with the queasy sensation that he had enjoyed the shock and horror which he professed so to abominate.

Most of Brady and Hindley's crimes were committed before the abolition of the death penalty. If anyone deserved to hang, was it not they?
The debate between advocates and opponents of a death penalty continued
in Britain until membership of the European Union (which bans capital
punishment in its member states) made it a non-issue. After abolition in
Britain, the rates of murder increased steadily. In 1957, there were fewer
than sixty offences committed which, under the term of the current legislation, would have merited death. By 1968, this number had crept up to
a little less than one hundred. By 2004, there were over nine hundred
murders a year.

In the case of Hindley and Brady, however, the arguments were less
about deterrence than about the need for 'closure'. They began their
career of torture and murder before hanging was abolished, so they knew
what they risked: it probably increased the thrill. As it was, they were
sentenced to life imprisonment, Brady to a psychiatric prison – Broadmoor
– and Hindley to a series of women's gaols. Hanging them would not
have brought back their victims. For some people, who certainly include
their victims' families, however, the ritual of violence, and the fact that
the story was given an ending, would have provided, if not consolation,
a degree of satisfaction.

A man for whom such sentiments were abhorrent was the 7th Earl of
Longford (1905–2001), who visited both Brady and Hindley in prison.
After Hindley became a Roman Catholic and professed her penitence,
Longford – himself a Roman convert – campaigned tirelessly for her
release, thereby guaranteeing that she spent her life behind bars. The
more he campaigned, the more the tabloid newspapers revealed stories
of her attempted prison escapes, and her affairs with lesbian wardresses,
while reminding the public of the enormity of her crimes.

Longford was a puzzling, lovable figure. Had he lived in the nineteenth century, he might well, like another 7th Earl, that of Shaftesbury,
have enjoyed a reputation as the philanthropist and human benefactor
that he undoubtedly was. It was not fair to claim, as did his detractors,
that he was interested only in celebrity criminals, and in seeing his name
in the newspapers (though his lust for publicity was part of his complex
nature). He spent all his available spare time, deep into his old age,
waiting on cold railway platforms to change trains, and scurrying across
England, to visit any prisoner who asked to see him. Many of them
were abusive to him. He never complained, believing quite simply that
he was obeying the Gospel injunction that inasmuch as we have visited
those who were sick or in prison, we have done so to Christ.[5] He had
been a don at Christ Church, Oxford – he taught politics, his colleague
Roy Harrod economics, to, among others, the future Chancellor of the

Exchequer, Nigel Lawson. Longford began as a Young Tory, but, having attended a rowdy Mosleyite rally at Oxford Town Hall, he was accidentally hit on the head by a chair and, when he came round, he was left wing. He had secretly become a Roman Catholic, under the influence of Father Martin d'Arcy SJ, without telling his clever, beautiful wife, Elizabeth, the biographer and historian. She saw him as Pierre in *War and Peace*. Others saw him, with his bald head often adorned by a patch of grubby Elastoplast, as at best a Holy Fool, at worst a deluded self-publicist. Whether or not it was true, there was an apocryphal story which appeared to sum up his paradoxical character: that of him going into a bookshop to protest that they had not displayed his book with sufficient prominence in the window. The book was a disquisition entitled *Humility*. Against this must be set the countless individuals to whom Longford provided their only hope of human contact when the criminal justice system seemed to have deserted them. In 1998 he caused a storm of protest among homosexual activists when, debating in the Upper House about lowering the age of consent for homosexuals, he said, 'if someone seduced my daughter it would be damaging and horrifying but not fatal. She would recover, marry and have lots of children . . . On the other hand, if some elderly, or not so elderly, schoolmaster seduced one of my sons and taught him to be a homosexual, he would ruin him for life. That is the fundamental distinction.'

Beside this extremely unfashionable point of view, which certainly damned him in the eyes of those in 1998 who knew best, must be set the actual experiences of those who knew him. At Longford's ninetieth birthday party at the House of Lords, Lord Montagu of Beaulieu said, with tears in his eyes, to a friend – 'When I came out of prison, no one would speak to me. I came to this place, and I was cut – until Frank came up and spoke to me.'[6] He had been regular in his prison visits to Montagu when, after a celebrated court case, his fellow peer had been sent to prison in 1953. The title of Montagu's autobiography, *Wheels Within Wheels*, alluded to his passion for veteran cars and the great collection of them at Beaulieu, his seat in Hampshire. It also, of course, alluded to the emotional and sexual complications of his reputation. He claimed in the book that he had been entirely innocent of the charges brought against him: 'I had no qualms or hesitation about protesting my innocence. On the other hand I believe it was entirely wrong that such charges should have been levelled against anyone at all.'[7] After his release from prison, Montagu went on to become a much-respected public figure, and as first chairman of English Heritage from 1983 onwards he did much to preserve the country's historic architecture and environment. Indeed, it was the brutality of his sentence which helped, very slowly, to change the law in Britain.

During the August Bank Holiday of 1953, Lord Montagu of Beaulieu, a young man aged twenty-seven, engaged to be married to Anne Gage, went swimming with his friend the film director Kenneth Hume. Some Boy Scouts had been camping in the grounds of Palace House on the Beaulieu River in Hampshire, which, together with his estate and his father's title, Montagu had inherited when aged three in 1929.[8]

The two asked the young boys to join them for a swim. In the course of the day, Montagu's camera was 'stolen' and there were subsequent suggestions that the camera was used for the purpose of blackmail. Montagu and Hume were charged by the local police with sexual assault upon the Boy Scouts. After the hearing at Lymington Magistrates Court on 7 November 1953, the case was heard a month later at Winchester Assizes. Montagu was acquitted of assault and not enough evidence had been produced to substantiate a second much more minor charge. The second charge, and Hume's case, would be heard by the judge at the following Assizes in March.

Montagu had undoubtedly antagonised the police. When the Boy Scouts made their initial allegations, Montagu had flown to France to explain matters to his fiancée but there had subsequently been a hare-brained scheme for Montagu to avoid trial by going to live in America. He later came to believe that the police had 'tampered' with his passport to make it look as though he had visited England during the time he was actually in America, and failed to give himself up.

By the time of the next Winchester Assizes much more serious evidence had been brought against him and his gay cousin Michael Pitt-Rivers and another gay friend, the journalist Peter Wildeblood. It appears that, a year before Lord Montagu had invited the Boy Scouts for a swim, Pitt-Rivers and Wildeblood had used the beach hut at Beaulieu for encounters with two Royal Air Force orderlies by the names of John Reynolds and Edward McNally. The police persuaded Reynolds and McNally to 'turn Queen's evidence' against Wildeblood, Pitt-Rivers and Lord Montagu, and they thereby had enough evidence with which to send the three to prison. The trial began on 15 March 1954 and by a strange irony *The Times* chose to report it in a column directly adjacent to an account of 'an exhibition of manuscripts, letters, books, and miscellaneous items associated with Walt Whitman', at the American Library in Grosvenor Square. While the American Ambassador Mr Winthrop Aldrich praised the lyrically homoerotic author of *Leaves of Grass*, Mr G. D. Roberts QC for the prosecution spoke of homosexuals as 'perverts' and 'men of the lowest possible moral character'. This salacious tale began in March 1958 with McNally on leave from the RAF at Ely meeting Wildeblood in Piccadilly Circus Underground Station; they 'smiled at one another and got into conversation'. McNally then came back to Wildeblood's flat where 'unnatural acts were committed mutually between them'. McNally returned for duty at the RAF, subsequently being posted to Blackpool, but he kept in touch with Wildeblood and held on to his highly prosecutable letters. In July he and a friend, John Reynolds, were introduced to Lord Montagu and invited to stay at the beach hut on the Beaulieu Estate. 'McNally . . . said that when he mentioned his friend Reynolds Lord Montagu asked him if he (Reynolds) was "queer". The witness replied that he was.'

The charges brought against Lord Montagu, Michael Pitt-Rivers and Peter Wildeblood were that they 'conspired together to incite John Reynolds and Edward McNally to commit acts of gross indecency with male persons'. Lord Montagu was further charged with having committed an offence with John Reynolds on 24 August 1952 and Wildeblood with having committed an offence on the same date with McNally.

Mr W. A. Fearnley-Whittingstall QC defending Lord Montagu said that were it not for recent events, 'Lord Montagu today would have been a happily married man. That must be a devastating thought. He was a useful member of the House of Lords and a kindly landowner, he was faced with a bitter future.'

Part of the offensiveness, as far as the court was concerned, was that, as Edward Montagu's sister later wrote, he had committed a terrible social impropriety by entertaining people of an inferior social class. Hence, in part, the fantasy that the three better-born men had needed to 'incite' the airmen to acts of indecency. There was undoubtedly a social, not to say political, dimension in the case; if it was not true to say that the police wanted to punish Edward Montagu in part for being a lord, there was probably an element of wishing to make an example of a well-known prosperous figure, *pour encourager les autres*. Lord Montagu himself always denied being homosexual at all. The case ended on 24 March with Wildeblood and Pitt-Rivers each being sentenced to eighteen months' imprisonment and Montagu to twelve. The judge, Mr Justice Ormerod, described the offences as 'serious', but said he was offering the most lenient sentences allowed by the law. A call by Wildeblood's lawyer, to the effect that he should be allowed a course of psychological medicine at the Middlesex Hospital, was rejected. Dr J. A. Hobson, a consultant physician, had given it as his view that 'Wildeblood was not a typical type [sic] of homo-sexual [sic]. There was a better chance than in most cases of homo-sexuality [sic] of curing him by treatment.' The plea, too, was rejected.

It had been a high-profile case, but by no means unique. Four hundred and eighty men were convicted in England and Wales during the three years ended March 1956 for homosexual offences committed with consenting adults in private. Most pleaded guilty, and most made written statements to the police admitting their offences. Inevitably, given the nature of the evidence and the difficulty of substantiating it, the police would have been unable to do their work without snooping, hiding in likely venues for gay 'cruising', such as parks or public lavatories; on occasion they posed as homosexuals and on occasion they indulged in such acts themselves before turning in their victim-partners.

But it was on 4 August 1954, while Lord Montagu was beginning to serve the fifth month of his prison sentence, that a committee was appointed by the government to submit a report on the law and practice relating to homosexual offences and prostitution. The chairman was a former public school headmaster (Uppingham, Shrewsbury) named John Wolfenden. He assembled a committee which included Canon Demant, the Anglo-Catholic moral theologian; Goronwy Rees, by then Principal of the University College of Wales in Aberystwyth; Lady Stopford, family doctor and magistrate; and others with legal and medical experience. Wolfenden had a double brief: to report on the law relating to prostitution and to look again at the question of homosexuality. 'For the sake of the ladies' on the committee, it was agreed that when referring to homosexuals they should say 'Huntley', and when talking of prostitutes they should say 'Palmer'– as in Huntley and Palmer's Biscuits.[9] Their all but unanimous opinion (James Adair, former Procurator General for Glasgow, dissented), published in the Wolfenden Report of 3 September 1957,[10] was that 'homosexual behaviour between consenting adults in private should no longer be a criminal offence'. Their report took ten years to be turned into law – the Sexual Offences Act of 1967. The Conservatives had dragged their feet over implementing Wolfenden and it was left to a courageous peer, 'Boofy' Arran, to introduce a bill calling for reform. The debate sparked some lively exchanges, with Lord Dilhorne ('Bullying-Manner') taunting the Archbishop of Canterbury about whether he favoured legalising the act of buggery, and the Chief Scout fearing the country would go the way of Greece and Rome,[11] quite a good way to go if you imagined the Greece of Alcibiades or the Rome of Caesar, it might be thought. (The Archbishop was a liberal in favour of reform, but he did not admit to their Lordships' House, as he once did to a private dinner when asked his view of homosexuality – 'Well.' Long, long pause. 'I tried it once.' Long pause. 'I didn't enjoy it. I didn't try it again.'[12]) After the Lords debate, it was inevitable that the law would change. Germany decriminalised homosexuality in 1913, Russia in 1917. England, by doing so in 1967, was nonetheless in advance of some European countries, especially those where the Roman Catholic

Church was dominant. (In Ireland, homosexuality was not decriminalised until 1993, a fact which perhaps lurks behind Captain Grimes's mysterious comment, in Waugh's *Decline and Fall*, that 'you can't get into the soup in Ireland, do what you like'.[13]) It was in 1973 that the American Psychiatric Association removed homosexuality from its official list of mental disorders.[14] The Church of England, in all its enlightened manifestations, had always known this, but in bringing the debate out into the open in the 1990s it smoked out some extraordinary bigotry within its own ranks and eventually caused the effective break-up of the worldwide Anglican Communion over the issue. So, it remained, throughout our times, a live issue, with many countries in the world, such as India and Uganda and Nigeria, retaining their ban on the activity.

Undoubtedly, the liberalisation of the laws governing sexual conduct brought to Britain a heady feeling of liberation. The old Tory world, which had been lampooned out of existence in 1964, was firmly knocked into its grave by the General Election of 1966, in which Harold Wilson won a second election victory. The 'planned economy' and the 'white heat of the technological revolution' would somehow pay the bills as public spending soared. The World Cup finals were held in England and England won. The football team, containing such figures as Bobby Charlton, Bobby Moore and Geoff Hurst, made everyone happy. Football is war without the blood. In a later, slightly more serious decade, the Argentine would be seen as a real enemy. In the World Cup of 1966 they were rivals, booted out in the quarter-finals. Alf Ramsey, the England manager, described the Argies as 'animals'. That cheered everyone up, too. For, though everyone was supposed to be left wing, and sexually liberated, a little bit of xenophobia never failed to make the British smile. It took their minds off the grim realities of war in other parts of the globe. General William C. Westmoreland, US Commander in Vietnam, told his troops 'to remove the people and destroy the villages'. While Bobby Charlton was restoring English *amour propre*, the Chinese Cultural Revolution, cheered on by young and not-so-young British lefties, was imprisoning the minds of millions, and leading to deaths and incarcerations which to this day are countless.

During the last summer of his life, playwright Joe Orton (1933–67) was walking from Islington to King's Cross with his friend the actor and comedian Kenneth Williams (1926–87) and talking of sex. '"You must do whatever you like," I said, "as long as you enjoy it and don't hurt anyone else. That's all that matters."' Williams quoted back Camus's line, 'All freedom is a threat to someone.' He described a visit to an East End pub at which young men had clustered around him. '"Kaw! Ken, it's legal now you know. And he started pulling his trousers down."' But

Williams would have none of it. '"You should have seized your chance," said Orton. "I know," Kenneth said, "I just feel guilty about it all." "Fucking Judaeo-Christian civilisation!" I said, in a furious voice, startling a passing pedestrian.' Both men were destined to die unnaturally.[15] Kenneth Williams took his own life in his bleak white flat near Great Portland Street Station in 1987. Orton was murdered by his lover, an unsuccessful actor named Kenneth Halliwell, two weeks after the conversation just quoted.

There was a studied frivolity, a need to see a passer-by *startled* as he denounced the Judaeo-Christian tradition. 'Cleanse my heart', he had prayed to a God in whom he did not believe, 'give me the ability to rage correctly.'[16]

An early, and highly successful, attempt to spread mayhem among the respectable classes had resulted in the twenty-nine-year-old Orton – described as a 'lens cleaner' and his friend, later murderer, Halliwell, aged thirty-five – being found guilty at Old Street Magistrates Court for stealing seventy-two public library books and 'wilfully' damaging a number of books, including the removal of 1,653 art books. The pair were sent to prison for six months. In the first volume of Emlyn Williams's plays the contents were amended to include dramas the Welshman never wrote, such as 'Knickers Must Fall', 'Up the Front', 'Up the Back' and 'Fucked by Monty'. Dorothy L. Sayers's mystery whodunnit would have surprised readers in the Islington Library by its blurb, beginning, 'When little Betty Macdree says that she has been interfered with, her mother at first laughs. It is only something that the kiddy had picked up off television. But when sorting through the laundry, Mrs Macdree discovers a new pair of knickers are missing she thinks again.'[17] Orton also delighted in spoof correspondences, often writing letters as 'Mrs Edna Welthorpe'. Sometimes Edna was avant-garde, as when she wrote to the Heath Street Baptist Church, trying to persuade them to stage a play called *The Pansy*, 'which pleads for greater tolerance on the subject of homosexuality'.[18] Sometimes she is more puritanical, even writing to denounce the immoral plays of Joe Orton, or Horton as she mistakenly called him on occasion. ('I myself was nauseated by this endless parade of mental and physical perversion.')

Orton suggested that his library pranks were an act of revenge upon librarians, though members of that profession were not above book abuse. Strangely enough, in the same year that Orton and Halliwell were sent down, 1962, the librarian poet Philip Larkin and his girlfriend Monica Jones were having a holiday at Haydon Bridge, near Hexham, Northumberland, during which they enjoyed systematically defacing a copy of Iris Murdoch's novel *The Flight from the Enchanter* – in the list of the author's previous publications could now be found 'UNDER THE NET her Garments'. Some originally innocent sentences were merely underlined – 'Today it seemed likely to be especially hard'. Others were altered so that, 'Her lips were parted and he had never seen her eyes so wide open' became 'Her lips were parted and he had never seen her cunt so wide open.'[19]

The defaced library books were Orton's first plays. The successes on the stage – *Entertaining Mr Sloane*, which was first presented in London at the New Arts Theatre on 6 May 1964, and *Loot* – at the Cochrane Theatre on 29 September 1966 – were an extension of the same anarchic wit, the same sense of the intolerability of conventions. By the standards of a later age they would seem overwhelmingly misogynistic. The discovery of a woman's dead body in *Loot* and her husband's outraged feelings that she is in the nude nudge us towards the idea that all conventions of morality are absurd. As Hal, the son of the woman, stuffs stolen money into her coffin he remarks, 'I shall accompany my father to Confession this evening in order to purge my soul of this afternoon's events.' 'It is at times like this I regret not being a Catholic,' says his friend. Hal retorts, 'Afterwards, I'll take you to a remarkable brothel I've found. Really remarkable. Run by three Pakistanis aged between ten and fifteen. They do it for sweets. Part of their religion. Meet me at seven. Stock up with Mars Bars.'

Though technical and comedic triumphs, nothing much lingered in the air after Orton's plays were staged. John Osborne, by contrast, was a writer no less refreshingly angry than Orton but his plays are much more closely observed, more morally intelligent. One of the finest of them, *Luther* – Albert Finney took the title role at the first performance in 1961 – dramatises the sense felt by practically all that generation, if they possessed any sensitivity to the state of things, that the status quo was intolerable. Osborne's *Luther* could be seen in retrospect as a man of the 1960s. His 'Here I stand; God help me; I can do no more, Amen' at the Diet of Worms, 1521, spoke to a generation that, as individuals, felt no personal commitment to the political programmes on offer. Osborne might have been considered an iconoclast with his first play, *Look Back in Anger*. Some of his contemporaries deemed to be Angry Young Men – Kingsley Amis, John Braine – managed to step seamlessly into the personae of Right-Wing Bastards in what seemed like no time at all. Braine, a librarian from Bingley, wrote a bestseller called *Room at the Top* which was obsessed by the injustice of the class system. Braine never stopped being class conscious but a single visit to the United States was enough to make him abandon left-wingery. Explaining his change of heart to Donald Soper, a Methodist preacher who identified the teachings of Christ with those of the Labour Party, Braine said that America had come as a revelation. Here was a country where it did not matter if your father was rich or poor. You had a chance to get on, regardless of class. 'And', added Soper, 'provided you aren't black.' Braine fixed his frog-like eyes, seen through thick spectacles, on to Soper's conceited, eager face. 'Of course I'm not black', he rasped in his strong Yorkshire accent.

Kingsley Amis's transition from member of the Communist Party to Garrick Club bore perhaps happened more gradually than Braine's conversion, but it was no less absolute. The Angry Young Men called themselves Fascist Beasts when they met for their lunches at Bertorelli's in Charlotte Street and the jokey application is better than 'Right Wing', still less 'Conservative'. Kingsley Amis remained class-chippy and godless, as did his great friend Larkin, who had never been tempted by any form of leftism. Osborne has much in common with them but was a toweringly more original and interesting writer. Just as Luther, in bold, colloquial language, rescued the Germans from formal religion (giving them back personal religion), so Osborne, greatest of the Angry Young Men, went on being angry as systems overpowered individuals. Where Luther had fought the Roman Church, Osborne punctured the pretensions of politics.

True nonconformity was a quality which Osborne saw as quintessentially English. In the 1960s there were many con artists purveying their Bohemian or anti-Establishment credentials who were in fact fiercely ambitious and cleverly opportunistic. They were the New Establishment in Waiting. Of such were the Beatles, never more New Establishment than when they pompously sent back the MBE which Harold Wilson, in a pathetic attempt to woo the younger voter, had recommended to the Sovereign should be theirs. Of such was John Mortimer, who combined the roles of fashionable QC with that of being a second-rate writer, and who would suck up to the New Establishment by his supposed daring in defending the obscene magazine *Oz* in 1971.

One of the most astute remarks ever made by Harold Macmillan was a reply to Anthony Wedgwood Benn in the House of Commons in 1960. Macmillan, then Prime Minister, had been persuaded by Hugh Trevor-Roper (later Lord Dacre) to stand for election as Chancellor of his old university, Oxford, against the former Ambassador to Washington, Sir Oliver Franks. After much intrigue and plotting of the sort which was Trevor-Roper's lifeblood, Macmillan won – by 1,976 votes to 1,697. (The electors are the MAs of the university.) A few days later, Wedgwood Benn congratulated Macmillan in the House, 'on having proved by his own tremendous victory in a ballot held in Latin, open for all to see, that the Establishment has nothing to learn from the Electrical Trades Union'.

And here was Macmillan's brilliant reply – 'Except that on this occasion, I think, the Establishment was beaten.'[20] Here, the 'Establishment' meant the Foreign Office Mandarin, the Liberal who appealed to the academic world. But Macmillan could see that the 1960s were going to be a time when the Old Establishment was replaced by a rival group of would-be Establishments. England would never be quite the same again.

John Osborne, likewise, could see that the true rebels during the 1960s were not those who grew their hair or made exhibitionistic boasts about their sexual lives, but those who saw the damage being done to the world by town planners, spivs, bad architects, businessmen and politicians who believed in Growth. These were the ones who were ruining England, and being actively encouraged by the political classes to do so. Anyone who objected to a Georgian high street being pulled to bits and replaced with brutalist multi-storey car parks, or who thought that Victorian terraced streets were preferable to asbestos-polluted high-rise blocks on the East German pattern, must bear the label of fuddy-duddy. Of such was the great John Betjeman. When Max Miller, the genius of English music hall, the master of double entendre, died in 1963 (his jokes were all about sex but he never said a 'dirty word' on stage), Osborne burst into a threnody: 'There'll never be another, as old John Betjeman says, an English genius as pure gold as Dickens or Shakespeare – or Betjeman come to that. What did Trollope say – muddle-headed Johnny? It's deep honesty that distinguishes a gentleman. *He*'s got it. He knows how to revel in life and have no expectations – and fear death at all times.'[21] Osborne's most poignant play, *The Entertainer*, was about a failed music hall entertainer, whose financial and emotional life implodes into chaos at the time of Suez.

Miller's ethnic origins were Romany. The long-suffering wife of this promiscuous man lived in Brighton but his fellow Anglican and devoted admirer Betjeman liked the fact that Miller was a stout high churchman who attended Saint Bartholomew's Church, Brighton (the tallest as well as one of the highest churches in the land), on 'the greater festivals'.[22]

Betjeman revelled in such jokes, knowing that they were celebrations of a vanishing England. The music halls, and the Church, were doomed, which was why he loved both. And he fought long and often lonely battles for such architectural wonders as James Bunning's Coal Exchange (demolished 1962) or the Arts and Crafts Bedford Park (which Betjeman saved from demolition in 1963). From his first emergence on to the social scene in the late 1920s, Betjeman had entranced such people as the Mitfords and the Guinnesses and the fading Irish aristocracy. Now, what had been reserved for drawing rooms in country houses, or Maurice Bowra's rooms at Wadham, could be enacted on the television and everyone in England fell in love with him. But only a few saw how deadly serious was his desire to save what was left of old England before the spivs pulled it down. There was a mindlessness about the 1960s, a sheer silliness, which could not see the consequences of policies such as architectural vandalism.

At Orton's funeral they played a tape of his favourite song, the Beatles' 'A Day in the Life': 'I read the news today, oh boy/About a lucky man who made the grade'.[23]

Many of the Beatles songs were about self-betterment, or about the fantasy, in the case of the Beatles themselves, of outsoaring provincial and class restrictions in order to hit the Big Time ('Paperback Writer', for example). No history of the period could overlook Beatlemania, though any history could afford to overlook the Beatles. They beat all records for sales in Britain and America.[24] For most of the decade, until in 1969 they announced that they were breaking up the group, they could be sure of mobs of screaming fans every time they checked into a hotel or airport or turned up at a gig. They also had their serious musical admirers. On 23 December 1963, the music critic of *The Times* praised their 'fresh and euphonious' guitars in the song 'Till There was You', their 'submediant switches from C major into A flat major' and the 'octave ascent' in 'I Want to Hold Your Hand'. The critic continued, 'One gets the impression that they think simultaneously of harmony and melody, so firmly are the major tonic sevenths and ninths built into their tunes, and the flat-submediant key-switches, so natural is the Aeolian cadence at the end of "Not a Second Time" (the chord progression which ends Mahler's "Song of the Earth").' Yet though the band produced some melodies which pass the memorability test – 'I Want to Hold Your Hand', 'She Loves You', 'Help!' once heard stay in the head – the secret of their success is that they are rock music's easy listening. The Beatles posed as rebels against class conventions and the supposedly stuffy mores of their elders, but their appeal was always to nice boys and girls, who would play their cherished Beatles LPs to their children when they paired off and settled down, enjoying the patronising sentimentality of 'Eleanor Rigby' and 'When I'm Sixty-Four'.

The four who composed the group came from Liverpool. John Lennon had attended Quarry Bank Grammar School, Paul McCartney was educated at Wilson Hall, Garston. Lennon, with a skiffle group called the Quarrymen, met McCartney at a church fete in 1957. McCartney brought along his friend George Harrison to join the Quarrymen. They went through a number of names – Johnny and the Moondogs, Long John and the Beatles, the Silver Beatles, before settling on the Beatles in 1960. They sometimes used a drummer called Tommy Moore, who was much older than they were. In the end, however, Moore left the band and returned to his work as a forklift truck driver in a bottling factory. Eventually they settled as a quartet when Richard Starkey joined them as drummer, with the name Ringo Starr. Their best career move was when they engaged Brian Epstein as their manager. He failed to sell them to Decca, but he did persuade George Martin, who headed the Parlophone label for EMI, to take them on for a year's contract. The first recording session was booked on 6 June 1962 at EMI's Abbey Road studios in St John's Wood, London.[25] This did not produce a single recording which the company wanted to use, but they eventually came up with 'Love Me Do', and their career was made. Three months later the song 'Please, Please Me', an anthem of the age, would take them to further heights. By 1964 they were so popular that crowds of four thousand waved them goodbye from Heathrow Airport on their first trip to America. The crowds waiting for them at the other end, in the newly renamed JFK Airport, exceeded any that had been seen there.[26]

It was in New York that they met Bob Dylan, who introduced them to smoking pot. Dylan was in every way a superior artist and performer. His songs, rasped out in that distinctive snarling voice and interrupted by jerky mouth organ recitatives, truly did herald something new in the world – 'The Times They Are a Changin'', 'Blowin' in the Wind', and countless others. The sung lyrics of Dylan are very nearly in the league of some of the great songs of the world, such as those of Robert Burns. The Beatles are pappy by comparison.

This fact, obvious to everyone else, was certainly not clear to the Beatles themselves, who, the moment they were famous, became invested with a risible degree of self-importance. Lennon was the most pretentious and self-regarding in this respect; the more he took drugs and made an exhibition of himself, the more he seemed to believe himself to be some kind of poet-sage or philosopher. Lennon's own self-importance, however, was as nothing to that of his second wife, Yoko Ono. Describing herself sometimes as a sculptress, sometimes as a film-maker, a naked Yoko invited journalists and cameramen into the honeymoon suite of the Hilton Hotel, Amsterdam, when the pair married. They lay in bed being photographed, and offering such useful pieces of advice to the world as 'Stay in bed' and 'Grow your hair'. They went further, and suggested that the violence which existed between South and North Vietnam, between the Arabs and Israelis, or between America and the Soviet Union, would evaporate were the politicians involved only to remove their trousers.

The pair's moral and political announcements, delivered *urbi et orbi*, were disconcerting. No crooners of a previous age would have considered it their place to make such statements. Dan Leno had not offered his thoughts to the world on the Schleswig-Holstein Question, or the Unification of Italy. Bing Crosby or Harry Belafonte would have been laughed off the stage if they had attempted to share with the audience their views on the legalisation of cannabis or the meaning of life. On 24 July 1967, the Beatles added their names to those of Graham Greene, R. D. Laing and others calling for the legalisation of pot. In August the same year they met the Maharishi Mahesh Yogi in India and became adepts of the wisdom of the East. Their need to impose their 'ideas' on the public were perpetuated by McCartney, who continued to be an advocate of animal rights and vegetarianism, long after Lennon had been assassinated (by Mark Chapman, 8 December 1980, in New York City), George Harrison had died of lung cancer (29 November 2001) and Ringo Starr had become a voiceover on animated versions of the Revd W. Awdry's *Thomas the Tank Engine* stories. They bequeathed to the world the annoying legacy that entertainers, rather than being humble enough to entertain, should inflict their half-baked views of economics, meteorology and politics to those who had been gullible enough to buy their recordings.

In an interview with Maureen Cleave in the *Evening Standard* in 1966, Lennon modestly announced that Christianity was dying out and that the Beatles were 'more popular than Jesus now'.[27] The remark was clearly not intended to be amusing. Many people in America and South Africa paid Lennon the compliment of melting down their Beatles records in protest.

The Rolling Stones from the south London suburbs were the more stylish answer to Liverpool's most famous quartet. Not just because they were southerners: the Stones were in every way more English than the Beatles, that is to say more capable of irony. Jagger's contortions on the stage, his overt sexuality, his exploitation of the bisexual signals which he gave out, both on and off stage, were all reversions to Lord Byron.

One legacy of the 1960s was that rock music, rather than being something which was reserved for parties, nightclubs and people who enjoyed that kind of thing, became the anthem and background music of every area of British life. There would never come a time when its music fell silent. People would hear it as the background music at airports and in shops, even in bookshops, where customers by definition want quiet; it would be played at children's parties instead of 'Ring a Ring o' Roses'. It was not deemed inappropriate at funerals. Trendy vicars of course incorporated it into their maimed liturgies. It provided the backing for films and advertisements. It was the most invasive of aural transformations ever suffered by the human race. And with that liberal tyranny, which was characteristic of that most intolerant decade, anyone who objected to it was labelled a fuddy-duddy.

The most remarkable musical productions to emerge from Liverpool during the decade were the early symphonic works of John McCabe (born 1939), but you would not have thought so if all you had heard of was the Beatles. When McCabe was growing up, Liverpool was a truly cultured place, its Walker Art Gallery, its concert halls, schools, library and university justly esteemed. They all continued, of course, but as the city collapsed around them, and it was redubbed a City of Culture, the kind of culture meant was really 'Popular Culture'. So, the 'music of the 1960s' for many people means the Beach Boys, Freddie and the Dreamers or Gerry and the Pacemakers.

The decade was in fact a memorable one musically. Shostakovich's 13th Symphony (1962) was a horrifying, moving depiction of the Stalinist Terror, evoked by a haunting bass solo, orchestra and chorus. Poulenc's *Gloria*, one of the most beautiful pieces in the whole repertoire of church choral music, was composed in 1959, and to the 1960s proper belong the operatic fantasy 'Votre Faust' and the *Couleurs croises* for orchestra (1967). In England, a great composer, Benjamin Britten, was producing such stupendous work as the Cello Symphony (1963), or the opera of *Death in Venice* (1973). A new star arose in the sky – John Tavener (born 1944) had the first performance of his extraordinary dramatic cantata *The Whale* in 1965. Michael Tippett not only continued to compose good work – the Second Piano Sonata (1962) and his opera *The Knot Garden* – but was a tireless promoter of musical performance. This was the great decade of Solti's conducting Wagner's *Ring* at Covent Garden. Malcolm Sargent was still conducting the annual Proms in the Albert Hall, with originality and brio.

In literature, the 1960s were a wonderful decade, too. Anthony Powell continued with his *roman-fleuve, A Dance to the Music of Time* – penning the best three volumes in the sequence, those relating to the war: *The Valley of Bones* (1964), *The Soldier's Art* (1966), *The Military Philosophers* (1968). V. S. Naipaul wrote his funniest and most tender novel, *A House for Mr Biswas* (1961); Geoffrey Hill (born 1932), perhaps the best poet of his generation, published *King Log* in 1968. John le Carré's *The Looking Glass War* of 1965 was rather more than just a spy thriller. In 1967 two brilliant comic miniaturists, Paul Bailey (with *At the Jerusalem*) and Beryl Bainbridge (with *A Weekend with Claude*), established their reputations. In 1969, George MacDonald Fraser had the inspired idea to write a series of novels about the British Empire in its heyday, with the Rugby School bully from *Tom Brown's Schooldays* as its hero. *Flashman* was published in 1969. But none of this, exactly speaking, was what people meant, in after times, when they spoke of the 1960s. Someone once met the young C. S. Lewis, pacing along Addison's Walk at Magdalen College, Oxford, his pipe ablaze. When asked the reason for his good humour Lewis replied that he had just discovered that the Renaissance had not happened. What he meant was that there had not been a great cultural break between the so-called Middle Ages and the age of Spenser and Shakespeare. Similarly, is it not possible to read the history of our times without thinking of the 1960s as the great watershed after which everything was different?

Pessimists tend to look back on the sixties as the time when Everything Came Unstuck. *Honest to God* destroyed the faith, and *Lady Chatterley* the morals, of the British. Libertarian libertine Woy Jenkins unleashed sexual depravity and pornography on an unwilling world. That is one picture. The optimists, who tend to be a little older, are sometimes those who remember the 1960s. They think that they spent the time with flowers in their hair, protesting against the Vietnam War, smoking pot and playing Beatles LPs. Perhaps they did so.

How can such things be measured? My suspicion is that British human beings had no more orgasms in the 1960s than they did in the 1860s or even than in the 1260s; that a brilliantly constructed farce by Alan Ayckbourn such as *Relatively Speaking* (first performed as *Meet My Father* in 1965) lasted just as well as some of the more obviously 'sixties' plays by Joe Orton. A few hundred, perhaps a few thousand, people changed, or thought they had changed, in the 1960s. But surely many more went on as they had always done.

If the 1960s was a time when Britain learned to fall in love with its future, it was also, this decade in which Churchill died, a time of nostalgia. When Harold Wilson launched an embarrassing campaign called 'I'm Backing Britain' to disguise from himself and his voters the effects of European membership, the BBC responded with a short six-part series. It began with a retired bank manager in a fictitious south coast town organising an 'I'm Backing Britain' luncheon, in 1968, and recollecting the days of 1940 when Backing Britain had meant being prepared to take up arms.

Dad's Army (such was the show's name) was a sitcom based upon the Home Guard. It ran for a total of eighty episodes until 1977. The scripts – not a dud among them – were by Jimmy Perry and David Croft, and they made superb use of some great character actors – above all Arthur Lowe as the bank manager and captain of the platoon – Captain Mainwaring – John Le Mesurier as his chief clerk and sergeant, John Laurie the undertaker, Arnold Ridley with a weak bladder, and Clive Dunn as Lance Corporal Jones, a very popular member of the cast but the only one who threatened to spoil things by overacting. There were some sublime moments, perhaps the best being those when the farcical and the heroic touched. In the episode called 'The Deadly Attachment', the captured captain of a German U-boat turns the tables on Mainwaring's platoon and holds Lance Corporal Jones hostage. He puts a grenade in the waistband of the old man's trousers.

> CAPTAIN: Seven seconds will give me plenty of time to get clear, but I think it is not enough time for the old man to unbutton his tunic.
> FRAZER: A terrible way to die.
> MAINWARING: You unspeakable swine. Now listen to me. I'm the Commanding Officer here, it's only right that I should have the bomb in my waistband.
> JONES: I will not allow you to have the bomb in your trousers, sir. Don't you worry about me, they can put twenty bombs in my trousers. They won't make me crack.
> MAINWARING: How can you hope to beat us? You see the sort of men we breed in this country?
> CAPTAIN: Yes, rather stupid ones.[28]

Dad's Army was so successful partly because it was a pastiche of the self-mockery of actual Second World War comedy, such as *ITMA*. (Some old-age pensioners 'remembered' the theme song, 'Who Do You Think You're Kidding, Mr Hitler', from their wartime days, though it had been commissioned specially for the series.) In fact there was something double-edged about *Dad's Army* and its success. In the episode just quoted, the languid Sergeant Wilson fails to prime the Mills bombs because he thinks they will be 'awfully dangerous'. He thereby saves Jones's life when the dastardly German plants the grenade on him. In 1968, however, many people were beginning to feel that Britain had come to feel like a pathetic old man with a bomb in his pants, a comedy hero with no future.

Others, more optimistic, felt that the change in the air was to be welcomed. The year 1968 was spoken of in after times by the baby boomers as if it had been one of those great dates in history, such as 1789, or 1848, in which a great revolution had occurred, not merely in the politics of nations, but in the human spirit. But to younger generations than theirs, it could not be seen as the real revolution of our times. Their salute of political heroes – Ho Chi Minh, Che Guevara and other leftists – seemed less like the dawn of a new age than the last shout of an old one. As they demonstrated, and pinned on their badges, and waved their little scarlet copies of *The Thoughts of Chairman Mao*, these supposed champions of a new liberty were unwittingly delaying the true revolution, which was the overthrow of the communist tyranny in Russia and Eastern Europe by the dissidents. When they thought that they were cheering on a bright future, they seemed to their children's generation to have been locked in a sinister historical past, which the things they most despised, free market capitalism and organised religion, would within little more than a decade eventually be destroyed. Chairman Mao killed infinitely more people than Hitler had done, and the system which had been strengthened by Stalin, enslaving the peoples of Eastern Europe, would be overthrown by the Poles, the Czechs, the Hungarians, the Bulgarians, the East Germans and the Russians who had known at first hand, and for decades, what it was like to live in a society governed by the incompetent tyrants of the Soviet Union.

Britain's year of revolution amounted to little more than a marijuana-induced party for spoilt students, the first generation not obliged to do military service or to earn their living as soon as they left school. Britain itself had, during the 1960s, become liberalised in its sexual behaviour, but this was more because of increased prosperity, and by the dissemination of cheap contraception by the medical profession and the pharmaceutical giants. But though it now had several hundred thousand immigrants from the Commonwealth, living largely in the poorer quarters of British cities, the country was fundamentally the same place in 1968 as it had been in 1958. It was still a monarchy. The institutions of Parliament, the judiciary and the Inns of Court, remained the same. The armed forces, though reduced, were still in place. Britain remained an independent archipelago. Industry remained hamstrung by the cold war between trades unions and management. If Great Britain's unity was under threat it was not from student demonstrations but from the centuries-old problem of Ireland. If its constitutional position, and its sovereignty, were to undergo a radical alteration, this would come not from the activities of the left, but from those new men of the Conservative Party who saw the political future of Britain not as a world empire, nor as an island fortress but as a johnny-come-lately in the European experiment.

Yet the 1960s as a whole, viewed retrospectively, polarised the British. The pessimists saw the decade as the period when everything began to unstick, when Britain undid itself, when the sniggering of the satirists and the misguided reforms of liberalism loosened the fabric of morals and social cohesion. The optimists saw the same changes and viewed them as the beginning of liberation. For the optimists, however childish the behaviour of students or iconoclastic playwrights, it was a period when Britain grew up. They no longer looked to the Lord Chamberlain to decide what they could see on the stage, nor to the Home Secretary and the police and the judiciary to tell consenting adults how to comport themselves in their intimate sexual lives. To the optimists, Roy Jenkins was the Home Secretary who allowed the mature British public to read what they wished, without the philistine interference of the Director of Public Prosecutions. To the pessimists, Jenkins was responsible for every corner-shop newsagent being filled with unsightly pornographic magazines. Optimists rejoiced that unhappily married people and homosexuals (sometimes the same) were no longer stigmatised. For the pessimists, stigma was a good thing, holding together the fragile but useful institution of family life. For the optimists, muddle was better than hypocrisy.

Whichever side of the argument you were guided by temperament to support, it became a commonplace as the years went by to regard the 1960s as the decade when everything in Britain changed. Philip Larkin's lines were regularly trotted out – 'Between the end of the Chatterley ban and the Beatles' first LP' – by readers who failed to see their irony: namely that for a provincial university librarian the revolutions in social and sexual mores with which the decade was associated had not really happened. For optimists, the quasi-revolutionary riots of the students of Paris in 1968, and the imitation demos which led to long-haired students occupying university campuses in Britain, there was a feeling of freshness in the air. In an echo of the Communist Manifesto, Paul Johnson, the editor of the leftist weekly the *New Statesman*, hailed *les événements* in Paris as a New Dawn: 'For what is happening there is of great importance not only to France but to the world. To be there is a political education in itself, to watch the birth-pangs (perhaps, soon, the murder or even suicide) of a new approach to the organization of human societies.'[29]

That was how it seemed to an intelligent left-wing commentator in the summer of '68. 'Here in Britain', he said, 'we have a stagnant economy, in which university students are told we must develop horror weapons in the cause of the export trade, and workers are stampeded by ignorance and demagogy into howling abuse at an even more exploited section of the population, the blacks. No wonder young people look for a fourth choice: and in Paris, it seems to me, they are beginning to find one.'[30]

It did not seem like that, however, to the majority of the English electorate. Perhaps dismayed by the stagnant economy, perhaps because they agreed with J. Enoch Powell's views of Pakistani and Indian immigrants, perhaps because they wanted to signal their instinctive feelings about inflammatory left-wingery such as was purveyed by the *New Statesman*, they voted Harold Wilson out, and the Conservatives returned to power on Waterloo Day, 1970.

PART FOUR

The 1970s

14

HeathCo

Alan Bennett's plays of this period captured the flavour of England being mysteriously lost. There is an atmosphere of inevitability about its dismantlement, and yet no one involved can completely understand why it has to be dismembered so fast, and so brutally. In *Habeas Corpus*, which opened at the Lyric Theatre on 10 May 1973 with Alec Guinness as the pathetic down-at-heel doctor who can't stop fumbling with the female patients, many of the familiar Bennett figures and themes were aired. The chorus was the charwoman, Mrs Swabb, originally played by Patricia Hayes, whose rendition of comical working-class characters became famous on television, and which belonged to a tradition of humour going back to Dickens. These women themselves, who were to provide Bennett with much of his stock in trade over the next thirty years, were part of the obsolescence. Their very names – Elsie, Edna, Hilda, Ena, Minnie – were passing out of use. *Habeas Corpus* was a bedroom farce in which otherwise respectable men found themselves running about on stage with no trousers on. The characters are all imprisoned in unsatisfactory bodies, or bodies which make unwanted jokes out of their lives. Wicksteed's sister Connie feels cheated by life because she is flat-chested, and much of the plot hinges on her ordering 'falsies'. The randy old men and the sex-starved middle-aged are almost wistful in their repeated allusions to the Permissive Society. Mrs Swabb, the expert, says, 'Me, I don't bother with sex. I leave that to the experts.' The play is a comedy, but it isn't without its message. Lady Rumpus, the colonial widow whose return to the old country sparks off the farcical train of the play's events, says, 'From end to end I've searched the land looking for a place where England is still England.'

Wicksteed exclaims, 'And now she's hit on Hove.'[1] John Osborne had entered comparable territory over the last decade or two of plays. Bennett's TV dramas unearthed a host of emotionally undernourished lives, but at the back of the story there was always this sense which Lady Rumpus had given off. That England was vanishing. The play in which this notion was given its best airing in Bennett's work was *Forty Years On*, whose first performance was given at the Apollo Theatre on 31 October 1968, with John Gielgud as the headmaster and Alan Bennett himself as a junior master called Tempest.

The occasion is the headmaster's last term at Albion House, a public school on the South Downs, a place whose proud traditions have descended into absurdity, and whose very future existence is in question. 'Albion' is, in the last strains of the drama, let out. 'A valuable site at the cross-roads of the world. At present on offer to European clients. Outlying portions of the estate already disposed of to sitting tenants. Of some historical and period interest. Some alterations and improvements neces-sary.'[2] If the allegory seems a bit heavy when read, it had a tremendous impact upon stage not only in its first West End run, but in its revivals. Bennett was one of those Englishmen intensely conservative in everything but politics. He was more than a little in love with Albion House, its arcane traditions, its unswervingly traditionalist, and on the edge of kinky, headmaster. The drama consists of a play within a play in which a more liberal master, Franklin, puts on a school play lampooning the traditional British readings of the First and Second World Wars, and of heroes such as Lawrence of Arabia. ('Speaking fluent Sanskrit he and his Arab body servant, an unmade Bedouin of great beauty, had wreaked havoc among the Turkish levies.'[3]) Yet there was a deep nostalgia in the play. The audi-ences who piled in to laugh at Bennett's jokes were as often conservative as they were revolutionaries. It captured the mood, as did the cartoon strip in *Private Eye* about England having been turned into a thrusting new company called HeathCo, of wistfulness about what was being thrown away.

'I do not suppose,' Lady Dorothy Macmillan remarked in the early 1960s, 'anyone realizes the overwhelming regard and affection my husband has for Mr Heath.' Many Tories shared Macmillan's high regard for this very competent Chief Whip, which was why, in their new system of choosing a party leader – election by fellow MPs – he comfortably beat his two rivals, after the resignation of Alec Douglas-Home. The votes were 150 for Heath, 133 for Reginald Maulding and 15 for J. Enoch Powell.

Of the three candidates, Powell was obviously the most inclined towards monetarism. But of the two candidates who had stood any chance of winning, Heath was the more right wing. That is, he stood for limiting the power of the trades unions, controlling inflation by interest rate rises, and pursuing the goal of joining the European Economic Community. (Being pro-Europe was right wing in those days.) Heath's voting record in the Commons was eloquent: on 13 December 1964 he abstained during the Abolition of Capital Punishment Bill. On 2 March 1965 he voted *for* Sir Cyril Osborne's bill to halt Commonwealth immigration; on 26 May 1965 he voted *against* Leo Abse's bill to implement the Wolfenden proposals, allowing consensual homosexual acts for men aged over twenty-one.[4] Moreover, Heath, with his non-public school background, would surely appeal to the wider electorate? He came from Broadstairs in Kent, where his enterprising father had risen from being a carpenter to running his own small firm, W. G. Heath, Builder and Decorator.[5] When still an undergraduate, at Balliol College, Oxford, he consulted the young Arnold Goodman, then working as a solicitor for Royalton Kisch, who had a seaside house near Broadstairs where he had employed W. G. Heath, about the possibility of suing the student paper the *Isis* for referring to his father as 'a jobbing builder'. This prickliness was kept well concealed, however. (Goodman, of course, dissuaded him from suing.) At Oxford, where he had been a music scholar, he excelled; he was President of the Union, and he later had a good, if slightly uneventful war, rising to be a colonel in the Royal Artillery. Thereafter, he had a number of occupations, including news editor of the *Church Times*, and a half-hearted attempt to work in a merchant bank.

Undoubtedly, he won the 1970 election (having lost the election of 1966) because of the association of the Conservative Party with Enoch Powell. No doubt Heath was genuinely repelled by racialist sentiments, but this cunning ex-Chief Whip knew that, after he had sacked Powell from the Shadow Cabinet in 1968, there were still very many Tories in the country at large who agreed with the Wolverhampton Prophet's views on immigration, and many backbench Tory MPs also. *Private Eye*'s cover for 16 April 1968 had a photograph of the unmarried Heath, a bubble coming from his mouth to say, 'Enoch may be talking balls, ducky, but there's no denying he's a vote catcher.'

Heath had been an assiduous Chief Whip, and as the old order of Macmillan and Home gave place to a more socially inclusive Conservative Party, he seemed an adventurous, unstuffy choice of pugilist to pit against the cleverness of Harold Wilson. If one Prime Minister, from the eleven Prime Ministers in our times, had a claim to have made an historic step, it was Edward Heath. He is the one out of the eleven without whom the history of our times would have been very distinctly different. He could easily have lost the leadership contest, and the Conservative Party could have been led by the lazy, genial slightly Eurosceptic Reggie Maudling, who would never have had the energy or political courage to push through Britain's entry to the EEC. Equally, Heath could have lost the election in 1970, in which case Harold Wilson, with his eye on the Eurosceptic left in his own party, would probably not have ventured entry either. As Hugo Young said in his magisterial history of Britain and Europe, from Churchill to Blair, *This Blessed Plot*, 'The most qualified "European" in Tory politics assumed the leadership of Britain at the time when the question of entry to Europe was ready for its final resolution.'[6] Yet, having negotiated British entry to Europe, Heath presided over a calamitous administration which was defeated humiliatingly, not by another party, but by the National Union of Mineworkers, whom he had challenged to a political contest not of its nor the nation's choosing. In a short spell in office, he reversed all the economic ambitions with which he had set out when he entered Number 10. He was cursed with very bad luck – above all the descent of the Irish situation from one of periodic violence to near civil war. At the end of his time he watched the price of oil rise as the result of a Middle Eastern war. But the worst of his fortunes was to have been born with his character – stubborn, and weirdly disengaged. So, although he was an honourable man and – unlike his successors in the role – never 'briefed' against Cabinet colleagues whom he did not like, he was incapable of geniality, feigned or otherwise. After the humiliations of the first 1974 election, for example, when he summoned his Cabinet (or ex-Cabinet), he had no word of encouragement for them or thanks for their support. 'In the Cabinet he would sit there glowering and saying practically nothing', remembered one colleague.[7] His 'outlets' were sailing and music, to both of which he devoted himself with a competitive fervour, though quite with whom the competition was being waged it was never clear. He was a world-class yachtsman, and it was typical of the man's defiant attitude to his snobbish critics that he chose to call his yacht *Morning Cloud* – the second word of which he always impenitently pronounced Clyeowd. It cost £7,450, a tidy sum for an MP with no private income, and with it he won the Sydney–Hobart Race and the Admiral's Cup. The second *Morning Cloud* was even bigger (it had a crew of eight) and even more expensive, competing honourably, though not winning, in the Fastnet Race. 'It was an unprecedented feat for a serving Prime Minister to have captained his national team in an international sporting event, let alone won it,' wrote his biographer John Campbell.[8] *Morning Cloud III*, a yet bigger yacht, was capsized near the Isle of Wight by two freak waves. Two of the crewmen were lost. It was an example of the capricious misfortune which dogged Heath, in politics, as in life.

His musical talent was, like his ability to sail, quite beyond the amateur average, but here, once again, the way he exercised that talent was devoid of charm. Each year at his constituency of Broadstairs he would conduct the Christmas carols. André Previn invited him to conduct a piece for a London Symphony Orchestra concert. Heath chose Elgar's 'Cockaigne' overture. Some musicians doubted whether he fully understood what was involved in conducting symphonic music – that is, mastering simultaneously all the musical parts and following them in the score. Heath's 'conducting' looked like a man merely waving his arms about while the players embarrassedly played the Elgar piece, waiting for Previn to return to the podium and conduct the Sibelius Violin Concerto. Heath devoted just one hour to rehearsing the performance, having had a two-hour Cabinet meeting on the morning of the concert and Prime Minister's Questions in the Commons. Yet his own memory was:

> I realized how fully the orchestra, together and as individuals, were responding to me. I felt I could do almost anything I wanted with them. Behind me, the concentration of the audience was intense. They, too, would follow wherever we led . . .[9]

The megalomaniac illusion of control, while actually failing to engage with the way the players were actually regarding him, is a metaphor for his life as a public servant. *Private Eye* snootily dubbed him The Grocer, presumably because he seemed to these public school boys like a man behind a shop counter as he told the nation about the likely effect of Europeanisation on the price of British bacon or cheese. But as so often Auberon Waugh's Swiftian cruelty touched the nerve of truth:

> Grocer, as anyone who has ever stood within ten yards of him will know perfectly well, is not human at all. He is a wax-work. Many are even beginning to suspect as much from watching his television appearances.
>
> This is the secret of the amazingly unattractive blue eyes, the awful, stretched waxy grin, the heaving shoulders and the appalling suntan.
>
> Even scientists now admit that something has gone wrong with the pigmentation . . . The stark truth now appears. Grocer the waxwork, like Frankenstein's monster before him, has run amok.[10]

The waxwork-quality of Heath, quite as much as his unmarried status, led to inevitable ribaldry whenever the question of his emotional or erotic preferences were discussed. Sub-editors no doubt deliberately introduced double entendres into a headline for a story concerning the night-time predatory prowls of homosexual parliamentarians on Hampstead Heath: MPs USE HEATH FOR SEX. The image of the waxwork being involved in actual sexual encounters would have been comic even before he turned into the obese, seemingly immortal curmudgeon of his many years on the back benches of the House of Commons. Inevitably, there was the suggestion that, at some earlier stage, he had been sexually active. Brian Coleman, a Conservative member of the London executive in the early twenty-first century, and himself a homosexual, claimed, in an article in the *New Statesman* of April 2007, that it was 'well known' in gay circles that Heath 'managed to obtain the highest office of state after he was supposedly advised to cease his cottaging activities in the Fifties when he became a Privy Councillor'. There was the inevitable huffing and puffing in response to this, with Ted Heath's successor as MP for Bexley and Sidcup, Derek Conway, saying, a little sadly, 'Ted was absolutely wedded to politics. He didn't have a great deal of personal companionship in his life but there are people who are capable of getting on with their lives without companionship.'

We shall probably never know for certain whether Ted Heath ever went cottaging, or ever had a companion. Though the only unmarried Prime Minister of our times, he is not the only one of whom the 'urban myth' does the rounds that he was a secret homosexual. Of Macmillan, it was always said that he was homosexual without completely realising it, and although this is a baffling analysis it makes sense of some of his more peculiar marital and political shifts and sways. Of at least two other Prime Ministers homosexual rumours abound. Of one it is said that he was arrested during his early career for 'cottaging', and having tried to give his two middle names to the police, rather than the surname, he was rescued from further embarrassment by a senior colleague. It is impossible to know if this is true or 'urban myth'. Of the other Prime Minister it has been said that he had a homosexual life as a student at university. If so, his friends were remarkably discreet about it afterwards. Whatever the truth of these things, it is a testimony to the fact that although Gay Pride marched every year in London, there were still many homosexuals in Britain at the end of our times who remained 'in the closet', and this was as true of politicians as of the rest of the population. If it is true that Heath and another, younger, Prime Minister, had both indulged in the cottaging habit, it would require the pen of Joe Orton to envisage the scene in the public lavatory in which they fortuitously might have met one another.

The character of politicians is as important as the ideals for which they claim to stand. In Heath's case, this was abundantly true, since the strategies and policies with which he earnestly set out in 1970 were all abandoned as soon as he encountered difficulties or opposition. It is not unfair to assume, as all primitive and myth-guided peoples have assumed, that bad luck itself is, as in the case of the prophet Jonah, a personal characteristic which men carry with them. No one suggests that Edward Heath wanted to lose his brilliant Chancellor of the Exchequer, Ian Macleod. Yet within five weeks of taking office, Macleod died of a heart attack. Thereafter, the nation's economic affairs were placed into the unwilling hands of the balding, dithering Anthony Barber, who seemed like a man playing the vicar in a suburban amateur dramatics society. It can hardly have been the case that the fortunes of Heath and his

'All political careers end in failure,' said J. Enoch Powell. But not that of the Rev. Ian Paisley, the only modern European to found both a church and a political party and to remain in charge of both until his dotage.

Dad's Army presented a reassuring self-image to the British of their semi-heroic, semi-comic past.

Germaine Greer's *The Female Eunuch* was a book which revolutionized the lives of millions of women.

Joe Orton's plays brilliantly succeeded in shocking the bourgeoisie, but left little trace.

Harold Wilson's failure to solve the Rhodesian crisis (he is pictured here with rebel Rhodesian Prime Minister Ian Smith) had disastrous consequences for the future of Africa.

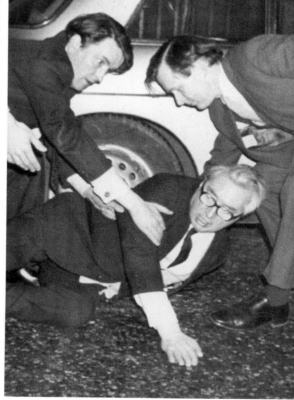

The Labour Foreign Secretary George Brown could guarantee happy work for cartoonists, headline writers and newspaper photographers as he staggered from one farce to the next.

The attempt by Jeremy Thorpe (*above*) to get rid of his former lover Norman Scott (*below left*) landed him in the dock of the Old Bailey. The emotional preferences of Ted Heath (*below right*) remained more mysterious. Here he appears to be greeting fellow sailors.

The horrifying crimes of the Moors Murderers, seen here leaving Chester Crown Court on 7 May 1966, shocked the world.

The Yorkshire Ripper, Peter Sutcliffe, eluded detection for years until he was found to possess a faulty vehicle licence.

The Earl of Longford, as a devout Christian, wanted Myra Hindley to be forgiven and pornography to be eliminated.

Margaret Thatcher's popularity on the world stage was reflected in her sunny relationship with President Ronald Reagan.

At home, Thatcher's policies caused violent dissension. Here miners' President Arthur Scargill is seen at a heavily policed picket. Below, Brixton in South London was aflame with riot. Here is a burnt-out pub after the second night of violence.

Nice Mr Major, and his even nicer wife, Norma, on the steps of Number Ten Downing Street.

Major's government was marred by Tory sleaze. Jeffrey Archer's performance on the stage of the Haymarket Theatre was as unconvincing as the various perjuries for which he was eventually sent to prison. Archer (*right*) is seen here with that much better actor Edward Petherbridge.

The murder of Stephen Lawrence was not only shocking in itself, but demonstrated the extent of violent racism on the South London streets and ingrained racialist attitudes in the Metropolitan Police Force.

Five youths accused of murdering Stephen Lawrence escaped prosecution in court, but failed to respond to the open accusation in the *Daily Mail*'s single-word headline: MURDERERS.

government depended entirely upon the skills of Macleod. There was no shortage of clever Cabinet ministers and civil servants working in Heath's administration. Nor on any logical level can the death of one man be an excuse for a whole government's absolute lack of willpower when confronted with the problems of the economy and industrial relations. Other external events, most notably in Ireland, would have knocked the stuffing out of many administrations, and certainly helped to deflect Heath from the course he had set himself before he was elected.

Yet in one area he would not be deflected, and it is to Heath that Britain owes, for better or for worse, its membership of the Common Market, as it was called then, the European Union as it became.

Membership was negotiated slowly and painfully after the rejection by General de Gaulle. The British political negotiator, sitting in the position that Heath had occupied under Macmillan, was now Geoffrey Rippon and the civil servant, in a way the mastermind behind the whole story of Britain's membership of the European Community, was Con O'Neill. The story of our times so far has been of Britain having suffered two severe blows – economic ruin at the end of the Second World War and international humiliation after the failed invasion of Suez in 1956. These cataclysms left the British uncertain of their identity. In a crisis, British politicians, like headless chickens whose muscular spasms still allowed them to scuttle aimlessly around the farmyard, reacted in one of two preconditioned ways. Those on the left behaved as if they wanted to revert to the shared austerities of wartime and of Attlee's Britain. The solution to all problems was to make of Britain an ever-more welfare-dependent, high-spending socialist state, in which industrial problems, social problems, education and health were all the responsibility of politicians and Whitehall bureaucrats. The reaction of the other headless chicken, the Tory chicken, was to hope that somehow or another, in spite of every economic indicator to the contrary, Britain could continue to be a world power, perhaps by emphasising its continued friendship with the British Commonwealth, which to these patriots was the old Empire in all but name, and perhaps by some sort of satellite relationship with America.

The European option seemed to Heath, as to his seventy or so pro-European allies in the Labour Party, led by Roy Jenkins, a way out of this rather bleak impasse. Britain need not be an austerity socialist state, becoming poorer by the year; nor need she be a pathetic satellite of America. She could become, instead, a partner in the European experiment, a grown-up modern nation. The two aims of any government are to secure the safety, and the prosperity, of its citizens. British entry into the European Economic Community seemed, to the optimistic pro-Europeans, to offer a chance of both.

It is impossible to say, of course, how Britain would have fared if she had not joined the Market in 1970. There have undoubtedly been some economic mishaps along the road, most notably the decision in the Thatcher government to link the pound sterling to the Deutschmark at an unfavourable rate when they joined the Exchange Rate Mechanism. Poverty still existed in Britain at the end of our times, as at the beginning, but not on a scale which would have been recognised as grinding poverty by those who had lived in the 1930s. There has been no war between France and Germany. The peoples of Northern Europe have lived without the fear of invasion, aerial bombardment or financial ruin, which had been their regular lot in the first half of the twentieth century. To this extent, the European experiment surely looks like a success. Perhaps for this very reason, however, for the great majority of the British, as our times advanced, the European Union became an object of loathing, and this inevitably had its effect on Ted Heath's posthumous reputation. In season and out of season, the old man remained doggedly proud of his achievement.

Some of the terms on which Britain entered were, even by the testimony of the most ardent Europhiles, 'disastrous'.[11] Of this the most conspicuous disaster perhaps was to sign up to the Common Fisheries Policy. By redefining what had hitherto been regarded as British waters, the negotiators did not merely put a lot of British fishermen out of business. They intruded upon something deeper. The water which surrounded the British archipelago was a friend as well as a guardian. To many British people, it felt like an ally against Britain's enemies. It was the element which had destroyed the Spanish Armada in its storms, and, in its calm, had allowed the 'little boats' to relieve the marooned British troops from the beach at Dunkirk in 1940.

Such was Heath's zeal to join the European Economic Community at any cost that he failed to see the emblematic nature of the Fisheries Policy. Of course, it could be argued, as the chief negotiator, Con O'Neill, continued to argue for decades afterwards, that, given the complexities of the issue, British fishermen got terms which were 'reasonable, advantageous and not too onerous'.[12] But Con O'Neill was a bureaucrat. Heath, as a politician, might have been expected to see what psychological effect this would have. From the moment Heath put his signature to the Treaty of Rome, and Britain joined the Common Market on 1 January 1973, the Fisheries issue was emblematic. For, what, in joining the Community, had Britain done? The issue for Westminster politicians and London journalists at the time was almost entirely seen as an economic one. Would it be to Britain's economic advantage to join? And the answer to this, when due allowance had been made for the Commonwealth, was yes, it would be very much to her advantage, though the share of the Budget to which O'Neill and his friends committed Britain to paying was steep – 8.64 per cent in the first year, rising to a staggering 18.92 per cent in 1977. The Labour Party continued to believe that Europe was a capitalist, anti-socialist club. That was the sum of their hostility to the project. There was very little talk of the matter of which the Common Fisheries Policy is emblematic, of British sovereignty. The One Nation group of Tories in 1962 had published a pamphlet, *One Europe*, which was 'little short of a federalist tract'. It was edited by Nicholas Ridley, a passionate supporter at this stage, of a United Europe, and J. Enoch Powell never denied writing 25 per cent of this document, which advocated 'the full economic, military and political union of Europe'.[13]

Opinion will always be divided between those who thought that the Treaty of Rome made perfectly clear its ultimately federalist aims, and those who believed that Heath somehow managed to hoodwink the British people into signing away their sovereignty and birthright. Repetitions of this argument would occur later in the century whenever Britain was asked to ratify a piece of pan-European legislation. Margaret Thatcher, for example, after signing the Single European Act, claimed that she did so not realising what it had contained – a strange claim for one who, in her days as Education Secretary in Heath's Cabinet, had been the keenest of Europeans. It is, as Alice's White Queen remarked, a poor sort of memory which only works backwards. As Britain became more and more uncertain about the nature of its own identity, and as it in effect began to break up in the closing years of the twentieth century, the belief grew that it had been Europe who was to blame. Europe became the scapegoat for something which was actually happening within. And it was then that the Eurosceptic belief hardened that Heath was the architect of British dissolution. It was not how things appeared at the time.

Ireland, at that stage, dominated most British thoughts much more than the question of sovereignty. The violence in the province of Northern Ireland grew much worse in the Heath years. From 13 dead in 1969, and 25 in 1970, it became infinitely bloodier: 174 in 1971, 467 in 1972, 250 in 1973 and 216 in 1974. Heath and his Cabinet cannot be blamed for the jubilation which broke out among the Ulster Protestants when the Conservatives won the election, even though that was one factor which explained the escalation of the violence. The idle Home Secretary, Reggie Maudling, had probably spoken for England when, after his first visit to the province, he remarked, 'What a bloody awful country!' – but the attitude did nothing to bring peace to Northern Ireland.[14] *Private Eye*'s cartoonist John Kent always depicted Reggie wearing a nightshirt and nightcap, and usually asleep. Brian Faulkner, who succeeded James

Chichester-Clark as the Prime Minister of Northern Ireland, tried to build bridges with the Catholics by offering the SDLP seats on various committees at Stormont, the Northern Irish parliament. But he made the catastrophic mistake of introducing internment for IRA suspects: 2,400 of these republicans were arrested in the six months up to April 1972, two-thirds of whom were released without charge. The resentment caused by the injustice of internment was something felt to the end, and the Westminster government was slow off the mark in doing what should have been done years before – they abolished Stormont and introduced direct rule of the province from Westminster – but not before Belfast, Londonderry and Newry had become battlefields in which British troops fought with Irishmen armed with automatic rifles and gelignite bombs.

The worst, and most emblematic, day of the Troubles in Heath's time was probably Bloody Sunday, in Londonderry, 30 January 1972. Marches had been declared illegal in the province but the demonstrators defied the order, and thirteen of them were shot dead by paratroopers. It was this catastrophe which finally persuaded Heath that direct rule from Westminster was the only option. Heath had acted decisively, and the levels of violence did fall off very considerably. After the 467 who died in 1972, the 250 in 1973 and 216 who died in 1974, though shocking and terrible statistics, are improvements.

It is obviously no accident that those who came to see the European Union as a threat to Britain's identity or sovereign independence were the same journalists and diehard parliamentarians who also thought that Ulster could go on being part of the United Kingdom. The Union was sacred to the likes of J. Enoch Powell, who, after putting himself beyond the pale in Heath's Conservative government, joined the Ulster Unionists and became the Member for South Down in 1974, or to T. E. Utley and his acolytes on the *Daily Telegraph*. There was a certain intellectual romance in continuing to believe in the unity of the old Kingdoms, when that unity was being so violently contested on the streets of Ireland. The truth was all much more complicated than these Unionists wanted it to be. One truth which slowly dawned on Powell was that most Unionists in Northern Ireland were not Unionists at all. Paisley was, Powell said, a Protestant Sinn Feiner, and that judgement was shown to be prescient when, after a quarter of a century of denouncing the Roman Catholic Church and the Irish Republican Army, Paisley settled down at Stormont to form an administration with those old Republican rebels Martin McGuinness and Gerry Adams. True Unionists, those who wanted Ireland, or the six counties, to be truly a part of Britain, with the same status as Warwickshire, were very thin on the ground, as every election showed. The High Tory journalists and politicians who argued the

Unionist position were simply ignoring the wishes of those who were involved in the conflict – and 'those involved' included, very much against their will, the people of England, Wales and Scotland. The huge majority of these took Reggie Maudling's view of Ireland and wanted to be shot of the 'bloody awful country'. Although the Irish Republican Army, and their supporters in America, who by bankrolling the fighters with 'Noraid' perpetuated the slaughter for a quarter of a century, persisted in seeing the struggle as one between Irish Independence and British Imperialism, very few British people, apart from the ideologues of the press, wanted the Northern Ireland experiment (an expedient hastily devised in the 1920s to stop the Civil War) to continue in the 1970s and 1980s. This was not 'giving in to terrorism'; it was simply what most people wanted. The bonds which held the peoples of the United Kingdom together were loosening, and the Irish story was helping them to loosen. Whether the 5.5 million Scots and 2.75 million Welsh wanted independence, or simply a little more say in their own affairs, without the patronage of being governed through a Welsh Office and a Scottish Office in London, was a matter which the unfolding decades might reveal. But as the century petered out, it was possible to see that all Britons had become uncertain of their own identity and that these movements for independence on the Celtic fringes were only one symptom, the bloodiest of symptoms, of that uncertainty which characterised the collective British self-perception throughout our times. In 1978, the communist Tom Nairn wrote:

> There are those who believe that this rump of the former empire will last forever, in an essentially unchanging evolution. Their number includes virtually all England, and a still formidable mass of allies in Scotland, Wales and Northern Ireland. On the other hand stands the growing opposition – within sight of being a majority in Scotland – which accepts the verdict a great part of the outside world passed on Britain long ago: that it is a matter of time before it founders. Its post-empire crisis is long overdue, and not even to be regretted.[15]

The paradox is that many of the keenest supporters of British membership of the European Community, as it would become, would probably have agreed with this analysis in its broad outline, even if they considered its stridency childish. Those who voted for Heath, and those who initially liked what he was doing, rejoiced at his apparent abolition of 'Butskellism' and his embrace of the modern. Reporting on his first speech as Prime Minister to the Party Conference at Blackpool in October 1971, Jean Campbell wrote for the *Evening Standard*, 'It was aggressive Toryism at last. A far cry from the defensive Toryism of Rab Butler which had shared room and board with Socialism for the last 22 years. Heath was pulling down the Butler boarding house . . . Instead he plans to build a skyscraper with self-operating lifts. When the speech ended the crowd went wild, and being accustomed to American conventions, I know a happy crowd when I see one.'[16]

Very typical of Heath's modernity, his skyscraper, was the decision to reorganise local government and to abolish many of the ancient counties of England. This was accomplished by a Heathite 'whizzkid'[17] named Peter Walker, who sought to rationalise what Heath's faithful biographer John Campbell scornfully calls 'the traditional patchwork of counties, county boroughs, on-county boroughs, rural and urban district councils and parish councils' . . . whose 'boundaries no longer reflected realities and some smaller counties were clearly unviable'.[18] So, away went Rutland and all the Welsh counties. Hereford was 'merged' with Worcestershire. Wales was carved up into districts, some with the names of ancient kingdoms which non-Welsh speakers have difficulty in pronouncing (Dyfed, Clwyd, Gwynedd). Away went the Assize Courts, and the judges' lodgings. In came supposedly more efficient County Courts. The ancient drama of the judge arriving in the county town with his clerk and hearing the most serious cases was removed. 'And where on earth is Avon?' asked Betjeman. Another bit of old England was lost.

The government of Heath came unstuck because of the trades unions. The historian Robert Blake mercilessly stated in *The Conservative Opportunity*, 'The Cabinet began with the intention of "getting government off people's backs", but, lacking any clear intellectual mandate to do so, somehow ended with an even larger number of public employees in the non-productive sector than ever before. It began with a determination to abandon lame ducks and avoid all forms of intervention in wage-fixing, but it ended by capitulating to the sit-in at Upper Clyde Shipbuilders and by trying to impose the most complete statutory wage policy ever attempted.'[19] This supposedly right-wing government had spent on average more than 30 per cent each year than the previous Labour government.

The volte-face over wages came about because Heath was unable to bring in the necessary legislation to curb the power of trades unions. He tried to do so.

Then, in October 1973, came the Yom Kippur War, followed by an oil embargo, and a fourfold increase in oil prices. It was the last piece of misfortune to assail the beleaguered Heath. A month after the war, the National Union of Mineworkers voted for a large wage increase – understandably enough since inflation was soaring, and retail prices alone had risen 10 per cent in the previous four weeks. The very men who might be able to help the country through the fuel crisis were set upon destroying it. On 13 December Colonel Heath declared that in order to save fuel, the country must be put upon a three-day week. In the weeks before Christmas, the country was cast into darkness, with electricity switched off and fuel supplies limited. It really felt as if the country, far from being in a state of temporary crisis, might have actually come to an end. Heath supposed that the miners were being influenced by their communist vice president Mick McGahey, rather than their rather right-wing President Joe Gormley. Sensing, probably wrongly, that the miners were attempting to make political capital out of the fuel crisis, and to bring down the elected government, Heath petulantly called an election in February 1972, with the single campaign slogan – 'Who governs?' The electorate were not sure of the answer to this question, but they had already seen who wasn't governing, or at least who wasn't governing very well. In spite of opinion polls assuring the public that the Conservatives were in the lead, the votes were inconclusive. The result was that although the Tories won more votes than Labour (just), the Labour Party won four more seats – Labour 301 and Conservative 297. There followed a humiliating farce in which Heath refused to concede defeat in the election, and walled himself up in Downing Street. Adding to the air of absurdity on one of the news bulletins that day, a large van arrived at the door of Number 10 to deliver a gargantuan quantity of lavatory paper; clearly the delivery was coincidental, but it suggested a determination by the Prime Minister to dig in for the long siege, and the inescapable mental image of his bulky, pink form seated on the lavatory and making use of the infinite rolls of Andrex did not endear him to the electorate. He tried to persuade the leader of the Liberal Party to come into the government. The Liberals had won fourteen seats and if they threw their vote behind the Conservatives there would still have been a chance of defeating the Socialists. But although tempted, the Liberal leader, Jeremy Thorpe, could not persuade his party, and so the three and a half years of HeathCo came to a humiliating end. His bitterness never abated, nor did the determination of his party to distance themselves from his mistakes.

It was at the Council of Clermont in November 1095 that Pope Urban II first made his announcement that the Christian West should march to the rescue of the beleaguered Christian East and the First Crusade had begun. A comparable moment in the history of monetarism occurred when Sir Keith Joseph addressed the Conservatives of Preston on 5 September 1974 with the message which he had only lately discovered for himself. The title of the speech, which was a rallying cry to free marketeers everywhere, was 'Inflation is caused by Governments' . . . 'Inflation is threatening to destroy our society . . . The distress and unemployment that will follow unless the trend is stopped will be catastrophic.'[20]

The doctrine to which Sir Keith Joseph had been converted was that it was not enough for governments to try to abate inflation by incomes policy if they themselves were not bold enough to switch off the tap: to stop printing more and more money, as successive 'consensus' British governments since the Second World War had tried to do. J. Enoch Powell had been preaching this doctrine for years and he remarked somewhat sourly, 'I have heard of death-bed repentance. Perhaps it would be more appropriate to refer to post-mortem repentance.'[21]

The words of the speech in Preston were spoken by Joseph, but they had been written by an in some ways unlikely friend, Alfred Sherman. Whereas Keith Joseph, the son of a Lord Mayor of London, had been brought up in the height of luxury in the house formerly belonging to the author of *Little Lord Fauntleroy*, and educated at Harrow, Sherman came from the East End, was an alumnus of Hackney Downs County Secondary, and had followed the Red Brigades to Spain. Yet it was Sherman who convinced Joseph that 'Keynes is dead. Dead.' An associate of Sherman's, who would play a vital role in the future of British Conservatism, was a businessman called John Hoskyns, one of the first to exploit the commercial potential of computers.

The monetarists took the view, which events would seem to have borne out in the late 1970s, that unless something were done to curb succeeding governments' lust for printing money, Britain would be bankrupted. They had arrived, to use the immodest but accurate title of Hoskyns's autobiography, *Just in Time*.

15

Women's Liberation

In June and July 1971, Court Two of the Old Bailey was thronged to witness the trial of Richard Neville, who had founded *Oz* magazine while a student at the University of New South Wales, and relaunched it in 1966, Jim Anderson, a former lawyer from Sydney, and Felix Dennis, an Englishman.[1] The previous year the three had published *Oz 28, the 'School Kids' Issue'*. The cover showed four naked females entwined in lesbian embrace, and with rats' tails dangling from their vaginas. The editorial content was largely written by appallingly self-important schoolchildren, and, as has been written, 'their juvenilia sits uneasily among adverts for penis magnifiers, "massagers" [dildoes], leather posing-pouches and Swedish porn books, magazines and films'.[2] At the end of a three-week trial, Neville was sentenced to fifteen months, with recommended deportation, Anderson to twelve months and Dennis to nine months. These sentences were squashed upon appeal, heard before the Lord Chief Justice, Lord Widgery.

Whereas the *Chatterley* trial had been about a book which was written with serious intentions, the *Oz* trial was a test of how far society had come to accept sexual liberation, and an abandonment of traditional restraints. The *Oz* defendants were charged with an offence which had not been used by prosecutors for 130 years: 'conspiracy to debauch and corrupt the morals of children and young persons within the realm and to arouse and implant in their minds lustful and perverted desires'. This had, in one sense, been the intention of the magazine, with its childishly priapic depiction of Rupert Bear. But the trial was memorable because it reminded many newspaper readers, who had not hitherto heard of *Oz* and would have been displeased by it, that they no longer quite knew how to define good and evil. The three young scallywags were defended by John Mortimer QC, an Old Harrovian with a high, drawly camp voice, but of heterosexual disposition, whose successful career as a barrister paralleled one as a middlebrow playwright. During the trial, Mortimer, in the words of Noel Annan, 'put forward three astonishing arguments. It was not possible, he said, to be a writer if you were prevented from exploring any area of human activity; obscenity could not be identified; and it was good for us all to be nauseated and outraged by what we saw and read – regardless apparently of the nature of the outrage.'[3]

Mortimer, whose pudgy expression and always dribbling lips, even in middle age seemed like an embodiment of moral as well as physical dilapidation, became one of those broadcasters who was everyone's darling – largely because of a successful TV drama series about an idealised version of himself at the bar – *Rumpole of the Bailey*. It would be possible to see Mortimer, and the gallery of witnesses he assembled as witnesses for the defence of *Oz* – such as Kenneth Tynan and George Melly – as similar demonstrations of the collapse of Western morals. Certainly, it is difficult to imagine any other society, at any other period of history, being presented with the arguments which Mortimer advanced in defence of the *School Kids' Issue of Oz* and taking them seriously. To that extent the trial was an emblem of 'something rotten in the state'. The actual participants, however, are not worth dignifying with the charge that they actually, in their own persons, changed anything. They were symptoms, not causes. Melly, another figure like Mortimer, who was depressing not because he was immoral but because he was second-rate (his particular area of non-expertise being jazz), continued to make gallant efforts to show off and shock people until he died. In case you did not get the message that he was unconventional, he wore scarlet trilby hats, and suits which would have been garish if sported by circus clowns. His only real distinction had occurred early in life, at Stowe School, Buckinghamshire, when he had been briefly fancied by the future journalistic genius Peregrine Worsthorne. 'The alternative society,' droned Melly from the witness box, 'is one that tries to invent or evolve its own lifestyle, which is usually in opposition to the official lifestyle.'[4] Hindsight makes not only these figures seem like clowns, but so, alas, also those who opposed them. Whereas Mortimer and his would-be bohemian, largely public school educated friends had made fools of themselves in the eyes of the intelligent majority by their behaviour in the Old Bailey, so too had those who defended 'the official lifestyle'. Lord Longford's Christian faith led him to conduct an inquiry into pornography, in which, poor old donkey, he led his researchers into striptease joints and brothels in several European capitals. (What had he *expected* to find in the Copenhagen red-light district?) His campaign against filth linked him up with some strange companions, such as Mary Whitehouse of the National Viewers and Listeners Association (founded 1965), a bustling, busy woman whose grin was rendered mirthless by too large false teeth, and whose obsession with rude words or suggestiveness in broadcasts were just as prurient, and no less offensive, than Neville's in the *School Kids' Issue*. She was dishonest, too, never fully admitting that all her lawsuits and campaigns were funded by Moral Rearmament. How else could the modest housewife and former schoolmarm, as she liked to present herself, have been able to bring expensive court cases, such as her ludicrous prosecution of *Gay News* for Blasphemous Libel in 1977? Moral Rearmament came back in 1971 under the new name of the Nationwide Festival of Light, and on the platform in Trafalgar Square was to be seen not only Whitehouse and Longford, but also that former Diogenes, the arch-mocker Muggeridge, who was, from now onwards, to the bewilderment of his old friends, seen as a sort of secular friar – Saint Mugg. His old friend Anthony Powell bemusedly examined a book published in 1987 called *My Life in Pictures* by Muggeridge. 'There is nothing against publishing 138 representations of oneself (Malcolm pondering on his own bust counting as two) in the interests of publicity, nor spending some hours of one's own time in prayer and meditation. What is hard on the reader is all the sanctimonious stuff about Christianity, RC conversion and Love of the Human Race, being exchanged by Malcolm for his former preoccupation with the world of Power, when a book of this self-promotional kind is purely an expression of one form of power: while should it really be necessary to be *photographed* praying and meditating, for the benefit of the public, especially if the material world has been forsworn?'[5]

The few show-offs on both sides of the argument about the Permissive Society were the sorts of people who would have been playing to the gallery at any era in history. At this particular moment, Melly and Mortimer were showing off that they had broader minds than anyone else (the slightly odious implication always being, especially in Mortimer's case, that they were nicer, too), and the Muggeridge–Whitehouse–Longford brigade quite literally advertising that they were holier than others. But the background of all this was a set of circumstances which was bound to have caused a 'sexual revolution'. That is: politics had quietened down and there was no longer any danger of a European war. There were more young men about whose primary concern could be chasing girls, not jobs, and being in no danger of having their amorous exploits interrupted by the recruiting sergeant. That hadn't happened in England since the eighteenth century. In addition to leisure and prosperity had to be added the quite extraordinary revolution in the lives of women, caused by improvement in obstetric techniques and the invention of oral contraceptives.

The improvement in medical care, and in general prosperity, during our times was reflected in the infant mortality rates. In 1945–49 the average rate of infant mortality in England and Wales was 39.2 per thousand, compared with 156 per thousand for the last decade of Queen Victoria's reign. By 1965–69, this had sunk to 18.5.[6] Until the mid-1970s all social policies assumed the dependency of a woman upon a man, but this was to change, with a number of legislative measures changing the status of women. The Equal Pay Act of 1970 was brought into force on 1 January 1976. This did not mean an instantaneous equality in the workplace. In 1970, women's pay was some 65.4 per cent, rising to 75.7 per cent in 1977, falling back again the following year, as male employers redefined women's jobs and downgraded their women employees.[7] Nevertheless, the Equal Pay Act was in place, and, gradually, women could regard themselves as the economic equals of males in society. The contraceptive pill had, at least theoretically, helped to make women more independent about their life choices. It was under the Conservatives, and at the behest of Keith Joseph, that the Pill became available on the National Health Service after a major parliamentary row over 'immorality at the taxpayers' expense'.[8] In fact, Joseph introduced free contraception for the very poor, and levied a normal prescription charge for the rest. The cost of the measure was £13 million. He was not moved by the arguments of some Catholic MPs that free contraception would lead to greater immorality; 'loose and casual people are not made loose and casual by the availability of contraceptives, whether free or for 20p'. For Joseph, the real problem was to 'break the cycle of deprivation' of which unwanted children were one manifestation.[9]

Birth control was a central political and social issue. The economy now depended upon mothers of young children being able to leave their children in someone else's care while they went out to paid work. Between 1971 and 1976 the proportion of children under five who spent time apart from their mothers rose from one child in six to one in four. The Education Secretary under Heath, Margaret Thatcher, made it her target in 1972 to provide 15 per cent full-time education for three- and four-year-olds, and part-time education for 35 per cent of three-year-olds, and 75 per cent of four-year-olds within a decade. These targets were never met, but they show that although the Conservatives continued to say that they were the party of the family, they did not wish to encourage mothers to stay at home and be mothers. The Conservative Sue McCowan admitted in 1975 that the result was 'latchkey children, truancy and juvenile crimes'. The previous year, Keith Joseph's expressed belief that too many poor mothers were breeding unfit children was deemed to be out of kilter with the benevolent spirit of the age.

'The balance of our population, our human stock, is threatened . . . A high and rising proportion of children are being born to mothers least fitted to bring children into the world and bring them up . . . Some are of low intelligence, most of low educational attainment. They are unlikely to be able to give children the stable emotional background, the consistent combination of love and firmness, which are more important than riches. They are producing problem children . . . Yet these mothers, the under-20s in many cases, single parents, from classes four to five, are now producing a third of all births.' This speech was followed by the predictable response in the newspapers: 'SIR KEITH IN STOP BABIES SENSATION'. A Labour MP glossed Joseph's solution to the problems facing society as 'castrate or conform'. Yet the children in Joseph's speech existed, even though he was challenged about his statistics. No one who chronicled the development of that generation over the next thirty years could deny that Joseph had been right to express his concern. After all, he was the Secretary of State for Social Services, and he was speaking to his brief.[10] But though he was undoubtedly right to draw attention to the rise, proportionately, of those in the lower intelligence and income ranges, there were also major changes taking place in the lives of women higher up the scale. If the stupidity and fecundity of the proles gave rise to appropriate concern in Whitehall, family life itself was changed more radically by the enterprise and cleverness of women who were not prepared to devote the best years of their life as housewives and nursery maids. The truth was that the values espoused by the Conservatives, more than those of the left, were doing damage to the traditional, basic structure of the family, in which the father was the breadwinner and the woman took charge of housework and child-minding. The Equal Opportunities Commission, whose Deputy Chairwoman was Elspeth Howe, another Conservative lady, admitted in 1978, 'The traditional single-role family, where the wife stayed at home and the husband went to work, is disappearing. As a society, we are right to worry about what is happening to women as they struggle to carry the double burden of their traditional duties and their role as workers.'[11]

If the aims of feminism had once been to allow women to pursue jobs, as well as be housewives and have babies, then it seemed as if the forces of the marketplace, the sheer need to pay bills, was bringing about the revolution which had in previous generations been a theoretical dream. In the early 1970s, when feminists spoke of 'liberation', it might have seemed, both to feminists and to the men who feared their progress, as if a campaign was being artificially waged to achieve their objectives. With hindsight, it perhaps seemed as if feminism had been the inevitable social and economic consequence of more efficient birth control, and the economic necessity, in many families, of young mothers seeking paid employment outside the home. In such a climate, it would have become inevitable that society would have changed, without the feminist prophets cheering on the sisterhood. In March 1971, between five hundred and a thousand women marched through a blizzard in London singing (with intended irony) 'Keep Young and Beautiful if You Want to Be Loved'. It was the first women's liberation demonstration in Britain, a rather tame affair compared with what was happening in the United States, with 50,000 women, in 1970, marching down Fifth Avenue in New York to commemorate the fiftieth anniversary of the Nineteenth Amendment (giving women the vote). The American songs were better too, such as:

> Oh do you remember Sweet Betsy the Dyke
> Who came from New Jersey on her motorbike,
> She rode across the country with her lover Anne,
> And said to all women, 'YOU KNOW THAT YOU CAN!'
> So leave all your menfolk and come on with us.
> If you don't have a cycle, we'll charter a bus.

American feminists were the first to popularise the notion that men could use their genitalia 'as a weapon to generate fear'.[12] 'Pornography is the theory and rape the practice' was another saying (by Robin Morgan) where, paradoxically enough, the vanguard of feminism met, if not exactly joining forces with, Lord Longford's campaign against pornography.

But for many women who grew up in the 1960s and 1970s, the totemic and life-changing figure was Germaine Greer.

The Female Eunuch was published in 1970. The author was a thirty-one-year-old lecturer at Warwick University. She claimed to be leading the second wave of feminism. The first was for parliamentary suffrage. 'Then genteel middle-class ladies clamoured for reform, now ungenteel middle-class women are calling for revolution.'[13]

As already indicated, the conditions in society were ripe for the feminist revolution. Economic circumstances would have demanded that more women, whether or not mothers, entered the workplace, and political and economic circumstances would have eventually determined that they were treated fairly and equally. But though an open door, it was not open very wide, and there can be no doubt that Greer's forceful heaves, and the eloquent way in which she skewered so many ancient male prejudices, had an explosive effect. Nothing was ever going to be completely the same after *The Female Eunuch*. She began with a bit of science, pointing out that of forty-eight chromosomes comprising a human individual, only one determines sex difference. In the short chapter on hair, she stated, 'Not so long ago Edmund Wilson could imply a deficiency in Hemingway's virility by accusing him of having crepe hair on his chest. The fact is that some men are hairy and some are not; some women are hairy and some are not . . . that most virile of creatures, the buck negro, had very little body hair at all.'[14] Greer devotes only an aside to the interesting question of female body-shaving: 'Men who do not want their women shaved and deodorized into complete tastelessness are powerless against women's own distaste for their bodies.' It is a very typical Greer sentence; while it registers disgust at men's arrogance, it exhibits as much contempt for women as it does for men. Did women shave or deodorise their bodies in order to please men, or to please themselves, or because they had been brainwashed by advertisers and cosmeticians? It would be interesting to know at what point during our times (and it surely was during our times) women began to shave their armpits. In communist countries, and sometimes in France, they continued to allow pubic hair to grow, even if it protruded from the bikini or swimsuit. In Terry Eagleton's *After Theory*, the post-Marxist professor wrote in 2003 that 'not all students are blind to the Western narcissism involved in working on the history of pubic hair while half the world's population lacks adequate sanitation and survives on less than two dollars a day'.[15] There are fifteen theses, at MA, M.Phil. or Ph.D. level, in the British Library database which include pubic hair in the title.[16] Whether they are as 'inconsequential' as the professor believes, one might take leave to doubt, since the question of *why* women shave their legs, armpits or pudenda, and whether this suggests, as Greer stated in 1970, 'women's own distaste for their own bodies', remains perhaps open. Much of the impact of Greer's classic was merely shock value: the Oz who dared to speak her mind when the Poms were too shy to talk about fucking or vaginas. 'Even the much-vaunted cervical smears are rarely given in our community. I first managed to get one when I went to the V.D. clinic in despair because my own doctor would not examine my vagina or use pathology to discover the nature of an irritation which turned out to be exactly what I thought it was.' These sentences in which the author puts her sex organs in the reader's excited face, while her brain outfizzed that of medical professionals, remained part of the ever-selling Germaine Greer formula for the next forty years. She wrote in the confidence that, although her doctor might have been too shy to look at her vagina, there would be many who would be only too happy to do so. But her lack of 'distaste', a favourite word, for her own body parts, was perhaps less feminist than simply Australian. Part of her success was to be built, as was that of her Cambridge-contemporary Oz, Clive James, playing up the Oz brashness for slightly more than it was worth, and then, to compensate, needing to remind the company that in spite of the directness of her approach, she was actually cleverer, and better read and more subtle-minded than her hearers, as well as infinitely less stuffy. (This, too, was very much Clive James's no less successful line of attack as he pursued the incompatible dual careers of polymath intellectual and cheeky chappy television chat-show host.)

These considerations aside, however, no history of our times would be complete without recognising the importance of *The Female Eunuch* as a liberating book. The exciting thing about it was not its appeal to violent radicalist feminists, but to the great majority of women, certainly those under fifty, who recognised the picture she drew of a paternalistic society, its conservative social stereotypes underpinned by the psychology of Freud, posited on the wish to subjugate and belittle half its population. 'Woman must have room and scope to devise a morality which does not disqualify her from excellence, and a psychology which does not condemn her to the status of a spiritual cripple.'[17] Writing six years before the enactment of the Equal Pay Bill, she pointed out that the average weekly pay for a woman in clerical or administrative work was £12 per week, compared with £28 per week for men in the same industries.

In her analysis of marriage, she seemed already, at thirty-one, to be writing herself out of the story of life-long relationships. 'Every wife who slaves to keep herself pretty, to cook her husband's favourite meals, to build up his pride and confidence in himself at the expense of his sense of reality, to be his closest and effectively his only friend, to encourage him to reject the consensus of opinion and find reassurance only in her arms is binding her mate to her with hoops of steel that will strangle them both.'[18] Many married couples would recognise the truth of her analysis. She punctured the 'middle-class myth of love and marriage' and mocked family life as 'mother duck, father duck, and all the little baby ducks'.[19] Many people of later decades, in the loneliness, exhaustion and poverty of bringing up children single-handed, might pine for the duck family and question Greer's adventurous assertion that 'there is no such thing as security'.[20]

Read at the time, *The Female Eunuch* felt like a liberation manual. Read with hindsight, its contextual and historical importance did not diminish, but its message seemed a little more blurred. Like revivalist evangelists, who depended upon their success in shattering the audience's sense of self-worth, in opening the sinner's soul to its need for redemption, Greer devoted the last third of her book to direct appeals to the feminine reader's heart. 'Women have very little idea of how much men hate them.'[21] Like the assertion that we are all sinners going to hell, it was not possible to prove or disprove. But here came a woman who had been vouchsafed a glimpse of the truth about life, illustrated with learned extracts from the Book of Genesis, Shakespeare's sonnets, and even contemporary songs. Bob Dylan was revealed as a woman hater every bit as noxious as John Milton. This last bit of Greer's book was the best. It assembled a great deal of evidence to illustrate misogyny, in literature, in medical practice, in the law, in common language and expressions. As always, her rhetorical tricks were as impressive as the range of examples she mustered. 'There are the cute animal terms like *chick*, *bird*, *kitten* and *lamb*, only a shade of meaning away from *cow*, *bitch*, *hen*, *shrew*, *goose*, *filly*, *bat*, *crow*, *heifer and vixen*, as well as the splendidly ambiguous expression *fox*, which emanates from the Chicago ghetto. The food terms lose their charm when we reflect how close they are to coarse terms like *fish*, *mutton*, *skate*, *crumpet* . . . Who likes to be called *dry-goods*, a *potato*, a *tomato*, or a *rutabaga?*'

Not many, one might conclude, but though most English-speakers in Britain have heard men and women use words such as cow and bitch to describe women, how many have ever heard or used the word tomato as a synonym of the feminine? It is a measure of how far and fast we all travelled in our times, however, that most of these synonyms had become obsolete by the end of the century, or if not obsolete, words such as *crumpet*, which were only to be used ironically. To refer to a woman as a *bird* by the end of our times would be as outmoded as to refer, as Greer does in the quotations from *The Female Eunuch* already cited, to the 'buck negro' or the 'cripple'.

At the end of her book, Greer would have convinced most dispassionate readers that the female sex had indeed been subjugated and humiliated in many subtle linguistic ways, and by the means of many quite crude religious and social structures which had by now become obsolete. She urged her female readers to *joy in the struggle*. 'Privileged women will pluck at your sleeve and seek to enlist you in the "fight" for reforms, but reforms are retrogressive. The old process must be broken, not made new. Bitter women will call you to rebellion, but you have too much to do. What *will* you do?' And so the book, brilliantly and provocatively, ended.

16

The Decline of the Roman Catholic Church

The dissolution of the Church of England during our times was an inevitability. That Church had originated in a time when its Erastian claims had known only one serious challenger, the Church of Rome, which had been seen off by the Penal Laws, which existed until 1829. While it tolerated the existence of Protestant sects, the central reason for the Church of England's existence was that any other religious body in England was superfluous. To be English was to be a member of the Church of England, unless one opted out. Hence the fact that nearly all primary schools were, throughout our times, Church schools. They were different in status from 'faith schools', run by Jews, Muslims or Catholics. Though – because – attached to the Church of England, they were also, *ipso facto*, state schools. The Church was part of the state. The Church of England was the religion of the monarch, and of the two older universities. It had periodic moments of spiritual revival, sometimes 'high', sometimes 'low' church, but its life had been bound up with the organism of the post-1660 nation state. That state was now unravelling. The aristocracy still existed, but they were no longer the 'governing class'. There was all but no squirarchy left, so that in those parishes where the living still had a patron – often the lord of the manor, who had been associated with the same area of England since the Norman Conquest – it seemed to many anomalous that a landowner, rather than a bishop, together with the church wardens, should choose the parson. The very word 'parson', familiar term for the parish priest since Chaucer, went out of use. Few quite realised it in the 1960s, but the last generation of literate parsons had been ordained. Those clerical families, such as had given birth to Jane Austen, the Brontë sisters, John Cowper Powys, etc, were a thing of the past. The large, draughty rectories – one in every parish, rural or urban – were also a vanished thing, as the Church began a policy of selling off its parsonage-houses, and rehousing the clergy in small, modern dwellings, which reflected the character and class of the new ordinands: no room for books, no room for eight children, all dressed in hand-me-downs; in short, they were no longer gentlemen's houses, and those gentlemen who would in a previous generation have taken orders were now drawn to other ways of life.

The organic unity of the Church of England, then, was threatened even before it had an Archbishop of Canterbury – Michael Ramsey – who candidly hated it, and who, by giving it its own parliament, the Synod, and cutting it loose from the Parliament, had sawn off one of its vital limbs. Hitherto, as has been stated already, there was a new sect, 'Anglicanism', which attracted fewer and fewer adherents.

Those who believed in Christianity as some ecstatic personal experience were drawn more and more to the Billy Graham religion, which had first been manifest in Britain in 1954, and which grew apace, until in many quarters it was seen as the only plausible version of Protestantism, sometimes flourishing in buildings belonging to the Church of England, but having little in common with the worship or beliefs of that organisation. Those who believed in an institutional form of Christianity looked, perhaps, to the parent Church from which the Church of England had broken away in the sixteenth century, namely that of Rome.

Those who had been drawn to the Roman Catholic Church in the past had often been under the impression that, unlike any other human institution, it was unchangeable. In fact, the Church of Rome had undergone many changes since the nineteenth century, when first the temporal power of the popes had been curtailed by the political unification of Italy, and then the Church had been shaken within by the crisis known as modernism, in which many so-called modernists – tentative believers in modern science, scholars prepared to accept some of the findings of textual scholars of the Bible, and others – were ruthlessly silenced or driven from the Church in the years before the First World War.

Though the liturgy appeared to be unchanging, even that had undergone some alterations in the twentieth century, with Pius X (Pope from 1903 to 1914), that great persecutor of modernism, introducing the custom of frequent Communion, for example, and Pius XII (Pope from 1939 to 1958) making a number of changes to the Mass. They were minor, and would not have been noticed by any but faddists. His successor, the Patriarch of Venice, Angelo Giuseppe Roncalli, was crowned in a magnificent ceremony on 4 November 1958, with ostrich feathers waved before him in the incense clouds, as a great medieval triple-crown was placed upon his head. No wonder Catholics the world over believed that the Church was the one rock in a changing world which would never alter.

In fact, the Roman Church was plunged, during and after the pontificate of Roncalli (he ruled as Pope John XXIII), into a crisis every much as divisive and bitter as those which in our time shook other institutions such as political parties and nation states. In 1962, Roncalli increased the number of cardinals to eighty-seven, making the Sacred College more international, and in the same year he opened the Second Vatican Council, on 11 October. The First Vatican Council (1869–70) had been a remarkable piece of backwoodsmanship, declaring the Pope himself to be infallible, and gallantly banging the drum of papal triumphalism as Garibaldi, Bismarck and others reduced the reality of the Pope's political power in Europe.

Some Roman Catholics, especially the converts, felt that the Catholic claim was of its essence Against the World. Not to have espoused the spirit of our, or of any, age, was one of the hallmark's of the faith's authenticity. That was certainly how Evelyn Waugh thought, for example. Other Catholics were troubled. Was it really appropriate to forbid Catholics to read works of literature merely because, like Charles Kingsley's *The Water Babies*, or Voltaire's *Candide*, they had found themselves on the lengthy *Index Librorum* of forbidden books? Was there not something a little crazy about the fact that you could not buy the Dublin masterpiece, *Ulysses*, in Dublin? (Until the *Index* was abolished, Catholics who went to university had to acquire special dispensations from their bishops to read books which were sometimes set texts for their examinations.) Were the Protestants, and others, who had studied the Bible in the spirit of textual criticism applied to other ancient texts – were they really at fault? Was the Roman Catholic teaching about the origin of human life, which was largely based on the trials and errors of Aristotle, who died in 322 BC, not to allow any more modern medical research to affect its thinking? Aristotle, for example, believed that the man who planted seed in a woman thereby planted the whole soul of a new being; he did not know that the seed on its own could not produce a baby, and therefore it made no sense to speak of the soul existing in the seed alone. Yet much of the Church's teaching on why some forms of sexual activity were allowable, others not, were posited on the idea that male masturbators, or homosexuals, for example, were wasting potential souls. (In its cruder form, as dished out in the confessionals, the belief existed that such 'impure' behaviour was spilling actual souls.)

More important than these esoteric questions, many Catholics questioned the right of the clergy to be asking them. Many had experienced in childhood abuse at the hands of priests and nuns – either sexual abuse or casual, systematic bullying. Though the full extent of this – surely the single greatest cause of the decline of the Roman Catholic Church in the West – would take some time to be acknowledged, it was part of the psychological story of why many men and women in the 1960s no longer felt inclined to accept everything which their parish priest or their Reverend Mother told them.

The Roman Catholic Church was, in fact, a seething cauldron of human grievance, waiting to bubble over. There were priests, and male and female members of religious orders who wondered how much, if anything, of the old doctrines they still believed, or whether they believed in the old way. The post-war world, as it reconstructed itself in Western Europe and the United States, discovered that it had lost, or discarded, the hierarchical, deferential way of viewing human society. Concepts of authority and obedience were changed, or abandoned. Inevitably, these changes in the secular sphere percolated to the Church. How possible was it, for a Roman Catholic of the 1960s, to accept teachings and practices simply on the authority of a bishop or an abbot or a pope? As Catholics became better informed about their own history, they came to realise that there had been hundreds of years, for example, when celibacy was not enjoined upon the priesthood. Was it still necessary to insist upon a married clergy? What of the struggles of the poor in Latin America, often against regimes which were brutal and unjust? Was it not part of the Church's mission to identify the Gospel with their aspirations? What of the Mass? Roman Catholic liturgical practice had evolved over many years. Viewed from the perspective of an historical scholar, as well as from that of a pastor trying to teach the faith in a parish, how could the bishops continue to justify, for example, the custom of giving Communion in one kind only (i.e., just the wafer) – a custom dating from a medieval fear of the Plague – if the congregation were allowed to sip together from one chalice? The old Mass, sometimes named after the Council of Trent ('Tridentine') but in substance a much, much older liturgy, was in Latin, and the more sacred parts of the texts were not recited audibly by the priest, but muttered rapidly at the level of a whisper. What opportunity did this give to the congregation to 'hear, mark and inwardly digest' God's word?

Questions which had been asked in the sixteenth century by the Protestant reformers were now asked by Catholic theologians. There is not much evidence that Pope John XXIII, an avuncular figure who kept an excellent table,[1] ever imagined that his Second Vatican Council would answer many of these questions. He spoke metaphorically of throwing open the Church's windows. He was a basically conservative figure. He continued to insist, for example, that seminarians were taught in Latin. It would seem likely that he merely intended, by initiating the Council, to institute minor liturgical changes, to remove some of the more obviously offensive or anomalous elements in Catholic teaching and practice, to reform the Breviary (the prayer book used in religious houses and said privately by priests), and above all to improve, if not actually to heal, broken relations with the churches of Eastern Orthodoxy. He died in 1963, while the Council was still in progress, and was replaced by a very different man, Giovanni Battista Montini, the Archbishop of Milan, who ruled (1963–78) as Paul VI. Pope John referred to Montini as a bit like Hamlet ('*un po' Amletico*') and there must have been many moments during his fifteen-year pontificate when Pope Paul could have echoed the Danish Prince's exclamation – 'O cursed spite – That ever I was born to set it right!' Montini was an intelligent man, the son of a liberal-minded, prosperous lawyer from Brescia who had got into trouble with the Fascists for his work as a political editor and parliamentary deputy. An Anglophile, Montini had English friends, and during the latter days of the Second World War had enjoyed nipping backwards and forwards between the Vatican (where he was secretary of state to Pius XII) to meet English friends in Rome, and swap talk with them about what was going on. He was the only Pope of modern times to have visited England in his youth, and as Pope he would receive the Archbishop of Canterbury, spontaneously giving Michael Ramsey his ring in a gesture which excited many of the High Church party into the belief that corporate reunion between the two Churches was imminent.

Paul VI it was who brought the Council to its conclusion in 1965, proclaiming an Extraordinary Jubilee (1 January–29 May 1966) to give the Church time to rejoice and meditate upon the very many decrees and deliberations which had been promulgated by the Council Fathers – archbishops, cardinals, monks and friars who had by then jetted back to their separate countries.

Apart from the multiplicity of difficult questions raised by a Church in a state of flux – what to do about the all but Marxist Social Gospel Catholics of South America or the all but fascist liturgical die-hard followers of Archbishop Lefebvre in France; what to do about the question of priestly celibacy; how to heal the breach with the Churches of the East and how to stop the flood of monks and nuns abandoning their vows – Paul VI was faced with two major questions: the questions with which the poor Hamlet-like Pope, with his bush-baby eyes and his worried, thin face, will forever by history be associated. One was how to interpret the Council's recommendations about changes to the Mass. The other was how to interpret the advice given him by a pontifical commission on the question of contraception, especially in the light of the invention of a contraceptive pill.

Die-hard conservatives could see that the answer to these questions was simple: change neither the liturgy nor the moral teaching of the Church. Aesthetes might call for relaxation of arcane sexual teaching, while retaining the liturgy for which Lassus, Palestrina, Haydn, Mozart and Beethoven had written their sublimest chords. Christians, of whom there were more and more among the ranks of the clergy, burned with the zeal which had once animated Luther and Zwingli, to share with their congregations the words of Scripture translated into the Jerusalem Bible. They longed for simpler forms of worship in which the laity could partake more fully. They were also aware, through their pastoral work, of the very great difficulties faced by the Catholic faithful who were trying to be loyal to the Church while surviving the strains and trials of married life.

Pope Hamlet agonised, and he knew that whatever he decreed, in either direction, would be greeted with dismay by some section of the Church or another. What he could not know, even though he was much more in touch with the world, and much more intelligent, than his predecessor, was the extent to which the collapse of the whole concept of authority in the Western world would lead to outright rebellion against him, not merely by the disgruntled laity, but also by the religious orders and the clergy. He opted to modernise the liturgy, and to be a conservative over the matter of contraception. His encyclical *Humanae Vitae*, which reasserted the impropriety of artificial birth control, made him an object of hatred throughout the world, with many who were Catholics, and an even larger number who were not, laying at his door Malthusian denunciations of callousness. The Pope was made responsible in the eyes of such critics for all the problems of overpopulation, including those felt in such areas as Muslim Nigeria or Communist China, which did not recognise his authority. Many felt there was some illogicality in the *Humanae Vitae* encyclical, since it repeated the traditional Catholic belief that it was allowable for couples to make love during the 'safe period'. This gave the lie to the notion that a purely Catholic sexual act must always be performed with the intention of procreation, or at least with the knowledge that procreation might result. How did such careful use of the safe period differ from taking a contraceptive pill? The lack of a good answer to this question drove many from the Church and caused others, gradually, to abandon any attempt to follow the specific guidelines of papal teaching about sexual morality. If it was possible for popes to make such muddled and irresponsible pronouncements, it was felt that there was no longer any need to heed what they said about, say, homosexuality or divorce, or sleeping with your steady partner before marriage. Catholics, in short, began slowly during our times to behave like everyone else, when it came to sex, and this would lead many to forsake, wholly or in part, the ways of behaviour which separated Catholics from others. 'They seem just like other people,' said Charles Ryder in Evelyn Waugh's Catholic masterpiece *Brideshead Revisited* (first published 1945, revised 1959). 'My dear Charles,' replied Sebastian Flyte, 'that's exactly what they're not – particularly in this country where they're so few' . . . 'Everything they think important is different from other people. They try and hide it as much as they can, but it comes out all the time.'[2]

For Catholics in Britain, as in the rest of the world, the *Humanae*

Vitae encyclical was a moment of crisis. One MP of a primarily Catholic constituency in Liverpool said, 'It was hoped in particular, that the novel biochemical function of the Pill, with its regulation of the natural menstrual cycle upon which the doctrine of the safe period had been founded, would enable the theological impasse to be circumvented without betraying the categories of traditionalist reasoning. For such Catholics, the crisis of faith was not provoked by those urging a comprehensive State family planning service, but by *Humanae Vitae* itself.'[3] One distinguished Catholic theologian, Charles Davis, felt this was the moment of truth, when he must leave the Church. 'The Roman Catholic Church contradicts my Christian faith because I experience it as a zone of untruth, pervaded by a disregard for truth.'[4] Once again, it was the encyclical which prompted him. 'One who claims to be the moral leader of the church should not tell lies,' he wrote in the *Observer*. Like many priests, Davis had his sympathies broadened by the experience of falling in love – in his case with a woman called Florence. 'I myself as well as other people have asked whether I should have left the church if I had not loved Florence or if Florence had been unable to follow me in my decision.' It prompted the limerick:

> Said Charles Davis, 'I view with abhorrence
> A Church without Biblical warrants.
> With Vatican II
> I'll have nothing to do.
> I stick to the Council/Counsel of Florence.'

Other priests remained, but they would not be silenced. A kindly Carmelite friar, Father Brocard Sewell, an expert on the 1890s and the personal friend of, among others, Christine Keeler and Sir Oswald Mosley, wrote to *The Times* to say that the encyclical had only intensified the distrust of the papacy which had been felt by the orthodox churches since the time of the Great Schism. He called upon the Pope to imitate the example of his thirteenth-century predecessor Celestine V and resign. Sewell was temporarily suspended, forbidden to say Mass or hear confessions, and sent as a punishment to Nova Scotia, where he continued his gentle researches into the by-ways of English literature. Other priests were not so fortunate, and of the fifty-seven who wrote to *The Times* to support him, many were sacked by their bishops and never reinstated.[5]

At the moment the Church was being disrupted by the row over *Humanae Vitae*, a young Liberal MP in Britain, David Steel – a future leader of his party – was introducing the Abortion Bill into the House of Commons. Up to fifty women a year in Britain were dying as a result of 'septic or incomplete abortions', and it was obviously quite wrong for the law not to recognise in some cases the medical need, and in all cases the woman's desire, to terminate pregnancy. In 1966–67 as the bill was passing through Parliament and becoming law, the current state of medical opinion was that twenty-eight weeks was the time when a foetus became viable. As midwifery and obstetric skills developed, this began to seem very late. Many children were born prematurely at this stage of the mother's pregnancy and survived to live healthily. There were survivals at twenty-two weeks, just as, more disturbingly, 'botched abortions', when the nature of the operation became clear: that it was the killing of a child.

Steel in later life came to feel that the law should be changed to limit abortion to the twenty-week period. He admitted that he had no notion, when bringing in the legislation, how many women would avail themselves of the chance to abort their babies, though he also noted the statistical fact that 'the rate of abortions in Britain is slightly lower than in Catholic France, Spain and Italy, and substantially lower in the U.S. where the subject is much more of a hot potato'.[6] The annual rate of abortions in Britain in the twenty-first century stands at over 180,000 per year.[7]

The abortion issue remained, perhaps, one of the few where Roman Catholics, together with some others for religious motives, differed from the majority. Most Britons came to feel that, even though the life inside the womb was one which could grow into a child, it was not quite of the same status as a child. They might mock Catholic explanations, based upon St Thomas Aquinas, of when a foetus develops a soul, but they would actually themselves be just as hazy about when (as David Steel showed with his shifting from twenty-eight to twenty weeks as the ideal cut-off point for abortions) a foetus became 'viable'. No one pretended this was an easy question. The Roman Catholic Church continued to hold a position which, until the Second World War, had been not only the majority view in Britain, but also the law of the land.

The matter of birth control was only the catalyst which hastened the process of disillusionment for many British Catholics. The Archbishop of Westminster, John Carmel Heenan, an uninspiring, conservative-minded man, was wholly unequipped, both intellectually and pastorally, to deal with the crisis, but it is doubtful whether anyone else could have prevented what happened – namely that the Roman Catholic Church lost about half its practising membership in England, Wales and Scotland, and that in Ireland, where many other factors needed to be taken into account, it would in many areas of life suffer almost complete wipeout.

It was a feature of our times that institutions began to question the very reason for their existence. Political parties and trades unions all underwent deep changes, and loss of active membership. Colleges and clubs which had continued for decades, sometimes for centuries, more or less unchanged asked themselves by what justification they limited their membership on grounds of gender, class or race. It is against this general background of institutional dissolution that the story of the Roman Catholic Church in our times must be read. Even when allowance has been made, however, for the fact that it was a period of change and upheaval in every sphere, the story of the Church's numerical decline, especially in Britain, is difficult to ignore. From 1965 to 1996, these are the statistics in England and Wales – Sunday Mass attendance fell from 1.9 million to 1.1 million. The number of priests fell from 7,808 to 5,732. Even more devastating are the statistics which reveal that the dogged 1.1 million who continued to attend Mass towards the end of our times were themselves ageing rapidly. The number of child baptisms over the period halved – 134,055 to 74,848 – and the number of Roman Catholic marriages fell from 46,480 (in 1960) to a mere 17,294 in the 1990s.[8] Then again, the statistics relating to Roman Catholic schools in England and Wales would not be encouraging to anyone intent upon the propagation of the faith. 'Faith' schools during our times retained their popularity among parents who wanted a disciplined and old-fashioned structure for the education of their children, regardless of theological observance. This would explain why the decline in attendance in Catholic schools, from 870,430 in 1980 to 808,774 in 1996, was comparatively small. The percentage of non-Catholic pupils in Catholic schools reflects this fact – only 3.5 per cent of non-Catholics in state secondary schools in 1980 but 17.7 per cent in 1996; and in the Independent Catholic schools, 50.4 per cent of non-Catholic pupils and 45.1 per cent of non-Catholic teachers.[9] It is clear that in this situation the extent to which the schools really are propagating Roman Catholicism is merely notional. There will be fluctuations in these statistics as more and more Eastern European Catholics, especially Poles, come to live in England, but the key statistic is little over 17,000 Catholic marriages per year.

The new Mass caused as much pain to some Catholics as the Pope's views on the safe period. 'The Vatican Council has knocked the guts out of me', Evelyn Waugh told a friend in March 1966. A month later, on Easter Day, he heard Mass for the last time, celebrated according to the old rite by his friend Father Philip Caraman SJ. Waugh then returned to his house at Combe Florey in Somerset and had a heart attack on the lavatory, where he died at luncheon-time. It was only one of the many instances of the ineluctable tendency of our times to deprive human beings of their dignity, and to turn potentially sad events into comedy.

Religions cohere on two levels, the ritual and the moral. In the 1960s, the words of the Roman Mass, which had been unchanged since the sixteenth century, and in effect unchanged for centuries longer, were rendered into the vernacular with the upsetting consequences which we observed at the opening of this chapter. At the same time, as the novels of David Lodge made wittily and abundantly clear, Roman Catholics began to ask themselves how much of their religion they had ever really believed. In the days of the Old Mass, the faithful at a small tin tabernacle, or in the largest cathedrals, could attend the ceremonies and know that they were at one, in word and action, with their Church throughout the world. Rather in the same way that Muslims, abasing themselves for prayer at the regulated intervals, continued to hear the same words, until the end of our times and beyond. For Catholics, however, the experience of church-going in our times became divisive, even for those who accepted the new liturgies; some congregations rejoiced in the chance to imitate the American Protestant tradition, with songs, handshaking, electric guitars and liturgical dance, while others felt that the past had been sold and yearned for the old ways.

Instead of being a focus of unity, the liturgy became a source of animosity and division. Institutions, secular as well as religious, need repetitious rituals to retain their sense of identity, which is why for many non-military-minded people there is still a virtue in the annual ceremonies of Trooping the Colour and laying wreaths at the Cenotaph at Armistice. Institutions also need to believe at least a substantial percentage of what they claim to believe. No adherent to a Church or a political party can ever have truly subscribed to every word of the manifesto, but when the discrepancy between aspirant and actual belief becomes too glaring, then institutions break up.

The destructive paradox of the Catholic civil war was that it was the most extreme conservatives who, in their hatred of the chummy new Eucharistic rite, were least willing to toe the new line. 'Let us offer one another the sign of peace,' said a Catholic priest in London at the moment in the rite when he hoped the congregation would shake hands. Jennifer Paterson, the cookery writer, visibly raised two fingers towards the altar.

Father Oswald Baker, in 1975, became the focus of recusancy when he refused to stop using the Tridentine Rite in his church at Downham Market, in Norfolk. The Bishop of Northampton, his diocesan, attempted to remove him, which had the effect of making Downham Market a place of pilgrimage for hundreds of disaffected Catholics. Baker made barbed comments about Masses which were enlivened by pop music and 'sensuous dancing girls'. He referred in one sermon to St John of the Cross, who was jailed by his superiors in the sixteenth century, and eventually released to become the Vicar General of Andalusia. 'These bishops,' said Baker, to an appreciative congregation, 'they will have their little joke.' His bishop appointed a new parish priest, who was obliged (since Baker and friends continued to occupy the church) to say Mass to a small congregation in the town hall. Baker was a devotee of the teaching of St Robert Bellarmine's teaching that a heretical Pope automatically loses his office. He therefore believed that the See of Peter, though apparently occupied in succession by Paul VI, John Paul I and John Paul II, was in fact empty. In 1984, he surprised a visitor by telling him, that the Pope 'is no more a Catholic than Ian Paisley – and no more Pope than Billy Graham'. Baker was in a minority, but it was a vociferous and numerous minority, which believed that 'the new Mass is a sacrilegious parody of the true Mass; it is sinful to take part in it'.[10]

To see the extent of Roman Catholic decline in England, however, it would have been necessary, not to visit the remote parishes of Norfolk, but to go to Liverpool. Liverpool, more than London, was the British Catholic capital. It was to Liverpool in the nineteenth century that the Irish Catholics had fled from the famine, and although many passed through Liverpool on their way to other sources of work, many stayed. The docklands of Liverpool remained for many travellers, until the 1960s, the natural point of departure for America.

Between 1968 and 1996, five docklands parishes closed.[11] Mass attendance sank to a fraction of what it was in the proud old days of Archbishop Richard Downey (Archbishop of Liverpool 1928–53), known as 'the ruler of the North', a hard-faced bigot who encouraged his clergy, preaching for the Catholic Evidence Guild, to stand on street corners and pour scorn on the Church of England. The Church of England bishop, Dr David, frequently complained to his RC counterpart that priests had 'terrorised' the non-Catholic wives of 'mixed marriages', 'using foul language, to tell them that their marriages were invalid and their children illegitimate; in one case a priest was said to have told a Catholic husband that he was quite free to leave his wife because they were not validly married'.[12]

Both Churches, the Church of Rome and the Church of England, doomed in our times to shrink in numbers, spent time and money constructing cathedrals.

The Protestant building was begun during the time of the second Bishop of Liverpool, Francis James Chavasse, a man whose anti-popish bigotry would have been a match for the anti-Protestantism of Archbishop Downey. As Rector of St Peter-le-Baily in Oxford, Chavasse was responsible for founding St Peter's Hall, a specifically evangelical college, designed to counteract the unmanly and Romish tendencies of Pusey

House. The parish church, later the college chapel, had a memorial window to Chavasse *fils*, also a Bishop (of Rochester), celebrating in emblematic form his career as an Olympic athlete and as a chain-smoker – he had an Episcopal ring which doubled as a cigarette-holder. Giles Gilbert Scott, a very young architect, was the grandson of George Gilbert Scott, who designed the Albert Memorial and St Pancras Station. His vast cathedral on St James's Mount, begun in 1901, was consecrated on 19 July 1924, but it was not completed until 1978, when the *Daily Telegraph* wrote:

> In such a setting, does not her Anglican Cathedral look like a huge anachronism? Even some of the devout seem inclined to apologize for it, on the grounds that money (all of it raised by private subscription be it noted) might have been better spent on works of mercy or on some more utilitarian place of worship.
>
> Such sentiments are wholly out of place. The Church proclaims her message by striving, as the architects of Liverpool Cathedral did, to build for as near to eternity as is humanly possible. We should surely by now have learned the error of supposing that Christian virtues will continue to flourish in a society which fails to nourish the faith from which they spring, and great ecclesiastical architecture is one of the most fertile sources of such nourishment. This Cathedral will stand, even to the eyes of the unbelieving, as a symbol of what patience and devotion can achieve in the face of endless difficulties and some catastrophes. It is a triumph and proclamation of hope.

The cathedral is in fact built at one end of Hope Street, at the other end of which the RCs erected a very different structure.

Liverpool itself, under the reforms of Peter Walker and Heath, became a questionable entity. As one social historian of the city put it, 'Inner urban decay and suburban sprawl melted Liverpool with Merseyside. In April 1974 the new metropolitan County Council of Merseyside was born, governing over 1½ million in an area of 250 square miles. Where once it was hard to define Merseyside, now it was hard to distinguish Liverpool.'[13]

Anyone who turned their back on the Protestant cathedral and walked towards the Roman Catholic one will have time, in their procession between the two buildings, to meditate on what had happened, not only to Liverpool, but to Britain since the older of the two structures was conceived. When the foundation stone of the Protestant cathedral was laid, Mr Gladstone had been dead for only three years. The fine Georgian terraced house in which he was born in Rodney Street still stands. When the cathedral was conceived, the great thriving industrial port of Liverpool stood at the centre of the British Empire. Riddled with poverty as Liverpool was in its dockland slums and elsewhere, Liverpudlians were 'universal merchants', bringing in American cotton, colonial tobacco, sugar, Midlands metals, Cheshire salt, Lancashire coal and textiles. It had founded its fortune, as Gladstone would guiltily remind himself, on the slave trade. It was the hub of commerce, and of the relentless efficient machine of manufacture and trade which made Britain tower over all its rivals in the world. In spite of the extreme poverty of the Irish working class here, it was a city of enormous pride. The great Mersey was overlooked by the majestic Exchange and Town Hall, and in the nineteenth century it had acquired a superb art gallery, an excellent university, all paid for by the voluntary donations of the rich, who lived here in some splendour.

Shipping went. By the time HeathCo had submerged Liverpool into 'Merseyside', the great old days of the Anchor Line, Brocklebank, Cunard, Lamport and Holt and the Ocean Steam Ship Company were over. Twenty-five thousand men worked in Liverpool Docks in 1963, compared, by the end of our times, with fewer than a thousand who, by means of improved technology, actually shift a bigger tonnage and make more profits.[14] Lancashire barely made any textiles any more, nor did Cheshire produce salt. Liverpool's reason for existence had been removed, partly by politicians, partly by circumstance. It was not surprising perhaps that the Militant Tendency (Trotskyite infiltrators into the ranks of the Labour Party) should have begun in the late 1950s and early 1960s, long before their destructive significance dawned on the minds of the National Executive of the Labour Party, to take seats on Liverpool City Council.[15] But at this date, the power of the Catholic Church in working-class Liverpool was greater than that of the Trotskyites. 'Caucusing for support within the Labour Group [on the Council] had long been a feature of city politics in Liverpool. In the 1950s and 1960s Jack Braddock and his allies formed one caucus, whilst "the left" and "Catholic Action" formed two others.'[16] The Protestant cathedral by the end of our times appeared as if it had been built in a ruin, and at the end of the twentieth century it symbolised something of which the *Daily Telegraph* might be expected to have approved, a defiant gesture of old values, which had been left behind by all around. Its mountainous height, its grandiose claims to be taken seriously, rose up in the surrounding wasteland, impressive but rather mad. Around its walls, as the faithful few gathered for the evening service, swarmed teenaged prostitutes, plying their trade.

Make the twenty-first-century pilgrimage through the desolation and dissolution which lies between the two buildings, however, leave behind the self-confidence of Edwardian England and you are confronted with an emblem not only of poverty-stricken, wrecked Liverpool Roman Catholicism but of the late 1960s in which it was finished. The original architect for the RC scheme was none other than the great Sir Edwin Lutyens, architect of Imperial New Delhi and of the Cenotaph in London. He had estimated the cost at £3 million. In 1955, the RC authorities authorised Adrian Scott to 'scale down the Lutyens design', but it was still too expensive. In the event, they chose Frederick Gibberd[17] to produce a completely different design, the gimcrack vulgarity known as 'Paddy's Wigwam', which was built on the cheap and within decades was showing severe signs of structural strain. This frail concrete eyesore, which lasted such a short time, was an architectural parable of the 1960s, and of the attempt of the Roman Catholic Church to move with the times.

Anthony Kenny, philosopher-priest, who was laicised and became the Master of Balliol, was only one of many who left the Church. He was laicised in 1963, and by 1970 Cardinal Heenan was ruefully remarking to another priest, 'The path which Tony trod has now become a high road.' Kenny was more eloquent than most, not least because he was so restrained in his account of loss of faith in the supernatural claims of the RC Church. 'It is true that many of the things which I objected to in Catholic practice have altered since the Vatican Council, and it is true that many priests will now cheerfully deny in the pulpit doctrines which I could only doubt in solitary guilt. But I am old-fashioned enough to believe that if the Church has been wrong in the past on so many topics as forward-looking clergy believe, then her claims to impose belief and obedience on others are, in the form in which they have been traditionally made, mere impudence.'[18]

17

The End of Harold Wilson

Harold Wilson had won a third election victory for the Labour Party, hitherto an unheard-of achievement in British politics. He had not expected to win. In the event of his defeat, he planned to go into hiding at the Golden Cross Hotel, Kirby, and to resign as party leader at once.[1] He had already signalled to colleagues that, in the event of a victory, he would not serve a full term. With his keenness for statistics and breaking records, he had some desire to break Asquith's record for length of office, and he was therefore prepared, once he became Prime Minister in March 1974, to stay on for another two years.[2] But, already at fifty-eight years old, he was feeling exhausted by the workload. He told Barbara Castle that the stress involved stomach pains,[3] which cannot have been helped by persistent pipe-smoking and by an ever-increasing intake of alcohol. 'Are we to be led by a neurotic drunk?' Anthony Wedgwood Benn had asked when George Brown stood against Wilson in the leadership election of 1963.[4] No, was the answer on this occasion; but by the time of his third administration, with the glass of brandy forever at his side, Wilson had turned into just that. He had lost his zest for infighting and intrigue, and his capacity for hard work. The first quarter of 1975, for example, involved eleven Cabinets, twenty-eight meetings with industrialists, twenty ministerial speeches, two visits abroad, one to Northern Ireland, where the situation was deteriorating, thirteen other public engagements at home. He did not find time for a single private or social engagement in the entire period.

The economic situation was bleak indeed. Ted Heath had asked the electorate the question 'Who Governs Britain?' Heath had maintained that miners' pay was 8 per cent above the average for industrial workers. During the election it emerged that he had made a mistake and that the pay was in fact 8 per cent *below*.[5] No wonder, when Heath had been humiliated, and ousted from leadership of his party, the first person whose name Margaret Thatcher recommended for a peerage should have been Joe Gormley, the leader of the National Union of Mineworkers. But for Wilson, as Prime Minister, the insoluble problem of the balance of payments was waiting for him as soon as he took office. Oil prices had quadrupled since the end of 1973; there was a record trade deficit in Britain; inflation stood at 15 per cent; there was decline in industrial production and a slump in living standards.[6]

Inevitably, given the discontent in the country at large, and the appalling state of industrial relations, the left weighed in to support the workers, and in so doing eventually to wreck the Labour Party. Wilson realised that, although he had won the election, his opponent Ted Heath had been right. The country could not afford to pay out money which it did not have, without the prospect of eventual ruin. It is out of such pain that successful political careers can be born. Anthony Wedgwood Benn, the former Gaitskellite Viscount Stansgate,[7] had come to realise that he was never going to impress Harold Wilson, but as Tony Benn the People's chum he stood a good chance of becoming the next best thing, a man who was perceived by the public as a conviction politician. He could become a rallying point for the disaffected left, the more so, since Michael Foot, the obvious guardian of the left's flame, had pledged loyalty to the leadership and become the Secretary of State for Employment. Wilson had thereby made the poacher into a gamekeeper, and turned the most eloquent possible advocate for the miners' and other workers' cause into the boss who would have to refuse them pay rises. It left the field for nuisance-making open to Benn. After the 1970 election, when Labour had expected to win, Tony Benn and Caroline, his very rich American wife, had been buoyant in mood. 'We've never been happier,' they told Susan Crosland. Benn now saw himself 'as the left-wing answer to Enoch Powell' calling in the wilderness. 'Enoch has more effect on the country than either Party,' said Wedgwood Benn, adding that he intended to make 'a major speech every three months'.[8] Wilson noted, as Wedgwood Benn embarked on this successful new piece of self-invention, that he immatured with age. The relentlessness with which Wedgwood Benn created this role for himself helped the party descend into the feuding which would all but destroy it.

Wilson, therefore, had formidable problems on his return as Prime Minister in 1974. But the warring of the left, both with itself and with the right of the party and the near-collapse of the economy, paled beside the everlasting problem of Marcia. In order to appease Mary, he had made the decision that they would no longer reside at Downing Street, but continue to live in their house in Lord North Street. But on the very day of the election, when he went to Number 10 to resume his office, Marcia went with him, and the front door had no sooner shut than she was shouting at him. 'Now you are back . . . you don't need me any more!'[9] From the Marcia angle, it had been a tense election. Things had been going well for Labour. J. Enoch Powell, as popular for his denunciations of Europe as for his hostility to Pakistani immigrants, had urged his supporters to vote Labour, to give them a chance to vote in a referendum to get Britain out of the Common Market. There had been the

8 per cent muddle over miners' pay, revealing that Heath had called the whole election on a false premise. So far, so good. And then the newspapers began to break the story of Marcia Williams's brother Tony Field, some slag heaps which had been bought on spec near Wigan, and sold to a dodgy property developer called Ronald Millhench. The *Daily Mail* had attempted to print a story before the election, which suggested that Wilson himself had been involved in the land speculation. The faithful Arnold Goodman issued writs and both the *Mail* and the *Express* were silenced. But by the time Wilson was Prime Minister the story was out.

Tony Field had indeed bought slag heaps at Ince-in-Makerfield, near Wigan, and a stone quarry. At a time when the Labour Party was formally committed to taking land into public ownership, Marcia's brother was responding to the property boom of 1971 and selling on his slag heaps, with planning permission attached, first to a group of companies run by one Victor Harper of Birmingham, who in turn sold on to Ronald Millhench, who also bought a larger neighbouring site without planning permission. It turned out that Tony Field sometimes used Harold Wilson's office, and that Millhench had stolen some of Wilson's personal writing paper. For this, and more serious offences, he was eventually to be gaoled in November 1974.

It was clear that the wisest course of action for Wilson would be to answer questions about the whole matter as lightly as possible in the House of Commons, and otherwise ignore it, and wait for it to blow away. This was the advice given to him by Joe Haines, and by his new policy adviser from the London School of Economics, Bernard Donoughue. Their advice was ignored, and Wilson ponderously rose in the Commons on 4 April to insist that Marcia's brother Field was engaged not in 'speculation' but 'land reclamation'. Thousands of column inches were now given to the matter in the press – over 6,000 inches between 3 and 11 April alone. Wilson and Marcia had unwisely declared war on Fleet Street, and the journalists were preparing their counterblasts. Only when Walter Terry, the father of her two children, threatened to take legal action were the papers prevented from splashing the (hitherto secret) existence of her illegitimate offspring all over the *Daily Express*. In the midst of the furore, Wilson played one of his boldest cards. Far from severing relations with Marcia, or putting a distance between the Prime Minister's office and her at the time of the press's obsession with slag heaps and reclamation, Harold Wilson recommended Marcia's name to the Queen, and she was created a Life Peer. Harvey Smith was a show jumper who had caused a stir when he stuck two fingers up to show his disapproval of some onlookers. Wilson, in recommending Marcia's name to the Queen, informed the monarch that he intended to 'do a Harvey Smith' at the press. Astonishingly, the Queen appears to have accepted this as a good enough reason for making Marcia into Baroness Falkender on 23 July 1974. It was often said during our times that the Queen 'never put a foot wrong'. Yet a conspicuous feature of her life as Head of State was the way in which she accepted recommendations for peerages, and eventually the complete rearrangement of the Upper House, without any apparent question. In this, she differed markedly from George V, who prevented Asquith from acting upon the threat to create five hundred Liberal peers to force through Lloyd George's Budget. There was no reason at all, constitutional or otherwise, why the monarch could not have questioned Marcia's right to become a pensioned legislator for the rest of her natural life; just as common sense and common decency should surely have prevented the Queen from ennobling Jeffrey Archer (perjurer, liar, cheat) or Conrad Black (shady businessman, asset stripper and eventually imprisoned fraudster) or the extraordinary gang of unworthies elevated by Tony Blair, having offered loans or gifts to the New Labour project. The Queen had many virtues but political courage was not one of them, and in allowing Parliament thus to fall further into disrepute she must be said to have 'put a foot wrong'.

Harold Wilson's final administration was marked – or marred – by appointments which seemed like bad jokes. Having done 'a Harvey Smith' to the press by allowing Marcia a peerage, he then did 'the same' to the Church. The time came for Michael Ramsey to retire as Archbishop of Canterbury. The idea was mooted that one of the great Chadwick brothers should immediately be appointed to Canterbury, even though neither of them was a Bishop. Henry Chadwick, a patristic scholar of brilliance, was Dean of Christ Church, Oxford, and his brother Owen was Professor of Modern History at Cambridge. Both would have brought distinction to the role of Archbishop; Ramsey had a low view of the Archbishop of York, Donald Coggan – the Cog – and allowed Wilson to know it. The Cog was the most senior evangelical churchman of his day, becoming Bishop of Bradford in 1956 and Archbishop of York in 1961. He had 'peaked' when becoming Principal of the London College of Divinity in 1944, and was quite unsuited for high ecclesiastical office. Nevertheless, the Prime Minister did not heed Ramsey's advice, and appointed the Cog,[10] or Donald Duck as *Private Eye* immediately christened him. Coggan was not without excellent personal qualities. He had a beautiful voice, and he was one of those strange individuals who could pick up a language almost immediately. He had only to attend a liturgy in Africa to grasp, by the end of an hour, the basic morphology of Hausa or Swahili. But he was not up to the task of public office. And by appointing him, Wilson then left the Archbishopric of York vacant. Three bishops in a row refused the offer to replace him. 'I am puzzled and concerned by the difficulties which have arisen. I fear that at least some of the story must be known to some of the Bishops and others. I therefore think that the person next approached will have to be told quite frankly that there have been these difficulties. I hope that you and the Archbishop of Canterbury will then be prepared to apply all decent pressure on that person to see a call to York as, among other things, a duty to be undertaken for the good of the church. Our next attempt must succeed.'[11] Astonishingly, all they could come up with was another dud – Stuart Blanch, an agoraphobic, who suffered a nervous breakdown in 1981,[12] having been the most undistinguished Archbishop of York in the 1,300 years or so of the province's history. But if the elevation of Donald Duck, Stuart Blanch and Baroness Falkender represented new 'lows' in the history of the Church and state, Wilson, the lover of Gilbert and Sullivan, had one final flourish up his sleeve before he left the stage.

Many of the G and S operettas contain jokes about the House of Lords. Perhaps these sank more deeply into Wilson's subconscious than the more earnest request, from the left of the Labour Party since its inception, to uproot or abolish the legislative rights of the peers. At every State Opening of Parliament, the peerage of England would be assembled in their robes of ermine and scarlet. As Wilson trudged from the Commons to the Lords, for his final State Opening, it is probably safe to guess that the merry airs of Sir Arthur Sullivan and the frivolous words of W. S. Gilbert were singing inside his tired head. The dingy wife Mary continued to be the 'martyr', regarding his return to office as Labour Prime Minister, not as a personal triumph for him, but as an inconvenience to herself. 'Of course I hate it. But then I always have. But I do my job.'[13] Marcia continued to supply strident 'noises off'. Week in, week out, Wilson had to be an embarrassed witness to such scenes as when, during the State Visit of the Prime Minister of Fiji, the food was not served the second everyone sat at table. Marcia strode out in front of everyone and yelled at Patrick Wright, the private secretary for foreign affairs, 'Don't you dare ever again allow people to sit down if their food is not ready to be served immediately.'[14] Her tirades and harangues against poor Harold never let up. He had never had any close friends. He was what Goodman called a philistine. It was hard to imagine into what comforting retreat he could crawl, without the help of alcohol and the semi-merciful humiliations of early dementia.

> As upon its lordly way
> This unique procession passes,
> Tarantara! Tzing! Boom!
> Bow, bow, ye lower middle classes!

Bow, bow, ye tradesmen, bow ye masses!
Blow the trumpets, bang the brasses!
Tarantara! Tzing! Boom!
We are peers of highest station
Paragons of legislation,
Pillars of the British nation![15]

We do not know when exactly he decided to resign, but he must have known that he was to do so, as he led the Commoners into the House of Peers for the last time. Was there anarchic playfulness in his mind? When a man is gripped with hatred for the women who are making his life a misery, he often realises that the worst punishment he could inflict upon them would be to give them precisely what they asked for. To poor Mary, he gave the quiet domestic life for which she had always begged: only now he was suffering from incipient Alzheimer's and was condemning her to be the nurse of a mental defective. He punished Marcia by making her friends into peers and knights, thereby alerting the world to their deplorable defects of character. Bernard Donoughue wrote of Marcia: 'He often indulged her wildest whims almost like a daughter . . . and equally, seemed to fear her like a fierce mother (as when he physically hid from her intimidating telephone calls) . . . Somehow over the previous twenty or so years, she had frightened Harold Wilson and reduced him to a dependence which was sometimes pathetic to observe.'[16]

Resignation honours lists were traditionally reserved for personal service to the Prime Minister. So it was that Harold Wilson, when he knew that he was going to lay down his office, made his first list, containing the names of the driver, Bill Housden, the cook Mrs Pollard, three of Marcia's long-suffering secretaries and some Number 10 civil servants. But there was another list, written on lavender writing paper, and it was this list with which Harold Wilson's name would be forever associated. If it was intended as some kind of anarchic joke, it could certainly be seen as effective, since after the ennoblement and glorification of the names upon it, it was impossible for anyone in Britain to take seriously either the honours system or the House of Lords.

Among the names on the list was Jacob Kagan, a textile manufacturer responsible for Wilson's awful 'signature' Gannex macs. He was a thug, known to offer physical violence to anyone, including women, who stood in his way. He approached the journalist Peter Jenkins asking him if he could procure women for him. He was eventually gaoled in December 1978 for serious currency offences.[17] Together with other Wilson peers, such as Lords Plurenden, Kissin and Schon, Kagan had trade interests in the Soviet bloc. Then there were the showbiz names. David Frost was written down for a peerage, though Arnold Goodman eventually persuaded Wilson to cross his name off the Lavender List.[18] Lew Grade and Bernard Delfont were there, and George Weidenfeld, implausible publisher, bon vivant, wheeler and dealer, all soon to be summoned into the Second Chamber and described in Her Majesty's words as her trusty and well-beloved friends.

Then there were knighthoods – for James Hanson and James Goldsmith, both of whom had given large sums to the Conservative Party. Goldsmith was apparently knighted for 'services to exports' even though his company, Cavenham Foods, had only 0.4 per cent of its sales overseas.[19] Then there was Eric Miller, the boss of the Peachey Property Company, a close friend of Marcia. Some people expected them to marry, especially when he offered to take her on a private visit to Israel – though this trip eventually fell through.[20] When Miller's wife protested against the relationship with Lady Falkender, Marcia went to bed, telephoning the Prime Minister in the middle of an important conference in Brussels to tell him that he must get in touch with Eric Miller at once and persuade Miller not to give her up, whatever his wife insisted. Miller was eventually offered only a knighthood. He shot himself in 1977, before a censorious DTI report was published which revealed his dodgy business dealings at Peachey Property.

On 27 May *The Times* described the list as 'a bizarre one for a socialist ex-Prime Minister'. The majority of honorands were 'capitalists of a tough risk-taking type' – i.e., Jews. 'Are they really his friends for whom he feels the warmth of personal gratitude?' Donoughue answered that with the information that Wilson himself said, on the day he left office, that he barely knew half of them. One of his Cabinet colleagues was quoted in the *Sunday Times* of 30 May 1976: 'A pity about Harold. Such a graceful exit – and then he had to do this on the doorstep.'[21]

18

Lucky Jim

On 16 March 1976, Harold Wilson suddenly announced that he was resigning as Prime Minister. He had developed advanced paranoia, a personal condition which spreads its sufferings to those in the sufferer's environs. For some years he had believed that the secret services were plotting against him – a theory borne out when the ex-MI5 officer Peter Wright published his sensational *Spycatcher* in 1986, revealing that some of his fellow intelligence officers believed Wilson to be a Soviet agent. They thought that Gaitskell had been murdered by the KGB so as to place 'their' man in Number 10 Downing Street. James Angleton, the American counter-intelligence chief, gave weight to the belief that Wilson was a Soviet agent. There was indeed a plot among MI5 officers to oust Wilson, but the men involved were comparatively junior and the upper echelons of the service quashed the conspiracy long before it took effect.[1]

Whether or not Wilson had any inkling of the plots themselves, or whether he had merely imagined the existence of them, his persecution mania caught on, and the press was slow to believe that there was nothing sinister in his resignation. They looked around feverishly for evidence of some secret wrongdoing which would subsequently 'come out'.

Wilson's wrongdoings as Prime Minister, however, were not concealed. They had been apparent for all to see – a dithering and indecisive foreign policy, and gross mismanagement of the economy. He had capped it all by ennobling a gang of scoundrels in his Resignation Honours List.

As happens with all but the most unusual of Prime Ministers, Wilson vanished without trace. His actual reason for resigning was that he had begun to recognise in himself the signs of incipient dementia. It was not for this reason, though, that he was forgotten so quickly. He simply had not added up to anything. His very great cleverness was all skin-deep, and the philistinism, which so troubled his friend and adviser Arnold Goodman, and the lack of interest outside politics, dealt its own cruel punishment. When the political life was over, Wilson's life and reputation were over, too, though he lingered on, a twilit existence, first on the back benches of the Commons, then in the House of Lords, and finally with his wife in a flat off Victoria Street. He who had once possessed a photographic memory for Treasury figures and Gilbert and Sullivan lyrics was now unable to remember his own name.[2]

Wilson's departure provided the Labour Party with an opportunity to choose a leader with more depth or integrity. It was one which it passed by. On the right of the party, Social Democrats Roy Jenkins and Denis Healey were both plausible leaders. They were well read, and well rounded in all senses, their Balliol bumptiousness being no obvious barrier to office. On the left, there was the colourful and intelligent figure of Michael Foot, who was eventually to have his turn as leader, and to demonstrate just how unelectable the left could become. Foot was by far the most powerful ally Margaret Thatcher had in her political career. His extreme stances on matters as varied as Europe, the armed forces and the economy would have guaranteed any Conservative leader the victory in a General Election. Denis Healey, a bruiser as well as an intellect, would have given Thatcher a run for her money. Woy Jenkins would have offered the middle classes what he would no doubt have considered a very civilised alternative to Conservative government. Instead, when Wilson resigned, the Labour Party elected the party apparatchik, the backroom fixer Leonard James Callaghan (1912–2005), a figure much less distinguished even than Wilson himself. He would manage to get into *The Guinness Book of Records* for two feats over which he had little control. Until the arrival of Gordon Brown, Callaghan was the tallest Prime Minister in British history (six foot one), and he turned out to be the longest lived. Apart from this pair of boring statistics, he had absolutely no distinction of character or of intellect. His attempts to compare himself with Baldwin[3] as a safe pair of hands in a crisis overlooked, first, his own record of extreme incompetence in any crisis, and, secondly, Baldwin's intellectual weight, shown not only in his political canniness but also in the eloquence and depth of his public speeches. Baldwin had his faults, and history has been strict with them – he treated the unemployed with indifferent contempt; he sacked a popular King on a trumped-up charge; he appeased, or appeared to appease, Hitler. Yet beside Callaghan, Baldwin was a giant. Callaghan, who had started out as a white-collar trades union official, was little better than a party hack. He always voted at his party's call and never thought of thinking for himself at all.

He had held three of the most senior offices of state. In 1964, as Chancellor of the Exchequer he began to borrow at reckless levels to stabilise reserves (there was the traditional run on the pound after any change of Labour leadership) and to finance unaffordable levels of public expenditure. He resigned when the pound was forced to devalue. He was also the Chancellor who approved of the joyless change from pounds, shillings and pence to a decimal currency, though this was not brought in until February 1971 by the relentlessly modernising Heath. As Home Secretary, Callaghan had brought in the Commonwealth Immigrants Bill, a typical fudge, seen by those who wished to limit immigration as entirely inadequate; liberal opponents, such as Ian Gilmour, Tory owner and editor of the *Spectator*, saw it as a measure to 'keep blacks out' – which it was. It was an Act which had the Callaghan hallmarks of being both inefficient and unenlightened. As Foreign Secretary, he had made no mark at all. No great enthusiast for the EEC, he had nonetheless led the campaign within the Labour Party for the Yes vote in 1975 which guaranteed continued British Membership of the European experiment.

Callaghan as party leader and Prime Minister was elected because he believed, rightly, that he could hold together the warring factions of left and right in his party, rather than because he would make a distinguished Prime Minister. Being possessed of no observable beliefs or principles, he found it easy to negotiate deals between left and right. Denis Healey, as Chancellor of the Exchequer, had the task of balancing the books. This was no easy undertaking, with a world recession in progress, the trades unions continuing to make crippling wage demands, the left of the Labour Party continuing to resist any 'cuts' in public expenditure and the Keynesian liberals in the party such as Antony Crosland, Foreign Secretary, being unsupportive of Healey for personal reasons. It took only a few months for the economy to unravel. Healey, like the finance minister of some emergent African nation, was obliged to go to the International Monetary Fund to secure a loan of $3.9 billion, without which Britain would have gone bankrupt. 'The disaster at Suez had revealed that without its Empire, Britain was no longer a major power except in the minds of its leaders. The IMF loan application suggested that the pioneer of the Industrial Revolution had become a charity case.'[4]

Healey it was, therefore, who, three years before Margaret Thatcher came into office, was compelled by financial pressure to adopt a strictly monetarist policy. The IMF loan came in three instalments, conditional upon £2 billion of cuts in public expenditure. A further £500 million was raised by selling most of British Petroleum shares, thereby effectively privatising BP.

Neither the Keynesians in the Cabinet such as Shirley Williams or Antony Crosland (who disliked Healey's bullying manners) nor the left-wingers such as Peter Shore or Michael Foot, could accept the reality of things, even after the IMF debacle. Figures such as Wedgwood Benn, Secretary of State for Trade and Industry, continued to believe that what Britain in its desperate economic plight most needed was more socialism. In 1974, Benn had pushed the Cabinet to accept investment in a workers' motorcycle cooperative in Meriden, a Midlands town near Coventry. The factory had been part of the Norton-Villiers-Triumph conglomerate and was doomed to closure until the workers formed their co-op. The civil servants who costed the enterprise could see that it was unviable, and said so in their reports. Benn, however, and his wife, Caroline, paid a visit to Meriden in 1974. 'It was a fantastic spectacle,' he told his diary. 'There was the freshly-painted factory with an old picket tent and brazier on the gate and a couple of bikes out front.'⁵ When he went round the factory, Benn found it was 'just like going round a Chinese factory – they were speaking with such confidence about their own skill and their work and how they wouldn't need many supervisors and so on'. When Benn left, the men sang 'For He's a Jolly Good Fellow', sentiments which, in time, the majority of Benn's countrymen came unaccountably to share. A few years later, Benn's successor Keith Joseph, in a Conservative government, wrote off the co-op's debts and the factory closed. It could not compete with its Japanese competitor Yamaha, which was producing motorcycles not with bands of happy Chinese-style workers, but with robots.⁶

The nation which had not only invented the Industrial Revolution but had also, in the 1840s, unleashed the triumphs of free trade upon a global economy, following the repeal of the Corn Laws, had forgotten its past. Trade and Industry was not in the hands of a man who showed the smallest glimmering of understanding that, with Japanese, and later Malaysian, and later still Indian and Chinese competition, the European labour markets would have to revolutionise their attitudes. Far from seeing the IMF as a warning signal, as a chilling message of realism, the British trades unions and their political allies continued to press for more wages, more public services, more welfare.

The so-called Winter of Discontent in 1978–79 doomed not merely Callaghan and his wretchedly undistinguished government, but also socialism in Britain as a viable option for any of the major parties. The socialists did not go away, but their attitude was well summarised by a young militant in the Brent constituency, Ken Livingstone, who in 1987 wrote *If voting changed anything, they'd abolish it.*⁷

While Healey and Callaghan tried to impose a 5 per cent wage rise, the winter saw strikes among rubbish collectors, gravediggers and hospital orderlies. In all the bigger towns, the garbage formed huge mountains, metaphors of what Callaghan and his cohorts had made of Britain. The dead lay unburied. Schools could not be opened because the caretakers were out on strike, as were cleaners, coal suppliers and cooks. In the post-war era there can never have been a time, even during the three-day week imposed by Edward Heath, when Britain felt closer to anarchy. Returning from an economic summit in Guadeloupe, Callaghan was asked at the airport, 'What is your general approach, in view of the mounting chaos in the country at the moment?' His answer was, 'Well, that's a judgement that you are making. I promise you that if you look at it from outside, and perhaps you're taking rather a parochial view at the moment, I don't think that other people in the world share the view that there is mounting chaos.' That very week, the lorry drivers achieved a pay rise of 20 per cent. Public sector unions such as NUPE and NALGO called for a twenty-four-hour general strike.[8]

The *Sun* newspaper, recently acquired together with *The Times* by the American-Australian tycoon Rupert Murdoch, summarised this waffly speech in the devastating headline: CRISIS? WHAT CRISIS? After a no-confidence debate in the House of Commons, Callaghan lost by one vote. He went to the country and if ever there was a feeling of retributive justice in a British election result it was on 3 May 1979 when Callaghan's disgraced government was removed from office and replaced by the Conservative administration of Margaret Thatcher.

The defeat of Callaghan, however, had one unfortunate consequence for Britain. His young Foreign Secretary, David Anthony Llewellyn Owen (born 1938), had been in the job scarcely two years. Owen had been appointed Foreign Secretary at less than forty years of age, following the sudden death of Antony Crosland.

This death left at large Crosland's simpering American wife, Susan, who continued to write prying, spiteful articles in the Sunday newspapers about other people's private lives. Crosland's death, however, enabled his Minister at the Foreign Office, David Owen, to take over. Owen was a world statesman. He, for example, was one of the first world leaders to see the dangers of a radicalised Islam, and he had supported the Shah of Persia against the Islamic revolutionaries. He had managed to negotiate peace in Rhodesia, and bring the nationalists to a negotiating table with the illegal white government. He had powerful charisma, high intelligence and real skills. Sadly, the Labour Party was no place for the likes of Owen. Inevitably, when Roy Jenkins and the others left to form the Social Democratic Party, Owen joined them, a disastrous career mistake. Had he stayed in the Labour Party, or crossed sides to the Conservatives, he had all the makings of one of the truly great Prime Ministers. He immediately saw that it had been a mistake to get mixed up with the likes of Shirley Williams and Roy Jenkins, and when they joined up with the Liberal Party, Owen ploughed his own lonely furrow, in the end being the only member of the Social Democrats – or possibly one of two since Andrew, 11th Duke of Devonshire, used to say that he continued to regard Owen as his party leader.[9]

Altogether, 1979 was an eventful year. It saw, for example, the dramatic murder of Earl Mountbatten of Burma (1900–79). It also saw a Privy Councillor put on trial for murder: Jeremy Thorpe, who, only a few years before, had been wondering whether to accept the Prime Minister's offer of a place in the Cabinet.

The Rt Hon. Jeremy Thorpe, with his hats at jaunty angles, his double-breasted, watch-chain-adorned waistcoats, and his crinkly, oily dark hair and shifty dark eyes was an allusion to an earlier age of English raffish-ness. 'The Card' and 'Gilbert the Filbert' were outmoded phrases which his appearance evoked. He looked like an Edwardian actor, on the verge of seedy, trying to exemplify those other obsolete words, rotter, scoundrel, cad. He was also a charmer. He was an Etonian and an Oxford man, ready with quips. It was he who had set the House of Commons in a roar, when Harold Macmillan sacked a handful of dud Cabinet Ministers, with the quip, 'Greater love hath no man, that he lay down his friends for his life.' It was a joke which returned to haunt him. For, laying down a friend – not to put too fine a point on it, having the friend killed in order to save his own political life – was what, to the Crown Prosecution Service, Thorpe had appeared to have done. He would be acquitted of the charge. But what did it say about England, that so many of his friends, fans and admirers appeared, whether he was found guilty or not, to condone the preparedness to commit a murder? The Thorpe affair revealed a certain amount about the life of Jeremy Thorpe. But it also revealed that many English people believed that it was permissible for public school-educated men to silence their more embarrassing former friends and lovers by any means at their disposal, including murder. If a class-less weirdo threatened an Etonian, then Eton must be allowed the final say and the weirdo must be humiliated and his words distorted and his character, if not his body, assassinated. Whatever the truth of the case, it was a dazzling example of how, when an Old Etonian finds himself in the soup, the other public school boys were prepared to close ranks and protect him, whatever the truth of the charges brought against him.[10]

The General Election of 1979 was held on 3 May. Jeremy Thorpe, Privy Councillor, formerly leader of the Liberal Party, and a man who, during the heady period of the Lib-Lab pact had been offered the post of Home Secretary by Harold Wilson, did not spend the day election-eering. He had stood down as a parliamentary candidate. With three other men – very rum coves all – he was in the dock of Court No. 1 at the Old Bailey, charged that 'on divers days between 1 January 1973 and 18 November 1977 in the county of Devon and elsewhere they conspired together and with others unknown to murder Norman Scott'. Thorpe was also charged 'that between 1 January 1969 and 30 March 1969 he unlawfully incited David Malcolm Holmes to murder Norman Scott'.

It was a curious case. During the committal proceedings at Minehead Magistrates Court the previous November, the country had been gripped by the full newspaper accounts of the prosecution case. The key witness was the alleged murder victim himself, Norman Scott, known previously as Josiffe. He had told the magistrates that he first met Thorpe before the changes in the law which allowed consensual sex between adult males. At the time of their first meeting, according to Scott, he was still a minor, which would have made Thorpe guilty of at least two serious offences at the very time when he was beginning his rise to political fame. When they met, Scott was working as a stable boy for a man whose real name was Norman Vater, but who styled himself the Honourable Brecht van de Vater. Vater was a friend of Thorpe's. Thorpe was already a Member of Parliament, and he is supposed to have told Scott on this occasion that if he ever needed help, he should get in touch. Not long afterwards, the stable boy had what was described as a nervous breakdown, and on leaving the clinic where he was treated, he called on Thorpe at the House of Commons. Scott alleged that he had had sexual relations in Thorpe's room at the Commons. And in a vivid, unforgettably graphic piece of evidence, he described being taken to spend a night in the house of Thorpe's mother, where he was given James Baldwin's gay novel *Giovanni's Room* to read in his camp bed, and then buggered on repeated occasions through the night. Later, he received a letter from Thorpe referring to his nickname, Bunny, which told him to clear off: 'Bunnies can and will go to France.'

On 24 October 1975, Scott had met one Andy Newton, who shot Scott's dog, a Great Dane named Rinka. This Newton, a professional hit man, was imprisoned for two years and charged with the unlawful possession of a gun with intent to endanger life.

When Scott went further, alleging that Newton had been hired by Thorpe, or, rather, by a strange gang of men on behalf of Thorpe, first to frighten him off, and then to kill him, the matter came to court. For the duration of the trial at the Old Bailey, in May 1979, the nation was gripped by the daily newspaper accounts. Thorpe gave no evidence, and never once spoke in the course of the proceedings, except to give his name. The prosecution, led by Peter Murray Taylor QC, took the jury through the story which was already familiar to newspaper readers who had, agog, read the committal proceedings – namely that Thorpe, having had a homosexual relationship with Scott in the early 1960s, became frightened that this would damage his political career, and took steps to shut Scott up. David Holmes, the sometime deputy treasurer of the Liberal Party, became convinced that the only way to achieve this end was to kill Scott. Through John Le Mesurier, not the widely loved comic actor of that name but a carpet dealer from South Wales, and George Deakin, a dealer in fruit machines, Holmes met Andy Newton, an airline pilot who was prepared to earn £10,000 as a hit man. The defence was conducted by George Alfred Carman QC, a tiny, chain-smoking heterosexual, domestically violent and much agitated man, who lived on his nerves. He had been at Cambridge with Thorpe and subsequently developed a high reputation for his skills at the Bar. Even Carman's skills, however, would not have been able to persuade the jury to acquit, had they not been more or less directed to do so by the judge, the Honourable Sir Joseph Donaldson Cantley. 'Remember, I have the last word.'

Thorpe was acquitted. At the time of the Stephen Ward trial, and suicide, in 1962, the public had seen the Establishment in the mode of attack. Under threat of exposure as a result of the indiscretions of Ward, and of the young women in his circle, the Establishment had savaged someone, destroyed his life, in an act of murderous hypocrisy which had sickened the public. In 1979, the Establishment was seen once again to be protecting its own, this time in defence mode. Lord Goodman issued a statement after the trial in which he said, 'In view of the observations from the learned judge and leading counsel relating to the individuals whose names were brought into the case without being parties or witnesses, it would be quite unnecessary for any further statement to be made by me except to reaffirm that there is not a scintilla of truth in any of the allegations that have been aired.' This statement, apart from provoking the obvious epistemological question – how would a scintilla of truth differ from the whole truth? – sat oddly beside the fact that everyone in Britain had heard, night after night on the television news, the statements of the witnesses and of the prosecution: viz. that Thorpe had siphoned off money given to him for Liberal Party funds to give to a professional hit man, who had shot Scott's dog and who alleged, together with some of Thorpe's former friends and colleagues called to the witness stand, that the intention had been to kill the unfortunate Scott. These allegations might or might not have had a scintilla of truth in them, but the interesting thing was that Carman did not produce any evidence to contradict them. They were passed over in silence until the judge effectively told the jury to acquit Thorpe.

It had been a lively year, since in addition to the Thorpe trial the public had also feasted on the excitement of Lord Mountbatten's assassination.

Mountbatten was regarded by the Royal Family, and especially by the Duke of Edinburgh and the Prince of Wales, as a fount of authority and wisdom. To 'Uncle Dickie' they turned in a crisis. But this elderly popinjay, with his offensively arrogant manners and his fondness for naval ratings, was not popular with the public. If they had to stomach Mountbatten at all, they preferred him in the fictitious film version of his Second World War exploits, *In Which We Serve*. In this moving picture, his sometime lover Noël Coward portrayed Mountbatten as a gallant sea captain. There was some truth in this, and the central incident of the film, in which Mountbatten lost his ship, HMS *Kelly* (called in the film HMS *Torrin*), is substantially true. Coward's laughably implausible attempt to play the happily married man with Celia Johnson was viewed with as much derision as was Mountbatten's improbable pretence to do the same with his wife, Edwina. Both had been promiscuous adulterers, sometimes, it was alleged, with the same man – e.g., Nehru.

It was a great pity that Antony Lambton never published his biography of Mountbatten, but he did publish a prolegomenon, which went into the question of Mountbatten's ancestry. Although he arrived as a boy cadet at Osborne Training College in May 1913 with a trunk inscribed, 'His Serene Highness the Prince Louis of Battenburg', Mountbatten was a very distinctly minor, not to say 'shabby genteel', royal personage. Heiligenberg, near Judenheim, a few miles south of Darmstadt in Hesse, was the closest thing his father ever had to a country house (they had no English seat). It has been described by Lambton as 'two bald houses opposing each other across a court, joined up by an ugly ballroom and other uninteresting buildings' – scarcely the romantic *Schloss* in which Mountbatten liked to pretend he had grown up. His closest claim to real grandeur in childhood was that an uncle by marriage, Prince Henry, was the brother of the Kaiser.

> His passionate wish to belong to the royal circle was a common characteristic of semi-royalties, who are often more concerned with 'position' and the importance of 'blood' than the heads of their families. Mountbatten's morganatic and uncertain ancestry made him desperately desire to be a trusted part of an inner circle which, when he was a young man, had reigned on the thrones of Europe east of the Rhine. Defending his birthright he collected, and then ignored and hid away, papers in his own archives, and created myths flattering to his vanity by romantically rewriting his family history. To his critics his obsession was and is ridiculous, but it should be balanced against his fearlessness and the greatest of all qualities in a leader, the ability to inspire those under his command.[11]

When Mountbatten's nephew Philip married the future Queen Elizabeth II it was the fulfilment of all Mountbatten's desire to control the destinies of the British Royal Family. As a boy cadet, he had witnessed the humiliation of his father, Prince Louis, who had so longed to become the First Sea Lord but was dismissed in the understandable wave of anti-German feeling which swept the country upon the outbreak of the First World

War. The family name of Battenberg was changed to Mountbatten, just as the House of Saxe-Coburg became the House of Windsor. ('Now,' the Kaiser had joked, 'I suppose we shall have the Merry Wives of Saxe-Coburg.') Mountbatten was so anxious to attend, and interfere in, the wedding of Philip and Elizabeth that, even though he was the last Viceroy of India, he rushed home for the event. It was for this trivial reason alone that he was so anxious to speed up Indian independence arrangements, leaving Greater India with the Partition of West and East Pakistan (the latter subsequently Bangladesh), with much avoidable slaughter and perhaps a million lives lost.

Prince Philip of Greece and Denmark had seriously entertained the idea that his bride would take his surname. Apart from the fact that it was without precedent in British royal history, the surname itself was ludicrous – Schleswig-Holstein-Sonderburg-Glücksburg. The Home Secretary of the time, Chuter Ede, suggested that he should take his mother's surname and be married as Lieutenant Philip Mountbatten. Pushed by 'Uncle Dickie', he had done his best to persuade the Royal Family that the future Queen should have the surname Mountbatten. This was roundly rejected, much to Philip's rage. He is supposed to have exclaimed, 'I'm nothing but an amoeba!' – by which he presumably meant that his only function in the constitutional scheme of things was as a stud to provide the monarch with heirs. In 1960, the Queen had declared, 'I and my children shall continue to be styled and known as the House and family of Windsor.' Yet by the time of Princess Anne's wedding in 1973, Mountbatten wrote to the Prince of Wales, 'her marriage certificate will be the first opportunity to settle the Mountbatten-Windsor name for good'. It was outrageous of Mountbatten to have asked the Prince of Wales to contravene a decision made by the Queen in Council, but the trick seems to have worked. After the wedding, in which Anne did indeed sign her name in the register as Mountbatten-Windsor, the Queen said that in future she wished her descendants to be known by the new name, having long wished, according to her press secretary, 'to associate her husband's name with their descendants'. Most people who gave much thought to such things, an admittedly diminishing band, recognised it as a mistake.[12]

Mountbatten, born 25 June 1900, was the age of the century. In August 1979, he and his family took a holiday off the coast of Ireland. Their twenty-nine-foot fishing boat *Shadow V* was left for long spells unattended in the little harbour of Mullaghmore while the party was ashore. On the 27th, Mountbatten went aboard with Lord and Lady Brabourne, Mountbatten's son-in-law and daughter, and their fourteen-year-old twin sons Nicholas and Timothy, together with Lord Brabourne's eighty-three-year-old mother Doreen. An Irish boy from the neighbourhood, Paul Maxwell, was also of the party. The bomb, which had been planted on the boat, went off just as they cleared the harbour. Paul Maxwell and Nicholas Knatchbull were killed, Doreen Brabourne was fatally injured, Timothy and his parents were badly injured. Mountbatten was killed outright.[13]

The IRA issued the half-witted declaration that it had carried out an 'execution', as a way of 'bringing emotionally home to the English ruling-class and its working-class slaves . . . that their government's war on us is going to cost them as well'. The murders merely exacerbated the intensely anti-Irish feeling in England which the IRA outrages always provoked. Princess Margaret, on a visit to Chicago two months after Uncle Dickie's death, got into trouble, when someone expressed sorrow at Mountbatten's murder, by replying that the Irish were pigs, a remark which some thought provoked the immediate departure of the Mayor of Chicago, Jane Byrne, from the party. Hasty denials were issued next morning, but no one was convinced. As for Dickie, Mountbatten's slavish biographer surely exaggerated when he wrote that 'the world mourned'. Mountbatten had not been loved, and except by Noël Coward fans he was not even much respected. *Private Eye* had discovered an easy target with its repeated suggestion that Mountbatten was not merely homosexual, but also a Soviet agent. Even if it was not quite true, he certainly did as much damage as many an enemy spy could have done. By gross mismanagement in India he was in effect, if not in intention, a mass murderer. By interfering, and giving disastrous advice to the Royal Family, he contributed to the very low esteem in which they had come to be held by the end of his life. They had their ups and downs in popularity after the Mullaghmore bomb exploded, but, on the whole, their fortunes have steadily improved.

As always, public feelings about the Royal Family, Establishment, the hierarchical structure of society and the inheritance of the past, were mixed. The Queen's Silver Jubilee in 1977 had occurred during a blazing hot summer. Street parties were held all over Britain, with bunting suspended from trees and lamp-posts, and children sitting at trestle tables eating egg sandwiches and drinking lemonade, much as they might have done in the year of the Coronation. These parties were quite spontaneous. No one was compelled to arrange them. Yet there was an air of defiance about them, as though the times were out of joint, and this expression of loyalty to the Queen was, paradoxically, itself an act of protest, against the state of Britain which the politicians had created.

A more strident form of protest against the existing order of things was punk. In the 100 Club, a small basement in Oxford Street, on Tuesday nights from 1976 onwards, the Sex Pistols performed their furious routines.[14] 'Anarchy in the UK' was one of their most famous numbers, screamed out by the author of the lyrics, Johnny Rotten, the stage name of John Lydon, an etiolated red-haired urchin who yelled at his squirming audience that he was the anti-Christ and he wanted to destroy everything. The audience bounced up and down, pogoing, and, in so far as thought was possible in minds blown with narcotics, they responded eagerly to Rotten's message, just as they thrilled to the sight of his friend Sid Vicious smearing himself with blood, or Siouxsie Sioux, a punk goddess with naked breasts protruding from her bondage outfits, and swastikas adorning her arms. For the Jubilee, Johnny Rotten wrote a version of 'God Save the Queen' which reached Number Two in the charts. The sleeve of the single disc was a Warholesque representation of Her Majesty with her eyes blocked by a collage reading God Save the Queen and her mouth pasted over with the words Sex Pistols. The lyrics equated the twenty-five years of her reign with a 'fascist regime'. Real fascism was now something which had retreated so far into the historical shadows that the word 'fascist' was used to denote more or less any form of hierarchy, any rule of law, any attempt to hold on to the concept of personal property, anything, in short, of which the speaker disapproved. The BBC awarded Rotten's 'God Save the Queen' the high accolade of banning it from any of its radio or TV stations.

The Sex Pistols' was a cry of horror, not from the absolute depths but from the stultifyingly boring fringes. The natural haunts of their fans were the soul-destroying purlieus and suburbs of London.

Siouxsie Sioux (of Siouxsie and the Banshees) was really a girl called Susan Janet Ballion (born 1957) from Bromley. John Lydon's background was 'lace curtains Irish'. His family lived in a council flat in Seven Sisters Road, Finsbury Park. Like Germaine Greer, Madonna, and many others in our times, Johnny found that a dysfunctional Catholic childhood had been the first brilliant career move.

The Catholic Church provided him with the props of Gothick horror, both against which to react, and with which to clothe his iconoclasm. It also inspired his most celebrated lyrics – the 'God Save the Queen' parody being almost word for word the same as the IRA's explanation of why they had blown Mountbatten sky high. Johnny Rotten, who had something of the artist about him, stood detached from the bizarre punk creation of which he was by far the most stylish representative. Punk was in any event always surrounded by irony and Rotten was a stylishly ironic exponent of it. Sid Vicious (other names John Beverley/John Simon Ritchie) was, by contrast, less an ironic exponent than an appalling object lesson of the movement's negativism. The child of a junkie, he appeared at the front of the band in a drug haze, mutilating himself and mouthing idiocies or making, sometimes feigned, puking sounds, sometimes trying to remember Lydon's lyrics. At the age of twenty-one he took up with a fellow heroin addict named Nancy Spungeon. The autumn of 1978 found them in New York, where, following in the footsteps of Dylan Thomas and Bob Dylan, they checked into the Hotel Chelsea on West 23rd Street. On 12 October, Nancy was found dead in the hotel room, lying under the bathroom sink with stab wounds in her stomach and a hunting knife at her side. When the police arrived, Sid admitted responsibility. After a spell in a psychiatric hospital he was sent to prison on Riker's Island. On 1 February 1979, he was released on bail, and found his mother, Anne Beverley, awaiting him. She gave him some heroin. Sid went to a friend's apartment in Greenwich Village and shot up. 'Jesus, son, that must have been a good hit,' said the mother when she saw her son lit up with the smack. He injected himself once more that night and died of an overdose. Anne was in the room next door. 'I'm glad he died,' said Sid Vicious's mother. 'Nothing can hurt him any more.'[15]

The commercial success of the Sex Pistols was a paradoxical fact given their desire to attack and defame the 'fascist' world of privilege and, presumably, of commerce. But the music industry knew that there was big money in the sheer offensiveness, not only of words, such as Rotten's 'God Save the Queen', but of the noise itself made by the great bands of the era. Synthesisers were invented in the late 1960s by Bob Moog, while he was studying engineering and physics at Cornell University, and thereafter the noisier the band, and the greater the scream of mindless rage they represented, the happier were the fans. On tour in 1972, the Rolling Stones fed their sound through massive banks of speakers hoisted high above the stage, guaranteeing deafening noise. Even this noise was as nothing to the volume produced by Led Zeppelin, described by Germaine Greer as the Wagner of rock music. They continued their mind- and ear-blasting career until 1980 when their drummer, John Bonham, drank himself to death. Huge sums had been generated by these assailants of the eardrums.

Vivienne Westwood and Malcolm McLaren, likewise, saw that there was money in punk chic. Their boutique at 430 King's Road selling rubber clothes, studs and bondage clothes fitted with buckles and straps, PVC which could be opened to reveal the genitalia, soon expanded into a multi-million-pound business. *Épater la bourgeoisie*, the old decadent rallying cry of the 1890s, now became immensely lucrative, creating not so much a bourgeoisie but an aristocracy of rock stars, clothes designers, film-makers and architects. Indeed, those attacking the system in Callaghan's Britain stood a much greater chance of making a good old-fashioned fortune than those trying to shore up conventional businesses while battling with the wage demands of trades unions. Youth was not merely in rebellion – against what it was never quite sure – it also had money to burn.

Monty Python's Flying Circus, which was first broadcast on BBC television in October 1969, and which continued until 1974, was a late flowering of surrealism, a televised version of the humour made popular by Harry Secombe, Michael Bentine, Spike Milligan and Peter Sellers in *The Goon Show*. It was a series of larky comedy sketches, in which, for example, a football match might be played between teams of the great German versus the Greek philosophers, or two young men in drag, impersonating charwomen, would go to Paris to meet Jean-Paul Sartre. The prodigious popularity of the series, and its long afterlife as a cult on American television, probably derived from its skilful flattery of the audience into thinking that they, too, enjoyed such juxtapositions of student essay subjects with the despised life of provincial middle- or lower-middle-class England which had been left behind when the actors themselves had gone to university. It was an undergraduate rag warmed up for general consumption. Some of the sketches, such as a man taking back a parrot to a pet shop because it was dead and had been dead when sold, became so much part of the common culture that pub bores could recite the whole of it to one another as a substitute for wit of their own. If compared with the sketches of *The Two Ronnies*, which were being aired during the same decade, most of the *Monty Python* sketches cannot be seen as funny at all. Compare the dead parrot sketch with, for example, the episode of *The Two Ronnies* in the hardware shop, where the customer, a taciturn Ronnie Barker, asks for 'fork handles' and is given 'four candles'.[16] The verbal ingenuity and the deadpan acting make this a small comic masterpiece. The best thing about the *Monty Python* show was the ingenuity of the graphics by the American Terry Gilliam. Had the sketches not been interrupted by Gilliam's visual jokes, nor accompanied by John Philip Sousa's march 'Liberty Bell', they would not have been so hilarious. Gilliam made the sketches into surreal circus, in which cut and pasted Victorian strongmen can lift the actors up like ants, or the foot from Bronzino's *Allegory with Venus and Cupid* descends upon the set to squash them. Heads blow off, and flowers burst from the gaping neck. Naked girls chase cardinals on tricycles, both crushed in turn by the descending foot, or by a nursery scrapbook cherub.

The Pythons themselves, a little like the *Beyond the Fringe* team of an earlier generation, came from the older universities. Terry Jones and Michael Palin were Oxford, Graham Chapman, Eric Idle and John Cleese were Cambridge.

They captured the mood of their generation by their expressed hatred of religion. Earlier generations had been prepared to leave alone the shattered shell of the Christian religion, but the Python team lived in an era when the Church was on the run, and Christianity itself seemed to many people to be fraudulent, even dangerous. Geza Vermes, a former Hungarian Roman Catholic priest then teaching at the University of Oxford and an expert on the Dead Sea Scrolls, published in 1973 a book called *Jesus the Jew*. It was an attempt to place Jesus in his historical setting. Few people have ever known more about first-century Palestine, its languages and religions than Professor Vermes, and his book had a great impact, seeming to many biblical scholars to destroy the plausibility of Christian beliefs that Jesus could ever have made the claims for himself which were made by later theology – above all that He was a divine being. Had Vermes, however, managed to create a more plausible Jesus than the figure of the Four Gospels? Many thought that he had, among them, presumably, the Pythons, whose *Life of Brian*, a spoof version of the life of Jesus, was designed as an assault upon the Christian religion. In a cowardly way, they covered themselves by asserting, in the first five minutes of the film, that Brian Cohen was a contemporary of Jesus, but in all the scenes which follow it is clear that Jesus himself was the object of their abuse. We have the Sermon on the Mount in which Brian's words, Blessed are the Peacemakers, is misheard as Blessed are the Cheesemakers, and it ends with a parody of the Crucifixion. Many theologians, religious teachers and priests at this period had come to accept the Vermes–Python version of Christian origins. 'Men said that Christ slept, and his saints' – the continuation of the *Anglo-Saxon Chronicle*'s despondent observation on the chaos of King Stephen's reign, would have made a fitting epitaph for the 1970s.

It was while the Pythons were filming an episode of *Monty Python* in Torquay that they came upon the ill-tempered hotelier, Donald Sinclair, who inspired one of the most enduring characters of the decade, Basil Fawlty. 'Could you call me a taxi, please?' Cleese asked him. 'A *taxi*?' 'Yes.' Sinclair emitted a deep sigh. Then through gritted teeth the grudging reply came, 'I *suppose* so.'

Cleese wrote the scripts of *Fawlty Towers* with his American wife Connie Booth. Their model was the Feydeau farce, but they outsoared their master. Each thirty-minute episode was a tightly wrought harmony of plotting, the different strands of the story coming together in an invariably hilarious catastrophe. Cleese played the irascible Basil, and Prunella Scales was his wife, Sybil, with an irredeemably common bouffant hairdo, and twangy south-eastern accent. Connie Booth, poised and beautiful, was Polly, the maid-of-all-work, and one of the many inspired things about the series was that (Booth, one suspects, being the real mind behind the comedies) never for one instance was any comic mileage made out of the fact that Polly is a meltingly beautiful blonde. No guest ever makes a pass at her and the termagant wife Sybil never suspects Basil of straying with Polly, though Basil once suspects Polly of indecent relations with someone who turns out to be an old family friend. They are all far too busy trying to train the idiotic Spanish waiter, Manuel, or coping with the disasters, nearly all of Basil's making, which befall their unfortunate guests. They stopped when the going was good, only making a dozen episodes, and it could be said that television knew no finer hour.

In one of the most electrifying episodes, an aggressive American stays at Fawlty Towers and is the first who is brave enough to confront Basil with the fact that the place is a dump. It leads to a minor rebellion in the ranks, with other guests, when challenged, admitting that the service, food and general standards of the hotel are lousy. You feel at this moment that it is a miracle that the hotel, like the marriage of its proprietors, has managed to survive. Luckily, by the next episode Basil is back in the semi-control, which is the most he ever exercises over life. With his regimental ties, sense of England going to the dogs, despair at the success of the trades unions, suspicion of the foreigner, but inability to be a good manager, Basil Fawlty was the archetypal Englishman of Callaghan's Britain. The wounded dignity, the feeling that the country was under threat, the despondent sense that nothing can be done to get them out of the mess into which Fate has dug them – these matched the mood of an electorate who watched powerless as the politicians caved in to union pay demands, and the economy lurched from one crisis to the next. (Basil is obsessed by strikes, especially by the car workers, and is wistfully envious, as he reads the newspapers, of the power and influence of Henry Kissinger.)

Johnny Rotten had said, at the time of the 1977 Jubilee, 'You don't write a song like "God Save the Queen" because you hate the English race. You write a song like that because you love them, and you're sick of seeing them mistreated.'

Some of the electorate, probably including the surviving Sex Pistols themselves, felt alienated by the entire political system. Some vainly believed that the creaking old system could serve them for their lifetimes: the series of industrial crises, labour disputes, high taxes. They offered corporate political and fiscal solutions to something which others felt to be not so much an economic as a moral malaise. The German guests in Torquay, treated to a gross series of insults by Basil Fawlty who is unsuccessfully trying not to mention the war, eventually stare at him, his head in a bandage from concussion, collapsed beneath a moose's head, which he had unsuccessfully tried to hang on the wall to add a bit of class to the hotel lobby. As the drunken Major leans over him to offer ineffectual help, the German asks, 'How did they ever win?' By the date of *Fawlty Towers* and Sunny Jim Callaghan it had indeed become unimaginable that Britain had ever been a country which could win a war or solve its own problems without intervention from the International Monetary Fund or injections of cash from America.

'There are times, perhaps once every thirty years, when there is a sea-change in politics,' said Callaghan to Bernard Donoughue. 'It does not then matter what you say or do. There is a shift in what the public wants and what it approves of. I suspect there is now such a sea-change – and it is for Mrs Thatcher.' The fatalism of the remark reveals what the electorate found so insufferable about, not only Callaghan's Labour Party, but also about the old Heathites of the Conservative Party: namely the suggestion that they, who had been elected to solve certain problems, were incapable of doing so. The only reason that they were turning to Mrs Thatcher in this view of events was that there had been a mysterious alteration in mood. It was about this time that the political cliché-mongers appropriated the beautiful Shakespearean phrase sea-change ('into something rich and strange' from *The Tempest*) and used the phrase simply to mean 'change'. At a similar date they raided, and thereby desecrated, the Apostle Paul, as translated in the Authorised Version of the Bible, and spoke of themselves grappling for 'hearts and minds', in their language, as a clichéd synonym for 'votes'.

Johnny Rotten in a sense spoiled the effect of his 'God Save the Queen' lyric by coming out from behind the screen and saying that he was sick of seeing the people of England mistreated. Mrs Thatcher could in a comparable sense be seen to have diluted her message, when she had won the election and became Prime Minister on 4 May 1979, by quoting the supposed words of Francis of Assisi – 'Where there is hatred may we sow love, where there is injury pardon, etc.' She had arrived at Number 10 Downing Street and her speechwriter Sir Ronald Millar had, on the spur of the moment, suggested the words for her. They were apt neither to herself nor to the times. Mrs Thatcher was the first politician in a generation to appeal to something visceral in voters. Her appeal to her admirers had something of what made punk attractive to fans of the Sex Pistols. To vote Thatcher was to issue a cry of rage. Where there was pardon, to sow injury, where there was love, hate. A vote for Thatcher was psephological pogoing, and to many of her followers she was the Siouxsie Sioux of politics, revealing things on the stage which had normally been reserved for the specialist market. Her fellow Somervillian and polar opposite Shirley Williams lost her seat at Hertford and

Stevenage. Callaghan said he was 'heartbroken'. Alas, Williams would return. All the old duds expressed their sadness at Callaghan's defeat. A. J. Ayer wrote to commiserate, and Sir Goronwy Daniel, Principal of the University College of Wales, Aberystwyth, made what must rank as a double-edged remark: 'You will surely be as highly esteemed by tomorrow's historian as you are by the great majority of today's public': it sounds like a compliment, until, read twice, it becomes the deadliest insult.

In fact, the Labour Party had polled its lowest result in a General Election since the debacle of 1931, a mere 36.9 per cent of the vote. The Conservative share was 43.9 per cent, and the final result, in terms of parliamentary seats, was Conservatives 339, Labour 268 and Liberals 11. Callaghan's biographer Kenneth O. Morgan, an Old Labour Welsh academic, was right to describe him as representing 'more clearly perhaps than any other living politician' the post-1945 consensus. 'He was the classic consensus man.'[17]

Of course nothing ever changes as radically as revolutionaries, or as story-tellers, would like. The old Heathites heavily outnumbered Margaret Thatcher in her Cabinet. The civil service remained the same. The benefits system still continued to underpin the lives of the unemployed and the sick and the old. But the Siouxsie Sioux of Grantham came not to bring peace but a sword.

The times were not auspicious for classic consensus men. Airey Neave MP had been one of Mrs Thatcher's keenest supporters and allies. He had escaped from the Colditz prisoner-of-war camp and lived, as a barrister, to take part in the post-war Nuremberg trials. As a fervently Unionist Opposition spokesman for Northern Ireland he had been blown up in his car as he was leaving the Houses of Parliament on 30 March. In Pakistan, President Bhutto, the closest thing Pakistan possessed to a Nehru-style Westernised liberal democrat, was executed for 'conspiracy'. In Iran, the Revolutionary court was ordering summary executions in a Robespierre-style bloodletting. Karol Wojtyla, elected Pope John Paul II on 16 October 1978, was on his way to Poland (his visit began on 2 June) in one of the most confrontational demonstrations against communism to take place since the Russian Revolution. But nor did he endorse the Western capitalism model of society. In his first encyclical, *Redemptor Hominis*, he deplored the ever-increasing gap between the rich and poor of the world, and criticised both the communists and the believers in free trade.

The Pope's political and economic ideas derived from his nineteenth-century predecessor Leo XIII and were of the kind sometimes labelled Distributism, popularised in England during Edwardian days by G. K.

Chesterton and Hilaire Belloc – a distrust of international finance, of companies and financial institutions, a belief that Small Is Beautiful.

Britain did not have the option to experiment with the Distributist belief that all society's ills would be solved if each family were given an acre and a cow. The left had failed to help the poor, yet in its blundering efforts to do so it had destroyed the economy. Thatcher would take the risk of making an American decision: to allow the lumpenproletariat to stew in its own juice while the Treasury attempted to save British industry from terminal decline, establish a culture of share and home-ownership, and increase prosperity for the fortunate 80 per cent. Could this ruthless programme be put through without calamitous social consequences? Was it possible so to control the money supply that unemployment was used as a weapon? And what compensation could be offered, in terms of real job creation, real improvement in education and training, for those who unfortunately suffered ruin in the first waves of the monetarist revolution – not through fecklessness, but simply because they happened to be employed in a dying industry, or an industry which the monetarist politicians had condemned to death? In times past, an angry underclass could be contained by press gangs and workhouses, institutions which no longer existed. The lunatic asylums were closing down, but could the prisons hold the numbers of dissidents if, in the face of rising unemployment and disillusionment, the young of the urban wastelands, in a punk gesture of despondency, and in order to fund their drug habits, turned to crime and plunder? The alternative to consensus is confrontation. What if the balance of civilised life in Britain turned out to be much more precarious than had formerly been supposed? From 1945, the politicians had lived with little worse than the dread that the trades union barons would turn nasty. They had never had to confront, as earlier generations had done, the possibility of the Mob erupting once more as a factor in British political life. With one part of herself, no doubt, Mrs Thatcher merely wanted a standard of middle-class decency to prevail, and to protect the interests of her natural constituents – the aspirant upper working classes, who would like to have owned their own homes; the old people with savings; the entrepreneurs trying to make something of small businesses, and labouring under bureaucratic laws and crippling taxes. With a deeper part of herself she felt instinctively that none of these benefits were to be had without a struggle. In her world-view the Labour Party, and Shirley Williams and A. J. Ayer and the Principal of the University of Wales, were merely hydra heads sprouting from the monster of anarchy who questioned the very validity of hard work, thrift or saving, who would undermine Britain itself.

In May 1978, Margaret Thatcher had been driving across Tehran with the British Ambassador, Sir Anthony Parsons. She remarked to him, 'Do you know, there are still people in my party who believe in consensus?' Parsons expressed surprise, suggesting that surely this was the belief of most British people, himself included. 'I regard them as Quislings, as traitors,' she replied. If she had her way – and given the power of the quislings in the Cabinet it was to be a big If – those traitors were to be smoked out as the first step in full-scale confrontation with the Enemy.[18]

PART FIVE

The Lady

19

'This Was a Terrific Battle'

'Ripper eleven, police nil!' was one of the chants at many football grounds in the north of England in the opening weeks of the 1979–80 season. Skinny, raven-haired, bearded Peter Sutcliffe, a former undertaker's assistant, had been hitting women over the head with hammers and stabbing them repeatedly with screwdrivers throughout the Callaghan years. He had taken amazing risks, and his victims, mostly, though not all, prostitutes, had often been attacked within hailing distance of other human beings. Wilma McCann, for example, in February 1977, had been found near the house of the disc jockey Jimmy Savile. She had been stabbed so violently in the stomach with a Stanley knife that her intestines had spilled out.[1] Yet 150,000 interviews, 27,000 house-to-house searches, and more than £3 million expended had failed to locate the killer. When Sutcliffe's friend Trevor Birdsall wrote a letter to the police identifying Sutcliffe, and saying, 'This man as [sic] dealings with prostitutes and always had a thing about them,' he was thanked for his cooperation but he heard nothing more from the police, and the constable on the desk who took his statement either failed to transcribe it or lost it. Sutcliffe was eventually found because he was driving with false number plates.

It was characteristic of the new Prime Minister that she was not content to allow the incompetence of George Oldfield's investigation to blunder on without her personal intervention. When Queen Victoria heard of the Whitechapel Murders in 1888, she wrote to Lord Salisbury, the Prime Minister, 'This new most ghastly murder shows the absolute necessity for some very decided action.'[2] In a rather comparable, but even more interventionist spirit, Margaret Thatcher announced to Willie Whitelaw, her leadership rival, whom she had appointed as Home Secretary, that she intended personally to take over the investigation of the Yorkshire Ripper case. He dissuaded her, and in the event, almost by chance, the Ripper was found without Thatcher donning the Miss Marple mantle.[3] She would have made a good bloodhound, however, and no one would have envied the Ripper had it been she who tracked down her prey.

Everyone agreed, when the years of Margaret Thatcher's premiership were over, that England had changed. How far she was personally responsible for changes, good and bad, opinion differed. Her admirers pointed to a Britain which was revived and richer. Antony Crosland, in his book *The Future of Socialism*, had written

> We need not only higher exports and old-age pensions, but more open-air cafés, brighter and gayer streets at night, later closing hours for public houses, more local repertory theatres, better and more hospitable hoteliers and restaurateurs, brighter and cleaner eating houses, more riverside cafés, more pleasure gardens on the Battersea model, more murals and pictures in public places, better designs for furniture and pottery and women's clothes, statues in the centre of new housing estates, better designed new street lamps and telephone kiosks and so ad infinitum.[4]

During Thatcher's three administrations, Giles Gilbert Scott's elegant neo-Georgian red telephone boxes were replaced, by a privatised telephone company (British Telecom), with ugly glass boxes, and there were no notable works of sculpture erected in housing estates, but the council houses in these estates became the property of the occupants, and many of the good things to which Crosland had looked forward did follow the enormous injection of wealth which Thatcher's reforms instigated. It was not socialism which made England have better restaurants and hotels. It was the availability of more private money. If you were lucky enough to survive the lurches of economic boom and bust which characterised the Thatcher years, if you managed to sustain mortgage repayments when interest rates were set at 15 per cent, if you held on to your property and your job when all about were losing theirs, then you, and the majority of Britons, would find yourselves citizens of a country which was more free and more prosperous. But the freedom and prosperity did not come free. Discarded with the true lumpenproletariat of people who could not find useful employment were many citizens who had the bad luck to be employed in industries which had simply died during the monetarist revolution. There were also many who were lured by the monetarist dream of becoming owners of their own house when they could not afford to do so, and there were those who bought into the share-holding democracy who watched their savings evaporate.

Those who hated Thatcher pointed to a Britain which was coarser, more philistine, which spent less money than other European countries on the arts and on libraries. It was a Britain in which the latent aggression which lurks beneath the surface of polite society came out into the open. It was in every sense a more violent society. Some of the violence had little to do with the Prime Minister and sometimes, as in the case of the successful crushing of the miners' strike, and the successful prosecution of war in the South Atlantic, it was Thatcher who was the Boudicca, leading the charge, the scythes on her chariot wheels cutting the legs off all who stood in her path.

It seemed appropriate, when poor old Betjeman died in 1984, that Thatcher should have chosen as her Poet Laureate the Little Englander from Hull, who hated abroad, and who cheered on her election victory – albeit fearing that she was 'much too left wing'.[5] 'How do you cut unemployment?' he asked. 'Cut unemployment pay!'[6] When asked to write some journalism, he replied, 'Thanks to the successive gangs of socialist robbers that have ruled us since the last war, now there is little incentive to make more than a certain amount of money annually.'[7]

Bald, myopic, bespectacled, awkwardly fat and tall, Larkin was technically one of the deftest lyricists of modern times. His melancholy, taut poems nudged towards the edges of life's limitations – 'first boredom, then fear'. ('What have you got to complain about?' was A. L. Rowse's shrill question when he met Larkin – 'You're tall, aren't you?'[8]) The metaphysics, more, surely than the deafness or the alcoholism, found the hard limit of Larkin's music. It could not go any further. 'Aubade', his terrified, controlled meditation upon death, was one of the greatest poems of our times. But it was a suicide note to his muse. He could not, would not, imagine himself outside the confines of his self-imposed limitations, both of opportunity and of imagination.

Ted Hughes was a very different figure, and, when Larkin turned down Margaret Thatcher's offer of the Laureateship, it was given to Hughes. Larkin, in point of fact, was the laureate of a different Britain. His fondness for drinking himself sozzled at the Hull branch of the British Legion, his hatred of London, his provinciality, all bound him to the Britain which had already died before he did. Hughes by contrast, who, Larkin said would in a happier age have been not the Poet Laureate but the village idiot, was an imagination which had engaged with the essential violence at nature's heart. To judge from the writings of the American feminists who held him guilty for the suicides of two women in his life, and who had deified his first wife, Sylvia Plath, Hughes was on a moral level with Peter Sutcliffe; he was the literary Ripper. His posthumous letters revealed a more troubled, sensitive figure than his published poems had suggested, a man who had been a good friend to his children and a patient enabler of other people's talents. In his best work, he invented a new theology. Crow, his perky twentieth-century Prometheus, was a Johnny Rotten of the ornithological world. His laughter torments his mother. He worships death. While God sleeps, Crow goes on laughing. When God wakes and tries to teach Crow to love, the bird retches.

He sees life as conflict:

> This was a terrific battle
> The noise was as much
> As the limits of noise could take.[9]

He is an electrically amplified beakful of amoral violence and cynicism. This notion of conflict being at the heart of existence fitted well with the Britain of the 1980s, and was as much a characteristic of the Queen's Prime Minister as it was of the Poet Laureate.

Lord Scarman began his report *The Brixton Disorders 10–12 April 1981*[10] with a candid account of what occurred: 'During the weekend of 10–12 April (Friday, Saturday and Sunday) the British people watched with horror and incredulity an instant audio-visual presentation on their television sets of scenes of violence and disorder in their capital city, the like of which had not previously been seen in this century in Britain. In the centre of Brixton, a few hundred young people – most, but not all of them, black – attacked the police on the streets with stones, bricks, iron bars and petrol bombs, demonstrating to millions of their fellow citizens the fragile basis of the Queen's peace. The petrol bomb was now used for the first time on the streets of Britain (the idea, no doubt, copied from the disturbances in Northern Ireland).' While expressing gratitude that no one had been killed, his lordship reported to the Home Secretary that 279 policemen had been injured, 45 members of the public injured, many vehicles damaged, 28 buildings gutted by fire. It is easy to imagine the reaction of every previous age to such acts of violence and destruction. The 1st Duke of Wellington or the 3rd Marquess of Salisbury would have settled the disturbances by use of the military and the perpetrators, if they escaped with their lives, would have been punished with the utmost severity. Such would have been the reaction anywhere else in the world – in America, Russia, Japan. Whatever the reason for the riots might have been, the acts of destruction themselves would have been deemed intolerable. Yet according to Scarman, one of the most senior of the Queen's judges, the fault for the riots lay, not with those who had stirred up the young hotheads, nor with the young men themselves who spent three days smashing windows, hurling bricks at police dogs, looting shops, and terrorising the peace-loving majority of their fellow citizens. Scarman did not go so far as to say that social conditions in Brixton excused the disorder; indeed he explicitly repudiated such a notion.[11] However, he made it perfectly clear that if 'social conditions' did not excuse, they at any event went some way to *explaining* the riots. The other factor was what Scarman called the 'policing problem'. Once again, in any other

The stormy relationship of the Prince and Princess of Wales, which would end in divorce, provided newspaper readers with something more interesting than the antics of politicians. Here
they are seen at Balmoral before their marriage, with their dog Harvey.

The Sex Pistols, in their most famous song, saw the reign of Queen Elizabeth II as 'a fascist regime'. There was in fact much in common between the rhetoric of punk and the angry revolt, championed by Margaret Thatcher, of the suburbs against Consensus Politics.

As Minister of Education, Mrs Thatcher – known as Milk Snatcher for her removal of free milk to primary school children – brought a splash of colour to the House of Commons.

The Falklands War shocked liberals but delighted the huge majority. Here the HMS *Invincible* receives a hero's welcome upon its return to Portsmouth harbour.

The bravery of Prince Andrew, who flew helicopters during the war, was widely admired.

During his premiership, Tony Blair behaved as if the Labour Party did not exist. What was more paradoxical was that so did the Labour Party. Seen here with Pope Benedict XVI, the religious-minded Blair eventually became a Roman Catholic.

Despite attracting some famous converts, the Roman Catholic Church in England slumped in membership during our times. The hideous 'Paddy's Wigwam', the RC Cathedral in Liverpool, was a gimcrack building with poor foundations. Some saw this as emblematic.

Islam grew apace during our times, with the minaret and the domed mosque becoming a feature of many British cities – as is shown in this Leeds street.

The religion of hate preached by extremist Islam led to the horrific slaughter of 7 July 2005. As many as 50 people were killed and 700 injured during these terrorist attacks.

Many came to share the views of Richard Dawkins (*left*) and Philip Pullman (*below left*) that religion itself was to blame for the ills of the world. Dawkins married the Honourable Sarah Ward, the former wife of space- and time-traveller Doctor Who, as played by Tom Baker (*below right*).

Would the United Kingdom survive? Alex Salmond of the Scottish Nationalist Party was strikingly successful in promoting severance.

Ian Paisley with Martin McGuinness. Having hated one another for a generation, the 'extremists' in Northern Ireland united in wishing to manage their own affairs without English interference.

Which would triumph at the end of our times? The technological miracles of Bill Gates (seen here with the Queen, who bestowed upon him an honorary knighthood, and his wife, Melinda) . . .

. . . or would 'old style religion' triumph? Osama bin Laden, the Napoleon of the Terrorist War on the United States, attracted more and more violent followers throughout the world.

era or clime such a phrase would refer to a supposed inadequacy of police resources – not enough water cannon, inadequate coshes or handcuffs, insufficient fire-proof uniform to enable officers to apprehend those throwing petrol bombs in what Scarman acknowledged had been 'a lively and prosperous place in the late nineteenth and early twentieth centuries'.[12] For Scarman, however, the police 'problems' were ones of attitude. The young rioters were apparently expressing frustration at police 'attitudes'.

No one would deny the data collected by Scarman in his report. The black young of Brixton were put upon by a racist police force. (And as Scarman told the Home Secretary, 'racially prejudiced or discriminatory behaviour is not at present a specific offence under the Police Disciplinary Code'.[13]) Many of them lived in conditions which would make anyone feel like hurling a petrol bomb; 25.4 per cent of the ethnic minority were unemployed. (Unemployment in the Brixton Employment Office stood at 13 per cent at the time of the riots.) Brixton had few recreational or sports facilities. Through no choice of theirs, they had been brought up in constricted flats in ugly tower blocks, and forced to attend lousy schools, taught by inadequate teachers unable to find employment anywhere else. Thirty-seven per cent of homeless households, waiting to be rehoused in substandard flats, were black.[14] What made the Scarman report remarkable was the way in which, in its liberal, paternalistic way, it infantilised the black community, and especially the black criminals.

Critics of Thatcher – and Lord Scarman's views of her are not difficult to conjecture – would say that the unemployment had come about as a direct result of her economic policies and that the job of the government was to improve the housing and living standards of all citizens. Thatcher, with a politician's disingenuousness, refused to take any responsibility for the riots which swept the inner cities that summer – Brixton in April, Toxteth, in Liverpool, in July, Moss Side in Manchester and again in Brixton itself. Hugo Young, Margaret Thatcher's biographer, who was of a Scarmanite political complexion, recalled her saying, as she contemplated the looting at Toxteth, 'Oh, those poor shopkeepers!'

Young wrote, 'A lot of Margaret Thatcher's character is expressed in that single phrase. It was a perfectly intelligible reaction. It just wasn't the first response that most people might have made when they saw rioters and police in pitched battle, and watched the disintegration of a run-down city. Later, seeing looters walking away with armfuls of merchandise, they may have felt for the shopkeepers too.' Young went on to remind his readers, yet again, of Thatcher's origins in a small grocer's shop, thereby implying that this was not merely where she still belonged, but also where her belief in the individual's duty to obey the law belonged.

Were shopkeepers, property owners, employers, the propertied classes necessarily at war with the unemployed or the dispossessed or un-possessed? The conventions of 'consensus' suggested not. Britons were all 'one nation' and it was in the interests of the propertied to appease the unpropertied with welfare, decent housing, chances of employment. The doctrines of monetarism went counter to the consensus. If Thatcher were to have abandoned her commitments to sound money, the consequences would have been dire to the country. While the painful medicine went down, however, it was inevitable that the young unemployed and unskilled should suffer the most. These, given the demographic nature of modern Britain, were the blacks. While she aspired to make Britain imitate the American success story – unrestricted growth of capital; entrepreneurs being loved, not attacked, by the state; financial services the key to economic boom – she was obliged to replicate the woeful divisions observable in all American cities. While the investment banker and the corporate lawyer grew ever richer, the poor blacks imprisoned in their ghettoes of hopelessness grew angrier. Brixton and Toxteth were Bonfires of the Vanities. 'The country briefly felt as though it was aflame.'[15]

Beleaguered shopkeepers deserved sympathy. So did the police who were caught in the crossfire of ideological battle. If angry, impoverished black boys setting fire to cities was one price to be paid for economic revival, it was not a price which the rich paid themselves. The police were the only representatives of government whom most poor people ever met. Post-Scarman, their jobs became more difficult. Section 66 of the Metropolitan Police Act 1839 laid down that 'a constable may . . . stop, search and detain . . . any person who may be reasonably suspected of having or conveying in any manner anything stolen or unlawfully obtained'. By extension, it was considered reasonable to stop and search anyone likely to be in possession of illegal narcotics. Clearly such a law was of great inconvenience to the muggers, drug-pushers and petty thieves of Brixton, and it was easy to stir resentment against clumsy attempts to police the area. The 'sus' laws were also hated – so called because of section 4 of the Vagrancy Act 1824, 'under which people can be arrested on suspicion that an offence is likely to be committed'.[16]

To an older generation, who had grown up in a culture of deference and whose males had done military service, the policeman had been a reassuring, admirable figure – 'the ideal male character'.[17]

The bobby, the local policeman, was recognised by the law-abiding working class as one of their own. Questioned by a sociologist for a book published in 2003, members of a tenants' association in south Manchester recalled 'the old bobby with the old helmet' . . . 'they had authority and you respected that authority. Like I say, they'd clip you round the ear hole, and you took it.' Another speaker in the same group made the point that the police were 'ordinary normal people. It could have been your father, your uncle.'[18] Older Britons remembered the time when they knew the local constable by name. Another witness from south Manchester, born in 1950, remembered, 'We had this respect for the police. And there was a fear of the police, and I think it was a healthy fear, because I think if anything it tended to give the police more authority. You would never deliberately be absolutely cheeky or foul-mouthed to a policeman. It just wasn't going to work . . . And of course if you went running to mummy and daddy with the idea of that policeman has just told me off, or "I've been arrested because", then you're back to being punished again, you got a back hander.'[19] In those days, a backhander was a slap received from, rather than a bribe given to, a policeman.

As the 1950s had receded, the crime rate had soared, 430,085 notifiable offences in 1955 rising 70 per cent to 743,713 in 1960: at this period public confidence in the police remained steady. As these figures grew at stratospheric rates, so public confidence in the police was dimmed. By 1970 the figure was 1.6 million. (In 1992, the *level of increase* in offences was greater than the *total* number of offences in 1950.) Between 1950 and 1993 thefts from motor vehicles increased twenty-eightfold, robberies forty-eightfold.[20] The law-abiding public began to question the competence, while the criminal or criminalised blatantly flouted the authority of the police. There were a disturbing number of suspicious deaths among detainees in police custody or in gaol. In 1982, when the Greater London Council was under threat of abolition by Margaret Thatcher, a monitor group calling itself INQUEST was set up to 'help friends and families of people who had died in police custody'. The death of Blair Peach, a schoolteacher in the largely Asian suburb of Southall on 23 April 1979, happened during a major clash between police and anti-fascist demonstrators. A strike by local Asian workers and shopkeepers had provoked an overreaction by the police – three thousand officers, the SPG, hoses, helicopters and riot gear. According to an anonymous pamphlet, *Policing Against Black People*, 'the police, according to eye-witnesses, went berserk and vans were driven straight at crowds of people, people were hit on the head with truncheons, mounted police charged and long batons were used'.[21] According to a *Daily Telegraph* reporter: 'Nearly every demonstrator we saw had blood flowing from some sort of injury: some were doubled up in pain. Women and men were crying.'

Blair Peach, a schoolteacher, died after being chased down the road and hit on the head with a truncheon by unidentified members of the SPG. Members of the SPG went to the Peoples Unite Centre in 6 Park View Road, which was being used as a first-aid post. They kicked down the door used by the medical unit and ordered everyone to get out. All those inside were forced down the stairs to run a gauntlet of police wielding truncheons. Virtually every item in the building was smashed to pieces, including PA equipment worth thousands of pounds. Clarence Baker, a member of Peoples Unite, was rushed with a fractured skull to intensive care, where he remained for several days fighting for his life.

This, together with so much of the other reporting of the Southall disturbances, overlooked the fact that the protesters, including Blair Peach, had gone out of their way to attack the police. Three thousand demonstrators had used concrete, smoke bombs and metal chairs, a fact that the pamphleteer chose to ignore. The death of Blair Peach – if indeed he was killed by a volunteer policeman, as alleged – was a very unfortunate accident whereas the breakdown in law and order, the chaos in which his death occurred, with acts of arson, looting and mass destruction, had all been planned and orchestrated by the demonstrators. The police were now in danger of being able to do nothing right. Individuals or groups in such a position begin, very often, to behave erratically.

A case in point occurred on 5 October 1985 when Floyd Jarrett, a black man, was taken to Tottenham police station, wrongly suspected of handling a stolen vehicle and (a matter which was never proven) of handling stolen goods. The police decided to search the home of the suspect's mother, Cynthia Jarrett. As the officers barged into the flat of this stout Jamaican lady, she was accidentally knocked over, and died of heart failure. A meeting was arranged at the West Indian Centre. The leader of Haringey Council, Bernie Grant, regarded by the readers of many newspapers as a dangerous agitator, was howled down when trying to address the Youth Association. He was said to be 'too white minded'. The police arrived at the estate, Broadwater Farm, sensibly armed with riot uniforms. This in itself was deemed to be 'provocative' from a crowd agog to be provoked. The riots followed the by now familiar pattern. These were not 'political' demonstrations in any but the most extended sense of the term. 'Many petrol bombs were thrown . . .' Leonardo Leon, looking from the Rochford block over the Griffin Road area, saw, 'People with bottles, then some people siphoning off fuel from cars, three or four people laughing, and putting cloth inside. There was a white cloth, a large piece, and they were tearing it apart and then putting it into the bottles, and throwing it. But of ten bottles they threw, one of them would actually light up and land in the road. All the others would just be nothing.'

This monstrous orgy of mindless violence, theft, vandalism and destruction was to claim a victim, the first policeman to be killed in a riot in

Britain since Cold Bath Fields in 1833 – when the National Political Union demonstrated for the 'Rights of the People' and the 'aristocracy of the working classes'. The Broadwater riots did not display the aristocracy of any class. Someone – they never found out who – was firing a shotgun into the crowds. Basement car parks had been flooded with petrol to be set alight when the police entered. (The same people who did this would complain that the police had 'provoked' the riots by wearing protective clothing.) From the inferno of burning shops and flats, the police were forced to retreat. PC Keith Blakelock fell on a grass verge and was set upon by a group of fifty rioters. There were calls to cut off his head, which was very nearly done, as the young man was kicked, stabbed, punched and hacked to death. Three men, later pronounced educationally subnormal, were arrested for the killing. Bernie Grant pronounced that the police had received 'a bloody good hiding'.[22]

20

Thatcher as Prime Minister

Margaret Thatcher embodied all that Victorian progressives might have hoped for when they championed the worthy causes of economic liberalism, free trade, education for all regardless of class and gender. Whereas the socialists within the Labour Party wished to perpetuate the class struggle, and the Social Democrats wanted to keep the class divide merely to change the identities of its contestants, Thatcher's revolution brought into being a Britain where class as such no longer mattered. Money mattered – it mattered more than it ever did. But all those very English things – things, paradoxically, which in her own person Thatcher almost parodied – deference, defining who you were by the way you spoke – as well as those non-Thatcherish things – a reverence for the past, romantic snobbery – were all blasted away by this very distinctive person, by far the most interesting Prime Minister of the post-Second World War years.

The times were ripe for her coming. In 1976, only a year after she became the party leader, the historian Robert Blake would say, 'the post-war consensus is dead and . . . Butskellism is extinct. The particular form of welfare state which came into being in the late 'forties and early 'fifties is simply not viable any longer. It has been collapsing through its own contradictions for the last ten years, certainly for the last five.'

Blake went on to say that the British political world then (1976) divided between 'those who wish to solve our ills by even more state intervention'. These he saw as 'the Wedgwood Benns' who would 'lead us to a socialist slum of an East European "people's democracy", in which, however, well-intentioned the authors may be, freedom, as we know it will become extinct'[1] and those – a much smaller number at this date – who believed that economic recovery – the prerequisite of any other form of recovery in those calamitous times – could only come about by diminishing bureaucracy, setting business free from government intervention, reducing taxes and making the notion of personal property – whether of those with modest means or of the rich – central to any other idea of law, public order and personal freedom.

Except to bigots this latter idea was by the end of our era accepted by almost all British politicians and a high proportion of the thinking adult population. Most British adults aspired, for example, to home-ownership.

Yet within Thatcher's own party – and especially in her own Shadow

Cabinet during her first administration – the home truths had not sunk in. These oafish men went on imagining that 'consensus' and 'corporatism', which had proved themselves so disastrous throughout the Heath–Callaghan years, would somehow save them. Thatcher's gender was seen as part of her 'extremism' in espousing an alternative which was subsequently adopted not only by all three British political parties, but throughout the formerly communist countries of Eastern Europe where she continued to be a heroine long after her political fall in Britain. Whereas her admirers, in America, Poland, Russia, and Czechoslovakia, saw her as a courageous innovator, her detractors saw her in caricature sexist and snobbish stereotypes. Whatever reasons people had for disliking her policies – or indeed for liking them – were blown up into mythic proportions by her sex and class. On the day she resigned, Richard Ingrams placed in the window of his Wallingford bookshop a novel by P. D. James, *An Unsuitable Job for a Woman*. Many of the jokes about her current during her premiership were primarily sex or sexist jokes, often recycled mother-in-law jokes in which she was seen as a ball-breaker. 'We've all heard about the fellow who broke into the Queen's bedroom, but have you heard about the fellow who broke into Margaret Thatcher's bedroom? He has a new career as a very promising soprano.' . . . 'What does PMT stand for? Prime Minister Thatcher' . . . 'Denis Thatcher went into a bookshop and asked the assistant, "Do you have a book called *How to Control Your Wife*?" "Our fiction section is upstairs, sir," smiled the assistant' . . . 'After all those years of marriage, Denis Thatcher is finally developing an attachment for his wife – it fits over her mouth' . . . These are all from the Irish 'comedian' Des McHale.[2] Paul Hogan, the Australian comic, just blatantly stated, 'When I tell the folks back home that the Poms have got a Sheila as a prime minister they go hysterical.' 'Traditionally, politics has been a male preserve, and I think we did all find it difficult coming to terms with a woman leader' – so said a nonentity member of Thatcher's first Cabinet, Jim Prior.[3]

In roughly the same era that the Church abandoned the symbolism of an all-male priesthood, Britain had elected its first female Prime Minister.[4] It had enjoyed a female Head of State for the previous quarter-century. The role of the monarchy and of this monarch in particular was so understated as at times to be unnoticeable. Thatcher was never unnoticeable. From the first, her confrontational manner awoke ancient mythological archetypes in the public psyche. Periods of history when the ruler has been female – Boudicca leading the Iceni in their fatal last stand against the Romans, Queen Elizabeth at Tilbury, or the Imperialist and capitalist expressionism of the reign of Victoria – have excited energy, aggressiveness, bravado. For much of the Thatcher era – and this decade is the

Thatcher Era in a way that none of the other eras into which my chronicle is divided can plausibly take its name from an incumbent Prime
Minister – political life, and the administrative life of Westminster, went
on as before. The civil service and the diplomatic service and the Palace
of Westminster continued in its all but self-perpetuating mechanisms.
Laws were debated and drafted in Parliament: budgets were drafted and
assigned to different departments, Secretaries of State and Ministers,
having hoped perhaps for this or that degree of expenditure, this or that
change, modified their expectations and laboured to complete the mounds
of paperwork which these aspirations engendered. The Thames still
flowed. Men and women still swarmed into London by morning and out
by evening on the same semi-efficient transport system, and in a great
many demonstrable ways Britain was more or less the same place at the
end of the era as at the beginning. But it did not *feel* the same. For the
politicians and the civil servants, immediately from the day she took
office, felt something had changed.

It was not long before the country at large became aware of it, too.
Two Margaret Thatchers took possession of public consciousness. One,
as has been noted, did so subliminally. This was the takeover of power, in
a phallic male world, by a priestess; the Queen of the Night had overthrown
Sosostris. This, Thatcher's mythic significance, programmed involuntary
responses of revulsion or admiration. But there was another Thatcher, of
whom everyone was aware, a figure of unconscious comedy, the bustling,
busy woman, a non-stop talker who shamelessly tongue-lashed Cabinet
Ministers, senior civil servants, foreign dignitaries – almost anyone except
underlings, to whom she was affectionate and polite. John Hoskyns, now
installed as a policy adviser at Number 10, kept a record of the hyper-
energy and irascibility, but also of the prodigious mastery of detail. The
entry for Tuesday 14 August 1979 is typical. 'Meeting at midday with
Angus Maude, David ****, Norman ****, self and Margaret. First half
hour or so disjoined and Margaret as ever, passionate at full throttle on
every tiny issue – and big ones too.'

Despite the preponderance of wets in her Cabinet, many of whom
hoped and assumed it would be possible to get rid of her after the
first setback, Thatcher set about the early stages of her capitalist revolution. She appointed as her Chancellor of the Exchequer a Welsh
solicitor by the name of Geoffrey Howe. He had been Solicitor General
in Heath's government and was a recent convert to the One True Faith
of monetarism. For nearly a decade, in various roles in Thatcher governments, he tolerated the rough edge of her tongue until his final act of
revenge, which helped to topple her . . . 'Called in to sit in on [the]
E[conomic Strategy Committee],' wrote Hoskyns in an ominous diary

entry. 'I was rather shocked at the way Margaret told off Geoffrey in front of E . . .'

Howe was a clever man. His soporific boringness, toneless voice and tediously pale grey suits concealed a competent operator and a fervent convert's zeal. Previous friends among the wets were appalled by Howe's first Budget. In order to reduce the growth of the money supply from around 13 per cent to 7–11 per cent he raised interest rates from 2 per cent to a staggering 14 per cent. He reduced the public sector borrowing requirement from 9.25 per cent to 8.25 per cent in 1979–80. This meant colossal cuts in public spending – some £1,400 million – in social welfare, the National Health Service and the unprofitable nationalised industries. Howe also radically reordered the tax structure, moving from an emphasis on direct to indirect taxation. When before the Budget Peter Jenkins, a *Guardian* journalist, asked Sir Ian Gilmour, Lord Privy Seal and leading wet, whether it was true that VAT would be doubled, Gilmour replied that there had been 'no question of any kind of Cabinet consultation' about the matter and that it was 'surely inconceivable that anything so silly could even be contemplated'.[5]

Prior whimpered, 'It was really an enormous shock to me that the budget was . . . so extreme.'[6] John Biffen, however, the Chief Secretary of the Treasury, responded, 'I do not deny that this is a severe package. The severity is made necessary by the situation we inherited.'[7]

In the same Budget, Geoffrey Howe reduced the highest rate of income tax from 83 to 60 per cent, and the basic rate of income tax from 33 to 30 per cent. This cost the Treasury over £4 billion in revenue, and, as the years unfolded, more tax revenue would be lost by the soaring numbers of unemployed, whose meagre dole money cost the tax-paying classes dear but was unable to stimulate the economy by spending. It was touch and go whether the medicine – what Denis Healey nicknamed sado-monetarism – would work.

Mrs Thatcher took on three principal enemies in the course of her eleven and a half years as Prime Minister. In the first of these two campaigns, she was decisively successful: when she confronted and over-came, first, the Argentinian invaders of the Falkland Islands, and secondly, the President of the National Union of Mineworkers – and, with him, the whole Marxian leviathan of organised labour which had demanded appeasement from the government classes since the Second World War. Her third foe was more amorphous. You could call them the chattering classes, an expression coined by her admirer the journalist Frank Johnson. You could call them the *bien pensants*. You could even call them the Establishment, or the New Establishment. Against these, she was never successful, and in the end 'they' got her. It is arguable that, with economic affairs in such a woeful state at the time of the IMF loan in 1976, some monetarist revolution would have been inevitable, whoever was the Prime Minister. Whether the 'Revolution' needed to take the sado-monetarist form, whether the medicine needed to have such drastic side-effects, is probably a debate for economists, all of whom would disagree with one another. One thing is sure – the 'Thatcherite' version of the revolution was the one which the British people experienced. And after it the old political, as well as economic, battle lines would never be the same again. Socialism, the attempt by socio-political means to overthrow global capitalism and replace it with corporatist state interventionism, was dead, seemingly forever. This happened in Thatcher's political lifetime. She regarded it as a phenomenon for which she should take some credit. In her time, the number of home-owners in Britain increased hugely, largely because of her policy that council tenants should be allowed to buy, at usually very favourable rates, their own flats or houses. This encouragement of the upper-working and lower-middle classes to give themselves a leg-up in the world and to escape the dependency culture of the state was a characteristic part of the Thatcher revolution. Equally characteristic was the lack of apparent concern by government for those who were unable, by temperament or financial hardship, to take advantage of these arrangements; or those who, through the periods of soaring interest rates, and boom–bust economic roller-coasters presided over by the Thatcherite Chancellors – Howe, Lawson and Major – found their houses repossessed, themselves repossessed. There was never enough adequate housing built, or acquired, to compensate for the sale of the council properties in the early 1980s, with the inevitable consequence in the later part of the decade that, for the first time in living memory, homeless beggars began to appear on the streets of big cities, their huddled, sleeping-bagged presence a disturbing reminder, to the consciences of their fellow citizens, that all was not quite right with the Revolution. While the spivs seemed to become richer and richer – in the City, in the service industries – the old manufacturing towns slumped into near-extinction. The primary British skill of the Industrial Revolution – making, or producing, commodities which other nations wished to buy – seemed to have deserted them. Two million jobs in the manufacturing industries were lost. Everyone in the world seemed able to make, or mine, or spin, or produce saleable goods more skilfully and more cheaply than could the British. And as the recessions grew, so did the unemployment queues, from 5.5 per cent in 1979 to 13 per cent by January 1983. Unemployment more than doubled in a single year, 1980–81, and by mid-1982 three million were out of work.

But fairness must allow the Lady her due, and record her two great victories. Without the first of these, the successful expulsion of Argentinian forces from the Falkland Islands in the South Atlantic, she might never have survived beyond her first term in office; the grievous social consequences of the monetarist revolution in its early stages would probably have lost her the election, and the wets in the party, who had always hated her, would have proceeded in the traditional Tory manner to assassinate their leader as soon as possible. But Margaret Thatcher was blessed in her opponents and enemies. Leopoldo Galtieri, who seized control of a junta government in Buenos Aires in December 1981, needed to establish popularity at home and to silence opposition. The Malvinas, known by the British as the Falkland Islands, were and are a remote and barren group of islands, inhabited by 1,800 people, 600,000 sheep and several million penguins. Ever since the British took possession of the islands, in 1765, their right to be there had been questioned. The Spanish had attempted to repossess them in 1769. Dr Johnson pointed out that West Falkland was a place 'thrown aside from human use, stormy in winter, barren in summer, an island which not even the southern savages have dignified with habitation, where a garrison must be kept in a state that contemplates with envy the exiles of Siberia, of which the expense will be perpetual'. Throughout the post-colonial period, someone at the Foreign Office had been forever on the point of moving papers about his desk and persuading the Foreign Secretary or the Colonial Secretary to hand over administration of the islands to the Argentines, but it had never quite happened, and this procrastination, interrupted by much sabre-rattling on both sides at moments of crisis, was what was destined to save Margaret Thatcher's career.

The Falklands invasion was, indeed, one of those great strokes of luck which come upon some politicians. At the time of Galtieri's decision, Thatcher was in all likelihood heading for political defeat, as the horrible effects of the monetarist revolution began to be felt. Then, in the early hours of Friday 2 April, news reached the Ministry of Defence in Whitehall that Argentinian troops had landed on the islands at Mullet Creek. A small force of British Marines was powerless against the Argentinian fleet, now moored off East Falkland, and a large fighting force, backed up by troop-carriers, guns and two Alouette helicopters. The Marines did what they could, firing 1,200 rounds of small-arms fire and they let off three 84mm Carl Gustav anti-tank rockets,[8] but surrender was the only course. Before long the officer commanding the Marines, Lieutenant Keith Mills, and the Governor of the Falklands, Rex Hunt, clad in full gubernatorial regalia of feathered hat and white uniform, had had no alternative but to surrender to the superior forces of General Oswaldo García. So far the casualties were four Argies dead. But what were the British government back in London going to do about the crisis?

Harold Wilson or James Callaghan would have attempted to get out of the problem by means of negotiation. Having consulted with the service chiefs, Margaret Thatcher knew that she was running a colossal risk if she were to attempt the retaking of the Falklands by force. It required the sending of a task force accompanied by tanker ships, supply ships and hospital ships. The journey would take weeks, giving the enemy the chance to build up their defences. Once arrived, there was the formidable task of landing on the islands and engaging with the Argentinians, who would by then have had probably eight weeks to dig themselves in, and who could hold the islanders hostage. Loss of life looked inevitable and victory by no means certain. When Thatcher told the Cabinet of the venture, only the Trade Secretary John Biffen, one of her monetarist supporters, dissented. The alternative was that the government, who had allowed the invasion to take them by surprise in spite of intelligence suggesting a build-up of Argentinian aggression, would have been forced to resign.[9]

During the subsequent war, between 2 April and 14 June 1982, 255 British and 650 Argentinian lives were lost. Perhaps the most controversial engagement of the campaign involved the sinking of the Argentinian ship *General Belgrano* by the British submarine *Conqueror*. Of all the events of the war, it was the one which was the most emblematic of the Prime Minister's character. Three hundred and sixty-eight young Argentinian lives were lost when the ship was sunk – outside the agreed exclusion zone. Thatcher was obliged to take the decision to sink the ship, and her executive courage impressed the military and naval top brass. They were not used to dealing with Prime Ministers who took such decisions so readily. Nor, in all the subsequent and highly predictable hullabaloo, did she show the slightest penitence. The following Christmas at Chequers, when showing composer Andrew Lloyd Webber and the film director David Puttnam (he of *Chariots of Fire*) round Chequers, she paused and said, 'This is the chair I sat in when I decided to sink the *Belgrano*.'[10]

The British public had not been able to enjoy anything like this since the Second World War, which most Britons were now too young to remember. When news of the sinking reached the the *Sun* on the night of 3 May, most of its journalists were on strike; it was three non-union staff who in fact thought up the headline which many thought typical not only of that newspaper but also of the Thatcher era: GOTCHA!

'I agree that headline was a shame,' said proprietor Rupert Murdoch. 'But it wasn't meant in a blood-curdling way. We just felt excited and euphoric. Only when we began to hear reports of how many men had died did we begin to have second thoughts.' In subsequent editions of the paper the headline was altered to the less catchy, and characteristically inaccurate, 'DID 1200 ARGIES DIE?'

Those who were 'horrified' by the headline would be those who eventually had the satisfaction of seeing Margaret Thatcher's political demise. They included the dons, and the clergy, and those who could see 'no future' for Britain outside Europe, who thought it would have been perfectly possible to continue with the consensus politics of the previous forty years, and somehow to work out the economic difficulties without the drastic monetarist remedy. These could be deemed liberal, or enlightened, Britain and, because they were unused to their voice not being heard in the land, they believed, correctly as it turned out, that it was only a matter of time before Thatcher and Thatcherism were eradicated. There was another group, however, who saw the Falklands War, and its enthusiastic reception in some circles in Britain, with an even heavier heart. This was the left, the old formal left, the communists of various colourings and their fellow-travellers. By means of the trades unions (some of them) – and with it the possibility of disrupted and disruptive organised labour; history and sociology departments in universities – and with them the possibility of student unrest; some of the back benches of the Commons, and their gang of fellow-travelling sillies in the media and the Church, the serious left had always known that, short of a revolution, they stood no chance of actually governing Britain. But they had sway and influence. The Falklands War was the first time they began to see that this influence was not merely on the decline. It was about to be eliminated – at first in Britain, and later across Eastern Europe – remaining eventually, by the end of our period, only extant in some parts of the United States, France and Northern Europe. 'The Falklands crisis represents a truly enormous setback for the Left and even for liberal attitudes in Britain. It has brought to the surface of the Right-wing press an hysteria and intolerance which must make one tremble for what might occur in a really serious crisis.'[11] The left saw immediately that, whatever the war's origins, its consequences would be electoral triumph for Thatcher. Many voters who would not have considered themselves especially belligerent felt that a fundamental principle had been established. Regardless of who should have been in charge of the Falklands/Malvinas at the beginning of 1982, they were, as a matter of law and fact, British sovereign territory. The Argentinian dictatorship had brutally invaded. Britain had responded legally, and with prodigious skill and efficiency. When the Argentinians surrendered Port Stanley on 14 June it was a moment not simply of relief; it was a vindication of right. That was how a majority saw matters at home in Britain. The grown-up stuff – that in this day and age we should not be solving international difficulties by means of warfare; that battleships were a thing of the past; that royal princes (Prince Andrew) flying helicopters in military engagements belonged to a vanished age – these protests only inclined the cheering readers of the *Sun* and the *Daily Telegraph* and the *Daily Mail* to feel that something truly miraculous had taken place. The military victory was not miraculous, for these voters had always believed in the skill and courage of the armed forces. It was the political will, and the executive courage of the Prime Minister, which they loved. Here was a real war, with casualties and ships being sunk and battles being fought. And it was being directed, not by an old man who had himself been a soldier; not by a uniformed Churchill in peaked naval cap, but by a suburban 'little woman', a person whom the vast majority of her supporters could recognise as 'one of them'.

The service of Thanksgiving at St Paul's Cathedral for Victory on 26 July infuriated the right wing by its conciliatory attitude, its expressions of regret for the young Argentinians slain, and its profession of hatred for war itself. In one of his 'Dear Bill' Letters, the fictitious Denis Thatcher wrote:

> I had taken the precaution of ingesting a few pretty stiff ones across the road in the Barbican Arms, and my recollection of the opening moments is not all that clear, but I realised as soon as the Proprietor made her entrance, in total silence without so much as a breath of applause, let alone the massed trumpeters or Cup Final cheering we had expected, that someone had blundered. When Runcie finally minced up into the pulpit and adjusted his frock, instead of rendering thanks to the great Bartender in the Sky for the sinking of the *Belgrano* and all his other mercies viz unexploded bombs, crass bungling by Argies, massacre at Goose Green etc., we got a lecture, would you believe, on the evils of war with the strong suggestion the whole episode need not have happened . . . M. inevitably was fit to be tied, shredded her programme, looked at her watch several times during the homily, and when it came to shaking hands with the Primate at the West Door, gave him a radioactive look that left him smouldering.[12]

The real-life Denis, however, had said that the sermon was 'better than expected', but this was 'more than could be said for the rest of the bloody service'.[13] The truth is that the sort of people who draft services in St Paul's Cathedral were never going to vote for Thatcher, or encourage Thatcherism; their lip-curling and disapproval, sensed throughout the Thatcherite ranks, was only one of many indications of disapproval which egged on the first-time home-owners and would-be purchasers of council houses, who found themselves the natural allies of the entrepreneurs, the moderate trades unionists who had had enough of being bullied by Marxists, and the old-age pensioners who did not mind it when interest rates increased the income from their savings in the building society. The sneering disapproval of those who considered themselves more sophisticated actually exacerbated the Thatcherites' taste for another battle.

In his diary, Alan Clark noted that, during the service held in Plymouth to commemorate the Falklands War, Dr David Owen had 'bellowed out the words', 'God who made Thee mighty, make Thee mightier yet'.[14]

The 1983 General Election was a foregone conclusion. It had been helped on its way, not merely by the war, but also by the short-term, or apparent, success of the monetarist economic miracle. On 30 March, 1981, three hundred and sixty-four academic economists had signed a letter to *The Times* stating, 'There is no basis in economic theory or supporting evidence for the Government's belief that by deflating demand they will bring inflation permanently under control and thereby introduce an automatic recovery in output and unemployment; present policies will deepen the depression, erode the industrial base of our economy and threaten its social and political stability.

'There are alternative policies.

'The time has come to reject monetarist policies and consider which alternative offers the best hope of sustained recovery.'

Nigel Lawson was to write proudly in his memoirs, 'Their timing was exquisite. The economy embarked on a prolonged phase of vigorous growth almost from the moment the letter was published. So far from launching the economy on a self-perpetuated downward spiral, the Budget was a prelude to eight years of uninterrupted growth and left our economic critics bewildered and discredited.'[15]

Lawson, as perhaps the most adventurous of Thatcher's Chancellors of the Exchequer, was bound to say this; and in his monetarist triumphalism he overlooked the fact that the despised academics in their letter to *The Times* got some things right: Thatcher, Howe and Lawson did help to exacerbate social problems by pursuing policies which destroyed manufacturing industry and increased unemployment. This, like the GOTCHA! attitude to the Argies, was very much what the fans wanted. For decades, the suburban classes had watched while members of big trades unions were able to clobber their bosses, especially those in the nationalised industries, by inflationary wage demands. In times of inflation, it was the middle classes, with mortgaged houses, who paid in higher interest rates for the short-term triumphs of the union barons. And for many such voters it was a chance to exact revenge on the collective bullyism of the left. The left, the numerically diminishing working classes, or as Auberon Waugh always referred to them, the 'working' classes, of course fought to maintain the status quo, as did the great liberal majority of academics, civil servants and their like. The knowledge that Thatcher intended to 'deal with' the unions was undoubtedly one factor in the electoral triumph of 1983, when she increased her majority by over a hundred seats – to 144.[16] True, because of the peculiarities of the British electoral 'first past the post' system, this figure concealed another fact – that Conservative *votes* had actually diminished in the election by 700,000. In 1983 only just over thirteen million people voted for Thatcher. Those who would belittle Thatcher's popularity point out that this was well less than half the possible adult electors. That somewhat misses the point. Thatcher never believed, and nor did her enthusiastic supporters, that she was loved by all of the people all of the time. Unpopularity, as well as popularity, was an essential ingredient in her political success. She was extremely fortunate, in her first two terms of office, in her enemies. The Thatcherites deplored not only the left, who were her natural enemies, but also the wets, the liberals, the consensus politicians, who wanted to hold back from a showdown.

And there was no doubt that a showdown was coming. Enter stage left the President of the National Union of Mineworkers, Arthur Scargill, a gift from the gods. In 1980, Derek Ezra, the chairman of the National Coal Board, had warned the government that unless it injected more cash into the ailing British coal industry there would have to be pit closures. A 'hit list' was leaked, the following year, of between twenty and fifty uneconomic pits which were ripe for closure, a leak which led to un-official strikes in Kent and South Wales, followed by a hasty retreat by Thatcher. She did not want to repeat the fate of Heath, who was seen off by the miners. When she took on the miners she would do so on her own terms, and, after years of preparation, when she had insured that sufficient supplies of cheap foreign coal had been imported, and the army and the police primed for the conflict. She also needed a less concil-iatory figure than Ezra at the NCB. For her role as general in the war against the working class, she chose the self-made Scots-American Ian MacGregor, who had already earned the nickname 'Mac the Knife' while running British Steel, and cutting the workforce by half. Was he a fit match for Scargill? Arthur Scargill, schooled in the Young Communist League, had remained in the party long after the Hungarian atrocities of 1956 had driven out tenderer souls. He first came to prominence in 1972 during the miners' strike, when he organised 'flying pickets' who had turned back the police at the Saltley Gate pits in the Midlands. Wearing a baseball cap, Scargill seemed willing to do Thatcher's work for her, coming on the television news night after night and mouthing threats against the police, verbal assaults on the management of the NCB and unapologetic, hectoring expressions of hope that a socialist paradise would soon spread from his own luxurious flat in the Barbican across the coal fields of England, Wales and Scotland until it made intrusions into the suburbs of Middle England.

'We had more people arrested at Saltley . . . than in the rest of the strike put together. I was the only official of the NUM arrested and subsequently convicted. It was incredible. I was taken to court for pick-eting and for organizing picketing . . . you will not get real control of the society in which we live, unless you commit and convince the working class of the need to struggle' . . . . . . 'If we get another Saltley then the whole picture can change from one where you have a peaceful road to one where you do not have a peaceful road.'[17] There was no doubting Scargill's ability as an orator and as an agitator. For a limited few (as in the case of his great enemy Thatcher) there was a great personal appeal. He was boyish in appearance, with a high, pink complexion, and an intelligent, bright pair of eyes. But the zest for going too far made him ultimately better suited as a political demagogue than as a union leader. Gormley had known exactly how to lure Ted Heath up to the edge of the heffalump trap: he did not even need to push. Scargill, who was a well-read Marxist, sensed a coming apocalypse. He wanted a battle. Thatcher therefore did not need to make her supporters' flesh creep with fear of the Red Peril; Scargill did the job for her.

Between the pair of them were the lives of tens of thousands of coal miners and their families, and of the towns and villages which were sustained by their earning power. In South Wales, in Yorkshire, Not-tinghamshire, Derbyshire and Kent, the miners were divided, most of the 25,000 Nottinghamshire miners, for example, being opposed to Scargill, realistic about the possible future of their industry and opposed to the strike. The dispute therefore became not merely (from Thatcher's perspective) a battle with the communists and wreckers; it became a civil war among the working class, with 'scabs' on the one hand and fool-hardy left-wing loyalists on the other. As the cruelly long months of the strike were extended, more and more miners, however much it stuck in their throats to do so, felt forced by economic hardship to return to work, even though crossing the picket lines to the cries of 'Scab! Scab!' from their fellow workers led to lasting wounds and breaches within families and communities.

Scargill had made three attempts, since becoming President of the NUM in 1979, to call for a national strike and on each occasion he was defeated by ballot. He would have been defeated again in 1984, but this time he did not call a ballot and merely called his union out on strike against the will of many – probably a majority – of his membership. MacGregor was not nearly as belligerent as either Thatcher or Scargill probably wanted him to be. The offer he had made to the miners was a £33,000 redundancy pay for a man aged forty-nine in the case of closed pits. Unlike Thatcher, and in common with most miners, MacGregor actually wanted to save jobs in the industry, and he did not have in mind any solution as draconian as, say, the Wilson government which, during the 1960s, closed more than two hundred pits.[18]

Thatcher's line, carefully dictated by her monetarist advisers, was that this was not a government versus miners dispute. That had been the mistake of Ted Heath in the old corporatist days. Governments did not negotiate with unions. Their bosses did – in this case the National Coal Board. All that was required of a government was to watch, and to support the police when the fisticuffs got out of hand.

The idea that the government were not involved, from the start, with the resistance to Scargill, was a fiction. As well as insisting that the Central Electricity Generating Board stockpiled cheap Polish coal at the power stations, the government had also made sure that the 'police' at the trouble spots were in fact members of the army wearing police uniforms. One of them told Tony Benn in 1986, 'I was in the army until last year, and during the miners' strike I was at Catterick Camp and we were regularly put into police uniforms and sent on to the picket lines. We didn't like it particularly . . . At Nottingham, of the sixty-four police-men in our group, sixty-one were soldiers and only three were regular policemen – an inspector, a sergeant and one bobby.' He said that the soldiers used were from the Military Police, the SAS and the Green Jackets.[19]

When, in the House of Commons, Thatcher insisted that the govern-ment was not intervening in the coal strike, Michael Foot, now resigned as the leader of the Labour Party, to be replaced by Neil Kinnock, rose from the back benches and said that she had 'lied to the House'. Most unusually, the Speaker did not ask him to withdraw the comment.[20] For the miners, both those who lost their jobs and those who attempted, by means of work and moderate negotiation, to keep them, the strike had brought nothing but anxiety and wretchedness. And in the end there was nothing which they, or MacGregor, or anyone else could do to make British coal competitive in the global marketplace. By the end of the century every mine in Britain would have closed.

As so often in Thatcher's career, the point of the war with Scargill was not its actual consequences but its mythic significance. Though her actual success in government owed much to her phenomenal grasp of detail (Quintin Hogg said that he had never known any other barrister who could master a brief, or a mass of government documents, with a more telling and thorough eye than she[21]), it was not the hard work and the detail which made the Thatcher magic successful in its glory days. She worked, by contrast, with a theatrical flourish; not with oratory – she was a leaden and boring speaker – but with the telling event, and with large emblematic gestures. The Argentinian forces might – just might – have been persuaded to leave the Islands by the intervention of some outside figure such as the President of Venezuela. But Thatcher's war showed that Britain was still capable of independent military action in the world. Likewise, Scargill's strike could have been averted by government, the NCB and the anti-Scargill miners uniting to express their common cause. But Thatcher had wanted, and achieved, a fight against what she called 'the enemy within'.

The 'police', in reality the army, who occasionally confronted the miners, were seen by Thatcherite television viewers as holding the pass against violent anarchy and communism. It was, to use the phrase of Denis in a 'Dear Bill' Letter – 'Comrade Scargill's fifty-nil defeat at the hands of my good lady the Grantham Mauler'.[22] The rest of the world could see the Iron Lady in action. This was the woman who, in her alliance with Ronald Reagan (first inaugurated as President of the United States in January 1981), in her championing of the Solidarity movement in Poland, in her persistent verbal onslaughts on the Soviet Union, had come to be seen, throughout Eastern Europe, as a real champion of the anti-communist cause. In Poland, Czechoslovakia, Russia, Bulgaria, Yugoslavia, they had actually been living for decades under governments which thought the things which Arthur Scargill thought. They did not regard her as a joke.

Moreover, she was manifestly a person of steely personal courage. In the middle of the miners' strike, on the night of 11 October, a bomb exploded at the Grand Hotel in Brighton, where she and the rest of the Conservative leadership were staying during the Party Conference. It was planted by the IRA 'because prisoners in Northern Ireland were being tortured'.[23]

There was no doubt that they had intended to kill Thatcher and as many as possible of her Cabinet. Five people were killed. John Wakeham, the Chief Whip, and Norman Tebbit were badly injured, and Tebbit's wife was paralysed for life. Thatcher would undoubtedly have been killed had it not been for the diuretic consequences of late-night whisky consumption. As Alan Clark put it in his diary: 'Mrs T had been saved by good fortune (von Stauffenberg's briefcase!) as she was in the bathroom. Had she been in the bedroom she would be dead.'[24]

She was determined not to allow the IRA the satisfaction of seeing her in any way rattled. She walked about among the rubble talking to reporters with a prodigious sangfroid and only a few hours later, with not a hair out of place, she stood in front of the packed Conference to deliver her speech as usual. 'It was an attempt not only to disrupt and terminate our conference . . . It was an attempt to cripple Her Majesty's democratically elected government.' There was something simply impressive about her demeanour on that day. Even her enemies were bound to see that.

Chesterton once said that Christianity had not been tried and found wanting; it had never been tried. The same could be said of Thatcherism. Although John Hoskyns, Keith Joseph and the inner cabal of monetarist mullahs who had tried to steer her in their direction, a combination of external events, the nature of the British economy and her own character made it ultimately impossible. She spent more on the Health Service, for example, than Harold Wilson, in his wildest or most extravagant dreams, would have promised. (Health spending rose by 32 per cent in real terms during the 1980s.[25]) The pure Thatcherite doctrine, taught by the guardians, was that it was their duty to get government off the backs of the people. But Thatcher, while convinced of this as a rhetorical device, was too bossy by temperament ever to wish to put it into practice. She was by nature an interventionist. She used her power to intervene in the economy just as much as Heath or Wilson had done – for example, it was at her personal insistence that high interest rates were imposed in 1980–81 on an economy already experiencing a high exchange rate and recession.[26]

The nationalised industries could be disbanded and sold off; the rates of income tax could be lowered; home-ownership could be encouraged and made more common. In the end, however, the bills for an unwieldy, centralised welfare system had to be paid: enormous sums of money had to be doled out to the National Health Service and 'benefits' showered down upon the old, the halt, maimed and blind, as well as upon the millions of unemployed put out of useful work by the monetarist experiment. Thatcherism, if by that is meant the pure word of monetarism, was not really any more a practical possibility in the messy, confused real world than doctrinaire Marxism was.

Thatcherism, however, meant something more than mere doctrine. It was a certain style.

For anyone as politically ambitious as Michael Heseltine, the question of Europe must sometimes have caused him worries. British membership of the European Economic Community was never very popular in the country at large and in the Conservative Party it was increasingly unpopular. In order to challenge the leadership of Thatcher, he would have to embrace opposite policies, and this meant, inevitably, adopting a vigorously pro-European stance. Not a good recipe for favour with the broadly anti-European public.

Thatcher herself, in common with almost all British politicians of the period, had in fact a very changeable attitude to the question of Europe. As a member of Heath's Cabinet, she had been not merely accepting of the EEC, she was a keen advocate; and certainly for most of the years of her premiership she supported economic membership of the community, while wishing to keep to a minimum any commitment to the more collectivist or pan-European dreams (things changed a little after she went into exile and became a focal point for the more hysterical Eurosceptic tendency). She forced the Single European Act through a reluctant House of Commons in 1986 but two years later expressed herself surprised by the intentions of Jacques Delors, President of the European Commission, wanting a 'fully fledged political spokesperson for federalism', with a single European currency and a Social Charter regulating workers' rights. In 1989, at a European Summit meeting in Madrid, Foreign Secretary Geoffrey Howe and Chancellor Nigel Lawson confronted her with an ultimatum. Unless she committed Britain to entering the ERM (Exchange Rate Mechanism) they would both resign. Subsequent events proved the wisdom of her reluctance to sign up to the scheme, but 'The Ambush before Madrid', as she called it, caught her on the hop and she was already beginning to lose her grip by then. Seeing the cataclysmic effect on savings and jobs which the collapse of the ERM caused in Britain she would have done much better to dispense with the services of Lawson and Howe, who both vanished into obscurity the moment they retired.

The European debate can be seen as an endlessly circular dispute between economic and political experts on the pros and cons of this or that vision of the future. But in Britain, where everything reduces itself to triviality, the question of Europe has always been a question of something else. The Establishment, the New Establishment, liked Europe because of, not in spite of, the fact that it is anti-democratic. The Little Englanders' objections to Europe were that its executive was unaccountable, that its bureaucracy was unnecessarily interfering, that its inner workings were profoundly corrupt and that its attempts at joint sovereignty, joint currency were unworkable. For the New Establishment, such considerations were 'embarrassing', 'negative'. While there were Establishment sceptics, there are not many. The Eurosceptics were seen as beyond the pale by the People Like Us who found Thatcher intolerable.

The European question both highlighted and tried to sideline the central paradox of Margaret Thatcher's political philosophy, and the position of Britain during her incumbency. A belief in free trade had always, since the old quarrels about it split the Tories in the 1840s, entailed the willingness to follow the market, regardless of narrow nationalism. While signing up to various documents on the continent of Europe undoubtedly diminished the sovereignty of the British Parliament, it could be said that these encroachments upon the national identity were often scarcely noticeable.

The great event, from an economic, and hence from a national and political viewpoint, in Thatcher's period as First Lord of the Treasury, was the abolition of fixed commissions in the London stock market. This was what was known as 'Big Bang', on 27 October 1986. Between 1979 and 1984, foreign firms had handled some 95 per cent of the £12 billion new overseas investments of insurance companies and pension funds generated by the North Sea oil boom. Something had to change and it was Thatcher's government, with its belief in allowing as much freedom to the market as possible, which made the inevitable decision. This enabled non-British firms to take over existing broking and jobbing houses in the City of London, and to create enormously rich conglomerates. Electronic dealing, now technically possible, brought to an end the arcane rituals of the stock market floor, men in top hats, bells ringing, and so on. The old *Forsyte Saga* – style banking firms and stockbroking families retreated before the invasion of American and European firms. By 1990, 154 of 408 Stock Exchange member firms were foreign, mostly Japanese, American, Swiss and French. By 1995, Barings, S. G. Warburg, Kleinwort Benson and Smith New Court had been absorbed into Dutch, Swiss, German and American banks. There had never been more money in the City of London in its history. And this created, in Britain itself, a class of super-rich city slickers, yuppies, Porsche drivers, second and third home-owners, crankers up of the housing market, competers for places in private schools, draughtsmen and women of a new social map, in which previous levels of income, and standards of living, seemed puny. But while it brought in untold wealth – wealth which would remain in Britain untaxed in many cases, until Gordon Brown's government laid down plans to charge 'Non Domiciled' (the so-called Non Doms) for their place in Britain – it could not be said to have left Britain unchanged. If Britain was less British at the end of our times than it was at the beginning, this was undoubtedly because of Europe, because of immigration, because of the Americanisation of popular culture and the cosmopolitanisation of eating habits. But a key factor, and one which actually played its part in all the foregoing, was Big Bang and the deregulation of capital. Not least, it had the effect of making London supremely more important, as a wealth producer, than anywhere else in Britain. As the manufacturing wealth of the North declined, as the mines of Scotland, Wales, Nottinghamshire and Kent were closed down, London became ever more the centre of British life. Provincial British and aspirant immigrants flocked to London if they could. 'Britain' was in the process of becoming a synonym for London, a multi-national, multi-racial city state, based in London, and largely indifferent to the fate of Manchester or Leeds.

There would inevitably be moments when the bubble burst. The story of Nick Leeson, born in a council house in Watford, reached its strange conclusion in 1995. Sitting in front of a computer screen in Singapore, the twenty-eight-year-old trader appeared single-handedly to bring down one of the most solid and ancient of banking dynasties – Barings – when he disastrously miscalculated and went on buying as the Nikkei index tumbled in February 1995. Yet, though he was, sociologically speaking, very much a product of his times (and he would not have been the sort of chap the Barings would entertain on a shooting party or at their London club), he was only doing what everyone in the City, since Big Bang, had hoped to do – making money not by solid investment but by gambling. 'Hedging' – protecting an open position in order to minimise risk – was an illusion of which Marx himself would have been proud, had he imagined it in the more apocalyptic pages of *Capital*. 'In layman's terms,' remarked the *Sunday Times*, as Barings went down, 'Barings' top team chose to smash through red light after red light in a craven chase for "easy" profits. Then, in the final moments, when it was clear that the next stop was a brick wall, they scrambled desperately to find someone, anyone other than themselves, to blame. Leeson, the oik from Watford, looked the perfect fall guy.'[27]

Though Leeson went down – literally – he went to prison while the 'top team' were 'sitting at home nursing their credibility back to pieces and always knowing what their friends were saying behind their backs'[28] – the ethos which destroyed him was not laid aside. The sheer venality, the savagery, the way that money gobbled and destroyed not only its greediest lovers, but also the entire culture which spawned it, was the theme of Martin Amis's most successful novel, *Money*. Significantly, it was set in New York. Like his friend Salman Rushdie, whose best novel, *Midnight's Children*, chronicled the lives of Indians born at the moment of national independence, the fecund imagination of Amis could not focus on the mother country. The revitalisation of London by Big Bang by the most 'patriotic' of Prime Ministers had mysteriously blown Britain sky high.

One of the early-warning signs that the New Establishment intended to fight back had been given in December 1984, when the ruling executive of Oxford University, the Hebdomadal Council, proposed the names of seven people whom it wished to honour with doctorates the following summer. There were some academics, Sir Geraint Evans, the former President Pertini of Italy and the Oxford graduate of Somerville College Margaret Hilda Thatcher, born Roberts. Normally, when the Hebdomadal Council proposes names for honorary degrees, the 2,500 or so Oxford teaching staff (the dons) allow the matter to proceed without protest. But they possessed a parliament where they could debate matters which they deemed important. And it soon became clear that they wanted to have their pathetic little moment of power. The seven previous British Prime Ministers had been honoured by Oxford with degrees, Attlee, Macmillan, Heath and Wilson within a year of taking office, and Douglas-Home and Eden receiving doctorates before they reached Number 10. The university had even given a degree to the bonehead Jim Callaghan. They were unable to stand back and consider the justice of promoting Thatcher. She was a person of high intelligence who had, in her way, shed glory on her old college, the more so since, while studying under science dons who were not merely left-leaning but actually communist, she had gone her own way and joined the University Conservative Association (OUCA), while being conscientious. 'I came to rate her as good,' said her tutor Dorothy Hodgkin, later a Nobel Prize winner. 'One could always rely on her producing a sensible, well-read essay.' Yet, when Thatcher returned to Somerville as Prime Minister, neither the former Principal, Janet Vaughan, nor Hodgkin would so much as consent to meet her. And now the university teachers en masse – if so petty a swarm could be described as a masse – voted against her being allowed an honorary degree by 738 votes to 319. All sorts of bogus justifications were produced for this exhibition of Lilliputian malice – Thatcher's supposed philistinism, or the government 'cuts' in expenditure on libraries, the 'arts' and so forth. As a matter of fact, Thatcher was no more philistine than many politicians, and she was considerably more intelligent. Whatever view might be taken of her politics, it was surely quite an achievement to have risen from modest origins to become the first woman Prime Minister; and it might have been thought that the university would have been big enough to see that her journey was unimaginable without Oxford, that she was indeed Oxford's daughter, and as such one who deserved an honour.

But the 738 ninnies who voted against her all supported that very influential class, the New Establishment. The vote to snub Thatcher showed them at their nastiest. The vote to appoint Roy Jenkins as Chancellor of the University a couple of years later, in March 1987, showed them at their most foolish. Puffed up, pompous and vacuous, Woy was the embodiment of all that these people would consider 'civilised'. This New Establishment had no more democratic mandate for determining the course of public affairs than had the Old Establishment of Etonians, senior bishops and civil servants, the army and the clubs. But the dismissal of Thatcher and the elevation of Woy to a position once occupied by the 1st Duke of Wellington and later Lord Curzon made it very clear, not merely that Thatcher, as a public figure, was living on borrowed time, but also that the New Establishment would never allow such a revolutionary phenomenon to happen again.

As a matter of fact, the political success of the Lady had been in large measure because the fastidious Woy, who, upon his return from the Continent, where he had served as a very well-dined President of the European Commission, could not dirty his hands any longer with engagement with the Labour Party. The formation of the Social Democratic Party, on the one hand, and, on the other, the unelectable hopelessness of the Labour leadership, made it very easy for the Conservatives to win elections in the 1980s. Woy had been an incompetent Home Secretary and a disastrous Chancellor of the Exchequer. But in his person, manner and friendships he appeared to stand for all the things which the New Establishment stood for, whereas Thatcher blatantly did not. When Jonathan Miller referred to her 'odious suburban gentility and sentimental saccharine patriotism, catering to the worst elements of commuter idiocy',[29] he was at least making clear where everyone stood. Britain was technically a democracy. The commuter classes – the majority of those working in the South East – might have supposed that they had enjoyed the supremacy of the trades unions and organised labour, in their alliance with leftist academics, for long enough; nor did they want, perhaps, to return to the days of being patronised by the Old Establishment or, before that, by the aristocracy. Perhaps this class – the class from whom H. G. Wells emerged and for whom he wrote – imagined that they might, just for once, be allowed their say. Their favourite newspaper, the *Daily Mail*, had made Mrs Thatcher politically. But the very expressions on the faces of such as Dr Jonathan Miller when that publication was mentioned would have been enough to remind the Pooters that their decade of whoopee was not to be allowed to last.

It would have been good for the New Establishment if a Social Democratic Party could have beaten the Conservatives outright; failing that, they realised that their best bet would have been that a Social Democrat fifth columnist such as Douglas Hurd or Kenneth Clarke could be fielded to defeat Thatcher in a challenge for the Conservative leadership. But they knew this was never going to be practicable. To defeat the

Lady, they would have to field a paradoxical candidate – not one of their own, but a maverick from the ranks of the spivs, a man who from his rise to riches through property speculation and motoring magazines might have seemed like the classic Thatcherite – and perhaps for this very reason became the snarlingly envious anti-Thatcherite Michael Heseltine.

The 'moderate' views of Heseltine – by which he meant a desire to return to the failed corporatist economics of the Heathite past, and his 'passionate commitment' to Europe – were more often heard among the sophisticated classes than the raw language of Thatcherism. To that extent his views went with his bought furniture and his Palladian house, Henford, near Banbury. Politicians who had *inherited* such houses tended, like Ian Gilmour, to be wets.

Michael Heseltine badly miscalculated his timing. Had he challenged Thatcher after the Westland affair he might at least have lived up to the image which he cultivated for the blue-rinsed ranks of Conservative rallies and conferences: namely, that of a swashbuckling man of courage. In fact, he had been too cowardly to risk losing the prize he so coveted. For years he had been preparing for the moment when he would become Prime Minister. In his absurd country house – absurd because he and his wife managed to transform a nice old Palladian seat into something with the gleaming, brand-new atmosphere of a 'country house' hotel – he had hung portraits of previous Prime Ministers such as Disraeli, giving the impression to any visitor that this was a mere waiting room for Chequers. For years he had plotted and smarmed and muttered his way round the smoking rooms and tea rooms of the Palace of Westminster. But although there were those who admired him for his supposedly compassionate Conservatism, others saw him merely as the spiv of spivs, a figure who made the lesser spivs such as Parkinson seem positively aristocratic. The result of the first ballot was a humiliation for Heseltine – Margaret Thatcher 204, Michael Heseltine 152, Abstentions 16. Had the Conservatives devised a sane method of electing their party leader, the Lady would have been safe. But she fell four votes short of the required surcharge of those entitled to vote.

When she heard the news she was in the Paris embassy. Twice in our period, a woman who bestrode the stage and dominated the British news was to meet her fate in Paris. Thatcher bustled out of the embassy and down the steps to say words which had been prepared for her in the event of this calamity – for no one who understood politics could fail to realise that a calamity is what it was. 'I'm naturally pleased that I got more than half the parliamentary party and disappointed that it's not quite enough to win on the first ballot so I confirm it is my intention to let my name go forward for the second ballot.'

But back in Westminster her Cabinet had decided that enough was enough. There was little doubt by now that the lobby fodder of the Conservative back benches had decided that Thatcher, once the election winner, was now a liability. They would desert her at the second ballot. Her most ardent supporter, Alan Clark, believed she'd be lucky to get '90 f***ing votes'.[30] Fairly obviously, the end had been reached, and when she summoned each of the Cabinet individually to give her advice, only the ultra-loyalists such as Cecil Parkinson and Michael Portillo told her to stay. Most of them told her to go. The next day she went to see the Queen and told her that as soon as the party had chosen a new leader she would herself resign.

She then went down to the House of Commons at a quarter past three to reply to an Opposition vote of censure of the government. No one who witnessed that scene could forget its drama. There must have been other women in the chamber of the Commons, but if so they did not seem visible. What was memorable was this small, immaculately dressed woman standing in the middle of a baying mob of males. Her old enemies Heath and Heseltine had already received cheers (from the Labour benches) as they entered the House to see the spectacle. But when she came in, things were different. The Conservatives cheered and waved their order papers, but the Labour members shouted 'Judas!' And justifiably so. Thatcher now stood in front of the party which had betrayed her and opposite the party which hated her, and she had never displayed herself so impressively.

'The Opposition's real reason [for the motion] is the leadership election for the Conservative Party, which is a democratic election according to rules which have been public knowledge for years. That is a far cry from the way in which the Labour Party does these things.'

She was asked about her visit to Europe.

Margaret Thatcher: Europe is strongest when it grows through willing co-operation and practical measures, not compulsion or bureaucratic dreams.

Alan Beith: Will the Prime Minister tell us whether she intends to continue her personal fight against a single currency and an independent central bank when she leaves office?

Dennis Skinner: No! She's going to be governor! (Laughter)

Margaret Thatcher: What a good idea. I hadn't thought of that. But if I were, there'd be no European Central Bank, accountable to no one, least of all to national Parliaments. Because the point of that kind of Europe with a central bank is no democracy, taking powers away from every single parliament, and having a single currency, a monetary policy and interest rates which takes all political power away from us. As my right honourable friend [Nigel Lawson] said in his first speech after the proposal for a single currency, a single currency is about the politics of Europe. It is about a federal Europe, by the back door. So I'll consider the honourable gentleman's [Mr Skinner's] proposal. Now where were we? I'm enjoying this. I'm enjoying this.

Michael Cartiss: Cancel it. You can wipe the floor with these people.

Later, Dennis Skinner shouted at the Conservatives, 'She's a better man than the whole pack of you!' In the morning, she had been unable to read her resignation speech to the Cabinet without breaking down, but now she was like a great diva, high on adrenaline, and there was tremendous poignancy in her final parliamentary hour.

The Cabinet performed their ritual assassination of Mrs Thatcher because of personal detestation. By the end, her judgement had deserted her and the riotous public reaction in April 1990 to her scheme to introduce a Poll Tax was only one indication of this fact. Had she resigned after eight or nine years in office, her standing would have been higher with the public. The truth is that the disloyal speeches of Ministers such as Geoffrey Howe – who resigned in a huff at an undignifiedly late stage, allegedly over 'Europe' – did not damage Thatcher in the eyes of her supporters. They merely showed up her Cabinet for the spineless and disloyal bunch everyone had always seen them to be. (As in the joke: Waiter at luncheon table when Thatcher was taking the Cabinet for a treat at the Ritz: 'Yes, madam, and what will it be?' Thatcher: 'I'll have a steak, please.' 'And for the vegetables, madam?' Thatcher: 'They'll have the same.')

None of the vegetables will be remembered. Thatcher always will, not merely as a Prime Minister, but as an emblem. She was not loved. She had never set out to be loved – this was part of her electrifying appeal.

Heseltine had toppled his enemy, but he was not to be given the satisfaction of replacing her as Prime Minister. For that there were too many people in the parliamentary party who hated him. The result of a second ballot for the leadership came two votes short of the required majority, but no one doubted that it would lead to the collapse of the other two candidates – Douglas Hurd 56 votes, Heseltine 131 and John Major 185. No one outside the world of political obsessives had much idea of who John Major was. He had been Foreign Secretary and Chancellor of the Exchequer in fast succession, but was he given these elevated offices of state because he was the obvious man for the job, or because the previous occupants of these posts had been unable to tolerate working any longer for Thatcher in her acrimonious decline? With his grey suits, grey hair,

grey smile and amiable, bespectacled face, John Major left no impression at all; he was not like the Thatcher favourites of earlier years, spivs
such as Parkinson or wide boys such as Archer. Yet, with what must have
been irrational optimism, when she heard of his election the former leader
burst into the room. She threw her arms around the new Prime Minister's
wife, Norma Major, and exclaimed, 'It's everything I've dreamed of for
such a long time. The future is assured; the future is assured.'[31]

PART SIX

Mr Major's Britain

21

Nice Mr Major

An exasperated scholar, Charles Dellheim, in an excellent book about the Thatcher years, wrote, 'Few Americans know, or care, what Ronald Reagan's father did for a living. But who in Britain does not know, and care one way or the other, that Margaret Thatcher is the daughter of a Grantham grocer?'[1]

If Thatcher's family background 'placed' her very firmly, what could the public expect of her pleasant-looking bespectacled successor, John Major, the youngest Prime Minister to date in the twentieth century? Here was no stereotype. Indeed, the Dickensian family background was something no one would have guessed from the grey suit, and the demeanour, which was that of a friendly bank manager. (He had worked for the Standard Chartered Bank, in the tricky section of development banking, chiefly in the area of facilitating investment in African countries, before moving over to the Corporate Affairs side of the business.[2]) Behind the grey suits and the smiles was the tragi-comic pathos of his father's life. In the bathroom of his parents' bungalow in Worcester Park, the young John Major could have opened a trunk – as his brother recalled – 'a large black one, with reinforced edges, containing such exotic items as a ginger wig, an evening cane and an opera hat, which as a child, I played with, popping it out and collapsing it over and over again. There were also greasepaints, band parts, false whiskers and a black jacket edged with silk. My sister Pat recalls a trapeze costume with a stars-and-stripes design, strongly suggesting that it dates from his time in America, and a photograph of Father wearing this costume.'[3]

John Major's father, born Tom Ball in the West Midlands in 1879, had emigrated to America when his father Abraham, a master bricklayer, went to seek work at the blast furnaces of Andrew Carnegie's steel works in Pittsburgh. Tom did not follow his father into bricklaying but, having taught himself acrobatics in the cellar (they by then had an independent builders' business), he left home to work as a trapeze artist in the circus. He subsequently pursued a career in vaudeville, performing in America, and in every town in England which possessed a theatre. His first wife, Kate Edith Grant, began her relationship with Tom as the other half of a music-hall double act, celebrated in its day as Drum and Major. It seems as if it were she who took 'Major' as a stage name: Kitty Major. They trod the boards with Dan Leno Junior, Marie Lloyd, Randolph

Sutton and many other household names. The Drum and Major act continued until well into the 1920s, with comedy routines and songs, some of them written by Kitty herself:

> And can you ever remember a Tommy,
> A Swaddie, a Tifly, or Jack,
> Hear a word said against Mother England,
> And not biff the foreigner back?

Towards the end of the marriage, Tom had formed an attachment to a young dancer named Gwen Coates, twenty-six years younger than himself. She was a brilliant dancer, who continued to be able to do the splits as an old lady. Terry Major-Ball, John's brother, tells us that 'Kitty died in June 1928, after a long illness as a result of an accident with a stage prop'. Unfortunately he did not expand. A year later, Tom Ball married Gwen Coates and in 1930, by the age of fifty-one, he had decided to give up his stage career. The pair began to have children – Aston, who died at birth in June 1929; Pat, described on the birth certificate as the child of an actor; and, in 1932, Terry, on whose certificate Tom has become a 'fuel agent', selling coke and coal. It was at about this time that Tom began to make garden ornaments, starting small in a spare bedroom of the bungalow, and eventually expanding into Major's Garden Ornaments – making gnomes out of plaster moulds. The business throve. 'Father had flourishing outlets all over southern England.'[4] The coming of war finished all that. 'Garden ornaments were the last thing people needed during the war. So he closed down the firm and went into Civil Defence, and Mother took a job in a library.'[5]

The last child, John Roy Major, was born on 29 March 1943. He had no memory of his parents having been interested in politics, though he assumed that they voted Conservative, 'if only out of admiration for Winston Churchill'.[6] When the future Prime Minister came into the world, his father was already sixty-four. The days of the flying trapeze and of music-hall routines were long over, shut away in the bathroom trunk. John Major grew up with elderly, loving parents who struggled with debt but proudly saw their clever son through Rutlish Grammar School in Wimbledon, where he did not work very hard but he enjoyed playing cricket. He left school at sixteen, and did a variety of jobs, including helping his brother Terry in a business very similar to Major's Garden Ornaments – Davids' Rural Industries. 'We didn't just turn out these other people's moulds, we made our own models. Terry was even better at it than I was, and my sister even more than him. Even today if you hand me a lump of clay, I will make you something rather good *and* make a mould out of it.'[7] Eventually, having been a clerk at the District Bank, he sat the exams for the Institute of Banking, and his career, such as it ever was, began.

Major's Jewish mistress, Edwina Currie, a sometime Junior Minister at the Department of Health, felt qualified to advise him about his wife, Norma – 'being half Jewish – he used to ask me about Jewish things, just at the end of the evening, as if he had been saving it up, something he wanted to know. And the most extraordinary moment was in the bath, when he asked if I believed in God. "Yes", I said, "but not in all the ritual. I had that stuffed down my throat as a child." He nodded and patted my back, as if satisfied, as if he's been asking himself the question a long time, and had now found a satisfactory formula.'[8] Currie's career came unstuck, not through her indiscretions about Major – these were published later as an exhibitionistic attempt to make some money – but because she had mishandled her Department's response to an outbreak of salmonella. By bossily, and quite needlessly, telling television viewers not to eat eggs, she managed to do such damage to the chicken farmers that kamikaze was required. (In all the rituals of resignation, she kept her humiliated cool, leaving her office at the Department, drafting her letter, and so on, until the moment when the Prime Minister, Margaret Thatcher, hugged her – 'gave me a cuddle', a phrase which, given the two participants, is slightly chilling – and 'it creased me for a minute'. She was soon back to her normal, brassy form. 'My trivial objective', she told her diary at the end of the same day, 21 December 1988, 'is to get to the end of this Parliament with a fur coat and some decent jewellery.'[9] She did this by a relentless campaign of self-publicity, writing various salacious novels which were supposedly autobiographical, and finishing up by publishing details of her relationship with Major. These did her no good, and him no harm at all. If anything, it increased his image among the British public that he was a normal, modern person. If, in the course of marriage to a much nicer woman than Edwina, he had been tempted to step aside, the public attitude was one of sympathy for the Majors, knowledge that such things sometimes happen in a marriage, and recognition that John and Norma Major were both behaving with dignity, whereas Edwina was not. John and Edwina had finished their affair before Major became Prime Minister, but her revelations must have prompted the historically minded to ask when was the last time that a Prime Minister found himself in a comparable position. Thatcher had married a man who had been previously married – a technical adultery in the eyes of some Churches; but though she had loved to flirt with her favoured spivs, she was no Catherine the Great, her interest in power for its own sake surely driving out other passions. Callaghan, though he fathered a well-known adulteress, the Baroness Jay, was not known for his extra-marital adventures, if he had any. There was gossip about Harold Wilson's baffling relationship with Marcia Falkender, but Wilson was not a conspicuously sexy person. Heath was Heath. Alec Home was obviously a loyal husband. Harold Macmillan was an undersexed cuckold. Eden, like Thatcher, broke the Church's marriage laws by remarriage after divorce, but was not obviously unfaithful to his second wife, Clarissa. Churchill was undersexed. Attlee's sexual nature, if existent, was unimaginable. Chamberlain, Baldwin and Ramsay MacDonald were hardly figures whose names are linked ineradicably with bawdry. For a figure comparable to John Major you have to go back in history to Lloyd George. John Major did not conduct himself with the exuberance of Lloyd George, but the knowledge that he had a sexual nature – that he was an attractive person – was a refreshing novelty in political life.

His new style of leadership, after Thatcher's combative approach, was perceived to be not merely nicer but (at first) more effectual. Most noticeably was this case in December 1991, when Major returned from the European Council at Maastricht, having personally negotiated three crucial opt-outs for Britain from the treaty which sought to bind the nations of Europe in an ever-closer political, legal and social union. First, he would not sign up to the Social Charter governing working conditions. Secondly, he would not sign up for a single currency, and the abolition of sterling. Thirdly, he would not commit Britain to federalism. The Foreign Office were amazed at Major's skill as a negotiator, and when he returned to tell the Commons there were cheers from the back benches. The election in the following year, which so many pundits predicted would be a disaster for the Conservatives, was a political triumph for Major. Fourteen and a half million people had voted Conservative, compared with the thirteen million who had voted for Thatcher in 1983. In his own constituency of Huntingdon, he had increased his personal majority from 27,500 to 36,000, one of the largest majorities in parliamentary history.[10] It was clear that this victory was not simply an answer to the question, 'Do you want Neil Kinnock to be Prime Minister?' Clearly, the profound electoral unattractiveness of the Labour dream ticket – Kinnock and Hattersley – made their contribution to the historic Conservative victory. But Major's personal rating was very high, and voters liked what he promised:

'I want a Britain where there is a helping hand for those who need it; where people can get a hand up, not just a hand out. A country that is fair and free from prejudice – a classless society, at ease with itself.' Yet, within months, Major was spoken of as the most disastrous Prime Minister in history; what went wrong?

First, there was a world recession, exacerbated in Europe by the reunification of Germany in November 1989. The German Budget moved from a surplus of $48 billion in 1990 to a deficit of $21 billion in 1991. Britain had been locked into the ERM, joining at a perilous moment when the pound sterling exchanged for 2.95DM, a rate which was never going to be easy for British business, and which in the gathering storm became ruinous for thousands of savers, importers and exporters. Understandably anxious to curb German inflation, Chancellor Kohl would not reduce the high interest rates in Germany. By September, the European markets were in turmoil, and on 16 September Britain was forced out of the ERM. Sterling had in effect been devalued by 10 per cent. In panic, the government – effectively, Major, his Chancellor Norman Lamont and the Governor of the Bank of England, reduced interest rates, bringing them down to 9 per cent (from a proposed 15 per cent) in one week. Savers, pensioners and businesses lost heavily, in many cases ruinously during the so-called Black Wednesday, while currency speculators such as the Hungarian-born George Soros made $1 billion in forty-eight hours. Major had chosen badly by appointing Norman Lamont as Chancellor of the Exchequer, and he also made a mistake in not sacking Lamont immediately after the fateful day. Black Wednesday not only created a country, overnight, which was very much the reverse of 'at ease with itself'. It opened up an unbridgeable fissure in the Conservative ranks. Thatcher, who had been against joining the ERM in the first place, and who had only been bullied into doing so by Lawson and Howe, could not restrain her harpie-squawks of triumph. She spent Black Wednesday on the telephone to her friends in Washington saying that she had been proved right.[11] A collective madness now descended upon the parliamentary party. There was no prospect at this juncture of Britain actually leaving the European Union, and it would have been hard to see how such a course could have improved the by-now-calamitous state of the British economy. Yet, to leave the Union was what the more impassioned of the Eurosceptics desired. In fact, the collapse of the ERM was a *felix culpa* for the British, proving Thatcher right in economic terms. Sterling could now find its natural level against other currencies, British businesses were now much more free and potentially more profitable. But Black Wednesday made many Conservatives wonder. The ERM calamity had happened because of Britain's involvement with the EU. The dread of losing British independence within the stultifying bureaucracy of a superstate led many people to think that the Prime Minister's skilful negotiations at Maastricht were not skilful enough. They wanted out. On the other wing of the party, the social democratically minded figures such as Kenneth Clarke, who became the new Chancellor, after the useless Lamont was eventually sacked in May 1993, or the genial Foreign Secretary Douglas Hurd, were understandably alarmed by the disloyalty of the sceptics, and by the silliness of some of their arguments. Their loftiness offended the majority of the public, whose doubts about the European experiment were legitimate and very far from the 'loony' figures such as John Redwood, the strange-looking Secretary of State for Wales.

The Conservative Party had, in the previous fifteen or twenty years, been through a series of exhausting transmogrifications. The doctrine-free alliance of the landed classes and the suburbs, which had kept the party in power for much of the twentieth century, had been violently disturbed by the Thatcher Revolution. Whether or not individual voters, or parliamentarians, embraced the sacred doctrines of monetarism, the Conservatives had become *the* party representing monetarist liberalism. It was not sure any longer who or what it was. It had sucked at the teats of its new wet nurse and drunk deep of the heady but potentially toxic draughts which she gave them. The enchantress seemed to lead them to victory and triumph, but when she no longer appeared able to do so, ritual sacrifice seemed the only way out. The massacre of the Money-Mother had been an act of gratuitous violence, but it had momentarily appeased the Fates. Now she returned from the dead, having lost what vestiges of political nous or personal niceness she might once have possessed. Like the witch at a christening, she wanted to curse the baby whom she had at first suckled as her natural heir. And she who had forced through British membership of the European Union now became the High Priestess of the Eurosceptic Cult, screeching her strange imprecations against each and every manifestation of 'compromise' from the government, and finding her words echoed by those of Major's Cabinet colleagues who sensed an electoral advantage in exploiting public concerns. It might have been supposed that this would have encouraged the true believers to embrace Europe, as the old right of the Conservative Party had done in the 1960s. Heath, after all, had been the candidate of the right in those days, and Thatcher had campaigned for a Yes vote in the referendum on British membership of the EEC, wearing a shirt emblazoned with the flags of the six member states. Black Wednesday, however, had been a demonstration of what happens if a free currency and a free country find themselves locked into currency agreements fixed by others. The enormous opportunities offered British businesses by membership of the largest free trade area in the world were balanced by the political and sometimes economic costs of 'Brussels'.

If the argument were being conducted on a purely intellectually level, it would have to be conceded that the existence of both sides was itself self-explanatory. There are indeed two sides to the question – is membership of the EU to Britain's advantage? For certain manufacturers, and certain financiers, the answer is very much yes; for others, who trade in other parts of the world or deal in non-European currencies, the economic consequences of membership are indifferent, and the political restraints could well seem tiresome. For the farmers and the fishermen, as General de Gaulle had long before warned, the Common Agricultural Policy favoured the French against the British farmer, the European against the British fishermen in countless ways.

Hence the divide. But the Conservative Party was suffering a collective identity crisis or nervous breakdown. Like a seventeenth-century Protestant sect breaking up into ever more fissiparous and esoteric groups, here Brownists, there Muggletonians, there Shakers, here Anabaptists, the parliamentary party splintered into ever more rancorous groupings: Tory Reform, Lollards, No Turning Backers, Bruge Groupists, Conservative Way Forwarders, 92 Groupers, Fresh Starters and European Foundationists.[12] Sensing that they wanted his blood, Major called the Eurosceptic rebels the Bastards. The most personable of the bastards, Michael Portillo, a blubber-lipped bisexual with rigorously combed-back hair, hid his intelligence in order to rouse the rabble, a low point being reached when he told the European Union, 'Don't mess with Britain', and claimed – his father had been a professor at the University of Salamanca – that European examination boards were less reliable than the good old British GCSE. But Portillo was too much of a coward to stand openly against his leader. Major smoked out the bastards in June 1995 by standing down as leader and inviting one of them to challenge him for the leadership. The gauntlet was picked up by John Redwood, christened by the press Vulcan because of a perceived resemblance to *Star Trek*'s Mr Spock. Major naturally won the contest. It was the most extreme case of 'No one will kill me, Jamie, to make you King.'[13] There was not much doubt, however, about the likely outcome of the next General Election. By the time that happened, Major was well into his eighth year as Prime Minister, a much longer run than many of his predecessors. The country was ready for a change. The nice decent man who negotiated Maastricht had evolved into a largely ineffectual Prime Minister who was blamed for Black Wednesday. He made catastrophic mistakes, such as allowing Michael Heseltine – whom he had appointed as President of the Board of Trade – to close thirty-one coal mines in one fell swoop with a loss of 30,000 jobs. ('A monumental cock-up' – said the Confederation of British Industry.[14]) The effects of the recession led to many natural Conservative supporters losing their houses through repossession. Even those who survived felt bruised by the experience. The newspapers, bored by more than eighteen years of government by the same party, began to play up the more absurd antics of Cabinet members, such as David Mellor, who had a three-month affair with a thirty-year-old actress, Antonia de Sancha (in a bugged telephone call he admitted to being 'seriously knackered' after a night with her[15]). The sleaze was not a journalistic invention. The career of Jeffrey Archer, liar, paymaster of a prostitute and convicted perjurer, should make that clear enough.

Jeffrey Archer was born in 1940, his mother a journalist, the first woman ever to work on the *Weston Mercury*. His father, whom Archer gave out was a First World War hero, decorated for valour, had in fact been a convicted fraudster and bigamist, who had travelled to New York at the beginning of the First War on his dead employer's passport and duped 'many well-known New York people'. The son would be a chip off the old block. His *Who's Who* entry was a better work of fiction than any of his novels which he so successfully persuaded the public to buy. He was down as educated at Wellington College – a Berkshire public school – whereas in fact he had merely been to school in the village of Wellington, Somerset. He studied as a gym teacher at the Department of Education in Oxford, but *Who's Who* readers were led to believe that Brasenose College was his *alma mater*. In 1966 he had married Mary Weeden, an ice-cold scientist. This was one of the best bits of luck he ever pulled off, for, as his career came unstuck, he discovered that this beautiful, mysterious person was far more prepared to share the financial rewards than she was to discard the moral disgrace of being Mrs, then Lady Archer. At twenty-nine, he became MP for Loughborough – Britain's fourth youngest MP. (He of course claimed to be the youngest.) Five years later, he came close to bankruptcy, having invested in a fraudulent Canadian cleaning firm called Aquablast. He decided, like Sir Walter Scott in comparable circumstances, to write his way out of penury. He had a genius, not for writing, but for self-promotion. Initially, the sales of the books were sluggish, but they were always written up and presented as if they were bestsellers on a level with *Gone With the Wind*. Little by little, people believed this, and the books sold. He re-entered public life, and Conservative political life, as a rich, popular author, much in demand on the circuit of speakers to Conservative luncheons, fetes and fund-raising evenings. By 1985, he had risen to become the deputy chairman of the party, even though Willie Whitelaw warned the Prime Minister, Margaret Thatcher, that Archer was 'an accident waiting to happen'.

In October 1986, sure enough, Archer resigned. 'I have been silly, very foolish. What else can I say?' He admitted arranging for a friend to pay Miss Monica Coughlan £2,000 in £50 notes, at a rendezvous arranged on Platform 3 of Victoria Station. The *News of the World* printed the story. The *Star*, however, had the temerity to suggest that Archer was not merely paying Miss Coughlan money out of the kindness of his heart but because he had had sex with her, and wished to offer hush money. He sued, and in July 1987 he was awarded £500,000 in damages. The judge, Mr Justice Caulfield, was so overwhelmed by the 'fragrant' beauty of Mary Archer that he could not conceive of a man married to her being tempted by 'kinky' sex, as had been alleged, with Miss Coughlan. The evidence given by Miss Coughlan, which included vivid descriptions of the spots on Archer's naked back, seemed convincing enough to many, but Caulfield effectively ordered the jury to find Archer not guilty. Mary Archer was worth more than her weight in gold. By January 1994, she was a member of the board of Anglia TV. Mysteriously Jeffrey Archer, who, it was claimed, knew nothing of an impending takeover of the company, cleared up a tidy £78,000 profit on buying and selling Anglia shares in a hurry – acting, naturally, on behalf of a friend. By 1997, Archer was speaking of himself as a plausible Conservative candidate for Mayor of London, but in November 1999, the *News of the World* was able to establish that Archer, in the libel trial of 1987, had persuaded a friend, Ted Francis, to lie about his whereabouts on the night in question. In some ways the interesting thing about the ensuing trial for perjury, in September 2000, was not the demeanour of the defendant, but that of the defendant's wife, who seemed to be on the edge of losing her cool, and who once actually called out and corrected evidence being given by another witness. Some of the evidence for Archer's defence consisted of a comparison between two desk diaries. One was a scuffed, well-used diary which appeared to have been the one in actual use in 1986. Another, much newer-looking diary for the same year, with only a few entries was, in Mary Archer's clear recollection, the one which had in fact been in constant use in the Archers' London flat. When her accountant came to be examined, he had difficulty in accounting for the half a million pounds in damages, which Mary Archer had said to a local newspaper had been donated to charity. Yet, it was not Mary Archer who was on trial, but Jeffrey, who, while the trial was in progress, had opened at the Theatre Royal, Windsor, with a play called *The Accused*. It transferred to the Haymarket in the latter days of Archer's own trial. He took the part of the Accused, his wooden acting in the theatre being neither more nor less convincing than his behaviour on political platforms over the previous twenty years. He liked to suggest that the play had transferred to the enormous West End theatre because of popular demand. The Haymarket was pathetically empty, whereas the court room at the Old Bailey full, to see him be sent down for four years on two counts of perjury and two of perverting the course of justice.[16] The question was not why he had been condemned, but why – given his obviously fraudulent character – he had been promoted within the political party by Margaret Thatcher, and, much more disgracefully, ennobled by the Queen at the recommendation of John Major. Poor Miss Coughlan's wad of money was very different from Miss Prism's handbag, in that other mishap on Victoria Station described by Oscar Wilde. Nevertheless, the words of Lady Bracknell hovered in the air as Major's government came unstuck. Losing one Minister through scandal was a misfortune, but having a whole pack of crooks as his colleagues and supporters began to look like carelessness.

When John Major became Prime Minister, Britain was involved in the Gulf War, but this was not a conflict of Major's making. Compared with his predecessors and his immediate successor, he was responsible for remarkably few deaths. His economic policy, following the debacle when Britain tumbled out of the ERM, was unexciting, which meant there were smaller dole queues, fewer strikes, and a higher level of personal prosperity than at any time in the nation's history. He came very close to helping the warring factions in Ireland find a peaceful way out of their ancient feud, and, indeed, handed an Irish situation on to his successor which was bound to end in peaceful negotiations. All in all, then, a successful term in office, and a good number of years at it, too – nearly eight. But by the end of the Major years, most journalists were writing John Major off as an embarrassing failure.

John Major was an apt Prime Minister for the times. In spite of the snobbish jibes directed at him by privately educated journalists, jibes which he understandably found vexing, he was more or less classless and, apart from a reassuring amiability when appearing on television, he was, in a good sense, characterless. The British had surely had enough of the cult of personality?

The country was no longer a great world power, but it had a sort of ex-great power status which meant it was necessary to have a Prime Minister who was courteous and good-humoured when meeting other world leaders. Major fulfilled this role admirably, as Thatcher most definitely had not. He was a patient negotiator – witness his winning the opt-out at Maastricht. But he was not pushing or needlessly aggressive. He seemed to be the perfect Prime Minister to express Britain's new status in the world – that of a prosperous ex–world power with an ambivalent attitude to the European Union of which it was a semi-detached member; a country with many of its old problems – corporatism, public inefficiency, too high taxes – but which was coming to terms with radical changes in its economic life and in its ethnic, social and demographic composition with resilience and inventiveness. Major presided rather appropriately over a period when the country wanted to cast aside the old divisive politics of unions versus new money. Something potentially rather interesting was happening to Britain, particularly to London. It was changing – into what, it was not quite clear. It had for a long time been clear that it would never revert to being a North European socialist state such as had been envisaged in 1945. It was therefore for the Labour Party to devise an alternative to state socialism. The trouble with being a Conservative at this date was that, intellectually, Conservatism had won, if not all, then a substantial number of the arguments. The former Eastern European communist states all yearned to become bourgeois liberal democracies such as Mrs Thatcher had championed. Britain, which combined a generous welfare system with burgeoning financial and services industries, was an attractive place not only to the majority of its own citizens but to many throughout the globe who wanted to come and work or live there. Yet, although Britain was more peaceful, more prosperous than it had ever been, there was a sense in many quarters that all was not well.

Major's government fell because it was inefficient, and because the Labour Party had eventually chosen a leader who did not frighten the electorate. But for those who had a responsibility to produce newspapers each morning, and for those who had an appetite to read them, the dullness of the Major years provided a challenge. Major's virtues, namely his unflappability and his understatedness, made him insufferably dull, especially to the cartoonists. Steve Bell of the *Guardian* envisaged him as always wearing Y-front underpants outside his trousers, while Patrick Wright and Peter Richardson devised *101 Uses for a John Major*. Major's expressionless face and his grey off-the-peg suits adorn each cruelly accurate drawing of their little book. The best of them show him standing dispassionately and dutifully being used as: an ironing board – Mr Major bends down while a woman places the board on his back; a toast rack – he kneels at a table, with the pieces of toast balanced on his fingers while a peppery old Tory rustles a copy of that morning's *Times*; a draught excluder – a trussed Major is wedged against the bottom of a door, and a lavatory paper holder – a polite, patient Major stands by holding the roll while another peppery Tory-looking character sits enthroned on the loo.[17] Something was necessary to fill the mythological gap after the demise of Mrs Thatcher. She had appropriated to herself the roles traditionally played not by ministers but by monarchs. And in Mr Major's gentle occupancy of Number 10 Downing Street it was inevitable that those who saw the world through the lenses of the newspapers and the television should have turned away from the dullness of politicians to the traditional stuff of story books and mythologies, princes and princesses. The newspaper proprietors and their readership were lucky, for this phase of political doldrums coincided with a period when, although the monarch was, as ever, leading a tastefully discreet existence, signing her state papers, exercising her corgis, following the horses and enjoying the companionship of a few carefully chosen, chiefly aristocratic ladies-in-waiting and courtiers, her heir was champing to be taken seriously, and to command the public stage.

21 January 1993

For the past 15 years I have been entirely motivated by a desperate desire to put the 'Great' back into Great Britain. Everything I have tried to do — all the projects, speeches, schemes etc. — have been with this end in mind. And none of this has worked, as you can see too obviously![18]

22

Prince Charles and Lady Di

In *Heir of Sorrows*, a running serial in *Private Eye*, the Prince of Wales was regularly lampooned. In this parody of romantic fiction, Charles's admiration for Sir Laurens van der Post, his love of health foods, his watercolours and his care for the environment, his passion for the cityscapes of England and for the preservation of old architecture, far from seen as admirable, were held up for ridicule, and were seen as contributory factors to his ever deeper estrangement from his wife. In one of the scenes, the Prince was summoned to the study of his terrifying father, the Duke of Edinburgh, who was sitting in front of 'a garish spread of the morning's newspapers' . . . 'This has gone far enough!' he bellowed, as if tearing a strip off some naval rating who had been caught asleep on the Watch.

> Charles felt helpless, as he always did. He hated these moments of confrontation. Desperately he groped in his mind for the advice of Sir Laurens.
>
> 'In moments of stress be still and build a bridge over troubled waters,' he had said, but it seemed of little avail as the Duke continued on his tirade.
>
> 'Your mother is very upset. And as for granny – well, she's hardly getting any younger, is she? We've worked bloody hard to keep this show on the road and now you're letting us all down, d'you hear?'
>
> The words stung Charles like the lash of a whip. 'I . . . er . . . terribly . . .' He began. But the Duke was in no mood to listen.
>
> 'It's up to you, boy, to bring her to heel before we end up as the laughing stock of Europe.'[1]

Were we to write down the virtues of Prince Charles, and his achievements, he would undoubtedly emerge as a, if not *the*, hero of this book. Unlike nearly all the career politicians who have dominated our story so far, this future Head of State took a wide, generous view, and had a much deeper knowledge, of the condition of Britain. The Prince's Trust, set up in 1976, was a practical response to the rise of crime and the growth of alienation among Britain's youth. 'Self-help schemes' were devised to rescue those young people who 'were destined for the scrap-heap before reaching adulthood'.[2] Within a decade of its inception, it

grew to a national organisation involving more than fifty regional committees, with over 1,000 volunteers. It dispersed more than £300,000 per
annum, and, unlike the government, it was able to dispense grants quickly
and without red tape to causes which were genuinely useful socially,
helping unemployed youth get training, encouraging young people to set
up businesses. More than 25,000 young people a year were helped by the
Trust, and it was recognised as a role model for state-funded organisations to help the nation's youth.

The Prince's Trust would have been a considerable achievement were
it the only thing which Charles had initiated. But he was also a responsible and intelligent opinion-former – as befitted a future Head of State –
about some of the issues of the day which could be seen as the most
vital. Long before politicians leapt on to the bandwagon, he was urging
people to wake up to environmental problems. He was a keen advocate
of organic farming years before it became fashionable. At Highgrove, his
Gloucestershire estate, he set up a food business which was a model of
its kind, selling excellent hams, bacon, biscuits and jams, full of good
flavour and hugely successful. Many other food suppliers imitated him.
He was often intelligent and interesting on the subject of food. During
a period when supermarkets and factory farms were homogenising and
Americanising the food supply, his was an early and clear-throated call
for more local produce, more seasonable fruits and vegetables, more celebration of the local and the near and the traditional. Nor did he, in this
respect, limit himself to home. While being a keen European, he spoke
out against the absurd EU regulations which threatened the very future
of French cheese by their insistence upon pasteurisation.

In 1984, addressing the Royal Institute of British Architects at their
Hampton Court dinner to celebrate 150 years of their existence, the
Prince spoke for England:

> For far too long, it seems to me, some planners and architects have
> consistently ignored the feelings and wishes of the mass of ordinary
> people in this country. Perhaps, when you think about it, it is hardly
> surprising as architects tend to have been trained to design buildings
> from scratch – to tear down and rebuild. Except in Interior Design
> courses, students are not taught to rehabilitate, nor do they ever meet
> the ultimate users of buildings in their training – indeed, they can
> often go through their whole career without doing so. Consequently,
> a large number of us have developed a feeling that architects tend to
> design buildings for the approval of fellow architects and critics, not
> for the tenants.

He continued, to the dismay of the assembled modernist-brutalist architects, to celebrate the joys of the small garden, the courtyard, the arch;
and he lambasted the wreckage of London's skyline, and singled out the
National Gallery extension as 'like a monstrous carbuncle on the face of
a much-loved and elegant friend'.[3]

As with the Prince's Trust, so in the matter of aesthetics, he put his
money where his mouth was. He established the Prince of Wales's Institute
for Architecture to teach students traditional methods of architecture,
the Prince of Wales Drawing School to teach draughtsmanship again to
a generation who could not find instructors in such basic skills at other
art schools. He established summer schools for teachers to explore ways
of helping them teach history and literature in schools which had lost
touch with both. Throughout this period, in which he took a more and
more active role representing the monarch in official engagements at
home and abroad, he also ran the Duchy of Cornwall, the chief source
of his income, as an enlightened landlord and businessman.

For all these virtues, and for many more, Prince Charles was much
admired, and much loved, by hundreds of thousands of British people. He probably always had a much bigger constituency of admirers
than any politician. He was a small 'c' conservative who, unlike the
party of the name, actually believed in conserving things – such as the
hunt, such as small rural communities, such as Georgian high streets,
and the Book of Common Prayer. In an age of arid secularism, he was
a gentle advocate of the spiritual dimension in life; and in a time of
increased intolerance, he remembered that he was destined to be not
merely the head of the Established Church (were it to survive, which
seemed ever less likely) but also the Head of a State which had within
it many of no faith, and many of non-Christian religious traditions.
It was particularly to Prince Charles's credit that in a period when
Islam was held in dread by the population at large, he spoke with well-
informed praise of the Islamic traditions, aesthetic, ethical, intellectual
and social.

Surely any country which had such a figure as its Head of State in
waiting would rejoice? Not since Prince Albert had there been in the
Royal Family a figure who had such public spirit and such a range of
talents. And when considered beside the Prime Ministers of Britain in
his grown-up lifetime, he towered above them all. But – and the previous
paragraphs of encomium have been waiting patiently for an inevitable
'but' – Prince Charles lived in strange times. One of the features of our
times was their ineluctable tendency to turn their events into farce and
its dramatis personae, however serious and worthy their intentions, into
clowns. It would be churlish to deny a single world of the praise which

we have heaped upon Prince Charles and his achievements. Equally, however, it would be sycophantic to suggest that this was the whole story.

At midnight on 30 June 1997, Britain handed back the sovereignty of its large major colony, Hong Kong, to the People's Republic of China. It was an emblematic moment in history, and it seemed all the more appropriate that it should have been happening after the landslide election victory of New Labour with its thrusting young leader, Tony Blair. The British Governor, Christopher Patten, a former Conservative Cabinet Minister of liberal disposition, had not enjoyed cordial relations with the Chinese. There were fears about the future of the colony, given the human rights record of the Chinese and the comparatively recent massacre (1989) in Tiananmen Square in Beijing. The ceremony itself, the lowering of the flag, with Governor Patten in a feathered hat, and in tears, was one which made it abundantly clear, to anyone who could possibly have doubted it, that the Imperial past was definitely over. Diplomatic niceties had to be observed, but many felt horrified by the murderous old communists taking over what had been the most vibrant capitalist island-economy outside Manhattan. When all the politeness was complete, everyone cheered Prince Charles when his comments on the occasion were leaked. In a letter-diary drafted to over a hundred friends, he described the Chinese tyrant leaders as 'appalling old waxworks' who engaged in 'an awful Soviet-style display' of goose-stepping at the ceremony. But, alas, these robust and wholly justified comments were spoiled by the 'round robin' he wrote to friends, complaining about being seated in business class on the plane. The decision to put him and his entourage in business class was a purely administrative one, designed for his convenience, so that he would not have to share with the much larger contingent of politicians on the plane. He tetchily said that he had 'noticed his seat was uncomfortable'. Everyone in the Western world knew that business class seats provide luxury beyond the wildest dreams of most inhabitants of this planet. Some of Prince Charles's subjects could remember from their history books that when Louis XIV was 'cut for the stone' (i.e., had a gallstone removed), he did not allow a single squeak to emanate from his royal lips when the surgeon's knife went in. An attendant lord-in-waiting felt the very faintest twitch of the King's hand as his insides were gouged out. That is kingly behaviour – not whingeing about seats on aeroplanes.

The contrast between the robust and admirable stance Charles took about the Chinese, and his self-pity over the plane seats, illustrates in miniature why his effectiveness as a communicator, and as a would-be Head of State, was curtailed. It was not simply the malice of newspaper journalists which found something truly extraordinary about Jeremy

Paxman's discovery about Charles and the boiled eggs – namely that when he returned from the hunting field the Prince liked to have seven boiled eggs lined up, in order from runny to hard, so that he can find one which was 'just right'. It was not possible to imagine Charles's mother going in for such pampered, silly extravagance.

Paxman observed at the time that Prince Charles has 'an Eeyoreish quality to him, this awful sense of being beleaguered, unloved and misunderstood. You want to help him – to tell him to snap out of it.'

The tetchy self-pity seemed to attract misfortune from the very first. Bad luck can be seen as something which happens to people, but it is often more properly regarded as a personal characteristic, like bad breath, which actually belongs to the person himself.

It is with both sides of the story in mind – Prince Charles's high virtues, and his innate tendency to self-pity and self-absorption – that one turns to what will always be seen as the central and most important aspect of his story: his marriage to Lady Diana Spencer. He was thirty-two at the time of the 'Fairy Tale wedding' in St Paul's Cathedral – which took place on Wednesday 29 July 1981.

As all the world would eventually come to learn, Charles was under immense pressure from his parents and their advisers to find a wife. Convention required that she be a virgin, and the law required that she be Protestant – or at least, not a Roman Catholic. (The law did not consider the possibility that the bride of a British sovereign might be Jewish or Muslim.) These requirements severely limited the field. There was, moreover, the awkward fact that Prince Charles was in love with a married woman.

Those members of the Royal Household who have kept as a souvenir *Ceremonial: The Marriage of His Royal Highness the Prince of Wales with the Lady Diana Spencer* must consider it to be a document so heavy with irony that it is as if penned by the Fates. It relates in punctilious and military detail the processional route from Buckingham Palace to St Paul's; at what hour the Sovereign's escort of the Household Cavalry will be in position on the South Side of the Forecourt in Buckingham Palace, which car will be transporting the King and Queen of Spain, and which the Prince and Princess of Liechtenstein; who will walk up the aisle behind The Rt. Hon. The Speaker, at what precise second the State Trumpeters will take up their positions in the portico, when the Earl Spencer will enter the Cathedral with his daughter on his arm, and when the fanfare will be sounded by the State Trumpeters as the Bride and Groom, newly married, enter the Quire from the Dean's Aisle. Then, there is the whole procession back again to Buckingham Palace for the Wedding Breakfast; the appearance of the Queen and the Bride and

Bridegroom on the balcony (1.10 approx). Finally, there is the departure of the pair at 4.00 p.m. (approx). 'The Bride and Bridegroom will depart from the Grand Entrance in a semi-State Landau, accompanied by a Travelling Escort of the Household Cavalry, under the command of Lieutenant-Colonel Andrew Parker Bowles, The Blues and Royals.'[4] It was with Colonel Parker Bowles's wife, Camilla, that Prince Charles was still in love.

Camilla Shand, a year older than the Prince, was the daughter of Major Bruce Shand, the Old Rugbeian son of the much-married architectural historian P. Morton Shand, the man who taught the young John Betjeman (while working with him on the *Architectural Review*) to admire the modernist works of Gropius and Le Corbusier. Bruce Shand (who won the Military Cross with bar) was in the 12th Royal Lancers (Prince of Wales's), and saw action during the Second World War in Belgium, France and North Africa. As befitted a cavalry officer, he was a keen horseman, a passion he passed on to his daughter. Camilla's mother was Rosalind Cubitt, the granddaughter of Alice Keppel, mistress of Edward VII. Legend has it that when Camilla Shand first met the Prince of Wales, at a polo match at Smith's Lawn in Windsor Great Park in the early summer of 1971, she reminded him of the fact that 'My great-grandmother was the mistress of your great-great-grandfather.' In some versions of the story, she added, 'So how about it?' When Gyles Brandreth asked her if there was any truth in the story, Camilla pulled a face and laughed, then shook her head.[5] Prince Charles's version of how they met was that they were brought together by one of his former girlfriends from undergraduate days, Lucia Santa Cruz, who thought that Camilla would be 'just the girl for him'.[6]

The passion between them was strong, but Charles did not want to commit himself to the relationship, and when he returned to his career in the navy she married Andrew Parker Bowles – on 4 July 1973. It was a marriage which produced two children, but it was interrupted by frequent adultery. When Lord Mountbatten was assassinated in 1979, Prince Charles turned in his grief to his old love, Camilla. The old sea dog would have found nothing strange in Charles seeking consolation with a married woman. He had once told a friend, 'Edwina and I spent all our married lives getting into other people's beds.'[7]

On the evening of the Queen Mother's eightieth birthday ball at Windsor Castle in 1980, Charles and Camilla spent the entire evening together on the dance floor, causing his date for the evening, 'Whiplash Wallace' (Anna Wallace), to exclaim: 'Don't ever, ever, ignore me like that again.'

The passion for Camilla remained undimmed a year later when he undertook what was in effect an arranged marriage to Diana Spencer.

When the betrothed pair appeared on television together on 24 February, Charles said, 'I am positively delighted and frankly amazed that Diana is prepared to take me on.' When pressed by a BBC interviewer, 'And in love?' Diana answered, 'Of course,' with a little giggle. Then Charles glossed, 'Whatever "in love" means.'[8]

It was an unfortunate bit of thinking aloud, which would be, like police evidence in a criminal case, taken down and used against the Prince of Wales in the years to come. There have since been endless retellings of the story. The traditional version tells of the innocent, virgin Sloane Ranger, daughter of an earl, working as a nursery-school assistant, and head over heels in love, desolated to discover a few days before the wedding that 'Gladys and Fred' (pet names given one another by the Prince and Mrs Parker Bowles) are still in love. This was the version fed to the public by the Princess herself in her television interview with Martin Bashir for the BBC programme *Panorama*. 'Well, there were three of us in this marriage, so it was a bit crowded.' A later, very clever piece of Dianology, by Tina Brown,[9] posited a variation on the traditional version by suggesting that, at the time of the marriage, Charles had fallen besottedly in love with his young bride, and that it was Diana Spencer herself who was manipulatively determined to become the Princess of Wales, even though she was not in love – 'whatever "in love" means'. Whether the Tina Brown picture, of a young blonde ruthlessly exploiting her sexual attractions and her charismatic personality for the purposes of self-promotion, is accurate, is a matter which future Dianologists will long debate. Perhaps all truly gripping biography entails a measure of self-portraiture.

The story was to end, or perhaps it would be more accurate to say to climax, in a death, on 31 August 1997. Diana, divorced from Charles, was in Paris with Dodi Fayed, the son of the Egyptian owner of Harrods, Mohammed Fayed, also the owner of the Paris Ritz. Fayed *père* went through the malicious farce, ten years after Diana's death, of insisting that she had been murdered at the behest of the Duke of Edinburgh, that she was pregnant at the hour of her death, that she was betrothed to his son Dodi. All these fictions had to be tested in an inquest, even though the truth had been established ten years before, by a French inquest: namely that she died as a result of an accident. In order to escape the attentions of the paparazzi, Dodi and Diana escaped from the Ritz and were driven at speed through the Pont d'Alma tunnel. Henri Paul, the driver hired by Fayed, had three times over the legal limit of alcohol in his bloodstream. There was a semi-collision in the underpass with a white Fiat Uno. The car containing Diana and Dodi collided with the side of the tunnel. She was still alive in the back of the car when a passing doctor tried to save her, but she died in La Pitié-Salpêtrière Hospital at 4 a.m. on Sunday 31 August 1997.

Did I say this was the end, or the climax of the story? It was the end of her life, but it was far from being the end of the Diana story. Her death, aged thirty-six, was met with a public response in Britain unmatched in our times, even by the death of Sir Winston Churchill. Indeed, it is hard to think of any death which has been received in such a way.

When Churchill died, there was a solemn, silent tribute, with thousands filing past his catafalque in Westminster Hall. A similar solemnity would meet the death of Queen Elizabeth the Queen Mother in 2002. The death of Diana was quite, quite different.

When the news broke, they streamed into London at a rate of six thousand people per hour.[10] Before long, the gates of Kensington Palace were covered with bouquets of flowers, teddy bears, Queen of Hearts playing cards, rosaries, children's drawings. People came to camp out. There were people in sleeping bags all down the Mall. Makeshift shrines were erected, with candles burning in front of Diana's picture. The crowds were not quiet in their grief. Howling, sobbing, gasping grief turned into mob hysteria.

Those old conservatives who had always been of the Prince's Party, and seen Diana as a dangerous, disruptive person, could not understand what was happening and dismissed it as a terrifying nonsense. When the crowds became angry and began to ask why the flag on Buckingham Palace was not flying at half-mast, the conservatives replied that in so far as a flag ever flew over the Palace, it was the royal standard; it was only ever flown when the Queen was in residence (she remained in Balmoral, with Diana's children) and it was never flown at half-mast. It was a symbol of the enduring monarchy. That was not a sufficient answer for the mob. 'Show Us You Care', screeched the *Daily Express* at the Queen. 'Your People are Suffering. Speak to us, Ma'am' – the *Mirror*.

As was shown in the (pretty accurate) film *The Queen*, in which the monarch was played by Helen Mirren, the court stuffpots were the last to pick up on the public mood, but Prince Charles had been sensitive to it from the beginning.

The Queen heeded advice, and spoke to the nation on television, with the French window open behind her and the mob more or less audible and visible behind her. When, at the funeral, Diana's brother Earl Spencer denounced the Royal Family, there was long and continued applause from the crowds outside Westminster Abbey.

In life, Diana had divided the British. To be of the Prince's Party, so-called, was to hate Britain becoming more touchy-feely; to regard the baring of the soul as an essentially bogus exercise for those who perhaps did not have much soul to bare. It was to see the Prince as a decent man, doing intelligent things to benefit society, rather than being a show-off who behaved like a celebrity queen. It was to deplore the manipulative way in which Diana wooed the media, briefed journalists, and, in the propaganda battle with the Prince, tried to have it both ways – claiming that Mrs Parker Bowles had wrecked her marriage, while herself conducting affairs with a string of ever less suitable partners. To be of the Princess's Party was to rejoice in her informality, and to feel that it did no harm at all for the British to learn to express their emotions a little more freely. It was also to feel that, while politicians seemed most to worry about the level of inflation and the balance of payments, it did the rest of the population no harm to be reminded that the homeless slept on the streets of London, that drug addiction among the homeless young was spiralling, that AIDS was killing hundreds of people. Nor did it do the military and political bosses any harm to be reminded, as Diana had done in her latter years, of the lunatic cruelty of landmines, which, left in the ground after conflicts were over, remained to deprive civilians all over the world of their limbs.

When he chose to marry her, neither Prince Charles nor Lady Diana Spencer could have known that she possessed the qualities which would electrify the world. Long before rifts between the married pair became apparent, and long before anyone thought of taking sides, she began to wow the crowds.

President Kennedy once joked, 'I am the man who accompanied Jacqueline Kennedy to Paris.' But he said it from the position of being the most powerful man, and one of the most promiscuous lovers, in the world. Prince Charles was unsure of himself, inwardly in need of friends to flatter him, older men to advise him, women to comfort him. 'At least I know my place now. I'm nothing more than a carrier of flowers for my wife.'[11] Anthony Powell was wise to say that it is envy, more often than jealousy, which breaks up marriages.

Diana was not a clever person in the intellectual sense of the word, but she possessed the quality which all truly great figures in history have, of knowing how to use her weaknesses to her own advantage. The fact (if it was a fact) that she was desolated by her husband's infidelity, that she felt cold-shouldered by the Royal Family, that she suffered from eating disorders and barely controllable mood swings, would, in a lesser person, have ruled her out of public life. Like other unhappy royal wives, she would have been seen somewhere near the back of the line-up on the balcony at the time of jubilees and royal weddings and, beyond a little light charity work, she would never have been seen out in public. Diana, even before she decided to tell all through the medium of Andrew Morton in his *Diana: Her True Story* (1992), reached out to the suffering hearts of other people by stripping naked her own. They sensed it, and it was this, combined with her quite extraordinary physical beauty, and by the animation of her face, and by the simply overwhelming personal charm which made her into, what she claimed she was, the Queen of Hearts. This was the moment when chaps in the Prince's Party, the hunting set, men in their clubs and Nicholas Soames, the rotund grandson of Sir Winston Churchill, would all reach for their sick bags — if in the circumstances the image is pardonable.

Undoubtedly, the interest expressed in the royal marriage both before and after Diana's death was as unwholesome as an eating disorder itself. Those of us who developed a compulsion to read and reread the story should have spotted the early warning signals when we first read Andrew Morton's book, and, having thrown up, started to gobble it up all over again. By the time we were binge-reading Lady Colin Campbell's *The Real Diana*, or the unforgettably nasty *The Housekeeper's Diary*, almost retching as we turned the pages, but unable to stop ourselves cramming in every last sordid detail, we were on a hopeless spiral. Even junk which was ready-spewed vomit before we read it, such as galloping Captain James Hewitt's caddish *Love and War* (spilling the beans about his affair with Diana) or the butler Paul Burrell's *The Way We Were*, could still lure us to spoon in their nauseating contents with slurping lack of control.

There is a danger, however, in confusing the obsession with its object. Because an obsession is unwholesome, this does not make its object unwholesome. The world was right to love Diana and, confused and unhappy as she was, she was a great force for good. The Royal Family, who had felt so threatened by the revolutions in taste and protocol which she effected, were her greatest beneficiaries. James Fox expressed an archetypically conservative viewpoint at the time of her death when he exploded, 'The people's heroine, why did we need one? It was celebrity culture meets the democratisation of the monarchy.'[12] Precisely. Without such ingredients, the monarchy would have been weaker. Diana paradoxically reminded people of why monarchy is a more satisfactory system of government than republicanism. It allows a focus upon persons, rather than upon institutions. It is cult of personality without any of its sinister or fascistic overtones. Diana needed, wooed, and received wild adoration. But the kind of 'democratisation of the monarchy' which James Fox so dreaded did not do any harm to the monarch herself, who drew forth from her people emotions which were different, but in many subjects no less deep: respect, reverence, and a sense which only a person, not an office, can embody, continuation with the past.

Archbishop Runcie, who had married Charles to Diana, was asked in 1993 whether the people of England would ever be able to tolerate

Charles's love for Camilla. The churchman in Runcie was disappointed that the Prince had clearly lapsed from the mainstream Anglicanism which he had practised as a very young man, serving the altar for Archbishop Ramsey at Lambeth Palace when he was being prepared for confirmation, and for Harry Williams, the Dean of Trinity College, Cambridge. Now, since the advent of Sir Laurens van der Post, the Prince seemed to want to be something called the defender of faiths. So, this coloured Runcie's outlook, no doubt, when he spoke of whether Charles would ever, after the divorce and the inability to abandon Camilla, be able to inherit the throne. Said Runcie in 1993, 'It depends whether the Prince wins his way with the British people over the next five to ten years. Also, it would quite help if he loved the Church of England a bit more.'[13]

Families are collectively haunted by skeletons in cupboards and events in their past. Looming over the Royal Family throughout Prince Charles's lifetime was the Abdication Crisis of 1936. Because of his desire to break the marriage laws of the Church and to marry a (twice) divorced woman, Edward VIII was forced to abdicate and banished into exile. His brother the Duke of York became the last King Emperor. George VI's wife, known throughout Elizabeth II's reign as the Queen Mother, would have been the mere Duchess of York, rather than a much-loved monarch, if her charming brother-in-law had been allowed to reign with Queen Wallis at his side. Yet there are factors more powerful than logic in human affairs, and in spite of the fact that it had brought her an Imperial Crown, and a manner of life in which she had visibly, and very charmingly, revelled, the Queen Mother continued to regard the Abdication as the ultimate betrayal, and the breaking of the Church's marriage laws as the one unpardonable royal sin. Throughout our times, nemesis returned, as if it were Wallis's revenge. First – Princess Margaret had to discard the man she loved, Group Captain Townsend, because he was divorced. Her own marriage to Lord Snowdon ended in divorce. Then, the Queen's children contracted marriages which unravelled – Princess Anne to a show-jumping captain called Mark Phillips, whose father worked for Wall's Sausages; Prince Andrew to the daughter of the raffish Major Ronald Ferguson, a horse-loving friend of the Duke of Edinburgh who was found out in a massage parlour called the Wigmore Club; and, much the most problematic from a constitutional viewpoint, there was the collapse of Prince Charles's marriage to Lady Di.

It was not until his beloved grandmother Queen Elizabeth died aged 101 that he could contemplate marrying Camilla. But the supreme irony of the whole matter was that without the 'Diana factor', without 'celebrity culture meets democratisation of the monarchy', he would never, as the supposed future Head of the Church of England, have been able to get married to a divorced woman and remain in the line of succession.

True, the Church had itself changed its own rules since Edward VIII's day. It allowed for divorced people to be remarried in church, and there were even bishops and priests who had been divorced and remarried. But it was surely Diana who posthumously helped to blow away the dark cloud of 1936. The monarchy is something more than 'celebrity culture', but it is celebrity culture in part. The unfortunate members of the Royal Family, who in earlier ages would have been protected against the intrusions of the press, were now made to suffer the kind of exposure which tortured, as well as enlivened, the existences of film stars and pop singers. But though this made them fair game, in the eyes of the paparazzi and newspaper editors, whenever they staggered half-tight out of a nightclub at 3 a.m., or attempted to have a discreet affair, it also made them less vulnerable to the legalists. The avid public expected celebrities to have love affairs and divorces. Indeed, the readers of celebrity magazines and tabloid newspapers would not have felt they were getting their money's worth unless the celebrities were seen to be dining at the Ritz with unsuitable partners. When Prince Charles and Camilla were eventually married, it was as if 1936 had never been. A few die-hards continued to say, nonsensically, that they would tolerate the marriage but that Camilla could never be the Queen of England. In deference to their views, perhaps, and in tactful recognition that the 'Princess of Wales' would, for a long time to come, always be, in most people's minds, Diana, Camilla was known as the Duchess of Cornwall. But everyone knew that if or when Charles became the King of England, his wife would become the Queen.

23

The Union

Was there a future for the United Kingdom in our times, or would the Union itself break? Since the setting up of the Irish Free State in 1922, it was a question the Welsh and the Scots must have asked themselves from time to time. Northern Ireland had been given devolved power (the Stormont Parliament set up in 1922) against its will. When that power was taken away in 1972 it had protested with even greater vigour. By the end of the conflict, the IRA would have killed 1,800, of whom 465 were soldiers of the British Army. Loyalists killed 990, government forces 363, the army killed 297, the UDR and Royal Irish Regiment 8, the RUC 55. In addition 40,000 had been injured – nearly 3 per cent of the population.[1]

The progress made by Mr Major in bringing this madness to an end led to a radically revised notion of devolution in all the regions of Britain. As Northern Ireland learned to make peace, with power-sharing across the Irish border and the slow process of making a democratic parliament for themselves in Stormont once again, Wales and Scotland were ready for devolution, too. Since the United Kingdom began there had been Celtic nationalists who wanted its dissolution but their aspirations could not seem realistic either on political or economic terms. British membership of the European Union altered that. Hitherto, membership of the United Kingdom provided the only umbrella by which these countries could survive. The existence of the European Union could offer the dream that Scotland could sit down in the Councils of Europe as an equal partner with France, that Wales, having cast off the English yoke, could be an independent member of the Union.

Whether in practice the EU would accept the applications of Scotland and Wales had not been tested. True, Ireland was an independent member and had done well out of it. But Spain, perpetually embattled by terrorists of the Basque separatist movement, would have resisted moves for an independent Wales, Cornwall or Scotland if this appeared to strengthen the arm of the terrorists on their own soil. Meanwhile, the Welsh could enjoy the slightly less impressive spectacle of their fellow countrymen exploiting British membership of Europe for all – and even for slightly more than all – it was worth. Anecdote began to circulate the cattle markets of West Wales of subsidised farmers writing down the extravagant shoe purchases of their wives in Freeman, Hardy and Willis in Swansea as 'agricultural wellington boots'. And there were jobs for the Welsh-speaking boys and girls in Brussels, translating every single piece of EU legislation and bureaucratic verbiage into Welsh.

Monolingualism in Wales had vanished by the time of the Second World War, and the numbers who spoke both Welsh and English was in steady decline – 909,261 in 1931, 714,686 in 1951, 656,002 in 1961, and 508,207 in 1981.[2] It was understandable that Welsh-language enthusiasts should have laboured to preserve their culture, with an expansion of Welsh-speaking schools, an increase in Welsh-language road signs and television programmes, a lavish grant (£300,000 pa in 1988) to the Welsh Books Council and an insistence on the use of Welsh in the professions. This lead to an influx of non-Welsh-speaking Welsh lawyers, businessmen and, to a smaller degree, clergy, to England.

Welsh nationalism as a political aspiration had, in the twentieth century, been focused at first around the figure of Saunders Lewis, founder and President of Plaid Genedlaethol Cymru. The chief aim of the movement was 'to take away from the Welsh their sense of inferiority . . . to remove from our beloved country the mark and the shame of conquest'. He saw the purpose of politics as the defence of civilisation. 'Civilization is more than an abstraction. It must have a local habitation and a name. Here its name is Wales.'[3] Just as de Valera and the Irish nationalists felt a natural kinship with the European right, so Saunders Lewis, who became a Roman Catholic in 1932, saw General Franco and Mussolini as the likely role models should Plaid Cymru ever find itself catapulted into power by an uprising of patriotic desire to undo the shame of Edward I's conquests. It was understandable that until the 1960s most Nonconformist Chapel – going farmers and professional people in Wales continued to vote Liberal, while the coal miners of Merthyr Tydfil and the steelworkers of Port Talbot remained staunch in their loyalty to the Labour Party.

But Plaid Cymru evolved, as all political parties do. The 3rd Marquess of Salisbury, had he risen from the dead and met his successor, would probably have been amazed that Mr Major was a Conservative Prime Minister, rather than a Radical. Tony Blair would find himself leading the party of Keir Hardie and Nye Bevan. Plaid Cymru, its early Catholic-fascist principles quietly abandoned, became the party of Welsh-speaking schools, and the translation of medical prescriptions and the Highway Code into the language of the *Gogynfeirdd*.

Gwynfor Evans, one of whose first political acts had been the formation of an organisation of Welsh pacifists at the National Eisteddfod of 1937,[4] became the leader of Plaid Cymru in 1945. There was something figurative about this gentle man capturing the parliamentary seat of Carmarthen on 14 July 1966. The by-election was fought following the death of Lady Megan Lloyd George,[5] the daughter of the last Liberal Prime Minister and in latter days a candidate for the Labour Party. Gwynfor, a law graduate of the University of Wales, Aberystwyth, farmed 300 acres at Llangadog. He was the father of seven Welsh-speaking children, a devout Christian, and a teetotaller. He seemed very different from the Free Wales Army, who modelled themselves on the IRA and enjoyed blowing up railway bridges. Nor did he advocate, as did the priest poet R. S. Thomas (who spoke Welsh with a patrician English accent), the torching of English holiday cottages in Wales. But he did concede that his election would not necessarily quieten the men of violence. 'It does not depend on us. It depends on the Government whether the people use violent means. The Government does not think anyone serious until people start blowing up things or shooting others.'[6]

Gwynfor's vision of Wales and Welshmen had been spiritual. At the beginning of 1980 two thousand members of Plaid Cymru vowed to go to prison rather than pay a television licence to an English-language broadcasting corporation. Gwynfor took the matter to Gandhian levels of heroism by announcing that he would fast unto death if a Welsh channel were not established. The government yielded before he even began his fast and the Welsh Fourth Channel (S4C) was launched on 1 November 1982.[7] Meanwhile, Gwynfor lost Carmarthen to the Tories, and Plaid Cymru had moved on to a position where, by the time of the setting up of a Welsh Assembly in 1999, it was mopping up the voters who in the past would have been natural Labour supporters. The Labour Party, by the time the Assembly came, had long since ratted on the ideals which had inspired the socialists of the coal mines and the slate quarries who had thrilled to the egalitarian rhetoric of Tom Jones of Rhymni (the trades unionist, not the singer) or Nye Bevan, or even of Megan Lloyd George.

One Welsh socialist more loyal than most to the dreams of Old Labour was Ron Davies, who was best known to the public at large (if known at all) for questioning the fitness of the Prince of Wales to ascend the throne and who asked how the Prince could allow his sons to indulge in field sports. A bright boy from the valleys, Ron had progressed from Bassaleg Grammar School, via Portsmouth Polytechnic, to the world of Welsh Labour politics, beginning with a seat on Rhymney Council, rising to take the safe Labour parliamentary seat of Caerphilly in 1983, and eventually to become the Welsh Secretary and the leader of the party in their new Assembly. Alas, on Monday 26 October 1998, only weeks into his new job, he went for a walk in the dark on Clapham Common, a well-known homosexual haunt, and encountered a man who robbed him at knife-point.[8]

Davies resigned his Cabinet post at once, in the hope at least of securing his future as Labour leader in the Welsh Assembly. 'In allowing myself to be placed in this situation, with people I had never met and about whom I knew nothing, I did something very foolish.'[9] Three days later, Davies gave a press conference referring to his 'moment of madness'.[10] Later he blamed 'a violent and emotionally dysfunctional childhood' for his difficulties. Quite what he had done, in what the madness consisted, or why he felt it necessary to resign, he did not explain. Later on, he came to 'blame the media' for what was seen by some as 'a personal tragedy'.[11] Most of his constituents continued to support him whatever form his particular madness had taken, but this was not enough to suppress the rise of his rival Rhodri Morgan, a Blairite placeman, to the position of First Welsh Minister. In August he and his wife, Christina, announced that they would be divorcing because of 'irreconcilable differences'.[12]

Was the establishment, at great expense and trouble, of a Welsh Assembly, itself a moment of madness, or the inevitable consequence of half-buried, violent and emotionally dysfunctional historical trauma? Or was it done because the Scots wanted some form of autonomy and it was deemed more judicious to offer the same to Northern Ireland, Wales and Scotland rather than seen to be pandering to Scottish separatists?

As Major's government lost strength, there was the possibility – indeed certainty – that in the Celtic countries the Conservatives would suffer electoral disaster. In the interwar years, 1918–39, the Conservatives had more MPs than any other party in Scotland.[13] In 1955 they had secured the majority of Scottish seats and a majority of the Scottish vote.[14] By 1987 there were a mere eleven Tory MPs, not enough to make up the necessary sixteen, which composes a parliamentary committee at Westminster. When bills relevant to Scotland came before the Westminster Parliament and reached the committee stage it became necessary to fill up the committees with English MPs. By 1997, the Scottish Tories were completely wiped out – without a single Westminster MP. Many factors contributed to the Conservative decline, though the chief of them could be summed up in the two words, 'Margaret Thatcher', whose attempt to impose the Poll Tax on the unwilling Scots was only the coup de grâce after a decade of high unemployment and financial hardship.

It was against this graph of psephological decline that the panicking rump of Scottish MPs in John Major's government began to make gestures of a distinctly un-Tory kind towards the Scottish nationalists. In 1995, Michael Forsyth succeeded Ian Lang as Scottish Secretary. A new slogan was introduced – 'Fighting for Scotland'.[15] ('Fighting for their lives' would have been more accurate.) One of the most distasteful, and ridiculous, acts performed by the Conservative Party at this time was the removal of the Stone of Destiny, or Stone of Scone, from the throne in Westminster Abbey. Forsyth, who was behind this piece of vandalism, and Major, who allowed it, both brought down ill luck on their heads. The throne of Edward the Confessor, and the stone beneath it, were all of a piece, inseparable. They were a symbol of the Union of the Crowns and Kingdoms long before these unions occurred as a matter of political fact. Edward I had removed the stone from Scotland in the thirteenth century. Until then, it had always been used as the coronation stone for Scottish kings. For Scottish separatists, naturally, they were viewed as symbols of English conquest. The Stone had been stolen by Scottish nationalists from Westminster Abbey in 1950, but at that stage the possibility of the Union being broken was entertained only by Celtic dreamers. By the time of John Major, this was no dream, but a political reality. The collapse of the Tory vote in Scotland left the way clear for the nationalists. It was to appease them that devolution was brought in. The matter was put to a referendum as soon as New Labour won the 1997 election. The referendum was held on 11 September. There was a 60.2 per cent turnout, compared with a turnout of 62.9 per cent in a referendum of 1979; 74.3 per cent of these voted for the proposition 'I agree that there should be a Scottish Parliament', and 63.5 per cent voted for the proposition 'I agree that a Scottish Parliament should have tax-varying powers'. It was open to those who wished to maintain the Union to vote against having a Scottish Parliament at all. Nevertheless, a mere 74.3 per cent of 60.2 per cent means that less than half of the population of Scotland did in fact vote for devolution. In Wales, a mere 50 per cent of 50 per cent voted for their assembly – i.e., no more than a quarter of the voters.

Nevertheless, once the devolutionary idea had been set in motion, it was inevitable that the Scottish separatists should move to greater triumphs. The inevitable consequence of this would one day be the break-up of the United Kingdom itself and the end of Britain as a political entity.

During the debates about Scottish devolution in the 1970s, the Labour MP for West Lothian, an Etonian named Tam Dalyell, had posed his famous West Lothian Question. After devolution, is it justifiable for Scottish MPs to vote in the Westminster Parliament on English domestic affairs? It was not permissible, after devolution, for English and Welsh MPs to vote on Scottish matters. The constitutional historian Vernon Bogdanor wrote, 'There is only one logical answer to the West Lothian question, but it is politically unrealistic: it is for Britain to implement legislative devolution all round, so becoming a thoroughgoing federalist state.'[16] But this was an optimistic point of view even in 1999, when it was published, for it was clear that the Scottish nationalists intended to take things much further than that, in which event there would be no centralised authority from which power could be said any longer to evolve. Almost contemporaneously with the Scottish nationalist success story is – by pure coincidence – the development of the Big Bang Theory in physics. (It was in 1979 that Alan Guth, of Stanford University, aged thirty-two, proposed his view that matter, electromagnetism, strong and weak nuclear forces, etc, all came into being milliseconds after the Bang.) Modern physics was a form of poetry, if not of theology, so strange as to be all but incomprehensible. One of the metaphors which it tried to use to describe the universe was that it was expanding. But Nobel Laureate Steven Weinberg noted, 'Solar systems and galaxies are not expanding, and space is not expanding.' Rather, the galaxies were rushing apart.

Rushing apart was a good metaphor of what was happening to Britain at the same period. It took poets to be able to comprehend the height and breadth of what was happening. Benjamin Zephaniah:

With my Jamaican hand on my Ethiopian heart
The African heart deep in my Brummie chest,
And I chant Aston Villa, Aston Villa, Aston Villa,
Believe me, I know my stuff.
I am not wandering dark into the rootless future
Nor am I going back in time to find somewhere to live . . .
I want to make politically aware love with the rainbow . . .
Dis is not an emergency
I'm as kool as my imagination, I'm, more caring than your foreign
    policy,
I don't have an identity crisis.

The Rastafarian poet might not have had an identity crisis. Many other Britons did. Many Scottish nationalists did want to wander drunk into the rootless future. And their desire to do so would plunge the British who did not share their desire, not into federalism, but into chaos. Wandering drunk into a rootless future was also the inevitable lot of the English and the Welsh if the Scots decided to go it alone and declare independence. And although the monarch was technically the Queen of Scots, as well as of the rest of her kingdom, it did not seem likely that Alex Salmond and his supporters in the National Party would wish to perpetuate her role. The Union, when it broke, would eventually bring not merely Britain, but also its monarchy to an end.

Part of the reason for the resurgence of the Scottish National Party was negative – the complete disillusion felt by the Scottish electorate for the Westminster-based parties, and for the patronising manner in which Secretaries of State for Scotland had (as it was perceived north of the border) known what was best for Scotland. Part of the reason was, no doubt, the political skill and personal charm of Alex Salmond, the leader of the party from 1990 onwards. By the time our period came to an end, it was too early to say whether an independent Scotland would enjoy a renaissance of cultural and national life, bestriding the world stage as an independent European nation, or whether, by contrast, it would become an inward-looking, puritanical, provincial, dull little country, incapable of recapturing the glory days of David Hume, Robert Adam, Adam Smith, Walter Scott and Francis Jeffrey. The British Empire had in many senses been the Scottish Empire, with many of those who settled in nineteenth-century Canada, New Zealand, Australia and the newly formed African states being Scottish, many of the best engineers, medics and colonial administrators being Scottish. In the nineteenth century, Dundee had been a world centre of the whaling trade; and of the jute industry which provided sacking for half the world's commodities. Glasgow was one of the greatest commercial centres in the world; and also one of the great manufacturing bases, where steam engines, machines for spinning cotton flax and wool were made. Above all, it was remembered as a hub of metal-working and of shipbuilding. No doubt two reasons for the pre-eminence of Glasgow were 'the abundance of skilled workmen and the low wages paid to them'.[17] But another reason was that, rather than being a small, inward-looking nation, Scotland, in partnership with England, was now part of the greatest Imperial adventure since Roman times. The Scottish *Sun* in January 1992 came out as a nationalist newspaper: 'The Scottish *Sun* has been thinking long and hard about what form of government would best serve our future. We have come to the inescapable conclusion that Scotland's destiny lies as an independent nation within the European Community. The political and economic union with England is now nearly 300 years old. It has served us well in the past, but as links with Europe strengthen, that union has become more and more unnecessary. The time has come to break the shackles. To collect our own taxes. To run our own lives. To talk to other nations in the world on our behalf. For too long – 300 years too long – we have thought of ourselves as a second class nation . . .'[18]

It is too soon to say whether the *Sun*'s self-contradictory prophecy will come to pass: self-contradictory because, in one breath, it says that the Union had served Scotland well in the past, and in the next that Scotland had thought of itself as a second-class nation. Historically, this was simply not the case. The period when Scotland was manifestly not a second-class nation, and was not regarded as one either by its own citizens or by others, was during the period of its Enlightenment, and during the heyday of Empire: i.e., when the Union was at its closest. Many Scots felt, after devolution, that their country had diminished, and become more provincial, more petty, more inward-looking.

In Northern Ireland, John Major was lucky enough to have history on his side. The Long War was exhausting all sides. The IRA's criminal activities made them deeply hated in working-class Catholic communities – the protection rackets, the knee-capping, the gangsterism. Crucially, its foreign backers in Libya and the United States were beginning to run out of cash, and at last America had a President, in Bill Clinton, who knew Britain (he was a graduate student at University College, Oxford) and who was prepared to stop the sentimental pro-Irish lobby in the US from giving money to Noraid. (Surveys had often showed that a majority of those donating money to this terrorist cause were under the impression that the IRA was the Army (official) of the Irish Republic, at war with an invading British force.) With an intelligent American President on the side of the Peace Process, the republican voters could feel reassured and, an almost equally weighty consideration, the self-importance of the Republican high command could be flattered. Not for them the kind of retirement they had witnessed being spent by IRA veterans in the 1950s and 1960s, undistinguished lives in the dingy outskirts of Dublin, poverty, whisky loosening the tongue to recall the bombing of pubs or shooting or border patrols, or to theorise about the Revolution, but with the evidence of failure all around their lyncrusta-coated parlours. They could see, if they played their cards right, careers as public speakers in America, perhaps even Irish senators. What was to prevent them by act or default from being awarded the Nobel Peace Prize?

These were the rewards which history might offer. 'It is time for the cycle of violence to be broken. We are prepared to break it,' Adams told Sinn Fein. And this in Dublin. Neither McGuinness nor Adams ever made any public acknowledgement of membership of the IRA and they continued to speak to the ends of their careers as if the violence was something quite outside themselves, something which they, in common with the American President and the new Prime Minister of Britain, who looked and sounded like a gentle bank manager, hoped would go away. 'Republicans want peace. We want an honourable peace, no papering over the cracks or brushing under the carpet the humiliations, degradations and injustices inflicted on us, by a foreign power.'[19]

So, John Major had history on his side. He began the Northern Ireland peace process. It was left to Tony Blair to finish it. Probably as a good Chief Whip, Major had already foreseen that they could allow the UUP and its leader David Trimble – i.e., the decent, sensible, pro-British, etc, etc – be the victims of the process. Hitherto, the British politicians had been unable to resist the impulse to impose decency and common sense upon the Northern Irish. Major, and Blair after him, allowed the leader of the 'mainstream' Unionists to be the one who was prepared, very, very tentatively, to talk about the possibility of power-sharing with the nationalists. Inevitably Trimble was represented to the Protestants as a trimmer.

There were the expected delays as the IRA, in ever less penetrable communiqués, spoke of 'decommissioning' their weapons. A few rogue explosions would continue to save their pride but their game was up. Major was the first British negotiator really to insist that the Northern Irish must solve their own problems. Their new political arrangements must be decided by a referendum. There were talks about talks about talks. Canadian inspectors came to inspect the caches of Libyan guns and explosives, Algerian rocket launchers and Russian[20] pistols which the maniacs had so expensively collected over the years. Boring 'framework documents' were drafted, read out, spat upon, agreed upon. Every now and then one of the negotiators would fall back on the old crackpot rhetoric to please their grass-roots supporters. But they were tired of killing one another. Mr Major, as reassuringly boring as a man from the Alliance and Leicester Building Society advising them about the respective merits of repayment versus interest-only mortgages, led all these fanatics, in spite of themselves, down the pathway of peace. His own personal doggedness and niceness were integral parts of the story, though perhaps the whole oddity of the situation did require, if it was to be brought to fruition, the skills of histrionic fraudulence in which Mr Major was lacking but with which nature had so liberally endowed his successor.

24

Stephen Lawrence

Mr Major, upon his becoming Prime Minister, had expressed the wish 'to see us build a country that is at ease with itself, a country that is confident'.¹ In almost every big speech from now on, the Prime Minister would allude to the 'two rooms in Brixton' from which he emerged to create the classless society. And when on another occasion he evoked an idyllic vision of an England in which men sipped warm beer while watching village cricket, and old ladies cycled to Holy Communion in the early morning mist, his experience as a Lambeth councillor had taught him that in his native south London there was an abysmal fissure between any such vision and the cruel reality of things. In local government as a young man he had a liberal record. In 1968 he had stood aside from the other Conservative candidates who had signed up to a leaflet entitled 'We Back Enoch, Don't You?' Nor did these die-hards, when offering themselves for election, even bother to approach Major to sign their pledge – 'We the undersigned call for a complete ban on all further immigration to the borough.'²

The other, and more poverty-stricken, parts of London, retained, in spite of much architectural wreckage, a rackety cohesion. South London, following much heavier wartime aerial bombardment than north, was rebuilt more brutally. Whereas north London had only one major thoroughfare, the M1, taking traffic out of the metropolis, south London became a sprawling mass of badly planned road systems attempting to convey traffic, in one direction to Kent, in another to Southampton, and often, it would seem from their chaos of traffic jams and road signs, to almost anywhere else other than where it happened to be, as though anyone finding themselves in Kennington or Lewisham or Camberwell had done so only by accident and was longing to get out again as soon as possible. Between the pockets of wealth in Clapham, Dulwich, Blackheath and Georgian Greenwich, there were the ruthlessly 'Corbusian slabs'³ of Loughborough Road, Brixton, the 'dour point blocks of Lambeth Walk'.⁴ South London was not at ease with itself. To cope with a huge increase in population, the boroughs had hurled up a chaos of gimcrack tower blocks and inadequate estates to house the growing numbers.

In the Borough of Greenwich alone, the GLC had created what was not merely an estate, but effectively a new town at Thamesmead on the

Erith Marshes. The 1960s also saw the rebuilding of two large hospitals in the brutalist manner in Greenwich, and an extension of the grammar school at Eltham.

As so often happened in London, prosperity and poverty juxtaposed. Greenwich threw up extremes – on the one hand the handsome big houses of the rich at Blackheath, on the other the urine-marinaded brutalist tower blocks of Woolwich. Eltham, on the further edges of Woolwich, had medieval roots. The Institute of Army Education was housed in Eltham Palace – the building dated from 1475, when it was inhabited by Edward IV, but the moated site was two hundred years older. The Royal Blackheath Golf Club was housed in Eltham Lodge, a fine banker's town house from the reign of Charles II. Beneath the more nondescript parts of Eltham High Street were the remains of Well Hall, a moated manor house which belonged in the earlier sixteenth century to Sir Thomas More's daughter, Margaret Roper.[5] It was in Eltham that Bob Hope and Frankie Howerd were born. Herbert Morrison lived there when a Cabinet Minister.[6]

Eltham had an ethnic minority population of around 13 per cent. Unemployment was way above the national average at this point. One household in five was seriously behind with utility bills. It was an area of London where the whites beneath or at the poverty line felt especially threatened. A misspelt scrawl on the church gate declared: 'Watch out coons, your now entering Eltham.'

Doreen and Neville Lawrence lived in a council house in Hanover Road, Woolwich. Neville was a builder, temporarily unemployed since the downturn in the housing market. Doreen was studying for a degree in humanities at the University of Greenwich. They had three children, the eldest of whom, Stephen, was preparing for his A-levels and wanted to be an architect. Doreen had been born in rural Jamaica in 1952. Her own mother was twenty-two when she came to England. 'Where we lived in Jamaica I don't recall seeing any white people.'[7] When Doreen went to school in England, '[I] was the only black child in the class. I don't recall anyone treating me badly or being racist towards me.'[8] Her children were among many blacks in their English schools.

The murder of their son Stephen, which took place in Well Hall Road, Eltham, was an event which revealed the fissures in British society. The eighteen-year-old schoolboy was standing at a bus stop with his friend Duwayne Brooks and three strangers, after 10.30 on the night of Thursday 22 April 1993. Duwayne heard a shout across the road – 'What? What? Nigger!'

The next five minutes, which were the last of Stephen Lawrence's life, happened very quickly. A gang of white youths had crossed the road to attack the two blacks. Duwayne saw the leading youth draw something long from inside his clothing as he crossed the road. This youth, the leader, lifted this object and brought it down on Stephen. The five attackers had found their prey and run off in a confused and terrifying instant. None of the four witnesses, including Duwayne, had a completely coherent memory of what happened, some remembering that Stephen was kicked to the ground and tried to ward off the blows, others remembering that he had fallen, while the attackers ran off down Dickson Road. Stephen had been stabbed twice, one blow cutting through two major nerves, a large vein and an artery before penetrating a lung; the other blow, which gashed the left shoulder, also cut an artery and a vein.[9] In spite of these injuries, Stephen Lawrence managed to stagger some 200 yards up the hill of Well Hall Road after his friend before slumping beneath a bright orange street light. Duwayne, terrified that the assailants might return, ran to a telephone kiosk, and dialled 999, reporting that his friend had been hit by an iron bar. By chance, an off-duty policeman, PC James Geddis, and his wife, Angela, returning from a prayer meeting, slowed their car and came to Duwayne's help. The ambulance arrived. The boys were taken to the Accident and Emergency Department at the Brooke Hospital, a mile or so up the hill; Stephen's parents Neville and Doreen Lawrence came anxiously to the hospital, but by the time they had done so, their son was dead.

This borough of London was no stranger to violence, nor to racism. In 1991 there had been two murders, of Rolan Adams and Orville Blair, which were thought to be racially motivated, and below the roundabout on Well Hall Road, in July 1992, a young Asian, Rohit Duggal, was murdered. This had been a knife murder by one Peter Thompson who was convicted of the crime at the Old Bailey.

What made the Lawrence case special was that no one was prosecuted for the crime in spite of the fact that no one appeared in much doubt about the identity of the killers. The inquest into Stephen Lawrence's death took place at Southwark Crown Court in February 1997. It had taken so long – getting on for five years after the murder – because of the failure of the Crown Prosecution Service to bring anyone to justice, followed by an unsuccessful private prosecution, brought by Neville and Doreen Lawrence, against five white youths with a known history of knife crime and racist abuse. The matter had been *sub judice* until the coroner's jury heard the evidence again and decreed – 'Stephen Lawrence was un-lawfully killed in a completely unprovoked racist attack by five white youths.'[10]

The next day the *Daily Mail* carried as its front-page headline a single word in two-inch-high letters: MURDERERS.

The Daily Mail today takes the unprecedented step of naming five young men as murderers. They may not have been convicted in a court of law, but police are sure that David Norris, Neil Acourt, Jamie Acourt, Gary Dobson and Luke Knight are the white youths who killed black teenager Stephen Lawrence. We are naming them because, despite a criminal case, a private prosecution and an inquest, there has still been no justice for Stephen, who was stabbed to death in a racist attack four years ago.

One or more of the five may have a valid defence to the charge which has been repeatedly levelled against them. So far they have steadfastly refused every opportunity to offer such a defence. Four have refused to give any alibi for that night in April 1993. One initially offered an alibi, but it did not stand up when police checked it out. This week the five refused to answer any questions at the inquest on Stephen, citing their legal right of privilege not to say anything which might incriminate them . . .

If these men are innocent they now have every opportunity to clear their names in legal action against *The Daily Mail*. They would have to give evidence and a jury in possession of all the facts would finally be able to decide.[11]

None of the five ever sued the *Mail* for libel. Doreen Lawrence was probably right to believe that an open accusation of murder in an English newspaper was 'unheard of'.[12] Neil Acourt, the prime suspect, had a history of stabbing, had been implicated in a stabbing incident in an Eltham Wimpy Bar; he appears to have been present at the knifing of a boy called Stacey Benefield by David Norris. The boys were run-of-the-mill south London miscreants whose upbringing more or less guaranteed a life of crime. (The Acourts' mother, Patricia, was the sister of Terry Stuart, convicted burglar and drug trafficker. Luke Knight was related to the East End gangster Ronnie Knight – and so on, and so on.)

Only a percentage of murders ever get solved. Nevertheless, to most observers the Lawrence story was particularly horrifying, not merely because a promising eighteen-year-old had been savagely massacred at a bus stop, but because the police could have done so much more to prosecute his killers. More than this, the first of the public inquiries into the Lawrence murder – that conducted by the Kent police force – uncovered a direct connection between 'unsatisfactory' policemen and the family of David Norris (which included Clifford Norris, whose big drugs racket had involved the corruption of a number of officers . . .[13]).

In the second inquiry into the case, headed by Sir William Macpherson – a former High Court judge – and submitted to the Home Secretary in

February 1999 – the incompetence of the police was mercilessly exposed, but it did not, as such, accuse the officers investigating the murder of corruption. Rather, it indicated that the catalogue of misjudgements, the failure to act on early tip-offs or to make early arrests, 'the botched surveillance, the failure to pursue leads swiftly and systematically; the mishandling of potential witnesses; the poor organization when the arrest finally came'[14] had been enormously exacerbated by one factor: race.

Unwitting racism can arise because of a lack of understanding, ignorance or mistaken beliefs. It can arise from well-intentioned but patronising words or actions. It can arise from unfamiliarity with the behaviour or cultural traditions of people or families from minority ethnic communities. It can arise from racist stereotyping of black people as potential criminals or troublemakers. Often this arises out of uncritical self-understanding born out of an inflexible police ethos of the 'traditional' way of doing things. Furthermore, such attitudes can thrive in a tightly knit community, so that there can be a collective failure to detect and to outlaw this breed of racism. The police canteen can too easily be its breeding ground.

In her book about her son's murder, Doreen Lawrence described walking down Well Hall Road after she had viewed her son's dead body and left the morgue. The spot where the murder happened is not, she emphasised, an obviously sinister place. Unlike the bleak estates of tower blocks which litter the poorer parts of south London, and unlike the working-class estate of council houses where the Lawrences themselves lived, 'Well Hall Road was a different world to the one we lived in. It all looked so Olde English . . . The streets all have poets' names: Rochester, Congreve, Lovelace. There is green in front of the houses, and plane trees line the road. Right opposite where Stephen finally fell down dying there is a Catholic church built in warm brown brick. It has the look of the 1920s, the look of an Agatha Christie film on TV rather than the gritty back streets of Woolwich or Peckham. If my son had not died there I would probably think it was a nice area, almost leafy and like a village . . . I couldn't believe that such an area could produce people who would commit such a horrific crime. But the Englishness was like a mockery now, and the fake old-world features a way of saying to me, You don't belong here in our little world, come here if you dare.'[15]

The Macpherson Report, and Mrs Lawrence, both saw a conservative, small 'c', old-fashioned England as itself colluding with the murder. The police had failed in imagination; but by extension, to use the old cliché mocked so mercilessly by the Peter Simple fantasies in the *Daily Telegraph*, we were all guilty. Sir Paul Condon, the Metropolitan Police Commissioner, was called upon by one member of the Macpherson

Inquiry panel, John Sentamu, then Bishop of Stepney, later Archbishop of York, to make a public confession of institutional racism. 'It seems to me, Sir Paul, that the door is open. It is like when Winnie Mandela was challenged in the Truth Commission in South Africa by Desmond Tutu to acknowledge that she had done wrong and she just did it and suddenly a whole burden of weight . . . melted away . . . If we are to go forward, I say to you now, just say, "Yes, I acknowledge institutional racism in the police" and then in a way the whole thing is over and we can go forward together. That is my question. Could you do that today?'

Sir Paul could not. Although there were calls for Sir Paul's resignation after the Macpherson Report was published, he stuck it out.

In Deptford, south-east London, ten million pounds were spent on an architectural centre in Stephen Lawrence's memory. The Turner Prize–winner Chris Ofili designed eight windows which cost £15,000 each. Within a week of the centre being opened in February 2008, these windows had been smashed by youthful local racists.[16]

The case of Stephen Lawrence was a shocking but unfortunately far from unique example of how little at ease with itself Mr Major's Britain was. Liberal commentary, from TV studio, leader article or lecture podium, found it easy to denounce the police as racist boneheads, and some of the officers concerned in the Lawrence investigation appeared to be parodies of a caricature, almost anxious to conform to stereotype.

The police were condemned by Macpherson as institutional racists. Racism in some form is very hard in most human beings to disentangle from a sense of their own identity, who they are in relation to others. Awareness is one thing, of course, and lack of impartiality, lack of manners, lack of common decency, are others. If the police behaved stereotypically towards black youths, it would only be fair to point out that a significant majority of street crime in London, involving muggings, stabbings, shootings, was perpetrated by black youths, themselves, it would seem, intent upon behaving according to stereotype.

In January 1998, the Runnymede Trust, 'an independent think-tank devoted to the cause of promoting racial justice in Britain', set up the Commission on the Future of Multi-Ethnic Britain. Under the chairmanship of Bhiku Parekh, Professor of Political Theory at the University of Hull, the Commission had over twenty members, including Yasmin Alibhai-Brown, Trevor Phillips and Andrew Marr. Its report, based on an extensive survey of 'the current state of multi-ethnic Britain'[17] painted a depressing picture of urban Britain, and there is a marked contrast between the architecturally wrecked, socially divided, crime and poverty-ridden cities they visited over a two-year period, and their bright hope that, by following their recommendations, it would have been possible for their fellow citizens to build 'a relaxed and self-confident multicultural Britain'.[18] They made, for example, two visits to Toxteth, scene of riots in 1981. On the first visit, they were pleased to find 'a group of local black activists working on youth sports and arts projects'. But when they returned to the 'Social Centre of Excellence' (a disused church) they found only dilapidation. Carved stones from the old building had been looted, and the vandals appeared to have triumphed.[19] Though hoping to build a mutually tolerant, 'vibrant' society, their innumerable witnesses told them of an atmosphere of unrelenting racial abuse and tension. 'I still don't feel British,' said one witness. 'Because I know we haven't been fully accepted. We still walk down the street and get called a Paki.'[20]

One of the Commission's fundamental premises was that 'Race, as is now widely acknowledged, is a social and political construct, not a biological or genetic fact' . . . 'There is more genetic variation within any one so-called race than there is between races.'[21] This would have been a point well made had they been arguing with some nineteenth-century prophet of racial differences such as Charles Darwin or Houston Stewart Chamberlain, or with their most sinister twentieth-century followers in the German National Socialist movement. Nearly all British citizens, however, in the twenty-first century used the word race interchangeably with what the Commissioners call ethnicity. Their pages are full of the statistics concerning Afro-Caribbean, Bangladeshi, Irish and other citizens. This is the sense in which the word 'race' was currently being used. Whatever word is used, the experience of the different groups was markedly different. It notes, for example, that, 'African-Caribbean children start school at the age of five at much the same standard as the national average. By the age of 10, however, they have fallen behind. The difference is greater than in English. At the age of 16 the proportion of African-Caribbean students achieving five higher-grade GCSE passes (grades A*–C) is considerably less than half the national average.'[22] Clearly crude racial theories do not explain this phenomenon and probably no one in the educational world, at the period under discussion, would have advanced them – though Charles Darwin would have done, and it was a curious feature of the age that many of the keenest progressives who wished to celebrate multi-culturalism were also fervent supporters of Darwinist assaults on religion.

Perhaps the single most depressing statistic in the Commission's findings came from the United States of America. At any one time since the 1960s, almost one in three of all African American males was either in prison or under some form of penal supervision.[23] The statistics are drawn from the American researcher Loïc Wacquant, and an article entitled

'From welfare state to prison state: imprisoning the American poor'. For whatever unhappy reason, a high proportion of Afro-Caribbean young males in Britain during the period looked as if they were going the same way. The British prison system would be asked to supply the service which in times past had been effected by the workhouse and the press gang.

How to promote a sense of belonging among the alienated, ethnically diverse peoples of Britain? That was the question the Commission set themselves. They turned to the wisdom of the works of Nigerian-born, bearded Ben Okri (born 1959) whose novel *The Famished Road* won the Booker Prize for fiction in 1991. Okri, a charming, smiling man, who celebrated the primitive joys of Nigerian rustics in his stories, while enjoying the hospitality of London *salonnières*, had written, 'Stories are the secret reservoir of values: change the stories individuals and nations live by and tell themselves and you change the individuals and nations . . . Nations and peoples are largely the stories they feed themselves. If they tell themselves stories that are lies, they will suffer the future consequences of those lies. If they tell themselves stories that face their own truths, they will free their histories for future flowerings.'[24]

In furtherance of their scheme of improvement, the Commission proposed 'rethinking the National Story'.[25] They proposed radically rethinking the notion that 'the British are an island race, their mentality shaped by a long and sturdy independence, free from foreign contaminations'.[26] It would be interesting to know how many schoolchildren of our times had been taught 'Our Island Story' as it was taught in schools and schoolrooms before the Second World War. Many otherwise well-educated students managed to get through school knowing almost no history at all by the standards of their grandparents: a smattering of the Tudors, a sortie into the First World War and for many that was about it. But the Commission on the Future of Multi-Ethnic Britain made it clear that if any school were to revive history teaching of the old sort – the dates of all the Kings and Queens of England, the Spanish Armada, the Civil War, Wolfe on the Heights of Abraham, Nelson at Trafalgar – they might be in danger of upsetting the project. There was not space in their book to spell out in detail what the alternative history of Britain might have been, though predictable hints are given – 'When I think of British history', someone wrote to us, 'I think of Oliver Cromwell's campaign of genocide in Ireland, the 1688 settlement and the crushing of Irish resistance it involved, the Gordon riots, the 1801 Act of Union, the Murphy riots, the Black and Tans', etc.[27] Praise is also given to a permanent exhibit at the National Maritime Museum in Greenwich depicting a 'Jane Austen-like figure sipping tea with a sugar-bowl on the table beside her. From beneath the floor at her feet a manacled black arm reached out as if from the hold of a slave ship, and as if to show the source of her comfort and wealth.'[28]

What is striking about the picture of Britain's past here is its negativity. If they had formed a basis for the National Curriculum, would the teachers have told the children, as earlier generations were told, that Cromwell, as well as being brutal to the Irish, was the hero of modern republicanism, and the builder-up of the British navy? Would they have been told that the 1688–89 'Glorious Revolution' saved Britain from becoming a Bourbon-style monarchical dictatorship, shackled to an intolerant Roman Catholicism? Would the terrible story of slavery have included the fact, of which many British people through generations have been proud, that it was the British who abolished the abominable slave trade, a trade originating in Africa, and perpetrated by Africans on their fellow Africans? And would the children have been taught to sing the words of that great anti-slaving anthem, 'Rule, Britannia!'? Whether they had or they hadn't, it would seem unlikely to have interested either the hoodlums who vandalised the Toxteth Social Centre of Excellence or the many, many persons of 'minority ethnic' origin who told the Commission that they did not 'feel British', that their loyalties and responses were not to some nebulous 'Britain', which was visibly breaking up around them, but to their own families and friends. Would not their testimony have been closer to Margaret Thatcher's candid admission that there was no longer such a thing as society?

PART SEVEN

The Project

25

New Labour

The 'career politician' was a phenomenon of our times, comparable to the career television presenter. Phillip Schofield left school at seventeen and worked as a bookings clerk at Broadcasting House in London. His family moved to New Zealand two years later, and he became a TV presenter for a programme called *Shazam!* Thereafter, he was imprisoned in the television. It was as if he was actually locked up inside the box. When he came back to England in 1985 he became a 'children's presenter', and between 1987 and 1993 he presented *Going Live!*. It was one of those programmes which take up the desultory Saturday mornings of children whose parents cannot be bothered to play with them or suggest they do something interesting. Schofield remained in television, moving on to present programmes for grown-ups. By the time he was co-hosting *Dancing on Ice*, he was said to have secured a £5 million two-year deal. His hair had turned white. He was already looking like an old man, the televisual equivalent of Dickens's Mr Dorrit, the 'Father of the Marshalsea', who had been in the debtor's gaol so long that it had come to feel like home. Schofield once presented *I'm a Celebrity . . . Get Me Out Of Here!*, one of the programmes in which a group of people are incarcerated together and spied upon by the cameras. By a supreme irony of language, these exercises in artificial group sadism were called 'reality shows'. Did something in Schofield scream 'Get me out of here?' or had he become the twenty-first-century equivalent of the figures on Keats's Grecian Urn, 'for ever piping songs for ever new', frozen in artifice?[1]

Career politicians inspired similarly disconcerting impressions. 'Lord Kinnock' had begun as an activist in the students' union at the University of Cardiff, and done nothing, nothing, nothing in his life except to be a politician, first as an MP, then as a European Fat Cat, then as a member of the House of Lords. Life whizzed past, for him, as for Phillip Schofield. Nothing happened, except the words which they read from their autocues.

Most politicians in the Blair era gave the impression of being like this, and although Tony Blair was obviously much more than that, he was a Phillip Schofield – like figure himself, a face to be seen on the television for a slice of most British people's lives, but fading as soon as he left it.

'You don't look or sound like a Labour MP.'

That was how Edward Heath addressed Tony Blair when they were first introduced in the House of Commons.[2] The words were not only perfectly true; they exactly summarise why Blair was so successful in defeating not merely the Conservative Party but also his own party, Labour. When he said the word 'sound' – SAYOWND – Heath would immediately have signalled to any listener that, for all the plumminess of his Oxford-educated tones, he remained the carpenter's son from Kent. Tony Blair, much more inclined than Heath to identify himself with another Carpenter's Son, defied social analysis, at any rate as far as his pronunciation of the English language was concerned. Much more a creature of artifice than Edward Heath, or than any previous Prime Minister, Blair could, by his voice, sometimes sound like a gorm-less rock singer – as a student he had played the guitar for a band called Ugly Rumours, and he would still, as Prime Minister, strum the instrument for recreation. As an orator, the new Prime Minister could sound like an evangelical preacher, as when he had offered his messianic vision to the Labour Party Conference of 1999 – 'A century of decline, 20 years of Conservative Government still not put to rights. Do you think I don't feel this, in every fibre of my being?' Like all rhetorical questions, this suggests to a sceptical ear the opposite answer to the one intended by the speaker; but at the time, his jerky, half tearful and verbless sentences made a great appeal. 'The frustration, the urgency, the anger at the waste of lives unfulfilled, hopes never achieved, dreams never realised. And whilst there is one child still in poverty in Britain today, one pensioner in poverty, one person denied their chance in life, there is one Prime Minister and One Party that will have no rest, no vanity in achievement, no sense of mission completed until they too are set free.' As time was to advance, his sense of himself as a saviour would extend beyond the one British child living in poverty to embrace the entire planet, as when he was able to offer salvation to the conti-nent of Africa (first at the G8 meeting in Gleneagles in 2005, and then at the Labour Party Conference). Being also a canny politician, as well as a Messiah, Blair's actual proposal for overseas aid, contained in his 2005 election manifesto, was 0.7 per cent of the Gross Domestic Product, a figure far higher than most British taxpayers would want, but scarcely the sacrificial giving which Blair probably believed, when on the podium and delivering his speech, that he was offering to the starving children of Darfur or Eritrea.

The electorate had perhaps thought they were sacking the dull bank manager and replacing him with a charming young man who was a little more, well, normal. Waking up on May Day 1997, many of the elec-torate, however, realised that they had chosen a person who was by no means run-of-the-mill. After the strange eight-year episode of the poor son of circus trapeze artistes and garden-gnomes makers, the British found themselves with a pop-star revivalist as Prime Minister. But both the personae – the Vicar of St Albion's as *Private Eye* was quick to dub him, and the Bono/Geldof side of Blair that liked wowing crowds and making big, global gestures – were distinctly part-time. He never stopped being an extraordinarily disciplined and relentlessly focused political operator.

Blair was just short of his forty-third birthday when he became the Prime Minister on 1 May 1997. He looked young for his age, and still possessed the well-scrubbed appearance of a public school prefect, the sort of boy who was never going to be a notable scholar but whose pleasant manners made him a favourite with the teachers and their wives. If prospective parents had come to the school, the housemaster's wife would have thought Blair could be trusted to show them round the squash courts and the science laboratories and make a 'good impression'. After Fettes, and St John's College, Oxford, at neither of which establishment he had shone, he was called to the Bar and joined Lincoln's Inn. He was never destined to become a great Chancery lawyer, but he had a quick mind, and a superficial plausibility. The ability to grasp one or two salient points in a case, and a boyish coquettishness of manner in front of the judge, would enable such a lawyer to put his case with success. He was never going to rise as high in the law as the woman he married, another barrister in the same chambers, Cherie Booth, the daughter of a drunken television actor called Tony Booth.

Superficiality is a tremendous advantage in a politician. Blair arrived on the political scene with no ideological 'baggage' beyond a slightly goofy students' union type of Christianity, which, as he sometimes blurted out to journalists, was the guiding principle of his life. (His minder and rather brutal press secretary, North Country journalist and bruiser Alastair Campbell, intervened on one occasion to tell interviewers, 'We don't do God.') Sometimes Blair would tell inquirers that the inspiration for his life had been the writings of a Christian socialist called John Macmurray, introduced to the undergraduate Blair by an Australian cleric, Revd Peter Thomson, seventeen years older than Tony and enjoying with the St John's undergraduate what might be thought a slightly odd friendship. 'There were people at university who got me into politics. I kind of got into religion, politics, at the same time, in a way,' he told the television chat-show host Michael Parkinson, declining to be viewed as a Christian socialist. 'It's a long time since anyone used the word socialist about me,' he said, in the same interview. It could be that Macmurray explains all; but in the case of the chameleon Blair it was never especially safe to take him at his word. When in the company of the bookish, he liked to allude to books. The editor of the *Spectator*, Matthew d'Ancona, told his readers, 'in private Blair was more inclined to talk about books, ideas and history, whether it was the theology of Hans Kung, the origins of neo-conservatism or the merits of de Gaulle. But he was clever enough to keep this mostly to himself.' So clever was he that he kept such intellectual interests a secret not only from the public, but from those close to him. One who shared a holiday with Blair and his wife and family noted that neither he, his wife nor any of his children had packed any books for a fortnight's holiday. When not swimming in the pool or playing tennis, Blair spent his time having anxious conversations on his mobile telephone.[3] Even Mr Major had read the occasional novel by Trollope, praising them for their wonderfully 'two-dimensional characters'.[4] Though he sat light to political ideology, Blair's religious views were often a source of interest. Those who set out to explain what motivated Blair, beyond fear of his hot-tempered and strong-willed wife, sought it in the influence of the Catholic Church. But how far was it possible to distinguish that Church from Cherie, who, as a working-class 'Scouse', had been brought up with regular visits to Mass and confession? Throughout his period in office, indiscreet Roman Catholic priests liked to hint that Blair was some form of crypto-papalist. The bizarre Father Michael Seed, a congenitally indiscreet Capuchin friar, said Mass in the house at Number 10 Downing Street, after Tony Blair was spotted receiving Holy Communion at RC altars and Cardinal Hume, the RC Archbishop, wrote to him telling him to desist. (Blair wrote back assuring the Cardinal that he would desist, but added – 'I wonder what Jesus would have made of it.' Interesting question.) The ecumenism of the Blair marriage seemed to go only one way. The Blair family never attended the Prime Minister's parish church near Chequers, preferring to attend the RC service at Great Missenden where the clergyman, a figure named Father Russ, speculated to the newspapers about the probable or likely date of Tony's 'reception' into that Church. And not merely reception. Blair had, claimed Father Russ, discussed with him the possibility of becoming a Roman Catholic deacon, a minor order only one down from the priesthood itself. After Blair's resignation, Sir Anthony Kenny remembered that 'The Emperor Theodosius was refused communion by the Bishop of Milan until he had done public penance for a massacre for which he was responsible. It is rumoured that in their farewell audience Pope Benedict rebuked Blair for his part in the invasion of Iraq. Perhaps his appointment as the quartet's [UN, US, EU, Russian] ambassador [to the Middle East] is meant to be his public penance. If so, we must hope that it has a favourable outcome.' After his resignation, Blair did formally submit to Catholicism. Lady Marchmain, the pious chatelaine of Brideshead in Evelyn Waugh's novel, explained to the puzzled narrator,

'When I married, I became very rich. It used to worry me, and I thought it wrong to have so many beautiful things when others had nothing. Now I realise that it is possible for the rich to sin by coveting the privileges of the poor. The poor have always been the favourites of God and his saints, but I believe that it is one of the special achievements of Grace to sanctify the whole of life, riches included.'[5] Once he was able, as a fully-fledged Catholic, to tap into this source of Grace, Blair lost no time in augmenting his prime ministerial pension. He took a post estimated at £2.5 million with the American bankers JPMorgan Chase; and another worth £500,000 per annum with the Zurich Financial Services Group to advise them on global warming issues.[6] This came on top of the seven-figure advance which he had collected for his autobiography, the seven-figure advance collected by his wife for hers, as well as her pay as a high-profile human rights lawyer, who could also command sums as high as £75,000 for speaking engagements. Christ taught that it was easier for a camel to pass through the eye of a needle than for a rich man to inherit the Kingdom of Heaven; but with the Blairs, all things were possible.

For some years previous, both Blair and Cherie had appeared to become more dependent upon the Catholic faith. Both the Blairs, however, were ever eclectic in their spiritual beliefs. Their generous souls accommodated not merely the theological complexities of the Nicene Creed, but also the sweet incense and mental aromatherapy of the New Age religion. For an exciting period, the Blair court had as its captivating Rasputin figure a former nude model named Carole Caplin. She first met Cherie at a fitness class in 1992 and by 2003 Cherie was paying her £3,500 for 'assistance with dress, fitness, and "lifestyle"'.[7] Carole's mother, Sylvia, introduced them to spiritualism. According to one source, in Mexico, 'the Blairs visited a "temazcal", a steam bath enclosed in a brick pyramid. It was dusk and they had stripped down to their swimming costumes. Inside, they met Nancy Aguilar, a new age therapist. She told them that the pyramid was a Mayan womb in which they would be reborn. The Blairs saw the shapes of animals in the steam and experienced "inner feelings and visions". They smeared each other with melon, papaya and mud from the jungle, and then let out a primal scream of purifying agony.'[8]

Like Father Russ and Father Seed, Carole was happy to blab to the greater world about the Blairs' dependency upon her spiritual counsels. Not only did Carole become Cherie's masseuse, but she gave details to the newspapers of her shared showers, and 'pampering' sessions to the newspapers. Within weeks of meeting Cherie she had persuaded her to divulge details of her life with Tony – 'Toblerone', as Carole soon came to call the Prime Minister.[9] Cherie, who had put her emotional energy into her career at the Bar and into her marriage, possessed few personal friends and was susceptible to Carole's charms. When Cherie's dependency upon Carole was at its height, the style guru accompanied the Blair family on their summer holidays. When Cherie, her own mother Gale Booth, Tony and the children borrowed a holiday villa near Le Vernet in the south of France from Sir David Keane, Carole came, too, bringing her sixty-seven-year-old mother with her. Carole came to dinner one day wearing a loose skirt and a diaphanous blouse. Cherie's mother, Gale, burst out at dinner with the comment, 'I don't think that outfit is appropriate dress at a family meal.' Sylvia and Carole protested that they could see nothing wrong with it, and both women continued to sunbathe all but naked by the pool, which so embarrassed one of Blair's sons that he and his friends were unable to use the pool.[10] Nobody supposed that Caplin had actually been the lover of either Cherie or Tony, but her public boasts that she chose Tony's clothes, even his underpants, and that she gave therapeutic massage to both the First Lord of the Treasury and to his wife caused inevitable titillation in the press. Poor Mr Major's indiscretions with Edwina Currie were an embarrassment to his admirers, but no Prime Minister in history had ever entertained such a figure as Carole, as not merely a spiritual helper, but by extension a financial adviser. Tony Blair even offered Carole's very welcome services to President Clinton during one of his visits to Chequers. Her massage technique had clearly made an impression on the susceptible President. When he visited the Labour Party Conference a little later in the year, Clinton told Blair, 'I wish I could have Carole again for that exercise.'[11]

As he came into office, Blair had made few specific commitments other than to keep to the same spending plans as the Conservatives over the first few years of government. The economy, about which he knew nothing, was handled, on the whole with admirable skill, by Gordon Brown, whose Treasury team extended more and more control over domestic policy and over the actual machinery of government, throughout Blair's decade in office. The largely right-wing press awaited, as did the defeated cohorts of the old left, to see whether, once in office, Tony Blair would show himself to have been Old Labour in disguise. But he had never had any interest in Old Labour, and his wary adversaries on right and left slowly began to realise he did not have any interests in right or left either.

One of the reasons that New Labour felt so modern was that the decline of the Tories under John Major, and the rise of the Blairites in the Labour Party, happened to coincide with one of the most prodigious changes of our times: personal computers became part of personal life.

When the geeky, bespectacled Bill Gates (born 1955) started Micro-Soft (the hyphen was dropped when it registered as a trade name in November 1976) computers appealed to very limited sections of the world's populace. They were of use in speeding up scientific research. They were super-counting machines. Only nerds would have wanted one in the home. Bill Gates changed that. By 1997, when Tony Blair came to power, most offices, libraries, hospitals and institutions in Britain were wired up to personal computers. The laptop swiftly followed, and it would soon become eccentric for private householders not to so be connected to the rest of the world. So rapid was the advance in computer technology that soon e-mail became the normal method of communicating with one another; and, whether in pursuit of pornography or scientific facts, of a cheap air flight or the time of the next train to Scunthorpe, the British, like everyone else in the world, 'surfed' the Web. The world became linked up, and yet separated, in one sweep. Anyone anywhere could tap into their laptop and communicate with anyone else, often with people they had never met, in 'chat rooms'. At the same time, those old-fashioned means of human communication – the arrival of the postman, the visit to the post office, the penning of a letter, the picking up of the telephone – became less necessary. Many became addicts – some to 'chatting', others to pornography, which was abundantly and mysteriously wafted to anyone who wanted it on the ether, some – children – to computer games. Many people wondered, as they watched their children with noses almost glued to the screen, their ears stopped with headphones, whether a profound shift in human experience was occurring, or whether Gates and the other boffins had invented the most perfect device for shutting children up. It is certainly questionable whether the universal availability of the Internet extended human liberty. That it changed life, however, cannot be questioned, and in the era when it became old hat to be socialist, it also became old hat to write a letter or look something up in a book, if you could hunch instead over the laptop.

The characteristic artists of the age were Damien Hirst (born 1965) and Tracey Emin (born 1963). Hirst's *The Physical Impossibility of Death in the Mind of Someone Living* sold for a sum which would previously have been considered expensive for an Old Master. It was a 14-foot tiger shark immersed in formaldehyde. (In 2007 he beat his own record, when *Lullaby Spring* sold for £50 million.) One mentions the money first, in relation to BritArt, since the sums commanded were an essential part of the phenomenon. Although he severed connections with Charles Saatchi in 2003, it was through Saatchi, the godfather of BritArt, that Hirst became a commodity. The Saatchi brothers, Baghdad Jews, had set up in business in the 1970s and been of invaluable help, as Britain's most colourful advertising agency, in promoting Mrs Thatcher, with the election poster 'BRITAIN ISN'T WORKING'. Saatchi and Saatchi became the world's largest advertising company, and the extent to which Charles Saatchi's prodigious collection of art was an extension of his work as an advertiser would always be a matter of discussion. Hirst's dead creatures (the shark in formaldehyde eventually leaked and had to be thrown away) were not metaphors for British dead past, nor for Labour's dead principles, but they came at an apposite time. The later work he did, in which arrangements of giant pharmaceuticals make allusions to Christian iconography, the white pill of healing with the Eucharistic host, ask to be jeered at by scoffers, but give the thoughtful pause.

Tracey Emin was easier for the philistines to guy since she was a woman, she was of foreign extraction (Turkish Cypriot on the father's side), and she resorted to that device which many women consider necessary as a way of crossing the barricades of male stuffiness – buffoonery. Germaine Greer and Jessica Mitford come to mind. Probably few had heard of Emin until 1997 when she appeared on a Channel 4 television programme, visibly drunk (she afterwards claimed an unwise mixture with painkillers on account of a cut finger). She abused the other panel members in the arty discussion, rose to her unsteady feet and tottered off, claiming she was going home to her mum. Thereafter, she was a famous character. She exuded sexual allure and charm, and, like many artists before her, she made her life her subject matter. She had been born in Croydon but brought up in Margate. At thirteen she was raped, or 'broken in' as the local boys called it. Her high intelligence and resourcefulness took her to Medway College of Design, where she met the arresting, overblown figure of Billy Childish and spent five years as his muse and concubine, posing naked for photographs while developing thoughts and artistic ideas which outsoared his by miles. Later she had a relationship with Carl Freedman, and it was during this period that her distinctive styles became marked. She was an extremely skilled draughts-woman, and her drawings would, at any era of art, have been esteemed. She was also interestingly involved with fabric appliqués and other embroidered works. She was witty and quirky – witness her neon signs *Is Anal Sex Legal?* and its companion piece, *Is Legal Sex Anal?* Her most famous art work was *My Bed*, which was acquired by the Tate Gallery and a tent, appliquéd with the names of those who could be included in its title *Everyone I Have Ever Slept With*. These included her twin brother, her granny and her aborted child, as well as sexual partners. Emin transcended the necessary absurd sounds and furies of the BritArt publicity machine. She seemed, miraculously, to be using all this stuff to do what art had always done – relating personal experience to the general culture. If that culture was in chaos and decline, and if many people felt the sort of confusions (and amusement) displayed by Emin in her work, she was doing the work of a public artist in a very strange era.

The older guard, of course, saw a different Britain, and responded in a different way. David Hockney had spent much of his creative life drinking up the Californian sunshine and splashing it down in unforgettable images of light and water. In the twenty-first century, partly influenced by Chinese art, partly seeming to revisit Van Gogh, but chiefly, surely, by homesickness for Yorkshire, he began to paint big splashy watercolour landscapes. To use a word like elegy for these pictures implies sadness, even soppiness. Hockney was a preternaturally robust personality, and the pictures of this time have full-square confidence. Yet many who saw the fields and skies, the rainy mornings of the valley in Lillington, the red trees of Woldgate in autumn, must have believed that Hockney, after long exile, was painting a Britain which they had almost forgotten existed: the rolled haystacks, the wild flowers, the telegraph wires stretching down country roads. Even the roofscapes, when he comes towards the suburbs, so pure and red against a blustery Yorkshire sky, seem to be Yorkshire unvisited by the mullahs. It is not a 'modern' picture of Britain, and many in after years would be surprised to know that the pictures had been executed when Tony Blair was Prime Minister.

Tony Blair wanted to be 'modern', and this more or less ruled socialism out. He wanted to appeal to the sort of men – publishers, architects, senior broadcasters – who drank fizzy mineral water, and who sat in expensive restaurants in their Paul Smith shirt sleeves. Not only did he want to appeal to business, the traditional enemy of the Labour Party, but he wanted to continue in the good graces of opinion formers (provided they were young, metropolitan and trendy). The 'views' and 'ideas' and 'opinions' which the left had cherished for so long, and which they loved to debate in impassioned form, were all dumped – the commitment to unilateral disarmament, the belief in nationalised industries. The local branches of the Labour Party, which used to choose the candidates for parliamentary election, were overridden and Blairite lobby fodder was sent down from London, whether the local party liked them or not. The poor old dinosaurs who liked thinking about such matters were never to be allowed to do so again in front of television cameras. The Labour Party Conference, which in the old days was under the impression that it formed party policy, was taken over ruthlessly by the spin doctors. There were, in effect, no more 'debates' in which union barons, each commanding block votes of millions, decided the contents of the party manifesto together with the socialist ideologues of the Parliamentary Party. Instead, there were to be 'focus groups', which could be conveniently ignored. The shape and pattern of the conferences now began to resemble brainstorming meetings of NatWest Bank executives on a short training course. Policy was now firmly in the hands of Tony Blair and a group of trusted friends. The left of the party hated Blair from the beginning, but they put up almost no fight against him, watching powerlessly as he, Gordon Brown and Peter Mandelson 'modernised' the party. Almost at once, the pure, 'straight kinda guy', as Blair had described himself, was mired in sleaze. He took his first family holiday after becoming Prime Minister at the villa of Signor Berlusconi. Bernie Ecclestone gave the Labour Party £1 million from Formula One racing which received large revenues from tobacco advertising. Tony exempted Formula One from the ban on tobacco advertising. He promoted his cronies and flatmates, and he unwisely put no check on his adorer and close adviser Peter Mandelson (Mandy).

Mandy, once in power, proved to be unfortunately accident-prone. Having secured the safe Labour seat of Hartlepool, he was able to find himself in the Cabinet. He wanted, needed perhaps, to live beyond his means. He was much the most social of the New Labourites. He liked dining out, he liked going to parties given by rich, fashionable people, regardless of their political persuasion. He liked Jamie Palumbo, Carla Powell (wife of Thatcher's Downing Street adviser Sir Charles). He liked escorting royal princesses, and became one in a long line of homosexuals who was pleased to be Princess Margaret's 'walker'. Such a life necessitated, in his view, a house where he could entertain, in a suitably fashionable part of London. This meant borrowing money for a house costing £475,000 – a sum way beyond his means. When Secretary of State for Trade and Industry, he borrowed £373,000 from a fellow Minister, Geoffrey Robinson. It emerged that Mandy had made a fatal error on his mortgage application form from the Britannia Building Society to supplement the loan from Robinson. Mandy had to go. Blair, however, retained an affection for him and gave him another chance, this time to become the Secretary of State for Northern Ireland. Mandy did not last much longer in this department, either, since it transpired that in 1998 he had personally intervened with Mike O'Brien, Immigration Minister, over a passport application made by the multi-millionaire businessman Srichand Hinduja. At the time of this conversation, Mandy had been responsible for the Millennium Dome, which contained the numinous area known as the Faith Zone, sponsored by Hinduja and his brother for the sum of £1 million. That quintessentially New Labour thing, the Millennium Dome had actually been the dream child of Michael Heseltine, when, as President of the Board of Trade, he liked to be called 'the President'. Not that it had originated with Hezza. It was as far back as 28 March 1989 that Bevis Hillier, biographer of John Betjeman, wrote to *The Times* with the suggestion, that 'it is not too late to start planning a British exhibition or festival to celebrate the year 2000? Like the Great Exhibition of 1851, it should have a cosmopolitan aspect rather than the insular character of the 1951 Festival of Britain. It should be a celebration of the western world's achievements. Not just a crowning manifesto of its own.'[12] Bevis sowed the seed, and Heseltine watered it. It was a typical Heseltine idea, based on the fallacy that by hiring a sufficiently trendy and expensive modern architect – Richard Rogers – and building an eyesore in a run-down urban area, they would achieve 'regeneration'. It was all to be paid for out of the National Lottery. At his pre-election conference speech Blair had told the bewildered party that they had 'a thousand days to prepare for a thousand years',[13] a typically New Labour phrase which provided the missing link between the language of the Third Reich and a cheap advertising jingle. When Blair's first Cabinet discussed the matter in June 1997, the majority, still thinking along Old Labour lines, believed that the Dome project should be shelved forthwith. If it was being paid for out of the Lottery, that was all the more reason to discard it, since the Lottery was a tax which exploited the gullibility of the poor; such money as it raised should be spent, it was argued, on worthy causes rather than on this piece of frivolity. They could not see, these old diehards, that New Labour was by definition frivolous. Seen from afar, the Dome gave the impression that a giant flying saucer might have landed from outer space on a bend in the Thames opposite Greenwich. Seventy-two giant pieces of fibreglass, coated in Teflon, made up the roof, surrounded by a framework of steel masts.[14] Bevis had sown. Hezza had watered. New Labour would bring forth the plant to glory. Egged on by Mandy, who saw the Dome as a symbol of the New Dispensation that was being brought into being, the Dome became the special responsibility of a former flatmate of Tony Blair's, Charlie Falconer, a genial lawyer who for no reason beyond his friendship with Tony found himself elevated to a peerage. The Dome was big. Its bigness made up for its emptiness, and so its bigness was often dwelt upon. Inside you could fit two Wembley Arenas, thirteen Albert Halls or one Eiffel Tower on its side. It was the largest dome in the world, twice the size of the Georgia Dome in the United States. The comparisons had the unfortunate effect of inviting . . . comparison. The Wembley Arena and the Albert Hall and St Peter's in Rome and all the other domes and great spaces which were smaller than Lord Falconer's great space had been built for a discernible purpose. The Crystal Palace of 1851, for example, which housed the Great Exhibition in Hyde Park, had attracted visitors from all over the world. Had it failed, the committee of public men who commissioned it had underwritten its costs. Blair's Dome was not paid for by any of those who sat on committees, and so prodigally ran up expense. One early enthusiast was the journalist Adam Nicolson, for whom 'the Dome was a catalogue of marvels, a cabinet of rarities, a circus of marvels' . . . 'a kaleidoscope of the very best that we could do'.[15] Others, as they stared at the finished result, the feebleness of the exhibits, the boringness of the 'zones', the tiny queues dwindling to nothingness as the whole project flopped so spectacularly, wondered if Nicolson's words did not provide an unintentional description of Blair's Britain. Was this Teflon-coated extravagance really 'the very best that we could do'? Perhaps it was.

The New Millennium was ushered in at Greenwich in a chaos, as the favoured guests queued for hours at Stratford East station in order to be allowed from the newly built underground station to the Dome. When they finally entered the symbol of Britain's regeneration, they were greeted by the uninspiring Archbishop of Canterbury, George Carey, cruelly dubbed 'Mr Blobby' by his own clergy, who intoned the Lord's Prayer. There was then a rendition of the Beatles' song 'All You Need Is Love', followed by a toe-curling jazzed-up version of the National Anthem.[16] The floor show, like the New Labour project itself, as it was to unfold in the coming years, was a strange mixture of the boring and the tawdry. As midnight struck Tony and Cherie linked arms to sing 'Auld Lang Syne'. On his right, his monarch permitted her fingers to be held, though she did not link, or swing, her arms with her neighbours. While they roared, 'We'll tak a cup o kindness yet', Elizabeth II's mouth remained rattrap-furious closed.

As in the case of Thatcher, and indeed of almost all Prime Ministers, Blair began by attempting to impose his will on domestic politics. Then, as this became messy and intractable, he turned his attentions to foreign policy and began to see himself, not without some justification, as a figure on the world stage.

The left watched and waited through ten years of Blair's premiership for any noticeable social engineering, or – to use a phrase popularised by David Shepherd, Bishop of Liverpool – 'bias to the poor'. They could wait in vain. Blair had no more interest in closing the poverty gap than had Thatcher. In the matter of constitutional reform, the radicals were to feel an equal sense of letdown. The historian Ross McKibbin, author of one of the best left-wing analyses of modern Britain, felt that at the end of his time as Prime Minister, 'Blair has had opportunities unavailable to any other Labour Leader, and has thrown nearly all of them away . . . the greatest of these opportunities would have been the democratic reform of the constitution.'[17]

Whether you agreed with McKibbin depended upon your perspective. If you were a Tory (feeling as disenfranchised by the antics of modern

Conservative parties as socialists were by New Labour) you might have felt that Blair's constitutional reforms went too far. Almost as soon as New Labour took power, they announced devolution for Scotland and Wales. Although neither country showed especial enthusiasm for the scheme, and in Wales it was all but necessary to fudge the referendum to make it seem as if a majority wanted a special Welsh Assembly, each country was fitted up with its own expensive legislature, and in the case of Scotland the setting up of the Parliament was but the first clear step on the road to nationalist independence and the breaking up of the United Kingdom. This was quite a radical change to have put into ineluctable effect within a year of taking office. Likewise, the introduction of an elected mayoralty to London was a significant change, even if central government held on to so many of the purse strings that the elected mayor (faced with a truly grotesque choice of candidates, Londoners opted for Ken Livingstone, former leader of the GLC) did not have anything like the spending power, hence administrative capacity, as the mayors of New York or Paris. The machinery was there for other elected mayoralties, if only the sluggish British could become more excited by 'democracy' and its processes. The truth is that from the time of the Chartists, only a very small percentage of the British electorate have been democrats, in the sense of wishing to be consulted about every change in or operation of the law. The system of representative government, by which voters send a local member to Parliament, to act and vote on behalf of all his constituents, regardless of political affiliation, had worked quite well until the Blair era, and for many voters it was preferable to the hectic political systems cobbled together in France and Germany after the Second World War. These voting systems, undoubtedly more democratic, were based on a proportional representation idea, rather than a first past the post system. Godfather Woy tried to persuade young Tony to adopt some such European scheme, but he never did so. In the matter of the House of Lords, the radicals were no doubt as disappointed as the Tories were outraged. In May 1997 there were 1,067 peers in the House of Lords. In March 2000 there were 682. In May 1997 there were 633 hereditary peers with voting rights. By March 2000 there were only 92, and these were subsequently abolished. The others were 564 life peers and 26 lords spiritual. Parties of the left – the Liberals under Gladstone, and even more under Lloyd George, and the Labour Party ever since its inception, had been talking about abolishing the system whereby hereditary peers automatically formed part of the legislature. It was Blair who actually did it.

Yet, in a brilliant short book, a young German scholar, Katrin Rohde, sees that Blair was never intent upon a revolution based on Thomas

Paine's *Rights of Man*. The pattern to seek in his administration is the essentially conservative one of Edmund Burke who, in opposition to Paine at the time of the French Revolution, saw that in order to be preserved, institutions needed constant minor reform. The plant which had been tweaked and pruned did not need to be uprooted.[18]

Blair's Britain was different from Mr Major's. If it was more modern to be governed by Tony's appointees, such as 'Lord' Falconer and 'Lord' Levy and 'Lord' Alli, rather than clever hereditary peers such as Max Egremont, Robert Salisbury, Conrad Russell, Garry Runciman or Andrew Devonshire, then British government had certainly become more modern. Hundreds of hours of parliamentary time were spent debating the issue of foxhunting. On Sunday 1 March 1998, a mass movement of the 'countryside' marched through the streets of London, almost matching the size of the protests against the government's wish to go to war against Iraq. Blair had no interest in the question of whether people should hunt foxes with hounds. He wanted, as often, two contradictory things – to please the dwindling country-dwellers and to appease those class-envious lefties who saw the hunt as one of the last bastions of old privilege to be swept away, like the hereditary peers in the House of Lords, to the dustbin of history. Blair, as a good Thatcherite, knew that soaring property prices in the 1980s had removed the last squires and parsons from the manor houses and parsonages of England and filled them up with yuppies, replacing the kitchen gardens with swimming pools, and erecting Colefax and Fowler festoons of fabrics in drawing rooms which had never previously known central heating. Meanwhile, in the villages and on the edges of fields, what had been affordable rented agricultural cottages became second homes for the white flight, those not yet fortunate enough to own old rectories and old manors, but who did not want their Boden-clad children to play in inner city recreation grounds, littered with used syringes and condoms. With the virtual extinction of cheap property to rent, and with a diminishing agricultural workforce, it was no surprise that the rate of suicides among the rural working classes soared. Thatcher had espoused Thatcherism knowing it would be hateful to the majority. The knowledge even gave her a certain satisfaction, just as predestinarian sects in the Protestant world enjoyed the warmth of inner assurance that those not elected to glory – a majority of the human race – would probably be damned. Blair, however, whose mind was drawn more instinctively to the doctrines of universal salvation preached by the Catholic Church, and who had the greasepaint in his blood, wanted to woo audiences and to be liked. He was a Thatcherite who lacked the one thing necessary to be a successful Thatcherite, namely the enjoyment of being hated. He wished to be seen as a man who took seriously the complaints of farmers and agricultural workers who had seen their quality of life eroded over twenty years, with more and more legislation coming from Europe; with mechanised conditions reducing those employed in agriculture; with the decline of country buses, schools, shops and post offices. 'I wouldn't live in a big city if I could help it,' he told *Country Life*. 'I would live in the country. I was brought up there, really.'[19] Really? At no time did Blair live in the country, spending most of his childhood in suburban houses on the outskirts of Durham, or at boarding school in Edinburgh. Yet he saw the foxhunting matter as something which could be offered to the left-wingers on his back benches, who were dismayed by his foreign policy and by the impenitent prudence of the Treasury. When, after spending hundreds of hours of parliamentary time discussing the question, what had been lost was not so much the hunt, as the spirit of live and let live. As it happened, nearly every hunt continued to go out with hounds during the season, some just about keeping within the limits of the law by drag-hunting, or by taking a gun with which to kill the fox when found; but most openly defying the law. But New Labour Westminster had shown that it was a government which wanted to boss, to impose the will of an urban and suburban majority upon the rural minority.

If this was their attitude to hunting, it was no surprise that they all took pleasure in banning smoking in public places. Their definition of the word 'public' took in bars and public houses, even if these were free houses owned by a publican who wanted his customers to smoke. They included private clubs, and offices and places of work, even if owned by one individual who permitted his workforce to smoke. As in the case of hunting, what was surprising was not so much the fact that so many Members of Parliament wished to mind other people's business. It was that the Conservatives and the Liberals, which some voters had supposed were parties which were meant to stand up for liberty of the individual, could not see that a matter of principle was at stake. Among public figures in Britain the painter David Hockney was alone in vociferous protest. Overnight, the pubs and clubs of England became less friendly places and within months many publicans faced bankruptcy. The bleak news was followed by news bulletins, dispatched without any questioning of their plausibility by BBC newscasters, about the 'improvements in public health' since the ban.

It was, then, a bossier, less tolerant Britain under Mr Blair. This should perhaps have made the British more capable of understanding the Muslims, who follow a scripture which is almost devoid of the narrative interest of the Hebrew Bible, and is largely injunctions and prescriptions. The Koran and New Labour's formidable reams of new legislation, governing every aspect of British life, could indeed be seen by students of comparative religion to have much in common. Both were essentially puritanical creeds, and though New Labour was not teetotal as such, it was undoubtedly a movement fuelled by white wine spritzers rather than Thatcher's malt whisky.

26

Tony's Wars

In foreign policy Blair was an impenitent interventionist. Mr Gladstone's agony on behalf of the Bulgarian hillsmen would – had Blair reached that far in mentor Woy's book on the Victorian statesman which was cobbled together from the work of Gladstone scholar Colin Mathew – have found an echo in the young Prime Minister's bosom. Almost as soon as he took office in 1997, Blair was given intelligence by the British Foreign Office which gave him grave cause for concern about the continuing menace of Saddam Hussein in Iraq.

Right-wing Republicans such as Donald Rumsfeld, Paul Wolfowitz and Richard Perle were urging a complete change of direction in foreign policy, what they called a Project for the New American Century. They argued that America would have the power to change the world for the better only if it were to take a much bolder leadership role in the years to come. It should dare to be interventionist. These neo-conservatives urged a regime change in Iraq, with the Shia exile Ahmed Chalabi, from a wealthy banking family, as the likely American puppet-president of a new democratic Iraq. Clinton resisted this suggestion, but as Saddam Hussein consistently refused to allow UN weapons inspectors into his country, and as US embassies in Kenya and Tanzania, on 7 August, suffered major terrorist attacks (224 killed), pressure was building on President Clinton to take a more aggressive attitude towards Iraq. After the embassy attacks in Kenya and Tanzania, Clinton authorised the punishment-bombing of a supposed terrorist base in Afghanistan and what was claimed to be a chemical weapons-related facility in Sudan. They in fact hit a veterinary pharmaceuticals factory. 'Everyone knew that what Clinton was doing was wrong, bombing that plant,' said one member of Blair's inner circle. 'But we also knew that supporting him was right.' While President Chirac of France and Kofi Annan of the United Nations made it clear that any further air strikes or military action by the USA were to be deplored, Britain alone remained supportive. Later that year, on 15 November, Clinton and Blair decided to use Tomahawk cruise missiles against Iraq. When asked by his secretary if he should cancel a game of tennis because of the impending air strikes, Blair replied, 'Can't let that squirt Saddam get in the way.'[1] By the end of Ramadan 650 sorties had been made by Allied bombers. Two hundred and fifty targets had been selected. No weapons of mass destruction seemed to have been found by these bombing raids, but Blair was pleased at having played a part on the world stage while the other European leaders held back. On 9 January he flew to Kuwait to thank the RAF pilots who had carried out the bombings, and proudly had himself photographed in the cockpit of a Tornado jet.[2]

In the next two wars which Blair conducted it seemed as if the case for interventionism was strong, if not overwhelming. President Clinton managed to broker a peace agreement in the Balkans on 21 November, 1995, after three and a half years of war and the deaths of 200,000. The British, guided by Douglas Hurd as Foreign Secretary, had been anti-interventionist, or 'hyper-realist' as the Americans called it. Bosnia had been left to suffer. Blair, once he came into office, was determined that the same should not happen in Kosovo. He dispatched his carrot-bearded Foreign Secretary Robin Cook to Belgrade to confront Slobodan Milošević and demand Kosovan autonomy. Threats of ethnic cleansing by Serbian forces, as had happened in Bosnia, were once again uttered. By August, 200,000 Kosovan ethnic Albanians had been driven from their homes. When a policy of intervention had eventually been decided, it was once again Britain and America who undertook the bombing – this time of Belgrade. There were some drastic mistakes, but Blair said, 'To those who say the aim of military strikes is not clear, I say it is crystal clear. It is to curb Slobodan Milošević's ability to wage war on an innocent civilian population.'[3] At first it seemed as if the American bombing of Serbia was rallying the people behind Milošević, but Blair, Robin Cook and Clare Short, the International Development Secretary in her 'lovely Brummie accent' – as Alan Clark called it – defended the bombings as an act of liberation – albeit a clumsy one. By the end of the war, there were 850,000 refugees, caused directly by the bombing, and most of the military targets had been missed. But when Blair visited Priština on 31 July, he was greeted by the liberated Kosovans as a saviour. As they chanted 'Tony, Tony', he could call out, 'We fought in this conflict for a cause and that cause was justice.'

Blair's third war was in Sierre Leone in which, with remarkably little loss of life, seven hundred entered Freetown, initially to evacuate foreign nationals after a *coup d'état* against the moderate Muslim government of Ahmad Tejan Kabbah. When eleven men of the Royal Irish Regiment, along with their local military liaison, were taken hostage, the SAS went in with Chinook helicopters. One British soldier was killed and twenty-five of the rebels. The rest of the hostages were rescued, and the Kabbah government restored. 'We welcome your excellency the peacemaker, we love you and respect you, trust and support you' read a sign hanging from a ramshackle school near Freetown airport when Blair revisited the country three years after its liberation.

Such messages were not hung out for Blair to read when he visited the Labour Party Conference or spoke to the trades unions. The office of Prime Minister is a lonely one, and, as successive occupants of the job had discovered, merely to lead a political party was to make most of your closest colleagues hate you. The more Thatcher had been loathed at home by her Cabinet, the more she saw herself as a liberator of eastern communist bloc countries, and a woman with a mission to the world. Blair had tasted early the heady excitements of being a world leader who could make a difference, in Kosovo and in Sierra Leone.

By the close of the second millennium, the Cold War had been won by the West. China had adopted capitalism and was well on the way to its phenomenal economic growth, making it a far greater world power than it had ever been in the days of its unbudgeable Marxism. The Soviet Union had broken up, and the subsequent wars in the Balkans had been brought to an end, very largely thanks to the interventionism of Prime Minister Tony Blair and President Bill Clinton in Kosovo. The new President of the United States, George W. Bush, had only been elected by a whisker, and there were those who questioned the very legality of his election. But elected he had been, and Blair was determined to follow Bill Clinton's advice to work alongside the Americans as he had done so successfully before.

The communist threat to American power had been overcome. Nothing else in the world, surely, could pose a comparable threat. One American historian believed that the world had seen the end of history. Hereafter, all that remained was for the rest of the world to adopt Western capitalism. The world had become, in effect, American.

Anyone contemplating what George Bush Senior had called 'the new world order' would see that there were flaws in the argument.

History does not end. No one predicted the speed with which the Soviet bloc would unravel. It was equally possible that the US economy could, as it had done in 1929, implode. Those Europeans who watched with dismay as McDonald's and Starbucks replaced their local cafés and restaurants would not necessarily have wept if, as could quite possibly happen, the United States themselves dissolved, as the nation states of the Soviet Union had dissolved.

If in Europe there were those who entertained feelings of generalised resentment against the spread of American food chains, American films, American music, American clothing, in the Middle East, and further east, there were more specific grievances felt against the United States and its influence. Many Muslims, in particular, saw in the United States nothing less than the Great Satan, a society which, for all its expressed belief in the teachings of Jesus, was grossly materialistic, and lost in a welter of pornography and sexual licence. Moreover, it was American money which armed, and maintained the existence of, Israel as an independent state. And the existence of Israel, especially in its post-1967 borders, was a cause of resentment far beyond the borders of that country itself – whatever those borders happened to be.

The growth of Islamism was something which the Western world noted with a mixture of indifference and incredulity. Had not the Islamic world always thrown up, from time to time, figures such as the Mad Mahdi whose followers murdered General Gordon of Khartoum? And then the Muslim Brotherhood, or the Mahdi, or whatever name it happened to possess in any one generation, faded away and the Muslim world resumed its peaceful, sleepy existence. That was the romantic idea, though ever since the West linked itself to dependence upon oil, and ever since large numbers of poor Muslims from the former Pakistan and elsewhere had migrated through the Western world, it was not a very realistic picture.

One fine day in the United States, 11 September 2001, four aeroplanes were hijacked by Islamist suicide-murderers. American Airlines Flight 11 from Boston to Los Angeles was diverted and flew into the North Tower of the World Trade Center in New York at 8.46 a.m., killing all on board and, within the building, an untold number. United Airlines Flight 175 Boston to Los Angeles was diverted and flew into the South Tower of the World Trade Center fifteen minutes later. The Twin Towers collapsed and the total casualties were almost 3,000 people. Meanwhile, American Airlines Flight 77 from Washington's Dulles airport to LA, also taken over by maniacs, was diverted, and, having flown in the direction of the White House, switched course and flew at the Pentagon at full speed, killing all 64 people on board and 125 Defense Department personnel. Donald Rumsfeld was in his office, but was uninjured, though he felt the impact of the crash on the building. A fourth flight, United Airways 93, left Newark, New Jersey, at 8.42 bound for San Francisco. Because the plane had taken off late, the flight controller was able to warn it, when in midair, of the danger of attack. It crash-landed in a field in Pennsylvania killing everyone on board.

It was after these events that the world became conscious of the words Al Qa'eda, a fanatical terrorist Islamist organisation, and of its evil genius, Osama bin Laden (born 1957), the seventeenth child of a Saudi construction engineer who had a total of fifty-seven children. Bin Laden money was 'new'. Osama's grandfather had been a penniless immigrant to Saudi from South Yemen, but the new money had bought for the bin Ladens the attributes and manner of life of European ladies and gentlemen. There were many bin Ladens in London. One of Osama's brothers had a nice house in Kensington Square. Osama, having led the life of a rich playboy, had recast himself in the model of a prophet. His long face, Jesus painted by El Greco, was soon to become one of the most famous of the age.

The morning after the 9/11 attacks, the band had assembled outside Buckingham Palace as it does every morning at the Changing of the Guard, and, when the music began, it struck up 'The Star Spangled Banner'. It was a spontaneous response to the tragedy, and representative of majority British opinion. Most people in Britain must have shared the feeling, of which the band music was a symbol, that the two great English-speaking peoples of the Western world, the United States and Britain, have a deep bond of friendship. The fact that many Britons perished on 11 September in New York was not the primary reason for the sense of shock and shared outrage in Britain. The British felt that the attack on America was an attack on their closest ally and strongest friend.

Such feelings in Britain are shot through with ambiguities and ironies, and in the weeks which followed the attack some of these ambiguities turned to expressions of outright anti-Americanism. There was even a perception, especially on the left, that 'the Americans' had in some sense 'had it coming to them'; that they 'deserved' or had been 'asking for' some such retributive act of violence against its innocent civilian population. Ever since the end of the Second World War, certainly since Suez, there has been a strong vein of anti-Americanism in the British psyche – 'over-sexed, over-paid, and over here'. But it would be easy to misread this. Many who would complain about the 'bloody Yanks' would also feel a natural kinship with them. Although the unfolding Iraqi crisis, the war and its aftermath, would allow anti-American feeling to be voiced by all the usual suspects, and it certainly increased anti-American feelings throughout the world, there was no notable increase in anti-Americanism in Britain, despite the best endeavours of the BBC, and some sections of the press, to whip such feelings into flame. Indeed, as the extent of the Islamist terror threat became clear, with explosions in the London transport system (see Chapter 27), there were increased feelings of solidarity with the Americans in their desire to go after the perpetrators of 9/11 and get 'em.

But how could such an elusive individual as bin Laden be found? And how would it be possible to distinguish between the need to get back at the mass murderers, and the need to construct a plausible Middle Eastern policy which would contain the rogue states?

The Americans had continued to receive intelligence about the dangers posed to world peace by Saddam Hussein, and a key source was the cousin of an aide to Ahmed Chalabi whose codename was Curveball. In the evidence gathered by the Presidential Commission on the reasons for pre-war misinformation guiding the Oval Office, it was stated that 'of all the disproven pre-war weapons claims from aluminium centrifuge tubes to yellowcake uranium from Niger, none points to greater levels of incompetence than those found within the misadventures of Curveball'.[4]

Curveball had originally surfaced in Germany, where he had persuaded his minders that he had worked as an Iraqi chemical engineer and supervised one of Saddam's mobile biological weapons labs. Curveball's real name was Rafid Ahmed Alwan. A 601-page report released in March 2005 by the US government conceded that Curveball and the CIA had been 'dead wrong' in all their pre-war assessments of the Iraqi situation.[5]

US relations with Saddam Hussein's Iraq had, broadly speaking, known three phases. There had been the phase, from September 1980, when this exceptionally brutal dictator had authorised the invasion of neighbouring Iran. For the next six years, America supported the Iraqis in their war against the Iranians. The war ended in a stalemate, and amazingly, Saddam survived it, in spite of uprisings by Kurds and Shias, which he suppressed with merciless severity. When Saddam invaded Kuwait in 1990, the Americans changed their view of him. He became a villain who was trying to steal oil. Following his humiliating defeat in the Desert Storm war it was a prodigious achievement on his part to survive. But he did so. The Israelis and their allies were never to forget that he launched scud missiles which landed in Tel Aviv. Economic sanctions over the next years brought Iraq to a state of near collapse. In 1998, a nationwide health survey of Iraqi children showed that 9.1 per cent were actively undernourished, 26.7 per cent undernourished and 22.8 per cent underweight. The health service was at the point of collapse. Iraqis were leaving their country in droves. In New Zealand alone, there were 30,000 Iraqi refugees, most of them highly skilled or professional.

There was every reason to hope that Saddam Hussein would be toppled by Iraqis, and that, when this happened, the West could repair the cruel damage inflicted upon Iraq by oil sanctions.

Then came Curveball's intelligence reports that Saddam possessed weapons of mass destruction. Six months after he became Prime Minister, Tony Blair had remarked to the Liberal Party leader Paddy Ashdown, 'I have now seen some of the stuff on this. It really is pretty scary. He is close to some appalling weapons of mass destruction . . . We cannot let him get away with it.'[6]

When Iraq had been invaded, and no WMD were found, it was easy to take the view that the fears had been foolish, or even that those intent upon a war with Saddam had simply invented, or at the very least exaggerated, the extent of the danger. It is only fair to stress that very many well-informed diplomats, politicians and observers of the Middle East, in the period from September 2002 to March 2003, believed in the existence of these weapons, and in the imminent danger of Saddam using them. Of course, the memory of those scuds in Tel Aviv, fired off towards the close of the First Gulf War, concentrated the minds of the pessimists. When a fifty-page document, 'Iraq's Weapons of Mass Destruction – the Assessment of the British Government' was published on 24 September 2002, there was mixed reaction. 'Chilling reading' for the *Jerusalem Post*. The *Financial Times*, however, found in the document 'no compelling evidence that immediate military action is needed'.[7]

Again and again, Blair told the House of Commons that there were two reasons why war was necessary in Iraq: that Saddam would not comply with UN Resolution 1441, and that he possessed weapons of mass destruction which could destroy the enemy within forty-five minutes. Both these claims were questionable. The Iraqis did respond to Resolution 1441 with a 12,000-page dossier which was never made public. We do not know what it contained. Nor had Tony Blair or George W. Bush ever demonstrated in what ways the government of Saddam Hussein was in breach of UN Resolution 1441. Unlike some Middle Eastern states – Israel, for example, which is also in breach of several UN resolutions – Iraq did at least permit weapons inspectors into their country, and none of the WMD were ever found. That said, the UN weapons inspectors who had visited Iraq on 25 November 2002 were unable to account for six thousand chemical aircraft bombs, seven Iraqi surface-to-surface missiles and two Russian scuds which were known to be in Saddam's arsenal, together with biological material capable of producing 26,000 litres of anthrax and 1.5 tons of VX gas. To exemplify the scale of the possible threat, the weapons inspectors noted that a mere 140 litres of VX could kill a million people.[8] In spite of this lingering threat, Kofi Annan stated that the war against Iraq was illegal.

The war against Iraq was the one event for which Tony Blair will undoubtedly be remembered by history. It was a war which turned into a catastrophe, plunging the peoples of Iraq into a civil conflict which would last for a generation, a conflict which killed well over half a million people.

Britain had never fought a war in the past which was based upon intelligence alone. As it became clear what George W. Bush intended, millions of people all over the world took to the streets to implore the governments of Britain and the United States to think again. The overwhelming argument against the war was not pacifist or anti-Zionist or anti-American, though people of these persuasions joined the millions who marched. Most British people believed, correctly as it turned out, that an aggressive war fought by Britain and America would make a bad situation in Iraq much worse: it would destabilise an already wretchedly volatile region; it would increase the likelihood of tension between Israel and her Arab neighbours, between pro- and anti-Western Arab states; it would strengthen the hands of the Islamist extremists throughout the world; and it would, indeed, seem to be a justification of the worst paranoid fantasies of Osama bin Laden. For, if the USA and Britain, in defiance of the United Nations and against the advice of France, Russia, China and most other people in the world, led an invasion force against the Iraqis, how else could poor Muslims respond, other than by acts of terrorism?

Why did Tony do it? He denied that in 2002, when staying with George W. Bush on his ranch at Crawford, Texas, he had prayed for guidance, even though Christian author Stephen Mansfield, claiming he owed his story to White House officials, says that both men did pray together; and this story is backed up by a writer on *Time* magazine, David Aikman. In March 2006, Blair told a British television audience, when asked why he had gone to war on Iraq, 'If you have faith about these things, then you realize that judgement is made by other people. If you believe in God, it's made by God as well.'[9] President Bush made no bones about having been guided by God to attack Iraq.

The Americans took responsibility for entering the northern parts of Iraq, and securing the northern city of Mosul, and Baghdad itself. The British troops, with immense skill and comparatively little loss of life, occupied Basra. The total Allied casualties for the war itself were 122 American and 33 British.[10]

Only a few pessimists had ever doubted whether the Americans and their allies would win the war itself. What was in doubt was what would constitute a victory. On 1 May 2003, George W. Bush announced that the war was over. But after that date, 20,000 American troops would be killed by the Iraqi resistance, and the country which they had come to liberate was in chaos. In Berlin at the end of the Second World War, the Soviet Army sent a senior Russian general to make sure that essential services would be restored for the civilian population once the war was over.[11] In Basra, the British Army did manage to restore the power stations, but in American-administered Baghdad there were long periods without water, gas or electricity. The police forces were in disarray. For years – not for weeks or months, but for years – it was unsafe to walk the streets. 'Paradoxically', wrote the journalist Patrick Cockburn,[12] who knew Iraq better than most over a period of over thirty years, 'Iraq became so dangerous that journalists, however courageous, could not rebut claims that most of Iraq was safe without being kidnapped or killed themselves.' Quite apart from the damage done to the stability of the Middle East as a whole, it had made America hated throughout the world. General William Odom, former head of the National Security Agency, the largest US intelligence agency, called it 'the greatest strategic disaster in American history'.[13]

The war and its aftermath showed New Labour in an ugly light. There was the affair of Dr David Kelly. He was a scientific civil servant who had met with a BBC journalist, Andrew Gilligan, to discuss the dossier asessing the threat posed by Saddam's WMD. There were no witnesses to the discussion between these two men and the only evidence for what was said were some hastily composed notes by the journalist. Kelly was among those who believed that Saddam had WMD and that they represented a threat. He knew Iraq and he knew about chemical weapons. Much of the pre-war excitement, as we have seen, had been caused by Tony Blair claiming in the Commons that Saddam could make use of WMD within forty-five minutes. It was assumed that this meant he could reach the nearest British troops or bases, that is to say Cyprus, within this time-span. In the course of talking to Gilligan, Dr Kelly appears to have conceded that it might have been possible that the 'forty-five minute claim' had been added to the dossier 'for impact'.

At 6.07 a.m. on the radio news programme *Today*, on 29 May 2003, Gilligan claimed that a British official who had helped to prepare the dossier now believed that it had been 'transformed in the week before it was published to make it sexier'. This was not what Kelly had ever claimed. In all the subsequent inquiry and the report written by Lord Hutton in January 2004, the BBC's editorial control was found to be 'defective' and Gilligan was censured for failing to be accurate. The chairman of the Governors of the BBC, Gavyn Davies, and Greg Dyke, the Director General, both resigned.

David Kelly, universally regarded as a man of intellectual seriousness and moral integrity, was given no support when the trouble broke. Quite the reverse. As soon as Gilligan made his unfounded, or at best highly exaggerated, claim on the *Today* programme, New Labour behaved with all the gentleness of Mafia thugs. Kelly's cover was blown and he was obliged to appear before the Intelligence and Security Committee of the House of Commons where he was given a mauling by a backbench bruiser (Labour) named Andrew Mackinlay, who mocked Kelly as a government 'fall guy'. Kelly went into hiding for a while to hide from the press, and when he returned home to Oxfordshire, his wife found him in a state of deep dejection. On 17 July 2003 he went for a walk, and next morning his dead body was found in some remote woodland. A coroner's verdict decided that he had committed suicide by cutting his wrist and taking an overdose of painkillers. Subsequently, this verdict was questioned, and it was suggested that Kelly had been murdered either by Iraqis or by the British security services. Whether or not the conspiracy theory is believed, New Labour had been shown in its nasty colours. The war was regarded by the huge majority of the electorate as a disaster, and the instinct of Blair's henchmen was to conduct a propaganda war with the press and the BBC and to find some scapegoats. Dr Kelly was indeed a 'fall guy'. His death was said to have been shattering to Blair, who considered resigning. 'Have you got blood on your hands, Prime Minister? Are you going to resign?' Blair was asked this by a *Mail on Sunday* reporter when his plane touched down in Tokyo. Most unusually, Blair was silenced, lost for words – ashen, exhausted, beaten.[14]

Had the Iraq war been, as Bush appeared to claim, part of the War on Terror? It was hard to see this as especially logical, since to quote the 'Iraq Options' papers produced by the Overseas and Defence Secretariat of the Cabinet Office of 8 March 2002, 'In the judgement of the JIC there is no evidence of Iraq[i] complicity with international terrorism. There is therefore no justification for action against Iraq based on self-defence to combat imminent threats of terrorism as in Afghanistan.'[15]

Saddam was a horrible dictator, but it was against international law to invade countries to depose their leaders merely because they were nasty to their own people. Many of the world leaders, certainly Robert Mugabe in Zimbabwe, could be seen as more worthy of such immediate attention.

There was at best a confusion, at worst a subterfuge, going on. The American neo-cons wanted to control Iraq and its oilfields. They also wished to teach rogue Arab states a lesson. It was certainly true psychologically that they would probably not have tried to sell such an idea to the American public had it not been for the assault on the World Trade Center and the massacre of over three thousand people in New York. But why this should have involved Britain, and why Blair should have been so anxious to go to war so quickly, remained a mystery. Was it a simple blunder, or had he in some mysterious way become an American neo-con? Certainly his contempt for British public opinion, and indeed for world opinion, became increasingly marked, as his hair became grey. His face was now so much televised that he regularly had lipstick and slap applied to his wrinkled skin. The eyes looked shifty and mad.

Tony and George Dubya's war had led to much agitation in the Middle East. There was still no suggested solution to the plight of Palestine. The Israelis felt threatened and embattled, especially by the rocket and mortar attacks from Lebanon into northern Galilee, and in the summer of 2006, Israel invaded Lebanon. The attacks on Lebanese civilians shocked the world, however much the world sympathised with the plight of Israelis frightened by Hamas. But what scandalised world opinion much more than an understandable Israeli aggression was the silence of Bush and Blair until 750 Lebanese civilians had been killed and many homes flattened. Under the jaunty headline LET'S HOPE SCOTLAND HASN'T ABOLISHED CAPITAL PUNISHMENT, Neil Mackay in the Scottish *Sunday Herald* on 6 August reported:

The Lebanese government is working behind the scenes to bring Tony Blair before the Scottish courts, charged with war crimes for aiding and abetting the Israeli onslaught against Lebanon.

Ali Berro, the Lebanese government's special adviser on legal affairs, is assisting Lebanese nationals living in Scotland, and their legal team, in their attempt to take the Scottish Executive and the UK government to court for allowing US aircraft to fly 'bunker-buster bombs' from America to Israel via Scottish airports.

Berro is providing the legal team, led by the Glasgow-based human rights lawyer Aamer Anwar, with detailed information about alleged Israel war crimes, and also forwarding information on the casualty rates of Lebanese civilians and the type of weapons being deployed by the Israeli army. In total, some 30 lawyers, including QCs, in Scotland and England are helping prepare the case against the government . . .

The team is accusing Blair of assisting Israel in carrying out war crimes against civilians, citing various pieces of international legislation, including the Geneva Conventions, which say that it is a war crime to aid and abet a nation carrying out attacks targeted against civilians.

Some 750 Lebanese civilians have died in the attacks – many women and children. Berro said: 'Human shreds are scattered amid the destruction.' He also outlined Israeli attacks on petrol stations, warehouses, electricity companies, places of worship, bridges, hospitals and ambulances.

Berro said the Israelis were using phosphorous bombs, and 'sending ultimatums to the inhabitants of villages, waiting for them to get out and then hunting them on their way to safety'.

International legislation, which Berro said was breached by Israel, included The Hague Convention, The 1948 Convention Against Mass Killings and The Geneva Conventions.

Azam Mohamad, one of the Scottish-based Lebanese nationals taking the case against the Scottish Executive and the UK government, said: 'We took this action as US aircraft are going through Prestwick Airport with bombs bound for Israel that will be used to shell our families. We want to stop those bombs.'

Mohamad, the director of Glasgow's Middle East Society, added: 'We are shocked that Tony Blair has allowed aircraft carrying bombs bound for Israel to come through this country. These weapons are illegal as they are used to kill civilians. I cannot find words to explain my unhappiness at Blair's decision. If we get a chance to take Tony Blair to court, we will do so.

'Blair is helping terrorism because what Israel is doing to Lebanon is terrorism – they are attacking and killing civilians. He is utterly in the wrong.'

It was presumably with a view to righting the effects of his Middle Eastern activities while Prime Minister that there emerged in his post-ministerial role Tony Blair, the peace-broker between Israel and Palestine. In this task, in so far as his other tasks as memoirist, banker, lecturer and expert on climate change permitted, he had an uphill struggle.

27

Islamists

In July 2007, Gillian Gibbons, a fifty-four-year-old teacher, left her job in Liverpool as deputy head of a primary school. Her marriage had come unstuck, she was a keen traveller and she wished to do some good in the world. Accordingly, she took a post as a teacher in Khartoum, at the Unity High School, a British school founded by a Church of England bishop in 1902, and catering for the children of expatriates and oil workers in the Sudan, as well as for the children of the Sudanese professional class. In September, when she began her new job, Gillian Gibbons met a teddy bear. It was brought in to class by one of the children, aged seven, and it was decided to make this toy the focus for a group diary. Each weekend a different child would take the bear home and write a diary of its impressions. This is standard practice throughout British primary schools. All that was needed was for the children to choose a name for the fateful stuffed creature. There were votes cast for Abdullah the Bear and Hassan the Bear, but in the end the children decided to name the toy Muhammad. An exercise book was selected for the creature's supposed reflections. A drawing of a bear was stuck on the cover, together with the legend, 'My name is Muhammad'. Alas! The drawing offended one of the more conservative teachers at the school who lodged a complaint with the theocratic civil authorities. None of the Sudanese parents, whose children wrote up the experiences of the controversially named toy, saw fit to complain. But in November 2007 the police seized the incriminating exercise book and interviewed the current guardian or tenant of the teddy. Drawing a bear, and adding the legend 'My name is Muhammad', infringed Sharia law. The school was temporarily closed and angry mobs gathered outside it shouting slogans. Sharia law had been adopted in the Sudan in 1983. There is no specific law in the Koran which forbids people to name toys after the Prophet. Although Islam is traditionally iconophobic, there is not even a specific injunction in the Koran against having pictures of Muhammad. As for whether an all-merciful God would consider Himself threatened by the drawing of a seven-year-old child, it is not worth inquiring. The unfortunate Gillian Gibbons was imprisoned, and the horrible prospect of the likely penalties for her crime – forty lashes – was gleefully rehearsed, both by the Islamist mobs in Khartoum and those other addicts of sadistic punishment, the British journalists at home. After a week in prison, she was released – 'pardoned' – but no British diplomat or politician was aggressive enough to suggest that it was not the teacher, but the Sudanese government, who had committed an offence.[1] Imagine Lord Palmerston's reaction to such an outrage!

Given the fate of Salman Rushdie's Japanese translator, or of those in different parts of the world who attempted to print or propagate matter which the adherents of Sharia law deemed offensive, it would be a brave publisher who commissioned an author to write the Adventures of Muhammad the Bear, but they would make for interesting reading. John Betjeman's Teddy, in *Archibald and the Strict Baptists*, had a taste for the more austere forms of Protestantism, and it might have been the case that the Khartoum bear had been an Islamist who resented its profane nomenclature at the hands of the infidel – or, as Islamists called the non-believers, the kaffir.

The very qualities which made Islamism so repellent to the rest of the world must be those which recommended it to its followers. Fourteen years before Gillian Gibbons imported the standard British primary school cliché of Teddy's Diary idea to the Unity High School, Khartoum, Auberon Waugh was noting, in his Way of the World column in the *Daily Telegraph*, 'In Pakistan, hundreds of religious enthusiasts have surrounded the district court of Gujranwale demanding that a 12-year-old Christian boy, Sulamet Masih, should be hanged for blasphemy. Never mind that the poor youth, accused of writing anti-Islamic slogans, was illiterate and unable, in fact, to write his own name.

'Much of the same problem arises for poor Bill Clinton, who has been called the most hated man in Islam since he received Salman Rushdie in the White House.

'I am sure that Clinton, like most of us, has never read a word of Rushdie's novels and probably thought he was a carpet salesman. That won't save either of them from the fundamentalists. In Egypt, the fundamentalists have taken to murdering anyone they suspect of being lukewarm towards the Mohammedan religion. Once again, they claim that under Islamic law, Muslims have the right to kill any apostate.'[2] Waugh knew whereof he spoke. Writing in *The Times* in the early 1970s, he jestingly referred to the baggy trousers worn by Turkish men in the days of the Caliphate. British soldiers used to call them 'Allah-catchers'. There were demonstrations by Muslims outside *The Times* building in Printing House Square. In Rawalpindi an angry mob, many of whom, it is safe to guess, were not readers of *The Times*, stormed the British Council building and burned the library to the ground. Far from being supportive of Waugh, *The Times* sacked him, and this was the usual pattern of behaviour, from employers and governments in our times, when faced with an angry Muslim mob.

One of the most ludicrous examples of the phenomenon occurred in September 2005 when a Danish newspaper, *Jyllands-Posten*, published some cartoons which depicted the Prophet. Strangely enough, in this instance, an Egyptian newspaper, *Al-Fagr*, reproduced the offending cartoons a month later without incident. But then some Danish imams began to circulate the cartoons on the Internet and to stir up the idea that these cartoons, not especially funny or skilful, were wounding the consciences of Muslims throughout the globe. There followed the usual grotesque and disproportionate reactions from radicalised Islam. Mass protests as far away as Nigeria, Libya and Afghanistan in which people were crushed to death. Barbaric cries for the cartoonist, or his editor, or both, to be beheaded, death threats issued, and loud shouts about blasphemy and the evils of the West. Terrified of the same thing happening to them, English newspaper proprietors and editors refused to reproduce the cartoons, so it was impossible for British readers to know what all the fuss had been about.

Thus intimidated by the blackmailing mobs, as was the blackmailers' intention, Western liberals tended to react in one of two ways. One reaction, perhaps the optimistic one, was to suppose that there was some grievance being suffered by the Islamists. Only remove this, it was supposed, and the mobs who called for the death of cartoonists or the flagellation of primary school teachers would fade away. This school of thought usually had no difficulty in identifying the 'causes' of the Islamists' outrage: they were American foreign policy, and the existence of the State of Israel.

Other liberals, perhaps the pessimists, tended to believe that it was pointless to apply the principles of John Locke and sweet reason to people who would be prepared to stir up mobs and murder on such manifestly trumped-up charges. This school of Western thought pointed to the deplorable ideas being peddled by the Islamists – hatred of homo-sexuals, subjugation of women, violent anti-Judaism – and asked by what right the Islamists dared to attempt to impose their perverted values upon the West while milking the Western democracies for bene-fits of all kinds. It was one thing to suppose that the West represented the Great Satan. It was another to choose to reside within the Great Satan's jurisdiction deriving free schooling and higher education, free or subsidised housing, and employment while choosing to denounce the countries which supplied these benefits. Certainly for Christians residing in countries which observed Sharia law, things were less rosy. For much of the loudest and most violent Islamism appeared to come, not from those who had the advantage of living under Sharia law, and watching their shoplifting neighbours having their hands cut off, and their blasphemous schoolmarms given the lash, but rather those who deliberately opted to live in the fag end of Christian democracies – Denmark, France, the United States.

Britain was the epicentre for much of the actual plotting of terrorism and violence by these people.

As the traveller of the twenty-first century stood in airports in long lines awaiting checkout and baggage searches, as such hitherto harmless items of luggage as toothpaste and shoes were X-rayed or actually confiscated, it was hard to work up much sympathy for the cause of Islamic fundamentalism. The times had changed. So much as one casualty was deemed by the touchy political classes to be a failure on their part. During the Second World War, diners at the Dorchester Hotel sawed their way through four-course dinners while outside the windows in Hyde Park the ack-ack guns fired at the aerial bombers of the Luftwaffe. Death by explosion on the streets of London claimed thousands of lives, but citizens continued to wait at bus stops, get on trains and crawl over the rubble, carrying their briefcases, with the admirable belief that one way of defeating the enemy was to maintain business as usual.

Half a century later, the Islamist terrorists had done terrible damage in many parts of the world. It was no longer possible for any one country to go it alone and simply to say that they would continue to travel about regardless of the bullies. International air travel was now so widespread, and so integral a part of the way the world chose to live, that the gung-ho bravery of the British during the Second World War, even if it had survived as part of the national character (which is questionable), would not have been allowed in the twenty-first century. If the airports in London had allowed passengers to get on and off aircraft without the tedium of searching and palaver, no other airport in the world would receive planes from Britain. So the Islamist blackmailers won that particular round of the game, having the satisfaction of seeing thousands of holidaymakers and innocent business travellers trudging through the security gates at the speed of snails. Because of political correctness, it was not allowable to wave through the majority of Caucasians, who clearly had no links with Islamic terrorism. Old ladies from Miami, well-scrubbed schoolgirls from Dusseldorf, Norwegian architects and retired civil servants from Hemel Hempstead were all treated as if their nail scissors and indigestion mixture were prime weapons in Al Qa'eda's arsenal.

As they stood there, asking themselves the old Second World War question, Is Your Journey Really Necessary?, these travellers must also have asked themselves, as everyone in the West has asked since the phenomenon began, why the Islamists were behaving in this odious manner, and what they hoped to gain by it. When Basque separatists blew innocent fellow mortals to pieces in Madrid, it was always clear what they wanted. Give them an independent Basque country and the bombings would stop. Though the IRA were far from being representative of the Irish, or of Republicans, still less of Roman Catholics, it was broadly speaking clear what they wanted. Few shared their desire for a Marxist Irish state, but there were enough in the United States and on the British mainland to share their wish to have a United Ireland for their activities to have a brutal plausibility. In these cases, terrorism was seen to be the only way that a small or impoverished group could hope to impose its will on the larger group. Terrorism was a word used when the poor were brave enough to wage war upon the rich. Or so it could be made to appear.

Islamism, or a belief in some world-wide Islamic nation or 'ummah', a revival of the Caliphate, these were hardly political ends which could ever be granted to the freedom fighters. The IRA had support among the working-class Roman Catholics of Northern Ireland because it was believed (wrongly) that they would eventually deliver a United Ireland. In fact they delivered a quasi-independent Ulster presided over by their arch-enemy Ian Paisley, with a couple of their token stooges as his quisling deputies. It isn't true that terrorism always works, even when it has quite specific aims. Without the IRA, it is quite possible that there would have been a United Ireland by negotiation.

But what would the Islamists have achieved, by bombing or by negotiating? Who would restore their Caliphate for them? Certainly not the Turks, who were anxious to join the European Union and escape from the religious maniacs. Nor would the Saudis, whose royal family enjoyed the benefits of unbounded wealth, based on the craven dependency of the Western powers upon oil. Nor would any other group, or head of state in the Arab world, or in the wider Islamic world, ever have been able to head such a Caliphate.

Standing in the airport, and trying to avoid illiberal suspicions about the more obviously Islamic of the fellow customers, the twenty-first-century traveller might stumble upon at least one plausible explanation for the horrific and ugly phenomenon of the Islamist threat. That explanation is the airport itself, the phenomenon of mobility. Our time was an era of migrations.

Britain, with its colonial past, was one of the first European countries to receive mass immigration from Islamic nations. Cheap labour was imported into the ailing British textile industry in such northern towns as Bradford, Burnley, Oldham and Rotherham. The mills could not compete with cheaper fabrics being manufactured in the Third World, and eventually this first generation of immigrants from Bangladesh and Pakistan found themselves unemployed.

As we have observed, the generation of old men who had grown up with a British Empire, and who were still occupying senior office until the 1970s, saw the question of immigration entirely in terms of colour. Even the learned J. Enoch Powell, who reckoned upon knowing the languages of the Asian immigrants whose arrival so dismayed him, was not on record as having worried about what was passing through the immigrants' minds. He made no mention, in all his talk of black men holding a whip hand over white men, of the possibility that Britain was importing tens of thousands of potential Muslim Guy Fawkeses. Melanie Phillips made a good point when she wrote, 'Virtually all concerns about this wave of immigration focussed upon the alleged racism or discrimination with which the host community in Britain was treating these newcomers. What went almost totally unnoticed was the enormous dislocation between the Muslim immigrants and the host society. These new arrivals came overwhelmingly from desperately poor, rural villages in places like Mirpur in Pakistan and Sylhet in Bangladesh. Many never thought they would stay permanently but expected to make some money and then return after a few years (not that this happened). So they remained umbilically connected to the culture of southern Asia. And what no one had realised was that religious life in Pakistan was in the process of becoming deeply and dangerously radicalised.'[3]

If it were simply a question of radicalised Islamists being imported from the more impoverished areas of Pakistan and Bangladesh, then an optimist could surely have hoped that within a generation or two in secularised, prosperous Northern Europe, all that religious extremism would surely have been educated out of them?

Sadly, such an optimist would have been proved wrong by events. You only had to listen to the recording of Mohammad Sidique Khan to realise that. He was apparently the ringleader in the 2005 London bomb plot. 'Our words are dead until we give them life with our blood. Therefore we are going to talk to you in a language you understand . . . We are at war and I am a soldier. Your democratically elected governments continuously perpetrate atrocities against my people and your support of them makes you directly responsible, just as I am directly responsible for protecting and avenging my Muslim brothers and sisters. Until we feel security, you will be our target. Until you stop the bombing, gassing, imprisonment and torture of my people, we will not stop this fight.' Though these words came from a young man wearing an Arab keffiyeh, they were spoken in a broad Yorkshire accent. This was the county of Alan Bennett, David Hockney, John Braine, J. B. Priestley! Mohammad Sidique Khan grew up in Dewsbury in the West Riding of Yorkshire.

In this same Dewsbury eighteen years earlier, the parents of twenty-six indigenous Yorkshire children were demonised by the chattering classes for their decision to withdraw their children from the local primary school, because the primary school had become largely Muslim.

What can be seen in the little town of Dewsbury is the enormous fissure which exists between the kind of people who might go out and bomb a train and the kind of people who want England, and Christianity, to continue as they existed before the immigrations began.

Mohammad Sidique Khan, aged thirty, blew himself up at 8.50 a.m. on 7 July 2005 at Edgware Road Station. Shehzad Tanweer (aged twenty-two and from Leeds) simultaneously blew himself up at Aldgate. Jamaican-born Jermaine Lindsay (nineteen, from Aylesbury) committed suicide at the same time on the underground train between King's Cross and Aldgate. Hasib Mir Hussain, eighteen, and from Leeds, was unable to detonate his bomb on the train, and so boarded a Number 30 bus and exploded it, and himself, in Tavistock Square just opposite the British Medical Association. Fifty-two people were killed in the explosions, not counting the four bombers; more than seven hundred were injured.[4] For a day, the transport systems were disrupted and it was impossible to get a signal on a mobile phone in the middle of London. On 8 July, Placido Domingo was singing *Siegfried* at the Royal Opera House. The organisers considered cancelling. Central London was still in a state of shock, and the public transport system was only just returning to normal. They decided to go ahead, even though it seemed unlikely that everyone who had bought a ticket would be able to attend. As things transpired, every seat was taken. No one allowed the bombers to spoil their evening of a stupendous performance of Wagner.[5]

If the bombers thought that they were cowing the public they were certainly wrong. But of all the strange social phenomena in Britain during our times, the existence of Muslim terrorists served most poignantly to highlight the fact that the British were by now living in parallel universes, failing to meet. British Intelligence suggested at the time that 16,000 British Muslims were engaged in, or supported (an important difference), terrorist activity. Three thousand Britons were believed to have passed through Al Qa'eda training camps, and several hundred had been primed to attack targets in Britain itself. Before she retired as Director of MI5, Eliza Manningham-Buller, daughter of 'Bullying-Manner', or Widmerpool (see p. 114), delivered a speech, on 10 November 2006, in which she said that the security service was monitoring 200 terror groupings or networks in Britain, 1,600 identified terrorists and 30 known terror plots. 'What we see at the extreme end of the spectrum are resilient networks, some directed from al Qaeda in Pakistan, some loosely inspired by it, planning attacks including mass casualty suicide attacks in the UK. Today we see the use of home-made improvised explosive devices; tomorrow's threat may include the use of chemicals, bacteriological agents, radioactive materials and even nuclear technology. More and more people are moving from passive sympathy towards active terrorism through being radicalised or indoctrinated by friends, families, in organised training events here and overseas, by images on television, through chat rooms and websites on the Internet. If the opinion polls conducted in the UK since July 2005 are only broadly accurate, over 100,000 of our citizens consider that the July 2005 attacks in London were justified.'[6]

This is a work of history, not of prophecy. It is beyond our scope to foretell how many of these potentially active terrorist cells resident in Britain at the time of writing will succeed in causing more major explosions, or launching a chemical attack on the population of British cities. Nor should one doubt Dame Eliza Manningham-Buller's words, even though they came from the Head of Intelligence. It was American intelligence agents who convinced diplomats and politicians in the West that Saddam had been hiding an arsenal of weapons of mass destruction, and so precipitated the disastrous Iraq War. Throughout the period of the Cold War, it was the intelligence agencies which persuaded both sides that the other intended imminent invasion, or nuclear war, though this never in fact took place. It is the business of intelligence agencies to make our flesh creep.

Compared with the Roman Catholic threats to national security in the seventeenth century, the Islamic ones in the twenty-first seemed comparatively slight. Though modern explosives could kill more people than those amassed by Guy Fawkes and friends, there was no figure in the Islamic world comparable to the Pope, or even to the King of Spain or the King of France, who might have gone so far as to conquer England had the religious terrorists at the start of James I's reign been successful. Compared with the Irish threats of the late twentieth century, the Islamic attacks were more vicious, in so far as they occurred without warning. It would have been rash, at that juncture of history, to suppose they would never be repeated. And the plague of their existence could not be solved by any obvious political means. Once the politicians had settled the Northern Irish problem to the semi-satisfaction of both sides, there was no reason why the IRA should keep up its bombings, even if Irish America had been prepared to pay Colonel Gaddafi any more dollars, and even if he could have laid his hands on any more Russian weaponry. The situation with the bombers of Leeds, Dewsbury and elsewhere was that their aims seemed so much more nebulous, and the sources of their weaponry more various. Besides, anyone prepared to be a suicide bomber did not need anything too sophisticated if they were prepared to die on a crowded underground train. Their bombs were home-made, not imported from Libya.

Pessimists would find little hope in a situation where so many British citizens — 100,000 or more — approved of the idea of such acts of mass slaughter. On the other hand, it is perfectly possible that 'extreme' Islamists, living as they did cut off from the rest of society, had a different way of answering opinion polls. It was a well-attested fact among pollsters that most British respondents give the answer which they believe is expected of them — always telling a researcher that they believed in God, for example, and claiming that such issues as Third World debt matter more to them than going on summer holidays, or saving for their old age. In private, sitting in front of their television sets, many indigenous Britons would express xenophobic and perhaps even murderous sentiments, which they would never have acted upon, and which they would not have revealed to an opinion poll. Maybe those of Muslim origin were more honest, and admitted to feelings of irrational and destructive hate which were often felt but seldom in the polite world expressed. In which case, they would be only marginally more likely than, say, angry old white pensioners, to have used themselves as suicide bombers on public transport.

Optimists might have discovered aspects of the Islamist phenomenon in Britain which gave grounds for hope. Most perpetrators of the atrocities, as opposed to their instigators, were young. The pessimists were right to ask why it took so long for the authorities to arrest Abu Hamza, for example, a terrible one-eyed creature with a hook for a hand, who preached murderous hatred at the North London Central Mosque in Finsbury Park before being arrested. The US government had accused him of membership of the Islamic army in Aden, the group responsible for bombing USS *Cole* in Yemen. At his mosque he received such dubious characters as Richard Reid, the 'shoebomber', and Zacarias Moussaoui, one of the 9/11 planners, as well as many other identified criminals. Even after the British authorities finally got round to stripping him of citizenship and deporting him to the US for trial, Hamza, though banned from preaching in the Finsbury Park mosque, was allowed to sit in an armchair blocking the pavement while his adoring congregation queued up to embrace him, and he was allowed to wow the crowds, still making inflammatory speeches in which he denounced Western politicians as corrupt homosexuals, and the Jews as criminals propping up a brigand state – of Israel. Three minutes spent by a Jewish rabbi making comparable comments about, say, Pakistan, would naturally have resulted in his arrest, and probably a riot of Muslims, expensively policed. Hamza was not finally gaoled until 2006, for inciting racial hatred and murder. By then his murderous message of hate had touched and inflamed many young fanatics. Nor was Hamza alone.[7]

Sheikh Abdullah al-Faisal was deported to his country of origin, Jamaica, from Britain on Friday 25 May 2006 after reaching the parole date in his prison sentence. He was found guilty of three charges of soliciting the murder of Jews, Americans and Hindus and two charges of using threatening words to stir up racial hatred in 2003, and after his appeal was sentenced to seven years in prison. In 2006 John Reid told MPs that al-Faisal had influenced Jermaine Lindsay, one of the 7 July suicide bombers.[8]

But optimists would be entitled to wonder – what if Jermaine had grown out of the influence of Abdullah al-Faisal? What if he had fallen in love, developed a sense of irony, had a family, made friends of another religious background, or none, and found that they made him laugh? Then, surely, the threat of Hamza, al-Faisal and the whole hellish pack of them would have evaporated. While it might be true that Islamic terrorists in some parts of the world are making what they see as the only military-political gesture they can against, let us say, the State of Israel's treatment of Palestinians, or the American occupation of Baghdad, the dignity of such a position cannot logically be ascribed to young fools brought up in comfort in Dewsbury or Aylesbury. Their alienation from their fellow citizens was terrifying, but it was a psychological as much as it was a political condition. If the Palestinians were granted East Jerusalem, or the Americans withdrew from Baghdad, there would have been some other grievance which angered them – some teddy bear with a blasphemous name. If this is true, then optimists can take heart from one of the most extraordinary books to emerge from the British Muslim experience: Ed Husain's *The Islamist*. Husain grew up in a Bangladeshi family in the East End of London. His father had been born in what was still British India and regretted the partition of the subcontinent after British withdrawal. Theirs was a poor but highly intelligent family and the Islam they practised was intense, spiritual and centred upon the mosque in Brick Lane which had started life as a Huguenot church and gone through a phase as a synagogue. In itself, this building was a parable of immigrant life in London over four centuries. Through the preachings of Fultholy Saheb, a sage whom he called affectionately Grandpa, Husain became something of an infant Samuel, travelling the country and learning to recite from the Koran in Arabic. All this was wholly spiritual and had nothing whatsoever to do with political extremists.

Ed Husain's book described how he rebelled against his parents and started mixing with 'radicalised' Islamists, not in the purely religious Brick Lane Mosque but in the East London Mosque. Here he began to pick up the ideas and mix with the enthusiasts for the various political groups who were campaigning for the Caliphate, 'ummah', and so on. When Husain's father gets to hear of it, he is appalled, wondering why, if a young man is interested in politics, he doesn't join the Labour Party. Significantly, Husain records that after he had become radicalised, although he spouted a lot of theological nonsense inwardly he had ceased to be religious. It is only after he had gone through his student years as a member of Hizb-ut-Tahrir, 'radicalising' whatever campus he happened to be attending, that he returned to sanity. At the end of the book, he had not abandoned religion – very far from it. But he had seen through 'Islamism' for the fraudulent and dangerous nonsense which his Muslim father had always told him it was.[9]

Three things appeared to save him. One was high intelligence. You can get sucked into this sort of thing if you are clever; but if you are clever, you will eventually argue your way out of it. Secondly, love of a good woman – he fell in love while at one of his colleges, with a beautiful Muslim woman, and after they were married they travelled in the Levant (Syria) and Saudi Arabia. Their experiences of the difference between the political and religious attitudes which existed in these places was further confirmation, if any were needed, that there was a huge difference between the attentive, tolerant, spiritual Islam found at, say, the tomb of St John the Baptist in Syria, where Christian nuns pray alongside Muslims, and the closed world of Saudi. The idea of 'ummah' is shattered when contemplating the realities of the actual Muslims who live in Islamic countries. Thirdly, what redeemed Ed Husain was his humour, gentle but definite. Only when he goes to Syria, for example, does he realise that many devout Muslims, men and women, do not dress in the clothes deemed essentially Islamic by the East End boy-members of Hizb-ut-Tahrir. The people who dress like that are the Christians.

Husain began his book with tender memories of the Sir William Burrough primary school in Limehouse. This was a place where inspirational white teachers and classroom assistants instilled in their pupils a sense of common belonging. 'It would take me more than a decade to understand what drove Ms Powlesland and Cherie. I was fortunate to have such marvellous teachers at such a young age. For later in life, when I doubted my affinity with Britain, those memories came rushing back.'[10]

As he described the rebellion against his good parents, and his attempts to distance himself from the multi-culturalism of his benign primary school, Husain drew a picture which very many Westerners would identify as quite familiar, from a psychological point of view. Extreme Islamism is a form of religious punk. Like punk, Islamism wanted to hurt, and it wanted to shock; but unlike punk it was humourless and deadly. Like punk, it was wholly aggressive, but, unlike punk, it did not possess the courage of its convictions. It used the odious trappings of hurt feelings, profound shock at a child's exercise book adorned with a teddy bear, or uncontrollable anger at the sight of a few cartoons. Islamism kept writing itself down as a spoilt psychopathic child, but the world is afraid of psychopathic children, especially when they reveal themselves to be capable of blowing up buses and trains. Hence the ludicrous spectacle in the early twenty-first century of kowtowing to Islamist bullies. They took it further – they actually anticipated the reactions of the bullies, as when a certain local council in Britain banned the use of a calendar which depicted a pig, in case of offence to Muslims. Performances of Marlowe's *Tamburlaine the Great* were censored at the Barbican Centre in London for fear of upsetting the Muslims, though the equally offensive – indeed far more offensive – *Jew of Malta* by the same playwright saw occasional revivals without any riots taking place outside the theatres.

The British public, in overwhelming proportions, knew exactly what was required. To the *Daily Telegraph*, a good flypaper for public opinion, often truer than focus groups, wrote a correspondent with the view: 'If the Muslim people are so upset with the ways of the west and the UK, if they dislike our laws so much why don't they go and live in a Muslim country and be ruled under Sharia law? This is not a racist comment as I believe we should all tolerate each other and our beliefs, as the English people have done for over 2000 years. We have allowed Jews, Hindus, Sikhs, Italians, Greeks, French, etc etc to come and live.

All have integrated and accepted the British way of life, without giving up their language or religion (I am from one of these minorities) yet come the followers of Allah and all hell breaks loose. They want special treatment, their own laws and the honour to blow themselves and innocent people up.'[11]

28

The Return of God

We began reflecting upon our times with a reading of J. R. R. Tolkien's *The Lord of the Rings*. At a distance of half a century since it first made an impact upon the imagination of its readers, it still seems the most powerful work of fiction of its age. In the last decade or so, the only book which rivals it in power and imaginative range is Philip Pullman's trilogy *His Dark Materials*. It begins with one of the central myths of our times, the disappearing child. This motif from the World of Faerie returned over and over again in the news reports of the last half-century. Folklore throughout the world, and throughout history, has externalised the fear of losing children by making them vulnerable to the witches, Little Folk, merfolk or gods who might apprehend them, take them for seven years, sometimes for ever. In the comparatively debased form which these stories take in newspapers, the predators are always paedophiles. These figures, who at the beginning of our times were regarded as a sinister joke, especially by children themselves, who knew that there were 'strange men' to whom it was unsafe to speak, became – after such horrors as the Moors murders – truly nightmarish projections. The paedophile was the embodiment of everything which our society took to be evil, matched only by the racist.

Every time the newspaper told the story of a disappearing child, the bucket was lowered into the well, stirring primitive responses which have been there since our fear of separation from our parents turned into Hansel and Gretel being kidnapped in the woods, or the 'little men' who stole Bridget for seven years long. Philip Pullman's trilogy began with such a theme. Children all over England are being taken by a sinister group popularly called the Gobblers – at heart, as we slowly discover, an ecclesiastical body called the General Oblation Board.

The adventures of Lyra Belacqua, the little girl allowed to grow up as a ragamuffin in a superbly archaic Oxford college, compose a rich narrative. The story takes her to the North, in the company of Gyptians – gypsy bargees whom she has befriended in Oxford – an armoured bear, an American adventurer in a hot-air balloon who seems to have flown in from the pages of Jules Verne, and some superbly sexy witches.

A central conceit to the whole myth is that fully rounded human beings have an alter ego, or soul, which is called a 'daemon', pronounced demon. When we are children, these daemons are constantly changing. Lyra, the heroine of the story, has a daemon called Pantalaimon. He takes many beautiful forms – a cat, a butterfly, a rat, a goldfinch – but he is always part of her. Grown-ups have fixed daemon forms. Pullman's daemon idea was suggestive of many deep thoughts, both about human souls and about our relationship with animals. The daemon is like a soul. The bears do not have them, a fact which increases our sense of their sturdy, northern sadness. In the first volume of the trilogy, it does not become entirely clear why the Gobblers are grabbing the children. But Lyra discovers this much. When they catch the children and take them to the northern laboratory, they separate them from their daemons. They want to get their hands on elementary particles, called simply 'dust' in that universe. Puberty, when your daemon becomes fixed, is also the time when your relationship with dust alters. Dust gives power.

Pullman's guiding genius is William Blake, and the General Oblation Board – the masterminds of the Gobblers – corresponds to the 'priests in black gowns' who bind with briars our joys and desires.

There is real Blakean lyricism in the wonderful descriptions of the Northern Lights. And the ragamuffin children of the Oxford bargees, and Lyra herself, at large in a Gormenghast version of an Oxford college, are essentially innocents; their 'daemons' are not sin-drenched burdens as for St Augustine, but instruments of light and joy. But though Pullman, like Blake, reworked Milton, and his angelology, in the service of his own mythological view of things, he did so in a spirit which was reflective of his age. And this is what marks Pullman off from Tolkien.

Tolkien's assembly of myth was a massive, tragic, dark bulwark against the spirit of the age. He saw the past itself, with all its heroism and all its mythology, being obliterated by the modern. Although a religious man himself, he buried overt religious reference in the myth, which is about wider and older themes than those which separate Homer from the Christian world.

For Pullman, however, as for so many liberals at the end of our times, religion was seen as a deadly force, an enslaver of the human spirit which has risen up as a surprise monster to threaten democracy and freedom, just when we might have hoped to have seen the end of superstition. A lesser myth-maker than Tolkien, Pullman cannot resist intruding into his story the views of any contemporary liberal newspaper columnist into a tale which seems everlastingly trying to be bigger than its author's narrow views. Hence, as the story goes on, its collapse into incoherence.

For example, at the beginning of the story we learn that no one in Lyra's universe can be separated from their daemon, an embodiment of soul which usually takes the form of an animal. But in the Virgilian journey to the world of the dead, undertaken by Will and Lyra in volume three, Lyra does leave her daemon behind, much to her and his sorrow. Then again, the whole book is posited on the notion that the Authority (God) does not exist; but we then *see* the poor old Authority, a doddering, decrepit old creature being borne aloft on a bier – a sort of Titurel from *Parsifal*. We seem to have strayed here from the Victorian atheism which underpinned volume one to the 'Death of God' theology of the 1960s. There are wonderful things in Pullman's story – the angels on both sides of the war, or tiny spy-creatures, the Gallivespians, who ride on dragon-flies; a splendid American hot-air balloonist; old Oxford bargees (the Gyptians); and the ever-beguiling Mrs Coulter, Lyra's mother, who starts as a wicked society hostess, secretly working for the church, and ends as a much more complicated figure, shaken by true maternal feeling into joining forces against religion.

Mrs Coulter's reignited passion for Lord Asriel is matched by the truly touching love between Lyra and Will, who, because they belong to different universes, are obliged in the end to part. There were no novels written in English in the last decade of our times to match this one for range, depth and passion. Yet future generations will surely see it not merely as a great, if flawed, work of the imagination, but also as an expression of contemporary liberal angst about the growth of religious fundamentalism.

From a Western European perspective, there is surely something para-doxical in this, since throughout the half-century which we have considered in this book, the institutional Churches, and especially the Roman Catholic Church and the Church of England, have declined in numbers and influ-ence. This has not been true, however, of religion when taken as a whole and viewed from a global perspective. Seen from a narrowly British perspective, Pullman might be thought to have chosen an odd moment to make the General Oblation Board, a sort of malign General Synod, into an instrument of terror. Not since St Augustine arrived in Kent in the late sixth century had the Church exercised less influence, for good or ill, upon the juvenile minds of the archipelago. Yet perhaps for this very reason, precisely because modern Europeans had become so secu-larised, the religious resurgence in our times seemed so alarming to the liberal mind.

'Whether we like it or not, the world is gravitating towards faith in the Almighty', wrote President Mahmoud Ahmadinejad of Iran in an open letter to President George W. Bush in 2007. Similar words had been spoken by Dr Billy Graham during his missionary journey to London in 1954. The difference is that, in those days, very few influential or intel-ligent people, even if themselves adherents to a religion, would have found the words credible. In Britain, as in Western Europe, institutional Christianity rapidly evaporated. The numbers of practising Catholics and

Anglicans was halved. Secularism was rampant. But to take a wider global viewpoint, as our times rolled onward into other times, the President of Iran's words were self-evidently true. When, in the early 1950s, Dame Ivy Compton-Burnett, one of the greatest English novelists of our times, heard that her friend Rose Macaulay had reverted to the habit of church-going, she expressed her exasperation, 'when for a lifetime she had been a perfectly sound agnostic, like everybody else'. It was something which puzzled many a liberal secularist in the opening decade of the twenty-first century who contemplated the religious frenzy which possessed the globe. Tony Blair had been a preacher on a tank.[1] His successor as Prime Minister, Gordon Brown, the son of the manse, quoted the Gospels in his first speech as Prime Minister to the Labour Party Conference. George Dubya was a born-again Christian. Unlike previous American Presidents, who saw their principal adversary as godless Marxism, Bush's greatest enemies were Islamists, who turned to Mecca in prayer as often as he clumsily thumbed the Epistles of St Paul. In Nigeria, where between 1990 and 2007, 20,000 people were killed in conflicts between Muslims and Christians, the Evangelical Church of West Africa doubled in number over the same period.

In Burma, the chief opposition to the repressive regime of Lt General Soe Win was led by Buddhist monks. In Guatemala, Pentecostals built the largest building in Central America, the 12,000-seater church of Mega Frater, which was not named, we must presume, in playful allusion to Orwell. The Yoido Gospel Church in Seoul, South Korea, boasted 830,000 members, a number which was growing, in 2007, at a rate of 3,000 per month. The number of Christians in China grew from 10 million in 1900 to 400 million in 2000 – and rising. In Russia, following the collapse of communism, not only were all the churches full on Sundays, but the monasteries and convents which had been so mercilessly destroyed by Lenin were rebuilt and bursting with aspirant monks and nuns. The proportion of people attached to the world's four biggest religions – Christianity, Islam, Buddhism and Hinduism – rose from 67 per cent in 1900 to 73 per cent in 2005, and according to the prognostications of *The Economist*, looked set to rise to 80 per cent in 2050.[2]

Was this what it had all been leading up to, as the intelligent sons and daughters of the Enlightenment tried to rebuild the world ruined by the mid-twentieth-century clash of European ideologies? The heirs of Bloomsbury had assumed that theology would vanish with the extension of education. Bertrand Russell's atheism had taught two generations to think as he did. A. J. Ayer's dismissal of religious questions as meaning-less had been as apparently devastating as his tutor Gilbert Ryle's dismissal of God Himself as a category mistake. The Church of England had done its bit to spread Enlightenment, with a Bishop of Woolwich in the 1960s trying to be Honest to a God in whom he could scarcely believe, and a Bishop of Durham in the 1980s wondering whether the Resurrection itself had been anything more remarkable than 'a conjuring trick with bones'. The Dean of Emmanuel College, Cambridge, had surely taken matters to their logical conclusion when, having mused on the ebb tide of *The Sea of Faith*, he wrote a book with the candid title *Taking Leave of God*. British primary schools were no longer teaching the children Bible stories but were giving them hazy versions of comparative religion, so that rather than having their heads filled with wonders which they would later dismiss as fables – Moses and the Burning Bush or Christ Walking on the Water – these progressive tots knew about Diwali and Ramadan and Yom Kippur, and, it could be hoped, by the kindly minded educational theorists, develop into mature beings who had the vague sense that religions, no more than social constructs, were phenomena out of which human beings progressed, when they came to learn about science. With no common mythology, they could learn to put their trust in the integrity of relationships, in intellectual sincerity, in respect for one another's differences. What else was religion, but, in the words of one of the most eloquent poems of our times:

> That vast moth-eaten musical brocade
> Created to pretend we never die?[3]

After half a century of 'perfectly sound agnosticism', it must have been galling, and worse than galling, for those who believed that human beings could simply be taught not to be religious, to watch the innumerable pairs of sandals and trainers cast off at the doors of mosques in every big British city, and to hear the jaunty strains of 'Sing Hosanna!' or 'Shine, Jesus, Shine' drifting from the packed doors of evangelical churches. No wonder some of the perfectly sound agnostics felt beleaguered, and, like religious people when beleaguered, began to say and write things which were no longer sensible.

The long-running British television series *Doctor Who* was a popular illustration of how science fiction provided an alternative metaphysic, comparable to, though not a substitute for, religious mythology. Dr Who was a Time Lord travelling through time and space in his Tardis ('Time And Relative Dimension in Space') which had the reassuring outward appearance of a police telephone box. These boxes became obsolete in reality so that the Doctor, by the time he was once again thrilling audiences in the early 2000s, had a dated rather than timeless quality whenever he fetched up on the planet earth. In the late 1970s and early 1980s he was played by an agreeably toothy actor called Tom Baker whose long face somewhat resembled that of the polymathic opera director Dr Jonathan Miller and whose long woolly scarves gave him the appearance of a fun-loving lecturer at one of the new universities which had sprung up in the real-life Britain of the period. At one stage his companion on his journeys in the Tardis was the Time Lady Romana, played by the Honourable Sarah Ward, daughter of the 7th Viscount Bangor. (Half)-sister-in-law of the biographer Sarah Bradford, she acted under the name Lalla Ward. Dr Who was not unlike a crude version of Christ, immortal yet apparently wholly human, who visited the planet to overcome evil. Baker and Lalla appeared in a number of adventures together, including *Destiny of the Daleks*, *City of Death* and *State of Decay*. The pair married for sixteen months, but separated, and it was at the fortieth birthday party of the science fiction writer Douglas Adams that she was introduced to a strikingly handsome and amusing biology don, a Fellow of New College, Oxford, named Dr Richard Dawkins. The same year Lalla and Dawkins were married.[4]

Dr Who had been fearless in his war on monsters, his most popular adversaries with television audiences being the Daleks, metallic dustbins covered in flashing lights who rolled along on castors pointing something like sink plungers at their victims with the throaty, agitated cry of 'Exterminate! Exterminate!'

Dr Dawkins was to become even more famous than Dr Who. He was one of the most successful popularisers of scientific ideas, occupying a position in our times comparable to that of Thomas Huxley in the time of Darwin, and, like Huxley, consumed not only with a zeal for scientific knowledge but also for the denunciation of superstition. In such elegant monographs as *The Selfish Gene, The River of Life* and *The Blind Watchmaker*, he explained the working of Charles Darwin's theory of the evolution of the species by natural selection, while never hesitating to point out that Darwin's theories, confirmed by twentieth-century discoveries about genetics, obviated the need for the mechanistic 'creator' envisaged by the cruder Deist philosophers of the seventeenth and eighteenth centuries. He devoted much of his intellectual energy, during his prime, to the demolition of such obsolete theological writers as Archdeacon Paley (1743–1805), whose *View of the Evidences of Christianity* defended a mechanistic idea of creation, owing more to Leibniz than to the Bible or the Church Fathers. Dawkins wrote as if he was unaware of the existence of William James (1842–1910), the pragmatist philosopher and psychologist who had concluded that Leibniz's God was 'a disease of the philosophy shop'.[5] James had a tentative belief in God, based on the widespread evidence that human beings had religious experiences. Whereas Dawkins preferred to concentrate on the nonsensical things which some religious people had written or said, and enjoyed seeking out proponents of intolerant and ugly theological points of view, James had pointed to the many cases where prayer or the awareness of God's presence appeared to bring courage, calm, a sense of wellbeing and an urge to be kinder.[6] (His brother Henry, an agnostic, had written in his notebooks, the sentence *Be kind, be kind, be kind*.)

A book which showed Dawkins at his most attractive and articulate was a volume of essays entitled *A Devil's Chaplain*. It contains a celebration of a great science teacher Frederick William Sanderson (1857–1922), who had been headmaster of Oundle School a generation or two before Dawkins himself picked up his infectious enthusiasm for science at the same establishment. It is a joyous essay, which celebrates the pleasures and duties of intellectual knowledge. Sanderson directed that the laboratories be left unlocked so that boys could go in at any time and work on their research projects. Dawkins longed for an educational system which, rather than making students cram for exams, inspired them with a thirst for knowledge, a passion for truth. Sanderson was an inspiration both in his own enthusiasm for science and in his ability to communicate it to others. Dawkins himself had this wonderful ability.

In the essay he quoted quite extensively from Sanderson's sermons in Oundle School chapel. One such paragraph summons up a cloud of scientific witness – 'Mighty men of science and mighty deeds. A Newton who binds the universe together in uniform law; Lagrange, Laplace, Leibniz in their wondrous mathematical harmonies.' And on the catalogue goes. Not surprisingly, Dawkins shortens the quotation a little and indicates his omissions in the traditional manner by the occasional . . .

There must have been readers of *A Devil's Chaplain* who felt tempted to turn from this essay to the compilation *Sanderson of Oundle*, put together by his grateful pupils. There they would have found the catalogue of great scientists, quoted by Dawkins – Faraday, Ohm, Ampère, Joule, Maxwell, Hertz, Röntgen. The words not quoted by Dawkins are that these scientists are 'all, we may be sure, living daily in the presence of God, bending like the reed before His will'.[7]

Nor did Dawkins quote Sanderson when he told the boys, 'We perish if we cease from prayer. Of course, true, earnest helpful prayer is difficult. It is difficult to fix the attention, difficult to know what to pray for, what to pray about. Perhaps the best way is to meditate with a notebook.'[8]

Sanderson the inspirational science teacher exclaimed, 'Thou, O God, dost reveal thyself in all the multitude of Thy works, in the workshop, the factory, the mine, the laboratory, in industrial life. No symbolism here, but the Divine God.'⁹ The 'biological purpose of man', thought Sanderson, was, 'to bring and maintain order out of the tangle of things; he is to diagnose diseases; he is to co-ordinate the forces of nature; he is above all things to reveal the spirit of God in all the works of God.' And education? 'The business of schools is through and by the use of a common service to get at the true spiritual nature of the ordinary things we have to deal with.'¹⁰

Some would consider it dishonest of Dawkins to have omitted these sayings in the account of his hero. Obviously, what Dawkins admired in Sanderson (the communicated enthusiasm for science) would have been admirable whether or not he himself shared the religious beliefs. But no one would guess from the account in *A Devil's Chaplain* that religious belief underlay all Sanderson's wonder at scientific discovery and all his faith in the curiosity, resourcefulness and healing creativity of human beings. 'Individuals are not hard Newtonian molecules. Individuals are like atoms under radium. The life within a man or a woman, a boy or a girl, is the most powerful, vital, complex, energetic thing there is. It cannot be treated as a "hard" molecule any longer. There are vast stores of energies to be liberated.'¹¹

It was clear from Dawkins's animated, handsome face, and from his laugh, and even from the arrogant contempt which fell from his lips or pen in anger that he did not believe, any more than had Sanderson, that human beings were hard Newtonian molecules. Ethical statements, denunciations of intellectual immorality, passion for liberty, animated much of Dawkins's rhetoric. In his accounts of life on earth, however, and his expositions of how natural selection operates, he never revealed by so much as a syllable that he considered himself, and other sentient beings, to be mysterious. Nor did he ever ask the question which had puzzled mankind at least as long ago as the pre-Socratics: what is Being itself? When we see, say, observe that we, or the Universe, are, rather than *are not* – what is it that we are saying? Instead, when he turned from the excellent explanations of science, which were his métier, to the area of metaphysical inquiry, Dawkins often gave the impression that these deep questions were scientific speculations about, say, the origin of the universe, or the origin of species. He answered What? questions with How? answers. *What is Man that thou art mindful of him?* was not a question which ever seems to have troubled him. What Wordsworth in *The Prelude* called 'a dark/Invisible workmanship' at work in each of us was central to the life-view of Sanderson of Oundle but apparently absent from that of Dawkins.

But so was it absent, apparently, from those 'fundamentalists' whom Dawkins attacked with such Huxleyan zeal. This is even odder. Readers

of Dawkins's bestseller *The God Delusion* will find that his bullets
reach a bull's-eye not when he is attacking what he understands as religion, but when he is demolishing those who themselves believe in the
'religions' he lambasts. In Emmanuel College, Gateshead, for instance,
one of the 'city academies' set up by Tony Blair for promoting higher
intellectual standards, Dawkins found an object worthy of his scorn.
The school was endowed by Sir Peter Vardy, a car salesman whose life
had been changed by the combination of becoming a very rich man and
conversion to neo-con American-style evangelicalism. It was Andrew
Brown, the *Independent*'s first religious affairs correspondent, who had
drawn attention to a lecture given at the school on 'The Teaching of
Science: A Biblical Perspective' in which the speaker, the head of science
in the school, spoke about the legendary narratives in Genesis as if
they were texts of a different order. Defence of the historicity of
Noah's Flood – a global catastrophe which took place 'in the relatively
recent past' – appear, from Dawkins's quotations in *The God Delusion*,
to be only part of a story which includes assertions from the science
teacher that the earth itself – contrary to all evidence from geology and
palaeontology – is also of recent origin.

Disputes between 'fundamentalists' or their subtler co-partners the
'creationists' and the debunking materialists became commoner in our
times as year succeeded year and not, as might have been predicted, less
common. Matters which some observers might have been thought settled
for good and all by Stanley Kramer's film *Inherit the Wind*, of 1960,
were more of a live issue than ever in the year 2008, both in the US and
in Britain. In that film Spencer Tracy played the role of a hard-bitten
lawyer coming to a Southern town to defend a schoolmaster accused of
teaching Darwin's theory of natural selection, the so-called monkey trials
of 1925. Maybe in 1960 the Southern backwoodsmen who professed
themselves outraged by a young teacher's scientific honesty seemed like
historical freaks. Kramer's film celebrates the passion for truth and
justice which the Spencer Tracy character exemplifies. But there is more
than a hint of patronage and swagger in the portrayal of the hayseed-
sprinkled hicks who actually believe in old-style religion. Kipling bid
the Christians

> Be gentle when the heathen pray
> To Buddha at Kamakara

They did not heed his advice. Nor did the modern unbelievers display
gentleness to the believers. The 'debate' which became louder and uglier
as the twenty-first century unrolled, was not really a debate: more a

species of trench warfare in which one side, only semi-visible to the other, hurled verbal abuse and occasional threats of actual violence. Dawkins quoted some of these poor crazies with evident relish in his book – such letters as this addressed to the author and director Brian Flemming, whose film *The God Who Wasn't There* had clearly hurt:

> You've definitely got some nerve. I'd love to take a knife, gut you fools, and scream with joy as your insides spill out in front of you. You are attempting to ignite a holy war in which some day I, and others like me, may have the pleasure of taking action like the above mentioned. However GOD teaches us not to seek vengeance, but to pray for those like you all.[12]

It is a happy accident that the English word *pray* (from Middle English *preien*, old French *preier* (Latin *precari*) should be a homophone for *prey* – (from Middle English *preye*, Old French *preie*, Latin *praeda*, booty). The Christian Bible itself ends with the alarming series of visions known as The Apocalypse in which all those of a different persuasion from the seer are made to perish everlastingly in a burning lake, and in which *civilisation* itself, the day-to-day life of the *civis*, is deemed to be in itself sinful (see especially the XVIIIth chapter of the Revelation of St John the Divine which exults over the desolation and fall of Babylon the Great): 'And the merchants of the earth shall weep and mourn over her; for no man buyeth her merchandise any more: the merchandise of gold, and silver, and precious stones, and of pearls, and fine linen, and purple, and silk, and scarlet . . .'. A great catalogue. So must the disciples of Osama bin Laden have exulted when they watched the mass murder of office workers in New York and imagined that they beheld the vengeance of the Almighty upon the unjust city.

Those who studied the alarming, and profoundly uncongenial fundamentalism of our times were bound to investigate the source and origin of all this violence and hatred. The ardent secularists took the view that religion was itself the poison from which the human race needed to be cleansed. While having some fun at the expense of Mother Teresa of Calcutta, Christopher Hitchens concluded in his diatribe that religion 'poisons everything'. 'What we' – the non-believers – 'respect is free inquiry, open-mindedness and the pursuit of ideas for their own sake,' he claimed. He called for a 'new enlightenment' which believed that 'the proper study of mankind is man, and woman'. He had little to say about the Anglican monks who had spearheaded resistance to apartheid in the 1950s, or about the phenomenon of the Peace and Reconciliation Committee in South Africa when apartheid came to an end and Christians led by Archbishop Tuto steered that country to majority rule without bloodshed. Nor did the Peace Now movement in Israel in which religious Jews played a striking role move him to moderate his tone, nor the Peace Movement in Northern Ireland, which was the impulse of practising Christians trying to build understanding in a community wrecked by the activities of neo-Marxist gangsters. The resistance to Hitler by Confessing Christians such as Pastor Bonhoeffer or the defence of Human Rights in Latin and Central America by heroic figures such as Archbishop Romeiro were conveniently passed by, as was the lifetime's witness for peace of the Dalai Lama or resistance to tyranny by the Buddhist monks of Burma. Nor were the works of aid agencies such as Christian Aid or CAFOD allowed to interfere with the argument that those who said their prayers were filling their minds, and presumably those whom they helped in famine and disaster, with poison. God, for Hitchens, was a Santa Claus–style invention, religion the *cause* of hatred and conflict in the world, the tool by which such evils as misogyny, child abuse and brainwashing kept the human race in the Dark Ages.[13]

If the first premises were accepted, that religion *causes* such abuses of human power as Al Qa'eda, or the Spanish Inquisition, who could have not sided with Hitchens and those who believed in 'open-mindedness for its own sake'? But what if he was using language lazily? What if by saying religion causes enslavement he was making a syntactical utterance of the same order as 'War causes nuclear weapons'? Human beings will always wish to exercise power over one another, and the invention of a 'Santa Claus' who shared all the xenophobic or misanthropic prejudices of the (usually collective) inventors was indeed toxic. It was unsurprising that the anti-Godders took this view of religious origin at a period in history when they had about them so many examples of those deluded by religious hatred. Hitchens's need to enlist Mother Teresa in the same brigade of murderous maniacs as Osama bin Laden, however, was revealing, as was Dawkins's suppression of the religious foundation of a great science teacher's ideas.

It would be frivolous to have denied that the anti-Godders had alerted their contemporaries, if such alert were needed, to a poison deadly indeed. Whether one considered the mental processes of the religious right in America, or of the radicalised Islam, or of the enraged Buddhists of Sri Lanka, or of the anti-Islamist Hindu nationalists in India, it was impossible to ignore the fact that religion appeared to be at the heart of very many of the world's most intractable political problems. Far from providing peaceable solutions to these problems, religion appeared to *be* the problem. One could indeed go the whole way with the anti-

Godders – religion *was* the problem – if, a very big if, religion connotes the closed mind, the implacable will, the ability to swallow nonsense and justify murder and suppression in the name of an invented Deity.

> The scientific work before the world is to co-ordinate, to *harness* the radio-active souls of men, just as we have to harness the energy of the atom. This is the stupendous work for which you boys are to be prepared: in the existence and needs of which you have to believe.
>
> And for this the centre of gravity must be changed. The viewpoint must be changed. Astronomy was once looked at from the earth as the fixed centre of vision. Through much conflict and many persecutions the viewpoint was changed to the sun – the sun a fixed star. Then the sun began moving. It is now changed to an 'atom', shall we call it, of light, moving with the velocity of 186,000 miles per second. And the new things must be viewed from that moving chariot of light . . .
>
> A new vision. A new Horeb and Sinai. A new Mount of Transfiguration. 'And after three days He took with Him His disciples, Peter, James and John, and went into a mount and was transfigured before them.' So, too, if we are to see a new world arise out of this conflict and strife, we also must go up into the mount – the new mount of vision.
>
> See, boys, that you make it after the pattern which hath been shown you on the Mount.[14]

The attitude of that kindly liberal Protestant headmaster towards science was very decidedly not that of any of the popular defenders of what might be called a scientific viewpoint from the middle of the twentieth to the beginning of the twenty-first centuries. Karl Popper has been mentioned as the advocate of an open society and the identifier of its enemies. He did not *invent* the open society. It has come about as a result of a number of factors, chief of which is economic growth. Popper was also concerned with the philosophy of science and in the more difficult area of trying to establish the objective truth of scientific statements. He tried to wrench the subjective element out of traditional epistemology which must always lead to the logical scepticism of Berkeley and Hume. (If your sole criterion is your own sense-perceptions, you cannot be said to *know* the laws of thermodynamics.) Popper, however, was as unable as anyone else has ever been to establish any criterion by which we could be said to know, beyond any shadow of doubt, that any statement, whether made by a scientist or not, is true.

The modern idolatry offered to 'scientific truth' goes back far beyond our times to the late seventeenth century, when the Cartesian philosophy threatened the very notion of objective knowledge. Unbelief in God began at this time, as did the deist conception of God – the idea of God as an inventor or mechanic who established the laws of nature and then retired to allow the universe to run itself. The pathetic need for certainty, in a world of unalterable, impersonal laws, led to the development of the 'scientific outlook', the need to claim that some concepts or objects were beyond dispute, were verifiable or falsifiable by some means other than sense-impression, so that they might be accepted as universal truths. From this superstition – the idea of 'science' being the sole arbiter of the verifiability of statements – sprang the slow death of religion(s). This was not, as scientists such as Thomas Huxley supposed, because scientific facts had been presented which disproved religious claims. It was because the human notion of truth had altered, and Christianity disastrously reacted by adopting the 'scientific' or 'materialist' outlook. Christians began to defend the Bible and its stories as if they were works of 'history' or 'science'. In so doing, whole generations of men and women, whether or not they believed in God any more, were seduced into thinking that these matters could be decided by 'scientific' investigation. Hence the truly ludicrous spectacle in our times of clever journalists or popularisers of Darwin thinking to set themselves up against the deep wisdom which had produced the Upanishads or the Book of Psalms or the works of Pythagoras.

A belief in 'science' as the sole arbiter of what is true must always resolve itself into a belief in force, in blind force. Before this idea, the nineteenth century fell prostrate, and from it emerged two of its most influential determinist prophets, Karl Marx and Charles Darwin. The writings of Marx were said to have been discredited in our times, although it only takes a crisis in the stock market or a run on a bank for his picture of Western man's dependence upon the vacillations of capital to seem mythologically true. Too much concentration on the failure of Marx's prophecies – that the revolution would first take place in the industrial heartlands of England, for example – can blind observers to how much Marx actually got right. Darwin got many things right, too, about the evolution of finches' beaks, about the breeding habits of earthworms and the expression of emotion in animals. That was only part of the reason why this great Victorian natural historian was deified in our times. He was placed on the throne once occupied by God, overseeing like a sad old bearded Jehovah the workings of a purposeless, blind process of procreation.

When confronted with this mythology, the Christian fundamentalists were stupid enough to question the *impersonality* of nature, or, more horrifyingly, they tried to personalise it, so that the blind force of nature which led to a child developing cancer became the act of a cosmic sadist.[15] Whether siding with the atheists who worshipped Darwin, or with one or another of the muddled 'creationist' standpoints, Western humanity found itself still in the Victorian 'semi-recumbent posture' of a worshipper at the throne of blind force.

For Simone Weil, 'the modern conception of science is responsible, as is that of history and art, for the monstrous conditions under which we live, and will, in its turn, have to be transformed, before we can hope to see the dawn of a better civilization'.[16] Her book *The Need for Roots* was first published in English in 1952, the year of Queen Elizabeth II's accession. Half a century on, it seemed a no less remarkable diagnosis of what had gone wrong – as undoubtedly something had gone wrong – in Western European society. Simone Weil, who had died aged thirty-four in 1943, was in England working with the Free French. It was they who commissioned this luminous genius to write a manifesto for what might bring regeneration to France after her defeat and occupation in 1940. Weil wrote *The Need for Roots* in her last months of life, and it is a frenzied, urgent book. T. S. Eliot, who wrote an introduction to its first English publication, said, 'I cannot conceive of anybody's agreeing with all of her views, or of not disagreeing violently with some of them.' He nonetheless urged readers to 'expose ourselves to the personality of a woman of genius, of a kind of genius akin to that of the saints'.

Weil made the connection – inescapable to anyone who has read his by now innumerable biographies – between Hitler and the nineteenth-century worship of science. She quoted *Mein Kampf*: 'Man must never fall into the error of believing himself to be the lord and master of creation . . . He will then feel that in a world in which planets and suns follow circular trajectories, moons revolve round planets, and force reigns everywhere and supreme over weakness, which it either compels to serve it docilely or else crushes out of existence. Man cannot be subject to special laws of his own.'

Simone Weil added, 'These lines express in faultless fashion the only conclusion that can reasonably be drawn from the conception of the world contained in our science.'[17] She added, 'Who can reproach him for having put into practice what he thought he recognized to be the truth? Those who, having in themselves the foundations of the same belief, haven't embraced it consciously and haven't translated it into acts, have only escaped being criminals thanks to the want of a certain sort of course which he possesses.'[18]

Simone Weil, as a French patriot and the daughter of a secularised Jewish family, had every reason to work ardently for Hitler's defeat, but she was able to see, as were her readers more than half a century after she wrote, that Hitler was Darwin's natural heir. The regeneration of post-war society could only, Weil believed, be achieved through a rediscovery by France – by Western society as a whole – of how it understands truth itself. She saw the defeat of France by Hitler not as the victory of a lie over truth, rather 'an incoherent lie was vanquished by a coherent lie'.[19]

As Queen Elizabeth II's reign drew to an end, the lies in which her subjects were asked to believe became, if possible, increasingly incoherent. The intellectual classes – taking that phrase broadly to include the academic world, the more intelligent writers and journalists – nearly all subscribed to the worship of blind force which Weil rightly diagnosed as impossible to detach from the modern view of science. To counteract this belief, to guarantee, as it were, that they would not turn into Hitler, the thinking classes and their pupils the political classes tried to invent a number of 'values' in which everyone was supposed to believe. After the elevation of Gordon Brown to the premiership, these values became *vah-lews* and his audiences were compelled to hear quite a lot about them without being left much wiser about how the *vah-lews* were to be defined or understood.

In denouncing 'the modern conception of science' Weil was tempted to denounce science itself. This was a mistake. If quantum physics was, as she claimed false, how are we to explain nanotechnology, silicon chips, computers – all of which owe their very existence to the pioneers of quantum physics?

Science did, however, take over from theology, or the Church, the role of intellectual dictator.

The science of genetics teaches us that we are the inevitable consequence of our inheritance. Scientific knowledge of our environment has led to what is, in effect, the chief alternative religion of our times, the belief that the planet itself is doomed by the failure of the human race to be its responsible custodian. The catalogue of loss – of rainforests, of flora and fauna – is presented as a new Myth of the Fall, with greedy Humanity raping the environment for short-term gain and thereby imperilling any chance of future happiness. Global warming is an alternative hellfire, with believers dividing, as in the old dispensation, between those who thought that by good works it is possible to be saved – that is by recycling milk cartons, reducing gas emissions and avoiding air travel – and those who believe that it is all too late, that the Chinese and the Americans are beyond persuasion, and that we shall all without doubt perish everlastingly. Another form of determinism which grips the modern mind is economic determinism. Though Marxist states have abandoned communism, Karl Marx nevertheless left the world with the belief that we are all the product of our economic and social environment. It would be very rare, perhaps impossible, to meet anyone of our times who did not believe this.

Religions have often themselves been forms of determinism, as the previous paragraphs would suggest. But they have also been ways of making the kind of illogical leaps out of the determinist circle, which modern physics appears to have made. Whereas genetics and economics follow deterministic patterns of thought, physics post the Big Bang Theory has been a story of surprises, of lurching out of systems, of inhabiting a universe which did not need to be the way it is, and which began its life in a completely weird series of throbs, leaps – no words can succinctly describe what it is that astronomy seemed to have been saying since the 1980s and 1990s.

This corresponds to those religious traditions and myths which, in the past, have insisted upon free will.

The struggle between free will and determinism is one of those philosophical conundrums which can never be adequately solved, which is why neat-minded people will always be determinists – it is easier. But determinism crushes the imagination, and almost all exciting developments in Western thought, Western art, Western music and literature over the last seven hundred years have been in one way or another an assertion of free will. Without free will, the human race has lost its moral purpose. Each generation, therefore, tries to escape its determinist straitjacket by some myth, or ritual, or grand gesture, which will give to us dignity, individuality, freedom. Those who hate religion will see it, and especially Islam and Evangelical Christianity, as the ultimate determinism. But is not the advantage of religion over irreligion (speaking of it merely as a life tool, and ignoring for a moment the question of whether 'it' is 'true' or 'false') that it sees every person as a soul, a person who carries about their own destiny? If this is the case, then the Muslims in their seemingly identical ranks, bowed to Mecca in prayer, may perhaps be closer to perfect freedom than a Western materialist who believes he is merely the product of genetic inheritance and economic circumstances. Ever since the Second World War, as Weil's *Need for Roots* makes plain, the human race has been trying not to live with the knowledge that if the blind determinisms of science and economics were the only truths, there should be nothing to prevent another archipelago of Gulags, another Belsen, another Dachau, another Auschwitz. The little spark, the 'irrational' little glow in the dark, the belief that each individual is of importance – it might not derive from religion, but when religion goes, it becomes very difficult to keep it alight.

29

Gordon Brown

After the death of its leader John Smith on 12 May 1994, the Labour Party had the chance to change direction completely and make itself electable. The only way that this could possibly happen was for it to abandon its left wing, and to become a party of Social Democracy, with a plausible economic policy, largely indistinguishable from that of the Conservatives. Hence, New Labour was born. There was more than one architect for the idea. Director of the London School of Economics Anthony Giddens, the author of *The Third Way*, was perhaps the theorist. Peter Mandelson had been the spin doctor. But the two heavyweight politicians who embraced the idea and made it their own had been Tony Blair and Gordon Brown. One of them was bound to succeed John Smith and put the Third Way into practice.

Smith's death had taken Brown by surprise, and he had been even more knocked off course by the speed and ruthlessness with which the Blair camp, a word which seems rather too apt, was directed by Mandy. By the time Brown had assembled his supporters in the House of Commons, he found out that the Blair bandwagon was unstoppable, and he felt 'betrayed, devastated'.

He did not have the courage to run against Blair. Had he done so, there were those, chiefly his Scottish fellow countrymen, who believed he would have stood a good chance of winning. But it was not in Brown's nature to take risks. 'Prudence' was his favoured fiscal and economic policy, and luckily for him it coincided with a period of stability in the world markets and economies which lasted for most of the time he was Tony Blair's Chancellor of the Exchequer. At first, licking his wounds, Brown directed his hatred against the mincing and absurd figure of Mandy. After they came into power, however, with Tony as Prime Minister and Gordon as Chancellor, Brown was unable to conceal his hatred of the Blairs, and their mutual detestation made for one of the most peculiar spectacles which public life had known for decades. The public had grown used to stories of Margaret Thatcher's Cabinet finding her difficult. But such legends paled beside the implacable, relentless feud which continued, in season and out of season, between the increasingly mad-seeming Blair and the not-obviously-much-saner Brown, with his dour manners and a tongue disconcertingly too large for his mouth.

The extent of the bad feeling between Brown and Blair astounded all who encountered the two men for the first time. A marked feature of it was the filthy language used by the Vicar of St Albion's ('I'm going to take no more shit from over the road' – i.e., from Brown). Brown believed, or let it be believed, that Blair had entered into a 'gentleman's agreement' over their 'dual premiership'; that he would stand down and allow his former friend, now his bitter enemy, to take over. Blair and the Blairites denied that any such 'gentleman's agreement' had ever taken place – as how could it between these non-gentlemen? One shrewd political observer, Andrew Rawnsley,[1] saw them as like the terrible twins Esau and Jacob, vying for power while even in their mother's womb. When Blair was talking big to his supporters, he pretended that he was on the verge of sacking Brown. Given the disloyalty of Brown and his acolytes, it was undignified of Blair not to have sacked him. But he did not dare, partly because Brown's power base in the Cabinet was so great, and partly because, for much of the decade of Blair's spell in office, it was indeed a dual monarchy, with Brown balancing the books in his counting house and Blair strutting the world stage. Brown, equally cowardly and just as painfully, locked into an abusive relationship which caused both parties more pain than delight, was too weak to resign or to stand openly against his leader.

Blair behaved towards Brown as Churchill had behaved towards Eden, endlessly teasing him with the possibility of his taking over, but never quite finding the moment when he was prepared to relinquish power. Brown and his friends had to wait before Blair had become extremely unpopular with the electorate (after the Iraq War) before they managed to stage a coup and extract his promise to stand down. Blair waited until he had done over a decade at Number 10, and then retired from office in order to convert to Roman Catholicism and to pursue a bewildering range of activities. Gordon Brown was at last able to hold the reins of power.

In the first few weeks he was popular. There was a palpable feeling of relief, both in the country and in the party, that Blair's hammy stage-acting had been replaced by the earnest seriousness of the Presbyterian dominie. But after only a few weeks, Brown became unstuck. First, at the Labour Party Conference, he made an ill-judged speech whose populism was at variance both with his serious character and the facts of the case. (He promised, for example, 'British jobs for British workers' – but how was this to be achieved in the current state of the European Labour Market?) His supporters, egged on by their cheerleader Ed Balls, now an education minister, urged him to capitalise upon his popularity and win a mandate from the electorate by going to the country. Fatally, Brown allowed it to be known that he was tempted by the idea and he took soundings, rather than quashing immediately the rumours that such an election might be called in the autumn of 2007. By the time he announced that there was to be no election, he had managed to look both opportunistic (considering such an election in the first instance) and cowardly (backing down when it looked probable that he stood a chance of losing).

Thereafter, Brown was revealed as a man, like the Prince of Wales, cursed with the one quality which makes public life unendurable: bad luck. For the first time in British history since the 1860s, there was a run on a bank: Northern Rock. Old Labour would have nationalised it on the spot. Anyone else of any sense would have allowed it to go bust. It had been borrowing and lending money it could not afford. But Brown's Chancellor, his former Treasury sidekick Alastair Darling, who was obviously His Master's Voice, dithered. They dithered with the taxpayers' money, eventually shelling out more to protect the shareholders and potential new owners of the bank than they had spent in the previous year on the entire military budget. Coming on top of a number of minor scandals, in which it became clear that his Cabinet colleagues had been vague about declaring donations when they had stood as his deputy leader, the public had decided that Gordon Brown was a less attractive proposition than he had seemed when he first came to office.

In the days of the Lilliputian battles between the Blairites and the Brownites, whose petty victories, on either side, were trumpeted in the columns of their fawning acolytes in the press, Brown was often described as a control freak. But economists, who are nearly always determinists of one sort or another, do not really believe in human beings, let alone Prime Ministers, controlling destiny. Andrew Glyn, for example, the Oxford Marxist, spoke in *Capitalism Unleashed* of the economic cycles of the previous half-century as if they were meteorological conditions over which human beings could exercise no restraint. In the 1950s, when the British had 'never had it so good', there was an unprecedented economic boom; there was low unemployment, inflation was easily containable and living standards expanded prodigiously. But this very prosperity, according to the Marxist analysis, led to a strengthening of the labour force and a high demand by larger numbers of people globally for finite energy sources. Therefore everything began to unravel. The price of oil went up, labour relations worsened as workers demanded to be compensated for inflation with yet more inflationary wages. Unemployment, at a level unseen since the 1930s, was the inevitable consequence. Then came the inevitable Reagan–Thatcher reaction. Interest rates were raised to punitive levels to curb inflation. Privatisation and deregulation freed the financial markets. Exchange rates floated. The economy revived itself. But no sooner had these inevitable decisions been taken than there was a cascade of surplus savings from the fast-growing economies of Asia. During this period, credit was seemingly unlimited. Unregulated by governments or by anyone else, the banks could lend money recklessly. With the advent of another recession, this was bound to be corrected by ruin.

All Gordon Brown's 'prudence' and control came to nothing as the world cascaded into recession. If he had allowed Northern Rock to collapse, the matter would have been a sorrow for its investors, but, instead, Brown and Darling committed themselves to a rescue which would cost every household in Britain the equivalent of a mortgage of £2,000. This would not be forgotten. Though the determinists might be right about the inevitability of economic cycles, electorates look at politicians and assess their steadiness under fire. Gordon Brown failed this test.

A central contention of Edward Gibbon's *History of the Decline and Fall of the Roman Empire* is that the essentially noble, civilised and pagan classical world debased itself by embracing the superstitions (as Gibbon saw them) of Christianity. When he reaches the life and career of Simeon Stylites (395–451), Gibbon abandons his normal irony and expresses his open contempt for the heroes of Christian monasticism. Contrast the writings, and lives, of the great Romans, with the ludicrous antics of the desert fathers, and in particular Simeon, who spent his life torturing himself on top of a pillar, and Gibbon's urbane, rationalist point is made: 'If it be possible to measure the interval, between the philosophic writings of Cicero and the sacred legend of Theodoret, between the character of Cato and that of Simeon, we may appreciate the memorable revolution which was accomplished in the Roman empire within a period of five hundred years.'[2]

Our span, in this book, has been shorter: a mere fifty-five years. It is tempting, however, to make similar comparisons as we appreciate the 'memorable revolution' which has taken place in Britain. We began the story with a Prime Minister in decay; but that Prime Minister was Winston Churchill. To compare even an ancient, sick, collapsed Winston Churchill with Gordon Brown would be a cruelty. But the comparisons would not get us anywhere. Go back a hundred years, however, to the time when Churchill was President of the Board of Trade in 1908, and the contrast will be sharper. Then we should find a political class composed of first-rate intellects; and in the fields of literature, music and the visual arts a similar level of excellence. Then you would be comparing the England of Lord Salisbury, Arthur Balfour and Lord Morley, with the England of Ed Balls and Jacqui Smith; the England of Edward Elgar with that of Harrison Birtwistle; the England of William Nicholson with the England of Gilbert and George; the

England of Henry James, Joseph Conrad, Thomas Hardy and George Meredith, with that of Ian McEwan and Martin Amis. Then Great Britain was the greatest power in the world. Compare it with the Britain of 2008, and the language of decline and fall becomes inevitable. The two world wars ruined Britain in much more than a financial sense. Culturally speaking, as we can now see, Britain had declined beyond redemption before the period covered by this book. We could draw Gibbonian comparisons between 1952 and 2008. For example, we could compare Evelyn Waugh, still writing novels when this book begins, and whichever contemporary novelist you would like to choose. It would be possible to continue in this vein, and to make a rhetorical case for the passage of the last half-century of British life having been a decline and fall; possible, but unhelpful. The Britain which saw Elizabeth II's Coronation and the Britain which will see her funeral are in reality two different, equally awful, places.

Coronation Britain was certainly not a very happy place, and it is doubtful whether even the most conservative inhabitants of Brown's Britain would truly rejoice if transported back to 1952, to a country where divorce was punitively difficult, where homosexuals could be imprisoned, where olive oil was sold in tiny phials at the chemist, and where table wine turned your teeth black. In all material senses, the Britain of 2008 is a much more plentiful and a much more interesting place than the Britain of 1952. Nor has there been a 'decline' in the sense that Gibbon chronicled in the history of the Roman Empire. Gordon Brown might not be Winston Churchill, but the politicians of the 1950s were not noticeably more impressive individuals than those of the 2010s. As for the general amenities of life, decline is, once again, not what we have to describe. True, British towns became uglier, smellier and more overcrowded in the period covered by this book; but compare the following in 1952 and 2008 – restaurant meals, in London and the provinces; provincial hotels; opportunities to hear operas and concerts generally; range of broadcasts; cost, and availability of telephones; price and range of raw food, and awareness of food and of dietary health; the standard of dentistry; the range and potentiality of pharmaceuticals and of surgical skills; the life expectancy of the old and of babies; the care for the disabled and the elderly, both residential and at home; the opportunities for higher education; the possibility of living, without the censure of the law or of your contemporaries, as a homosexual, a lesbian, a transsexual; the possibilities of cheap travel, anywhere in the world . . . When you consider all these things, it is impossible to think of the last half-century as a decline. But at some stage along the journey, Britain ceased to be a society. Margaret Thatcher spoke in simplified terms to a woman's illustrated weekly, but her contention that 'there is no such thing as society' became true in our times. There was a multiplicity of societies, all wondering how they could best live together without actual hostility breaking out between them.

One very obvious indication of how confused the governments of the twenty-first century felt about being British was to be found in their immigration policies. In 2005, the Home Secretary introduced a system whereby potential immigrants to Britain would be assessed upon their usefulness. 'High-skill workers' – doctors and engineers, for example – could enter Britain without a job offer. Those at a slightly lower level of skill, for example teachers and nurses, would be allowed to come, but only for a limited period, and only if the labour market was short of their particular skills. Those who applied for permanent residency would be required to pass simple English language tests.

Far from being reassured by these measures, most members of the British public were horrified to have it so clearly spelt out that such simple entrance requirements had not been in place for the previous fifty years. While all this tough talk was emerging from the Home Office, the news had broken that the government actually had no idea how many illegal immigrants there were in the country, nor how many escaped asylum seekers, nor how many criminal immigrants who had been released, or who had escaped, from prison. With all its love of statistics and minding the business of the law-abiding and tax-paying population, the government could not keep tabs on migrants. And no wonder, since, quite apart from the numbers of asylum seekers and immigrants from the rest of the world, Britain had signed up to the enlargement of the European Union. When this measure was introduced in 2004, France, Germany, Italy, the Netherlands, Spain – indeed all the bigger and richer countries in Europe – saw that to allow unlimited movement of workers from Eastern Europe would create chaos in the labour market, not to mention putting intolerable burdens on services such as hospitals, public transport and housing. Sweden and Ireland had their own reasons for not fearing an overwhelming invasion of migrant workers, and they alone (apart from Britain) allowed open entry to migrant workers from the new member states. For Britain to do so was little short of insanity. 'Far more workers came into the UK than was originally anticipated,' admitted the New Labour guru Anthony Giddens[3]: around 420,000 from Eastern Europe, this on top of the numbers of asylum seekers and illegal immigrants in the same period. By 1 January 2007, the government had changed its mind about an 'open-door' policy, and decreed that Bulgaria and Romania, when they joined the Union, would not be granted the same privileges of unlimited access. The EU expressed its 'disappointment' at the British decision, but made no suggestion as to where the extra buses, extra underground trains, extra flats, extra hospital beds and extra schools were to be found to accommodate all these extra people.

No doubt the Polish plumber and the Czech bricklayer were cheaper than their British equivalent. It was strange for a Labour Party – even a New Labour Party – to be so blatant about importing cheap labour on this scale, with the inevitable depletion in wages and living standards for the majority. No doubt it was also embarrassing to see how much more hard working and how much more skilful were the workers trained under communist regimes than under fifty years of 'consensus' politics. Certainly, the arrival of the Poles, particularly in London, with their eager, intelligent faces, their willingness to work fifty-hour weeks mending the lavatories and building the kitchens of the British middle classes, made the indigenous poor seem all the more pathetic.

The underprivileged of Brown's Britain were not poor as the inhabitants of Victorian slums had been poor. But because they ate the consoling junk food beloved by American proles, they came to resemble them, waddling from Iceland to Burger King or Dunkin' Donuts in their huge blue jeans, pushing their obese tots in groaning strollers. The intelligent among these tots stood less chance than their British working-class equivalents in 1952 of rising through education and shaking off the constraints of their upbringing; this was partly because their upbringing and education (constant television, computer games, overcrowded inner city schools where few graduates were brave enough or unworldly enough to want to teach) was unlikely to train them in the gifts of concentration which would make such a life change possible.

In 1944, when drafting his Education Act, R. A. Butler recognised that there would be a strong case for abolishing private education. Had he done so, and had at least a proportion of the good teachers from the private sector remained in the system, and had that system resisted some of the educational theories which plagued teachers' training establishments from the 1960s onwards (for example, the abolition of phonic techniques when teaching children to read), then it might have resulted in a more cohesive society. Every now and then, even late in our times, an old optimist would surface, wishing that the iniquity of division could be abolished. Alan Bennett, for example, when in his seventy-fourth year, called for private schools to be brought to an end. 'It is the paying. It is the fact that you can buy advantages for your children over and above their abilities, which seems to me to be wrong. It's a fissure that runs right through English society and you don't get that in France. In France, state education is the best. It should be the same here. If the state schools were the best, if you had to compete to get into them and their education was better than what was on offer privately, then the whole nature of education would be transformed.'⁴ Such an optimistic viewpoint presupposed that the same educational values and ideas would have obtained in 2008 as were current when Bennett himself enjoyed the benefits of an old-fashioned grammar school education in the 1940s. When Antony Crosland expressed the wish to abolish 'every fucking grammar school in England', however, he ushered in a mob of theorists who questioned the very standards of excellence which enabled school-children, regardless of income bracket, to prosper. Alan Bennett's notion of clever children *competing* with one another to get into the 'best' schools would have been anathema to the egalitarians of the 1970s, when Iris Murdoch, for example, a lifelong leftist, abandoned her commit-ment to Labour after streaming was abolished in state schools and the theorists insisted upon mixed-ability classes for languages and mathe-matics. As she said at the time, 'you don't have mixed-ability football teams'. Had Antony Crosland and Shirley Williams *made* the state schools better than the private sector (as in France), then there would have been no problem, since the great majority would then presumably have patronised the state schools. The fact that so many parents choose to subsidise state schools through tax, and then to spend a large amount of their taxed income on private education, was not a sign of their innate selfishness. It was an indictment of the gross incompetence of genera-tions of politicians.

In any case, what might have been an economic or political possibility in 1944 was never going to be a possibility in the twenty-first century. As many as a quarter of London primary school children by this date were educated privately. One-tenth of the schools in England, Wales and Scotland were private (2,261 schools compared with a little over 20,000 primary and secondary schools in the maintained sector⁵). Even if the political will and courage had existed to abolish 'every fucking' private school, in the way that the grammar schools were similarly abolished in a previous generation, it is hard to see how the economy could pay for the thousands of teachers, and hundreds of thousands of pupils, who would need to be absorbed into the maintained system. Yet Alan Bennett and the good-hearted optimists were of course perfectly correct to say that the division between those educated privately and those not so lucky was 'a fissure that runs right through English society'.

As Belloc wrote:

> For the hoary social curse
> Gets hoarier and hoarier
> And it stinks a trifle worse
> Than in the reign of Queen Victoria.

Optimists would dig up the drains and try to get to the source of the odour. Pessimists would think that a stink was not worse than the chaos which would thereby ensue. 'Leave ill alone' had, in a quite different context, been the 3rd Marquess of Salisbury's advice a century and more earlier. At the end of our times, the good intentions of the educational theorists of the 1960s and 1970s had ended in disaster, with a higher proportion than ever of privately educated children being admitted to the better universities, and landing the better jobs. The underclass or lumpenproletariat therefore grew in our time; and its clever members had even less chance of escaping it. Its benign members could still be pampered and condescended to, from cradle to grave, by the benefits system. But the crashing boredom of life for the lumpenproletariat meant that more and more of its members sought variety through narcotic abuse, alcohol and the diversions of criminal activity which could pay for the former indulgences. The world of 1952 thought that badly behaved young people could be knocked into shape – by compulsory military service, or by corporal punishment at the hands of teachers, parents or the police. Those options were no longer open to the (in some ways) kindlier world of 2008, even if it were supposed that such methods would be effective. Though politicians and sociologists tried to persuade anyone who could listen that there were optimistic solutions to the problem, the pessimists had long since begun to behave as if British cities of the twenty-first century were like American cities of a quarter of a century before. Rather than attempting the radical, kindly solutions provided by such as the Prince's Trust (through education, youth training or family counselling), many British people in 2008 took the 'American' solution – of better burglar and car alarms, more vigilance when walking in city streets after dark, and care not to stray into those shadowy areas where the wild things walked. Every now and then the news would tell of yet another knifing, shooting or strangling. Few really believed that the New Labour promise, to be 'tough on crime, tough on the causes of crime', was any more than an empty phrase.

The relationship between crime and narcotic abuse was evident, but the political class did not dare to draw the obvious conclusions. Prohibition of drugs in Britain had been no more effective than had been the prohibition of alcohol in the United States in the gangster era. In both cases, the criminalisation of the substance merely made the suppliers into barons, figures of power. Had any government had the courage to decriminalise drugs it would at least have been able to deprive the pushers, the pimps, the suppliers small and large, of their power and money. It would never do so, for fear of the popular press. When Richard Brunstrom, Chief Constable of North Wales, said that the recreational drug ecstasy was 'far safer than aspirin', he spoke no more than the simple, scientific and statistical truth.[6] Yet every teenager who died as a consequence of taking an ecstasy tablet while out clubbing had died an avoidable death; and the popular press would not allow the politicians to forget it.

Regrettable as drug-related deaths were for the families concerned, it was the social menace posed by the drug users who did *not* die which was noticeable in early twenty-first-century Britain. The use of crack cocaine soared. From 1985 to 1987 cocaine-related hospital emergencies rose from 23,500 to 55,200.[7] The need to satisfy the urge for crack was as intense as the effects of the drug itself: the resulting rise in crime was simply consequential, but, as the medical statistic just quoted shows, as well as the nuisance of a million stolen purses, smashed car windows, the vandalised phone boxes, one has to take note of the time and money at Accident and Emergency units expended by doctors and nurses on these individuals.

Nor was cannabis, the recreational drug of preference for baby boomers and the middle classes, as safe as its adepts hoped. Fifteen per cent of cannabis sold on British streets in 2002 was skunk, a super-strength resin which, medical opinion said, accounted for a quarter of all cases of schizophrenia in 2007. The 15 per cent of 2002 had soared to 80 per cent in 2008. There were an estimated five million cannabis smokers in Britain at this date.[8] That is a lot of people risking, not the slow wits and silliness of the Bob Dylan dopehead generation, but the outright and seemingly incurable madness of the skunk-minded. In such circumstances, the government's vigilant attacks on cigarette smokers looked to some citizens like fiddling while Rome burned.

Comparable, and related, to the question of crime, and of the social alienation which it both reflects and brings to pass, is the whole story of immigration to Britain. Those who governed Britain in the first two decades covered by this book tended to be old men. They had grown up when the British Empire, whatever virtues it had possessed, was ingrained with racialist ideology. The chief thought in their minds, once the immigrations from former Commonwealth countries began, was of racial contamination. The rival ideology was the optimistic idea of multiculturalism, which by the end of the period we have been considering had been largely abandoned by some of our social engineers. Trevor Phillips, for example, Chairman of the Commission for Racial Equality, announced in April 2004 that multi-culturalism was no longer 'useful' because it 'encouraged separateness between communities'. On a day when British Muslims were holding one of their regular protests and burning the Union flag outside Regent's Park Mosque in London, Phillips said, 'What we should be talking about is how we reach an integrated society, one in which people are equal under the law, where there are some common values'. Against the 'extremist' ideas of the radical Islamists, Phillips proposed that there was an urgent need to 'assert a core of Britishness'. Being British meant that everyone, including the Muslims, had to 'work by the rules of British people – and that excludes terrorism'.[9]

The advantage of the 'multi-cultural' idea was that it enabled everyone to feel at home in their own language, religion, dress codes and eating habits without being imposed upon by the government. It was, after all, successive British governments who had allowed, or actively encouraged, immigration over the previous half-century; happy to do so when it provided cheap labour in an expanding economy; worried by the number of brown faces it might assemble in one place in such towns as Leicester or Bradford; and only noticing several generations later that behind the brown faces and the statistics were actually human beings with sets of beliefs, religious and political attitudes which might not sit easily with modern British secularism.

How do you impose 'a core of Britishness' upon people who are only British in the sense of possessing a passport, and who perhaps do not want someone else's so-called values thrust upon them? What are these values, in any case? 'Democracy and the rule of law' is the answer which some would give. Yes, but . . . As we have seen several times in the previous pages, and in the two volumes which preceded this history – *The Victorians* and *After the Victorians* – Britain was only ever a partial democracy. Its parliamentary system and its civil service had both fully evolved long before the franchise was extended to all adults. The General Election is an opportunity for the British electorate to express preferences, and to change the make-up of Parliament, but it leaves the civil service untouched, the police and the judiciary untouched. Only established or 'acceptable' political viewpoints are offered at the ballot box, and those who wish, for example, to be governed by greens, by communists, by fascists, by Islamic fundamentalists or others – and this represents a substantial part of the electorate if added together – have no chance, no chance whatsoever, of seeing a candidate with their viewpoint elected to Parliament. Even the Liberal Democrats, who receive a high share of the votes, elect only a few dozen members to Westminster.

Britain remained a country governed by those who thought they knew best. In the nineteenth century this was a coalition of aristocrats and the professional classes, with a growing professional civil service. In the last fifty years, the aristocracy was slowly replaced by a different Establishment, of university graduates and career politicians, who were no less adamant that they did not need too much advice from the headstrong populace. The populace might think it wanted capital punishment, or an escape from the bureaucracy of Europe, but the governing classes always knew better.

Confronted with the spectre of Irish terrorism in the period 1970–95, this Establishment contorted itself into any number of positions until Tony Blair had the brilliant idea of giving the 'extremists' in Northern Ireland what they actually claimed to want: namely, power. He made them share it, a Dantean joke which worked. It would be less easy to do the same with the Islamic terrorists, since it was not in the power of the New Establishment to reinvent the Caliphate and bring to pass an Islamic world government – even if the New Establishment were to want such a thing. So it fell back on the rather lame belief that it must assert British-ness – at the period in history when it was hardest to define what so nebulous a concept might mean. A substantial number of Scots, at the identical period, wanted to break up the Union, and they look, as we bring our tale to a close, as if they will succeed. If they do so, where will it leave Wales? Britishness is apparently not so desirable a quality that all the British want to share in it.

Nor could the British fall back, as could the Poles, for example, at a time of national identity crisis, upon their 'core values' reflected in a shared religion. Although the world in general appeared, by the end of our period, to be becoming more religious, there was not much sign of this happening in Britain itself. Indeed, the Church of England by law established never looked more like breaking up altogether in a series of Lilliputian squabbles. To the outside world, which did not share its preoccupation with the legitimacy, or otherwise, of homosexual bishops or female priests, these appeared ever more arcane.

In October 1972, when he was MP for Plymouth, Alan Clark went to the high school to give a talk to the students.

'A girl, a slim dedicated Marxist, asked me why I was like I was, what motivated me. "Because I am British," I said, "because I want to advance and protect the British people." "So, what's so special about the British?" she answered. "What makes them so different from everybody else?" Well I could have answered that what makes them so different from anyone else, is the capacity they seem to have for producing at every level of society, people like yourself who ask a question like that.'[10]

Everything in history evolves, and one of the things which has evolved and changed in our times in Britain has been the concept of the nation state. It is regarded in all the circles to which Alan Clark alludes with smiling contempt or with actual abhorrence. President Woodrow Wilson's idea, promulgated with some happy, and some disastrous, results after the First World War, was that peoples should express their collective identity by the formation of nation states. In our times, we witnessed the urge for such identity, in the Baltic states, in Central Europe, in the Balkans, in the Middle East. The concept of a Jewish homeland turned into the right of the State of Israel to exist as an independent nation. Two little strips of land on either side of it, occupied by Arabs who were formerly citizens of Egypt and Jordan (and before that of the Ottoman Empire) were deemed to be a suitable starting point for a Palestinian state, presumably as a *quid pro quo*. Montenegro and Bosnia and Serbia emerged in our times, not as independent states, wishing to escape the violence of history, but as would-be nations, as did Latvia, Lithuania, Poland, Czechoslovakia . . . And naturally enough, Ireland and Scotland had the same need to express their collective identity as *nations*. The dangers of nationalism, which hardly needed to be explained to Europeans after the Second World War, did not deter the Russians and the French from becoming more rather than less nationalistic as the era wore on.

But, Britain, and more especially England, was somehow deemed to be different. Although Gordon Brown spoke with eloquent lack of meaning or substance about 'Britishness' and 'core vahlews' and 'British jobs for British workers', voters could see through the rhetoric. He meant that if the Scottish nationalists were to succeed, his position, and that of all the other Scottish MPs at Westminster, would be untenable.

What he actually thought about Britain was revealed in a symbolic action which had been performed before he became the Prime Minister. As Chancellor of the Exchequer, he was responsible for coinage, and before he left that position he approved of a new set of British coins. For the first time since the reign of Charles II, the figure of Britannia had been removed from them.

The helmeted figure of Britain's tutelary deity, clutching her trident as she sat with a lion at her feet, had first appeared on a Charles II farthing. It was at the time when modern British history was beginning. The country had been through a devastating civil war. Religiously and politically divided, it now came together in an era of extraordinary creativity. The Book of Common Prayer of 1662, the origins of modern science in the Royal Society, the architecture of Wren and, a little later, the political rationalism of John Locke, began the story of modern Britain. Britannia was its emblem. During the eighteenth century, as the country expanded, both industrially and colonially, Britannia became the symbol of its emerging self-identity. The separate quarters of the kingdom – Ireland, Wales, Scotland and England – were all one. The skills and arts of all its peoples contributed both to its colossal commercial success in the nineteenth century, and to its expansion throughout the world. Thomson's old ditty 'Rule, Britannia!', set to music by Thomas Arne, was an anti-slaving song, which expressed the innocence, the exuberance, the confidence in their own rightness of the British people in the ascendancy.

Gordon Brown sent Britannia packing. It was a small thing, but it signalled the end which any observer had seen coming for decades, the strange dissolution of Britain itself, not merely (as Scotland's independence seemed ever more likely) as a political entity, but as an idea. Britannia no longer ruled the waves. But this was not simply because her shipbuilding industry was decades-long dead, and her navy in decline; it was not merely because her last major colony had been restored to the monstrous and ever-expanding power of China; it was not merely because there was a European Union and a United States which were both bigger and more powerful than she was. It was because Britannia had, at some point during our times, ceased to exist. She had become a missing person. The families of such characters rehearse, over and over, the last day they saw their beloved daughter, husband, mother; how they waited for the return which never came. Such was the state of anxiety and heartbreak of certain conservative romantics as our times came to an end. They strained their ears and eyes for signs of a return: none came. For such as these, almost the most intolerable thing about the loss was that there were others in the family who, bloated by illegal narcotics and American junk food, sat in front of the television in the downstairs room and did not notice that she had gone.

Notes

Introduction
1. Aleksandr Solzhenitsyn, *A Warning to the West*, p. 45.
2. See A. N. Wilson, *God's Funeral*, John Murray, 1999.

1 Old Western Man
1. Tolkien, p. 283.
2. Quoted White, *Tolkien: A Biography*, p. 200.
3. Carpenter, *Tolkien*, p. 43.
4. Ibid., p. 228.
5. 'De Descriptione Temporum', in Lewis, pp. 1–14.
6. Taylor, *English History*, p. 600.
7. Ibid.
8. Popper, *The Open Society and Its Enemies*, pp. 176–7.
9. Ibid., *Unended Quest*, p. 198.

2 Space and Spies
1. Lindsay, p. 28.
2. Ibid., p. 48.
3. Ibid., p. 22
4. Ibid., p. 238.
5. Scott and Leonov, p. 241.
6. Annan, p. 235.
7. Muggeridge, *The Infernal Grove*, p. 211.
8. *Guardian*, 14 September 2002.
9. Wodehouse, *The Inimitable Jeeves*, p. 125.
10. *Sunday Times*, 24 February 2008.
11. Massingberd, *The Daily Telegraph Fifth Book of Obituaries*, p. 106.
12. Wharton, p. 103.
13. Bennett, *Single Spies*, p. 18.
14. Ibid., p. vii.

3 Other Gods
1. White, *The Fruits of War*, p. 121.
2. Oakes, p. 73.
3. Spurling, p. 289.
4. Cooper, p. 202.
5. David, *Italian Food*, p. 25.

6. David, *A Book of Mediterranean Food*, p. 13.
7. To the author.
8. Massingberd, *The Daily Telegraph Fourth Book of Obituaries*, p. 156, for this, and subsequent details about Cradock.
9. MacCarthy, p. 221.
10. Ibid., p. 232.
11. Hickman, p. xix.
12. Auberon Waugh, *Will This Do?*, p. 91.
13. Hickman, p. 58.
14. Marx, p. 712.
15. *The Times*, 8 February 2008.
16. Compton-Burnett, p. 9.
17. Charlie Gillett, Five Styles of Rock and Roll, in Heylin, *The Penguin Book of Rock & Roll Writing*.
18. Wikipedia.
19. Dors, *For Adults Only*, p. 25.
20. Flory and Walne, p. 205.
21. Colquhoun, p. 71.
22. Ibid., p. 74.
23. Ibid.
24. Ibid., p. 71.
25. Pollock, p. 120.
26. *The Economist*, 22 May 1954.
27. Duncan-Jones, p. 93.

4 A Portrait of Decay

1. Muggeridge, *Like It Was*, p. 463.
2. Moran, p. 557.
3. Berthoud, p. 218.
4. Ibid., p. 216.
5. Gilbert, *Winston S. Churchill*, Vol. viii, p. 1086.
6. Berthoud, p. 219.
7. Ponting, *Churchill*, p. 760.
8. Ibid., p. 760.
9. Ibid., p. 761.
10. *Journal for Historical Review*, March/April 1999.
11. Ponting, *Churchill*, p. 769.
12. Ibid., p. 757.
13. Quoted Pimlott, *The Queen*, p. 279.
14. Ibid., p. 280.
15. Moran, p. 722.
16. Colville, *The Churchillians*, p. 171.

5 Suez

1. Thorpe, p. 524.
2. Moran, p. 440.
3. Thorpe, p. 418.
4. Ibid., p. 453.
5. Ibid., p. 468.
6. Ibid., p. 471.
7. Ibid., p. 478.
8. Lloyd, p. 172.
9. Thorpe, p. 516.
10. *The Times*, 1 November 1956
11. Ibid., 6 November 1956.
12. Ibid.
13. Cole C. Kingseed, *Eisenhower and the Suez Crisis of 1956*, Louisiana State University, Baton Rouge, 1995, p. 140.
14. Steven Z. Freiberger, *Dawn over Suez: The Rise of American Power in the Middle East, 1953–1957*, Ivan R. Dee, Chicago, 1992, p. 266.
15. Colville, *The Fringes of Power*, p. 670.
16. Goodhart, p. 4.
17. Ibid., p. 7.
18. Turner, p. 433. See also Robertson, p. 76, and Lloyd, *Suez, 1956: A Personal Account*, passim.

6 Supermac

1. Malcolm Muggeridge, quoted Horne, *Macmillan*, Vol. 2, p. 122.
2. Alan Clark, *The Tories*, p. 313.
3. Ibid., p. 384
4. Horne, *Macmillan*, Vol. 2, p. 140.
5. Horne, ibid., p. 160.
6. Clark, *The Tories*, p. 311.
7. Tolstoy, p. 327 – and passim for exposé of the disgraceful story of the handing of White Russians to the Red Army in 1945.
8. Quoted Clark, *The Tories*, p. 329.
9. Horne, p. 554.
10. Ibid., p. 555.
11. Quoted Hogg to author.
12. Ibid.
13. Quoted by Alastair Forbes to the author.
14. Quoted Robert Rhodes James, *Bob Boothby: A Portrait*, Hodder & Stoughton, 1991, p. 121.
15. Massingberd, *The Daily Telegraph Fourth Book of Obituaries*, p. 280.
16. Pearson, p. 157.

17. Quoted Rhodes James, *Bob Boothby*, p. 416.
18. Ibid.
19. Massingberd, *The Daily Telegraph Fourth Book of Obituaries*, p. 283.
20. Rhodes James, *Boothby*, p. 419.
21. Reg and Ron Kray, p. 42.
22. Rhodes James, *Boothby*, p. 114.
23. Horne, p. 276.
24. Ibid., p. 93.
25. Richie, pp. 716–18.
26. Horne, p. 194.
27. Ibid., p. 422.
28. *The Times*, 11 January 1960.
29. Fisher Papers, Lambeth Palace Library, Vol. 251 f. 95.
30. Dorril, p. 610.
31. Horne, p. 319.
32. Lamb, *The Macmillan Years*, p. 407.
33. Horne, p. 423.
34. Lamb, *The Macmillan Years*, p. 439.
35. Ibid., p. 434.
36. Horne, p. 268.
37. Lamb, *The Macmillan Years*, p. 501.

7 Mental Health and Suicides

1. Carpenter, *That Was Satire, That Was*, p. 121.
2. Larkin, 'Church-going', *Collected Poems*, p. 59.
3. Andrew Scull reviewing Michel Foucault, *History of Madness*, TLS, 23 March 2007
4. Quoted Busfield, p. 28.
5. *TLS*, 2 April 2007, p. 17.
6. See Foucault, p. 112.
7. Slinn, p. 314.
8. Shepherd, p. 223.
9. To the author.
10. Canetti p. 153.
11. By Richard Titmuss – Timmins, p. 212.
12. Timmins, p. 209.
13. Heffer, p. 282.
14. Sedgwick, p. 77.
15. Ibid., p. 6.
16. Quoted Massingberd, *The Daily Telegraph Fourth Book of Obituaries*, p. 56.

17. The judgement is that of Dorothea Krook, Plath's favourite teacher at Cambridge, quoted Janet Malcolm, p. 54.
18. Malcolm, pp. 120–1.
19. Plath, p. 387.
20. Ibid., p. 395.
21. Alvarez (quoted Malcolm, p. 42).
22. Feinstein, pp. 142–3.
23. Hughes, *Letters of Ted Hughes*, p. 524.
24. Sylvia Plath, 'Daddy'.
25. *Church Times*, 16 November 2007.
26. *The Times*, 9 November 2007.

8 *Lady Chatterley* and *Honest to God*
1. Rolph, p. 4.
2. H. Montgomery Hyde, *Other Love: An Historical and Contemporary Survey of Homosexuality in Britain*, Heinemann, 1970, pp. 213–14, quoted in an interesting paper by A. D. Harvey, 'Hotting up Homophobia', which he was kind enough to show to the author.
3. Quoted A. D. Harvey, p. 6.
4. Rolph, p. 17.
5. Levin, p. 305.
6. *The Trial of Lady Chatterley*, privately printed 1961, p. 72.
7. *Daily Sketch*, 9 October 1961.
8. Wodehouse, *Meet Mr Mulliner* (The Bishop's Move), p. 90.
9. Ramsey Papers, Lambeth Palace Library, Vol. 50, f. 238.
10. Ibid., f. 132.
11. Ibid., f. 157.
12. Robinson Papers, Lambeth Palace Library, Lambeth MS 4359 f. 3.
13. Margaret Ramsey to author.
14. De-la-Noy, pp. 136–7.
15. Ibid., p. 139.
16. Ramsey Papers, Vol. 3, 6 August 1966.
17. Ibid., f. 221, 19 January 1967.
18. Ibid., f. 86.
19. De-la-Noy, pp. 143, 144.

9 Profumo and After
1. Oswald Mosley, *My Life*, Nelson, 1968, p. 244.
2. Ibid., p. 240.
3. Phillip Knightley and Caroline Kennedy, *An Affair of State*, Jonathan Cape, 1978, p. 46.

4. Ibid., p. 57.
5. Wayland Young, p. 3.
6. Quoted Knightley and Kennedy, p. 93.
7. Wayland Young, pp. 15–16.
8. Ibid., p. 26.
9. *DNB*, Oxford University Press, Vol. 58, p. 833.
10. *The Times*, 9 March 2006.
11. Wayland Young, p. 34.
12. Ibid.
13. Ibid.

10 Enemies of Promise

1. Sampson, *Anatomy of Britain*, p. 175.
2. Wayland Young, p. 14.
3. Massingberd, *The Daily Telegraph Fourth Book of Obituaries*, p. 209.
4. Baston, p. 327.
5. Sampson, *Anatomy of Britain*, p. 89.
6. Douglas-Home, p. 14.
7. Bernard Crick, *The Reform of Parliament*, Weidenfeld & Nicolson, 1966, p. 133.
8. *Annual Register*, 1999, p. 17.
9. Dominic Hobson, *The National Wealth*, HarperCollins, 1999, p. 531.
10. Ibid., p. 40.
11. Heard by the author three or four times.
12. *Private Eye*, No. 67, 10 July 1964.
13. Ibid., No. 71, 4 September 1964.
14. Ibid., No. 73, 6 October 1964.
15. Ibid., No. 302, 4 July 1973, p. 19.
16. Kenneth Young, *Sir Alec Douglas-Home*, J. M. Dent & Sons, 1970, p. 192.
17. Ibid., p. 205.
18. Carpenter, *That Was Satire, That Was*, p. 281.
19. Peter Collier and David Horowitz, *The Kennedys*, Secker & Warburg, 1984, p. 170.
20. Alistair Forbes, quoted ibid.
21. Charlotte Mosley, ed., *The Mitfords: Letters Between Six Sisters*, Fourth Estate, 2007, p. 359.
22. Horne, *Macmillan*, Vol. 2, p. 483.
23. Phillip Knightley and Caroline Kennedy, *An Affair of State*, Jonathan Cape, 1987, p. 197.
24. Ibid., p. 206.

11 The 14th Mr Wilson

1. King, p. 59 (18 February 1966).
2. Pimlott, *Harold Wilson*, p. 334.
3. Paterson, p. 165.
4. Brivati, *Lord Goodman*, p. 128.
5. Donoughue, *The Heat of the Kitchen*, pp. 200–201.
6. Annan, p. 221.
7. Foot, p. 150 – the echo being from Marx's *Capital* that 'capitalist production develops technology only by sapping the original sources of all wealth – the soil and the labourer'.
8. Pimlott, *Harold Wilson*, p. 304.
9. Clarke, *Hope and Glory*, pp. 284–6.
10. F. R. Leavis, 'The Significance of C. P. Snow', *Spectator*, 9 March 1962.
11. Ibid., p. 302.
12. *DNB*, Oxford University Press, 1980, p. 788.
13. PREM, 13/10.
14. Meredith, p. 46.
15. *Annual Register*, 1965, p. 105.
16. Ramsey Papers, Lambeth Palace Library, Vol. 86, f. 84.
17. Massingberd, *The Daily Telegraph Fourth Book of Obituaries*, p. 165.
18. Ramsey Papers, Vol. 86, f. 84.
19. Ibid., Vol. 87, f. 100.
20. Ibid., Vol. 86, f. 86.
21. Meredith, pp. 60–61.
22. Ibid., p. 368.
23. Foot, p. 214.
24. Pimlott, *Harold Wilson*, p. 393.
25. Foot, p. 185.
26. Ibid., pp. 216–17.
27. *Sunday Times*, 7 May 1967, quoted Foot, p. 213.
28. Paterson, p. 194.
29. Ibid., pp. 282–5.
30. Ibid., p. 214.
31. Ibid., p. 216.
32. Winder, p. 289.
33. Shepherd, p. 223.
34. Ibid., p. 325.
35. Ibid., p. 365.
36. Ibid., p. 354.
37. Foot, p. 327.

12 Ireland

1. Pimlott, *Harold Wilson*, p. 407.
2. *Sunday World*, 17 March 1985, quoted Bruce, p. 221.
3. 'In our area we did more or less as we liked . . . knew all the Roman Catholics and kept close watch on them. Sometimes some of the lads gave them a roughing up – I'm not saying that went on a lot but the politicians never complained then.' Vox pop quoted Mulholland, p. 62.
4. S. Wilson, p. 40.
5. Bruce, p. 227.
6. Gladstone Papers May 1886. BL Add MS 44772. f. 82 9; Bodganor, p. 19.
7. W. S. Churchill, *The World Crisis: The Aftermath*, Thornton Butterworth, 1929, p. 319.
8. House of Commons Debates 5th series, Vol. 129, cols 1279–80, 18 May 1920.
9. Ibid., cols 1289–90.
10. Callaghan, p. 15.
11. Bruce, p. 196.
12. Ibid., p. 199.
13. Utley, p. 31.
14. Mulholland, p. 78.
15. Stetler, p. 162.
16. The author.
17. Neumann, p. 63.
18. Utley, p. 72.
19. Moloney, pp. 9–10.

13 The 1960s

1. Duncan Staff, *The Lost Boy*, Bantam Books, 2007, p. 114.
2. Ibid. p. 136.
3. Ibid., p. 141.
4. Pamela Hansford Johnson, *On Iniquity*, Macmillan, 1967.
5. Matthew xxv: 39.
6. The author.
7. Montagu of Beaulieu, *Wheels Within Wheels*, Weidenfeld & Nicolson, 2000, p. 107.
8. *Debrett's Peerage and Baronetage*, p. 891.
9. Wikipedia – Wolfenden Report.
10. Wikipedia.
11. Annan, p. 134.

12. Private information.
13. Evelyn Waugh, *Decline and Fall*, p. 38.
14. American Gay Rights Movement, a Timetable. www.infoplease.com/ipaA0761909/html.
15. John Lahr, ed., *The Orton Diaries*, Methuen, 1986, p. 251.
16. Joe Orton, *Head to Toe*, quoted as epigram for John Lahr's *Prick Up Your Ears*, Allen Lane, 1978.
17. Lahr, *Prick Up Your Ears*, p. 95.
18. Lahr, *The Orton Diaries*, p. 274.
19. Andrew Motion, *Philip Larkin: A Writer's Life*, Faber & Faber, 1993, p. 319.
20. Sampson, *Anatomy of Britain*, p. 216.
21. A. N. Wilson, *Betjeman*, p. 258.
22. Jonathan Cecil to author.
23. Lahr, *Prick Up Your Ears*, p. 336.
24. Fact recorded in *Recording Industry Association of America*, 1999, 11 October, that the Beatles were 'the best-selling musical act of all time in the United States'.
25. Hunter Davies, *The Beatles*, Heinemann, 1968, p. 178.
26. Bob Spitz, *The Beatles*, Little, Brown, 2005, p. 322.
27. Maureen Cleave, 'How Does a Beatle Live', *Evening Standard*, 4 March 1966.
28. Jimmy Perry and David Croft, *Dad's Army*, Elm Tree Books, 1975, p. 45.
29. *New Statesman*, 7 October 1968.
30. Ibid.

14 HeathCo

1. Alan Bennett, *Habeas Corpus*, Faber & Faber, 1973, p. 14.
2. Ibid., *Forty Years On*.
3. Ibid., p. 39.
4. *Private Eye*, No. 65, 6 August 1965.
5. John Campbell, *Edward Heath: A Biography*, Jonathan Cape, 1993, p. 6.
6. Hugo Young, *This Blessed Plot*, p. 215.
7. Campbell, *Edward Heath*, p. 486.
8. Ibid., p. 499.
9. Edward Heath, *Music: A Joy for Life*, Sidgwick & Jackson, 1976, p. 176.
10. *Private Eye*, 30 July 1971.
11. Young, *This Blessed Plot*, p. 232.

12. Ibid., p. 233.
13. Ibid., p. 241.
14. Campbell, *Edward Heath*, p. 425.
15. Tom Nairn, *The Break-up of Britain. Crisis and Neo-Nationalism*, New Left Books, 1977, p. 194.
16. Quoted Campbell, *Edward Heath*, p. 312.
17. Ibid., p. 378.
18. Ibid., p. 379.
19. Robert Blake, *The Conservative Opportunity*, quoted Morrison Halcrow, *Keith Joseph: A Single Mind*, Macmillan, 1989, p. 54.
20. Halcrow, *Keith Joseph*, p. 72.
21. Ibid., p. 74.

15 Women's Liberation

1. Unless otherwise stated, all information about the *Oz* trial comes from Grove, *A Voyage Round John Mortimer*, pp. 246–64.
2. Ibid., p. 247.
3. Annan, p. 146.
4. Grove, p. 255.
5. Powell, p. 18.
6. Elizabeth Roberts, *Women and Families: An Oral History 1940–1970*, Blackwell, Oxford, 1995.
7. Sheila Rowbotham, *A Century of Women: The History of Women in Britain and the United States*, Viking, 1997, p. 413.
8. Timmins, 1995, p. 121.
9. Stephen Ingle and Philip Tether, *Parliament and Health Policy*, Gower, Farnborough, Hampshire, 1981.
10. Morrison Halcrow, *Keith Joseph: A Single Mind*, Macmillan, 1989, p. 83.
11. Rowbotham, p. 407.
12. Susan Brownmiller, *Against Our Will*, Secker & Warburg, 1975.
13. Greer, p. 11.
14. Ibid., p. 37.
15. Terry Eagleton, *After Theory*, Allen Lane, 2003, p. 6.
16. Louise Thondeur, 'A history of pubic hair, or reviewers' responses to Terry Eagleton's *After Theory*', in *The Last Taboo: Women and Body Hair*, edited by Karin Lesnik-Oberstein, Manchester University Press, 2006.
17. Greer, p. 115.
18. Ibid., p. 161.
19. Ibid., p. 219.

20. Ibid., p. 239.
21. Ibid., p. 249.

16 The Decline of the Roman Catholic Church

1. Father Charles-Roux told the author that he had eaten with all the Popes since Pius IX and that John XXIII's table, and cellar, were prodigious.
2. Evelyn Waugh, *Brideshead Revisited*, p. 87.
3. Edwin Brooks, *This Crowded Kingdom*, C. Knight, 1973, p. 110.
4. Charles Davis, *A Question of Conscience*, Hodder & Stoughton, 1967, p. 64.
5. Trevor Beeson, *Priests and Prelates*, Continuum International Publishing Group, 2002, p. 224.
6. *Guardian*, 6 July 2004.
7. Department of Health Statistics – e.g., in 2005, 186,400.
8. Michael P. Hornsby-Smith, *Catholics in England 1950–2000*, Cassell, 1999.
9. Ibid., pp. 246–8.
10. *Daily Telegraph*, 14 July 2007.
11. Hornsby-Smith, p. 65.
12. Peter Doyle, *Mires and Missions in Lancashire: The Roman Catholic Diocese of Liverpool 1850–2000*, The Bluecoat Press, Liverpool, 2005, p. 72.
13. P. J. Waller, *Democracy and Sectarianism: A Political and Social History of Liverpool 1868–1939*, Liverpool University Press, Liverpool, 1981, p. 186.
14. Peter Kilfoyle, *Left Behind: Lessons from Labour's Heartland*, Politico's, 2000, p. 3.
15. Ibid., p. 39.
16. Ibid., p. 106.
17. See Frederick Gibberd, *Metropolitan Cathedral of Christ the King, Liverpool*, The Architectural Press, London, 1968.
18. Anthony Kenny, *A Path from Rome*, Sidgwick & Jackson, 1985, p. 43.

17 The End of Harold Wilson

1. Austen Morgan, p. 433.
2. Ziegler, *Wilson*, p. 468.
3. Ibid., p. 468.
4. Pimlott, *Harold Wilson*, p. 255.
5. Ibid., pp. 405–6.

6. Ibid., p. 416.
7. Ibid., p. 241. Benn voted for Gaitskell to be leader in 1955.
8. Susan Crosland, p. 210.
9. Donoughue, *The Heat of the Kitchen*, p. 146.
10. Ziegler, *Wilson*, p. 417.
11. Ibid., p. 418.
12. *DMB*, Vol. 6, Oxford University Press, 2004–8, p. 148.
13. Ziegler, *Wilson*, p. 408.
14. Donoughue, *The Heat of the Kitchen*, p. 215.
15. Ian Bradley, ed., *Iolanthe*, Act 1, *The Complete Annotated Gilbert and Sullivan*, Oxford University Press, 1996, p. 375.
16. Donoughue, p. 200.
17. Ibid., p. 194
18. Ibid., p. 195.
19. Ibid., p. 195.
20. Ibid., p. 195.
21. Ibid., p. 199.

18 Lucky Jim

1. Pimlott, *Harold Wilson*, p. 491.
2. Ibid., p. 571.
3. Kenneth Morgan, *Callaghan*, p. 240.
4. John Hoskyns, *Just in Time: Inside the Thatcher Revolution*, Aurum Press, 2000, p. 89.
5. Benn, p. 114.
6. Hoskyns, p. 92.
7. Morgan, *Callaghan*, p. 112.
8. Ibid., p. 272.
9. To author.
10. Details of the Thorpe case, unless otherwise stated, from Auberon Waugh, *The Last Word*.
11. Lambton, p. 71.
12. Ibid., p. 87.
13. Ziegler, *Mountbatten*, p. 422.
14. Sounes, *Seventies*, p. 282.
15. Ibid., p. 391.
16. Ronnie Barker, *All I Ever Wrote: The Complete Works*, Sidgwick & Jackson, 2001, p. 124.
17. Morgan, *Callaghan*, p. 423.
18. Hugo Young, *One of Us*, p. 278.

19 'This Was a Terrific Battle'

1. Gordon Burn, *Somebody's Husband, Somebody's Son*, William Heinemann, 1984, p. 12.
2. A. N. Wilson *The Victorians*, Hutchinson, 2002, p. 527.
3. Hugo Young, *One of Us*, p. 311.
4. Antony Crosland, *The Future of Socialism*, p. 76.
5. Larkin to author.
6. Ibid.
7. Anthony Thwaite, ed., *The Selected Letters of Philip Larkin*, Faber & Faber, 1992, p. 701.
8. Larkin to author.
9. Hughes, *Collected Poems*, p. 222.
10. HMSO, 1981.
11. Scarman Report, p. 14.
12. Ibid., p. 4.
13. Ibid., p. 87.
14. Ibid., p. 5.
15. Young, *One of Us*, p. 238.
16. *OED*.
17. Gorer, p. 310.
18. Loader and Mulcahy, p. 70.
19. Ibid., p. 75.
20. Ibid., pp. 4, 22.
21. London, Institute of Race Relations, no date, p. 77.
22. All details of the Blair Peach killing and the Tottenham riots, Bloom, pp. 455 ff.

20 Thatcher as Prime Minister

1. Blake, *Conservatism in an Age of Revolution*, p. 37.
2. Quoted Des McHale, *The World's Best Maggie Thatcher Jokes*, Angus and Robertson, 1989, p. 32.
3. Prior, pp. 13–14.
4. Eleven women of the Protestant Episcopal Church were ordained priests in Philadelphia in 1974. Although it was not until 1992 that the Church of England authorised female ordination, it was widely accepted as desirable at this period.
5. Gilmour, *Dancing with Dogma*, p. 58.
6. Prior, p. 119.
7. *Guardian*, 14 June 1979.
8. Hastings, p. 94.
9. Ibid., p. 97.

10. Hugo Young, *One of Us*, p. 277.
11. Ibid., p. 401.
12. Ingrams and Wells, p. 155.
13. Young, *One of Us*, p. 282
14. Alan Clark, *Diaries*, 10 September 1982.
15. Lawson, p. 98.
16. Young, *One of Us*, p. 324.
17. *The Times*, 26 June 1984.
18. Keenan, p. 3.
19. Tony Benn, *The End of an Era: Diaries 1980–1990*, Hutchinson, 1992, p. 479.
20. Young, *One of Us*, p. 370.
21. Quintin Hogg conversation with author mid-1980s.
22. Ingrams and Wells, p. 258.
23. Benn, *The End of an Era*, p. 380.
24. Alan Clark, *Diaries*, p. 99.
25. Johnson, p. 95.
26. Ibid., p. 253.
27. *Sunday Times*, 28 February 1995.
28. Leeson, p. 354.
29. Young, *One of Us*, p. 411.
30. Watkins, p. 9.
31. Anderson, p. viii.

21 Nice Mr Major

1. Dellheim, p. 141.
2. Edward Pearce, pp. 44–5.
3. Major-Ball, p. 31.
4. Ibid., p. 45.
5. Ibid.
6. Edward Pearce, p. 5.
7. Ibid., p. 8.
8. Currie, pp. 248–9.
9. Ibid., p. 102.
10. Junor, p. 251.
11. Ibid. p. 266.
12. S. Ludlam, 'The Spectre Haunting Conservatism' in Ludlam and Smith, p. 99.
13. Charles II's taunt to his brother James, when Duke of York.
14. Junor, p. 274.
15. Ibid., p. 267.

16. *Guardian*, 19 July 2001.
17. Wright and Richardson.
18. Dimbleby, p. 493.

22 Prince Charles and Lady Di

1. Krin, p. 15.
2. Dimbleby, p. 237.
3. Ibid., pp. 316–17.
4. *Ceremonial*, p. 32.
5. Brandreth, p. 46.
6. Ibid., p. 178.
7. Ibid., p. 205.
8. Tina Brown, *The Diana Chronicles*, Century, 2007, p. 124.
9. Ibid.
10. Ibid., p. 412.
11. Quoted ibid., p. 166.
12. Ibid., p. 414.
13. Carpenter, *Robert Runcie*, p. 221.

23 The Union

1. Mulholland, p. 93.
2. John Davies, p. 644.
3. Ibid., p. 591.
4. Ibid., p. 595.
5. *The Times*, 2 July 1966.
6. Ibid., 16 July 1966, p. 10.
7. John Davies, p. 680.
8. *The Times*, 28 October 1998.
9. Ibid., p. 1.
10. Ibid., 21 June 1998, p. 3.
11. Ibid., 4 November 1998, p. 23.
12. Ibid., 28 August 1999, p. 3.
13. T. M. Devine, *The Scottish Nation, 1700–2000*, Allen Lane, 1999.
14. Bogdanor, p. 132.
15. Devine, p. 615.
16. Bogdanor, p. 228.
17. Devine, p. 261.
18. Peter Lynch, *SNP: A History of the Scottish National Party*, Welsh Academic Press, Cardiff, 2002, p. 197.
19. Clarke and Johnson, p. 188.
20. Dillon, p. 432.

24 Stephen Lawrence

1. Seldon, *Major*, p. 131.
2. Ibid., p. 29.
3. Cherry and Pevsner, p. xvi.
4. Ibid., p. 330.
5. Ibid., p. 421.
6. Cathcart, p. 21.
7. Lawrence, p. 21.
8. Ibid., p. 24.
9. Cathcart, p. 71
10. Lawrence, p. 171.
11. *Daily Mail*, 14 February 1997.
12. Lawrence, p. 173.
13. Cathcart, pp. 184, 185, 203, 362.
14. Ibid., p. 405.
15. Lawrence, p. 74.
16. *The Times*, 15 February 2008.
17. *Commission on the Future of Multi-Ethnic Britain*, Profile Books, 2000, p. viii.
18. Ibid., p. x.
19. Ibid., p. 88.
20. Ibid., p. 58.
21. Ibid., p. 63.
22. Ibid., p. 146.
23. Ibid., p. 132.
24. Ibid., p. 323, quoting Ben Okri.
25. Ibid., p. 14.
26. Ibid., p. 18.
27. Ibid., p. 16.
28. Ibid., p. 159.

25 New Labour

1. Schofield information – Wikipedia.
2. Tony Blair's tribute to Edward Heath in the Commons, July 2005.
3. Private information.
4. In a speech given to a dinner of the Trollope Society.
5. Evelyn Waugh, *Brideshead Revisited*, p. 122.
6. *Evening Standard*, 28 January 2008.
7. Beckett and Hencke, p. 273.
8. Quoted ibid., p. 279.
9. Paul Scott, p. 162.
10. Ibid., p. 149.

11. Ibid., p. 150.
12. *The Times*, 28 March 1989.
13. Rentoul, *Tony Blair*, p. 555.
14. Julia Dawkins, p. 1.
15. Nicolson, p. 249.
16. Rentoul, *Tony Blair*, p. 556.
17. Quoted Riddell, *The Unfulfilled Prime Minister*, p. 33.
18. Rohde, p. 219.
19. Rentoul, *Tony Blair*, p. 442.

26 Tony's Wars
1. Kampfner, p. 31.
2. Ibid., p. 35.
3. Ibid., p. 44.
4. Quoted Coates, p. 11.
5. *The Times*, 14 March 2008.
6. Seldon, *Blair*, p. 84.
7. Ibid., p. 137.
8. John Keegan, *The Iraq War*, Knopf, New York, 2004, p. 111.
9. *Independent*, 4 March 2008.
10. Keegan, p. 204.
11. The comparison is made by Patrick Cockburn, *The Occupation*, Verso, 2007, p. 82.
12. Ibid., p. 7.
13. Ibid., p. 4.
14. Seldon, *Blair*, p. 220.
15. Henry Porter, *Observer*, 5 November 2006.

27 Islamists
1. *The Times*, 7, 9, 12 November 2007.
2. *Daily Telegraph*, 4 December 1993.
3. Ibid., p. 108.
4. *The Times*, 8 July 2005.
5. Keith Warner (director) to author.
6. Phillips, p. 280.
7. Burleigh, p. 117.
8. Ibid., p. 213.
9. Ed Husain, *The Islamist*, Penguin Books, 2007, p. 173 and passim.
10. Ibid., p. 216.
11. *Daily Telegraph*, 7 August 2007.

28 The Return of God

1. Spurling, p. 509.
2. *The Economist*, 'In God's Name: A Special Report on Religion and Public Life', 3 November 2007.
3. Larkin, p. 190, 'Aubade'.
4. Wikipedia, and *Debrett's Peerage and Baronetage*, Macmillan, 1995, p. 90.
5. Ralph Barton Perry, *The Thought and Character of William James*, Vol. II, Little, Brown, Boston, 1933, p. 33.
6. William James, *Writings, 1902–1910*, The Library of America, New York, 1987, p. 435.
7. *Sanderson of Oundle*, p. 205.
8. Ibid., p. 194.
9. Ibid., p. 202.
10. Ibid., p. 211.
11. Ibid., p. 216.
12. Richard Dawkins, *The God Delusion*, p. 217.
13. See Hitchens, p. 183.
14. *Sanderson of Oundle*, p. 217.
15. 'The Cosmic Sadist, the spiteful imbecile'. The images occur in C. S. Lewis writing as N. W. Clerk, *A Grief Observed*, Faber & Faber, p. 27.
16. Weil, p. 227.
17. Ibid., p. 229.
18. Ibid., p. 230.
19. Ibid., p. 231.

29 Gordon Brown

1. Rawnsley, p. 76.
2. Gibbon, p. 236.
3. Giddens, p. 95.
4. *Daily Telegraph*, 17 February 2008.
5. *Whitaker's Almanack*.
6. *Daily Telegraph*, 4 January 2008.
7. www.streetdrugs.org.
8. *Daily Telegraph*, 7 February 2008.
9. Mike and Trevor Phillips, p. 201.
10. Alan Clark, *Diaries*, Vol. 2, *Into Politics*, p. 198.

Bibliography

The place of publication is London, unless otherwise stated.

———— *Ceremonial. The Marriage of His Royal Highness the Prince of Wales with The Lady Diana Spencer, etc*, by Appointment to Her Majesty the Queen, Printers, 1981

———— *Commission on the Future of Multi-Ethnic Britain*, Profile Books, 2000

———— *Sanderson of Oundle*, Chatto & Windus, 2003

Acheson, Dean, *Present at the Creation: My Years at the State Department*, Hamish Hamilton, 1970

Adeney, Martin, and Lloyd, John, *The Miners' Strike, 1984–5: Loss without Limit*, Routledge & Kegan Paul, 1986

Ali, Tariq, *Bush in Babylon*, Verso, 2003

————, *Streetfighting Years*, Verso, 2005

Allsop, Kenneth, *The Angry Decade: A Survey of the Cultural Revolt of the Nineteen-fifties*, Peter Owen, 1958

Alt, James E., *The Politics of Economic Decline*, Cambridge University Press, Cambridge, 1979

Alvarez, Al, *The Savage God: A Study of Suicide*, Weidenfeld & Nicolson, 2001

Amory, Mark Heathcoat, ed., *The Letters of Ann Fleming*, Collins Harvill, 1985

Anderson, Bruce, *John Major: The Making of the Prime Minister*, Fourth Estate, 1991

Andy Warhol Museum (staff of, eds), *Andy Warhol: 365 Takes*, Thames & Hudson, 2004

Annan, Noel, *Our Age*, Weidenfeld & Nicolson, 1990

Appleyard, Bryan, *Richard Rogers*, Faber & Faber, 1986

Arblaster, Anthony, *The Falklands: Thatcher's War, Labour's Guilt*, Socialist Society, 1992

Arbus, Diane (estate of, eds), *Diane Arbus: Revelations*, Jonathan Cape, 2003

Arnason, H. H., *A History of Modern Art* (3rd edn), Thames & Hudson, 1986

Aronson, Theo, *Princess Margaret: A Biography*, Michael O'Mara Books, 1997

Ascoli, David, *The Queen's Peace*, Hamish Hamilton, 1979

Ashworth, William, *A History of the British Coal Industry*, Vol. 5, *1946–1982*, Clarendon Press, Oxford, 1986

Bacon, Roger, and Eltis, Walter, *Britain's Economic Problems: Too Few Producers*, Macmillan, 1976

Bailey, Paul, *An English Madam*, Jonathan Cape, 1982

Bain, G., *The Growth of White Collar Unionism*, Clarendon Press, Oxford, 1970

Barker, Elizabeth, *Britain in a Divided Europe, 1945–70*, Weidenfeld & Nicolson, 1971

Barker, Rodney, *Education and Politics, 1900–51*, Clarendon Press, Oxford, 1971

Barnes, Richard, *The Who: Maximum R&B*, Plexus, 2000

Barnett, Corelli, *The Audit of War*, Macmillan, 1986

Barnett, Joel, *Inside The Treasury*, André Deutsch, 1982

Bartle, John and King, Anthony, *Britain at the Polls, 2005*, Congressional Quarterly Press, Washington, DC, 2006

Bartlett, C. J., *The Long Retreat*, Macmillan, 1972

Baston, Lewis, *Reggie: The Life of Reginald Maudling*, Sutton Publishing, Stroud, 2004

Baxter, John, *Stanley Kubrick: A Biography*, HarperCollins, 1998

Baylis, John, ed., *British Defence Policy in a Changing World*, Macmillan, Basingstoke, 1977

Beckett, Frances, and Hencke, David, *The Blairs and Their Court*, Aurum, Press, 2004

Beer, Sam, *Modern British Politics*, Faber & Faber, 1965

——, *Britain Against Itself: The Political Contradictions of Collectivism*, Faber & Faber, 1982

Benn, Tony, *The Benn Diaries*, Arrow, 1996

Bennett, Alan, *Forty Years On*, Faber & Faber, 1969

——, *Single Spies*, Faber & Faber, 1989

——, *Forty Years On and Other Plays*, Faber & Faber, 1991

Benson, Mary, *South Africa: The Struggle for a Birthright*, Penguin Books, Harmondsworth, 1966

Berthoud, Roger, *Graham Sutherland: A Biography*, Faber & Faber, 1982

Bevins, J. R., *The Greasy Pole*, Hodder & Stoughton, 1965

Biskind, Peter, *Easy Riders, Raging Bulls*, Bloomsbury, 1999

Björkman, Stig, *Woody Allen on Woody Allen*, Faber & Faber, 1995

Blake, Robert, *Conservatism in an Age of Revolution*, Churchill Press, 1976

——, *A History of Rhodesia*, Methuen, 1977

——, *The Conservative Party from Peel to Thatcher*, Heinemann, 1985 edn

————, and Patten, John, eds, *The Conservative Opportunity*, Macmillan, 1976

Bloom, Clive, *Violent London*, Sidgwick & Jackson, 2003

Bockris, Victor, *Lou Reed: The Biography*, Hutchinson, 1994

Bogdanor, Vernon, *Devolution in the United Kingdom*, Oxford University Press, Oxford, 1999

————, and Skidelsky, Robert, eds, *The Age of Affluence*, Macmillan, 1970

Booker, Christopher, *The Neophiliacs*, Collins, 1969

Bosworth, Patricia, *Diane Arbus: A Biography*, Knopf, New York, 1984

Bowie, Angela, with Carr, Patrick, *Backstage Passes: Life on the Wild Side with David Bowie*, Cooper Square Press, New York, 2000

Boyer, Paul S., ed., *The Oxford Companion to United States History*, Oxford University Press, New York, 2001

Boyle, Andrew, *The Climate of Treason*, Hutchinson, 1979

Bradley, Ian, *Breaking the Mould? The Birth and Prospects of the Social Democratic Party*, Martin Robinson, Oxford, 1981

Bradley, Simon, and Pevsner, Nikolaus, *The Buildings of England: London 1: The City of London*, Penguin Books, Harmondsworth, 1999

Brady, Robert, *Crisis in Britain*, University of California Press, Berkeley, 1950

Brando, Marlon, *Songs My Mother Taught Me*, Century, 1994

Brandon, Henry, *In the Red: The Struggle for Sterling, 1964–1966*, André Deutsch, 1966

Brandreth, Gyles, *Charles and Camilla*, Century, 2005

Briggs, Asa, *Sound and Vision: The History of Broadcasting in the United Kingdom*, Oxford University Press, Oxford, 1979

Brittan, Samuel, *The Treasury under the Tories, 1951–1959*, Penguin Books, Harmondsworth, 1964

————, *Left or Right: The Bogus Dilemma*, Secker & Warburg, 1968

————, *Steering the Economy: The Role of the Treasury*, Secker & Warburg, 1969

————, *How to End the Monetarist Controversy*, Secker & Warburg, 1981

————, *The Role and Limits of Government*, T. Smith, 1983

Brivati, Brian, *Lord Goodman*, Richard Cohen Books, 1999

Brown, Craig, *The Private Eye Book of Craig Brown Parodies*, Private Eye/Corgi, 1995

Brown, E. H. Phelps, *The Origins of Trade Union Power*, Oxford University Press, Oxford, 1983

————, *Inegalitarianism and the Origins of Inequality*, Oxford University Press, Oxford, 1988

Brown, George, *In My Way*, Victor Gollancz, 1971

Bruce, Steve, *Paisley: Religion and Politics in Northern Ireland*, Oxford University Press, Oxford, 2007

Bruce-Gardyne, Jock, *Mrs Thatcher's First Administration*, Macmillan, 1984

Buckley, David, *Strange Fascination: David Bowie: The Definitive Story*, Virgin, 2001

Burgess, Anthony, *A Clockwork Orange*, Penguin Books, Harmondsworth, 1972

Burk, Kathleen, *The First Privatisation*, Historians' Press, 1988

Burleigh, Michael, *Sacred Causes*, Harper Perennial, 2006

Busfield, Joan, *Managing Madness: Changing Ideas and Practice*, Hutchinson, 1986

Butler, David, and Sloman, Anne, *British Political Facts, 1900–1979*, Macmillan, Basingstoke, 1980

——, *British Political Facts since 1979*, Macmillan, Basingstoke, 2006

Butler, R. A., *The Art of the Possible*, Hamish Hamilton, 1971

Butt, Philip Alan, *The Welsh Question*, University of Wales Press, Cardiff, 1975

Byrd, Peter, ed., *British Foreign Policy under Thatcher*, Philip Alan, Oxford, 1988

Cairncross, Alec, *Anglo-American Economic Collaboration in War and Peace, 1942–1949*, Clarendon Press, Oxford, 1982

——, *Years of Recovery: British Economic Policy, 1945–51*, Methuen, 1985

——, *'Goodbye Great Britain'*, Yale University Press, New Haven, Connecticut, 1992

—— and Eichengreen, Barry, *Sterling in Decline*, Blackwell, Oxford, 1983

Callaghan, James, *A House Divided: The Dilemma of Northern Ireland*, Collins, 1973

Calvocoressi, Peter, *The British Experience, 1945–1975*, The Bodley Head, 1978

Campbell, Beatrix, *Iron Ladies*, Virago, 1987

Campbell, John, *Nye Bevan and the Mirage of British Socialism*, Weidenfeld & Nicolson, 1987

Canetti, Elias, *Party in the Blitz*, Harvill Press, 2003

Carpenter, Humphrey, *J. R. R. Tolkien: A Biography*, George Allen & Unwin, 1977

——, *Robert Runcie: The Reluctant Archbishop*, Hodder & Stoughton, 1996

——, *That Was Satire, That Was*, Victor Gollancz, 2000

Carroll, E. Jean, *Hunter: The Strange and Savage Life of Hunter S. Thompson*, Dutton, New York, 1993

Castle, Barbara, *The Castle Diaries, 1974–1976*, Weidenfeld & Nicolson, 1980

———, *The Castle Diaries, 1964–1970*, Weidenfeld & Nicolson, 1984

Cathcart, Brian, *The Case of Stephen Lawrence*, Viking, 1999

Cherry, Bridget, and Pevsner, Nikolaus, *London: South*, Penguin Books, Harmondsworth, 1983

Churchill, Randolph S., *The Rise and Fall of Anthony Eden*, MacGibbon & Kee, 1959

Clark, Alan, *Diaries*, Weidenfeld & Nicolson, 1993

———, *The Tories: Conservatives and the Nation State*, Weidenfeld & Nicolson, 1998

———, *Diaries*, Vol. 2, *Into Politics*, Weidenfeld & Nicolson, 2000

Clark, William, *From Three Worlds*, Sidgwick & Jackson, 1986

Clarke, Liam, and Johnson, Kathryn, *Martin McGuinness: From Guns to Government*, Mainstream, 2001

Clarke, P. F., *Hope and Glory*, Allen Lane, 1996

Coates, Ken, *Not Fit to Be Prime Minister*, Socialist Renewal Fourth Series, Number 5, Nottingham, 2005

Colley, Linda, *Britons*, Yale University Press, New Haven, 1992

Collingwood, R. G., *The Idea of Nature*, Oxford at the Clarendon Press, 1945

Colquhoun, Frank, *Harringay Story: The Official Record of the Billy Graham Greater London Crusade, 1954*, Hodder & Stoughton, 1955

Colville, John, *The Churchillians*, Weidenfeld & Nicolson, 1981

———, *The Fringes of Power: Downing Street Diaries*, Hodder & Stoughton, 1985

Compton-Burnett, I., *More Women Than Men*, Victor Gollancz, 1933

Cook, Chris, and Ramsden, John, eds, *Trends in British Politics since 1945*, Macmillan, 1978

Cooper, Artemis, *Writing at the Kitchen Table*, Michael Joseph, 1999

Coppola, Eleanor, *Notes: On the Making of Apocalypse Now*, Faber & Faber, 1995

Cosgrave, Patrick, *Thatcher: The First Term*, The Bodley Head, 1985

Crick, Bernard, *George Orwell: A Life*, Penguin Books, Harmondsworth, 1980

Crick, Michael, *Scargill and the Miners*, Penguin Books, Harmondsworth, 1985

Crosland, Antony, *The Future of Socialism*, Jonathan Cape, 1956

———, *The Politics of Education*, Maurice Kogan, Harmondsworth, 1971

Crosland, Susan, *Tony Crosland*, Jonathan Cape, 1982

Crossman, Richard, *Diaries of a Cabinet Minister*, 3 vols, ed. Janet Morgan, Hamish Hamilton, 1975–7

——, *The Backbench Diaries of Richard Crossman, 1951–64*, ed. Janet Morgan, Hamish Hamilton and Jonathan Cape, 1981

Crouch, Colin, *Class Conflict and the Industrial Relations Crisis*, Humanities Press, New York, 1977

Currie, Edwina, *Diaries 1987–1992*, Little, Brown, 2002

Curtis, William J. R., *Modern Architecture Since 1900* (3rd edn), Phaidon, 1996

Dahrendorf, Ralf, *On Britain*, BBC, 1980

Daniel, Clifton, ed., *America's Century*, Dorling Kindersley, 2000

Danziger, Nick, *Danziger's Britain*, HarperCollins, 1996

Darwin, John, *Britain and Decolonisation: The Retreat from Empire in the Postwar World*, Macmillan, Basingstoke, 1988

Davenport, Nicholas, *Memoirs of a City Radical*, Weidenfeld & Nicolson, 1974

David, Elizabeth, *A Book of Mediterranean Food*, Penguin Books, Harmondsworth, 1955

——, *Italian Food*, Penguin Books, Harmondsworth, 1963

Davies, Christie, *Permissive Britain: Social Change in the Sixties and Seventies*, Pitman, 1975

Davies, John, *A History of Wales*, Allen Lane, 1993

Davis, Sharon, *Stevie Wonder: Rhythms of Wonder*, Robson Books, 2003

Davis, Stephen, *Hammer of the Gods*, Pan Books, 1995

Davis, William, *Three Years' Hard Labour: The Road to Devaluation*, André Deutsch, 1968

Dawkins, Julia, *Spirit of the Dome*, Faygate Publishing, Bexleyheath, Kent, 2002

Dawkins, Richard, *A Devil's Chaplain*, Weidenfeld & Nicolson, 2003

——, *The God Delusion*, Bantam Press, 2006

Decharne, Max, *King's Road: The Rise and Fall of the Hippest Street in the World*, Phoenix, 2005

De-la-Noy, Michael, *Michael Ramsey: A Portrait*, Collins, 1990

Dellheim, Charles, *The Disenchanted Isle*, W. W. Norton, New York, 1995

Dempster, Nigel, *HRH The Princess Margaret*, Quartet Books, 1981

Devlin, Bernadette, *The Price of My Soul*, André Deutsch, 1969

Dickens, Norman, *Jack Nicholson: The Search for a Superstar*, Signet, New York, 1975

Dillon, Martin, *The Dirty War*, Hutchinson, 1990

Dimbleby, Jonathan, *The Prince of Wales*, Little, Brown, 1994

Donoughue, Bernard, *Prime Minister: The Conduct of Policy under Harold Wilson and James Callaghan*, Jonathan Cape, 1987
———, *The Heat of the Kitchen*, Politico's, 2003
———, *Downing Street Diary*, Jonathan Cape, 2005
Dorril, Stephen, *Blackshirt*, Viking, 2006
Dors, Diana, *For Adults Only*, W. H. Allen, 1978
———, *Diana Dors' A–Z of Men*, Macdonald Futura, 1984
Douglas-Home, William, *Old Men Remember*, Collins & Brown, 1991
Draper, Robert, *The Rolling Stone Story: The Magazine That Moved a Generation*, Mainstream, Edinburgh, 1990
Drew, Philip, *Sydney Opera House: Jørn Utzon*, Phaidon, 1995
Driberg, Tom, *Ruling Passions*, Jonathan Cape, 1977
Driver, Stephen, and Martell, Luke, *New Labour* (2nd edn), Polity, Cambridge, 2006
Duncan-Jones, Austin, *Butler's Moral Philosophy*, Penguin Books, Harmondsworth, 1953
Duran, J., McCarthy, W., and Redman, G., *Strikes in Postwar Britain*, George Allen & Unwin, 1983
Dylan, Bob, *Lyrics 1962–1985*, Paladin, 1988
Eatwell, Roger, *The 1945–51 Labour Governments*, Batsford, 1979
Eden, Sir Anthony, *Full Circle*, Houghton, 1960
Eisenman, Peter, with Graves, Michael, Gwathmey, Charles, Hejduk, John and Meier, Richard, *Five Architects*, Oxford University Press, New York, 1975
Elbaum, Bernard, and Lazowick, William, eds, *The Decline of the British Economy*, Oxford University Press, Oxford, 1986
Elliott, Marianne, *The Catholics of Ulster. A History*, Allen Lane, 2000
Elsom, John, *Postwar British Theatre*, Routledge & Kegan Paul, 1976
Evans, Robert, *The Kid Stays in the Picture* (revised edn), Faber & Faber, 2003
Falkender, Marcia, *Inside Number Ten*, Weidenfeld & Nicolson, 1972
———, *Downing Street in Perspective*, Weidenfeld & Nicolson, 1983
Farson, Daniel, *Gilbert & George*, HarperCollins, 1999
Feinstein, Elaine, *Ted Hughes: The Life of a Poet*, Weidenfeld & Nicolson, 2007
Fleming, John, Honour, Hugh and Pevsner, Nikolaus, *The Penguin Dictionary of Architecture* (3rd edn), Penguin Books, Harmondsworth, 1980
Flory, J., and Walne, D., *Diana Dors: Only a Whisper Away*, Cassell, 1988
Foot, Paul, *The Politics of Harold Wilson*, Penguin Books, Harmondsworth, 1968
Foote, Geoffrey, *The Labour Party's Political Thought: A History*, Croom Helm, 1985

Foster, Hal, with Hughes, Gordon, eds, *Richard Serra*, The MIT Press, Cambridge, Massachusetts, 2000

Foster, R. F., *Modern Ireland, 1600–1972*, Allen Lane, 1988

————, *The Free Economy and the Strong State: The Politics of Thatcherism*, Macmillan, Basingstoke, 1988

————, *Luck and the Irish*, Allen Lane, 2007

Foucault, Michel, *Discipline and Punish*, Granta, 1977

Freedman, Lawrence, *Britain and Nuclear Weapons*, Macmillan, Basingstoke, 1980

————, *Britain and the Falklands War*, Blackwell, Oxford, 1988

Friedman, Martin, *Hockney Paints the Stage*, Thames & Hudson, 1983

Frum, David, *How We Got Here: The '70s: The Decade That Brought You Modern Life – For Better or Worse*, Basic Books, New York, 2000

Fyvel, T. R., *Intellectuals Today: Problems in a Changing Society*, Chatto & Windus, 1968

Galbraith, John Kenneth, *Ambassador's Journal: A Personal Account of the Kennedy Years*, Paragon House, New York, 1988

Gamble, Andrew, *The Conservative Nation*, Routledge & Kegan Paul, 1974

Gardner, R. N., *Sterling–Dollar Diplomacy*, Clarendon Press, Oxford, 1956

Gibbon, Edward, *The History of the Decline and Fall of the Roman Empire*, ed. David Womersley, Allen Lane, The Penguin Press, 1994

Giddens, Anthony, *Over to You, Mr Brown*, Polity, Cambridge, 2007

Gilbert, Martin, *Winston S. Churchill*, Vol. vii, *Road to Victory (1941–5)*, and Vol. viii, *Never Despair (1945–65)*, Heinemann, 1986, 1988

Gilmour, Ian, *Inside Right: A Study in Conservatism*, Hutchinson, 1977

————, *Britain Can Work*, Martin Robinson, Oxford, 1983

————, *Dancing with Dogma: Britain under Thatcherism*, Simon & Schuster, 1992

Glees, Anthony, *Exile Politics During the Second World War*, Clarendon Press, Oxford, 1982

Goodhart, Sir Philip, *A Stab in the Front: The Suez Conflict 1956*, The Conservative History Group, Windsor, 2006

Gorer, G., *Exploring English Character*, Cresset Press, 1995

Gormley, Joe, *Battered Cherub*, Hamish Hamilton, 1982

Goulbourne, Harry, *Race Relations in Britain since 1945*, Macmillan, 1998

Gray, John, *Black Mass*, Allen Lane, 2007

Greer, Germaine, *The Female Eunuch*, McGibbon & Kee, 1970

Grimsley, Johnson Rheta, *Good Grief: The Story of Charles M. Schulz*, Ravette Books, 1990

Grobel, Lawrence, *The Hustons*, Bloomsbury, 1990

Grove, Eric, *Vanguard to Trident: British Naval Policy since World War Two*, The Bodley Head, 1987

Grove, Valerie, *A Voyage Round John Mortimer*, Viking, 2007

Gupta, P. S., *Imperialism and the British Labour Movement, 1914–1965*, Macmillan, 1975

Guralnick, Peter, *Careless Love*, Little, Brown, 1999

Gwyn, W. B., and Rose, Richard, *Britain: Progress and Decline*, Macmillan, 1980

Hackett, Pat, ed., *The Andy Warhol Diaries*, Simon & Schuster, 1989

Haines, Joe, *The Politics of Power*, Jonathan Cape, 1972

Hall, Stuart, and Jacques, Martin, *The Politics of Thatcherism*, Lawrence & Wishart, 1983

Hall, Tony, *King Coal*, Penguin Books, Harmondsworth, 1981

Halsey, A. H., *Changes in British Society*, 3rd edn, Oxford University Press, Oxford, 1985

——, *British Social Trends Since 1900*, Macmillan, Basingstoke, 1988

Harris, José, *William Beveridge: A Biography*, Clarendon Press, Oxford, 1977

Harris, Kenneth, *Attlee*, Weidenfeld & Nicolson, 1982

Harris, Robert, *The Making of Neil Kinnock*, Faber & Faber, 1984

Harrison, Martin, *Trade Unions and the Labour Party Since 1945*, Allen & Unwin, 1960

Harvie, Christopher, *No Gods and Precious Few Heroes*, Edward Arnold, 1981

Haseler, Stephen, *The Gaitskellites*, Macmillan, 1969

Hastings, Max, *The Battle for the Falklands*, Michael Joseph, 1983

Hattersley, Roy, *A Yorkshire Boyhood*, Hogarth Press, 1983

Healey, Denis, *The Time of My Life*, Michael Joseph, 1989

Heffer, Simon, *Like the Roman*, Weidenfeld & Nicolson, 1998

Heilpern, John, *John Osborne: A Patriot for Us*, Chatto & Windus, 2006

Henderson, Nicholas, *The Birth of NATO*, Weidenfeld & Nicolson, 1982

Hennessy, Peter, and Seldon, Anthony, eds, *Ruling Performance: British Governments from Attlee to Thatcher*, Routledge & Kegan Paul, 1987

Hennessy, Peter, *Cabinet*, Blackwell, Oxford, 1986

——, *Whitehall*, Secker & Warburg, 1989

——, *Never Again*, Jonathan Cape, 1992

——, *Having It So Good*, Allen Lane, 2006

Hernon, Ian, *The Blair Decade*, Politico's, 2007

Hewison, Robert, *In Anger: Culture in the Cold War, 1945–60*, Weidenfeld & Nicolson, 1981

Hewison, Robert, *Too Much: Art and Society in the Sixties, 1960–75*, Methuen, 1985

Hey, Tony, and Walters, Patrick, *The New Quantum Universe*, Cambridge University Press, Cambridge, 2005

Heylin, Clinton, ed., *The Penguin Book of Rock and Roll Writing*, Penguin Books, 1992

Heylin, Clinton, *Bob Dylan: Behind the Shades: The Biography – Take Two*, Viking, 2000

Hickman, Tom, *The Call-up: A History of National Service*, Headline, 2004

Hitchens, Christopher, *God Is Not Great: How Religion Poisons Everything*, Twelve, New York, 2007

Hockney, David, *David Hockney by David Hockney*, Thames & Hudson, 1977

———, *That's the Way I See It*, Thames & Hudson, 1993

Hodgson, Peter E., *Theology and Modern Physics*, Ashgate, Aldershot, 2005

Holmes, Martin, *The First Thatcher Government, 1979–1983: Contemporary Conservatism and Economic Change*, Wheatsheaf Books, Brighton, 1985

———, *The Labour Government, 1974–1979: Political Aims and Economic Reality*, Macmillan, 1985

Honeyford, Ray, *The Commission for Racial Equality*, Transaction Publishers, New Brunswick, 1998

Hopkinson, Tom, *Of This Our Time*, Hutchinson, 1982

Horne, Alastair, *Macmillan*, Vol. 1, *1894–1956*, Macmillan, 1988

———, *Macmillan*, Vol. 2, *1957–1986*, Macmillan, 1989

Howard, Anthony, *RAB: The Life of R. A. Butler*, Jonathan Cape, 1987

———, *Crossman: The Pursuit of Power*, Jonathan Cape, 1990

———, *Basil Hume: The Monk Cardinal*, Headline, 2005

———, and West, Richard, *The Making of the Prime Minister*, Jonathan Cape, 1965

Howard, Michael, and Lous, William Roger, eds, *The Oxford History of the Twentieth Century*, Oxford University Press, Oxford, 1998

Howell, David, *British Social Democracy*, Croom Helm, 1976

Hughes, Ted, ed. Paul Keegan, *Collected Poems*, Faber & Faber, 2003

———, ed. Christopher Reid, *Letters of Ted Hughes*, Faber & Faber, 2007

Hurd, Douglas, *An End to Promises*, Collins, 1979

Hutber, Patrick, *The Decline and Fall of the Middle Class*, Associated Business Programmes, 1976

Hylson-Smith, Kenneth, *The Churches in England from Elizabeth I to Elizabeth II*, Vol. III, *1833–1998*, SCM Press, 1998

Ingham, Bernard, *Kill the Messenger*, HarperCollins, 1991

Ingrams, Richard, and Wells, John, *The Best of Dear Bill*, Private Eye/André Deutsch, 1986

Irving, Clive, Hall, Ron, and Wallington, Jeremy, *Scandal '63: A Study of the Profumo Affair*, Heinemann, 1963

Jackson, Brian, *Working Class Community*, Routledge & Kegan Paul, 1968

Jagger, Mick, *According to the Rolling Stones*, Weidenfeld & Nicolson, 2003

Jay, Douglas, *Socialism in the New Society*, Longmans, 1962

——, *After the Common Market*, Penguin Books, Harmondsworth, 1968

——, *Change and Fortune: A Political Record*, Hutchinson, 1980

——, *Sterling*, Sidgwick & Jackson, 1985

Jenkins, Peter, *Mrs Thatcher's Revolution*, Jonathan Cape, 1987

Jenkins, Peter, *The Battle for Downing Street*, Charles Knight, 1970

Jenkins, Roy, *A Life at the Centre*, Macmillan, 1991

Johnson, Christopher, *The Economy Under Mrs Thatcher*, Penguin Books, 1991

Jones, Jack, *Union Man*, Collins, 1986

Judt, Tony, *Post War: A History of Europe since 1945*, The Penguin Press, New York, 2005

Junor, Penny, *John Major: From Brixton to Downing Street*, Penguin Books, 1996

Kampfner, John, *Blair's Wars*, Free Press, 2003

Katz, Ephraim, *The Macmillan International Film Encyclopedia*, Macmillan, 1998

Kavanagh, Dennis, *Thatcherism and British Politics*, Oxford University Press, Oxford, 1987

Kay, W. D. *Defining NASA: The Historical Debate over the Agency's Mission*, State University of New York Press, Albany, 2005

Keegan, William, *Mrs Thatcher's Economic Experiment*, Allen Lane, 1984

Keeler, Christine, *The Truth at Last*, Sidgwick & Jackson, 2001

Keenan, Joe, *Scargill's Strike*, British and Irish Communist Organisation, Belfast, 1984

Kellas, James, *The Scottish Political System*, Cambridge University Press, Cambridge, 1989 edn

Kennedy, Ludovic, *The Trial of Stephen Ward*, Victor Gollancz, 1964

Kenny, Mary, *Goodbye to Catholic Ireland*, Sinclair-Stevenson, 1997

Keynes, Milo, ed., *Essays on John Maynard Keynes*, Cambridge University Press, Cambridge, 1975

King, Cecil, *The Cecil King Diary, 1965–1970*, Jonathan Cape, 1972

Klein, Naomi, *The Shock Doctrine*, Allen Lane, 2007

Kogan, David, and Kogan, Maurice, *The Battle for the Labour Party*, Maurice Kogan, Harmondsworth, 1982

Kogan, Maurice, *The Politics of Education*, Maurice Kogan, Harmondsworth, 1971

Kragh, Helge, *Quantum Generations: A History of Physics in the 20th Century*, Princeton University Press, New Jersey, 2002

Kramnick, Isaac, *Is Britain Dying? Perspectives on the Current Crisis*, Cornell University Press, Ithaca, NY, 1988

Kray, Reg and Ron, *Our Story*, Sidgwick & Jackson, 1988

Krin, Sylvie, *Heir of Sorrows*, Penguin Books Private Eye, 1987

Kynaston, David, *The Financial Times: A Centenary History*, Viking, 1988

——, *The City of London: A Club No More*, Chatto & Windus, 2001

——, *Austerity Britain*, Bloomsbury, 2007

Lamb, Richard, *The Failure of the Eden Government*, Sidgwick & Jackson, 1987

Lamb, Richard, *The Macmillan Years, 1957–1963. The Emerging Truth*, John Murray, 1995

Lambton, Antony, *The Mountbattens*, Constable, 1989

Larkin, Philip, *Collected Poems*, The Marvell Press and Faber & Faber, 2003

Lawrence, Doreen, *And Still I Rise*, Faber & Faber, 2006

Lawson, Nigel, *The View from Number 11*, Bantam Press, 1992

Leavis, F. R., *Nor Shall My Sword*, Chatto & Windus, 1972

Ledwidge, Bernard, *De Gaulle*, Weidenfeld & Nicolson, 1982

Leech, Kenneth, *Youthquake: The Growth of a Counter-Culture through Two Decades*, Sheldon Press, 1973

Lees-Milne, James, ed., *The National Trust*, Batsford, 1945

Leeson, Nick, *Rogue Trader*, Warner Books, 1996

Levin, Bernard, *The Pendulum Years*, Icon Books, 2003 (originally published Jonathan Cape, 1970)

Lewis, C. S., *Selected Literary Essays*, Cambridge University Press, Cambridge, 1969

Lindsay, Hamish, *Tracking Apollo to the Moon*, Springer-Verlag, 2001

Livingstone, Ken, *If Voting Changed Anything, They'd Abolish It*, Fontana, 1987

Lloyd, Selwyn, *Suez, 1956: A Personal Account*, Jonathan Cape, 1978

Loader, Ian, and Aogan Mulcahy, *Policing and the Condition of England*, Oxford University Press, Oxford, 2003

Longford, Francis [7th Earl of] and McHardy, Anne, *Ulster*, Weidenfeld & Nicolson, 1981

Ludlam, S., and Smith, M. J., eds, *Contemporary British Conservatism*, Macmillan, 1996

Lydon, John with Keith and Kent Zimmerman, *No Irish, No Blacks, No Dogs*, Plexus, 2004

Lyons, F. S. L., *Ireland Since the Famine*: Weidenfeld & Nicolson, 1971 edn

Lysaght, C. E., *Brendan Bracken*, Allen Lane, 1979

MacCarthy, Fiona, *Last Curtsey*, Faber & Faber, 2006

MacKillop, Ian, *F.R. Leavis: A Life in Criticism*, Allen Lane, 1995

Macmillan, Harold, *Memoirs*, Vol. iv, *Riding the Storm. 1956–1959*, Macmillan, 1971

———, *Memoirs*, Vol. v, *Pointing the Way. 1959–1961*, Macmillan, 1972

———, *Memoirs*, Vol. vi, *At the End of the Day. 1961–1963*, Macmillan, 1973

Maddison, Angus, *Phases of Capitalist Development*, Oxford University Press, Oxford, 1982

Magee, Brian, *Popper*, Fontana/Collins, 1973

Mailer, Norman, *The Prisoner of Sex*, Signet, New York, 1971

———, *The Executioner's Song*, Hutchinson, 1979

Major-Ball, Terry, *Major Memories of an Older Brother*, Duckworth, 1994

Malcolm, Janet, *The Silent Woman: Sylvia Plath and Ted Hughes*, Knopf, New York, 1994

Moloney, Ed., *A Secret History of the IRA*, Allen Lane, 2002

Manso, Peter, *Mailer: His Life and Times*, Simon & Schuster, New York, 1985

———, *Brando: The Biography*, Hyperion, New York, 1994

Margach, James, *The Anatomy of Power*, W. H. Allen, 1979

Margolis, Jonathan, *Close Encounters*, Orion, 2003

Marley, Rita, with Jones, Hettie, *No Woman, No Cry: My Life with Bob Marley*, Pan, 2005

Marquand, David, *The Unprincipled Society*, Jonathan Cape, 1988

Marr, Andrew, *The Day Britain Died*, Profile Books, 2000

———, *A History of Modern Britain*, Macmillan, 2007

Marwick, Arthur, *The Sixties*, Oxford University Press, Oxford, 1998

———, *Social Change in Britain, 1920–1970*, Birkbeck College, 1970

———, *Culture in Britain since 1945*, Blackwell, Oxford, 1991

Marx, Karl, *Capital*, Everyman, Dent, Dutton, 1957

Massingberd, Hugh, ed., *The Daily Telegraph Book of Obituaries*, Macmillan, 1995

———, ed., *The Daily Telegraph Second Book of Obituaries. Heroes and Adventurers*, Macmillan, 1996

———, ed., *The Daily Telegraph Third Book of Obituaries. Entertainers*, Macmillan, 1997

———, ed., *The Daily Telegraph Fourth Book of Obituaries. Rogues*, Macmillan, 1998

———, ed., *The Daily Telegraph Fifth Book of Obituaries. Twentieth Century Lives*, Macmillan, 1999

Matlock, Glen, with Silverton, Peter, *I Was a Teenage Sex Pistol*, Virgin, 1996

Maudling, Reginald, *Memoirs*, Sidgwick & Jackson, 1978

Maynard, Geoffrey, *The Economy under Mrs Thatcher*, Oxford, 1988

McCabe, Bob, ed., *The Pythons Autobiography*, Orion, 2003

McKeen, William, *Hunter S. Thompson*, Twayne, Boston, 1991

Medhurst, Kenneth, and Moyser, George, *Church and Politics in a Secular Age*, Clarendon Press, Oxford, 1988

Mercer, Derrik, ed., *Chronicle of the 20th Century*, Longman, Harlow, 1988

Meredith, Martin, *The Past Is Another Century*, Pan Books, 1980

Miles, Barry, *Paul McCartney: Many Years from Now*, Vintage, 1998

Miliband, Ralph, *Parliamentary Socialism*, Allen & Unwin, 1961

Miller, Jim, ed., *The Rolling Stone Illustrated History of Rock & Roll*, Picador, 1981

Milward, Alan S., *The Reconstruction of Western Europe, 1945–51*, Methuen, 1984

Moore, Richard, *Escape from Empire*, Clarendon Press, Oxford, 1983

Moran, Lord, *Winston Churchill: The Struggle for Survival, 1940–65*, Constable, 1966

Morgan, Austen, *Harold Wilson*, Pluto Press, 1992

Morgan, Kenneth O., *Rebirth of a Nation: Wales 1880–1980*, Clarendon Press, Oxford, 1981

———, *Labour People: Leaders and Lieutenants, Hardie to Kinnock*, Oxford University Press, Oxford, 1987

———, *The People's Peace, British History, 1945–1989*, Oxford University Press, Oxford, 1990

———, *Modern Wales: Politics, Places and People*, University of Wales Press, Cardiff, 1995

———, *Callaghan: A Life*, Oxford University Press, Oxford, 1997

———, *Michael Foot: A Life*, Harper Press, 2007

Morris, Jan, *Conundrum*, Faber & Faber, 1974

Morton, Andrew, *Diana: Her True Story*, Michael O'Mara Books, 2003
———, *Diana in Pursuit of Love*, Michael O'Mara Books, 2004
Muggeridge, Malcolm, *The Infernal Grove*, Collins, 1973
———, *Like It Was*, Collins, 1981
Mulholland, Marc, *The Longest War: Northern Ireland's Troubled History*, Oxford University Press, Oxford, 2002
Nairn, Tom, *The Enchanted Glass: Britain and Its Monarchy*, Radius, 1988
Neumann, Peter, R., *Britain's Long War: British Strategy in Northern Ireland, 1969–1988*, Palgrave Macmillan, Basingstoke, 2003
Nicholson, Vivian, and Smith, Stephen, *Spend, Spend, Spend*, Fontana/Collins, 1977
Nicolson, Adam, *Regeneration*, HarperCollins, 1999
Norman, Philip, *Symphony for the Devil: The Rolling Stones Story*, Linden Press, New York, 1984
North, Richard D., *Mr Blair's Messiah Politics, or What Happened When Bambi Tried to Save the World*, The Social Affairs Unit, 2006
Nossiter, Bernard, *Britain: A Future That Works*, Houghton Mifflin, Boston, Massachusetts, 1978
Nunn, Heather, *Thatcher, Politics and Fantasy*, Lawrence & Wishart, 2002
Oakes, Philip, *Tony Hancock*, Woburn Press, 1975
Okri, Ben, *Birds of Heaven*, Phoenix, 1996
Osborne, John, *The Entertainer*, Faber & Faber, 1957
———, *Inadmissible Evidence*, Faber & Faber, 1965
Ottey, Roy, *The Strike: An Insider's Story*, Sidgwick & Jackson, 1985
Owen, David, *Face the Future*, Jonathan Cape, 1981
———, *A Time to Declare*, Michael Joseph, 1991
Parker, John, *Elvis: The Secret Files*, Anaya Publishers, 1993
Parkin, Frank, *Middle Class Radicals*, Manchester University Press, Manchester, 1968
Parris, Matthew, *Chance Witness: An Outsider's Life in Politics*, Viking, 2002
———, and Maguire, Kevin, *Great Parliamentary Scandals*, Robson Books, 1995
Paterson, Peter, *Tired and Emotional: The Life of Lord George Brown*, Chatto & Windus, 1993
Paxman, Jeremy, *Friends in High Places. Who Runs Britain?*, Michael Joseph, 1990
———, *The Political Animal: An Anatomy*, Michael Joseph, 1990
———, *The English: A Portrait of a People*, Michael Joseph, 1998
Pearce, Edward, *The Quiet Rise of John Major*, Weidenfeld & Nicolson, 1991

Pearce, Joseph, *Solzhenitsyn: A Soul in Exile*, HarperCollins, 2000

Pearson, John, *The Rise and Fall of the Kray Twins*, Weidenfeld & Nicolson, 1972

Penrose, Barrie, and Courtiour, Roger, *The Penrose File*, Secker & Warburg, 1978

Perry, Jimmy, and Croft, David, *Dad's Army*, Elm Tree Books, 1975

Peston, Robert, *Brown's Britain*, Short Books, 2005

Phillips, Mike, and Phillips, Trevor, *Windrush: The Irresistible Rise of Multi-Racial Britain*, HarperCollins, 1998

Pimlott, Ben, *Hugh Dalton*, Jonathan Cape, 1985

——, *Harold Wilson*, HarperCollins, 1992

——, *The Queen*, HarperCollins, 2001

Plath, Sylvia, *The Journals of Sylvia Plath, 1950–62*, Faber & Faber, 2000

Plowden, William, *The Motor Car and Politics*, The Bodley Head, 1971

Pollock, John, *Billy Graham: Evangelist to the World*, Harper & Row, San Francisco, 1979

Ponting, Clive, *Breach of Promise: Labour in Power, 1964–70*, Hamish Hamilton, 1988

——, *Churchill*, Sinclair-Stevenson, 1994

Popper, Karl, *The Open Society and Its Enemies*, Vol. I, Routledge & Kegan Paul, 1945

——, *Unended Quest*, Fontana, 1982

Porter, Roy, *A Social History of Madness*, Weidenfeld & Nicolson, 1987

——, *Madness: A Brief History*, Oxford University Press, Oxford, 2002

Powell, Anthony, *Journals, 1987–1989*, Heinemann, 1996

Prior, Jim, *Balance of Power*, Hamish Hamilton, 1986

Puzo, Mario, *The Godfather*, Arrow, 1991

Pym, Francis, *The Politics of Consent*, Hamish Hamilton, 1984

Ratcliff, Carter, and Rosenblum, Robert, *Gilbert & George: The Singing Sculpture*, Thames & Hudson, 1993

Rawnsley, Andrew, *Servants of the People*, Penguin Books, 2001

Rentoul, John, *Me and Mine: The Triumph of New Individualism?*, Unwin Hyman, 1989

——, *Tony Blair, Prime Minister*, Little, Brown, 2001

Rhodes James, Robert, *Anthony Eden*, Weidenfeld & Nicholson, 1986

Rice-Davies, Mandy, *The Mandy Report*, Confidential Publications, 1964

Rich, Paul, *Race and Empire in British Politics*, Cambridge University Press, Cambridge, 1986

Richards, Jeffrey, *Films and British National Identity*, Manchester University Press, Manchester, 1997

Richie, Alexandra, *Faust's Metropolis: A History of Berlin*, Carroll & Graf, New York, 1998

Riddell, Peter, *The Thatcher Decade*, Blackwell, Oxford, 1989

———, *The Unfulfilled Prime Minister*, Politico's, 2005

Robertson, Terence, *Crisis: The Inside Story of the Suez Conspiracy*, Hutchinson, 1965

Robinson, John A. T., *Honest to God*, SCM Press, 1963

———, *The New Reformation?*, SCM Press, 1965

Rohde, Katrin, *Die britischen Verfassungsreformen unter Tony Blair 1997 bis 2001*, Uni-Edition, Berlin, 2003

Rolph, C. H., ed., *The Trial of Lady Chatterley*, Penguin Books, Harmondsworth, 1961

Rosecrance, R. S., *Defense of the Realm: British Strategy in the Nuclear Age*, Columbia University Press, New York, 1968

Ross, Robert, *Monty Python Encyclopaedia*, Batsford, 2001

Roth, Andrew, *Enoch Powell*, Macdonald, 1970

———, *Heath and the Heathmen*, Routledge & Kegan Paul, 1972

———, *Sir Harold Wilson, Yorkshire Walter Mitty*, Macdonald and Jane's, 1977

Rothwell, Victor, *Britain and the Cold War, 1941–1947*, Jonathan Cape, 1982

Rous, Lady Henrietta, ed., *The Ossie Clark Diaries*, Bloomsbury, 1998

Runciman, David, *The Politics of Good Intentions*, Princeton University Press, Princeton, NJ, 2006

Sampson, Anthony, *Anatomy of Britain*, Hodder & Stoughton, 1962

———, *The Changing Anatomy of Britain*, Hodder & Stoughton, 1982

Samuel, Raphael, *The Lost World of British Communism*, Verso, 2006

———, Blomfield, Barbara, and Boanas, Guy, eds, *The Enemy Within: Pit Villages and the Miners' Strike of 1984–5*, Routledge & Kegan Paul, 1986

Savage, Jon, *England's Dreaming: Anarchy, Sex Pistols, Punk Rock, and Beyond*, St Martin's Press, New York, 2001

Scarman, Lord, *The Brixton Disorders 10–12 April 1981*, HMSO, 1981

Scharpff, Paulus, *Geschichte der Evangelisation*, Brunnen-Verlag, Giessen und Basel, 1964

Schlesinger, Peter, *A Chequered Past*, Thames & Hudson, 2003

Schulman, Bruce J., *The Seventies: The Great Shift in American Culture, Society, and Politics*, Da Capo Press, New York, 2001

Schulz, Charles M., *Peanuts Jubilee: My Life and Art with Charlie Brown and Others*, Penguin Books, Harmondsworth, 1976

Schumacher, Michael, *Francis Ford Coppola: A Filmmaker's Life*, Crown, New York, 1999

Scott, David, and Leonov, Alexei, *Two Sides of the Moon: Our Story of the Cold War Space Race*, Simon & Schuster, 2004

Scott, Paul, *Tony and Cherie*, Pan Books, 2006

Sedgwick, Peter, *Psycho Politics*, Pluto, 1982

Seldon, Anthony, ed., *Conservative Century: The Conservative Party since 1900*, Oxford University Press, Oxford, 1994

————, *The Heath Government: A Reappraisal*, Longman, 1996

————, *Major: A Political Life*, Simon & Schuster, 1997

————, *The Blair Effect*, Simon & Schuster, 2001

————, *Blair*, Simon & Schuster, 2004

————, *Blair's Britain*, Cambridge University Press, Cambridge, 2007

————, *Blair Unbound*, Simon & Schuster, 2007

Service, Robert, *Comrades: Communism. A World History*, Macmillan, 2007

Shanks, Michael, *The Stagnant Society*, Penguin Books, Harmondsworth, 1963

Shepard, Sam, *The Rolling Thunder Logbook*, Penguin Books, Harmondsworth, 1978

Shepherd, Robert, *Enoch Powell*, Hutchinson, 1996

Sherman, Dale, *Urban Legends of Rock and Roll*, Collectors Guide Publishing Inc., Ontario, Canada, 1990

Shuckburgh, Evelyn, *Descent to Suez: Diaries, 1951–56*, Weidenfeld & Nicholson, 1986

Skidelsky, Robert, ed., *Thatcherism*, Chatto & Windus, 1988

————, *The World after Communism*, Macmillan, 1995

Slinn, Judy, *Abbott Laboratories in the UK*, Granta, 1989

Smith, Ian, *Bitter Harvest*, Blake, 2001

Snow, Philip, *Stranger and Brother*, Macmillan, 1982

Solzhenitsyn, Aleksandr, *One Day in the Life of Ivan Denisovich*, Penguin Books, Harmondsworth, 1963

————, *The Oak and the Calf*, Collins, 1980

————, *The Gulag Archipelago* (abridged), Harvill Press, 2003

Sounes, Howard, *Down the Highway: The Life of Bob Dylan*, Grove, New York, 2001

————, *Seventies: The Sights, Sounds and Ideas of a Brilliant Decade*, Simon & Schuster, 2006

Spurling, Hilary, *Ivy*, Richard Cohen Books, 1995

Stacey, Nicolas, *Who Cares*, Anthony Blond, 1971

Stephenson, Hugh, *Claret and Chips: The Rise of the SDP*, Michael Joseph, 1982

Stetler, Russell, *The Battle of Bogside*, Sheed & Ward, 1970

Summers, Anthony, and Dorril, Stephen, *Honeytrap: The Secret Worlds of Stephen Ward*, Weidenfeld & Nicolson, 1987

Taylor, A. J. P., *English History, 1914–1945*, Clarendon Press, Oxford, 1965

———, *A Personal History*, Hamish Hamilton, 1983

Tebbit, Norman, *Upwardly Mobile*, Weidenfeld & Nicolson, 1988

Tevis, Walter, *The Man Who Fell to Earth*, Bloomsbury, 1999

Thatcher, Margaret, *The Downing Street Years*, HarperCollins, 1993

———, *The Path to Power*, HarperCollins, 1995

Thomas, D. M., *Alexander Solzhenitsyn: A Century in His Life*, St. Martin's Press, New York, 1998

Thompson, Brian, *Clever Girl*, Atlantic Books, 2006

Thompson, Harry, *Richard Ingrams, Lord of the Gnomes*, Heinemann, 1994

Thompson, Hunter, S., *Hell's Angels*, Penguin Books, Harmondsworth, 1967

———, *Fear and Loathing in Las Vegas*, Paladin, 1972

———, *The Great Shark Hunt*, Picador, 1980

Thorpe, D. R., *The Life and Times of Anthony Eden*, Chatto & Windus, 2003

Thurlow, David, *Profumo: The Hate Factor*, Robert Hale, 1992

Timmins, Nicholas, *The Five Giants: A Biography of the Welfare State*, HarperCollins, 1995

Titmuss, Richard, *Essays on the Welfare State*, Allen & Unwin, 1958

Tolkien, J. R. R., *The Return of the King*, Allen & Unwin, 1955

Tolstoy, Nikolai, *Stalin's Secret War*, Jonathan Cape, 1981

Towne, Robert, *Chinatown*, Faber & Faber, 1998

Trudeau, G. B., *The Doonesbury Chronicles*, Holt, Rinehart & Winston, New York, 1975

———, *Flashback: Twenty-Five Years of Doonesbury*, Andrews & McNeel, Kansas City, Missouri, 1995

Turner, Barry, *Suez, 1956*, Hodder & Stoughton, 2006

Tyler, Rodney, *Campaign*, Grafton Books, 1987

Utley, T. E., *Lessons of Ulster*, J. M. Dent & Sons, 1975

Vaizey, John, *In Breach of Promise*, Weidenfeld & Nicolson, 1983

Verrier, Anthony, *The Road to Zimbabwe*, Jonathan Cape, 1986

Vickers, Hugo, *Alice, Princess Andrew of Greece*, Hamish Hamilton, 2000

Walters, Alan, *Britain's Economic Renaissance*, Oxford University Press, Oxford, 1986

Watkins, Alan, *A Conservative Coup*, Duckworth, 1991

Waugh, Auberon, *Biafra: Britain's Shame*, Michael Joseph, 1969
———, *In the Lion's Den*, Michael Joseph, 1978
———, *The Last Word*, Michael Joseph, 1980
———, *A Turbulent Decade: The Diaries of Auberon Waugh*, Private Eye/André Deutsch, 1985
———, *Another Voice*, Firethorn Press, 1986
———, *Will This Do?*, Century, 1991
Waugh, Evelyn, *Decline and Fall*, Chapman & Hall, 1947 (first published 1928)
———, *Brideshead Revisited*, Penguin Books, Harmondsworth 1999 (first published 1945)
Webb, Peter, *Portrait of David Hockney*, Paladin, 1990
Weil, Simone, *The Need for Roots*, Routledge & Kegan Paul, 1952
Welsby, Paul A., *A History of the Church of England, 1945–1980*, Oxford University Press, Oxford, 1984
Wharton, Michael, *The World of Peter Simple*, Johnson, 1973
Wheatcroft, Geoffrey, *Absent Friends*, Hamish Hamilton, 1989
———, *The Strange Death of Tory England*, Allen Lane, 2005
Wheeler-Bennett, J. W., *King George VI*, Macmillan, 1958
Wheen, Francis, *Tom Driberg, His Life and Indiscretions*, Chatto & Windus, 1990
———, *How Mumbo Jumbo Conquered the World*, Fourth Estate, 2004
White, Michael, *Tolkien: A Biography*, Little, Brown, 2001
———, *The Fruits of War*, Simon & Schuster, 2005
White, Timothy, *Catch a Fire: The Life of Bob Marley*, Omnibus, 2000
Whitehead, Phillip, *The Writing on the Wall: Britain in the Seventies*, Michael Joseph, 1985
Wiener, Martin, *English Culture and the Decline of the Industrial Spirit, 1850–1981*, Cambridge University Press, Cambridge, 1981
Williams, Philip, ed., *The Diary of Hugh Gaitskell, 1945–56*, Jonathan Cape, 1983
Williams, Philip, *Hugh Gaitskell*, Jonathan Cape, 1979
Wilmut, Roger, ed., *Monty Python's Flying Circus: Just the Words*, Vol. 1, Methuen, 1999
Wilson, A. N., *Betjeman*, Hutchinson, 2006
Wilson, Harold, *The Labour Government, 1964–1970: A Personal Memoir*, Weidenfeld & Nicolson, 1971
———, *Final Term: The Labour Government, 1974–1976*, Weidenfeld & Nicolson, 1979
———, *Memoirs, 1916–1964: The Making of a Prime Minister*, Weidenfeld & Nicolson, 1986
Wilson, S., *The Carson Trail*, Crown Publications, Belfast, 1981

Winder, Robert, *Bloody Foreigners: The Story of Immigration to Britain*, Little, Brown, 2004

Winter, J.M., ed., *The Working Class in Modern British History*, Cambridge University Press, Cambridge, 1983

Wodehouse, P. G., *Meet Mr Mulliner*, 1927, reprinted Everyman Library, 2000

———, *The Inimitable Jeeves*, Everyman, 2007 (first published 1923)

Wood, Lee, *The Sex Pistols Diary: Sex Pistols Day by Day*, Omnibus Press, 1988

Worswick, G. N., and Ady, P., eds, *The British Economy, 1945–50*, Clarendon Press, Oxford, 1952

———, eds, *The British Economy in the Nineteen-fifties*, Clarendon Press, Oxford, 1962

Wright, Patrick, and Richardson, Peter, *101 Uses for a John Major*, André Deutsch, 1993

Wright, Peter, *Spycatcher*, Viking, 1986

Yorke, Ritchie, *The History of Rock and Roll*, Eyre Methuen, 1976

Young, Hugo, *One of Us*, Macmillan, 1989

———, *This Blessed Plot*, Macmillan, 1998

Young, Michael, *The Rise of the Meritocracy*, Penguin Books, Harmondsworth, 1958

Young, Wayland, *The Profumo Affair: Aspects of Conservatism*, Penguin Books, Harmondsworth, 1963

Youngson, A. J., *Britain's Economic Growth, 1920–1966*, Allen & Unwin, 1967

Ziegler, Philip, *Mountbatten*, Collins, 1985

———, *Wilson*, Weidenfeld & Nicolson, 1993

Index

INDEX